APIL Guide to Catastrophic Injury Claims

Second Edition

APIL Guide to Catastrophic Injury Claims

Second Edition

Grahame Aldous QC, 9 Gough Square, General Editor
Stuart McKechnie, 9 Gough Square
Jeremy Ford, 9 Gough Square
Terry Lee, Russell-Cooke Solicitors

With specialist contributions from

Lucy Wilton, Russell-Cooke Solicitors, on Costs and Funding
Andrew Molyneux on Adult Neuro-Radiology
Udo Kischka on Neurological Rehabilitation
Richard Cropper on Periodical Payment Orders
Nicholas Leng on Traumatic Brain Injuries
Maggie Blott on Birth Brain Injuries
Brian Gardner on Spinal Cord Injuries
Maggie Sargent on Care
Sellaiah Sooriakumaran on Prosthetic Rehabilitation
Martin Baggaley on Psychiatric Injuries

JORDANS

TABLE OF CASES

References are to paragraph numbers.

TABLE OF STATUTES

References are to paragraph numbers.

TABLE OF STATUTORY INSTRUMENTS

References are to paragraph numbers.

TABLE OF ABBREVIATIONS

ADR	alternative dispute resolution
AEI	average earnings index
AFB	automatic forearm balance
AFO	ankle foot orthosis
APIL	Association of Personal Injury Lawyers
ASHE	annual survey of hours and earnings
ASHE 6115	annual survey of hours and earnings, occupational earnings for care assistants and home carers
ASIA	American Spinal Injury Association
ATE insurance	after the event insurance
AvMA	Action Against Medical Accidents
BABICM	British Association of Brain Injury Case Managers
BICMA	Bodily Injuries Claims Management Association
BMA	British Medical Association
BTE insurance	before the event insurance
CAA	constant attendance allowance
CAD-CAM	Computer-aided design and computer-aided manufacturing
CBT	Cognitive behavioural therapy
CEDR	Centre for Effective Dispute Resolution
CFA	conditional fee agreement
CFS	chronic fatigue syndrome
CMC	case management conference
CPR	Civil Procedure Rules
CQC	Care Quality Commission
CRAG	Charging for Residential Accommodation Guide
CRBs	criminal record checks
CRU	Compensation Recovery Unit
CRU certificate	certificate of recoverable benefits
CT	computerised tomography
CTB	council tax benefit
CTC	child tax credit
DAI	diffuse axonal injury
DLA	Disability living allowance
DSM-IV-TR	Diagnostic and Statistical Manual of Mental Disorders, 4th edn, Text Revision of the American Psychiatric Association

DWP	Department for Work and Pensions
ECHR	European Convention on Human Rights
EEG	electroencephalography
EL	Employer liability
emw	early morning wakening
ENT	ear, nose and throat
ERNIC	Employer's National Insurance
ESA	employment and support allowance
FSA	Financial Services Authority
GCS	Glasgow Coma Scale
HB	housing benefit
HMRC	HM Revenue and Customs
HPC	Health Professions Council
HSSASSA Act 1983	Health and Social Services and Social Security Adjudications Act 1983
IB	incapacity benefit
ICD 10	International Classification of Diseases, Version 10 of the World Health Organisation
ICSI	intra-cyto-plasmic sperm injection
IIDB	Industrial injuries disablement benefit
ILF	Independent Living Fund
ILGS	index-linked government securities
INA	independent needs assessment
IS	income support
JSB	Judicial Studies Board
LEI	legal expenses insurance
LSC	Legal Services Commission
ME	myalgic encephalopathy
MND	malingered neurocognitive disorder
MRI	Magnetic resonance imaging
MTBI	mild traumatic brain injury
NA(AR) Regulations	National Assistance (Assessment of Resources) Regulations 1992
NAA 1948	National Assistance Act 1948
NASDAB	National Amputee Statistical Database
NHSLA	National Health Service Litigation Authority
NICE	National Institute for Clinical Excellence
NICs	national insurance contributions
OCD	Obsessive compulsive disorder
ONS	The Office of National Statistics
PC	pension credit
PCS	post-concussional syndrome
PIQ	performance IQ
POI	perceptual organisation index
PPAM aid	post-amputation pneumatic amputation mobility aid
PPO	periodical payment order

PSI	processing speed index
PTA	post-traumatic amnesia
PTB	patellar tendon-bearing
PTSD	post traumatic stress disorder
RA	Retrograde amnesia
RCJ	Royal Courts of Justice
RPI	retail prices index
RPI	retail prices index
RSC	Rules of the Supreme Court
RSC	Rules of the Supreme Court
RTAs	road traffic accidents
RTM	round table meeting
SACH	solid ankle cushion heel
SCI	spinal cord injury
SIGAM	special interest group in amputee medicine
SS(RB)A 1997	Social Security (Recovery of Benefits) Act 1997
TBI	traumatic brain injury
TICCS	The Injury Care Clinics
TMR	targeted muscle reinnervation
VAI	ventilator assisted individuals
VCI	verbal comprehension index
VIQ	verbal IQ
WMI	working memory index
WTC	working tax credit

INTRODUCTION

Once again we have chosen to avoid the lawyers' normal desire to define and categorise when it has come to the subject matter of this book. We have not offered a definitive definition of catastrophic injuries. What we are dealing with in this book are the cases of serious injury that will warrant large awards of compensation, where a claimant's life has been changed for ever. In many personal injury claims the award compensates a claimant for a period of injury and disability until they are able to make a full, or substantial, recovery and return to life as it was before with no, or no major life changing, disability. In the sorts of cases we are dealing with here that is not the case. We are considering here claimants whose lives will never return to anything like the normality that they knew before their injury, and where the award they receive will condition to a large extent the quality of life that they and their families have until death.

Even though some individual awards of damages for catastrophic injury are now exceeding £20 million, litigation of this kind is not immune from the current changes in costs management (see Chapter 4). For substantial claims of this sort, however, it will still be proportionate to spend time and money preparing cases properly. We look forward to encouraging the courts to share this view in order to ensure that claims of this sort are considered fully and properly, and that the principle of full compensation is not eroded.

The courts remain active in this area and this edition considers a number of recent decisions, including the seminal judgment on damages of Mrs Justice Swift in *Whiten v St George's Healthcare* and the Court of Appeal's views on the impact of cost budgeting rules in *Mitchell v News Group*.

We have avoided discussions in terms of people's lives being ruined as we remain constantly humbled by the stoicism of clients who face disability with enormous bravery, and display such positive outlooks that our own modest grumbles with life are put into the shade. What we have learned from, and with, those clients we have sought to share with you in this book.

We have not attempted to cover the whole of the law of personal injuries in this book. We have sought to emphasise the particular aspects of personal injury litigation that relate to catastrophic injury claims. The book proceeds from dealing with the immediate aftermath of a client's traumatic experience and the impact on their family through the processes of gathering evidence, both lay and expert, and assembling and valuing a claim to presenting it in court or for settlement and dealing with the award of damages. We are very grateful for the updated contributions from leading medical experts in their fields on the specific areas of Care and Case Management, Traumatic Brain Injury, Spinal Cord Injury, Psychiatric Injury, and Prosthetic Rehabilitation for amputees. We are also pleased to welcome new contributions to this edition in the fields of Birth Brain Injury, Adult Neuro-Radiology and Neuro-Rehabilitation.

For those who want to see the whole process from beginning to end the book can be read straight through, but for most readers we appreciate that it will be a book for reference and for dealing with particular queries. Thus we have designed the book so that for each topic on which the reader seeks advice they will find a relevant passage supported by reference to the law and practice in that area.

Once again, a large number of people have made this work possible. We are grateful to them all, including the named contributors. We would also like to thank Natasha Kirk of Russell-Cooke Solicitors and Cheryl Prophett for their assistance. Sadly, one of our former contributors, Peter Andrews QC, was unable to assist with this edition, but we thank him for his contributions in the past. We welcome Jeremy Ford and Lucy Wilton to the panel of legal contributors. You will find short biographies for the principal contributors in the Appendix.

We have endeavoured to state the law as at 1 December 2013.

Grahame Aldous QC

9 Gough Square
London EC4A 3DG

CHAPTER 1

FIRST STAGES

1.1   INTRODUCTION

In a catastrophic injury claim the working relationship between the client and their family and the lead solicitor with conduct of the claim will be a complex and lengthy one. A lot of information will have to be exchanged and complex levels of mutual trust will need to be established. In this chapter we consider the first stages of taking on a catastrophic injury claim.

A catastrophic injury not only brings about a pause in the claimant's life activities, but changes them forever and they will need to come to terms with the loss of their previous life and the new reality that they face for the future. The exact extent of this change is likely to be still unclear at the time when a solicitor is first instructed to bring a claim. As a result the solicitor will not only be a legal adviser, but also a companion on a voyage of discovery of a new life that will bring highs and lows. In cases of serious head injury it is rarely sensible to attempt a final prognosis until at least two years post-injury and in that time the efforts made at rehabilitation can produce profound improvements, but also profound despair as realisation dawns on the extent of permanent changes.

The impact of such changes affects more than just the injured client. The family will often feel that they have lost a loved one and found a stranger who they barely recognise. This sense of bereavement and rediscovery can be painful and they will need support too if the claimant is to get the care and support they need. Further, in the case of a child who has suffered catastrophic injuries, this can have a profound and negative effect upon the family as a whole and in particular on the relationship between the child's mother and father. Particular stress points can be anticipated. For example, a discharge home from hospital can produce feelings of elation, which can then descend into depression as the reality of the change wrought by the injuries becomes apparent in the home setting and under the stresses of daily home life. A legal adviser can become a single constant in a sea of changing carers and emotions helping clients through the highs and lows.

Any legal adviser dealing with a catastrophic injury claim needs to be alive to the emotional stresses that are involved in this process and to factor them into their dealing with the claim. Ultimately the litigation process results in a financial award. The process of dealing with catastrophic injury claims involves more than money and that needs to be recognised without forgetting the limitations on what litigation can achieve. Very often the family may demand greater justice; expressing a desire to ensure the prosecution of those involved or that steps be taken to prevent others suffering in the same way.

These issues need to be addressed in order that the claimant and their family can move on, but again they should not be allowed to distract from an effective claim for adequate compensation. A defendant who has been hounded in the press or the criminal courts may not respond as positively as one might wish when asked in a settlement meeting to take a reasonable approach to an offer. As ever, there is a balance to be found.

Without establishing liability there will be no award of damages and so any practitioner must first of all focus upon the issue of liability before dealing with issues regarding quantum. It would be inappropriate, and ill-judged, for a practitioner to undertake significant work in relation to quantum of a claim before supportive evidence regarding liability, or an admission of liability, is obtained. When considering breach of duty, however, it is important to consider at the same time whether, or to what extent, the loss and injury was caused by any breach of duty that may be established before incurring large costs on breach of duty evidence.

At the first meeting the claimant, or the claimant's family, will have a large number of questions including how much compensation is likely to be paid; when is the compensation likely to be received; how involved in the litigation do they need to be; will there be a cost involved in recovering the compensation and if so, how much will that cost be? However, judges repeatedly warn that 'the assessment of damages is not, and never can be, an exact science. There are too many imponderables'.[1]

The difficulty in assessing fair and proper compensation accurately is underlined by the comment of Lord Scarman in *Lim Poh Choo v Camden & Islington Area Health Authority*:[2]

> 'There is only one certainty; the future will prove the award to be either too high or too low.'

The introduction of periodical payments has gone some way to allay the fears expressed by Lord Scarman but the management of compensation monies must be based upon the premise that adequate compensation has been recovered which will provide for the victims needs for the remainder of his or her life. In addition, the introduction of provisional payments does, in certain cases, provide an opportunity for a claim for damages to be reopened at a subsequent date, if a particular supervening event occurs, and for additional compensation to be paid.

---

[1]   *Hunt v Severs* [1994] 2 AC 350 at 365, [1994] PIQR Q60 at Q71, per Lord Bridge.
[2]   [1980] AC 174 at 188, [1979] 2 All ER 910 at 914, HL.

For many people whose lives have been irrevocably changed by a traumatic event the idea of embarking on the strange, stressful process of litigation, dealing with lawyers for the first time in their lives, can all seem too much to contemplate. They will require patient explanation and comforting about what is involved and what can be achieved without raising undue excessive expectations that will lead to later disillusionment.

Thus, the catastrophic injury practitioner is expected to accomplish a difficult mission. The litigation will involve the demanding task of assembling the complex factual and expert evidence which is required for a substantial award, against a background of limited financial resources. Also relevant is the tension between the desire of the victim, or victim's family, to see an end to the litigation and the need to ensure that the claim is adequately, professionally and appropriately investigated so that all heads of claim are properly quantified. This is a time-consuming process.

At any stage in this process, a defendant is able to make a formal, 'Part 36', offer to settle, thereby threatening the claimant with an adverse costs order. The claimant can now deploy the same tactic against the defendant by making an offer to settle. Pursuant to CPR, r 36.14(1)(b) and (3), where a claimant obtains a judgment against a defendant which is at least as advantageous as an offer made by the claimant under Part 36, the court will (unless it considers it unjust to do so) order that the claimant is entitled to:

- interest on the whole or part of any sum of money (excluding interest) awarded at a rate not exceeding 10% above base rate for some or all of the period starting with the date on which the 'relevant period' expires;
- costs on the indemnity basis from the date on which the relevant period expired;
- interest on those costs at a rate not exceeding 10% above base rate; and
- an additional amount, which shall not exceed £75,000, calculated by applying the prescribed percentage set out below to an amount which is:
  - up to £500,000 – 10% of the amount awarded; or
  - above £500,000 and up to £1,000,000 – 10% of the first £500,000 and 5% of any amount above that figure.

The practitioner must also be wary of delay which can be construed as 'unnecessary' in order to avoid adverse judicial comment at trial and the risk of a penalty by way of reduced interest if it is considered by the judge that the action has not been brought to trial within a reasonable period of time. In such circumstances the cautious practitioner should consider proceeding by way of a split trial in circumstances where liability is still in dispute and also consider the advantages to be gained by use of interim payments.

What is clear is that, whether the claim is successful or not and whether adequate compensation is recovered, this will determine the way in which the injured person lives the remainder of his or her life. In an ideal judicial system there should be a significant degree of predictable certainty about the sum of money which the claimant would be likely to recover, should the action proceed to trial. However, it is accepted that predictability is never entirely attainable.

The assessment of damages for pain, suffering and loss of amenity has been to a significant extent regularised and made more predictable by the Judicial College Guidelines (formerly the Judicial Studies Board Guidelines). However, within the analysis and assessment of various heads of claim, which is dominated by uncertain chances and contingencies of an unknown nature, the opportunities for disagreement between the claimant and the defendant on the proper quantum of damages for a particular injury are obvious and real.

That potential for disagreement is magnified in catastrophic injury claims. In these cases there are a multiplicity of separate heads of damage, all of which are capable of creating discrete disputes and the likelihood of disagreement increases in such claims since there are large sums at stake.

In the past there was arguably critical judicial comment as the level of compensation claims increased. Thus, in *Lim Poh Choo v Camden & Islington Area Health Authority*[3] Lord Denning said:

> 'The Judge awarded nearly £250,000.00. It is a staggering figure.'

In the intervening years the defendants have more and more frequently faced claims well in excess of £1m and we have become accustomed to settlements and awards in multimillions of pounds.

Thus, the catastrophic injury claim is no longer the exceptional case that it once was. Personal injury practitioners must now expect regularly to confront the challenge which is posed by a claim which involves injuries of the utmost severity. What is vital is that the practitioner recognises that such claims not only involve additional effort and commitment, but they give rise to unique features which the practitioner must bear in mind at all times so as to avoid adding to the claimant's woes by providing inadequate service.

The focus of this chapter is upon the issues which need to be considered and addressed when first embarking upon a claim for catastrophic injuries and, first of all, upon the initial contact between the solicitor/practitioner and the victim and/or the victim's family. Of all meetings it could properly be argued that this is the most crucial since it will not only be a fact-gathering exercise but, perhaps more importantly, will, hopefully, create a bond of trust and confidence.

In addition, it is crucial that, at the earliest opportunity, a number of vital areas of discussion are dealt with which have to be considered and, if necessary, actioned following that initial meeting.

---

[3]   [1978] 3 WLR 895; [1979] 1 All ER 332, CA.

Whilst the following list is not exhaustive (it never can be since each case involving catastrophic injuries is different) the preliminary matters to be covered with the prospective client are likely to include the following:

- the basis on which liability may be established;
- the identity of the potential defendants and the depth of their pockets, either in terms of assets or insurance;
- issues of jurisdiction for any potential claims;
- the possible funding methods available to cover the client's legal costs, including whether they might have the benefit of legal expenses cover, trade union or other employers' assistance or legal aid and, if not, what other options may be available;
- the capacity of the claimant and whether this needs to be addressed separately by the commissioning of expert evidence;
- limitation and whether the relevant limitation date will influence the likely timeline and timescale for the litigation process, particularly up to commencement of proceedings;
- funding facilities which can enable the claim to be driven forward;
- the information to prepare the preliminary master statement of the claimant, as well as, if appropriate, statements of family members, friends and/or work colleagues;
- the details of the claimant's injuries and the nature of medical evidence, specifically a lead medical report needed to particularise the nature and extent of those injuries;
- discussion of the claimant's current care needs and what he or she is receiving. To include whether the services of a case manager are required and, if so, to undertake what activities. Also to consider the claimant's accommodation requirements in the light of his or her disabilities;
- whether the claimant would benefit from any form of rehabilitation and whether the Rehabilitation Code should be implemented;
- whether any application should be made for assistance, including assessment, by any other agency such as local authority, social services, the Department for Work and Pensions, the NHS etc;
- what benefits are being paid and whether the client should be referred for advice about applying for additional benefits;
- whether an early application for an interim payment should be made once defendants are notified of the claim, so as to provide financial funds for necessary outlays on behalf of the claimant;
- whether there are any other services that could, and should, be applied for (e.g. from any charitable organisation);
- setting up a structure for receipt of information and documents to enable a draft preliminary schedule of losses to be prepared prior to issue of proceedings.

The aim is to develop further, and in more detail, the various items of agenda on this checklist during the remainder of this chapter.

1.2   THE ROLE OF THE SOLICITOR/PRACTITIONER

Solicitors who have never dealt with catastrophic injury cases may never have ventured very far into their client's more personal affairs. They may perhaps have advised the client to consider setting up a form of trust, for example to protect their eligibility for means-tested benefits, or they may have suggested a review of the client's estate planning (although obviously such matters should be referred to other specialist solicitors).

However, the role of the practitioner who acts for a claimant in a catastrophic injury case will be different from that which may be adopted in other, standard, personal injury actions.

The solicitor may not merely be focusing upon the claim itself (although this will, of course, remain their primary concern). They may also be providing assistance and support to the injured person and their family in a number of ways and these activities will not normally be of concern in cases involving minor or moderate injuries.

The very nature of the claim predicates a client who will have suffered an accident or event leading to injuries of the utmost severity, which will have destroyed his or her ability to lead an independent existence and which have caused not only great suffering but also, in all likelihood, signalled the end, or a major curtailment, of employment. The injured claimant will also commonly have experienced significant psychological shock as a result of the accident, its aftermath and its consequences. The family of the claimant will have suffered from the event and its aftermath as well.

Whilst the courage and inner strength of the claimant and the family may become apparent, the practitioner must anticipate that his or her perceived role will be more than just a provider of legal advice. Whilst the practitioner must not be seduced into acting as some form of untrained social worker or trauma counsellor, they must deal with the claimant and the claimant's family in a sympathetic, understanding manner. They must also, however, balance an emotional connection to the claimant and the claimant's family with the need to provide objective advice on difficult matters. They must provide clear and dispassionate views on issues regarding the quantification of the claim, such as recoverability of outlays and expenses, the need to mitigate losses, duplication or overlap of claims, etc.

What is required is a sympathetic and caring approach to the claimant, balanced with the need to provide an efficient and objective preparation of a claim to achieve the ultimate aim of fair and adequate compensation.

A feature of these claims is their longevity. Such claims routinely take several years to complete, often for entirely appropriate reasons. The practitioner will often need to provide encouragement and support, not only to the claimant but also to members of the family, especially in those cases where delays are inevitable; for example when the claimant is undergoing a period of rehabilitation, or where time has to be allowed to pass so as to enable a medical expert to reach a position where a reliable and confident medical prognosis can be provided.

The need for encouragement is more pronounced in those cases where members of the family are providing the claimant with the required care and other means of support, including financial support.

Thus a relationship of mutual trust should be fostered and every reasonable effort must be made in order to ensure that such trust is not betrayed. The victim of catastrophic injuries should not have to suffer the emotional disappointment and distress of seeing his or her claim prejudiced by inept management or handling. If the practitioner feels unable to provide the necessary commitment or generally does not have the necessary expertise, then the victim would be better represented by one who can provide that commitment and who possesses the necessary expertise.

It is important for solicitors to understand the limits of their own abilities. Unfortunately it is by no means uncommon for a claim arising from catastrophic injuries to be commenced by a seemingly competent solicitor and then to be pursued part way before either the practitioner himself or the claimant realises that the practitioner is out of his depth. There is then a parting of the ways. The claimant then, hopefully, instructs an experienced catastrophic injury practitioner, but damage may already have been done.

It may be that inappropriate experts (and inappropriate counsel) have been instructed. It may be that inadequate or damaging reports have been disclosed to the defendants; the claim strategy misdirected or subject to unnecessary and unacceptable delay and/or incurring of costs and using up limited funding. It may be that negotiations have opened with the other party at a gross undervaluation of the claim. A second practitioner taking such a claim over, no matter how experienced, will have real difficulty in hauling such a case back on to the right track.

The sympathetic practitioner will need to anticipate the claimant's difficulties and provide appropriate help. A quadriplegic claimant, for example, will have the very greatest difficulty in writing or using a keyboard. A simple and reliable line of communication must be set up and maintained. A key requirement is that the claimant has a direct line of communication to the practitioner by email. The claimant should be kept informed of all the significant stages of progress in the case or, if the victim has suffered disabling brain damage, the family must be given the appropriate progress reports. Of course if the action is being conducted in the name of a litigation friend, by reason of the claimant's disability (due either to minority of age or to mental incapacity), then they should be kept informed of progress.

The practitioner must provide assistance and support to the injured person and their family in a number of ways that are ancillary to the formulation of the claim itself. Those activities could potentially involve:

- contact with the local social services agency in order to check the extent of care and other therapy support and, where appropriate, to procure or increase such input;
- examination of the adequacy of accommodation and consideration of whether adaptations should be sought through the local authority;
- consideration of whether help from any other source should be sought, such as a charity or support network;
- analysis as to whether there is a need for an interim payment and if so, how much and how this would be used;
- review of the benefits being received (or not) so as to ensure that all appropriate help through the social security scheme is made available;
- consideration of whether any legal mechanisms can be used in order to protect or improve the injured person's financial position, for example by setting up a personal injury trust.

The whole area of receipt of benefits is complex and some might say convoluted, see Chapter 19. Specialist welfare benefit advice may be required to assist the claimant and/or the claimant's family in receiving all appropriate social security benefits.

The practitioner should also explain to the victim or the claimant's family the Compensation Recovery Unit recoupment provisions at an early stage so that they are aware that a deduction will be made at the stage of settlement of the claim in order to provide recoupment to the Department for Work and Pensions (DWP).

Furthermore, at an initial stage the victim may be assisted by a programme of psychological counselling. The legal practitioner should not adopt the role of an amateur counsellor but may probably suggest that the victim seeks appropriate and skilled help regarding psychological counselling through his or her general practitioner.

Bearing in mind the longevity of such claims, it is not at all surprising for the practitioner to find that the claimant and the claimant's family suffer from low morale during the course of the pursuit of the claim to trial. The reactive depression may first be engendered by the traumatic effect of the injuries and their aftermath, and then exacerbated by the nature of the legal process which follows, including delay which may arise quite properly.

The litigation of catastrophic injuries cannot always be swift if adequate compensation is to be secured, but inappropriate or unnecessary delay is erosive of even the bravest of victim's determination. Moreover, a protracted process can become a campaign of attrition between the opposing sides of the litigation. One may find the victim and member of the family at a low ebb because the initial legal service provided was inadequate. Against this background a strategy for maintaining client confidence is essential in claims of catastrophic injuries.

The strategy of care to be provided by the practitioner will include:
- the provision of clear and authoritative advice on the broad principles of quantum assessment at an early stage, including perhaps a warning that, in catastrophic injury compensation claims, the sky is not the limit;
- the formulation, with the client, of the long-term plan of action which will be coupled with a proposed timetable;
- an explanation of the role of the expert witnesses and that, although there may seem to be a never-ending procession of appointments with a host of experts, the process is a vital and necessary part of the litigation to enable the relevant heads of claim to be analysed, assessed and costed. Further, it is important to emphasise the primary duty of an expert is not to the claimant who instructs him/her but to the court and so the expert is expected to provide input entirely independently of any sympathy that he or she may feel for the claimant;
- an explanation of the proposed role of counsel in the case and the intention to work with counsel as a team, utilising their expert input from an early stage;
- provision of regular progress reports as the various milestone stages in the case are reached;
- the delivery of key documents for consideration and, if appropriate, approval such as medical reports, quantum reports, schedule of losses, counsel's advices, particulars of claim and the disclosed evidence from the other side.

With the conscientious implementation and maintenance of such a programme, the client is likely to feel both confident in the litigation progress and confident in the competence of his or her instructed solicitor.

In addition to achieving and maintaining successful client care, the practitioner must institute a timetabled management structure in order to ensure the regular and constant progress of the litigation towards the goal of a contested quantum trial. In particular, the action should be pursued with the philosophy that 'the case will go to trial'. Preparing a case in the hope that it will settle is not sufficient preparation at all. It is likely to lead to inadequate preparation. Of course a claim may settle at a fair and proper figure but this will only be achieved if the other side is persuaded of the claimant's preparedness for a fight and that the claimant's practitioner makes it clear to the other side that he is preparing the case on the basis that it will proceed to a trial.

Standard procedures such as information sheets, client questionnaires and diary reminders continue to have their place in all claims but in complex catastrophic injury cases of high value the practitioner will normally find that the management of the claim and the quantification exercise cannot be managed by means of a standardised case management system. Regular personal input is essential. Key requirements for an efficient system of progression may include:

- access to a comprehensive and updated database of source organisations, medical experts, non-medical experts and counsel;

- a strategic plan and detailed timetable of the milestones for the intended progress of the case with provision for regular, personal reviews as to the actual progress made;

- a diary (normally computerised) which will provide timely warnings for primary time-limits, the intended milestones, compliance with court orders and reminders for the receipt of reports and return of papers from various sources including counsel and instructed experts;

- a flexibility to react as developments occur;

- a readiness to seek help as and when required from counsel and the instructed experts;

- a genuine commitment in order to ensure that the case is pursued diligently to trial within an appropriate timescale;

- an acceptance of the need to adopt a mutually supportive team approach, with the practitioner understanding that a central role to ensure success is the appropriate management of the evidence, selection of suitable counsel and members of the team and coordination of the formulated strategy;

- a recognition of the need, not only to provide the necessary expertise as a practitioner and to manage the team, but also to display the necessary perseverance to bring such a claim from inception to conclusion.

Thus the solicitor/practitioner may find themselves undertaking a different (and expanded) role to that which they are used to. The solicitor should not lose sight of his obligation to act only within the ambit of his own expertise. However, it is certain that in catastrophic injury cases the solicitor's functions will be far wider and more all-encompassing than would normally be the case.

1.3 CONTACT WITH CLAIMANT AND THEIR FAMILY

1.3.1 Impact of injuries

The effect of catastrophic injuries will, of course, primarily impact upon the victim. However, the award of damages for pain, suffering and loss of amenity for that victim will not have the centre stage as it often does in claims involving minor or modest injuries. This head of the damages is unlikely to form the major element of the final award.

Catastrophic injury claims are routinely those where the valuation is well in excess of £1m. Where catastrophic injuries are suffered, the award of damages for pain, suffering and loss of amenity is unlikely to exceed £257,750 (this figure may need to be revised upwards) (the upper end of the bracket set out for 'very severe brain damage' and quadriplegia in the Judicial College Guidelines).[4] The spotlight will be on the proper and adequate quantification of the claim for the claimant's rehabilitation needs and routinely the largest claim, in financial terms, is for care.

The uniqueness of catastrophic injury claims is apparent from the outset, since the practitioner should meet their client and where relevant, the client's family, and invariably will have many meetings before the conclusion of the case. In some instances, personal injury claims are dealt with from inception to conclusion without the practitioner meeting his client. Instead they deal with the client through systems involving checklists, case management frameworks and communication by way of letter, email and the occasional telephone call. Catastrophic injury claims cannot be managed by the normal personal injury claims management systems that practitioners often use for routine claims where injuries are minor or moderate.

In cases involving catastrophic injury the initial meeting will very often take place not at the practitioner's office, but at the injured person's home, or occasionally elsewhere, such as in hospital or residential rehabilitation centre. It is essential that in such cases the practitioner sees and examines at the outset the environment in which the injured person lives, the make-up of and dynamics of the family, the support that is available and the appropriateness and security of the area where the home is based.

The practitioner must investigate and identify not only the devastating effect upon the injured person but also the impact that the injuries have upon the family and others who are close to the victim. That impact could be felt financially, emotionally and even, occasionally, culturally.

The health of a wife who has provided continuous care over a prolonged period without respite will need to be investigated. She may be suffering from concealed care fatigue and, although professing to be ready, willing and able to provide 24-hour care in the future, in reality will be unable to cope with the demands required of her catastrophically injured husband. A carefully planned and commercially provided care regime will enable the spouse to reclaim part of her own life and also spend more quality time with her husband, the victim.

Furthermore, a spouse may experience progressive back pain as a result of transferring his or her partner into and out of a wheelchair, but will often be reluctant to admit that there is a possible medical problem. Thus the practitioner will have to obtain information from various members of the

---

4   Judicial College Guidelines for the Assessment of General Damages in Personal Injury Cases (Oxford University Press, 11th edn, 2012).

injured person's family which could impact directly upon the formulation of the claim including, in particular, the care claim.

The injured person's family and friends can also provide a sense as to how the victim used to be prior to the index event. They can also provide insight into what the injured person's future might have held, for example in the area of employment/career, had the index event not occurred.

Whilst appropriate experts provide valuable input on such issues, the courts are often more impressed by the evidence of members of the injured person's family and friends. As well as family members, work colleagues and friends may be able to testify in a direct and credible way as to the injured person's achievements and progress up to the time of the index event. Clearly such witnesses will also need to provide details of any services that they have provided or are providing to the injured person, particularly in the area of gratuitous care.

Often the claimant (contrary to popular belief) will try to mask the full extent of his or her injuries and the consequential requirement for support. However, this should be addressed in the evidence of those close to the victim. Another difficulty, whilst not specific to those suffering catastrophic injuries or their families, is the emotional reaction to what has occurred. That emotional reaction can have a cataclysmic consequence upon the claimant and his or her family and friends.

Of course in most, if not all, cases involving personal injuries, the solicitor will be faced with their client's anger, or distress, regarding their injuries and how those injuries came about. It is not uncommon for a client to express a strong desire to hold someone, or some agency, to account and to 'have their day in court' in order to do so.

At the outset of the case, when the practitioner has his first meeting with the client and when the long-term effects of the injuries may be unclear, this may perhaps be more important to the victim than obtaining monetary compensation for the injuries suffered.

However, the instances in which clients will actually achieve any public condemnation of what has occurred, or even an apology, will be few and far between and currently tend be limited to claims involving allegations of clinical negligence, or where a mediation has allowed a settlement that looks outside of the litigation process.

Whilst, in cases involving catastrophic injuries, the emotional impact of the case may well be heightened for the client and the family, the paramount consideration in the practitioner's mind must be the practical and financial needs arising from those injuries. Hence there is a risk that the potential gulf between the client's goals in the litigation and those of the solicitor can become wider in cases involving catastrophic injuries.

A key consideration at the first point of contact will therefore be to explain the principle of compensation to the client and, if applicable, their family. The explanation should be frank about the limits of what can be achieved so as not to set up unrealistic expectations. The need for evidence has to be explained. Claimants sometimes cannot understand that they have to prove their claim as it seems so obvious to them. They sometimes feel that the need for them to prove their claim means that it is they, rather than the defendant, who is on trial. They should be encouraged, from the very early stages, to keep a record of what expenses have been and are being incurred as a result of the alleged negligence and also, perhaps, to provide a written account of how they feel the injuries have affected their lives.

Although this might change over time, for better or worse, it is important that the solicitor and, ultimately, the court, be informed about the impact that the injuries have had from the outset. Further, taking a statement of this kind at this stage may help the client or their families to feel engaged with the litigation process and understand that their own personal perspective is of importance.

The practitioner will give advice, as best they can with limited information, as to the likely award of damages for pain, suffering and loss of amenity, emphasising that this is likely to form a relatively minor part of any final settlement or award. Thus a client should be advised from the outset that, if their claim is successful, their future needs will largely be determined by the commissioning of expert evidence.

1.3.2 First instructions/evidence

1.3.2.1 *Statement evidence of and on behalf of claimant*

The point of departure for a catastrophic injuries compensation claim is often an initial statement of evidence from the potential claimant. Where the client has suffered severe brain damage and he or she cannot provide sensible information in any logical way, then statements of evidence will have to be obtained from the spouse, the parents, members of the family, close friends or even work colleagues. The importance of such statement evidence from those other than the victim him or herself has already been stated above and will normally be useful in any event.

However, once the practitioner finds that the claimant cannot give a coherent statement of evidence, or there are concerns about the ability of the claimant to provide instructions, understand advice, take informed decisions or manage their own affairs the question of capacity should be addressed at once and the issue should if possible be resolved prior to the issue of proceedings.

Where the claimant has capacity and is able to give a coherent statement of evidence, that statement should have regard to the particular circumstances of the claimant's pre-accident history and post-accident lifestyle and each statement will be unique but will probably be structured in order to include all or some of the following information:

- details of past history including family and marital background, education, qualifications, employment record and career path, sports, pastimes, leisure pursuits and social activities;

- pre-accident career intentions and aspirations (or educational and career aspirations in the case of a younger claimant);

- pre-accident domestic circumstances and family plans, for example, intentions in respect of children and family arrangements;

- the material accident and the injuries suffered, the post-accident treatment, operations and process of rehabilitation (a subjective account by the claimant of the pain and suffering can provide a very useful cross-check with the medical reports which are to be obtained in due course);

- a concise description of the residual, physical and any psychological disabilities and how they affect the claimant's everyday activities. The medical evidence will provide detailed accounts concerning the consequences of the injuries but, again, the claimant's subjective account will provide a useful cross-check For example, the medical report may not address the psychological or emotional consequences of impaired sexual activity;

- the extent and duration of the care, assistance and supervision which has been provided, who has provided it and how long during the day and any care provided at night;

- what effect, if any, the traumatic event and its consequences have had upon the spouse, family and friends of the injured person;

- the consequences of the injuries upon the ability to undertake gainful employment and upon the claimant's pre-accident employment potential;

- details of all past expenses incurred by the injured person, the family and close friends; this will include help in the home and in the garden, DIY maintenance and decorating. Any gratuitous assistance should also be recorded together with details of any expenditure, either formal or informal, for such services;

- the claimant's proposals for future medical treatment including the expected aims and objectives of such treatment and how it is anticipated these will be achieved;

- the claimant's intentions and plans for future care, aids and equipment, transport and accommodation, setting out in detail where he or she would wish to live if money were available, what kind of care plan he or she would envisage and details of input the claimant would adopt if monies were available to provide for such services;

- details of social security benefits which have been or are being received together with details of any assistance provided by the local social services department of the local authority (to include any therapy/care input, adaptations to the home, etc); any aids and equipment provided or loaned without charge from any source including relevant treating hospital, charity, etc; provision of any visiting nursing care and any charitable assistance received;

- a self-assessment of the claimant's morale and any other, perhaps less obvious, consequences affecting either the claimant or the claimant's immediate family.

In the case of a claimant who is not sentient and is therefore unable to provide the necessary information directly, a statement (or statements) will be required from the spouse and/or from other members of the family. One person alone may not be able to provide a comprehensive picture, but the same topics as suggested above should be considered.

As already stated, it will be necessary to obtain additional statements from family, friends and where appropriate, work colleagues. Again, the statements will be tailored to the individual circumstances of the victim. They will supplement and corroborate the evidence of pre-accident and post-accident lifestyle. They will provide a further perspective as to the impact of the injuries upon the victim as well as the victim's family and friends and the impact upon their career plans and intentions.

Again, whilst each case will generate individual statements, it is suggested that such statements may include the following matters:

- the career and employment history of the witness, with information as to past and current net earnings;

- where appropriate, details of the contact the witness had with the claimant prior to the accident, his perspective of the claimant's character, activities and aspirations;

- details of the provision of any gratuitous care, identifying what form it has taken, over what period of time and whether provided during the day and/or at night, including a careful estimate of the actual time expended;

- the witness's perspective on care and accommodation requirements and plans for the future in the light of the claimant's disabilities and needs, both in the short and long term. This is a subject which usually requires the most sensitive handling. A spouse or a parent may wish to provide actual hands-on care for as long as she or he is physically able to do so, but the practitioner should be alive to the likely onset of care fatigue in the short term and the physical incapacity due to age or infirmity in the longer term. The experienced nursing or care expert, to be subsequently instructed on behalf of the claimant, will take these potential factors into account and, where appropriate, recommend a phased regime for the future in any event;

- whether the family member suffers from any existing disability which now inhibits, or will in the future prejudice, the ability to provide care or assistance. This may include whether any disability or injury has arisen already as a result of providing assistance for the claimant, such as a bad back from lifting an injured claimant;

- details of any relevant expenses and purchases incurred and losses suffered since the accident by the witness which have arisen as a result of the claimant's injuries;

- an overview from the witness's perspective of any anticipated problems relating to care, accommodation, mobility, transport, therapy aids and equipment and medical treatment;

- a lay person's view as to whether, and if so to what extent, the claimant's character has changed since the index event.

The initial statements of both claimant and witnesses should be regarded as first drafts of the statements which will later be exchanged pursuant to Part 32 of the Civil Procedure Rules (CPR). For further guidance on the use of witness statements in proceedings see Chapter 6.

The witness statements to be served must:

(a)   be intended for use at the trial itself; and

(b)   relate to issues of fact to be addressed by that witness at trial.

The statement must eventually contain all the relevant matters which will need to be covered at trial because, without leave of the court or the consent of the other parties, no new evidence can be led during examination in chief of the witness (save for new matters which have arisen since service).

Statements which are to be served in accordance with the CPR must:

(a)   be dated and signed by the intended witness (unless the witness is unable to read or sign the document, in which case the statement must contain a certificate made by an authorised person certifying that the document and statement of truth have been read to and understood by the person signing it and that that person signed/made his mark in the presence of the authorised person) and include a declaration by him or her that the contents of the statement are true to the best of his or her knowledge and belief; and

(b)   sufficiently identify any documents referred to therein.

The witness statement should be expressed in the first person and should state:

(a)   the full name of the witness;

(b)   his or her place of residence, or if making the statement in a professional, business or other occupational capacity, the address at which he or she works, the position which he or she holds and the name of his or her firm or employer;

(c)   his or her occupation, or if he or she has none, his or her description; and

(d)   the fact, if it be the case, that the witness is a party to proceedings, or is the employee of such a party.

The statement should represent the evidence in chief of the witness in his or her own language. In terms of format, the statement should follow the chronological sequence of the material events and be divided into numbered paragraphs, double-spaced, on one side of the paper only.

The statement served in accordance with Part 32 of the CPR will be included in the court bundle which is to be lodged with the court shortly before trial.

The witness statements of the claimant and other witnesses are likely to progress through two or more drafts. A party should identify those witnesses whose statements it is proposed will be relied upon in the directions questionnaire, as well as a summary of the issues they will address.[5]

The first draft may include both relevant and irrelevant matters. The latter may include areas of weakness, doubts about the prospects of success in the litigation, anticipation of cross-examination and inadmissible evidence.

The final draft, from which the irrelevant material has been excised, will be in a form which complies with the CPR and be capable of exchange.

There is, however, no requirement that the party must in the witness statement disclose all the admissible evidence which is known to him; and even less that he should disclose all available items of information, knowledge and belief which possibly concern the material topics of litigation.

The statements for exchange need only include the evidence which the party desires to adduce at trial. There is no necessity to reveal to the other side at exchange potentially damaging evidence which would normally be discovered by the process of cross-examination. Anything which a party does not wish to disclose may be withheld, though of course the court must not be misled. It may, however, be better to deal with any obvious weaknesses or potential problems in the witness statement as evidence in chief rather than expose the claimant to cross-examination on the points unaided by a prior opportunity to provide a coherent account.

The initial statement should be edited into a form which complies with the CPR and which expresses the anticipated evidence in chief of the witness. This draft should be approved by the witness and signed by him or her. The non-exchanged material may conveniently form a privileged supplemental statement, which need not be signed.

The preparation of the initial statement in a formal manner has a number of advantages. It is far easier to undertake the task of obtaining a full and comprehensive statement at an early stage rather than wait until the latter stages of the litigation when memories will have become dimmed with the passage of time. The statement can be updated on a regular basis to the moment of exchange. Moreover, the signed statement will, subject to the CPR and the Civil Evidence Act 1995, be directly admissible as evidence in the event that the witness dies or becomes incapable of being traced prior to trial.

---

[5]   CPR, PD 26 2.2(3).

In some cases it can be of assistance to serve a series of witness statements that will each have the benefit of being more contemporaneous with the events described, and which may show the progress of a condition, or lack of it. However, care should be taken to ensure that the claimant has permission to rely on more than one witness statement.

The court may exercise control over statements by:

- identifying or limiting the issues to which factual evidence may be directed;
- identifying the witnesses who may be called or whose evidence may be read;
- limiting the length or format of witness statements.[6]

1.3.2.2   Documentary evidence

At the outset the practitioner should gather together all relevant documents that the claimant or his or her family have available. These will include:

- documents in support of any expenses incurred including travel expenses and outlays;
- utility bills for gas, electricity and similar expenses for a period of a year or so before the index event and for the period after the claimant has returned home;
- similarly, household accounts for telephone expenditure;
- any medical records that the claimant or his or her family have in their possession, including from the treating hospital, rehabilitation unit, therapy clinics, etc;
- any documents from the local authority regarding the provision of any support (e.g. adaptations, care, therapy, etc);
- any documents received from the social security office providing details of benefits paid.

Whilst it is not necessary for all expenses to be validated by documentary evidence, it is useful to have a voucher or receipt to confirm any significant outlay that has been incurred.

The victim or his or her family should also be asked to keep a careful record of expenses incurred in the future, with details to be sent to the solicitor/practitioner on a regular basis together with documents in support. The documents which support the claim for past expenses and losses will, of course, be retained and listed for the purposes of subsequent disclosure.

The information contained in the household accounts will be of assistance in the task of assessing the *additional* household costs which are attributable to the consequences of the injuries. Many spinally-injured victims feel the cold

---

6   CPR, r 32.2(3).

much more than the able-bodied and accordingly, heating bills will be higher after the accident. In addition, those who are largely confined to their homes will spend more on heating and other household outlays than otherwise. Similarly, the telephone as a means of communication after an accident is a vital resource which commonly leads to increased bills. For additional guidance as to the preparation of documentary evidence see Chapter 6.

It is also useful at the outset to arrange for photographs of the inside and outside of the house to be taken which can provide useful insights as to the inadequacies of the accommodation, bearing in mind the nature of the claimant's injuries and the consequential need for either adaptation to the home or a move to alternative accommodation.

The practitioner will also use the opportunity at the first meeting to arrange for the claimant, or where appropriate the claimant's litigation friend, to complete and sign appropriate forms of authority which will enable the practitioner to obtain documentary records from other sources including treating hospitals, rehabilitation units, general practice, local authority, etc.

It is also useful at an early stage for the victim or the victim's family to prepare a care and attendance diary which can cover a period of some six weeks or thereabouts. It should be prepared by a close member of the family who is providing any gratuitous services such as care. The diary will be a valuable indicator of the extent and type of care that has been provided and can highlight in particular care that is provided during the night.

Subsequently the diary can be compiled for a similar two-week period on a regular basis, perhaps every nine–twelve months. It will provide a snap-shot of the family care from the lay-perspective and will assist the nursing or care expert in the preparation of the formal care report. A gallery of pre-accident and post-accident photos may help to provide literal snapshots of the effects of the accident.

The mechanism of the diary will, in addition, provide an indication of any special or unforeseen difficulties which affect the claimant and/or his or her family. The practitioner will then be alerted and able to take the appropriate action, either by way of supplementing the relevant statements or investigating the cost of remedying the problem and so including the cost in the claimant's schedule of losses.

1.4 FUNDING

This section will need amendment in the light of the latest funding changes that have been made.

The issue of funding is dealt with in more detail in Chapter 4, however, at the outset, when the solicitor/practitioner meets with the claimant and/or his or her family, it is inevitable that from the very start they will be very anxious as to how the litigation will be funded, how much it will all cost and who will pay.

It is the duty of the solicitor to discuss and advise upon the appropriate form of funding for the claim in the event that the solicitor is satisfied that the case is one that should proceed.

Further detail as to the detailed requirements (often complex, onerous and confusing!) will be provided later but, in summary, the following funding sources should be considered:

- 'before the event' (BTE) insurance;
- public funding;
- funding under a conditional fee agreement (CFA);
- funding under a damages-based agreement (DBA), though see health warnings currently attached to this form of funding, set out in Chapter 4;
- funding through a trade union membership;
- private client funding.

The practitioner will need first of all to check whether there is any policy of insurance that provides BTE insurance cover for legal expenses. He should see the policy itself and not simply take at face value any statement to the effect that 'there is a policy of insurance but legal expense cover is not included'. It should be borne in mind that the victim may be eligible under a policy of BTE insurance, even if the policy is not issued in his or her name (eg if a son is living at home and his parents have a policy of insurance on the home that provides legal expense cover for residents or if the claimant is a passenger in a vehicle which carries a policy of insurance providing BTE cover).

The practitioner should make the necessary enquiries to find out if the claimant will be eligible under the legal aid scheme to receive public funding support. However, this support has now been markedly reduced. Public funding is only available for clinical negligence cases that satisfy very limited criteria, namely neurological injuries that occur in utero, during delivery or within 8 weeks of their birth. In addition, there are further limitations: the claimant will have to satisfy the necessary financial criteria (in the current circumstances this will normally be satisfied unless, for example, a trust fund has been set up for the infant claimant) and the Legal Aid Agency (which administers the legal aid scheme) needs to be satisfied that the claim has sufficient prospects of success to justify the expenditure of public money to investigate and, if necessary, pursue the claim.

The practitioner should also make enquiries to find out if the claimant is a member of a trade union which provides legal funding or assistance for the claim in question. An enquiry should be made with the trade union as to whether they will provide indemnity cover for the claim in question, or any form of financial assistance in relation to the legal costs.

If other options are not available or are considered to be inappropriate (although practitioners should in the latter instance cover themselves by recording on the file why the other arrangements are not considered to be in the client's best interests) the solicitor can consider acting under a CFA or DBA. Before entering into such an agreement, the practitioner, or others at his practice, should undertake a risk assessment to determine if it should be offered and if so, on what terms (eg requiring the claimant to pay disbursements).

If no other funding facility is available the claimant can agree to pay the solicitor's fees for undertaking work on his or her behalf as a private client. This would obviously entail covering not only the solicitor's profit costs but also the disbursements and would additionally leave the client open to the risk of being ordered to pay some of the defendant's legal costs, in the event they fail to beat a Part 36 offer. However, it is to be hoped that if investigations into a claim were to be commenced under a private retainer that arrangement could be reviewed once initial investigations into liability were complete.

It is often the case that a trade union or BTE insurer will have their own panel of solicitors who they will want to deal with the case on behalf of the claimant. This can give rise to serious difficulties where the claimant is unhappy about using the services of a practitioner who he or she has not met. It may be that the practitioner he or she wishes to instruct has been strongly recommended to him or her as a specialist in dealing with catastrophic injury claims but the trade union or BTE insurers insist that panel solicitors must be retained if the claimant wishes to avail him or herself of the benefits of the policy.

1.5 CAPACITY

When meeting a client with catastrophic injuries for the first time, it is likely that the solicitor is going to have to form a view regarding the injured person's capacity. This exercise may appear to be relatively simple; where a client has suffered a catastrophic brain injury, one might all too readily assume that the victim cannot possibly have capacity for the purposes of conducting the litigation or indeed running their own affairs.

The issue of 'capacity' under the current law will be dealt with in more detail in Chapter 3, however, capacity is, nevertheless, an issue that has to be addressed by the practitioner at the outset and, if necessary, they should obtain expert evidence from a suitable clinician (normally a consultant psychiatrist) to provide a view as to the claimant's capacity within the context of the Mental Capacity Act 2005 (MCA).

The sensible solicitor will be cautious about drawing too quick a conclusion about capacity based upon their own, non-medical, perception of the client's medical or psychological condition. Certainly the pervading theme of the MCA is that a person should be given all possible assistance to ensure that they are able to make what decisions and perform what functions they can, rather than having the decisions made and functions performed on their behalf by a litigation friend.

As the MCA recognises, the issue of capacity is not one to be approached in a blunt or 'broad brush' manner but discretely, looking at the nature of the activities to be undertaken, the assistance that can and should be made available to the victim in relation to these and bearing in mind the presumption of capacity that the MCA proclaims.

Further, as the MCA recognises, an individual's capacity may fluctuate over a period of time and they may have capacity to deal with certain matters and make certain decisions but not others. These considerations require that capacity is kept under review as the litigation unfolds, with the commissioning of up–to-date medical input when required.

In cases where it is considered that the injured person does lack capacity, or where this is obviously the case, as with minors, the solicitor will need to discuss with the immediate family, or friends, who should act as litigation friend. Where the victim is under a disability then the action for damages can only be brought on his or her behalf by an individual acting as litigation friend. This is not an optional element of procedure but a requirement.

In many instances the choice may be simple; a child's mother or father or an adult's spouse or partner may be willing and able to take on this role. However, this decision is not one to be taken lightly and without a true understanding of the concept and responsibilities of the role of litigation friend. Where the litigation friend is also responsible for caring for the person who has the catastrophic injuries, the additional burden of fulfilling the role of litigation friend can be too much to cope with.

This can prove problematic for the solicitor running the litigation, for example as a result of difficulty in obtaining clear instructions. Similarly, if the litigation friend is acting as principal carer, this runs the risk that they maybe unwilling to accept expert and/or legal advice which runs contrary to their own perception of their loved one's abilities and needs. That difficulty may become extreme, acute and crucial if the litigation friend will not accept their legal team's advice to accept, on behalf of the claimant, an offer put forward to settle the case.

However, these considerations will not usually outweigh the benefits of having a litigation friend who knows the injured person well and who is likely to want to be involved in the proceedings in any event. It would only be in relatively rare circumstances that it would be preferable to seek the assistance of an outside party, such as the Official Solicitor, to act as litigation friend. This may be appropriate, for example, if the infant claimant's parents have separated and there has been a breakdown of relationship between the parents, including the institution of any family proceedings which are likely to give rise to lack of cooperation and/or conflict of interest, particularly if any new relationship has commenced involving either parent.

Nevertheless, one must not forget the duties imposed upon the litigation friend and, by extension, the ethical obligations of the solicitor under CPR Part 21. Pursuant to CPR, r 21.4(3), a person might act as litigation friend if they:

(a)   can fairly and competently conduct proceedings on the protected party's behalf;

(b)   have no interest adverse to that of the protected party; and

(c)   undertake to pay any costs the protected party might be ordered to pay in relation to the proceedings (subject to the right to recover these from the assets of the protected party).

These responsibilities should of course be brought to the attention of the putative litigation friend before they are appointed.

A person can become a litigation friend without the need for a court order, by filing a certificate of suitability stating that they satisfy the conditions specified in CPR, r 21.4(3). However, this must be done at the time the claim is made[7] and the certificate must be served upon everyone upon whom the claim form must be served.[8]

It is highly unusual for the Court of Protection to have any involvement in the affairs of the victim when the solicitor sees the claimant and his or her family at the outset unless there are pre-existing funds in need of administration. The Court of Protection will only become involved when it becomes clear that compensation will be received, at which stage it will be necessary for the appropriate steps to be taken to apply for the appointment of a deputy.

Unless, therefore, the Court of Protection had become involved at an earlier stage, for example, if insurance monies became available as a consequence of the index event, then the practitioner will not have any direct contact with the Court of Protection at the outset but only if and when any compensation monies were to be paid. The Court will become involved if the claimant does lack capacity under the MCA and there is an early admission of liability which prompts or leads to a request for an early interim payment on behalf of the claimant. In these circumstances an application will have to be made to the Court of Protection for the appointment of a deputy since any monies received, including by way of an interim payment, should be paid into the Court of Protection and there administered and managed for the benefit of a claimant who is under a disability as a result of mental incapacity.

The practitioner can of course seek guidance from the Court of Protection if there appears to be a doubt about the claimant's capacity, but it would appear

---

7   CPR, r 21.5(3).
8   CPR, r 21.5(4).

to be expected that in those circumstances the practitioner would obtain appropriate medical evidence upon capacity, in order to determine whether the claim should be pursued on behalf of the claimant by a litigation friend or by the claimant in his or her own right.

Of course it is possible, and indeed common, for a member of the family to be appointed deputy. This can be a spouse of an injured husband or wife or a parent of an injured child.

Whilst the role of the Court of Protection is dealt with elsewhere in more detail, it is important to emphasise that the obligations and responsibilities of a deputy are considered to be far more onerous following the implementation of the MCA. This has contributed to the growth in some firms of Court of Protection and deputyship departments which offer specialist deputy services to their own and other firms. The additional duties and responsibilities they have to undertake have not always been followed by an equivalent recognition that the real costs that are involved in acting in the capacity of professional deputy should be recoverable, but such claims should now form a properly evidenced part of any claim in which they arise.

1.6   EXPERTS' AND INITIAL REPORTS

Experts' reports are a cornerstone of any personal injury or clinical negligence claim but the quantity and complexity of the evidence obtained is particular to catastrophic injury cases. Both medical and non-medical experts will need to be engaged so as to provide a full picture of the injuries suffered, to identify the areas of need and estimate the costs of providing for those needs. Also, as the claimant's condition develops and progresses in the future, either for the better or worse, so the needs of the claimant will have to be considered where appropriate, on the basis of a series of phases. Detailed guidance on the use of experts is to be found in Chapter 7.

It is important to note at this point that, pursuant to CPR, r 35.4, not only is the court's permission required to rely upon expert evidence in a particular field but the court also has the power to specify the issues which the evidence should address (CPR, r 35.4(3)). Practitioners should also bear in mind that the court has the power to limit the amount of a party's expert's fees and expenses that may be recovered from any other party (CPR, r 35.4(4)). The 'overriding objective' of the Civil Procedure Rules has been amended to emphasise the need for courts to deal with cases justly 'and at proportionate cost'[9] and, pursuant to CPR, r 1.4(2)(h) the court must consider 'whether the likely benefits of taking a particular step justify the costs of taking it'. Practitioners must therefore choose their experts judiciously.

It would not be unusual for there to be a constellation of injuries, for example to the head, limbs and various internal organs. Medical evidence will need to be

---

[9]   CPR, r. 1.1(1).

provided from a number of disciplines in order to provide details as to the nature, extent and effect of these different injuries, but initially as a first step it can be helpful to obtain a 'lead' expert's report in order to get an overview of the injuries and the likely areas of concern. Generally speaking, the lead medical expert will not only provide the initial overview report upon the claimant's injuries, treatment, present state and prognosis, but will also provide views as to the claimant's life expectation, as well as guidance as to the other medical reports that should be obtained so that a full picture of the claimant's injuries can be provided. Similarly, the lead medical expert should also provide guidance as to the non-medical (quantum) experts' reports that should be obtained in order to provide a full picture of the claimant's needs as well as the costs of providing for them.

There should be a symbiotic relationship between the medical and non-medical experts, in that the latter should have regard to the former when drafting their reports. A nursing or care expert cannot provide a reasoned analysis of the injured person's future care requirements if they do not know the medical perspective as to how the claimant's condition is likely to progress. Similarly, the medical experts should then review the quantum reports in order to confirm whether they can support the assessments and recommendations that are made in relation to provision for the injured person's needs in the future.

A further, very important, consideration at the outset is to consider whether a case manager should be appointed/retained. A case manager can perform a vital role in assisting the victim, and the victim's family, in dealing with other organisations, agencies and individuals who can, or should, provide support for the victim in a number of areas including facilities, therapies, services and finance. Whilst the role of a case manager is dealt with in Chapter 8 the practitioner should consider at the outset the advantages of engaging the services of a case manager who can provide practical assistance and support which can not only assist, but accelerate, the victim's rehabilitation, progress and provision of financial support.

The range of quantum reports which may be required is also extensive. The usual raft of non-medical reports would include:

- care (including gratuitous care – to include any case management requirements);
- occupational therapy (including aids and equipment);
- physiotherapy; and
- accommodation.

The following may be obtained more infrequently, but are nevertheless indispensible in certain cases:

- a report from an expert in the field of assistive technology, i.e. specialist equipment which would enable the claimant to control their environment and thereby maximise their independence and quality of life;

- a report regarding speech and language therapy, including swallowing ability;
- a report from a dietician regarding the claimant's nutritional/dietary needs;
- a report dealing with the claimant's podiatry and/or postural requirements, linking them to their mobility and transport needs;
- a report dealing with employment to cover the claimant's likely career, progression and earnings if the accident/event had not occurred and to cover any residual earnings capacity.

The identity of a 'lead' medical expert will vary depending upon the nature of the injuries suffered by the victim. If, for example, the injury is confined to the spine, then the medical team leader is likely to be a spinal injuries consultant. In cases of severe cerebral damage, the relevant function may be performed by a consultant neurologist with experience of head injury rehabilitation. In cases of hypoxic-ischemic brain injury at birth leading to cerebral palsy, the role may be undertaken by a consultant paediatric neurologist.

It is important to identify the tasks to be performed by the lead medical expert. He or she will not only be the expert providing the preliminary medical report on diagnosis, treatment and prognosis. The lead expert will be asked, in addition, to give an overview of the case and to assist the practitioner in the identification and management of the medical and non-medical evidence to be required. This potential wider commitment should be indicated to the lead expert from the outset in the practitioner's initial letter of instruction.

The advantages of using the team leader approach is that the action, in respect of the expert evidence, should progress forwards in an agreed and predictable fashion and in a series of logical steps, namely:

- the primary core medical report, which provides evidence of the principal injuries, the history of the treatment given, the symptomatology, the present condition and a preliminary prognosis;
- further medical reports which flow from the lead medical report, such reports being commissioned from other suitable medical specialists as advised by the team leader, so that a complete picture of the injuries and disabilities, both physical and psychological, is obtained;
- further specialist reports to include any particular investigations that the team leader recommends, for example, electroencephalography (EEG), magnetic resonance imaging (MRI), computerised tomography (CT) and intensive psychological testing, to include behavioural therapy;
- paramedical therapy reports, identifying the claimant's needs in various areas, including care, physiotherapy, occupational therapy, speech therapy and conductive therapy, as suggested or approved by the lead expert;
- additional commentary reports from the lead medical expert dealing with, and approving or otherwise commenting upon, the various non-medical experts' reports which are commissioned as the litigation proceeds;

- a commentary report upon the schedule of special damages and future losses and expenses prepared on behalf of the claimant, as well as reports and schedule prepared and disclosed by the defendant;
- a search of the medical literature with a view to supporting the expert's opinions on matters in dispute from published textbooks or validated research.

Considerable caution should be exercised before obtaining any medical report from the claimant's own treating clinicians for the reasons discussed in Chapter 7 which include:

(1) the treating clinician will often, for reasons of professional pride, provide a more optimistic assessment of the disability and prognosis than in fact may be the case;

(2) the treating medical experts may be unable, or unwilling, to attend conferences, participate in joint discussions, or attend the eventual trial;

(3) the clinician may lack the necessary experience in the preparation of medico-legal reports (although the CPR declaration should avoid this) and providing a persuasive opinion on a key issue such as expectation of life;

(4) the treating clinician may also lack the necessary experience of dealing with the 'cut and thrust' of a meeting with his or her opposite number (who is likely to be a highly experienced clinician instructed on behalf of the defendant) and may have no, or inadequate, experience of giving evidence 'first hand' in the witness box at a trial.

The experts should see the claimant's pre-accident general practice records as well as any post-accident medical notes. The expert should also be provided with copies of the statements of evidence which had been taken from the claimant and members of his or her family.

The role of the practitioner will be to act as case manager, marshalling the necessary medical and non-medical experts, ensuring that there is no duplication or overlap in the assessments, identifying any differences of opinion that need to be resolved and, ultimately, preparing a substantial (and lengthy) schedule of special damages and future losses.

Rather than having a schedule which is perhaps one or two pages long, schedules in cases involving catastrophic injuries will run to many pages. Further guidance is offered Chapter 16 as to the preparation of schedules of loss, but they should set out not only the bare figures, but also the basis upon which the claims are made and the expert evidence upon which reliance is placed.

The schedule will also provide a narrative which will set out the background to the index event and the consequences that followed, both for the claimant and the claimant's family, and will provide in the text explanatory details as to the circumstances under which specific items of claim are advanced and the basis upon which broad heads of claim are founded.

The practitioner has the responsibility for the initial selection of each of the experts, for ensuring that each expert is carefully instructed as to the necessary evidence which is sought and that the reports are presented in a form which allows disclosure. They are also responsible for the updating of the reports during the course of the litigation, and for the management of the experts into a unified and coherent team which has a common view, so far as possible, as to the claimant's needs and the scenario which provides him or her with an appropriate support package for the future.

Inevitably, such cases will often require the use of a number of conferences involving both medical and non-medical experts. These are often crucial to ensure that the expert evidence is credible, supportive and reflects the claimant's disabilities as well as providing a detailed assessment of the needs and the costs of providing for them. A conference can also be used to iron out any difference of opinion between experts and provide clarification where there is overlap or duplication of the assessments made.

Again, the input of the claimant him or herself or where appropriate, the claimant's family, is essential so that the claimant or the family are made fully aware as to the input provided by the various experts and are given the opportunity to discuss the reports and raise any concerns or queries that they may consider appropriate, including where they disagree with an expert's conclusions as to the claimant's needs. Such problems can often be resolved by a timely conference involving the claimant him or herself.

As part of the solicitor's role he must inform the claimant, or his or her family, at the outset as to the likely nature of the medical and non-medical expertise that will be commissioned to provide reports in the case.

The practitioner must adopt strategic planning in relation to the selection and management of the expert witnesses. Access to a database of experts is required. A number of sources can be accessed including:

- Association of Personal Injuries Lawyers' expert database;
- Law Society Directory of Expert Witnesses;
- UK Register of Expert Witnesses; and
- the Academy of Experts.

Counsel experienced in personal injury litigation often compile their own expert lists and can provide useful input, particularly with regard to experts who have given evidence recently in court. Similarly, solicitors experienced in the field may be prepared to assist by recommending experts. An experienced proposed lead medical or non-medical expert who is unable to assist can often suggest the services of a colleague with whom the expert has worked previously. However, an expert who has not previously been instructed can properly be asked for information as to their background qualification, expertise and court experience. This may enable the practitioner to decide if the expert has the appropriate qualifications and experience for the material task.

The advantage of keeping one's own database up to date is self-evident. It may no longer be appropriate to instruct those experts whose reports are noted as being inadequately prepared, whose approach is seen to be partisan or otherwise seeking to act as an advocate rather than an independent specialist, or whose charged fees have become significantly beyond the level recoverable on costs assessment.

The expert, medical or non-medical, who is asked to provide a report outside his field of expertise, should decline the instruction. Accordingly, the practitioner's preliminary letter of enquiry should identify the area or areas of practice which the chosen expert will have to address. The witness must be asked directly if the proposed subject for the report falls within his particular area of expertise, and if it does, when he last practised in that subject. Failure to take this elementary step may well lead to the expenditure of irrecoverable costs if the report proves to be of little or no litigation use. Further guidance on instruction of experts is set out in Chapter 7.

Having regard to the gravity, and often protracted timescale of the litigation, the experts who are selected should not only be clear, cogent and credible in the contents of their reports, but should also be willing to assist the practitioner in a number of continuing respects as the claim progresses towards trial. This continuing assistance will include:

- clarification of reports submitted;
- attending conferences with counsel;
- updating reports as required;
- dealing with any request for further information that the other side may serve in relation to input from a particular expert;
- conducting literature searches as requested, for example, in respect of medical papers and articles on the expectation of life of the catastrophically injured;
- participation in joint discussions with experts of like discipline instructed by the other side and the preparation of joint statements;
- not only attendance at trial but also a reasonably co-operative attitude towards demands for pre-trial conferences and the amplification of information in response to last minute requests of solicitor or counsel.

In conclusion, the choice of the expert witnesses in a catastrophic injuries claim remains one of the most important aspects of the overall management of the case by the practitioner.

1.7   COUNSEL

At the outset when the practitioner discusses the future strategy regarding the claim, it is anticipated that he will include reference to the use of the services of counsel.

Certainly another feature of catastrophic injury claims is that they require the use of counsel's services at a far earlier stage than normal and counsel's services are not used on a sporadic basis but, far more often, as part of the 'team' approach. It may be that some counsel find the role of being a team player a difficult one to adopt and, accordingly, the selection of the appropriate counsel is just as important to the success of the case as is the choice of the appropriate medical and non-medical experts.

It is simply not enough for counsel to settle the necessary statements of case and to provide an advice on quantum at an advanced stage of the case. Equally, if leading counsel is to be instructed, then leading counsel should be part of the teamwork approach to the litigation and simply briefing leading counsel for the trial itself will seldom, if ever, be the best approach.

Initially an experienced and capable junior counsel will be selected to form part of the legal team. They must be prepared to provide clear advice, either orally or in writing, be happy to be contacted on a regular basis (e.g. by e-mail) if specific queries arise and be ready to create and maintain a positive relationship with the client and the client's family. Thus, counsel should be prepared to attend a conference at the home of the claimant, rather than expecting all conferences to take place at counsel's chambers. Certainly far more progress can be made in the case where the claimant and his or her family are asked to provide information in the more familiar surroundings of their own home, than in the somewhat daunting environment of counsel's chambers.

Counsel will also, in all probability, be involved at an earlier stage in the proceedings than is normally customary in standard personal injury claims. Counsel should be asked to advise upon strategy for the litigation as a whole as soon as is practicable, so that the instructed solicitor has a clear perspective on the lines of investigation and enquiry to be undertaken, the issues to be addressed and agreement as to the experts to be retained.

Issues to be considered at an early stage would include:
- whether the claim should proceed by way of a split trial;
- whether an early interim payment should be sought and, if so, how much and what should such an interim payment be used for;
- the scope of the medical evidence to be obtained (e.g. whether a report should be obtained from a clinical psychologist, a neuropsychologist or consultant psychiatrist, etc.);
- strategic issues regarding quantum evidence (e.g. whether an approach should be made to the defendant to obtain quantum reports from any single joint experts);
- the need for any early conferences in order to address and, if possible, resolve any differences of opinion or areas of duplication that arise between the medical and/or non-medical experts;
- whether a claim for provisional damages should be advanced and, if so, on what basis;

- whether any or all of the damages, in the event of a successful claim, should be made up by way of periodical payments and, if so, to what extent.

In addition, counsel can advise upon an appropriate timetable for the interlocutory stages of the litigation, assist in the selection of the medical and non-medical experts, give guidance as to the appropriate heads of damage to be pursued and give advice as to the core evidence that will be required.

The instruction of leading counsel in such cases, to work with junior counsel, is a less common occurrence than in the past. This may be because there are costs restrictions (e.g. in public funding cases), or because many cases settle at a round-table meeting where the services of leading counsel are not utilised.

In those cases where it is clear it will proceed to trial, and where the services of leading counsel are certain to be required, it is suggested that leading counsel should first be instructed long before delivery of the brief for trial. The carefully prepared and properly conducted consultation between leading counsel, the other members of the legal team and the expert witnesses, at or around the setting down for trial stage can be extremely productive in achieving a successful long-term preparation for trial. Often, however, the solicitor representing the claimant will not be in a position to make the decision or not have the funds to retain the services of leading counsel until far closer to the trial date, which raises obvious and real difficulties in securing the services of suitable leading counsel and providing him with sufficient time to make an impact upon the strategy in preparing the case effectively for the trial itself.

Consideration should be given to whether leading and junior counsel are to be selected from the same set of chambers, which has a number of clear advantages.

1.8 LIMITATION

In catastrophic injury claims it is not uncommon for the claimant, or his or her family, not to seek legal advice or assistance for a significant time after the date of the index event. This can be for a number of reasons including the quite understandable need to concentrate upon the claimant's treatment, rehabilitation and recovery. In cases involving catastrophic injuries that process can take a considerable period of time, even several years. For this reason it is important to be clear about when limitation may become an issue.

In this chapter we do not seek to provide a detailed recitation of all the various statutes and case-law that have a bearing upon the relevant limitation date in given circumstances but, rather, to provide a broad guide. It is hoped that this will assist the practitioner in getting to grips with this issue as part of the first contact with the victim or the victim's family.

1.8.1   The starting point

Usually, the limitation period in personal injury claims will expire 3 years from the date on which the cause of action accrued *or* the date of knowledge, if later, of the person injured[10] (cf accidents on ships or aircrafts at **1.8.5** for applicable shorter limitation periods). If the injured person dies before this period expires, the limitation period for claims brought by a personal representative under the Law Reform (Miscellaneous Provisions) Act 1934 and/or the Fatal Accidents Act 1976 will be 3 years from either the date of death or, if later, the date of the personal representative's knowledge.[11]

1.8.2   Date of knowledge

When the injuries occur as a result of a specific event then the practitioner can calculate the 3-year anniversary, which will be the relevant limitation date (subject of course to whether the claimant is under a disability – see further below). However, in many cases the injuries occur not as a result of a specific index event but as a consequence of a drawn out process and thus it may be that:

•   the injuries themselves occurred over a period of time; or

•   the injuries occurred as a result of an index event, but knowledge of the injuries was not gained when that event occurred.

Those who undertake clinical negligence work will be used to receiving instructions some years after the treatment complained of has been completed. They will therefore routinely need to enquire as to when the claimant gained the requisite knowledge for the purposes of the Limitation Act 1980.

Given the importance of this issue, it is considered useful to summarise here the elements which make up 'knowledge' in these circumstances. The claimant must have knowledge of the following facts:

(1)   that the injury was significant;

(2)   that the injury was attributable in whole or in part to the act or omission which is alleged to constitute negligence, nuisance or breach of duty;

(3)   the identity of the defendant; and

(4)   if it is alleged that the act or omission was that of a person other than the defendant, the identity of that person and the additional facts supporting the bringing of an action against the defendant.[12]

It is important to note that 'knowledge' will include knowledge which the claimant might reasonably have been expected to acquire from facts observable or ascertainable by him or her, or from facts ascertainable by him or her with

---

[10]   Limitation Act 1980, s 11(4).

[11]   See Limitation Act 1980, s 11(5) and (6) in relation to the Law Reform (Miscellaneous Provisions) Act 1934 and s 12 in relation to claims under the Fatal Accidents Act 1976.

[12]   Limitation Act 1980, s 14(1).

the help of medical or other appropriate expert advice which it is reasonable for him or her to seek.[13] However, if that knowledge was ascertainable only with the help of expert advice then the claimant will not be fixed with that knowledge provided that he or she has taken reasonable steps to seek and, where appropriate, act on that advice.[14] The courts take a fairly strict approach to the objective test of knowledge, but they do so because there is scope for the subjective elements to be taken into account in the exercise of discretion where appropriate, see *Whiston v London Strategic Health Authority*.[15]

Bearing the above factors in mind, the cautious practitioner should question the client carefully regarding the earliest date on which they realised that they might have suffered a significant injury which could be attributable to negligence or some fault on the part of another. Equally significantly, they should enquire as to how the client came to reach that conclusion. It may also be necessary for the practitioner to obtain documentary evidence, such as medical records, in order to shed light on when the client may have acquired the requisite knowledge (eg, by receipt of a letter) that would cause the limitation period to start to run.

Whilst it may seem that it should be obvious whether or not an injury was 'significant' for the purposes of acquiring knowledge, especially in catastrophic injury cases, the practitioner must bear in mind that the limitation period does not necessarily run from the moment the claimant knew this. It is still necessary, as set out above, for the claimant to have knowledge that the injury was attributable to the act or omission which is alleged to constitute negligence, breach of statutory duty, etc.

Whilst not involving catastrophic injuries, the question of what constituted 'significant' injuries was considered by the House of Lords in the case of *A v Hoare*,[16] which dealt with six appeals where claims of sexual abuse had been made. The claims had previously been held to be statute-barred.

The House of Lords applied s 14(2) of the Limitation Act 1980 by first of all considering what the claimant knew about his or her injury. They then turned their attention to whether any 'objective' knowledge could be inferred under s 14(3) and finally asked whether a reasonable person with that knowledge would have considered their injury sufficiently serious to justify issuing a claim.

Knowledge of the identity of the defendant is often relevant in clinical negligence claims, for example where there are multiple potential defendants or issues of vicarious liability. In those circumstances the 3-year limitation period will run from the date on which the claimant acquired knowledge of the defendant's identity (as well as the other facts referred to above), or from when they might reasonably have been expected to do so.

---

[13]   Limitation Act 1980, s 14(3).
[14]   Ibid.
[15]   [2010] EWCA 195.
[16]   [2008] UKHL 6.

1.8.3   The court's discretion

Section 33 of the Limitation Act 1980 gives the court the discretion to allow an action to proceed even though the limitation period has expired. This discretion can be exercised wherever 'it appears to the court that it would be equitable to allow an action to proceed', having regard to any prejudice that this might cause to either party.[17]

However, there are various factors to which the court must have regard in making their decision, namely:

(1)   the length of and reason for the delay;

(2)   whether the evidence adduced by either party is likely to be less cogent than if the action had been brought within the limitation period;

(3)   the conduct of the defendant after the cause of action arose, including the extent to which they responded to requests reasonably made by the claimant for information or documentation;

(4)   the duration of any disability of the claimant arising after the date on which the cause of action accrued;

(5)   the extent to which the claimant acted promptly and reasonably once he had the relevant knowledge;

(6)   the steps taken by the claimant to obtain expert advice and the contents of that advice.[18]

As is generally the case in a personal injury claim, the burden of proof falls upon the claimant; they must provide reasons why the limitation period ought to be disapplied, bearing in mind the above factors.

Following the decisions in *Horton v Sadler*[19] and *Leeson v Marsden and another*,[20] made by the House of Lords and the Court of Appeal respectively, practitioners should note that it may be possible to issue new proceedings against a defendant where the original claim has not been served in time. However, it should be borne in mind that the discretion to do so still lies with the court alone and that they will take into account all the circumstances of the case, including the factors referred to above. This should not be relied upon as a 'get-out' clause and service should be effected properly and within the necessary time frame.

1.8.4   Claimants under a disability

It may often be the case that those suffering from catastrophic injuries may be considered to be under a disability. If this was the case as at the date when the cause of action accrued, the action can be brought at any time before the expiry

---

[17]   Limitation Act 1980, s 33(1).
[18]   Limitation Act 1980, s 33(3).
[19]   [2006] UKHL 27.
[20]   [2008] All ER(D) 147.

of 3 years from the date when they ceased to be under a disability.[21] 'Disability' would cover those under the age of 18 and/or those who are considered not to have capacity under the MCA.

Therefore, in practical terms, a child has until the age of 21 to commence a claim for damages arising from personal injury. A person lacking capacity, and who was in that position when the cause of action accrued, must start proceedings within 3 years of the date on which they acquired capacity.

Whilst it is clear when a claimant is a minor, the question of capacity is often complex and may be uncertain. The MCA recognises that an individual's capacity to manage his or her property and affairs gives rise to a far more sophisticated analysis than has typically been the case in the past. Further observations in relation to this issue will be dealt with in Chapter 3.

1.8.5 Further UK exceptions to the 3-year rule

Practitioners should also bear in mind that there are different limitation periods for accidents which occur on ships or aircraft.

1.8.5.1 *Passengers on ships: the Athens Convention*

The Athens Convention[22] relating to the Carriage of Passengers and their Luggage by Sea is incorporated into UK law by, and can be found in, Sch 6 to the Merchant Shipping Act 1995. It relates to passengers under a contract of carriage. It does not cover crew members working on a ship under a contract of employment with the ship-owner. Article 16 of the Convention imposes a time-limit for personal injury claims of 2 years from the date of disembarkation. The Convention itself applies to international carriage by sea, but its provisions are also applied to domestic carriage by sea, ie, voyages to and from UK ports that do not visit another country in between, by the Carriage of Passengers and their Luggage by Sea (Domestic Carriage) Order 1987. The 2-year time-limit under the Athens Convention can only be extended by a declaration of the carrier or by agreement of the parties after the cause of action has arisen, but any such declaration or agreement must be in writing. The suspensive provisions of the Limitation Act 1980, including the discretion to extend time under s 33, do not apply to the Athens Convention limit, see *Higham v Stena Sealink*.[23] Thus even a claim by a child will be caught by the 2-year time limit.

1.8.5.2 *Ship incidents and collisions: the London Convention*

The other 2-year time-limit in shipping cases in the UK arises out of s 190 of the Merchant Shipping Act 1995. This applies a 2-year time-limit to claims against

---

[21] Limitation Act 1980, s 28(1) and (6).
[22] For further guidance on the Athens and London Conventions see Grahame Aldous QC and Linda Nelson *Work Accidents At Sea* (9 Gough Square Publishing, 2008).
[23] [1996] 1 WLR 1107.

the ship or her owners in respect of damage or loss caused by the fault of that ship to another ship, its cargo or freight or any property on board it or for damages for loss of life or personal injury caused by the fault of that ship to any person on board another ship. The common situation to which s 190 applies is injury resulting from collision between ships. A collision need not actually occur, however, so long as it is a 'two ship' incident. Thus, if somebody on board one ship is injured when they are knocked over, or a rope parts, due to the wash of a passing ship that is travelling too fast, then a claim will be subject to the 2-year time-limit under s 190. In the case of a person injured on one ship with a claim against the owners or operators of that same ship s 190 will not apply.

Where loss of life or suffering of injury is not coincidental with the causative maritime incident, time runs under s 190 from the time the injury is suffered. In *Sweet v RNLI*,[24] a lifeboat man started to have psychiatric symptoms a month after a collision and by 6 months after the collision they had developed into a recognised psychiatric condition. It was held that time started to run only once an injury had commenced and the date when that occurred was ordered to be tried with the medical issues.

Unlike the Athens Convention, under s 190 the UK court has power to extend time for bringing proceedings to such extent and on such conditions as it thinks fit. The discretion will usually be exercised by the Admiralty Court, as generally the action will be one that is required to be brought in the Admiralty Court under CPR Part 61 and accordingly the county court may not be a court having jurisdiction to extend time. Unlike s 33 of the Limitation Act 1980, the s 190 discretion is unhindered by lengthy criteria or specified matters to be taken into account and s 190 simply provides a wide discretion. An example of the discretion being exercised can be found in *Santos v The Baltic Carrier and the Flinterdam*.[25]

1.8.5.3   Passengers on aircraft: the Warsaw and Montreal Conventions

Insofar as aircraft and hovercraft passenger claims are concerned, the Warsaw[26] and Montreal[27] Conventions state that there is again a 2-year limitation period from the date of the accident.

---

24   TLR 22/2/2002.
25   [2001] Lloyd's Rep 689.
26   Warsaw Convention (1929) Regulating Liability for International Carriage of Persons, Luggage or Goods performed by Aircraft for Reward.
27   Montreal Convention (1999) for the Unification of Certain Rules for International Carriage.

1.8.6 Foreign limitation periods

Where an accident happens abroad the limitation period applicable in the area in question may apply by reason of the Foreign Limitation Periods Act 1984.[28] Where a UK court has to apply foreign law, it is a question of fact for the court to find what the applicable foreign law is, and the court must then apply the relevant law as it finds it would be applied in the country in question. In reaching its finding of fact as to the applicable foreign law the court may be assisted by expert evidence. The expert evidence can come from any suitable source and does not necessarily have to come from someone qualified to practice in the country in question.

Section 4 of the Civil Evidence Act 1972 provides that:

'(1) It is hereby declared that in civil proceedings a person who is suitably qualified to do so on account of his knowledge or experience is competent to give expert evidence as to the law of any country or territory outside the United Kingdom, or of any part of the United Kingdom other than England and Wales, irrespective of whether he has acted or is entitled to act as a legal practitioner there.

(2) Where any question as to the law of any country or territory outside the United Kingdom, or of any part of the United Kingdom other than England and Wales, with respect to any matter has been determined (whether before or after the passing of this Act) in any such proceedings as are mentioned in subsection (4) below, then in any civil proceedings (not being proceedings before a court which can take judicial notice of the law of that country, territory or part with respect to that matter)—
(a) any finding made or decision given on that question in the first-mentioned proceedings shall, if reported or recorded in citable form, be admissible in evidence for the purpose of proving the law of that country, territory or part with respect to that matter; and
(b) if that finding or decision, as so reported or recorded, is adduced for that purpose, the law of that country, territory or part with respect to that matter shall be taken to be in accordance with that finding or decision unless the contrary is proved:
Provided that paragraph (b) above shall not apply in the case of a finding or decision which conflicts with another finding or decision on the same question adduced by virtue of this subsection in the same proceedings.

(3) Except with the leave of the court, a party to any civil proceedings shall not be permitted to adduce any such finding or decision as is mentioned in subsection (2) above by virtue of that subsection unless he has in accordance with rules of court given to every other party to the proceedings notice that he intends to do so.

(4) The proceedings referred to in subsection (2) above are the following, whether civil or criminal, namely—

---

[28] For comprehensive guidance on international conflicts of law see, *Dicey and Morris on the Conflict of Laws* (Sweet & Maxwell, 13th edn, 2004).

(a)   proceedings at first instance in any of the following courts, namely the High Court, the Crown Court, a court of quarter sessions, the Court of Chancery of the county palatine of Lancaster and the Court of Chancery of the county palatine of Durham;

(b)   appeals arising out of any such proceedings as are mentioned in paragraph (a) above;

(c)   proceedings before the Judicial Committee of the Privy Council on appeal (whether to Her Majesty in Council or to the Judicial Committee as such) from any decision of any court outside the United Kingdom.

(5)   For the purposes of this section a finding or decision on any such question as is mentioned in subsection (2) above shall be taken to be reported or recorded in citable form if, but only if, it is reported or recorded in writing in a report, transcript or other document which, if that question had been a question as to the law of England and Wales, could be cited as an authority in legal proceedings in England and Wales.'

A party who intends to put in evidence a previous relevant finding on a question of foreign law under s 4(2) of the Civil Evidence Act 1972 must follow the procedure set out in CPR, r 33.7. That provides that notice of the intention must be given to the other parties. The notice must be given not later than the latest date for serving witness statements, or not less than 21 days before the hearing at which he proposes to put the finding in evidence if there are no witness statements. The notice must specify the question on which the finding was made and enclose a copy of a document where it is reported or recorded.

1.8.7   Limitations on the amount of damages

There are circumstances as a result of various conventions to which the UK may be a party where the amount of damages may be 'capped' at a maximum sum. Whilst for most claims this may be academic as a result of increases in the limits, for catastrophic injury claims the issue of whether the right to limit damages can be challenged may become crucial, and for that reason it should be addressed early on.

The UK has traditionally accepted a right for ship-owners and aircraft operators to limit the amount of damages that can be claimed against them and has implemented in UK law various international conventions setting the limits and the circumstances in which they can be relied on. The conventions that most commonly arise are the Warsaw and Montreal Conventions in relation to air accidents and the London and Athens Conventions in relation to accidents at sea.[29]

The right to cap claims under the Warsaw, Montreal, London or Athens Conventions can only be defeated, or 'broken', if it can be shown that the loss resulted from some personal act or omission committed with the intent to cause

---

[29]   For further guidance on the Athens and London Conventions see Grahame Aldous QC and Linda Nelson *Work Accidents At Sea* (9 Gough Square Publishing, 2008).

such loss, or recklessly and with knowledge that such loss would probably result. That is a deliberately difficult burden.

A number of cases under the Warsaw Convention, provide some useful guidance. The knowledge that damage would probably result does not necessarily have to be knowledge of the precise damage which actually occurred, but it must be of the same kind: see *Goldman v Thai Airways International Ltd.*[30] The requirement for knowledge is subjective. It requires an actual knowledge on the part of the relevant person at the moment at which the relevant act or omission occurs. It is not sufficient if the relevant person is aware that if a certain risk materialises, damage would probably result: see *Gurtner v Beaton.*[31] An appreciation or awareness at the time of the conduct in question that such conduct will probably result in the type of damage that is caused is required: see *Nugent v Michael Goss Aviation Limited.*[32]

In *Margolle v Delta Marine Co Limited,*[33] Mr Justice Gross held that it was likely that only truly exceptional cases would give rise to any real prospect of defeating an owner's right to limit under the 1976 London Convention. That case involved a fishing boat that was in the habit of crossing the Channel separation zones in breach of the Collision Rules whilst the skipper was asleep below. His Lordship thought that that might be a truly exceptional case and there was a real prospect of the right to limit being defeated. Accordingly he allowed the matter to go to trial. Such cases will, however, be rare. In *The Bowbelle,*[34] Sheen J described the right to limit as 'almost indisputable', and in *The Leerort,*[35] Lord Phillips stated that 'when a claim is made for damages resulting from a collision it is virtually axiomatic that the defendant ship-owner will be entitled to limit his liability'.

A ship-owner seeking to exercise the right to limit merely has to establish that the claim falls within the wording of the applicable Convention, and will incur the costs of establishing the necessary facts. Once they have established those facts then they are entitled to a decree limiting liability unless the claimant proves the facts required to 'break' the limit. If the claimant chooses to contest the right to limit and fails in the attempt then they will be at risk as to the costs of doing so: see *The Capitan San Luis.*[36]

1.9 TIMESCALE

The solicitor/practitioner must, from the outset, give clear advice to the claimant and, where appropriate, the claimant's family as to the likely timescale of the litigation and why an extended timescale is not only likely, but necessary.

---

[30] [1983] 1 WLR 1186.
[31] [1993] 2 Lloyd's Rep 369.
[32] [2000] 2 Lloyd's Rep 222.
[33] [2002] EWHC 2452 (Admlty).
[34] [1990] 3 All ER 476.
[35] [2001] 2 Lloyd's Rep 291, 295.
[36] [1994] 1 All ER 1016, per Clarke J.

Claims arising from catastrophic injuries will tend, generally, to have a longer timescale than those which arise from less serious injuries. Of course, no matter how complex or difficult, the action will be subject to the normal 3-year period of limitation from the date when the cause of action accrued or the relevant date of knowledge (Limitation Act 1980, ss 11 and 14), save and except where the claimant has been continuously under a disability by reason of infancy or incapacity, in which case the limitation period does not commence until the disability ceases.[37]

The practical task of investigating a complex case and gathering the necessary lay documentary and expert information from many different sources (including experts who themselves may seek to set their own relaxed timetables) is expensive and time-consuming.

However, an early settlement of such a claim will not always be in the best interests of the victim, despite the often repeated judicial mantra, that justice delayed is justice denied.

For example, a child, although catastrophically injured at birth, will for the first years of life be entirely dependent upon others. It is only as the child grows, and the motor functions and intellectual ability become capable of measurement, that the true extent and nature of the injuries, physical and psychological, become apparent. An accurate assessment, in all probability, may well not be possible until the child reaches the age of perhaps 8 years, or thereabouts.

Similar considerations may apply to accident victims who have suffered a prolonged period of unconsciousness after the initial trauma and for whom rehabilitation may take a number of years. Similarly, spinally injured victims may well have to undergo a lengthy period of rehabilitation at a suitable spinal centre before their injuries have reached a 'plateau' at which time discharge can be achieved and a reliable assessment of both injuries and prognosis can be provided.

For such victims a settlement too early after injury may understate the true compensation value of the claim because the extent of the disability has not been properly or sufficiently comprehended and a reliable prognosis has not been provided.

It is in such circumstances that the merits of a split trial become apparent, where the issue of liability and causation can be dealt with as a separate and preliminary issue which, if found in favour of the claimant, can enable interim payments to be provided so as to provide for the claimant's needs (including accommodation, care, etc) until final quantification of the claim can be reliably undertaken.

It must not be forgotten that a client and their family may be hoping for a swift resolution, particularly where there is a pressing financial need. They must

---

[37]   Limitation Act 1980, s 28.

therefore be apprised of the potential timescale as soon as possible as well as being advised why this type of case might take so long to come to fruition.

Expert evidence will, of course, be relied upon in determining when a claimant's injuries have reached a stage where the claimant's condition is sufficiently stabilised to allow their future requirements to be assessed and a confident prognosis to be given.

It often takes a period of up to 2 years and possibly longer before an injured person reaches the stage where their condition is stable, where rehabilitation has maximised their recovery and where a reliable opinion can be given as to prognosis. It is therefore not unusual, or unreasonable, for claims involving catastrophic injuries to take 3 or even 4 years before reaching a conclusion.

This delay, of course, will lead to significant financial stresses and strains, particularly as the injuries are such that it is overwhelmingly likely that the injured person will have ceased work and thereby have lost their employment income. Whilst receipt of benefits may provide some financial assistance, it is highly unlikely that they will provide adequate support for the injured person's needs whilst the litigation is ongoing.

This underlines the importance of interim payments in cases where liability has been admitted or established. These can provide a lifeline for the injured person's cost of living expenses and, indeed, can provide funds to set up a support package (including suitable accommodation) until a final quantification of the claim can be made. Further guidance on interim payments can be found in Chapter 5.

1.10 CATASTROPHIC INJURY LITIGATION – PRE-ACTION PROTOCOLS

The overriding objective of the CPR is to enable the relevant court to deal with cases justly and at proportionate cost. This includes, as far as practicable:

(a) ensuring that the parties are on an equal footing;

(b) saving expense;

(c) dealing with the case in ways which are proportionate:
   (i) to the amount of money involved;
   (ii) to the importance of the case;
   (iii) to the complexity of the issues; and
   (iv) to the financial position of each party;

(d) ensuring that it is dealt with expeditiously and fairly;

(e) allotting to it an appropriate share of the court's resources, whilst taking into account the need to allot resources to other cases; and

(f) enforcing compliance with rules, practice directions and orders.

Thus, it is clear that the overriding objective provides some justification for the outlay of the significant costs involved in undertaking the complex investigations routinely required in catastrophic injury cases, but that proportionality is still a factor to be borne in mind.

Adopting a planned and structured approach to each catastrophic injury case will help to strike the right balance between thoroughly investigating the case and progressing it expeditiously. The current pre-action protocols provide a broad framework for all personal injury claims. There are three at present:

- Pre-Action Protocol for Personal Injury Claims;
- Pre-Action Protocol for the Resolution of Clinical Disputes; and
- Pre-action Protocol for Disease and Illness Claims.

None of the current pre-action protocols *specifically* address catastrophic injury cases. This is not to suggest, however, that appropriate pre-action conduct should be ignored in catastrophic injury cases. The protocols need to be complied with where they apply, and their spirit needs to be followed even where they do not.

Solicitors who are conducting catastrophic injury claims (for claimant or defendant) are expected to follow the relevant pre-action protocol, where a greater emphasis is placed upon co-operation. This is enhanced and underlined by the Rehabilitation Code 2007 as well as the draft Multi-track Code.

A court's case management powers do not operate prior to the commencement of proceedings but the court will need to be satisfied, where proceedings are commenced, that the parties *have* complied with the requirements of the relevant protocol.

Pre-issue settlement discussions and other forms of alternative dispute resolution (ADR) ought to be planned and executed whenever possible, as the court sees itself as a forum of last resort.

1.10.1 Aims of the protocols

The first pre-action protocol dealt with the management of personal injury claims and was produced as part of Lord Woolf's *Access to Justice* report (1996). A group representing both claimants and defendants produced it with the following aims:

- more pre-action contact and co-operation between the parties;
- earlier and more comprehensive exchange of information;
- more effective pre-action investigation by both sides;
- to enable the parties to be put into a position where a fair settlement can be achieved, thus avoiding litigation;
- to ensure the proceedings run to the timetable set by the court and efficiently, should litigation become necessary;

- to promote the provision of medical or rehabilitation treatment so as to address, in a practical way, the claimant's needs.

Whilst there has been anecdotal evidence of defendants paying nothing more than lip-service to the aims of the various protocols, it is generally agreed that there has been a greater degree of co-operation between the parties since the protocols have been introduced. However, it is also a fair comment, and criticism, to say that defendants have been more cautious to recognise and operate within the aims of the protocols, the greater the valuation, or potential valuation, of the claim.

Although the protocols appear designed primarily for cases of lower value, it was always intended by the working party that the spirit of the protocol should be followed in higher value claims also. The parties will therefore be expected to comply with the relevant protocol so far as is possible, such as disclosing documents and information, making early admissions, considering early ADR, etc. Thus a claim should not be issued prematurely when a settlement is being actively explored by the parties.

Certainly, since the introduction of the protocols, there has been far more co-operation between the parties. This has required the claimant's lawyer to carry out far more work at the outset of the case. The claimant's solicitor may have the power to control the timetable and the work he undertakes in the period before a protocol letter of claim is sent but he must remember that it is quite likely that at a later stage the work he has undertaken and the time spent in that phase may be subject to scrutiny, criticism and a penalty in costs.

1.10.2 Practice

It is perfectly permissible under the spirit of the CPR to send correspondence to potential defendants with the purpose of notifying them of the claim, providing what information the practitioner has and inviting those defendants to provide relevant pre-action disclosure before a formal letter of claim can be prepared. If the practitioner is not sure as to who is the likely defendant against whom the claim will be pursued, then it would be sensible to notify *all* potential defendants so that they can notify their insurers where appropriate and commence investigations, but they are not *required* to do so and may simply refer the practitioner to the relevant protocol.

If a defendant is simply provided with early notification of the claim before a detailed letter of claim is sent, the timetable for the defendant to provide a response does not start to run.

The protocols recognise the need for early disclosure of relevant documents on the part of the defendant (eg, copies of the claimant's medical records in a clinical negligence claim and his or her occupational health records in a claim arising from disease or illness). The claimant's solicitor will also identify if any additional records are considered relevant (eg, clinical protocols) and must, in any event, specify which documents, or categories of documents, are considered relevant.

Once this documentation has been obtained and the claimant's solicitor has completed his own investigations (including the taking of statement evidence), he will then be in a position to decide whether an effective letter of claim can be dispatched or whether expert evidence should be commissioned beforehand.

If proceedings are subsequently commenced, the court will expect the relevant protocol to have been complied with and where this has not been achieved then the non-compliant party will be expected to provide an explanation and may be visited with a penalty, including a penalty in relation to costs.

1.10.3   Letter of claim

The protocols provide for the claimant to write a detailed letter of claim to the defendant as soon as is practicable after the medical records and other evidence has been analysed. However, they do not require the content of the letter of claim to plead a case as it is recognised that the case is likely to develop and change as more evidence becomes available. Thus, the practitioner has a relatively wide discretion in deciding when it is best to send the formal letter of claim.

Nevertheless, the letter of claim must contain the following:
* sufficient details of the accident to enable effective investigations to be undertaken;
* the allegations of fault/blame;
* sufficient information to enable the defendant to place a broad value on the case;
* if relevant, the identity of other potential defendants;
* details of funding arrangements where appropriate. Practitioners should note that as of 1 October 2009 they became obliged to provide more detailed information regarding the existence of an ATE policy to the defendant. This includes information regarding the level of indemnity and whether the premiums are staged. This information *must* be provided to the defendant, pre- or post-issue, within a maximum of 7 days from the policy being incepted *or* must be enclosed within the letter of claim (where the relevant funding arrangement was entered into before 1 April 2013). Failure to do so may result in non-recovery of the ATE premium(s). Where funding arrangements were entered into on or after 1 April 2013 in personal injury claims, it would appear that these notice requirements would no longer apply, due to the fact that the claimant will not ordinarily be able to recover their ATE insurance premium and/or any success fee from their opponent. However, in clinical negligence claims it is still possible to recover that proportion of the ATE premium which relates to

the liability experts' reports and so, in order to protect their position, practitioners should comply with the aforementioned notice requirements in connection with such policies;

- an invitation to the defendant to consider rehabilitation where the claimant is still suffering from the effects of his or her injuries;
- identification of documents, or categories of documents, which are considered to be relevant to the action;
- details of the claimant's earnings, where relevant; and
- in road traffic accident cases, details of the hospital where the claimant has been treated and whether a police report has been obtained or is awaited.

It is, of course, essential that the letter of claim is approved by both the client and, where possible, any expert who has provided input before it is dispatched to the defendant. The expert in these circumstances should state clearly that he supports the allegations that are contained within the letter of claim.

The claimant should also set out in the letter which records have been received and offer to disclose these to the other side.

In cases involving catastrophic injury, it will not be possible for the claimant's solicitor to provide any more than a broad indication of value. The preliminary schedule should include, insofar as possible:

- details of special damages incurred to date;
- details of losses which are continuing; and
- heads of claim for future losses.

The letter can invite the defendant to admit liability or agree to a form of mediation in order to endeavour to settle the claim amicably. The claimant's solicitor can also provide broad details of injuries or, with his client's permission, disclose any medical evidence already received, dealing with injuries, condition and prognosis.

The practitioner can invite the defendant to consider instructing other medical and/or non-medical experts to undertake examinations and assessments of the claimant on a single joint basis.

1.10.4 Protocol response

Pursuant to the personal injury protocol, the defendant or his or her insurer has 21 days to acknowledge receipt of the letter of claim and if he or she fails to do so, then the claimant can proceed to issue proceedings without any penalty. Defendants routinely argue that there are omissions from the letter of claim which prevent the timetable from starting to run. The claimant's solicitor must do all he can to avoid such a criticism and not to allow such arguments to divert him from the reasonable progression of the case.

The defendant then has a further 3 months, again in personal injury claims, to investigate the claim and to provide a detailed response to the letter of claim. In a clinical negligence claim, the defendant is entitled to a period of 4 months in which to investigate matters and provide its letter of response, to run from the date on which the letter of claim was served. The NHS Litigation Authority requires that the letter of claim be copied to them as well as being sent directly to the trust.

In the letter of response, if liability is denied then the defendant must set out his detailed reasons for that denial, including any dispute as to the factual events as set out in the letter of claim. It is not sufficient simply for a defendant to deny the factual content contained in the letter of claim or the allegations advanced but must provide a full response, identifying any areas of dispute and the grounds for so doing.

Defendants must also supply copies of documents which are likely to be relevant to the issues between the parties and must give reasons as to why any disclosure is refused. In the absence of agreed disclosure of relevant documents, the claimant's solicitor will have to consider an application for pre-action disclosure.

If the defendant intends to admit liability then he or she must do so clearly. The words used must not be capable of misunderstanding. If primary liability is admitted but the defendant wishes to raise any allegation of contributory negligence then he or she must do so clearly, setting out in the letter of response reasons for any allegations of contributory negligence.

In the letter of response the defendant can make a full admission, an admission of primary liability but raising allegations of contributory negligence, an offer to settle the case or an offer of liability. If the defendant does make an admission of liability, the claimant's solicitor should ensure that this represents an admission both in relation to breach of duty and causation.

1.10.5 Medical reports

The protocols require the parties to use expert evidence economically. One way of providing economy is the use of single jointly instructed experts. Detailed guidance as to the use of such experts is set out in Chapter 7. Where a single joint expert is thought to be appropriate (most usually with respect to condition and prognosis and/or non-medical quantum experts) the claimant should nominate one or more medical experts and invite the defendant to agree to their joint instruction. Under the Personal Injury Protocol, the requirement is that all such experts ought to be joint but the complexity of a particular catastrophic injury case will often make this inadvisable for all of the experts. If the nomination is contained in the letter of claim then the 14-day period does not run until the 21 days for the acknowledgement has expired. Of course if the defendant does object to any nominated expert then it must be prepared to justify this at a later stage. An agreed nomination is not, of course, the same as an agreement to jointly instruct that expert and so care should always be taken in that regard to avoid prejudicing your client's case. It would not appear unreasonable for a defendant to ask for sight of the CV of a nominated expert before making a decision.

If a defendant does not object to a nominated expert, this does not transform them, once instructed, into a single joint expert whose report would accordingly be available to both parties. This highlights the importance of specifying whether you are nominating an expert or inviting the defendant to jointly instruct one.

The clinical negligence and disease protocols are stated to be less prescriptive on expert evidence and so provide greater flexibility. As stated above, the current climate is to encourage rehabilitation and the parties should consider this possibility as early as possible. Whilst use of the Rehabilitation Code is not mandatory, its use is encouraged and, following the Code, it is clear that any medical report obtained for rehabilitation purposes shall not be used in the litigation.

Non-compliance on the part of a claimant includes:
- not providing sufficient information to the defendant;
- not following the procedure required by the protocol.

Non-compliance on the part of a defendant includes:
- not making a preliminary response to the letter of claim within the time fixed for that purpose by the relevant protocol;
- not making a full response within the time fixed for that purpose by the relevant protocol;
- not disclosing documents required to be disclosed by the relevant protocol.

The sanctions include costs (potentially on an indemnity basis) for the issuing of proceedings which would have been unnecessary if there had been compliance.

1.11   PRE-ACTION PROTOCOLS: CONCLUSION

The key concept in catastrophic injury litigation is the early exchange of information where it is possible to do so. *Halsbury's Laws of England, Practice and Procedure* (vol 37)[38] succinctly summarised the role of pre-action conduct and the protocols as follows:

> 'Pre-Action Protocols are statements of understanding between legal practitioners and others about pre-action practice and which are approved by a relevant practice

---

[38]   4th edn, 2001 re-issue.

direction. Pre-Action Protocols outline the steps parties should take to seek information from and to provide information to each other about a prospective legal claim.'

The handling of catastrophic injury cases may require a degree of departure from the precise wording of the pre-action protocols – but not from their spirit. As long as a practitioner acts within the spirit of pre-action conduct and acts to protect his client's interests then modest departures are acceptable and are unlikely to attract costs penalties later in the case.

1.12 ANONYMITY ORDERS

The general rule under CPR, r 39.2 is that the names of parties to an action are included in orders and judgments of the Court and that hearings are open to the public. Thus members of the public, including the press, can obtain details about cases heard in court, including approval hearings, and publish those details. CPR, r 39.2(3), however, allows the court to hold a hearing, or any part of a hearing, in private where publicity would defeat the object of the hearing or damage confidentiality of information (including personal financial matters), or where privacy is necessary to protect the interests of any child or protected party or where the court considers it to be necessary in the interests of justice. Under CPR, r 39.2(4) the courts have power to order that the identity of any party or witness must not be disclosed if it considers non-disclosure necessary in order to protect them and under CPR, r 5.4C the court may make an order limiting the right of non-parties to inspect and copy documents on the court file.

It is unusual for orders to be made in personal injury actions that hearings should be held in private, but the courts do regularly use the powers to anonymise proceedings, normally by requiring the claimant to be known by letters only (eg *AXB v Defendant Ltd*), and to limit inspection of the court file, normally by requiring an application to be made to the court, in the Royal Courts of Justice to the Senior Master or other specified Master, before a non-party can inspect the court file. Such applications are often made in advance of an approval hearing, but can be made at any stage of the proceedings.

An application for an order that the names of the parties or the subject matter of the action be kept private is, however, a derogation from the principle of open justice and an interference with the rights of freedom of expression of the public at large. Accordingly the court needs to balance in each case the claimant's right to respect for private and family life under Art 8 of the European Convention of Human Rights and the right of the public, including the press, under Art 10 to freedom of expression in reporting cases before the courts.

The press place considerable emphasis on being able to publish the names of parties to litigation because a story about particular individuals is much more attractive to readers than a story about unidentified people. This is why reporters ordinarily seek to highlight the human interest in a story, and this is restricted by the granting of an anonymity order.

There has been a spate of decisions on the issue of anonymity. Some of them concerned anonymity for people who had been accused of terrorism and/or were subject of control orders, but the Supreme Court took the opportunity to consider the balancing exercise that the courts must undertake, see *In Re Guardian News & Media Limited*[39] and *Secretary of State for the Home Department v AP*.[40] Other cases have concerned parties seeking to restrain publication of what is said to be private and confidential information, see *DFT v TFD*,[41] a decision of Sharp J, and *Gray v UVW*[42] and *JIH v News Group Newspapers Ltd*,[43] both decisions of Tugendhat J.

Tugendhat J has been particularly active in considering the issues that arise when granting anonymity and he turned his attention to cases where anonymity had been sought at the application for the Court's approval to a settlement of a claim brought by a protected party in *LK v Sandwell & West Birmingham Hospitals NHS Trust*[44] and *JXF (a Child suing by his Mother and Litigation Friend KMF) v York Hospitals NHS Foundation Trust*.[45] In both cases anonymity was granted to the claimant, but not to the defendant. It was emphasised, however, that the court should scrutinise applications carefully, and that to achieve this applications should be supported by evidence and by a skeleton argument referring the court to the authorities. In *JXMX v Dartford and Gravesham NHS Trust*[46] Tugendhat J held that it was inappropriate to grant anonymity for approval hearings as a matter of routine and based on a formulaic application without special features, but he granted permission to appeal to the Court of Appeal so that the issue of what judges should do when faced with applications for anonymity of approval hearings could be considered by that court.

In *Sandwell* Tugendhat J held, at para 6, that:

'The test under 39.2 is a test of necessity. It is not uncommon in applications for approval of settlements of personal injury claims for anonymity orders to be made, but it is certainly not, or should not be, considered a normal order, or an order where the parties can expect the court to simply endorse an agreement the parties may have reached. There are many vulnerable claimants whom it is necessary to protect. For example – and this is only an example – protection may be from the unwanted attentions of people who, having heard of a large sum of money, want to somehow or another persuade the claimant to part with that money. There are

---

[39] [2010] UKSC 1.
[40] [2010] UKSC 26.
[41] [2010] EWHC 2335 (QB).
[42] [2010] EWHC 2367 (QB).
[43] [2010] EWHC 2818 (QB).
[44] [2010] EWHC 1928 (QB).
[45] [2010] EWHC 2800 (QB).
[46] [2013] EWHC 3956.

other risks. These very large sums of money are paid in order to enable the claimant and the claimant's carers to acquire expensive equipment. There are risks to claimants and their carers inherent in attempts to acquire and keep safe expensive equipment.

But whether or not an order under CPR 39.2 is necessary – and I emphasis the test – will depend on the facts of each case, An application ought, therefore, to be supported by evidence and by argument. The Court should be provided with the argument in a skeleton form, separate from the approval advice. The skeleton will be expected to refer to the guidance given in the cases decided by the Supreme Court.'

In *JXF* Tugendhat J described the process that the court had to go through, at paras 18–19:

'There are therefore two questions for the court to consider before making an anonymity order based on the need to protect Convention rights. The first question is: are the Art 8 rights (or any of the Convention rights) of the applicant engaged at all? In the case of the claimant in a personal injury action, his or her Art 8 rights will often be engaged, to a greater or lesser extent, because of the sensitivity of the medical or financial information under discussion.

If the Claimant's Art 8 rights are engaged, then the second question for the court is: is there sufficient general, public interest in publishing the report of the proceedings which identifies the Claimant to justify any resulting curtailment of his right and his family's right to respect for their private and family life?'

CHAPTER 2

REHABILITATION

2.1 INTRODUCTION

If steps can be taken to bring the claimant back towards a recovery then both the claimant and the potential defendants benefit. In this chapter we consider what rehabilitation can mean for catastrophic injury claimants and how the Rehabilitation Code can be applied. The concept behind the Rehabilitation Code is one of mutual benefit and, so long as both sides enter into an arrangement with and for the benefit of both parties, all should be well. The danger with rehabilitation is that it may lead to delay and early intrusion by the defendant without gain to the claimant if, in the end, this mutual self interest breaks down. For that reason rehabilitation needs to be approached positively and proactively, without deflecting from the preparation of evidence for, and progress of, a claim.

2.2 A PROACTIVE APPROACH

Rehabilitation has been defined as being 'a process of active change by which a disabled person achieves optimal physical, psychological and social function'.[1] Comprised within this definition is 'vocational rehabilitation', this being 'whatever helps someone with a health problem stay at, return to, and remain in work'.[2]

Accordingly, it can be seen that rehabilitation ought to be in the best interests of every injured person. Indeed, one cannot envisage any circumstances where rehabilitation is contraindicated.Certainly early rehabilitation has been shown to be hugely beneficial to a client's physical and mental recovery from his or her injuries.

Thus, it is crucial that a solicitor is proactive in his approach and the client's needs are assessed at the earliest practicable opportunity. The client and his or her family must be consulted right from the start and their expectations managed carefully. Two key issues in particular must be discussed:

- the type of rehabilitative treatment; and

---

[1]   *Rehabilitation Standards* (The UK Rehabilitation Council, December 2008).
[2]   Gordon Waddell, A Kim Burton, Nicholas AS Kendall, *Vocational Rehabilitation: What works, for whom and when?* (The Stationery Office, 2008).

- the provider of such treatment.

Of course rehabilitation cannot be provided unless appropriate funding is in place or if the rehabilitation can be provided free of charge, for example by the National Health Service.

Each client will have a different perspective on his or her injuries and, in particular, the path to recovery and indeed whether any recovery is possible. Thus, it is important to explain as fully as possible to the client exactly what rehabilitation is and what it can (and cannot) achieve.

The client's quality of life and his or her wishes and expectations in relation to rehabilitation should be discussed. There are a wide range of rehabilitation options providing various therapies including nursing care, physiotherapy, occupational therapy and practical input with regard to issues such as the need to make adaptations to accommodation.

The client needs to be clear that rehabilitative treatment is not always restricted to that which can be funded by the state and therefore the various alternative funding options should be discussed and explained. This process can be lengthy but the client needs to be aware of all their options.

In summary, once it is agreed that a rehabilitation programme should be considered, the aim should be to arrange for an independent needs assessment (INA) to be carried out. The defendant insurer, or 'compensator' as they are termed in the code, should then consider whether to pay for the recommendations provided in the INA report.

Once agreement has been reached and payment has been organised, then treatment begins. When final damages are ultimately awarded the cost of rehabilitation will be taken into account as an interim payment, so long as that cost is reasonable.

The client should also be made aware of the possible physical, psychological and emotional benefits of rehabilitation and the ability (obligation) to mitigate their losses by receiving rehabilitation and thus recovering faster and/or to a more optimum, pre-accident, level.

2.2.1   Independent needs assessment (INA)

An INA will explore the suitability of various types of rehabilitation and the extent to which that rehabilitation is required. A solicitor must ensure that the person carrying out the assessment is properly qualified. It is likely to be a specialist nurse, occupational therapist, or someone holding a professional 'rehabilitation' form of qualification. The purpose of the assessment is to address the client's circumstances and to provide preliminary recommendations on rehabilitative steps. Routinely such reports are relatively inexpensive to commission and will be provided simultaneously to both parties when provided under the Code. In liability-admitted cases there may be an advantage for the claimant practitioner to commission the INA privately if funds permit, outside the Rehabilitation Code, in order to ensure that the assessment is done quickly and under their control.

2.2.2 Case managers

Case managers play a major role in a client's rehabilitation in catastrophic injury cases and therefore should be brought on board as early as possible, often from the outset. The role of a case manager is to assess and/or provide treatment for clients suffering from such injuries. However, their role is varied and will depend upon the facts of each case and the nature of the injuries suffered.

A case manager may be involved in a range of activities including: planning, implementing, coordinating and monitoring services provided, as well as analysing various options for the claimant's treatment. The case manager is likely to liaise with other agencies and individuals to ensure that the claimant's needs are identified, assessed and properly addressed. A case manager will also ensure that the programme for rehabilitation is actually implemented and, where appropriate, subject to regular review.

Thus, a separate INA may not be required where a case manager is instructed at an early stage. Additionally, the solicitor should be wary about instructing a case manager who carried out the INA, as their partiality may be compromised. It must also be remembered that a case manager's duty is to the client and not to the solicitor or defendant insurer.[3]

A case manager should provide a summary of preliminary conclusions, for example, an estimate of the timescale, details of the proposed rehabilitation and justifications for this, as well as an estimate of the costs.

The Case Management Society UK develops consistent professional standards of best practice and conduct for case managers and provides training programmes for its members. Most rehabilitation providers belong to this organisation.

2.2.3 Contact with the defendant

Contact should be made with the defendant and/or his or her insurers as soon as possible as this may facilitate, or accelerate, early recovery. The issue of rehabilitation and its funding should be canvassed at this stage.

---

[3] *Wright v Sullivan* [2005] EWCA Civ 656, CA.

2.2.4   Counsel's opinion and rehabilitation

It has already been stated that, as part of the 'team' approach, it is essential that in catastrophic injury cases the services of appropriate counsel are retained as soon as possible and often from the outset. Certainly catastrophic injury cases should always benefit from the early involvement of counsel.

Some counsel may not be as familiar as some solicitors with the role of the Rehabilitation Code or its detailed provisions, since their involvement is not usually from the outset of a case and the Rehabilitation Code is intended to be implemented at the earliest stage possible (subject, of course, as to the claimant's medical status).

Nevertheless, it is important that counsel does have a good understanding of the role and aims of the Code as well as the action to be taken under that Code. This will aid the planning of the legal case and the input that counsel can provide in relation to important matters of strategy, such as the need to proceed to a swift trial upon the issue of liability (split trial), or the need for an early application for an interim payment.

Counsel must also understand which parts of the Code are within and outside the litigation process and how the Code fits into the process of a personal injury claim.

Ultimately, if the reasonableness of the rehabilitation costs is disputed by defendants, then counsel will be called upon to argue the claimant's case in relation to any outlay incurred in a rehabilitation programme.

2.2.5   Care and nursing

This area is often the most important priority. It is self-evident that appropriate care and nursing can maximise recovery, increase morale and self-esteem and optimise independence. Appropriate care and nursing can also provide not only a direct benefit to the claimant but also close members of the family or friends who may well have been providing the claimant with substantial care. These family members and friends will normally be untrained in the provision of care, including nursing care and support, and may have themselves suffered physical and/or psychological consequences due to the stresses and strains of looking after a catastrophically injured claimant which can often demand heavy physical input from carers.

The stages of recovery as a result of rehabilitation may vary considerably and therefore adjustments to the treatment should be carefully planned, with close monitoring of the claimant's progress and any change to the anticipated medical prognosis.

It has been noted that often, generous personal injury settlements are not being used to help claimants live as they would want, but rather as practitioners and carers believe they should be living.[4] Focus needs to be put on the individual needs and desires of the injured person, particularly when the injury is neurological. Special consideration must be made to accommodate the fact that many brain-injured claimants lack the capacity to make rational decisions concerning their intellectual and social needs.[5] Claimant solicitors and the professionals involved in providing rehabilitation must consider the many nuances of a claimant's anticipated care needs beyond the traditional perceptions of 'symptom reduction' and 'looking after'.[6]

The appointed case manager is usually the most appropriate person to organise the treatment as he or she will have the level of experience and expertise necessary to understand the needs of the client and respond to them. However, it is possible that the advice of a separate occupational therapist may be necessary, often to work in conjunction with the case manager.

The case manager, or other appointed expert, will need to have access to all existing reports/assessments and might need to discuss the claimant's needs with experts from different disciplines. A meeting with the client and his or her family will be arranged, and possibly a meeting with those providing medical treatment as well. The report will provide conclusions on the existing care currently provided, the client's ability to cope with the difficulties posed by his or her injury, and an assessment of the level of care required in the future. Where appropriate, that assessment must look at the future level of care required on the basis of a phased approach, ie, as the claimant's condition and reliance upon nursing/care input changes (either for the better or worse). In addition, health and safety issues, including appropriate risk assessments, have to be undertaken.

Ultimately the report should set out in detail any domestic assistance required, the nursing and care plan, as well as any equipment needed in the home. Accompanying these recommendations should be details of anticipated costs, timescales and suggested providers.

2.2.6   Accommodation

In many cases the client's accommodation is no longer suitable following catastrophic injury and adjustments will need to be made in order to provide the client with a fully accessible and comfortable home following his or her return from hospital or a rehabilitation unit. In addition, where appropriate, those adaptations must remove any hazards or risks in the layout of the home

---

[4]   Bruce Scheepers, Mark Thorneycroft, Allan Perry-Small, 'Personal Injury Law and Severe Head Injury: Helping Millionaires to Lead Impoverished Lives?' (2009) *Journal of Personal Injury Law*.

[5]   Bruce Scheepers, Mark Thorneycroft, Allan Perry-Small, 'Personal Injury Law and Severe Head Injury: Helping Millionaires to Lead Impoverished Lives?' (2009) *Journal of Personal Injury Law*.

[6]   Bruce Scheepers, Mark Thorneycroft, Allan Perry-Small, 'Personal Injury Law and Severe Head Injury: Helping Millionaires to Lead Impoverished Lives?' (2009) *Journal of Personal Injury Law*.

which, whilst not posing a threat to an able-bodied person, will pose a threat to a person catastrophically injured, such as a person who is wheelchair-bound.

If the client's long-term accommodation needs are unclear at first, then a number of short-term alterations/adaptations to the property can be made, for example, installing stair handrails or lowered light switches. Such measures can and should be undertaken quickly and are relatively inexpensive. The case manager or occupational therapist will be able to advise on such measures following a visit to the client's home and then organise workmen to carry out the alterations. Again, where appropriate, a risk assessment should be undertaken.

Long-term requirements may subsequently become necessary which would include substantial adaptations to a home, or even plans to construct a purpose-built property. Of course, these will only be undertaken when it is reasonably clear that such work is necessary. An accommodation expert (architect or surveyor) will usually be required to carry out the assessment. It is possible that grants may be obtained from the local authority to assist towards the outlay.

When considering an expert's report on this matter it is important to ensure that recommendations in the report are focused on the overall objective of maximising the client's potential for independent living, although the detailed particulars will depend upon the nature and extent of the injuries suffered.

Provision for a carer's accommodation should also be discussed where necessary. In addition, there should be a detailed section dealing with costs, including possible maintenance and/or replacement costs.

2.2.7   Mobility

Mobility within the home is a significant consideration. Simple alterations, such as those outlined above, can have a huge effect on claimants achieving independence (albeit possibly not full independence). When trying to obtain complex equipment such as specialised wheelchairs, the waiting time may be considerable. It is commonly the case that a catastrophically injured client has to wait an unnecessary length of time before specialised equipment becomes available, which inevitably leads to a reduction in morale and an increase in the support and care that the client has to receive from his or her family and friends.

There are a number of Disability Living Centres across the country. These are specialised centres offering free advice in respect of equipment and products which help people make a more informed choice that should aid easier, and more independent, living.

In terms of transport, it is possible for a driving assessment to be carried out which will identify any difficulties the client experiences with his or her driving ability and will recommend aids or adaptations which could ensure that such problems are overcome.

2.2.8 Physiotherapy, osteopathy and chiropractice

Where physiotherapy, osteopathy or chiropractic treatment is deemed necessary, it is important that this continues after the client's discharge from hospital or rehabilitation unit. Such input can be hugely beneficial and should be considered as part of the client's overall treatment plan.

Where there are soft tissue injuries, an assessment of the client's needs must, if at all possible, be made within a few weeks of the injury occurring. Practitioners providing such therapy services must be members of the relevant professional bodies. Details on this can be found via the Chartered Society of Physiotherapists, General Council of Osteopaths or British Chiropractic Association.

Routinely the client will undergo an initial assessment before a programme is devised and treatment is commenced. A treatment plan should then be prepared by the lead medical expert, which details the number of sessions recommended and the content and objective of the sessions.

2.2.9 Vocational therapy

Returning to work can have a huge impact upon a client's morale and self-esteem. In many catastrophic injury cases, however, a return to work is not possible. If a return to work is anticipated then it is crucial to get a vocational or employment rehabilitation expert onboard as soon as possible. Such an expert can provide guidance and advice as to whether, with appropriate support, the claimant can return to his or her pre-accident work, or, if not, what work he or she should be capable of undertaking, if necessary, after undergoing a programme of vocational rehabilitation.

Employers should also be contacted, where appropriate, in order to discuss adaptations to the workplace required as a result of the claimant's injuries. Employers may need to be reminded of the duties placed upon them under the Disability Discrimination Act 1997.

First, a detailed assessment of the client's experience and qualifications, aspirations and current physical and mental state should be carried out. The pre-accident employer will then meet with the vocational assessor to discuss whether a return to work is suitable and any recommendations to be made such as adaptations, personal support, etc.

If it is decided that a return to work at the pre-accident place of employment is not possible, then other local jobs, training schemes or work experience placements, ought to be considered. Where appropriate, a discussion should take place with the claimant as to whether he or she should undergo a period of enhanced educational training, eg, to provide improved educational qualifications, so as to assist the claimant in his or her search for alternative employment.

An additional, more detailed, assessment can be carried out if the likelihood of finding suitable employment is low. There are a number of centres around the country which can carry out such assessments and measure ability in a work environment in terms of speed, ability, coordination, confidence, motivation and communication.

2.3   PSYCHOLOGICAL THERAPY

The psychological impact of a serious accident can be debilitating. However, claimant solicitors are often of the opinion that clients 'slip through the net'[7] when it comes to psychological rehabilitation.

Unlike physical injuries, claimants' psychological problems can often remain unaddressed throughout the litigation process until a much later point. Some of the reasons suggested for this disparity are the stigma attached to psychological injury, the ignorance of claimant solicitors to the various avenues of support available, and additionally the failure of medical practitioners to take into consideration the potential funding opportunities available to claimants, whether that be via interim payments or under the Rehabilitation Code.[8] However, often the main barrier to claimants receiving the psychological help they need is their own reluctance to discuss the trauma and the impact it has had on them.

Claimant solicitors need to be aware of these difficulties if they are to effectively accommodate those claimants less able to make their psychological needs known.

2.3.1   Finding a suitable rehabilitation provider

Selecting a suitable 'rehabilitation provider' to assess and/or provide treatment for a client can be a difficult task. There are certainly increasing numbers of providers in the UK who are offering their services and there are a wide range of services available, ranging from individuals offering specific services to large organisations that offer to provide and arrange treatment across the range of disciplines.

---

7   Angus Lyon, 'Psychological Rehabilitation After Trauma (or Mr Dickens' Neurosis)' [2009] *Journal of Personal Injury Law*.

8   Angus Lyon, 'Psychological Rehabilitation After Trauma (or Mr Dickens' Neurosis)' [2009] *Journal of Personal Injury Law*.

At the outset it is important to bear in mind that the provision of rehabilitation and rehabilitation services is a largely unregulated area in the UK.

However, there is a concern that a number of agencies and individuals who have emerged into the market in recent times are not sufficiently experienced, do not have the appropriate qualifications to provide the breadth of services they claim they can provide, or cannot supply the specialist input that a catastrophically injured claimant will require. The solicitor must therefore make all necessary enquiries to ensure that the individual or agency selected to provide rehabilitation input does have the appropriate qualifications and can provide the nature and range of services offered.

The solicitor must not therefore simply accept a provider's statement/assertion of expertise or excellence, or their claims of success, without proof or validation.

It is unfortunate that there is no single register available in which all UK rehabilitation providers are listed. It can be difficult to know where to start looking. Obviously, careful consideration of the type of treatment required is necessary and research into local providers must be carried out in detail and assiduously.

The following organisations are often useful avenues for help:

- The Association of Personal Injury Lawyers (APIL): APIL have collated a database of rehabilitation providers which is contained in a directory and is updated on a regular basis. Each organisation will provide details of their location, background information regarding the individual or organisation concerned, details of the categories of injuries that fall within their expertise and the nature of the therapy input that can be provided.

- Bodily Injuries Claims Management Association (BICMA): this organisation's website contains a 'rehabilitation service providers register' of approximately 90 providers and it is possible to search the register by location or contact name. Across the different providers, a fairly wide range of rehabilitation services are available including care, physiotherapy, occupational therapy, spinal injury rehabilitation and chiropractors.

- The Injury Care Clinics (TICCS): although there is no public directory of providers on this organisation's website, this is a very useful source which offers advice about recommended rehabilitation providers. It also undertakes, through its own services, an initial assessment report on a catastrophically injured claimant.

- Rehab Window: there is an extensive register of rehabilitation providers available on this organisation's website and a search of the providers can be carried out by geographical location and also within the following categories: medical, functional, vocational, psychological, or an integrated assessment service can be provided.

- NHS Patient and Liaison Advisory Service: since initial treatment of the client's injuries is routinely likely to take place in hospital, it is possible that members of staff at the NHS will be able to recommend good local providers. Certainly personal recommendations can be invaluable when trying to find a suitable rehabilitation provider.

Following receipt of an award of damages (interim or otherwise), the claimant effectively becomes a purchaser of rehabilitation services. Once the practitioner has identified the need for a rehabilitation provider, that practitioner then has to establish whether it is appropriate to allow any particular provider to assess and/or treat the client. It is hoped that the following points for consideration will assist the practitioner in undertaking this task.

(1) *Qualifications held by the provider* – if using a larger agency or organisation, a solicitor ought to check that the person who will actually be assessing and/or treating the client has the appropriate expertise and qualifications to do so. Consideration of his or her CV is normally a good place to start. Given the largely unregulated area of rehabilitation, there are, in practical terms, few 'rehabilitation' qualifications available. It may be, therefore, that the provider who offers the service may have qualified into a different area which is inappropriate for the specific rehabilitation input that the client needs. This must be checked by the practitioner to ensure that the qualification of the provider is appropriate for the input that the claimant requires. In addition, the provider must also have in place adequate and comprehensive professional indemnity insurance. In many cases, expertise in a specific, discrete area and the provider's current scope of practice may carry more weight than the provision of formal qualifications, but an additional endorsement, for example by way of a personal or professional recommendation (from counsel or another expert), should be sufficient. Ultimately, the solicitor will have to decide whether the individual or agency concerned are the correct source for the rehabilitation assessment and/or provision of rehabilitation input for their client.

(2) *Competency* – in a largely unregulated sector, solicitors ought to bear in mind that catastrophically injured clients need protecting. Potential providers ought to be able to readily provide experts with a document demonstrating both the ongoing services that they will provide and the specific set of skills and expertise they possess which will allow them to provide a proper and appropriate service. These details should include: available training programmes and supervision processes; how employees and agents are screened for their suitability; evidence that they can provide modern, client-focused telephonic and internet-based communication skills; provision of accurate and clear costings; details of the area, or areas covered and the relationships that they have with other local organisations (including employers). Bearing in mind the likely length of time that rehabilitation input will be required; the provider should ideally be located within a reasonable distance of the client in order to ensure convenience, proportionate travel costs and reliability of attendances.

(3) *Success stories* – an expert ought to be asked to confirm how successful a particular provider is. This helps to satisfy the claimant and the claimant's

family that they are not simply being abandoned once the practitioner's direct input into the case concludes. The details provided should include: total number of cases dealt with; the ratio of cases where a client has successfully maintained their rehabilitation objectives; examples where significant improvements have been made to a client's life; drop-out ratio; specific examples of satisfied and dissatisfied clients. It should be stressed that this is not simply a data collection exercise – it is both necessary and proportionate to protect the claimant's interests as fully as is reasonably possible.

(4) *Regulatory standards* – there are now very few instances where a provider can justify not knowing their exact statutory and regulatory safeguards and requirements. The exact obligations will of course depend upon the type of rehabilitation service being provided and every provider ought to be able to provide full details, evidencing their compliance. Particular attention should, however, always be given to a provider's safeguards for ensuring the protection of the client's personal information and for securing their informed consent to treatment where necessary. In addition, it goes without saying that the provider must supply clear evidence of their ability to safeguard the client's health and safety.

The Rehabilitation Code 2007 sets out a timeline to be followed and the practitioner must carefully consider (and seek the appropriate assurance) that the provider is able to comply with the timetable. This may be difficult where the provider has a large list on their current client base.

The provider must also demonstrate to the practitioner that they have an efficient system of working and that they have appropriate backup where necessary and will be willing to provide regular updates on progress with regard to any assessment or rehabilitation input.

The practitioner must bear in mind that the provider's primary duty is to the client and, therefore, they must disclose any business relationships or agreements they have with others, as well as the nature of their relationship.

The provider should also provide a detailed estimate of costs and keep the client and the client's practitioner informed of any cost levels which are reached so that, if appropriate, they can be reviewed and, if necessary, increased.

2.4 REHABILITATION AND THE MULTI-TRACK CODE/PROTOCOL

The various personal injury protocols apply to all personal injury claims, including those claims which involve catastrophic injuries. There are no 'special rules' within those protocols for claims which have caused catastrophic injuries.

Cases involving catastrophic injury require special skill, commitment and dedication. They involve, from the claimant's practitioner, input and attributes that he or she will not find in the normal run of personal injury cases.

In short, such cases are different and need to be managed differently.

As a consequence of the recognition of this factor that the Multi-track Code has been constructed as a separate protocol to deal with claims involving more serious injuries.

The Multi-track Code was originally launched as a pilot scheme which was intended to facilitate the more effective case management of personal injury claims which have a value in excess of £250,000. It is not correct to state, therefore, that the Code is, strictly speaking, a 'catastrophic injury' Code and it does not apply to clinical negligence or asbestos claims.

A claim may have a value well in excess of £250,000 if the injuries suffered are moderate but have either impeded or prevented a high-earner from returning to work at the level enjoyed before the accident occurred. If the claim for loss of earnings alone is in excess of £250,000, then it will fall within the proposed Multi-track Code, even if the injuries cannot be described as 'catastrophic'.

The original pilot was published in March 2008 and commenced in July 2008. It was later extended to allow more detailed feedback as it was considered that an insufficient number of cases of the necessary value and complexity were completed within the first year of the pilot.

The Multi-track Code was piloted over a period of 3 years from 2008 to 2011, when its effects were evaluated and presented to stakeholders and Jackson LJ on 12 October 2011. The Code received overwhelming support upon review and it was recommended that it be applied widely as a result.[9] Jackson LJ commented on the code in his review of civil litigation costs:

> 'I support the aims of the Code and welcome the progress that has been made in that regard. The process is becoming less adversarial: there is earlier access to rehabilitation and greater structure is being achieved in cases from an earlier stage.'[10]

The use of the Multi-track Code is voluntary. Practitioners who wish to use it must register with APIL. There are some 32 claimant firms participating in the pilot. Not all defendant insurers have joined the pilot scheme but those that have include AXA, Liverpool Victoria, Norwich Union, RBS, Zurich and the MIB. The Code cannot be used for cases which were notified to insurers before 1 July 2008.

---

[9]   Suzanne Trask, David Fisher, 'The Multi-track Code' [2012] *Journal of Personal Injury Law*.
[10]   Published in January 2010.

Upon receipt of instructions, the claimant solicitor must notify the named contact at the participating defendant insurer that the solicitor has a case which falls within the criteria of the Multi-track Code and log the case details on to the monitoring system. These details are updated as the case progresses. The solicitor will then agree a suitable timetable and case plan (called a 'route map') which is intended to resolve the case. In order to be effective, this ought to cover:

- how liability issues are to be approached;
- how to maximise the claimant's rehabilitation; and
- whether (and when) interim payments are to be made.

The stated purpose of the Code is to improve the system for seriously injured claimants by improving the effectiveness of bringing a claim. Collaboration between the parties, and promoting early rehabilitation, is a key aspect of this. Rehabilitation is, of course, the focus of the Rehabilitation Code 2007 (para B.1). Accordingly, applying the Multi-track Code would appear to be a useful way of improving the practitioner's chances of assisting his client sooner than might otherwise be the case.

In summary, the aims of the Code are to:

- ensure the process of claiming compensation is more efficient and less antagonistic;
- ensure early interim payments are made by defendants;
- ensure admissions are treated as binding;
- aid claimant solicitors by promoting the prompt payment of disbursements and base costs; and
- aid insurers with a commitment to the early notification of claims.

Accordingly, the persuasiveness of the Code lies in the attractiveness of its provisions to both sides. These include the following:

(1) The provisions of the Code are 'claimant centred' (Introduction). Thus, by agreeing to use it, defendants ought not to be singularly promoting their interests. Any arrangements made are subject to liability being established by the claimant and so liability must be among the claimant solicitor's primary issues.

(2) The need for collaboration is prevailing. There is no room within the Code for adversarial behaviour and, indeed, avoidance of such behaviour is necessary in order to promote the Code's usefulness. The provisions of the Code are not to be used to gain any sort of tactical advantage by either side (Introduction). Both sides are expected to work together 'in an environment of mutual trust and collaboration' and formal offers of settlement are expressed to be prohibited, unless negotiation has failed (Objectives).

(3) The need for collaboration should not be used as a tool to extend liability investigations unreasonably. It is considered that liability ought to be

resolved within 6 months of the first notification of the claim, whether by 'agreement or, if necessary, trial' (Objectives, sub-para v) following prompt discussions as to how liability is to be investigated (Objectives, sub-para ii). This necessarily depends on the nature of the case but attempts should be made to reach agreement as to what evidence is necessary in the absence of an admission being made (Objectives, sub-para ix, x and para E.3) together with a set of identifiable review dates within the route map itself (paras 1.2 and 4.2). Paragraph 4.2.2 specifically provides that the commencement of proceedings does not suspend the Code and so consideration ought to be given to using it throughout the life of the case – it is not simply a pre-action protocol. Useful checklists are to be found in Guideline E of the Code.

(4)   An essential requirement of the Code is that the claimant solicitor provides notification of the claim within 7 days of receiving instructions (paras 3.1 and 3.3). There is no need for a formal letter of claim at this stage (para 3.2) and the letter should be marked as being entirely 'without prejudice' (para 3.3). This letter should (inter alia) highlight the claimant's rehabilitation needs (para 3.3).

(5)   The period following the early notification of the claim is akin to a combined investigation of the case with a view to reaching agreement over the likely issues. Regular contact and 'stock takes' are promoted and unilateral investigations frowned upon (The Code, 1. The Collaborative Approach – An Outline). The defendant's representative is expected to take instructions on his or her client in time to have a constructive meeting with the claimant's solicitors within 28 days of receiving the initial letter (para 4.1).

The success of the Code is dependent on parties genuinely wanting to promote collaboration, because the Code itself is otherwise unenforceable. The Introduction to the Code makes it clear that any failure to comply with the Code should be taken into account by a judge later in the case. Thus, there is no mandatory penalty if the Code is ignored.

Further, whilst technical legal points are not within the spirit of the Code, it ought to be borne in mind that there is no guarantee that the Code offers 'without prejudice' protection and the ready (and documented) exchange of information is required to maximise its effectiveness.

It will certainly not be suitable for every catastrophic case to be pursued within the framework of the Code, for the reasons given above. The Code's Introduction makes it clear that it does not override a solicitor's duty to act in his client's best interests.

Any documents produced by the client's clinical case manager should be promptly disclosed to the defendant's legal representatives, unless they are privileged. Where redaction has occurred, the defendants can make representations regarding the redaction, including why it has occurred.

Further, any admissions made may still be resiled from later on during the claim, although it is strongly implied (para D.4.2) that certainty is required. The prudent practitioner should therefore carefully balance the need to protect his client with the need to facilitate the early resolution of the case and the client's rehabilitation needs.

2.5 THE REHABILITATION CODE 2007

2.5.1 Introduction

The aim of the Rehabilitation Code ('the Code') is to promote the use of rehabilitation and early intervention in the compensation process so that the injured person makes the best, and quickest, medical, social and psychological recovery. The starting point must be the aim of compensation, which is to place the victim in the position he or she would have been 'but for' the injury.

The Code applies to all personal injury claims, including those where the claimant has suffered injuries of a catastrophic nature.

2.5.2 Historical background

The Code was launched in 1999 and was subsequently updated by the rehabilitation working party in 2003 and also in 2007. A number of changes to the 2003 Code have been made, including:

- 'A timetable setting out the key stages in implementing care, starting with an immediate needs assessment'; and
- greater flexibility – 'The new Code is also less prescriptive, allowing more flexibility for the parties to take into account the individual circumstances and the need to the Claimant'.[11]

In addition, a summary of the new Code has been published (the 'Rehab-Lite' version). The full text of the Code and the 'Rehab-Lite' version are reproduced at the end of this chapter.

2.5.3 Key provisions of the Rehabilitation Code 2007

The Code is a voluntary Code for use in all personal injury and clinical negligence claims. It eschews the adverse serial nature inherent in litigation in favour of promoting early collaboration between the parties (para 2.5).

The stated aim of the Code is to promote the use of rehabilitation and early intervention in the compensation process. The Code recognises the purpose of a compensation payment (para 1.1). Accordingly, although the Code only refers to the Personal Injury Protocol, this ought not to dissuade one from using it with the clinical negligence disease or draft Multi-track pre-action protocols.

---

[11] Bodily Injuries Claims Management Association (BICMA).

However, one does not have to use the Code. It was recognised that the aims of the Code can be achieved without necessarily strictly adhering to the formal terms of the Code. Accordingly, it is open to the parties to agree an alternative framework so as to achieve the early rehabilitation of the claimant (para 1.2). Accordingly, the Code is not a 'new procedural Code' in the way that the Civil Procedure Rules 1998 were. The Code simply attempts to provide a practical and effective framework for helping the victims of injury to receive rehabilitation input, thereby improving their condition and their independence. It leaves ample room for an experienced solicitor's pre-existing practices to remain justified and relevant, as long as those practices assist the objective of rehabilitation.

The Code provides a useful framework within which claimants, their legal advisers and the defendant's representatives can work together, so as to ensure that the needs of the injured claimant are assessed at an early stage (para 1.3). It is not necessary to wait until liability has been admitted (para 2.5). Therefore, the Code can be used to assist the catastrophically injured client before an interim payment is available, as the costs of the report and treatment are not recoverable from the claimant, even if his or her case later fails (para 7.3).

However, addressing rehabilitation needs before liability is admitted does require the agreement of the defendant's representatives and so raises the same practical difficulties as obtaining an early interim payment does in cases where liability is likely to be contested. In such cases it can be helpful to point out that the case can still be defended notwithstanding the provision of rehabilitation and questions of 'cost' are secondary to the concept of 'value'. It can also be useful to point out to the defendant that, the sooner rehabilitation is commenced, the more likely it is that the claimant's condition and prognosis will improve, ultimately leading to a mitigation of the claimant's losses which will be to the financial benefit of the defendant, or defendant's insurer, who ultimately pays damages.

However, there is no inherent right to rehabilitation and the Code does not apply if no agreement (on either liability or the use of the Code) can be reached. Furthermore, the defendant is not obliged to pay for rehabilitation treatment that has not been caused by the index event (para 5.5).

This practical difficulty is most likely to arise in clinical negligence cases where, even if breach of duty appears clear-cut, there is likely to be an argument raised by the defendant regarding causation of all, or part, of the claimant's disabilities.

This is not to say that the Code and the Civil Procedure Rules (CPR) are completely separate. For the collaborative nature of the Code to be practical and, therefore, useful, the emphasis is placed on providing the proposed defendant with enough information to allow them to make a 'proper decision' about the 'need for intervention, rehabilitation or treatment'. To achieve this, the Code states that the claimant solicitor 'must comply' with the requirements of the Pre-Action Protocol for Personal Injury Claims, to provide 'full and adequate details of the injuries sustained by the claimant, the nature and extent of any, or any likely, continuing disability and any suggestions that may have already been made concerning the rehabilitation and/or early intervention'. However, there is no need to obtain a medical report and it is perfectly permissible to identify a need for rehabilitation before experts are instructed (paras 2.6 and 2.7).

One may ask at this point, how is the catastrophic injuries solicitor to address this? As with any personal injury case, it effectively comes down to how likely it is that liability will be established. The defendant's representatives are less likely to recommend that their client pays for rehabilitation if they do not believe they were responsible for the claimant's injuries.

Unlike a claimant who receives an interim payment, he or she will not need to repay the costs of rehabilitation if his or her claim ultimately fails.

Liability is, naturally, dependent upon the facts of each individual case and these, of course, vary. However, the facts of each case are demonstrated and proven by the evidence for them and, inevitably, in a case involving catastrophic injuries, the solicitor will undertake far more detailed investigations than the norm. These should allow the claimant solicitor to investigate adequately what remedial treatment the claimant is receiving, whether that treatment is adequate, and what further treatment should be provided. Undertaking this careful analysis ought to minimise the risks of recommending rehabilitation treatment that is inappropriate or misdirected and enable the appropriate focus to match the available resources to the claimant's needs.

There is no bar to the solicitor in obtaining an assessment report, so long as the solicitor believes it is necessary. The solicitor may, however, prefer to wait until the letter of claim has been dispatched and the letter of response received, although the authors recognise that this is often counterproductive, given the customary delays that occur during the pre-action protocol phase, particularly the delays before a letter of response is received from the defendant or their insurers.

Certainly it is sensible, and compliant with the Code, to raise the issue of rehabilitation under the Code at the outset with defendants. In a clinical case, it could be made at the time when the solicitor makes a preliminary request for copies of the claimant's medical records.

The claimant solicitor is obliged to consider:

(a) from the earliest practicable stage; and

(b) in consultation with the claimant, the claimant's family, and, where appropriate, the claimant's treating physician(s), whether it is likely, or possible, that early intervention, rehabilitation or medical treatment, will improve their present and/or long-term physical and mental well-being (para 2.1).

It is also necessary for the claimant solicitor to consider whether there is an immediate need for aids, adaptations, adjustments to his or her employment (to enable him or her either to keep his or her existing job, or to obtain suitable alternative employment with the same employer, or retrain for new employment) or other matters that would seek to alleviate medical problems caused by, and related to, disability.

If there is, then it is necessary to communicate with the defendant as soon as practicable about any such rehabilitation needs (para 2.3). Claimant solicitors are not, however, required to reach these decisions without using the input of suitably qualified doctors and so questions of rehabilitation can often be dealt with as part of one's usual pre-issue investigations and preparation of the case.

However, it should be noted that once the defendant's representatives have confirmed that they believe a case 'might' be suitable for rehabilitation, the claimant solicitor is expected to advise the claimant of this 'immediately' (para 3.3). Since the inception of the Code, there has been anecdotal evidence of defendants representatives attempting to pre-empt investigations by offering rehabilitation directly to victims, or writing to claimant solicitors well before their initial investigations have been completed on the basis of the defendant's obligation to consider rehabilitation at 'the earliest practicable stage' (paras 3.1 and 3.2).

Although the Code promotes the need to agree the choice of the rehabilitation provider and assessor, it also allows the use of a rehabilitation provider linked to either party (with the agreement of the other side) although neither party may insist on using one particular provider of rehabilitation services. Any objection, however, should be made within 21 days of receiving the suggestion (paras 4.2, 4.3, 4.4 and 5.1).

This ought not to pose any significant problems to a solicitor who is experienced in dealing with catastrophic injury claims. The purpose of the Code is to promote the appropriate rehabilitation of the claimant, rather than to promote rehabilitation in general, or a particular rehabilitation provider. It can be readily incorporated into the solicitor's case plan and the claimant's best interests, as can any reasonable objections that the solicitor has. Indeed, the assessment itself can be legitimately superseded by the claimant solicitor if he has already obtained suitable medical evidence (para 4.1) as is often the case with a catastrophic injury claim.

If one does wish to proceed to have an assessment for rehabilitation under the Code, the defendant is required to respond to a reasonable rehabilitation request within 21 days and is not entitled to use its obligations to extend its response time under the Pre-Action Protocol for Personal Injury Claims (paras 3.4 and 3.5).

Consideration should also be given as to whether the assessment to be undertaken is going to be suitable. The Code necessarily covers all personal injury claims and so the stipulated 14-day time-limit for arranging the assessment appointment (under para 5.4) may justifiably be changed to a more convenient one which fits in with the claimant's needs. There is no need to agree an appointment which is not suitable for the claimant and telephone appointments (which are permitted under para 5.2) should not be used in catastrophic injury cases, unless there are exceptional circumstances.

The suitability of the contents of any report obtained should also be carefully considered. There is no set format for the instruction, although agreement should be sought for the means of instruction (para 5.1) and this can include the letter of instruction. The suggested format of the rehabilitation report is set out by para 5.2 and this may need amendment for the particular catastrophic injury suffered by the claimant. The format will need to be considered individually, bearing in mind the circumstances of the case and the injuries caused. The broad topics are:

(1) the injuries sustained by the claimant;

(2) the current disability/incapacity arising from those injuries. Where relevant to the overall picture of the claimant's needs, any other medical conditions not arising from the accident should also be separately annotated;

(3) the claimant's domestic circumstances (including mobility, accommodation and employment) where relevant;

(4) the injuries/disability in respect of which early intervention or early rehabilitation is suggested;

(5) the type of intervention or treatment envisaged;

(6) the likely cost; and

(7) the likely outcome of such interventional treatment.

Although the report is not intended to be used as part of the litigated case, it can be, if all parties agree in writing (para 6.2). This can be advantageous to the claimant and the practitioner should consider using the report within the litigation framework, bearing in mind the amount of work the practitioner has put in to preparing the case at the stage when the report is received. The practitioner should bear in mind that a complicated 'suite' of symptoms can, nevertheless, be followed by a change in clinical status and disabilities over a period of time, in which event a report commissioned at an early stage of a claimant's treatment may ultimately be superseded, either wholly or in part and, indeed, may be misleading, for example if an overoptimistic prognosis is given.

It should also be borne in mind that the assessor undertaking the activity will usually not be called as a witness in the litigation and the notes and documents prepared pursuant to the assessment are not disclosed (para 6.3). This is a relevant consideration in deciding whether to request a rehabilitation assessment in the first place. However, the notes and documents prepared as part of the subsequent treatment are disclosable and so these can be shown to the experts instructed on behalf of the claimant (and defendant) (para 6.4). This does allow the adequacy of the report's recommendations to be kept under review.

Thus, the catastrophic injury solicitor who is confident of success in the claim may well be tempted to respond to a defendant's refusal, or reluctance, to comply with the Rehabilitation Code by seeking an early interim payment in order to pay for the appropriate rehabilitation assessment and subsequent treatment or therapy. Indeed, it is possible that a defendant may be willing, or persuaded, to make an early interim payment generally which can then be utilised for the purposes of providing rehabilitation input for the catastrophically injured claimant.

The claimant's practitioner, however, must bear in mind that the approval of the High Court (not the Court of Protection) will be required in respect of any interim payment for a claimant who is under a disability and that approval will be required for any interim payment which is offered before proceedings are commenced.[12]

2.6   FUNDING OF REHABILITATION

In catastrophic injury cases it is very likely that the NHS will provide some form of rehabilitation, which will be at no cost. However, the scope of such rehabilitation may well be limited and private funding might become necessary to continue, or extend, rehabilitation after the initial stage of treatment has concluded. It is important for a solicitor to ensure that a good relationship between the NHS provider and insurer is maintained and regular feedback in respect of the client's progress is provided.

Some clients may have a private health insurance policy, sometimes provided through their employment contract. If so, the policy must be carefully checked to see if it covers any form of rehabilitation input. The practitioner must also bear in mind that the policy may contain an obligation to refund payment of rehabilitation services if, and when, an award of damages is made.

As soon as it has been established that rehabilitation of a certain type is necessary, a solicitor should contact the defendants, or their insurers, to inform them of this need and to invite them to make an interim payment, on a voluntary basis, in order to accommodate the cost of this treatment.

Of course, such an approach is only likely to be successful if the solicitor is confident of establishing liability. Waiting for a decision on this would be

---

[12]   CPR, r 25.6.

unnecessary. A situation where a defendant is persuaded at such an early stage that liability is almost certain to be found in favour of the claimant (even if there is a likelihood of a finding of contributory negligence) is not one that practitioners come across every day. Defendants routinely 'hedge their bets' by refusing to be drawn at an early stage upon the issue of liability, but it is only by persuading a defendant of the strength of the claim that they will be persuaded to provide financial support for the provision of rehabilitation treatment at an early stage.

Thus, a good working relationship between the claimant solicitor and defendant, or his or her insurers, is often a key to the provision of early treatment by the use of a judicious and adequate interim payment from a defendant. It is our experience that maintaining a firm, but non-confrontational, relationship increases the likelihood of a payment being made.

Of course, if such a payment is made, then when final damages are awarded, any payments for such rehabilitation will be taken into account and deducted from the final award. However, a defendant who successfully establishes contributory negligence on the part of the claimant will not lead to a refund of rehabilitation costs. In addition, funds provided under the 2007 Rehabilitation Code cannot be contested on the grounds of unreasonableness.

If no agreement is reached in relation to the extent of treatment required then an INA can be made in order to assess the client's requirements on a 'without prejudice' basis. Where proceedings have been commenced, such assessments can be funded by way of earlier interim payments which are achieved under a formal order of the court.

It is, of course, possible for a client to fund his or her rehabilitation out of their own financial resources, but it is our experience that it is rare for a client to have sufficient funds to do so.

It is also possible that a rehabilitation provider who is persuaded that the claim is a strong one, will provide the necessary services by way of rehabilitation assessment and treatment on the basis that payment of their fees will be deferred until either:

(a)   an interim payment is made; or

(b)   the final award is secured.

However, such an arrangement will give rise to obvious difficulties in the event that the claim concludes unsuccessfully and, in those circumstances, the practitioner himself may find that they have to pay the rehabilitation costs.

A client can also seek funding from a charitable source, but it is fair to say that it is rare for a charity to provide funding for rehabilitation, although there are a number of charities who can provide guidance and advice to claimants who have suffered a catastrophic injury. This support can, in certain circumstances, include specific services which the claimant may well find not only useful, but vital. These charitable organisations include:

- *Aspire*: Aspire works with people with spinal cord injury to create opportunity, choice and independence for disabled people in society.
  www.aspire.org.uk

- *Headway*: Headway works on a national and local basis to promote understanding of all aspects of brain injury and its effects, as well as providing information to support and services to help brain injury survivors and their families.
  www.headway.org.uk

- *Spinal Injuries Association*: the Spinal Injuries Association is a national, user-led charity which offers support to individuals who have become spinal cord injured and their families, from the moment the injury or illness occurs and for the rest of their lives.
  www.spinal.co.uk

- *The Child Brain Injury Trust*: this Trust is a UK-wide charity offering support and information on acquired brain injury in children. It supports children, parents, siblings, relatives and professionals.
  www.cbituk.org

- *The Backup Trust*: this Trust runs a variety of services for adults and young people that encourage self-confidence, independence and motivation following a spinal cord injury.
  www.backuptrust.org.uk

- *Back Care*: this is a national charity that helps people manage and prevent back pain by providing information and support, promoting self-help, encouraging debate and funding research into better back care.
  www.backcare.org.uk

A discussion of rehabilitation services provided by the government in order to assist a return to work is beyond the scope of this book. However, it may be of assistance to mention that the first point of contact should be the client's local Job Centre Plus, as there are a number of schemes and training programmes which might be available. An assessment of a client's vocational capabilities will be made by a specially trained member of staff, usually a disability employment adviser.

It is clear that early provision of rehabilitation will, in almost all cases, be very beneficial to the client and, where appropriate, his or her family. The opportunity to make informed decisions about the suitable methods of treatment and to have sufficient time to test various options of rehabilitation, if necessary, by trial and error, can be invaluable.

2.7　LOCAL AUTHORITY/SOCIAL SERVICES PROVISION

There are numerous statutes and regulations relevant to considerations of state funded rehabilitation. Some impose specific duties and others merely contain a general guide. However, the practitioner must be aware of the legislation and, where appropriate, advise the claimant accordingly where it is considered that such services can, and should, be implemented. With that backdrop, the following legislation is perhaps the most relevant:

- NHS and Community Care Act 1990, s 47 – the local authority must undertake an assessment of the needs of apparently disabled persons in order to ensure that disabled people are able to access rights to state provision. This is the 'trigger' to obtaining formal assistance. Examples of social services provided would include laundry services, housing adaptations, transport, or residential care. It is important to bear in mind the availability of services is dependent upon the resources of the local authority and the standard of services may vary depending upon locality. In the current economic climate one would anticipate that the response from local authorities would be restrictive rather than sympathetic. There is no guarantee that any such provision will remain in force for the remainder of your client's lifetime.

- Chronically Sick and Disabled Persons Act 1970, s 2 – the local authority has a legal obligation to provide certain services to disabled persons which include home help, holidays, meals and telephone services.

- National Assistance Act 1948, s 21 – under this Act, the local authority has an obligation to provide suitable accommodation for a person who is disabled.

- Community Care (Direct Payment) Act 1996 – local authorities are able to make direct cash payments to disabled persons so that they can purchase care services directly for themselves.

It should be pointed out that if a local authority provides such services free of charge, a claim cannot be raised in respect of such services. The decision as to whether to charge for such services (apart from residential care) is one for the local authority to make and will depend on whether it is reasonable, in all the circumstances, to make that payment and whether the claimant has sufficient means to pay for the services.

The practitioner must also bear in mind that the social services department of the local authority may seek to recover costs from the client, even where state provision is approved and provided. Therefore, it might be useful to consider whether insurer indemnities are appropriate in ensuring that the client's damages are not reduced as a consequence.

Although a comprehensive examination of the various benefits available to clients who have suffered catastrophic injuries is beyond the scope of this book, it is useful to point out that the following benefits may be of assistance:

- incapacity benefit;
- severe disablement allowance;
- industrial disablement benefit;
- industrial injuries benefit;

- disability living allowance (care component, mobility component);
- disability working allowance.

The legal issues that have come before the courts over the past few years have centred upon whether (and to what extent) the provision of these services amounts to double recovery. Whilst the position now appears to be settled in favour of claimants, it remains prudent to write to the local authority to seek confirmation as to whether they will be able to provide the requisite services for the rest of the claimant's life. It is likely to be a rare situation where such confirmation can be provided and the correspondence is helpful evidence of the need for a more comprehensive care regime.

ANNEXES

The 2007 Rehabilitation Code

Introduction

The aim of this code is to promote the use of rehabilitation and early intervention in the compensation process so that the injured person makes the best and quickest possible medical, social and psychological recovery. This objective applies whatever the severity of the injuries sustained by the claimant. The Code is designed to ensure that the claimant's need for rehabilitation is assessed and addressed as a priority, and that the process of so doing is pursued on a collaborative basis by the claimant's lawyer and the compensator.

Therefore, in every case, where rehabilitation is likely to be of benefit, the earliest possible notification to the compensator of the claim and of the need for rehabilitation will be expected.

1. Introduction

1.1 The purpose of the personal injury claims process is to put the individual back into the same position as he or she would have been in, had the accident not occurred, insofar as money can achieve that objective. The purpose of the rehabilitation code is to provide a framework within which the claimant's health, quality of life and ability to work are restored as far as possible before, or simultaneously with, the process of assessing compensation.

1.2 Although the Code is recognised by the Personal Injury Pre-Action Protocol, its provisions are not mandatory. It is recognised that the aims of the Code can be achieved without strict adherence to the terms of the Code, and, therefore, it is open to the parties to agree an alternative framework to achieve the early rehabilitation of the claimant.

1.3 However, the Code provides a useful framework within which claimant's lawyers and the compensator can work together to ensure that the needs of injured claimants are assessed at an early stage.

1.4 In any case where agreement on liability is not reached it is open to the parties to agree that the Code will in any event operate, and the question of delay pending resolution of liability should be balanced with the interests of the injured party. However, unless so agreed, the Code does not apply in the absence of liability or prior to agreement on liability being reached.

1.5 In this code the expression 'the compensator' shall include any loss adjuster, solicitor or other person acting on behalf of the compensator.

2. The claimant's solicitor

2.1 It should be the duty of every claimant's solicitor to consider, from the earliest practicable stage, and in consultation with the claimant, the claimant's family, and where appropriate the claimant's treating physician(s), whether it is likely or possible that early intervention, rehabilitation or medical treatment would improve their present and/or long-term physical and mental well being. This duty is ongoing throughout the life of the case but is of most importance in the early stages.

2.2   The claimant's solicitors will in any event be aware of their responsibilities under section 4 of the Pre-Action Protocol for Personal Injury Claims.

2.3   It shall be the duty of a claimant's solicitor to consider, with the claimant and/or the claimant's family, whether there is an immediate need for aids, adaptations, adjustments to employment to enable the claimant to keep his/her existing job, obtain suitable alternative employment with the same employer or retrain for new employment, or other matters that would seek to alleviate problems caused by disability, and then to communicate with the compensators as soon as practicable about any such rehabilitation needs, with a view to putting this Code into effect.

2.4   It shall not be the responsibility of the solicitor to decide on the need for treatment or rehabilitation or to arrange such matters without appropriate medical or professional advice.

2.5   It is the intention of this Code that the claimant's solicitor will work with the compensator to address these rehabilitation needs and that the assessment and delivery of rehabilitation needs shall be a collaborative process.

2.6   It must be recognised that the compensator will need to receive from the claimant's solicitor sufficient information for the compensator to make a proper decision about the need for intervention, rehabilitation or treatment. To this extent the claimant's solicitor must comply with the requirements of the Pre-Action Protocol to provide the compensator with full and adequate details of the injuries sustained by the claimant, the nature and extent of any or any likely continuing disability and any suggestions that may have already have been made concerning the rehabilitation and/or early intervention.

2.7   There is no requirement under the Pre-Action Protocol, or under this code, for the claimant's solicitor to have obtained a full medical report. It is recognised that many cases will be identified for consideration under this code before medical evidence has actually been commissioned or obtained.

3.   The Compensator

3.1   It shall be the duty of the compensator, from the earliest practicable stage in any appropriate case, to consider whether it is likely that the claimant will benefit in the immediate, medium or longer term from further medical treatment, rehabilitation or early intervention. This duty is ongoing throughout the life of the case but is most important in the early stages.

3.2   If the compensator considers that a particular claim might be suitable for intervention, rehabilitation or treatment, the compensator will communicate this to the claimant's solicitor as soon as practicable.

3.3 On receipt of such communication, the claimant's solicitor will immediately discuss these issues with the claimant and/or the claimant's family pursuant to his duty set out above.

3.4 Where a request to consider rehabilitation has been communicated by the claimant's solicitor to the compensator, it will usually be expected that the compensator will respond to such request within 21 days.

3.5 Nothing in this or any other code of practice shall in any way modify the obligations of the compensator under the Protocol to investigate claims rapidly and in any event within 3 months (except where time is extended by the claimant's solicitor) from the date of the formal claim letter. It is recognised that, although the rehabilitation assessment can be done even where liability investigations are outstanding, it is essential that such investigations proceed with the appropriate speed.

4. Assessment

4.1 Unless the need for intervention, rehabilitation or treatment has already been identified by medical reports obtained and disclosed by either side, the need for and extent of such intervention, rehabilitation or treatment will be considered by means of an assessment by an appropriately qualified person.

4.2 An assessment of rehabilitation needs may be carried out by any person or organisation suitably qualified, experienced and skilled to carry out the task. The claimant's solicitor and the compensator should endeavour to agree on the person or organisation to be chosen.

4.3 No solicitor or compensator may insist on the assessment being carried out by a particular person or organisation if [on reasonable grounds] the other party objects, such objection to be raised within 21 days from the date of notification of the suggested assessor.

4.4 The assessment may be carried out by a person or organisation which has a direct business connection with the solicitor or compensator, only if the other party agrees. The solicitor or compensator will be expected to reveal to the other party the existence of and nature of such a business connection.

5. The Assessment Process

5.1 Where possible, the agency to be instructed to provide the assessment should be agreed between the claimant's solicitor and the compensator. The method of providing instructions to that agency will be agreed between the solicitor and the compensator.

5.2 The assessment agency will be asked to carry out the assessment in a way that is appropriate to the needs of the case and, in a simple case, may include, by prior appointment, a telephone interview but in more serious cases will probably involve a face to face discussion with the claimant. The report will normally cover the following headings:
1.   The Injuries sustained by the claimant.

2.   The current disability/incapacity arising from those Injuries. Where relevant to the overall picture of the claimant's needs, any other medical conditions not arising from the accident should also be separately annotated.

3.   The claimant's domestic circumstances (including mobility accommodation and employment) where relevant.

4.   The injuries/disability in respect of which early intervention or early rehabilitation is suggested.

5.   The type of intervention or treatment envisaged.

6.   The likely cost.

7.   The likely outcome of such intervention or treatment.

5.3   The report should not deal with issues relating to legal liability and should therefore not contain a detailed account of the accident circumstances.

5.4   In most cases it will be expected that the assessment will take place within 14 days from the date of the letter of referral to the assessment agency.

5.5   It must be remembered that the compensator will usually only consider such rehabilitation to deal with the effects of the injuries that have been caused in the relevant accident and will normally not be expected to fund treatment for conditions which do not directly relate to the accident unless the effect of such conditions has been exacerbated by the injuries sustained in the accident.

6.   The Assessment Report

6.1   The report agency will, on completion of the report, send copies onto both the claimant's solicitor and compensator simultaneously. Both parties will have the right to raise questions on the report, disclosing such correspondence to the other party.

6.2   It is recognised that for this assessment report to be of benefit to the parties, it should be prepared and used wholly outside the litigation process. Neither side can therefore, unless they agree in writing, rely on its contents in any subsequent litigation.

6.3   The report, any correspondence related to it and any notes created by the assessing agency to prepare it, will be covered by legal privilege and will not be disclosed in any legal proceedings unless the parties agree. Any notes or documents created in connection with the assessment process will not be disclosed in any litigation, and any person involved in the preparation of the report or involved in the assessment process, shall not be a compellable witness at Court. This principle is also set out in paragraph 4.4 of the Pre-Action Protocol.

6.4   The provision in paragraph 6.3 above as to treating the report etc as outside the litigation process is limited to the assessment report and any notes relating to it. Any notes and reports created during the subsequent case management process will be covered by the usual principle in relation to disclosure of documents and medical records relating to the claimant.

6.5   The compensator will pay for the report within 28 days of receipt.

6.6 This code intends that the parties will continue to work together to ensure that the rehabilitation which has been recommended proceeds smoothly and that any further rehabilitation needs are also assessed.

7. Recommendations

7.1 When the assessment report is disclosed to the compensator, the compensator will be under a duty to consider the recommendations made and the extent to which funds will be made available to implement all or some of the recommendations. The compensator will not be required to pay for intervention treatment that is unreasonable in nature, content or cost or where adequate and timely provision is otherwise available. The claimant will be under no obligation to undergo intervention, medical or investigation treatment that is unreasonable in all the circumstances of the case.

7.2 The compensator will normally be expected to respond to the claimant's solicitor within 21 days from the date upon which the assessment report is disclosed as to the extent to which the recommendations have been accepted and rehabilitation treatment would be funded and will be expected to justify, within that same timescale, any refusal to meet the cost of recommended rehabilitation.

7.3 If funds are provided by the compensator to the claimant to enable specific intervention, rehabilitation or treatment to occur, the compensator warrants that they will not, in any legal proceedings connected with the claim, dispute the reasonableness of that treatment, nor the agreed costs, provided of course that the claimant has had the recommended treatment. The compensator will not, should the claim fail or be later discontinued, or any element of contributory negligence be assessed or agreed, seek to recover from the claimant any funds that they have made available pursuant to this Code.

The Rehabilitation Code is endorsed by many organisations, including:

Association of British Insurers

Association of Personal Injury Lawyers

Bodily Injury Claims Management Association

Case Management Society of the UK

Forum of Insurance Lawyers

International Underwriting Association

Motor Accident Solicitors' Society

To download the Code, go to www.iua.co.uk/rehabilitationcode.

Rehab 'Lite'

The 2007 Rehabilitation Code – Making a real difference to injured people

The Rehabilitation Code provides an approved framework for injury claims within which claimant representatives and compensators can work together. Whilst the Code is voluntary, the court Pre-action Protocol provides that its use should be considered for all types of personal injury claims. The objective is to ensure that injured people receive the rehabilitation treatment they need to restore quality of life and earning capacity as soon as possible and for as long as the parties believe it is appropriate.

The important features of the Code are:

1   the claimant is put at the centre of the process

2   the claimant's lawyer and the compensator work on a collaborative basis to address the claimant's needs, from first early notification of the claim and through early exchange of information

3   the need for rehabilitation is addressed as a priority and sometimes before agreement on liability. Fixed time-frames support the Code's framework

4   rehabilitation needs are assessed by those who have the appropriate qualification, skills and experience

5   the choice of rehabilitation assessor and provider should, wherever possible, be agreed by the claimant lawyer and the compensator

6   initial rehabilitation assessments can be conducted by telephone or personal interview, according to case type and the resulting report should deal with matters specified in the Code

7   the claimant is not obliged to undergo treatment or intervention that is considered unreasonable

8   the compensator will pay for any agreed assessment of rehabilitation needs and must justify a refusal to follow any of the rehabilitation recommendations

9   the initial rehabilitation assessment process is outside the litigation process

10 where rehabilitation has been provided under the Code, the compensator will not seek to recoup its cost, if the claim later fails in whole or part.

The new 2007 Code simplifies the original version, first published in 1999, at the same time as underlining the important principles. It has the support of all the important stakeholders in the claims process including the ABI, IUA, APIL, FOIL, MASS, the Civil Justice Council and major insurers.

To download the full version of Code, go to www.rehabcode.org

For enquiries, email rehab@iua.co.uk

Time scales

Claimant Solicitor	• Duty of every claimant to consider from the earliest practicable stage in consultation with the claimant/their family and if appropriate treating physicians the need for rehabilitation
	• Give earliest possible notification of the claim and need for rehabilitation
	• Where the need for rehabilitation is identified by the compensator, the claimant solicitor shall consider this immediately with the claimant and/or the claimant's family
Compensator	• Shall equally consider and communicate at earliest practicable stage whether the claimant will benefit from rehabilitation
	• Where the need for rehabilitation is notified to the compensator by the claimant solicitor, the compensator will respond within 21 days
Parties	• Consider choice of assessor and object to any suggested assessor within 21 days of nomination
Immediate Needs Assessment	• Assessment to occur within 14 days of referral letter
	• Provide report simultaneously to parties
Compensator	• Pay for report within 28 days or receipt
	• Respond substantively to recommendations to claimant solicitor within 21 days of receipt of report

CHAPTER 3

CAPACITY AND THE COURT OF PROTECTION

3.1 MENTAL CAPACITY ACT 2005: THE PRACTICE FOR PROTECTED PARTIES AND THE IMPLICATIONS FOR PERSONAL INJURY LITIGATION

The Mental Capacity Act 2005 (MCA)establishes the law and practice concerning persons who lack the capacity to make decisions, providing a detailed framework that is designed both to empower and protect vulnerable persons. It makes clear who can take the decisions that matter on their behalf, in what circumstances and how to put the decision-making into practice. The Act was born out of a new approach to the issue of capacity, the philosophy being that those who suffer a disability shall be assisted to live normal lives and make choices about their lives to the greatest extent possible. Its provisions came into effect from 1 October 2007.

At the same time the Court of Protection became a specialist court of record, enjoying the powers of the High Court, with power to determine all issues relating to people who lack capacity. It has its own judges and procedure and it is governed by the Court of Protection Rules 2007.[1] It has the power to make declarations, decisions and orders affecting people who lack capacity and make decisions for, or appoint deputies to make decisions on behalf of, people lacking capacity to do so themselves.

Neither the MCA nor the Court of Protection Rules directly govern a civil court dealing with a party who lacks capacity. This is governed by CPR Part 21. However, Part 21 expressly requires a civil court to adopt the statutory definition of capacity within the MCA (CPR, r 21.1(2)), the rule defining a person who lacks capacity to conduct proceedings as a 'protected party' and a party who lacks capacity to manage and control money recovered by him or on his behalf or for his benefit in the proceedings as a 'protected beneficiary'.

The Public Guardian is a statutory office empowered to support the work of the Court of Protection, in particular supervising deputies. Practitioners must also be familiar with the Mental Capacity Act 2005 Code of Practice ('the Code') as

---

[1] As very slightly amended by the Court of Protection (Amendment) Rules 2011 which now provides for a court officer to exercise the jurisdiction of the court in defined circumstances, amending rule 7.

they have a duty to have regard to the Code under s 42(4) of the MCA when dealing with people who lack capacity. This would include solicitors and counsel engaged in litigation involving a protected party and/or a protected beneficiary.

Pursuant to s 1 of the MCA, the following five guiding principles apply:

- a person must be assumed to have capacity unless it is established that he lacks capacity;
- a person is not to be treated as unable to make a decision unless all practicable steps to help him to do so have been taken without success;
- a person is not to be treated as unable to make a decision merely because he makes an unwise decision;
- an act done, or decision made, under the MCA, for or on behalf of a person who lacks capacity must be done, or made, in his best interests;
- before the act is done, or the decision is made, regard must be had to whether the purpose for which it is needed can be as effectively achieved in a way that is less restrictive of the person's rights and freedom of action.

3.2   THE DEFINITION OF A PERSON WHO LACKS CAPACITY

Section 2 of the MCA defines mental incapacity as follows:

> 'a person lacks capacity in relation to a matter if, at the material time, he is unable to make a decision for himself in relation to the matter because of an impairment of, or a disturbance in, the functioning of, the mind or brain.'

It matters not whether the impairment or disturbance is permanent or temporary and the definition is unequivocally both issue specific and time specific. Merely because a person lacks capacity in respect of one issue and at one period of time does not necessarily mean that they lack capacity on other issues or for all time.[2] By s 3 of the MCA[3] a person is unable to make a decision for himself if he is unable:

- to understand the information relevant to the decision; or
- to retain that information; or
- to use or to weigh that information as part of the process of making the decision; or

---

[2]   Those who assess a person's capacity must consider the person's social, economic, and cultural background, as well as their pre-morbid character, family situation and full medical history. A person's incapacity can be masked by the available support or the unquestioning acceptance of advice. Overprotection can also prevent the person from demonstrating a resumption of capacity. Variable capacity can be seen where the person also suffers from substance abuse, alcohol abuse, or depression. Such a person should be regularly reassessed, certainly at key stages of development or change, such as the end of a period of rehabilitation, or when a recovery from depression has occurred.

[3]   The functional test.

- to communicate his decision (whether by talking, using sign language or any other means).

A person is not to be regarded as unable to understand the information relevant to a decision if he is able to understand an explanation of it given to him in a way that is appropriate to his circumstances (using simple language, visual aids or other means).

The fact that a person is able to retain the information relevant to a decision for a short period only does not prevent him from being regarded as able to make the decision.

The information relevant to the decision includes information about the reasonably foreseeable consequences of (i) deciding one way or another, or (ii) failing to make the decision.

Any question as to whether a person lacks capacity within the meaning of the MCA must be decided on the balance of probabilities and the burden of establishing incapacity falls on the person asserting it.

3.3   CAPACITY TO LITIGATE

Personal injury practitioners must make a careful investigation of issue and time specific capacity when first acting for any person with serious neurological and/or cognitive damage and thereafter at key stages of the litigation such as issue of proceedings and settlement of liability and/or damages.

A protected party must conduct the litigation by a litigation friend acting on his behalf and special rules apply for the court approval of any proposed settlement in the proceedings. A protected party, acting alone and without a litigation friend, whether as the result of his lawyer's ignorance or otherwise, cannot bring an effective claim or make a binding settlement.

When considering whether a litigant has capacity to litigate, there is a two-stage test to be adopted:

(1)   Is an impairment of, or disturbance in the functioning of the mind or brain, established?

(2)   Is this sufficient to rebut the presumption that the party has capacity?

Paragraphs 4.32 and 4.33 of the Code make it clear that pre-MCA case-law may remain relevant to assessments of capacity and, despite being required to use the statutory definition of capacity within the MCA, the Courts continue to take guidance from the seminal pre-MCA capacity cases of *Masterman-Lister v Brutton & Co*[4] and *Bailey v Warren*,[5] cases which implicitly anticipated the provision of a statutory definition of capacity.

---

[4]   [2002] EWCA Civ 889.
[5]   [2006] EWCA Civ 26.

In making any assessment of capacity practitioners will be reliant upon expert medical evidence, usually from the neuro-psychiatrists and neuro-psychologists. It cannot be over emphasised that one-line assessments of capacity should be avoided. Experts must adopt the test of capacity as set out in the MCA, initially highlighting that they are aware of the presumption of capacity before considering the individual criteria in s 3(1) of the MCA. They should also consider the issue of capacity to litigate separately from the issue of capacity to manage and control money recovered.

A factor in determining whether a party has capacity to litigate will be the type and complexity of the litigation. This was neatly summarised in the first instance decision of *Sheffield City Council v E*:[6]

> 'Someone may have the capacity to litigate in a case where the nature of the dispute and the issues are simple, whilst at the same time lacking the capacity to litigate in a case where either the nature of the dispute or the issues are more complex.'

However, when considering the conduct of discrete proceedings, although the test is time and decision specific, it would be an error to judge matters on too piecemeal a basis. In *Bailey v Warren*[7] a litigant who had an ability to understand what was meant by a 50/50 liability split, but lacked ability to understand the concept of damages that resulted from the split, lacked true capacity to conduct the proceedings. This need to consider the entire proceedings, not severable parts of the same litigation, was reaffirmed by the Court of Appeal in *Dunhill v Burgin* (see below).[8]

It is common for there to be a dispute between the claimant and defendant concerning the issue of capacity, the court's ultimate finding on the issue of capacity having a considerable bearing on the value of a claim given the necessity for a protected party/protected beneficiary to claim the future costs of the Court of Protection. A decision on capacity will either be considered at a preliminary hearing or at the trial of the action.

A far more difficult situation arises when a claimant receives conflicting assessments of capacity from different expert specialisms instructed on their behalf. Guidance for such a circumstance was given by Stanley Burnton J in *Lindsay v Wood*.[9] In that case counsel for the claimant, because of the conflicting medical evidence, had felt unable to take a positive stance on the issue of capacity and since the burden of establishing incapacity is on the person asserting it, and nobody was asserting it, Stanley Burnton J detected an forensic imbalance. Consequently, he suggested that consideration should be given to seeking an order from the Court directing the Official Solicitor to consider the

---

6   [2005] 2 WLR 953 at 964.
7   [2006] EWCA Civ 51.
8   [2012] EWCA Civ 397.
9   [2006] EWHC 2895.

evidence, to appoint his own medical expert if he sees fit, and to appear and make such submissions as he considers appropriate at a hearing of the issue on capacity.

Given that such an approach has potentially significant cost implications, parties have in practice sought to overcome the situation proportionately by instructing a further expert to examine the claimant. Such an approach was adopted in the first case to be decided post-MCA, *Saulle v Nouvet*.[10]

On the trial of a preliminary issue the court was required to determine whether the claimant had the capacity to manage his own property and affairs, and to conduct the litigation. He had sustained a severe brain injury in a road traffic accident. The defendant admitted liability. The claimant suffered from an impaired memory, having difficulty in processing information. Frustration led to aberrant, and occasionally, violent behaviour. On his discharge from hospital the claimant lived with members of his family. They gave evidence that he proved to be a difficult person with whom to live.

However, he had an income from the proceeds of an insurance policy and managed his own bank account and credit card. He had instigated savings and payments for the support of his son, born to his former partner, and had voluntarily maintained those payments. He could use a computer at a basic level. He had, since the accident, travelled on holiday on his own. His sister had managed the litigation for him. He had a good relationship with his solicitor.

All but one of the expert medical witnesses agreed that, although his cognitive and intellectual functions and his memory were significantly impaired, he was not deprived of his capacity in law.

The court held that CPR, r 21.1(2) as amended made clear that the new statutory definition of capacity should be adopted in deciding whether a person was a protected person, and if so, whether he was a protected beneficiary for the purpose of managing and controlling any money recovered in the proceedings.

The claimant had a significant support network of people who were able to advise him and explain matters to him and his good relationship with his solicitor was relevant. The court held that on the evidence there were times when he was able to make decisions and other times when he was so affected by his adjustment disorder and his grief reaction as to become irrational and aggressive. During the latter periods he would probably lack capacity if he were to attempt to make an important decision; however, there was no evidence that he had ever sought to do so while in that mental state and he had enough control over himself to take important decisions at times when he was properly able to do so.

---

[10] [2007] EWHC 2902 (QB).

The court determined that the presumption of capacity was not displaced. The preliminary issue was found in favour of the defendant. The cost of the special procedure in the Court of Protection was not required to be put in place. Importantly, however, the judge did recognise that the claimant's capacity may not persist in the future and he mooted that the court might award a discounted lump sum in respect of the risk of deterioration in the claimant's condition that might require him to seek the assistance of the Court of Protection.

The courts have since considered the issue of capacity in a number of additional decisions. In *V v R*[11] the court also tried the issue of capacity to conduct the litigation as a preliminary issue. The claimant suffered multiple injuries in a road traffic accident, including a closed head injury causing traumatic brain injury. Liability was conceded as was, at that time, the claimant's inability to manage her own financial affairs, but the issue of capacity to litigate was disputed, the experts instructed by the defendant opining that the claimant had capacity to litigate, with only the claimant's neuro-psychiatrist asserting that the claimant lacked this capacity. The Court heard oral evidence from the respective neuro-psychiatrists, evidence focusing on the claimant's distractibility; her difficulty in following complex conversations and instructions; her impulsivity and forgetfulness; and her difficulty initiating actions. Overall cognitive abilities were fine but attention and consideration of new information was difficult resulting in the claimant becoming stuck when moving from one task to another. As a result the claimant's neuro-psychiatrist formed the view that the claimant's difficulties using and weighing the necessary information to give instructions or to conduct legal proceedings meant that, on the balance of probability, she lacked litigation capacity. Having considered all the evidence, including the fact that the claimant had hitherto conducted the litigation; had produced a detailed witness statement in the proceedings; and was likely to continue to receive support and assistance from her family with decision-making, the judge was not persuaded that the claimant lacked capacity to litigate.

The substantive assessment of damages in *V v R* is reported as *Verlander v Rahman*.[12] The trial took place just over a year after the Court had found that the claimant had litigation capacity. By then, whether the claimant had capacity to manage her own financial affairs was in dispute. Having considered in detail the extent to which the claimant used money entrusted to her, the judge was not convinced that the claimant was actually managing her own money and he was concerned there was a considerable risk that she would 'blow' any award, her impulsivity preventing her from properly weighing the necessary information to make a decision about her money. Accordingly, the presumption of financial capacity was rebutted although the judge specified that this was not a permanent incapacity, suggesting that her capacity should be reviewed after 2 years.

---

[11] [2011] EWHC 822.
[12] [2012] EWHC 1026.

The issue of borderline capacity was considered further in *Loughlin v Singh and Others*.[13] The claimant was 12 years of age when suffering a comminuted depressed frontal fracture of the skull and left subdural haematoma. As a result the claimant's powers of motivation; initiation and organisation were greatly reduced. Although his IQ was well preserved, outside a structured setting he struggled to utilise his intelligence. The parties were in dispute as to whether the claimant lacked capacity to litigate or manage his property and affairs and the arguments were finely balanced, the judge ultimately finding that the presumption of capacity had been rebutted because he preferred the evidence of the claimant's neuro-psychiatrist. That expert had accepted, in line with the defendant's experts, that so long as the claimant had the capacity to recognise that he needed appropriate guidance and assistance, and the capacity to take and act upon such advice and assistance, the claimant could be treated as having capacity in the legal sense but on this issue, he had suggested that the claimant was unlikely to know when to seek advice due to a lack of insight.

This case is also of significance given the *obiter* comments of Parker J on the issue of disclosure to the Court of Protection when parties make an application. The court made it clear that the Court of Protection must be provided with all available medical evidence relevant to the issue of capacity when being asked to make a finding on capacity and/or when appointing a deputy. This would include all medical reports obtained on behalf of the proposed protected party regardless of whether that report has been disclosed as part of any litigation process (see *Annex* to the judgment of Parker J). This has already led some defendant insurers to request sight of the evidence supporting such an application and it is likely to be a fertile ground for argument in the future.

3.4 THE LITIGATION FRIEND AND THE CPR

The CPR deals with the appointment and role of the litigation friend in the civil court proceedings. Part 21 and PD 21 mirror the provisions of the Court of Protection Rules 2007.

A protected party must conduct his claim by a litigation friend acting on his behalf in the proceedings.[14]

The Court may appoint a litigation friend in the claim if and as required, or the intended litigation friend may proceed without a court order provided he certifies that he can fairly and competently conduct proceedings on behalf of the protected party, has no interest adverse to that of the protected party and undertakes to pay any costs which the protected party may be ordered to pay in relation to the proceedings, subject to any right he may have to be repaid from the assets of the protected party.[15]

---

[13]   [2013] EWHC 1641.
[14]   CPR, r 21.2.
[15]   CPR, r 21.4–8.

A deputy appointed by the Court of Protection under the MCA with power to conduct proceedings on behalf of the protected party is entitled to be the litigation friend.[16]

Any step taken in the proceedings before the protected party has a litigation friend has no effect, unless the court orders otherwise.[17] Upon application, the Court may bring the saving provision into play by a specific order that retrospectively validates the previous, unauthorised part of the proceedings.

A litigation friend who incurs expenses on behalf of a protected party is entitled on application to recover the amount paid or payable from any money recovered or paid into court to the extent that it has been reasonably incurred and is reasonable in amount.[18]

3.5   BEST INTERESTS

Any act done, or decision made, on behalf of someone who lacks capacity, must be done or made in their best interests and not by way of substituted judgment. By s 4 of the MCA the person doing the act or making the decision must consider all the relevant circumstances. These may include the wishes of the protected party as far as they can be ascertained.[19]

Specific regard must be had to the likelihood of a person having capacity in relation to the matter in the future; to encouraging self-participation in the decision; to the protected person's past and present wishes and feelings as far as reasonably ascertainable; to the beliefs and values that would be likely to influence the person's decision; to the views of others closely connected with the person, including a court appointed deputy; and whether the purpose for which any act or decision is needed can be as effectively achieved in a manner less restrictive of the person's freedom of action.

A person's capacity, or lack of it, cannot be established simply by reference to their age or appearance, or by a condition or aspect of behaviour which might lead others to make unjustified assumptions about capacity.[20]

Crucially, no one is to be labelled as lacking capacity only by reason of a particular medical condition or diagnosis. The determination of capacity must be individual specific as well as both issue and time specific.

---

[16]   CPR, r 21.4(2).
[17]   CRP, r 21.3(4).
[18]   CPR, r 21.12.
[19]   HH Judge Marshall QC, a nominated circuit judge of the Court of Protection, in *Re S and S (Protected Persons) v P* [2009] WTLR 315 (20 November 2008); and Lewison J in *Re P* [2009] EWHC 163 (Ch). The judge stressed that the goal of the enquiry was not what P 'might be expected to have done' but what was in his best interests. This is more akin to the 'balance sheet' approach than to the 'substituted judgment' approach. The wishes of P were just one, albeit an important, element in the balancing exercise.
[20]   Mental Capacity Act 2005, s 2(3).

Consideration of a claimant's best interests can permeate decision-making within a litigation context. This was demonstrated in *Sedge v Prime*[21] where a court, when considering the size of an interim payment predicated on a claimant's trial of community-based living, had regard to the results of a best interests meeting that had taken place amongst the claimant's care team. That decision had been made without considering the medico-legal expert evidence and had not been influenced by the presence of legal advisers to either party (see further Chapter 5 Interim Payments).

3.6   COMPROMISE AND SETTLEMENT

It is trite law that no compromise or settlement of a protected party's claim for damages may be validly concluded, or a defendant's offer under CPR Part 36 accepted, unless and until, the formal approval of the civil compensation court has been obtained. Without such approval, neither side is obliged to consider the compromise as binding or enforceable.[22]

On behalf of a protected party the discrete code of procedure under CPR Part 21 must be followed (see below). Any proposed settlement, compromise or payment, including voluntary interim payments, must be approved in order to achieve bipartite validity.

Where, before proceedings on behalf of a protected party are begun, an agreement is reached for the settlement of the claim and the sole purpose of proceedings is to obtain approval, the Part 8 alternative procedure for claims should be made and should include a request for court approval.

Where the proposed settlement or compromise for a protected party includes an order that the damages or part of them are to be made by periodical payments, PD 21, CPR, r 41, and PD 41B should be followed.

Where money is recovered by or on behalf of or for the benefit of a protected party, the money must be dealt with in accordance with the directions given by the Court and not otherwise. Before giving directions, the Court should first consider whether the protected party is a protected beneficiary.[23]

---

[21]   [2012] EWHC 3460.

[22]   CPR, r 21.10: where a claim is made on behalf of a protected party no settlement, compromise or payment (including any voluntary interim payment) and no acceptance of any money paid into Court shall be valid, so far as it relates to the claim by, or on behalf of the protected party without the approval of the Court. The rule will be strictly interpreted: *Dietz v Lennig Chemicals* [1969] 1 AC 170, [1967] 2 All ER 282). See also *Drinkall v Whitwood* [2003] EWCA Civ 1547 and *Brennan (a protected party) v (1) Eco Composting Limited (2) J Bascombe Contractors Limited* [2006] EWHC 3153 (QB), the latter confirming that interest only runs from the date of approval.

[23]   A protected party who lacks capacity to manage and control any money recovered by him or on his behalf or for his benefit in the proceedings: CPR, r 21.1(2)

The importance of an early assessment of capacity and the need for approval was highlighted by the case of *Dunhill v Burgin*.[24] There settlement was initially agreed at the door of the court, in the sum of £12,500, in 2003. The judge was not asked to approve that settlement and 'some time later' doubts began to emerge about the claimant's capacity. In February 2009 the claimant (acting by a litigation friend) issued an application in the original proceedings seeking a declaration that she did not have capacity at the time of the purported settlement and applying for the order to be set aside and directions given for the future conduct of the claim, a claim the parties now contended was worth between £800,000 and £2m on a full liability basis.

At first instance Silber J held that the claimant did have capacity to enter into the compromise agreement. On appeal, however, it was considered that he had looked at the issues too narrowly, being concerned only with the actual transaction leading to the compromise rather than considering whether the claimant had the necessary capacity to conduct proceedings. The question had to be whether a claimant had the capacity to litigate, a compromise being an inseparable part of proceedings as a whole.[25] The court must then consider what might have been required from the claimant if the litigation had been conducted differently. With proper advice the claim would never have been advanced for the limited sums pleaded and the claimant lacked capacity to give proper instructions for, or to approve, the particulars of claim. She further lacked capacity because she had no insight into the compromise, being unaware of the vast sum she was giving up. Had she been recognised as a protected party, the compromise she entered into would never have been approved by the court.

At a second preliminary issue hearing the defendant sought to argue that CPR, r 21 was inapplicable in this case because the defendant did not know that the claimant lacked capacity, an argument based on the common law position in contract that to set aside a contract it must be proved by the party asserting a lack of capacity that the other contracting party was aware of his lack of capacity.[26] If CPR, r 21 did not apply, there was no requirement for the compromise to be approved and the settlement could not be reopened. Bean J found that the CPR governed the conduct of litigation and therefore the Civil Procedure Rules Committee was entitled to promulgate a rule which conflicted with the general law of contract.[27] A correct interpretation of CPR, r 21 confirmed that a party who in fact lacks capacity to conduct proceedings is protected by the need for the compromise to be approved even if (s)he has not been declared as lacking capacity and is not acting with a litigation friend.

---

[24]   [2012] EWCA 397.
[25]   Considering *Masterman-Lister v Brutton & Co* [2002] EWCA Civ 1889 and *Bailey v Warren* [2006] EWCA Civ 51.
[26]   See *The Imperil Loan Company Ltd v Stone* [1892] 1 QB 599.
[27]   Cases of *Re Grosvenor Hotel, London (No 2)* [1965] Ch 1210 and *Vinos v M&S* [2001] 3 All ER 784 considered.

Clearly, settlement of a claim on behalf of a protected party must be approved but does the issue of capacity need to be decided before a court can approve a settlement on behalf of a child? This point arose in the case of *Rebecca Coles v David Perfect and Others*.[28] In this case the claimant suffered a very severe head and brain injury in a marine accident when aged 14 years old. Neither party asserted that she lacked capacity and the medical evidence was equivocal but the judge was being asked to approve a settlement without first giving a determination on the issue of capacity. He found that the court had an inherent jurisdiction to approve settlement and that, if settlement was approved and it was later found that the claimant lacked capacity, the effect of CPR, r 21.10 will not render the settlement invalid because she is not a declared protected party at the time of approval, it will remain valid because approval would have been obtained from the court.

Although this case is authority that approval can be given despite the issue of capacity having not been determined, it should be noted that the court treated the defendant as having limited its total liability for the accident under the Merchant Shipping Act 1995. Accordingly, the limit of the total liability was £1.439m and the claimant had accepted an offer of £1.37m, the maximum the defendant was obliged to offer this claimant given that it was required to meet a claim for the difference by another young girl injured in the same accident. As such, the court would have been aware that even if the claimant was found to lack capacity it would not have sounded in increased damages. It is probable that a court will be more concerned to decide the issue of capacity before approving any settlement in more conventional cases, given the increased damages reflecting the future costs of the Court of Protection that are likely to result if a claimant is found to lack capacity.

3.7 CPR PART 21 AND PRACTICE DIRECTION 21

Before the Court gives directions for the control of money recovered by or on behalf of the protected party, it must first determine whether the protected party is also a protected beneficiary.

Practice Direction PD 21 provides that only a Master, a designated civil judge or his nominee should normally hear applications for the approval of a settlement or compromise involving a protected party.

Paragraph 5 of PD 21 provides a comprehensive list of the documents to be obtained and put before the Court for the approval of a settlement or compromise on behalf of a protected party before the issue of proceedings.

Paragraph 6 of PD 21 provides a comprehensive list of the documents to be obtained and put before the Court for the approval of a settlement or compromise on behalf of a protected party after proceedings have been issued.

---

[28] [2013] EWHC 1955.

Paragraph 8.1 of PD 21 provides that directions for the control on money recovered or accepted on behalf of a protected party may include a direction that certain sums be paid directly to the protected beneficiary, his litigation friend or his legal representatives for his immediate benefit or for expenses paid on his behalf.

Paragraph 8.4 of PD 21 provides that where the protected beneficiary is in receipt of publicly funded legal services, the damages fund will be subject to a first charge under s 10 of the Access to Justice Act 1999 and an order for the investment of money on the protected beneficiary's behalf must contain a direction to that effect.

Paragraph 10 of PD 21 provides detailed guidance on the investments made on behalf of a protected beneficiary.

3.8   THE PRINCIPAL FUNCTIONS AND PRACTICE OF THE COURT OF PROTECTION

The Court of Protection has a wide jurisdiction that relates to the whole MCA. As we have seen, it deals with both property and financial affairs as well as health and welfare decisions. The resolution of complex or disputed cases about capacity or best interests is an important part of its regular business. The Court is based in London (near the Royal Courts of Justice), but regional hearings may be authorised before nominated district or circuit judges sitting at Bristol, Cardiff, Birmingham, Newcastle and Manchester/Preston. The senior judge of the Court remains Judge Denzil Lush.

The powers and responsibilities of the Court include the following:

(1)   the determination of whether a person lacks the capacity to make a particular decision on a matter of fact at a particular time;

(2)   declarations concerning the lawfulness or otherwise of any act done or yet to be done in relation to a protected person;

(3)   single, one-off, orders; for example, an order authorising the execution of a statutory will or an order for the sale of a house and the investment of the net proceeds of sale;

(4)   the appointment of a deputy to take individual decisions in relation to the matter upon which the protected person lacks the capacity to make the decision;

(5)   granting potential parties, not automatically entitled, to make application to the court.

By s 15 of the Act, the Court may make a declaration:

(a)   whether a person lacks capacity to make the specified decision;

(b)   whether a person lacks capacity to make decisions on a specified class of matters; and

(c) concerning the lawfulness, or otherwise, of any act done, or yet to be done, in relation to that person.

3.9 VULNERABLE PERSONS: THE INHERENT JURISDICTION OF THE HIGH COURT

Despite the wide remit of the Court of Protection, the inherent jurisdiction of the High Court to make declarations relating to adults has probably been preserved. In *Re SA (Vulnerable Adult with Capacity: Marriage)*[29] Munby J held that the inherent jurisdiction of the Court can be exercised for the protection of vulnerable adults even though they do not lack the capacity to make the decision in question.

The inherent jurisdiction may be invoked wherever a vulnerable adult is, or is reasonably believed to be, for some reason deprived of the capacity to make the relevant decision, or disabled from making a free choice, or incapacitated or disabled from giving or expressing a real and genuine consent. The cause may be, but is not for this purpose limited to, mental disorder or mental illness.

3.10 DEPUTIES

The Court of Protection is specifically authorised to make decisions about a person's personal welfare or his property and affairs on his behalf where that person lacks capacity. In the alternative, the Court of Protection may appoint a person (a deputy) to make decisions on the protected person's behalf in relation to the particular matter or matters.

When deciding whether it is in the person's best interests to appoint a deputy, the Court of Protection must have regard to the principles that:

(a) a decision by the Court is to be preferred to the appointment of a deputy to make decisions;

(b) the powers conferred on the deputy should be as limited in scope and duration as possible; a deputy, for example, will be unable to refuse consent for life-sustaining healthcare treatment.

The Court of Protection (via the Office of the Public Guardian) supervises the Court-appointed deputies.

Personal welfare includes place of residence, contact with specified persons, and the giving or refusing of consent for healthcare treatment. Family matters and relationships are specifically excluded from the definition of personal welfare.

Moreover, some types of decision are so personal to the person concerned that another can never make that decision for them, even though the person concerned lacks capacity. Section 27 of the MCA makes clear that decisions

---

[29]   [2005] EWHC 2942 (Fam), [2006] 1 FLR 867.

about marriage or civil partnership, sexual relations, divorce on the basis of 2 years' separation, consent to adoption, parental responsibility, voting, mental health treatment, and consent under the Human Fertilisation and Embryology Act 1990 on behalf of a person who lacks capacity all fall outside the scope of the MCA. Applications to the Court of Protection on these issues are not entertained.

3.11 THE COURT OF PROTECTION RULES 2007

By virtue of s 51 of the MCA, the Rules of the Court make provision for:

(1) the manner and form of commencement of proceedings;

(2) the parties to be notified and to be made parties;

(3) the allocation of business;

(4) the exercise of jurisdiction by officers or other staff of the Court;

(5) the appointment of a suitable person, who may be, with his consent, the Official Solicitor, to act on behalf of the person to whom the proceedings relate;

(6) the disposal of an application without a hearing;

(7) proceeding with a hearing in the absence of the person to whom the proceedings relate;

(8) the proceedings to be in private and for the exclusion of specified persons when sitting in public;

(9) the admission of evidence and procedure at hearings;

(10) the enforcement of orders and directions made by the Court.

The Court of Protection Rules 2007 provide a comprehensive, detailed and wide-ranging code of practice on all the matters within the jurisdiction of the Court, including the overriding objective and active case management. By the Civil Procedure (Amendment) Rules 2007, Part 21 and PD 21 of CPR (children and protected persons) were amended in order to harmonise its vocabulary with the Court of Protection Rules.

3.12 APPLICATIONS TO THE COURT OF PROTECTION

By Part 8 of the Court of Protection Rules 2007, the Court's permission is required to start proceedings under the Act, except where the application is made by the Official Solicitor; is made by the Public Guardian; concerns the protected person's property and affairs (the pre-MCA jurisdiction); or is subject to specified exceptions.[30]

---

[30] Court of Protection Rules 2007, rr 50, 51 52 and 53. The procedure for making and for determining applications for permission is governed by rr 54–60.

3.13 HEARINGS

The general rule is that the hearing be held in private. Only the parties, the protected person, any person acting as a litigation friend, any legal representative and any court officer may be entitled to attend.[31]

In relation to a private hearing, the Court may make an order authorising any person or class of persons to attend the hearing or part of the hearing; or excluding any person, or class of persons from the hearing or a part of it.

3.14 LITIGATION FRIEND AND/OR DEPUTY

The Court of Protection, by Part 17 of the Court of Protection Rules 2007, has the power to appoint a litigation friend[32] at any stage in the proceedings if the protected party, the relevant person or any other person with sufficient interest lacks the capacity to conduct the proceedings himself.

Any person may act as a litigation friend if he can fairly and competently conduct proceedings on behalf of the protected party or the relevant person, and has no interest adverse to the protected party.

The Court may appoint a litigation friend either on its own initiative or on the application of any person, but only with the consent of the person to be appointed.[33]

The Rules[34] also permit litigation friends to act without a court order (on the filing of the appropriate certificate of suitability).

The Court has the power to order that a named person may not act as a litigation friend and to order a change of litigation friend. The Rules lay down the procedure where the appointment of a litigation friend comes to an end and where the protected party ceases to lack capacity.[35]

If the action for damages on behalf of the protected party proceeds without a litigation friend the steps taken in the proceedings have no validity unless the court orders otherwise. The litigation friend in the action may also be appointed a deputy for the proceedings in the Court of Protection, but they exercise very different and separate functions.

---

[31] Court of Protection Rules 2007, r 90.
[32] Court of Protection Rules 2007, r 143. The order may only be made with the consent of the person to be appointed the litigation friend. By r 141, a protected party (if a party to the proceedings) must have a litigation friend. CPR, r 21.2(1) also specifies that a protected party must have a litigation friend to conduct proceedings on his behalf.
[33] Court of Protection Rules 2007, r 143.
[34] Court of Protection Rules 2007, r 142.
[35] Court of Protection Rules 2007, Part 17, rr 144–149.

3.15   APPEALS

An appeal from any decision of the Court of Protection lies to the prescribed higher judge of the Court and ultimately from a High Court judge of the Court to the Court of Appeal.[36]

An appeal cannot be made without permission, save for a committal to prison.

Permission to appeal will only be granted where there is a real prospect of success or other compelling reason.

An order on paper alone without a hearing or notice may be corrected on an application for reconsideration.

3.16   FEES AND COSTS

Sections 54 and 55 of the MCA make provision for fees and costs. The applicable fees are now provided in the Court of Protection Fees Order 2007[37] and the Public Guardian (Fees, etc) Regulations 2007,[38] as slightly amended.[39]

Where the proceedings concern the protected person's property and affairs the general rule is that the costs of the proceedings, or that part of the proceedings that concerns his property and affairs, shall be paid by the protected person or charged to his estate.[40]

Where the proceedings concern the protected person's personal welfare, the general rule is that there will be no order as to the costs of the proceedings or of that part of the proceedings that concern his personal welfare.[41]

3.17   FEES AND COSTS IN THE COURT OF PROTECTION

All applications to the Court of Protection are decided by the judicial members of the Court.

An application fee (£400) is payable by the applicant on making an application under Part 9 of the Court of Protection Rules 2007 (how to start proceedings). The payment must be made on the initial application to the Court to assume jurisdiction and thereafter on every subsequent application to vary an existing order.

---

[36]   Court of Protection Rules 2007, r 172.
[37]   SI 2007/1745.
[38]   SI 2007/2051.
[39]   Court of Protection Fees Order 2009 and Public Guardian (Fees etc (Amendment) Regulations 2009.
[40]   Court of Protection Rules 2007, r 156.
[41]   Court of Protection Rules 2007, r 157.

Where initial permission to start proceedings is required under Part 8 of the Rules (permission), an application fee (£400) is payable by the applicant on making the application for permission.

An appeal fee (£400) is payable by the appellant on the filing of an appellant's notice under Part 20 of the Rules (appeals). The fee will be refunded if the protected person dies within 5 days of the appellant's notice being filed.

A hearing fee (£500) is payable by the applicant where the Court has:

(a) held a hearing in order to determine the case; and

(b) made a final order, declaration or decision.

A hearing fee (£500) is payable by the appellant in relation to an appeal where the Court has:

(a) held a hearing in order to determine the appeal; and

(b) made a final order, declaration or decision in relation to the appeal.

A fee (£5) for a copy of a court document is payable at the time the request is made by the person requesting the copy.

By art 8 of the Court of Protection Fees Order 2007 applicants, and those protected within the jurisdiction of the Court, are, as of right, exempt from fee payments in respect of applications, appeals, hearings and copy documents if they are in receipt of a qualifying means-tested benefit, provided a relevant award of damages in excess of £16,000 has not been disregarded for the purpose of determining eligibility for the benefit. An application to the Court is likely to be required if the exemption is not initially allowed. A similar exemption is provided by reg 9 of the Public Guardian (Fees etc) Regulations 2007 for fees relating to the appointment of deputies and their supervision.

In the alternative to exemption, the Court of Protection fees pursuant to the Fees Order 2007 and/or the Public Guardian fees pursuant to the Fees Regulations 2007 may, in the exercise of discretion, be reduced or remitted in the exceptional circumstances of the particular case that involved undue hardship.[42]

Reductions and remissions will be granted on a discretionary basis, but only with evidence of exceptional circumstances. Any application for a reduction or remission of the Court fees will be considered by the Lord Chancellor. Any application for a reduction or remission of the fees for deputies will be considered by the Public Guardian. Evidence of the relevant income, expenditure and capital assets of the protected or other party will be required. A partial remission is likely to be the starting point and a full remission given only if the applicant or other relevant party could not pay any part of the fee.

---

[42] By art 9 of the Court of Protection Fees Order 2007 and by reg 10 of the Public Guardian Fees Regulations 2007 respectively.

The Court of Protection fees (and the Public Guardian fees, as below) will be increased, from time to time, in line with inflation

3.18   FEES RELATING TO DEPUTIES AND THEIR SUPERVISION

As we have seen, a deputy may be appointed by the Court of Protection to make financial and personal welfare decisions on behalf of a person who lacks the capacity. The deputy must be aged 18 years or more and must consent so to act. He undertakes a serious responsibility on behalf of the person who lacks capacity and is to be treated as his agent in relation to anything done or decided within the scope of his appointment.

The deputy is entitled to be reimbursed for his reasonable expenses in discharging his functions and, if the court so directs when appointing him, to remuneration for discharging them, from the property of the person who lacks capacity.

Deputies are often appointed from the protected party's immediate family. Whether they act alone or together with or without the assistance of a professional deputy, their role will include:

(a)   liaison with the Court of Protection for approval of expenditure;

(b)   preparation of the annual Deputy account;

(c)   completion and filing of tax returns;

(d)   ensuring tax affairs are up to date;

(e)   dealing with requests for capital expenditure;

(f)   approving investment proposals;

(g)   payment of bills, fees, and other regular payments;

(h)   overseeing and arranging contracts for care;

(i)   liaising with the protected person and their family;

(j)   ensuring the protected party is in receipt of applicable state benefits;

(k)   preparing and regularly reviewing income and expenditure budgets; and

(l)   liaising with the Court of Protection in respect of annual visits by the Court appointed visitor.

When the Court of Protection appoints a deputy, a key function of the Public Guardian will be to act as a regulator, monitoring the deputyship and ensuring that the deputy acts in the best interest of the person who lacks capacity.

Most deputies are expected to be supervised by a range of activities that reflect the need for 'light touch' supervision, characterised by:

•   training and coaching opportunities;

•   assistance from an easily accessible customer support and advice service;

•   a requirement to provide an annual account or report to the Office of the Public Guardian;

- confirmation of a security bond as directed by the Court;
- the provision of short-term advice on specific questions of concern.

Where the assessment of the Public Guardian determines that a greater degree of supervision is appropriate, additional activities will be undertaken:

- enhanced support for deputies;
- an initial visit, followed by further visits as required;
- the calling for records and other documents;
- additional financial assessment during the initial period of accounting;
- periodic review by the Office of the Public Guardian.

The Public Guardian (Fees etc) Regulations 2007, as amended,[43] lays down a schedule of fees for the appointment and supervision of deputies.

The Public Guardian determines the level of supervision to be required, pursuant to his function under s 58(1)(c) of the Act. The available levels of supervision are delineated by reg 8(3). Although the initial regime was characterised by four grades of supervision, on 1 October 2011 these were scaled back to only two levels of supervision, general or minimal, a minimal level of supervision being appropriate when assets were less than £19,500. The annual administration fee for general supervision is £320 reducing to £35 for minimal supervision.[44]

An initial fee of £100 is payable by the protected person where the Court appoints a deputy. The fees relating to deputies may be exempt from payment in certain qualifying fiscal circumstances or, alternatively, may be reduced, or remitted, where the Public Guardian accepts that payment would involve undue financial hardship.[45]

3.19 FEES RELATING TO THE COURT REPORTING SERVICE

Section 49 of the MCA provides for the Court to order a report on a matter or matters, relating to a person who lacks capacity, in order to assist in the determination of a case. An impartial report may be sought from the Public Guardian, a Court of Protection visitor, and from other bodies such as local authorities or the NHS wherever the Court decides that this would be helpful.

The Public Guardian sets up and then manages the independent Court Reporting Service. A fee will be charged where the Court asks the Public Guardian or a Court of Protection visitor to report. The fee compromises of

---

[43] See the Public Guardian (Fees etc) (Amendment) Regulations 2009, 2011 and 2013.

[44] Supervision where the value of the assets the deputy has been appointed to manage is less than £19,500 (rising to £21,000 on 1 April 2014) and there are no other factors that indicate a higher level of supervision would be appropriate.

[45] Public Guardian (Fees etc) Regulations 2007, reg 10. See the similar provisions in the Court of Protection Fees Order 2007, above.

two elements: the actual cost of preparing the report and an administrative handling charge, payable on completion of the hearing.

3.20   THE LEGAL COSTS OF APPLYING TO AND ATTENDING COURT

By the Court of Protection Rules 2007, the parties to a case will each fund their own costs, but with a wide discretion for the Court to order that the costs, including any court fees incurred, paid from the estate of the person who lacks capacity.

The Court also has the power to make costs orders against other parties where they have acted unreasonably or not in the best interests of the person who lacks capacity.[46]

3.21   APPROVAL OF SETTLEMENT AWARDS FOR DAMAGES BY THE SENIOR JUDGE OF THE COURT OF PROTECTION

Before 1 October 2007 the Master of the Court of Protection was often invited on behalf of a patient (using the former term) to approve a proposed financial settlement in ongoing civil proceedings. The invitation would supplement the application for formal approval in the civil court to made under CPR, r 21.

By s 96(1)(i) of the Mental Health Act 1983, the Master of the old Court of Protection had power, as he thought fit, to give directions or authority for the conduct of legal proceedings brought in the name of the patient or on his behalf.

With the introduction of the new regime, the Civil Practice and Procedure Rules Committee determined that the informal reference for approval by the Master of the Court of Protection was an unnecessary duplication of effort, and Judge Lush implemented this change and stopped considering proposed settlements of claims.

3.22   HEADS OF POTENTIAL LOSS AND EXPENSE TO FORM PART OF THE CLAIM FOR DAMAGES

A checklist of potential heads of expense and damage for the protected party under the authority of the Court of Protection includes:

---

[46]   Court of Protection Rules 2007, r 159: the Court may depart from the general rule if the circumstances so justify, and in deciding whether departure is justified, the Court will have regard to all the circumstances, including the conduct of the parties; whether a party has succeeded on part of his case, even if he has not been wholly successful; and the role of any public body involved in the proceedings.

(1) the anticipated fee for applications and for subsequent applications for variation;

(2) the anticipated fees for appeals against the decision of the Court;

(3) the anticipated fees for hearings and appeals;

(4) the anticipated fees for the appointment and supervision of the deputy;

(5) the fees charged by the Court for its asset management and other allied functions;

(6) the anticipated, reasonable out of pocket expenses of the deputy;

(7) the anticipated, reasonable fees of a professional deputy;

(8) an allowance for the gratuitous deputy services provided by a non-professional deputy;

(9) the anticipated, reasonable fees for any professional services required by a deputy;

(10) the anticipated fees for legal services arising from the representation of the claimant in the Court;

(11) the anticipated cost of any security bond[47] demanded by the Court of Protection;

(12) the costs of a statutory will application;

(13) the winding-up costs of the protected party's affairs on death; and

(14) a contingency for additional management costs to accommodate unforeseen upheaval.

Both past and prospective fees and expenses should be claimed on behalf of the protected party and evidence will ordinarily be provided by a specialist solicitor which considers the reasonableness of past expenditure as well as identifying likely future expenses and the annual costs of the same.

However, even where the damages for future pecuniary loss for care costs are awarded as periodical payments with an earnings based indexation, future expense for Court of Protection fees and similar are likely to be calculated either on a 2.5% multiplier–multiplicand basis or using periodical payments indexed at RPI.

The expense of specialist investment advice and management, over and above the Court of Protection fees, will not be recoverable.[48]

---

[47] A deputy has to provide an annual account and give a security for performance. There have been inconsistent decisions regarding the level of security required. *In the matter of H (a minor and an incapacitated person)* Court of Protection no 1141874 a district judge imposed a security of £750,000 on a professional deputy on which the annual premium would be £1,500. The case was transferred to HH Judge Marshall QC, a nominated Court of Protection circuit judge for reconsideration and guidance (15 October 2009). The Court should make an objective assessment of the risk of future default. The judge reduced the required security bond required from £750,000 to £150,000. The likely annual cost was estimated at £375–£460 per annum.

[48] *Page v Plymouth Hospitals NHS Trust* [2004] EWHC 1154 (QB), [2004] PIQR Q68.

3.23   THE ROLE OF A PERSONAL INJURY TRUST?

As can be seen above, the costs of administering an award of damages for a protected beneficiary through the appointment of a deputy are likely to be significant. In cases where damages have been substantially reduced, for example as a result of a large deduction for contributory negligence, can the Court of Protection authorise the creation of a personal injury trust in the alternative? This issue was considered by HH Judge Marshall QC in *SM v HM*.[49] In a very detailed judgment guidance is given on the factors to be considered in deciding whether to authorise the creation of a bare trust.

HM was 7 years of age at the time of the application having suffered cerebral palsy as a consequence of injuries sustained at birth. She was likely to lack capacity upon attaining the age of 18 and it was agreed that the Court of Protection has jurisdiction over her property and affairs notwithstanding her minority. Proceedings were brought against the relevant NHS trust for damages, the claim being compromised (and approved) with a £450,000 gross lump sum and periodical payments of £25,000 per annum until 18 years, rising to £50,000 per annum thereafter. This compromise represented a significant discount on the potential value of the claim but it was approved after advice from leading counsel that prospects on liability were less than 50%.

It was appreciated that administering the damages through a personal injury trust, rather than by appointing a deputy, could save in the region of £1,500 per annum. HM's mother made an application to the Court of Protection for authority to set up the proposed trust but at first instance, DJ Ashton refused the application on the grounds that it was not in HM's best interests for her damages to be administered otherwise than by the Court of Protection.

On appeal, it was accepted that the day-to-day management of the award required a management structure operable outside the court structure and that as a matter of law a settlement could be used as an alternative to a deputyship (s 18(1)(B) of the MCA). The Court must bear in mind what is in HM's best interests and that deputyship should be taken as the norm. The burden therefore lay on an applicant to demonstrate a clear and significant advantage in the use of a trust.

Consideration was given to the limits and protection afforded by either regime as well as the extent of supervision and the financial advantages and comparative expenses. Of primary importance would be the existence of a willing and trusted family member to be trustee. The court was persuaded on balance and on the facts of that specific case that the proposed structure and terms of the trust provided suitable protection; there were costs savings; and there was a devoted parent who would make an able, energetic and responsible trustee. Throughout the judgment however, it was reiterated that the deputyship regime was the gold standard and should be taken as the norm. It was not, therefore, open for defendants to argue in future personal injury cases

---

[49]   Court of Protection no 11875043/01 (04/11/11).

that the costs of deputyship could be avoided by a claimant because a personal injury trust could be used as a cheaper effective alternative.

CHAPTER 4

COSTS MANAGEMENT AND FUNDING

4.1   INTRODUCTION

On 1 April 2013 a raft of reforms was brought into effect in relation to funding and costs in civil litigation in England and Wales. This followed Lord Justice Jackson's Review of Civil Litigation Costs, which was completed in 2009, with the final report published in 2010. In the foreword to that report, Lord Justice Jackson stated that his proposed programme of reforms was 'designed to control costs and promote access to justice'.

Many, though not all, of Lord Justice Jackson's suggested reforms were implemented by changes to the Civil Procedure Rules (CPR), and by statute in the Legal Aid, Sentencing and Punishment of Offenders Act 2012 (LASPO). These changes have collectively been referred to as 'the Big Bang' by some practitioners and included the following changes of particular relevance to catastrophic injury claims:

- Various reforms to civil procedure have come into effect which will have a bearing on recoverable costs in catastrophic injury claims, including the 'new' proportionality test and the court's extended costs management powers such as costs budgeting.

- Public funding, or 'legal aid', is no longer available for the vast majority of clinical negligence claims.

- Where a claimant instructs a legal representative under a conditional fee agreement (CFA) on or after 1 April 2013, and the claim is successful, the success fee will not be recoverable from the defendant. However, the client can be required to pay such a fee to the legal representative (up to a maximum of 100% of the representative's base costs and subject to a new cap of 25% of the client's damages for pain, suffering and loss of amenity and past pecuniary losses).

- Where a claimant takes out a policy of after the event insurance ('ATE insurance') on or after 1 April 2013, and the claim is successful, they will not be able to recover the insurance premium from the defendant. There is a limited exception in relation to any part of the premium, in clinical negligence cases, which relates to the costs of the experts' reports regarding liability.

- A claimant can now instruct a legal representative on a contingency fee basis, under what is known as a damages-based agreement (DBA).
- Qualified one-way costs shifting (QOCS) will apply to most proceedings including a claim for damages for personal injuries (including clinical negligence claims) or claims arising from a person's death, save where a 'pre-commencement funding arrangement' was in place before 1 April 2013 (see section on QOCS below for more detail). This means that, subject to the relevant exceptions, claimants will not have to pay their opponent's costs where their claim does not succeed.

This chapter will identify the cost management reforms introduced by the Jackson inspired reform of the CPR and the key reforms of the funding of those costs ushered in by LASPO and will consider practice points arising from these in the context of catastrophic injury claims. This will include a brief overview of the solicitor's ethical obligations when advising their client about funding and costs.

The chapter will also touch upon other methods of funding, which have not been directly affected by LASPO though some of which may become more prevalent as a result, including before the event insurance and third party funding. However, given that the requirements of the respective insurers or other funders are likely to vary quite widely, only general guidance can be provided on these topics.

In light of the relatively long duration of many personal injury actions (and catastrophic injury claims in particular) funding arrangements entered into before 1 April 2013 will continue to be of relevance for some time to come. This chapter will therefore summarise the 'old' funding models and some issues that can potentially arise from these.

Whilst private retainers were, and remain, a possible method of funding in relation to catastrophic injury claims, these will rarely be considered appropriate given the very high costs involved in investigating and pursuing such claims (although arguably QOCS will reduce the costs liability to which claimants may be exposed). Consequently, no detailed consideration will be given to the requirements of private retainers in this chapter.

4.2   COSTS MANAGEMENT AND PROPORTIONALITY

As of 1 April 2013, the 'overriding objective' of the CPR has been amended to emphasise the need for courts to deal with cases justly 'and at proportionate cost'.[1] Proportionality does not, however, relate solely to the costs of the litigation as compared to the damages recovered. Cases should, so far as is reasonably practicable, be dealt with in ways which are proportionate to the

---

[1]   CPR, r 1.1(1).

amount of money involved, the importance of the case, the complexity of the issues and the financial position of each party.[2]

The court must seek to give effect to the overriding objective when exercising its powers under any of the CPR or when interpreting these rules.[3] It is also required to 'actively' manage cases and this is stated to entail not only 'fixing timetables [and] otherwise controlling the progress of the case', but also 'considering whether the likely benefits of taking a particular step justify the costs of taking it'.[4] To further this objective, the court has been given enhanced costs management powers and its ability to monitor and control the parties' recoverable costs has been increased.

A key aspect of the move towards greater court oversight and management of litigation costs is the implementation of the new costs budgeting rules, which apply to all multi-track cases commenced on or after 1 April 2013, save those in the Admiralty and Commercial Courts and some Chancery Division and Technology and Construction/Mercantile Court cases (recent judicial comment suggests these exceptions may not last). All parties to multi-track personal injury or clinical negligence actions commenced on or after this date (except for litigants in person) will therefore be required to file and exchange such budgets.

Budgets must be filed at court by the date specified in the notice of allocation to track or, if no date is specified, 7 days prior to the first case management conference.[5] The date for filing the budget cannot be varied by agreement of the parties[6] and failing to meet this deadline will have disastrous results for the party and the legal representative concerned, in that they will be treated as having filed a budget which includes only the applicable court fees.[7] Budgets must be in 'Precedent H' format (see the annex to Practice Direction 3E), unless the court orders otherwise.[8]

The court is able, at any time during the case, to make a 'costs management order' which records the extent to which the parties' budgets are agreed between the parties and record the court's approval of any budgets (or parts of these) which are not agreed 'after making appropriate revisions'. This process is not supposed to amount to a detailed assessment of costs, but rather the court is obliged to consider whether the costs in the budget fall within the range of reasonable and proportionate costs.[9]

Where a costs management order has been made, the court will thereafter control the parties' budgets in respect of recoverable costs.[10] This can be done

---

[2]   CPR, r 1.1(2)(c).
[3]   CPR, r 1.2.
[4]   CPR, r 1.4(2)(g) and (h) respectively.
[5]   CPR, rr 3.12 and 3.13.
[6]   CPR, r 26.3(6A).
[7]   CPR, r 3.14.
[8]   Paragraph 1 of Practice Direction 3E.
[9]   Paragraph 2.3 of Practice Direction 3E.
[10] CPR, r 3.15.

at discrete costs management conferences[11] or when making any case management decisions. Indeed, the court is required to have regard to the available budgets when making such decisions and to take account of the costs involved, whether or not a costs management order has been made.[12]

If a party considers that there have been 'significant developments' in the litigation, such as to justify amending their previously filed budget, they must submit the revised budget to the other parties for agreement.[13] If no agreement can be reached then the party has to file the revised budget at the court with a note of the changes made and the reasons for those changes, as well as the objections of the other parties.[14] The court can then approve, alter or reject the proposed changes, having regard to any significant developments which have occurred since the date when the previous budget was approved or agreed.[15] The approved budget must then be re-filed and served, with the order approving it.[16]

In cases where a costs management order has been made and the court comes to assess the costs payable by one party to the other on the standard basis, the CPR state that the court must have regard to the receiving party's last approved or agreed budget for each phase of the proceedings and not depart from this unless satisfied there is a good reason to do so.[17] The court must also, when it comes to make a standard assessment of costs, apply CPR, r 44.3(2), which states that the court must:

'•   Only allow costs which are proportionate to the matters in issue. Costs which are disproportionate in amount may be disallowed or reduced *even if they were reasonably or necessarily incurred*[18] [our italics]; and
 •   Resolve any doubt which it may have as to whether costs were reasonably and proportionately incurred or were reasonable and proportionate in amount in favour of the paying party.'[19]

As previously, where costs are to be assessed on the indemnity basis, the court will resolve any doubt as to whether costs were reasonably incurred or reasonable in amount in favour of the receiving party.[20]

The fact that costs may not now be recoverable from a defendant, even where they were necessary in order to progress the case or were otherwise incurred entirely reasonably, on the grounds of disproportionality is a hugely significant (and some would say disturbing) development for those who represent

---

[11]   CPR, r 3.16.
[12]   CPR, r 3.17(1) and (2).
[13]   Paragraph 2.6 of Practice Direction 3E.
[14]   Paragraph 2.6 of Practice Direction 3E.
[15]   Paragraph 2.6 of Practice Direction 3E.
[16]   Paragraph 2.7 of Practice Direction 3E.
[17]   CPR, r 3.18(a) and (b).
[18]   CPR, r 44.3(2)(a).
[19]   CPR, r 44.3(2)(b).
[20]   CPR, r 44.3(3).

claimants. A definition of 'proportionality' is set out in CPR, r 44.3(5), which states that costs are proportionate if they bear a reasonable relationship to:

- the sums in issue in the proceedings;
- the value of any non-monetary relief in issue in the proceedings;
- the complexity of the litigation;
- any additional work generated by the conduct of the paying party; and
- any wider factors involved in the proceedings such as reputation or public importance.[21]

CPR, r 44.4 provides further guidance as to the factors to be taken into account when deciding whether costs were proportionately and reasonably incurred and proportionate and reasonable in amount. As previously, these will include the conduct of the parties both before and during proceedings and the complexity, difficulty or novelty of the questions raised.[22]

For cases and work done before 1 April 2013, the old CPR, r 44.4(2)(a) still applies. This stated that, '[w]here the amount of costs is to be assessed on the standard basis, the court will – (a) only allow costs which are proportionate to the matters in issue and (b) resolve any doubt which it may have as to whether costs were reasonably incurred or reasonable and proportionate in amount in favour of the paying party'. Parties who are going to have to file a costs budget may wish to consider separating out the costs which were incurred before and after 1 April 2013, given the different tests which, at least in theory, will be applied on assessment.

Given the recent nature of the reforms, it is not yet clear how the courts will apply the new procedural rules and there is obviously some prospect of satellite litigation, either where parties have fallen foul of the rules or where they wish to seek clarification of the court's approach.

As concerns the recoverability of costs where a party has exceeded their costs budget, there have already been some applications arising from the pilot schemes for costs budgeting which were in place prior to 1 April 2013 and some consideration is given to these below, insofar as they might have a wider impact following LASPO.

In the case of *Henry v News Group Newspapers Limited*,[23] which fell under the Defamation Proceedings Costs Management Pilot Scheme, the claimant's bill of costs exceeded her approved costs budget and the parties agreed to apply to the court for a decision as to whether the budget could be departed from. When this issue was heard by the court, the judge (Senior Costs Judge Hurst) stated that he was in no doubt that there would be a strong argument on detailed assessment that the claimant's costs were reasonable and proportionate.

---

21 CPR, r 44.3(5)(a) to (e).
22 CPR, r 44.4(3).
23 [2013] EWCA Civ 19.

However, he observed that the relevant practice direction[24] was in mandatory terms and that the objective was to manage the litigation so that the costs were proportionate and so that the parties were on an equal footing. If one party were to be unaware that the other's budget had been significantly exceeded they would no longer be on an equal footing and the purpose of the costs management scheme would be lost. The judge went on to conclude that there was no good reason to depart from the approved budget and he consequently disallowed £268,832 of the claimant's costs, before any success fee was added.

The claimant appealed to the Court of Appeal and that court's leading judgment was given by Lord Justice Moore-Bick, who stated that it was implicit in the practice direction that the approved costs budget was intended to provide the framework for a detailed assessment and that the court should not normally allow costs which exceeded those budgeted for each section. However, he noted that the practice direction also accepted that there could be good reason to depart from the budget and, in deciding whether this was the case, it was relevant to consider the objectives of the costs management scheme. These, in his view, were twofold:

- to ensure that the costs incurred in connection with the proceedings are proportionate to what is at stake; and

- to ensure that one party is unable to exploit superior financial resources by conducting the litigation in a way that puts the other at a significant disadvantage.

Lord Justice Moore-Bick concluded that in this case there was no inequality of arms, neither party being 'financially embarrassed', and that failure to comply with the requirements of the practice direction was just one of the factors that the court could take into account in deciding whether costs in excess of the budget should be awarded. Other factors, which he appears to have found more compelling, were as follows:

- Both parties had exceeded their budgets and yet neither had gone back to court to revise these.

- If the budget were not departed from then the claimant would not be able to recover the costs of the action and Lord Justice Moore-Bick found this to be an important factor, given that the court was persuaded that the costs were reasonable and proportionate.

- The defendant's solicitors had failed to register any protest when they were informed of the amount of costs incurred by the claimant, prior to reaching a settlement.

Lord Justice Moore-Bick did, however, note that his judgment related only to the practice direction arising from the defamation costs management scheme and that the rules (which were yet to come into effect) relating to costs management in multi-track claims would be different in some key respects. He stated that '[r]ead as a whole [the latter] lay greater emphasis on the importance

---

24   Practice Direction 51D (the Defamation Proceedings Costs Management Scheme).

of the approved or agreed budget as providing a prima facie limit on the amount of recoverable costs'. He also observed that where budgets are approved by the court and revised at regular intervals the receiving party is unlikely to persuade the court that costs which exceed the budget are reasonable and proportionate.

This is a theme which was taken up by the Technology and Construction Court in the case of *Elvanite Full Circle Limited v Amec Earth and Environmental (UK) Limited.*[25] In this case, the parties each filed a costs budget and the claimant's was approved at £317,333.25 and the defendant's at £264,708. The defendant's budget was subsequently revised and approved at £268,488 at the pre-trial review but at no other time did the parties make an application to the court to revise the budgets.

The defendant did, however, send a revised budget to the claimant and the court a month before trial, which included costs totalling £531,946.18. The claimant objected but also advised the defendant that its own anticipated costs had increased to £372,179.53. After the claimant's claim was dismissed and the defendant's counterclaim was allowed (though only in one respect), the parties disagreed as to the costs recoverable by the defendant and this fell to be decided by Mr Justice Coulson, who held that:

- If the defendant had wanted the court to approve the changes to its costs budget then this approval should have been formally sought and it was not enough simply to file a revised budget at court.

- Such an application should have been made immediately when it became apparent that the original budget costs had been significantly exceeded by more than a minimal amount.

- The application here should have been made before trial and this was expressly required by the relevant practice direction.[26] Otherwise this would no longer be a budgeting exercise but would instead be based on the actual costs incurred.

- If the defendant were to be allowed to revise its budget now, the claimant would be faced with a personal liability for costs (over and above the available ATE insurance indemnity) of up to a quarter of a million pounds, as opposed to the amount it faced under the existing costs management order (namely £18,488.00). This would be unjust and contrary to the case management rules.

- Turning to the issue of whether there was good reason to depart from the approved budget, Mr Justice Coulson observed that by far and away the largest item in respect of which the defendant had exceeded its budget was in relation to the experts' fees. No good reason had been given to justify the increased costs, save in one discrete respect.

---

[25] [2013] EWHC 1643 (TCC).
[26] Practice direction 51G – Costs Management in Mercantile Courts and Technology and Construction Courts Pilot Scheme.

Neither of the above cases is directly relevant to the costs budgeting rules which now apply, with limited exceptions, to all multi-track cases. As referred to by Lord Justice Moore-Bick in *Henry v News Group Newspapers Limited*, albeit in *obiter* remarks, the rules which came into force on 1 April 2013 explicitly state that an approved costs budget will place a limit on recoverable costs,[27] though there is some scope for departing from this where there is good reason to do so. There appears to be little doubt that what constitutes 'good reason' will be a much-vexed topic for the courts over the coming months or even years.

In relation to the ramifications of breaching the more technical rules relating to costs budgeting, the Court of Appeal's judgment in *Andrew Mitchell MP v News Group Newspapers Limited*,[28] was handed down on 27 November 2013 and is a cautionary tale for litigation lawyers. This was an appeal by the claimant, Mr Mitchell, against two decisions of Master McCloud relating to his costs budget.

The claimant's solicitors had failed to file his costs budget 7 days or more before the first case management conference and he was therefore taken by Master McCloud to have filed a budget including only the applicable court fees. The claimant appealed this initial decision of Master McCloud on various grounds, which were dealt with by the Court of Appeal in the Master of the Rolls' leading judgment, before it went on to consider the issue of relief from sanctions.

It is worth reiterating that the new CPR, r 3.14, which came into effect on 1 April 2013, states that 'any party which fails to file a budget despite being required to do so will be treated as having filed a budget comprising only the applicable court fees'.

The claimant argued that Master McCloud should not have applied CPR, r 3.14 to his claim at all, given that the proceedings were governed by PD 51D, which continued to apply to defamation claims issued before 1 April 2013. The claimant therefore argued that the new costs budgeting provisions set out in CPR, rr 3.12 to 3.18 did not apply to his action.

The Court of Appeal held that Master McCloud was entitled to apply CPR, r 3.14 'by analogy', notwithstanding the fact that PD 51D governed the proceedings, as 'this represented the considered view of the Civil Procedure Rules Committee as to what constituted a proportionate sanction for failure to file a costs budget in time unless the court otherwise ordered'.[29]

The claimant had also argued that CPR, r 3.14 was intended only to bite on those parties which failed to file a costs budget *at all*, rather than those who filed a budget outside the requisite timeframe. The Court of Appeal again

---

[27]   CPR r. 3.15.

[28]   [2013] EWCA Civ 1526.

[29]   Paragraph 27 of the Master of the Rolls' judgment [2013] EWCA Civ 1526.

rejected this submission, stating that 'the mischief at which CPR 3.13 and 3.14 are directed is the last-minute filing of costs budgets'.[30]

Finally, in connection with CPR, r 3.14, the claimant argued that the decision of Master McCloud to treat him as having filed a costs budget which included only court fees was not in accordance with the overriding objective, in that it was disproportionate. The claimant argued that the breach was minor and easily remedied, that it had caused no prejudice to the defendant (but would of course prejudice the claimant) and that it would have no lasting effect on the litigation.

The Court of Appeal held that the claimant had been unable to ask the Master to make an alternative order as concerns the budget because his solicitors had not produced evidence which might have persuaded the Master to adopt this course. The Court of Appeal added that the considerations which might allow the courts to make an alternative order would likely be the same as those which were relevant to the issue of whether to grant relief from sanctions under CPR, r 3.9, which the Master of the Rolls then moved on to consider in his judgment.

The Master of the Rolls noted that CPR, r 3.9(1) now provides that:

> 'On an application for relief from any sanction imposed for a failure to comply with any rule, practice direction or court order, the court will consider all the circumstances of the case, so as to enable it to deal justly with the application, including the need –
> (a)   for litigation to be conducted efficiently and at proportionate cost; and
> (b)   to enforce compliance with rules, practice directions and orders.'

The Master of the Rolls contrasted this new evocation of the rule with the previous CPR, r 3.9(1), which had explicitly required the court to consider a multiplicity of factors, including the interests of the administration of justice, whether the failure to comply was intention, whether there was good explanation for the failure and the effect which the failure and the granting of relief would have on each party.

The Master of the Rolls stated that the reference to dealing with the case 'justly' under the new CPR, r 3.9 was a reference back to the overriding objective. He said that the Court of Appeal accepted that it was obliged to consider all the circumstances of the case when deciding whether to grant relief from sanctions, but opined that other circumstances should be given less weight than the two factors specifically referred to in CPR, r 3.9 (ie, the need to conduct litigation efficiently and at proportionate cost and to enforce compliance with rules, practice directions and orders).

---

[30]   Ibid, para 30.

The Master of the Rolls then went on to endorse, on behalf of the Court, some of the remarks made by his predecessor as Master of the Rolls in the latter's implementation lecture on the Jackson reforms. Amongst these was a statement that:

> 'Parties can no longer expect indulgence if they fail to comply with their procedural obligations. Those obligations not only serve the purpose of ensuring that they conduct the litigation proportionately in order to ensure their own costs are kept within proportionate bounds. But more importantly they serve the wider public interest of ensuring that other litigants can obtain justice efficiently and proportionately . . .'

The Court of Appeal placed considerable emphasis on the effect that the claimant's default had reportedly had upon the court system and, by extension, other court users generally. The Master of the Rolls, in his judgment, pointed out that the initial costs management conference in the *Mitchell* case had had to be adjourned and Master McCloud then had to accommodate this at a time when she would otherwise have been dealing with asbestos-related disease claims.

The Court of Appeal went on to provide guidance regarding the new approach which should be taken by the courts and drew a distinction between various different scenarios, ie:

(a)   Where non-compliance can properly be regarded as trivial, the court will usually grant relief provided the application for relief is made promptly. 'Trivial' breaches would, according to the Court of Appeal, potentially include failures of form rather than substance and narrowly missing a deadline but otherwise complying with an order's terms.

(b)   Where non-compliance cannot be said to be trivial, the defaulting party will need to convince the court to grant relief and if there is good reason then the court will be likely to decide that relief should be granted. For example, if the party or their solicitor was suffering from a debilitating illness or was involved in an accident which led to the default then, depending on the circumstances, this could constitute good reason.

(c)   However, if no good reason can be provided for a default which is not in itself considered to be trivial then parties cannot expect to receive relief from sanction. For example, 'mere overlooking a deadline [*sic*], whether on account of overwork or otherwise, is unlikely to be a good reason'.[31]

The Master of the Rolls went on to say that applications for an extension of time made before time has expired will be looked upon more favourably than applications for relief from sanction made after the event.

The Court of Appeal then applied this bracing new approach to the circumstances arising in the *Mitchell* case and found that the claimant's defaults were neither minor nor trivial and that there was no good excuse for these. The

---

[31]   Paragraph 41 of the Master of the Rolls' judgment [2013] EWCA Civ 1526.

defaults had resulted in an abortive costs budgeting hearing and an adjournment which had serious consequences for other litigants. The claimant's appeal against the decision to refuse relief from sanctions was therefore dismissed.

By its own admission, the Court of Appeal in this case intended to send out 'a clear message' to litigators that a change in culture is going to be enforced by the courts, whereby legal representatives should 'become more efficient and will routinely comply with rules, practice directions and orders'.[32] The Master of the Rolls, however, acknowledged that this cultural shift is almost bound to give rise to contested applications and satellite litigation whilst the boundaries of the changes are explored.

4.3 FUNDING AND THE SOLICITORS REGULATION AUTHORITY CODE OF CONDUCT 2011

The Solicitors Regulation Authority Code of Conduct 2011 ('the SRA Code') has been in force since 6 October 2011 and sets out mandatory outcomes which must be achieved by solicitors, as well as 'indicative behaviours' which may serve this end. The SRA Code contains several provisions relating to funding and costs, most of which are set out in Chapter 1 of the code, which relates to 'client care'.

On 1 February 2013 new Scheme Rules were implemented for the Legal Ombudsman, which included an increase in the amount of compensation the Ombudsman could order a legal practitioner to pay, up to £50,000. Furthermore, breaches of the SRA Code may not only result in complaints and disciplinary action against a solicitor but also potentially in the need to pay civil damages to the client. In the case of *Hollins v Russell*,[33] the Court of Appeal confirmed that professional rules were civilly enforceable as though they were statutory duties. Clearly, therefore, a legal practitioner must guard against breaching the SRA Code or risk heavy financial consequences.

Whilst the SRA Code is less prescriptive than the code which preceded it (the Solicitors' Code of Conduct 2007), the required client care outcomes mean that solicitors will need to be assiduous in advising their clients about costs and funding. This exercise has perhaps become even more complex given the diversity of funding arrangements now available and the number of statutory provisions and procedural rules which apply to them.

According to the SRA Code, the key outcomes which need to be achieved in relation to costs and funding are as follows:

- O(1.1) – You treat your clients fairly.
- O(1.2) – You provide services to your client in a manner that protects their interests in their matter, subject to the proper administration of justice.

---

[32] Ibid, para 60.
[33] [2003] EWCA Civ 718.

- O(1.6) – You only enter into fee agreements with your clients that are legal and which you consider are suitable for the client's needs and take account of the client's best interests.
- O(1.12) – Clients are in a position to make informed decisions about the service they need, how their matter will be handled and the options available to them.
- O(1.13) – Clients receive the best possible information about the likely cost of their matter, both at the time of their engagement and when appropriate as the matter progresses.

The relevant indicative behaviours that solicitors might employ in meeting these goals include:

- IB(1.13) – Discussing whether the potential outcomes of the client's matter are likely to justify the expense or risk involved, including any risk of having to pay someone else's legal fees (a costs-benefit analysis).
- IB(1.14) – Clearly explaining your fees, and if and when they are likely to change.
- IB(1.15) – Warning about any other payments for which the client may be responsible.
- IB(1.16) – Discussing how the client will pay, including whether public funding may be available, whether the client has insurance that may cover the fees and whether the fees may be paid by someone else (such as a trade union).
- IB(1.17) – Where you are acting for a client under a fee arrangement governed by statute, such as a conditional fee agreement (CFA), giving the client all relevant information relating to that arrangement.
- IB(1.18) – Where you are acting for a publicly funded client, explaining how their publicly funded status affects the costs.
- IB(1.19) – Providing the information in a clear and accessible form that is appropriate to the needs and circumstances of the client.
- IB(1.20) – Where you receive a financial benefit as a result of acting for a client, either:
  - paying it to the client;
  - offsetting it against your fees; or
  - keeping it only where you can justify keeping it. This is where you have told the client the amount of the benefit (or an approximation if you do not know the exact amount) and the client has agreed that you can keep it.
- IB(1.21) – Ensuring that disbursements included in your bill reflect the actual amount spent or to be spent on behalf of the client.

Clearly, solicitors should therefore be providing the client, or potential client as they may then be, at the outset with a summary of the funding options available to them and a brief description of the relative merits of these for the particular client. Whilst it is not obligatory for a client who has before the event insurance or who is eligible for legal aid to utilise these methods of funding, a solicitor who did not at least enter into a discussion about these may well fall foul of O(1.6) and O(1.12), given that the alternative options may involve the client shouldering some of the costs burden.

As concerns CFAs and DBAs, there is no requirement in the relevant legislation (including the Conditional Fee Agreements Order 2013 and Damages-based Agreements Regulations 2013) for a practitioner to inform their client how the success or contingency fee has been arrived at, though of course the agreement must set out what the percentage fee is. The practitioner need not say whether a risk assessment has been carried out or what the factors in that assessment were.

However, we would again suggest that the SRA Code provisions referred to may make it sensible for a practitioner to provide some advice to their client as to why they consider a success or contingency fee at a certain level is justified. Practitioners should also bear in mind that a client can apply to court under s 70 of the Solicitors Act 1974 for a solicitor's bill to be assessed, including the success fee, and again it may be of assistance to the solicitor to show that they provided an explanation for this to the client before the retainer was entered into.

4.4   LEGAL EXPENSES INSURANCE

As already stated above, solicitors have an obligation to only enter into fee agreements with clients that are suitable for the client's needs and take account of their best interests (O(1.6) of the SRA Code). Solicitors must also ensure the client is in a position to make an informed decision about the service they need and the options available to them (O(1.12)). Failing to at least discuss whether the client has the benefit of legal expenses or before the event (BTE) insurance could arguably be a breach and so this should be raised with them before other funding arrangements are entered into.

BTE cover could be contained in a discrete legal expenses policy, or else be included as part of another form of insurance. Identifying whether a client has BTE cover can be a complex task and will involve looking at the scope of the policy, both in terms of the applicable areas of law (for example some policies will exclude clinical negligence claims) and the period of cover, as well as the level of indemnity.

It can be difficult for a client to determine, even after consulting their insurers, whether they have the benefit of BTE cover for their particular case. For example, there may not be any one discernible 'event' giving rise to the claim and so, in order to determine whether the claim is covered, it will be necessary to look at when the cause of action accrued.

It is submitted that the sensible practitioner will not leave the issue of whether BTE is available solely to the client and insurers to determine and that they should at least offer to liaise with the insurers directly, particularly where there is any doubt as to the type and duration of the cover available. Whether they or the client liaise with the insurers, the solicitor should document what investigations have been made and what communications have been had with the insurers before moving on to another funding arrangement.

Where it is determined that the client *does* have the benefit of appropriate BTE cover in relation to the case, the solicitor should liaise with the insurer to ascertain their terms of appointment and confirm whether the insurers will allow the client to instruct the solicitor under the policy. It is not at all unusual for insurers to dictate that clients must use a particular firm of 'panel' solicitors if they are to utilise their BTE cover, at least in relation to the initial investigations.

This has long been a matter of concern to non-panel solicitors, who may feel that their potential client's freedom of choice is being infringed and (less altruistically) that the solicitors themselves are being denied the opportunity to take on potentially interesting and valuable work. It is not considered appropriate to go into a detailed analysis here of whether or not insurers are entitled to dictate the client's choice of solicitor. However, in brief summary:

- Regulation 6(1) of the Insurance Companies (Legal Expenses Insurance) Regulations 1990[34] ('the Regulations') states that where under a legal expenses insurance contract recourse is had to a lawyer (or such other person having such qualifications as may be necessary) to defend, represent or serve the interests of that insured in any inquiry or proceedings, the insured shall be free to choose that lawyer (or other person).

- However, the European Court of Justice in *Eschig v UNIQA*,[35] when interpreting the European Council directive which was implemented by the Regulations,[36] observed that Article 4(1) restricts the right to freely choose a legal representative to 'inquiries and proceedings'. BTE insurers tend to place reliance on this to say that their insured is only entitled to freely choose their solicitor if and when proceedings are issued, but that the insurers can require use of their panel solicitors in the pre-issue stage.

- The Financial Ombudsman Service (FOS) set out its position regarding the interpretation of the regulations in Ombudsman News: Issue 26: Legal Expenses Insurance (March 2003), stating that in the absence of clear guidance from the courts it would not require an insurer to offer the insured a free choice of solicitor at the start of the claim. However, the FOS indicated that it will expect insurers to agree the appointment of the insured's chosen solicitors in cases involving large personal injury claims or claims that are necessarily complex (such as clinical negligence claims).

---

[34]   SI 1990/1159.

[35]   Case C-199/08.

[36]   EU Council Directive 87/344/EEC on the co-ordination of laws, regulations and administrative provisions relating to legal expenses insurance.

Practitioners wishing to deal with a catastrophic injury claim should therefore consider drawing the BTE insurers' attention to the FOS guidance if the insurers argue that panel solicitors should be used. If the insurers continue to hold out, practitioners can consider referring the matter to the FOS.

If these measures fail, or if the existing cover is considered insufficient or inappropriate for some other reason, the practitioner can explore with the client whether there are any steps which could be taken to offset these problems. For example, if the problem is the amount of the indemnity available then they could consider using the BTE insurance and then applying for top-up indemnity at a later stage.

If no such solutions are available, or suitable, the practitioner can discuss with the client whether an alternative type of funding arrangement would suit their interests better. It may, for example, be possible for the practitioner to enter into a CFA for the investigative stages and then seek to use the BTE cover if and when proceedings are issued.

The client would have to be carefully advised about the financial implications for them of choosing not to use their BTE insurance. It is possible for a practitioner to act for a client under a CFA with no success fee, either with or without provision for the client paying any shortfall in the base costs recovered from the defendant. These options should be borne in mind when advising a client about their options, should they have BTE insurance but not wish to use it for any reason.

However, even if a CFA with no success fee or enforcement of the shortfall against the client is offered, the premium for any ATE insurance taken out on or after 1 April 2013 would be payable by the client instead of the defendant (save in relation to any part that relates to obtaining experts' reports in clinical negligence cases). This is of course unless the solicitor's firm was willing to pay this.

Practitioners should therefore ensure that they document the reasons for entering into an alternative form of funding arrangement, when BTE was available. They should also record what discussions were had with the client regarding this issue.

Where, in clinical negligence cases, a client is considering taking out ATE insurance where BTE insurance is already available, solicitors should confirm with the potential ATE insurers what they would do if the proportion of the premium relating to liability experts' reports was challenged by the defendant. It should be clarified whether they would then seek payment of this from the client, as of course this may have a bearing on the client's decision about whether to opt for a funding arrangement other than their existing BTE insurance.

4.5 'THIRD PARTY' FUNDING

This is probably not a method of funding that the majority of practitioners specialising in personal injury and clinical negligence claims will ever have utilised and, given its current rarity, this chapter will not cover third party funding in any detail. However, some commentators speculate that third party funding may become more common, due to the potentially beneficial effects on practitioners' cash flow, and as such we consider that it merits some consideration here.

Third party funding, which is also sometimes referred to as 'third party litigation funding', involves a non-party agreeing to pay some or all of the claimant's legal costs in return for a proportion of any damages they recover. Financial assistance provided by trade unions could potentially fall under the heading of 'third party funding', though where unions make a charge for their legal advice or support to members this will not usually involve their seeking a proportion of any damages.

Third party funding could involve the funder agreeing to bear the whole of the claimant's costs, including the legal representatives' fees and any disbursements. Alternatively, it could be combined with other methods of funding, such as CFAs or DBAs (in relation to which see below). For example, the legal representatives might agree to act under a CFA in relation to their respective fees and the third party funder could be responsible for the claimant's disbursements, should the claim not succeed.

In the latter circumstance, the third party funding would, in effect, act as a form of ATE insurance but instead of paying an insurance premium the claimant would agree to pay part of their damages to the third party funder in the event of a successful claim. It seems questionable whether this carries any additional benefit to claimants in areas of law where ATE insurance is quite readily available, as would currently appear to be the case with personal injury and clinical negligence claims. However, there is a risk that ATE insurance may become more difficult to come by, once insurers see what returns they are getting on their post-LASPO policies and have a chance to consider the economic viability of these.

There are some aspects of third party funding which arguably render it a risky proposition, both for claimants and for funders. For example:

- The legal doctrines of 'maintenance' and 'champerty' militate against arrangements whereby litigation is funded by third parties, if there is an element of impropriety which amounts to 'wanton' interference in the disputes of others with or without a division of the damages. If a funding arrangement breaches these principles then it will be unenforceable, which obviously would not be good news for the third party funder, who would be unable to seek payment of any agreed sums from the claimant even where the claim succeeds. It would also be unfortunate for the claimant, since the indemnity principle would dictate that as they have no obligation to repay any sums to the third party funder they would not be able to recover the relevant costs from the defendant.[37]

- As will be seen below, 1 April 2013 saw the advent of qualified one-way costs shifting (QOCS) in relation to funding arrangements entered into on or after that date. However, if the proceedings include a claim made for the financial benefit of a person other than the claimant or a dependant under the Fatal Accidents Act 1976, an order for costs can be made against that other person if the court thinks it would be just to do so.[38]

- There is therefore a risk of adverse costs orders being made against third party funders, though the case of *Arkin v Borchard Lines Limited and others*[39] would suggest that this would be limited to the amount of the costs they had paid, as was held to be the case in that instance by the Court of Appeal where a defendant sought their costs from the third party funder. The court, however, indicated that if the agreement had been found to be in breach of the doctrine of champerty liability could have been unrestricted.

- In the case of *Germany v Flatman*,[40] the Court of Appeal recently considered whether the funding of disbursements in a personal injury action by a claimant's solicitor justified an order for costs being made against them. This is of course a slightly different issue to whether a third party funder might be subject to an adverse costs order, but the case nevertheless provides some helpful guidance as to when a third party costs order (whether against a solicitor or another) could be made. It was suggested by the Court of Appeal that the funder would have to have substantially controlled and benefitted from the proceedings, to the extent that they became 'a real party', before an order of costs should be made against them. Paying disbursements would not, in and of itself, give rise to a liability to an adverse costs order.

Whilst, in light of the above, it would appear that third party funding may be a legitimate option in connection with personal injury and clinical negligence claims, it is submitted that this is not without risks. If such funding were to be considered, the precise nature of the arrangements would need to be carefully considered and the practitioner would need to guard against any suggestion that the third party funder could be said to be 'controlling' the litigation.

4.6 PUBLIC FUNDING ('LEGAL AID')

LASPO brought in substantial changes in relation to legal aid in almost every area of law, including clinical negligence. Prior to 1 April 2013, legal aid could be sought in relation to clinical negligence actions, but claims relating to other

---

[37] See for instance *Hughes v Kingston upon Hull City Council* [1998] EWCA Civ 1731.
[38] CPR, r 44.16(2).
[39] [2005] EWCA Civ 655.
[40] [2013] EWCA Civ 278.

forms of 'negligently caused injury, death or damage to property' were already excluded from such funding by the Access to Justice Act 1999,[41] save for in exceptional circumstances.

Prior to 1 April 2013, applicants for legal aid would have to satisfy the Legal Services Commission (which as of the aforementioned date has been abolished and replaced by the Legal Aid Agency) that their claim had sufficient merit to warrant funding this from the public purse. This would involve some consideration of the estimated costs of pursuing the action, as against the potential damages to be obtained (the 'costs/benefit' analysis).

The applicant would also have to pass a stringent means test and, unless they received certain benefits which would automatically render them financially eligible or were under 16 years of age with no regular income or significant capital, would have to submit detailed information and supporting documents regarding their finances.

Where claimants pursuing clinical negligence claims were successful in obtaining legal aid prior to 1 April 2013, their certificates will remain in effect (at least pending any reassessment of the merits of the case or the client's means), due to the transitional arrangements set out in the Legal Aid, Sentencing and Punishment of Offenders (Consequential, Transitional and Saving Provisions) Regulations 2013. Any financial reassessment will be made under the legislation which preceded LASPO, ie, the Community Legal Service (Financial) Regulations 2000 (as amended) or the Civil Legal Aid (Assessment of Resources) Regulations 1989, depending on the statute under which the original legal aid certificate was issued.

However, pursuant to s 9(1) of LASPO, from 1 April 2013 legal aid will only be available in relation to those civil legal services set out in Part 1 of Sch 1 to that act (and only then if the person applying for legal aid qualifies financially). Paragraph 23(1) of Part 1 of Sch 1 of LASPO states that civil legal services in respect of claims for damages relating to clinical negligence which caused a neurological injury to an individual, as a result of which they are severely disabled (whether physically or mentally[42]), may still qualify for legal aid, provided the following conditions are met:

- The clinical negligence occurred either:
  - whilst the affected person was in his or her mother's womb;[43] or
  - during or after the affected person's birth but before the end of the following period:
    - o if the person was born before the beginning of the 37th week of pregnancy the period of 8 weeks beginning with the first day of what would have been that week;[44] or

---

[41] As per Sch 2 to the Access to Justice Act 1999.
[42] Paragraph 23(5) of Part 1 of Sch 1 to LASPO.
[43] Paragraph 23(2)(a) of Part 1 of Sch 1 to LASPO.
[44] Paragraph 23(2)(b)(i) of Part 1 of Sch 1 to LASPO.

○ if the person was born during or after the 37th week of pregnancy, the period of 8 weeks beginning with the day of their birth;[45] *and*

- the services are provided to the affected person or, where they have died, to their personal representative.[46]

Other than as referred to above, since 1 April 2013 legal aid has been abolished for all personal injury and clinical negligence claims, save where these can be established as 'exceptional cases' pursuant to s 10 of LASPO. This section permits legal aid to be granted where:

- it is necessary to make the civil legal services available to the individual under Part 1 of LASPO because failure to do so would be a breach of their rights under the European Convention on Human Rights (within the meaning of the Human Rights Act 1998) or any rights of the individual to the provision of legal services that are enforceable European Union rights;[47] or

- it is appropriate to do so in the particular circumstances of the case, having regard to any risk that failure to do so would be such a breach.[48]

In order to qualify for exceptional cases funding, the applicant would also need to qualify under the relevant means criteria (s 10(2)(b) of LASPO).

The key resources when it comes to ascertaining whether a client, or a potential client, would be financially eligible for legal aid are the Civil Legal Aid (Financial Resources and Payment for Services) Regulations 2013 ('the 2013 Regulations') and the Legal Aid Agency Civil Representation Guide to Determining Financial Eligibility for Certificated Work 2013 ('the Guide' – currently in its first version). The Director of Legal Aid Casework must apply the former and have regard to the latter when determining whether an individual is financially eligible for civil legal aid services.

The aspects of the 2013 Regulations and the Guide which are of particular relevance to this publication are as follows:

- Where an application for legal aid is made on behalf of a child or someone incapable of managing their own affairs, a certificate will be issued in the name of the protected party and it is their resources which will be assessed, not those of the litigation friend who is bringing the proceedings on their behalf.[49]

- An application by a child must be made on their behalf by a person aged 18 or over.[50]

---

[45] Paragraph 23(2)(b)(ii) of Part 1 of Sch 1 to LASPO.

[46] Paragraph 23(3) of Part 1 of Sch 1 to LASPO.

[47] Section 10(3)(a)(i) and (ii) of LASPO.

[48] Section 10(3)(b) of LASPO.

[49] Paragraph 1 of section 3.3 of Legal Aid Agency Civil Representation Guide to Determining Financial Eligibility for Certificated Work 2013 version 1.

[50] Paragraph 1 of section 10.1 of the Guide.

- Applications submitted on behalf of children or 'patients' within the meaning of the Mental Health Act 1983 (the authors do not know why the guidance falls back into using the outdated term of 'patients' rather than 'protected parties' here) should be submitted by someone of full age and capacity and they should sign the relevant application and means forms.[51] In clinical negligence cases, the application must be made by the person who is, or proposes to be, the litigation friend for the child or protected party.[52]

- Funding for legal representation must be refused where alternative funding is available to the individual on whose behalf the application is being made and there are other persons or bodies which can reasonably be expected to bring or fund the case.[53] Section 6.9 of the Guide explicitly states that an interest under a trust could be considered to amount to such funding though this will presumably depend upon the extent of the child or protected party's interest.

Where legal aid is granted and the person receiving the funding subsequently has a change in their financial circumstances, they are obliged to inform the Legal Aid Agency of the change.[54] The Director for Legal Aid Casework will then make a further determination as to whether they are financially eligible for legal aid, pursuant to reg 20 of the 2013 Regulations.

Section 7.5 of the Guide states that capital received in connection with the incident giving rise to the dispute (eg interim payments received during the litigation) will not automatically be disregarded when it comes to assessing a person's financial eligibility for legal aid. Instead, this is at the discretion of the Director for Legal Aid Casework.[55] The Guide goes on to say that 'in general' such capital will be disregarded unless, having regard to the amount and purpose of the payment, the Director is of the view that the legally aided individual can afford to proceed without legal aid. If so, then the Director can withdraw legal aid or else seek a capital contribution from the legally aided person.[56]

Clearly, this is something that must be considered when advising the legally aided person, or their litigation friend, as to whether or not it is sensible to apply for an interim payment on account of damages during the course of the case. Where an interim payment of this kind is to be sought, the claimant or their litigation friend must be advised that they (or the legal representative on their behalf) will be obliged to inform the Legal Aid Agency if such a payment is received as it will represent a change of financial circumstances, even if there are plans to spend the money in the near future.

---

[51] Section 10.2 of the Guide.
[52] Articles 30(2) and 30(4) of the Civil Aid (Procedure) Regulations 2012.
[53] Article 39 of the Legal Aid (Financial Resources and Payment for Services) Regulations 2013.
[54] Article 18 of the 2013 Regulations.
[55] Article 42 of the 2013 Regulations.
[56] Paragraphs 2 and 3 of section 7.5 of the Guide.

The representative should, when notifying the Legal Aid Agency of an interim payment, make representations setting out why they feel this should be disregarded for the purposes of assessing the legally aided person's continuing eligibility for legal aid. For example, the interim payment may have been obtained in order to cover the immediate needs of the claimant, such as the need for more suitable accommodation or to put in place an appropriate care regime. It is to be hoped that the Director for Legal Aid Casework will exercise their discretion in the claimant's favour in such circumstances.

In cases where their client is receiving legal aid, practitioners should now have recourse to the new Legal Aid Agency Clinical Negligence Funding Checklist (dated April 2013) when applying for an increase to the costs limitation under the legal aid certificate. This document sets out the maximum costs for each stage which the Legal Aid Agency is likely to pay, should the case be unsuccessful, and these can be revised downwards in accordance with the costs/benefit ratios set out in the Civil Legal Aid (Merits Criteria) Regulations 2012, ie:

- 1:4 for cases where the prospects of success are estimated to be between 50% and 60%;
- 1:2 where the prospects are estimated at between 60% and 80%; or
- 1:1 where the prospects are estimated at 80% or more.

The Checklist also sets out the information which the legal representative will need to provide to the Legal Aid Agency in order to obtain an increase in the costs limitation at each of the various stages. Practitioners should of course keep a watchful eye over the costs they have incurred and apply for increases in the costs limitations whenever this becomes possible under the Checklist, as the Legal Aid Agency is highly unlikely to pay a higher level of costs than those explicitly allowed for under the certificate, even if these related to work which it was reasonable and/or necessary to carry out.

4.7 CONDITIONAL FEE AGREEMENTS (CFAS)

4.7.1 CFAs entered into before 1 April 2013

Where a CFA was entered into between a client and a legal representative before 1 April 2013 then, as long as the statutory requirements which then applied were complied with, a claimant who succeeds with their personal injury claim can seek to recover not only their representative's base costs and disbursements from a defendant but also a 'success fee'. A success fee is a percentage uplift, calculated using the solicitor's or barrister's base costs and *not* the amount of damages received.

The corollary to this type of agreement was that, under a CFA, the client would not have to pay the legal representatives' base costs if the claim did not succeed. However, the unsuccessful client would usually still be liable to pay the disbursements arising in relation to their claim and they could also be ordered to pay the defendant's costs of the action (including profit costs, counsel's fees and disbursements), pursuant to what was then the general rule that the losing party will pay the winning party's costs.[57] These 'adverse' costs could be substantial and so the solicitors would generally advise the client to take out a policy of ATE insurance to cover them, either at the outset of the case or once supportive evidence had been obtained.

ATE insurance would also generally provide cover in relation to the risk that the claimant could be ordered to pay some of the defendant's costs in the event that they failed to beat an offer that the defendant had made under Part 36 of the CPR, though it is worth noting that some ATE policies would only do so to the extent that such costs exceeded the claimant's damages. In other words, the claimant might have to apply some or all of their damages towards the costs that they were ordered to pay the defendant pursuant to Part 36, with the ATE insurers only covering any shortfall.

Before 1 April 2013 (as indeed has been the case since the LASPO reforms) it was possible for both a solicitor and a barrister to act under a CFA in relation to a personal injury or clinical negligence claim, though the barrister's CFA would be entered into with the solicitor rather than the client. Save in relation to claims where fixed success fees applied (in relation to which see further below), where their CFAs were entered into before 1 April 2013 the solicitor and barrister could each charge a success fee of up to 100% of their base costs.

4.7.2   Fixed success fees

Given that no CFAs entered into after 1 April 2013 will be subject to fixed success fees (and those CFAs to which these apply will already have been entered into), this chapter will not provide any detailed consideration of this topic. Practitioners wishing to review the relevant provisions relating to fixed success fees should consult what were formerly CPR, rr 45.17 to 45.19 (relating to fixed uplifts in road traffic accidents) and the old CPR, r 45.22 and Parts IV and V of CPR Part 45 (in relation to employer liability cases). These provisions continue to have force where a CFA to which fixed success fees applied was entered into before 1 April 2013.[58]

It is worth noting that, in certain cases, it is possible to apply under the old CPR, r 45.18 for an alternative percentage uplift in road traffic accident cases to be applied during the pre-trial stage. The old CPR, r 45.18(2) stated that such an application could be made where:

- the parties agree damages or the court awards damages in excess of £500,000;[59] or

---

[57]   CPR, r 44.3(2)(a) relating to 'pre-commencement' funding arrangements.
[58]   CPR, r 48.1 and para 1.2 of the Practice Direction to Part 48.
[59]   CPR, r 45.18(2)(a).

- the court awards damages of £500,000 or less but would have awarded damages greater than £500,000 if it had not made a finding of contributory negligence;[60] or
- the parties agree damages of £500,000 or less and it is reasonable to expect that if the court had made an award of damages, it would have awarded damages greater than £500,000, disregarding any reduction the court may have made in respect of contributory negligence.[61]

Pursuant to the old CPR, r 45.18(4), if the court is satisfied that these circumstances apply then it must either assess the percentage increase or make an order for this to be assessed. However, practitioners considering applying for an increase in the uplift should bear in mind CPR, r 45.19(2). This states that where the court assesses the appropriate uplift but finds it to be no more than 20% or no less than 7.5% then the allowable percentage uplift will remain at 12.5% and the applicant will have to bear the costs of the application.

4.7.3 Statutory requirements of a pre-1 April 2013 CFA

In order to be enforceable, a CFA entered into before 1 April 2013 had to comply with the provisions of ss 58 and 58A of the Courts and Legal Services Act 1990 (CLSA), as amended by ss 27 and 28 of the Access to Justice Act 1999. In summary, the relevant provisions were as follows:

- A CFA was defined as 'an agreement with a person providing advocacy or litigation services which provides for his fees and expenses, or any part of them, to be payable only in specified circumstances'.[62]
- Litigation and advocacy services were defined in s 119 of the CLSA as follows:
  - litigation services meant any services which it would be reasonable to expect a person who is exercising, or contemplating exercising, a right to conduct litigation in relation to any proceedings, or contemplated proceedings, to provide;
  - advocacy services meant any services which it would be reasonable to expect a person who is exercising, or contemplating exercising, a right of audience in relation to any proceedings, or contemplated proceedings, to provide.
- A CFA provided for a success fee if it provided for the amount of any fees to which it applied to be increased, in specified circumstances, above the amount which would be payable if it were not payable only in specified circumstances.[63] In the usual course of events, the 'specified circumstances' in which the success fee would be paid would be where the claim had been won. The definition of 'winning' the claim had to be set out in the CFA.
- A CFA entered into before 1 April 2013 had to be in writing, as in fact is still the case following the LASPO reforms.

---

[60] CPR, r 45.18(2)(b).
[61] CPR, r 45.18(2)(c).
[62] Section 58(2)(a) of the CLSA.
[63] Section 58(2)(b) of the CLSA.

- The CFA had to specify the success fee which would be charged in the event of success and this could not exceed 100% of the legal representative's base costs (pursuant to the Conditional Fee Agreements Order 2000).

Failing to satisfy these obligations could result in the CFA being unenforceable. For example, in the cases of *Jones v Caradon Catnic Limited*[64] and *Oyston v Royal Bank of Scotland*[65] the courts held that the respective legal representatives' CFAs were unenforceable where they had fixed success fees at 120% (in the former instance) and 100% plus a bonus if damages beyond a certain amount were recovered (in the latter).

Where a practitioner becomes aware that there is an error in a CFA or else there is something that they wish to alter, they can seek to vary the agreement by entering into a deed of variation with the client. However, it is important that the reasons underlying the change and the effects of this are explained to the client, both orally and in writing, before the deed of variation is entered into. It is also important to point out that the court has held that a CFA that would otherwise be unenforceable cannot be 'saved' by varying it after judgment has been given (*Oyston v Royal Bank of Scotland*[66]). This may also be the case where a variation is agreed after a settlement has been reached.

4.7.4 CFAs entered into on and after 1 April 2013

The Legal Aid, Sentencing and Punishment of Offenders Act 2012 (Commencement No 5 and Saving Provision) Order 2013 brought into effect s 44 of LASPO on 1 April 2013. This section amended ss 58 and 58A of the CLSA. The definition of a CFA remains unchanged, being 'an agreement with a person providing advocacy or litigation services which provides for his fees and expenses, or any part of them, to be payable only in specified circumstances'.[67]

Section 58(2)(b) of the CLSA goes on to state that a CFA provides for a success fee if it provides for the amount of any fees to which it applies to be increased, in specified circumstances, above the amount which would be payable if it were not payable only in specified circumstances. It also confirms that references to a success fee, in relation to a CFA, are to the amount of the increase.[68]

As with CFAs entered into before 1 April 2013, where a legal representative acts under a CFA and the claim succeeds they can seek to recover their base costs and disbursements from the client's opponent. Where the case does not succeed, the legal representative will normally be entitled to payment of the disbursements their client has incurred either from their client or from the

---

[64]   [2005] EWCA Civ 1821.
[65]   [2006] EWHC 90053 (Costs).
[66]   Ibid.
[67]   Section 58(2)(a) of the CLSA.
[68]   Section 58(2)(c) of the CLSA.

client's ATE insurers (if any), though these (like profit costs) may be made conditional on the outcome of the case.

However, s 58A of the CLSA, as amended by LASPO, states that a success fee will no longer be recoverable from the opponent in civil litigation, unless the success fee relates to a pre-commencement funding arrangement (ie, one entered into before 1 April 2013). This is supplemented by s 58A(6) of the CLSA, which now states that a costs order may not include any provision requiring the payment by one party of all or part of a success fee payable by another party under a CFA.

The recoverability of the success fee from a defendant in personal injury and clinical negligence claims has therefore been abolished and, where acting under a CFA which was entered into with a client on or after 1 April 2013, a legal representative must instead look to their client if they wish to seek a success fee. This is not, however, to say that a success fee *must* be charged if a legal representative is to act under a CFA. Indeed, there are many other forms which a CFA may potentially take, including the following:

- a CFA with no success fee and without the client paying any shortfall in the base costs and disbursements recovered from the defendant, if the case succeeds;
- a CFA with no success fee but with the right to enforce any shortfall in the base costs and disbursements recovered from the defendant against the client, if the claim succeeds. Such an agreement is sometimes colloquially referred to as a 'CFA lite';
- a CFA with the client to pay a discounted hourly rate if the claim does not succeed and to pay an enhanced hourly rate (and potentially a success fee) if the claim succeeds. Given the potentially high costs involved in investigating and pursuing a catastrophic injury claim, it is likely that such agreements will be rare in those cases. It is also worth noting that, in such circumstances, a success fee is likely to have to be fixed at a relatively modest level, given that much of the risk to the legal representative has been obviated.

There is some speculation that where a solicitor has already entered into a CFA with a client before 1 April 2013 but counsel is instructed under a CFA on or after that date, it may still be possible to seek to recover counsel's success fee from the defendant. However, so far as the authors of this chapter are aware, this suggestion has not yet been tested and of course defendants are likely to challenge it.

It is suggested that care therefore needs to be taken when entering into a CFA with counsel that provides for recovery of a success fee from the defendant in these circumstances. The legal representatives must ensure that provision is made as to what will happen should this agreement be considered unenforceable (eg, a separate and alternative CFA could also be entered into, providing for recovery of a success fee from the client). The effects of this would need to be discussed with the client, before the CFA with counsel is entered into, particularly if they are potentially to be called upon to pay counsel's success fee or any shortfall in their base costs.

The Conditional Fee Agreements Order 2013 revoked the Conditional Fee Agreements Order 2000 but duplicated its provisions, with the result that the criteria which previously had to be satisfied in order for a CFA to be enforceable must still be met. In other words, it must:

- be 'an agreement with a person providing advocacy or litigation services which provides for his fees and expenses, or any part of them, to be payable only in specified circumstances';[69]

- be in writing;[70] and

- specify the success fee which will be charged in the event of success, which must not exceed 100% of the legal representative's base costs.[71]

However, s 58(4A) and (4B) of the CLSA, inserted by s 44 of LASPO, set out additional conditions which a CFA entered into on or after 1 April 2013 must comply with if it is to be enforceable, ie:

- the CFA must state that the success fee is subject to the maximum limit;[72]

- it must express the maximum limit as a percentage of the descriptions of damages awarded in the proceedings that are specified in the agreement;[73] and

- the percentage must not exceed the percentage specified by the Conditional Fee Agreements Order 2013 or calculated in a manner specified by that Order;

- the descriptions of damages may only include descriptions specified by the Conditional Fee Agreements Order 2013.

In relation to personal injury and clinical negligence claims, art 5(1)(a) and (2) of the Conditional Fee Agreements Order 2013 dictate that, in proceedings at first instance, the success fee must be capped at 25% of the damages the client obtains for pain, suffering and loss of amenity and for pecuniary loss, other than future pecuniary loss, net of any sums repayable to the Compensation Recovery Unit. If the claim proceeds to an appeal (whether made by the client or by the defendant), the legal representative is free to charge a success fee of up to 100% of damages for pain, suffering and loss of amenity and past pecuniary loss, net of CRU-recoverable benefits.[74]

Any success fee charged by counsel will need to be included in the caps referred to, as well as the solicitor's success fee. The way the success fee is to be 'split' between the respective legal representatives may ultimately prove a bone of

---

[69]   Section 58(2)(a) of the CLSA.

[70]   Section 58(3)(a) of the CLSA.

[71]   Section 58(4B) of the CLSA and art 3 of the Conditional Fee Agreements Order 2013.

[72]   Section 58(4)(c) of the CLSA and art 5 of the Conditional Fee Agreements Order 2013.

[73]   Ibid.

[74]   Articles 5(1)(b) and 5(2) of the Conditional Fee Agreements Order 2013.

contention between them, particularly where one representative has put the success fee at a higher level than the other. The best way of dealing with this would seem to be for the representatives to confer regarding risk assessment when counsel is asked to consider entering into a CFA and, ideally, for some procedure to be agreed as to what should happen if a dispute arises at conclusion of the case.

Notwithstanding the cap, there is obviously the potential for the legal representatives' success fees to have a significant impact on the damages a client can expect to recover as a result of bringing legal proceedings. Whilst any damages that the client may recover to provide for their future needs (which are of particular importance in catastrophic injury claims) are safeguarded, those practising in this area know that damages for pain, suffering and loss of amenity (PSLA) and past losses are often of key importance in establishing an appropriate contingency fund.

In recognition of this concern Lord Justice Jackson recommended that general damages for PSLA, which he described as 'not high at the moment',[75] should be increased by 10% to make up for the proposed shift in the burden of success fees. The Court of Appeal took the unusual step of giving prospective judicial guidance to implement this change in *Simmons v Castle*,[76] making provision for general damages for PSLA to increase by 10% in cases decided after 1 April 2013.

This increase will not, however, apply where the client and legal representative entered into a CFA before 1 April 2013, in relation to which the success fee remains recoverable from the defendant.[77] Pre-April 2013 claimants funded by legal aid or private funding will, however, benefit from the increase in PSLA. Bereavement damages were not covered by the Court of Appeal guidance, but the statutory damages under the Fatal Accident Act were increased by 10% to £12,980 by the Damages for Bereavement (Variation of Sum) (England and Wales) Order 2013.

Practitioners may still feel somewhat squeamish about seeking any sizeable success fee from a client in a catastrophic injury case. However, any remaining qualms should hopefully be assuaged by undertaking a detailed assessment of the risks involved in the litigation and then ensuring that the effect of the proposed agreement and the various alternative funding options are discussed with the client. In cases which appear to have strong prospects of success, practitioners will probably have to become used to potential clients using their bargaining power to seek a modest, or indeed a 'nil', success fee.

As referred to above, there is no statutory requirement that a legal representative must inform their client how they have come to fix the success fee at a certain level or to provide them with a copy of the risk assessment.

---

[75]   Jackson Final Report Ch 10, para 5.6.
[76]   [2012] EWCA Civ 1039.
[77]   *Simmons v Castle No 2* [2012] EWCA Civ 1288.

However, given that clients for whom practitioners act under CFAs following 1 April 2013 are likely to become increasingly interested in the costs of the litigation, we would suggest that it may represent good practice to do so.

Again, it is worth remembering that the client has the right to request that the court assess the amount of the success fee at conclusion of the case,[78] as well as the right to raise conduct issues under the SRA Code if they feel they haven't been appropriately counselled about costs and funding. Practitioners should therefore take steps at the outset, and as the case progresses, to demonstrate that they have considered and acted upon their client's best interests and entered into an appropriately full discussion as to how these can be met.

4.8   DAMAGES-BASED AGREEMENTS (DBAS)

Prior to 1 April 2013, legal representatives in personal injury and clinical negligence claims were not permitted to act for a client under any form of contingency agreement as these were prohibited for contentious business, save for employment and some other tribunals which are not of relevance here. However, s 45 of LASPO amended s 58AA of the CLSA to allow DBAs in contentious business, except for criminal and family proceedings.

A DBA is defined in s 58AA of the CLSA as an agreement between a representative and a client which provides that the client will make a payment to the representative if the client obtains 'a specified financial benefit'. The financial benefit in question will usually be a sum of damages payable by their opponent and the payment to be made to the legal representative will be a percentage of those damages. If the claim does not succeed then the representative's fees and, depending on the scope of the agreement, their disbursements, will not be paid but the client is still responsible for paying any costs they might be ordered to pay to the defendant.

As set out below, given that QOCS will now apply, save in limited circumstances, to personal injury and clinical negligence claims where a CFA or DBA has been entered into on and after 1 April 2013, the only defendant costs that the majority of claimants could be called upon to pay would relate to failing to beat a defendant's Part 36 offer. This risk can potentially still be covered by an ATE policy, but the premium for this will be payable by the client if the claim succeeds.

The Damages-Based Agreement Regulations 2013 ('the DBA Regulations') set out the requirements which must be complied with if a DBA is to be enforceable:

- Regulation 4(1) of the DBA Regulations states that the DBA must not require the client to pay anything other than:

---

[78]   Section 70 of the Solicitors Act 1974.

- 'The payment', which is defined as 'that part of the sum recovered in respect of the claim for damages awarded that the client agrees to pay the representative, and excludes expenses but includes ... counsel's fees';[79]
  - o any expenses incurred by the representative, net of any amount that has been paid or is payable by another party.[80]
- 'Expenses' are defined in reg 1(1) of the DBA Regulations as disbursements incurred by the representative, not including counsel's fees.
- Regulation 4(2) of the DBA Regulations states that DBAs relating to personal injury and clinical negligence proceedings at first instance must not provide for a payment to the representative which is more than 25% of the 'sums recovered' by the client, including VAT. The 'sums recovered' are general damages for pain, suffering and loss of amenity and damages for pecuniary loss other than future pecuniary loss, net of any sums repayable to the Compensation Recovery Unit.[81] Where a claim proceeds to an appeal, whether this appeal is made by the claimant or the defendant, no limit is set and therefore the representative can charge up to and including 100% of the sums recovered by the client.
- A DBA must be in writing.[82]
- Regulation 3 of the DBA Regulations states that a DBA must specify:
  - the claim or proceedings or parts of them to which the DBA relates;[83]
  - the circumstances in which the representative's payment, expenses and costs or part of those are payable;[84] and
  - the reason for setting the amount of the payment at the level agreed.[85]

If any of these requirements are not met, the DBA will be unenforceable and even if the claim succeeds the representative will receive no payment.

It is worth noting that the legal representative's contingency fee must be based on the sums ultimately recovered by the client and not the damages awarded or agreed. If the damages are reduced by contributory negligence, the representative's contingency fee will be based on the net sum, after the reduction for contributory negligence has been applied. If, in a more extreme scenario, the defendant turns out to be insolvent and damages are only recovered in part, or not at all, this too will affect what the representative can recover.

When the DBA Regulations were released in draft form, shortly before 1 April 2013, there was a feeling amongst many practitioners and legal commentators that these failed to address certain fundamental points and that there were

---

[79] Regulations 4(1)(a) and 1(2) of the DBA Regulations 2013.
[80] Regulation 4(1)(b) of the DBA Regulations 2013.
[81] Regulation 4(2) of the DBA Regulations 2013.
[82] Section 58AA(4)(a) of the CLSA.
[83] Regulation 3(a) of the DBA Regulations 2013.
[84] Regulation 3(b) of the DBA Regulations 2013.
[85] Regulation 3(c) of the DBA Regulations 2013.

ambiguities in the way aspects of these were drafted. The fear is that this could lead to disputes or even satellite litigation, even if the DBAs appeared to comply with the regulations. Nonetheless, the DBA Regulations were then brought into effect, without amendment.

The following represents only a brief summary of some of the concerns that have been raised in relation to the current DBA Regulations:

- It is unclear whether legal representatives can seek to protect their position by entering into two agreements with the client, one of which is a DBA or a DBA relating to some of the fees, with the remainder being paid under either a private retainer or at a reduced hourly rate irrespective of whether the claim succeeds.

- The DBA Regulations do not specify whether legal representatives acting under a DBA will be immune from adverse costs orders made against them (as opposed to against the client), as they are when acting under CFAs.

- It is not clear whether an ATE premium is an expense which falls outside the 25% cap.

- The DBA Regulations do not contain any provisions about terminating a DBA in a personal injury or clinical negligence claim. There is a concern that a client could decide to terminate the DBA at any stage and that the legal representative may not then have any right to claim the percentage payment, or even their expenses, should the claim subsequently succeed.

Since 1 April 2013, the Ministry of Justice has confirmed that it intends to revise the DBA Regulations. In view of this, and the uncertainties arising from the existing regulations, it is submitted that practitioners should be extremely wary of entering into a DBA before the DBA Regulations are amended. They should probably nonetheless bring DBAs to their clients' attention as a possible method of funding, given that O(1.12) of the SRA Code dictates that a client must be able to make an informed decision about the service they need, how their matter will be handled and the options available to them.

4.9   RETAINERS ENTERED INTO AT A CLIENT'S HOME OR PLACE OF WORK

The Cancellation of Contracts made in a Consumer's Home or Place of Work etc Regulations 2008 ('the 2008 Regulations') came into force on 1 October 2008 and may affect retainers (whether private, CFA or DBA) which a solicitor enters into with their client. Regulation 5 of the 2008 Regulations states that the legislation applies to contracts, including consumer credit agreements, 'between a consumer and a trader which [are] for the supply of goods or services to the consumer by a trader' and which are made:

- during a visit by the trader to the consumer's home or place of work, or to the home of another individual;[86]

---

[86]   Regulation 5(a) of the 2008 Regulations.

- during an excursion organised by the trader away from his business premises;[87] or
- after an offer made by the consumer during such a visit or excursion.[88]

There does not appear to be any question but that, under the 2008 Regulations, a solicitor is a 'trader' and a client would be considered a 'consumer'. Practitioners must therefore have regard to their obligations under the 2008 Regulations where they are proposing to enter into any funding agreement with the client (including a CFA or a DBA) at or following a meeting with the client which takes place away from the practitioner's offices.

Regulation 7 of the 2008 Regulations sets out the relevant obligations as follows:

- The trader must give the consumer a *written* notice of his right to cancel the contract within the cancellation period (which is fixed at 7 days) and such notice must be given at the time the contract is made, except where the contract is entered into pursuant to an offer made by the consumer during a relevant visit or excursion (in which case the notice must be given at the time the offer is made by the consumer).[89]
- The notice must be dated, indicate the right of the consumer to cancel the contract within the cancellation period, be easily legible, contain the information set out in Part 1 of Sch 4 to the 2008 Regulations and include a cancellation form in the form set out in Part 2 of that Schedule (in the form of a detachable slip). It must also indicate that a related credit agreement will be automatically cancelled if the contract for goods and services is cancelled.[90]
- Where the contract is wholly or partially in writing, the notice must be incorporated in the same document (so must therefore be encompassed within the CFA, DBA or other retainer document).[91] The notice of the right to cancel must then be set out in a separate box in the agreement, under the heading 'Notice of the Right to Cancel' and it must be given as much prominence as any other information in the contract or document apart from the heading and the names of the parties or any handwritten information.[92]
- If the consumer serves a cancellation notice within the 7-day period the contract is cancelled.[93] The notice need not follow the form of the cancellation notice set out in the agreement (or in Part 2 of Sch 4 to the 2008 Regulations)[94] though it must be served on the trader or another person specified in the agreement as being a person to whom the

---

[87] Regulation 5(b) of the 2008 Regulations.
[88] Regulation 5(c) of the 2008 Regulations.
[89] Regulation 7(2) of the 2008 Regulations.
[90] Regulation 7(3) of the 2008 Regulations.
[91] Regulation 7(4) of the 2008 Regulations.
[92] Regulation 7(5) of the 2008 Regulations.
[93] Regulation 8(1) of the 2008 Regulations.
[94] Regulation 8(3) of the 2008 Regulations.

cancellation notice can be given.[95] The 'deemed date' of service differs in the 2008 Regulations to those which practitioners will be used to under the CPR, in that the cancellation notice will be deemed to have been served on the day it was sent, whether by post or by electronic mail[96] and whether actually received or not.

Parts 1 and 2 of Schedule 4 to the 2008 Regulations go on to state, in detail, what information needs to be contained within the 'Notice of the Right to Cancel' section of the agreement, including the cancellation notice which has to form part of this. Practitioners should read these provisions carefully and ensure that their retainer documents are fully compliant.

It is not possible to contract out of the 2008 Regulations and, if they fail to provide notice to their clients of their right to cancel pursuant to reg 7 of the 2008 Regulations, a practitioner is guilty of a criminal offence, the penalty for which is a fine.[97] There is a limited defence of 'due diligence' where it can be proved that the commission of the offence was due to the act or default of another and that the person being prosecuted took all reasonable precautions and exercised all due diligence to avoid the commission of such an offence by himself or any person under his control.[98]

Practitioners should remember that, where the client cancels a contract within the 7-day cancellation period, the solicitor will not be able to recover the costs of any work carried out during that time unless:

- the contract stated that the client could be required to pay for this; and
- the client gave their written permission for such work to be carried out during the cancellation period.

Practitioners should therefore be wary of carrying out substantial amounts of work during the cancellation period, where the 2008 Regulations apply to their retainer agreement with the client.

4.10   AFTER THE EVENT (ATE) INSURANCE

As referred to above, where a client and their legal representative entered into a CFA prior to 1 April 2013, the client would commonly be advised to take out ATE insurance to cover their disbursements and the defendant's legal costs, which they could be ordered to pay in the event the claim did not succeed. Such insurance would often also cover them in the event they had to pay some of the defendant's costs as a result of failing to beat a Part 36 offer, though this might only cover any shortfall in those costs once the client's damages had been set against them (this would depend on the policy terms).

---

[95]   Regulation 8(4) of the 2008 Regulations.
[96]   Regulation 8(5) and (6) of the 2008 Regulations.
[97]   Regulation 17 of the 2008 Regulations.
[98]   Regulation 18 of the 2008 Regulations.

It was normally possible for claimants in personal injury and clinical negligence claims to obtain ATE insurance on the basis that the premium for this would be both deferred (ie, payable only following conclusion of the case) and conditional upon success (ie, payable only if the claim was won). Where policies were taken out before 1 April 2013, claimants would be able to seek to recover the premium from their opponent, though the amount of the premium was sometimes subject to challenge by defendants.

Section 46 of LASPO abolished the recoverability of ATE insurance premiums from defendants in all personal injury (as distinct from clinical negligence) cases, save where such insurance had been taken out prior to 1 April 2013. It also inserted a new s 58C into the CLSA, stating that recovery would be permitted in clinical negligence cases only to the extent that the premium relates to the costs of any experts' reports in respect of such negligence. The Recovery of Costs Insurance Premiums in Clinical Negligence Proceedings (No 2) Regulations 2013 specified the circumstances in which this exception would apply as follows:

- the financial value of the claim must exceed £1,000;[99]

- the relevant ATE policy must insure against the risk of incurring a liability to pay for an expert report relating to liability or causation in respect of clinical negligence;[100] and

- the amount of the premium that can be recovered under a costs order cannot exceed the premium in respect of the liability to pay for an expert report or reports relating to liability or causation.[101]

Clearly this aspect of funding is yet another which the solicitor will have to consider and discuss with their client at the outset of the case. Where the solicitor has entered into a CFA or a DBA on or after 1 April 2013, the costs risk to which the client could be exposed is, save in the exceptional cases where QOCS will not apply (see further below), limited to paying their own disbursements and some of the defendant's costs if they fail to beat a Part 36 offer made by that defendant.

However, these costs could be significant and whilst a client is unlikely to welcome having to pay an insurance premium from their damages when their claim succeeds, this is often going to be preferable to their being called upon to pay costs out of their own pocket where the claim does not succeed. This is something that the solicitor will have to weigh up and discuss with the client before any ATE insurance is taken out.

4.11 QUALIFIED ONE-WAY COSTS SHIFTING (QOCS)

The new CPR, rr 44.13 to 44.17, which came into effect on 1 April 2013, introduced QOCS in relation to most proceedings which included a claim for

---

[99] Regulation 3(1)(a) of the 2013 Regulations.
[100] Regulation 3(1)(b) of the 2013 Regulations.
[101] Regulation 3(2) of the 2013 Regulations.

damages for personal injuries, a claim under the Fatal Accidents Act 1976 and/or a claim under the Law Reform (Miscellaneous Provisions) Act 1934.[102] QOCS will not, however, apply where there are 'pre-commencement funding arrangements' in place in relation to the proceedings, as defined by CPR, r 48.2, including:

- a CFA in relation to the proceedings entered into before 1 April 2013;[103]

- an ATE insurance premium taken out in relation to the proceedings before 1 April 2013;[104] or

- an agreement with a membership organisation, made before 1 April 2013, to meet the costs of the other parties to the proceedings.[105]

The effect of QOCS is that orders for costs made against a claimant may be enforced without the permission of the court only to the extent that the aggregate amount in money terms of such orders does not exceed that of any orders for damages and interest made in favour of the claimant.[106] This means that where a claimant is wholly unsuccessful in their claim they should not have to pay anything towards the defendant's legal costs, save in the circumstances referred to below.

There are some exceptions to the application of QOCS even in post-LASPO funding arrangements. Orders for costs made against the claimant can be enforced to the full extent of such orders where the proceedings have been struck out on the following grounds:

- the claimant has disclosed no reasonable grounds for bringing the proceedings;[107]

- the proceedings are an abuse of the court's process;[108] or

- the conduct of the claimant or a person acting on the claimant's behalf and with the claimant's knowledge of such conduct is likely to obstruct the just disposal of the proceedings.[109]

Orders for costs against a claimant can also be enforced to their full extent, though the permission of the court is required, where:

- their claim has been found to be fundamentally dishonest on the balance of probabilities.[110] No definition is given of the term 'fundamentally dishonest' in the CPR; or

- the proceedings include a claim which is made for the financial benefit of a person other than the claimant or a dependant within the meaning of s 1(3) of the Fatal Accidents Act 1976 (other than a claim in respect of the

---

[102] CPR, r 44.13(1).
[103] CPR, r 48.2(1)(a)(i)(aa) and (bb).
[104] CPR, r 48.2(1)(a)(ii).
[105] CPR, r 48.2(1)(a)(iii).
[106] CPR, r 44.14(1).
[107] CPR, r 44.15(a).
[108] CPR, r 44.15(b).
[109] CPR, r 44.15(c).
[110] CPR, r 44.16(1).

gratuitous provision of care, earnings paid by an employer or medical expenses) or a claim is made for the benefit of the claimant other than a claim to which this section applies and the court thinks that it is just to do so.[111]

Orders for costs can also be made against someone other than the claimant, where the proceedings include a claim for the financial benefit of that other person (other than a dependant under the Fatal Accidents Act 1976).[112] This is, however, subject to CPR, r 46.2, relating to costs orders against non-parties, which provides that the non-party must be added as a party to the proceedings for the purposes of costs only and must be given a reasonable opportunity to attend a hearing at which the court will consider the matter further.[113]

As referred to above, CPR, r 44.14 provides that an order for costs against a claimant can be enforced up to the value of any order for damages and interest obtained by that claimant. This means that if a claimant fails to beat a Part 36 offer made by the defendant, either by way of an award made at trial or by way of a settlement agreed between the parties, the claimant can be ordered to pay the defendant's costs from the end of the 'relevant period' under Part 36.

It will be clear that the risk of a claimant having to pay a defendant's costs has been substantially reduced, but not extinguished, where they have entered into a funding arrangement after 1 April 2013. A practitioner should consider whether the remaining risk should be covered by the claimant taking out an ATE insurance policy, though as already mentioned the premium for such a policy will not be recoverable from the defendant save for any portion relating to experts' reports on liability in clinical negligence cases.

The terms of any ATE insurance which the claimant might be considering taking out will need to be carefully considered. Whilst insurers will usually be prepared to offer cover in relation to any adverse costs arising from failure to beat a Part 36 offer, it is more doubtful whether they will be prepared to do so in circumstances where a claim is struck out on the grounds referred to in CPR, r 44.15 (as they may argue that the claim did not enjoy reasonable prospects of success). ATE insurance policies which will cover adverse costs in the event of a claim having been found to be 'fundamentally dishonest' will be vanishingly rare, probably non-existent.

---

[111] CPR, r 44.16(2).
[112] CPR, r 44.16(3).
[113] CPR, r 46.2(1).

CHAPTER 5

INTERIM PAYMENTS

5.1 INTRODUCTION

Interim payments form a significant part of catastrophic injury litigation. The claimant will have a variety of needs that may have to be addressed quickly, including care and assistance, equipment, transport, medical expenses and accommodation. A case manager will probably be required. Lost income may need replacing. Most catastrophically injured claimants cannot wait until the conclusion of their claim for damages. A proportion of those damages will be required in advance if possible.

Interim payments can also take on a tactical role in the conduct of litigation overall. The payments can be used to put an appropriate regime in place to address the claimant's needs. If the regime works and has a beneficial impact then the costs will be known rather than a matter of speculation and thus easier to calculate. It may also be much harder for the defendant to argue that the regime or the costs incurred in meeting those needs are unreasonable. For this reason alone many defendant insurers refuse to make substantial interim payments before proceedings have been issued, and even then have to be ordered by the court to make payment.

In this chapter we consider when orders for interim payments can be obtained from the court and the practical approach to be taken with interim payments in catastrophic injury cases: when they should be sought, the conditions that need to be satisfied and the pitfalls that should be avoided.

5.2 TIMING

Under CPR, r 25.6(1) a claimant cannot apply for an order for an interim payment before the end of the period for filing an acknowledgement of service applicable to the defendant against whom the application is made. Therefore, unless proceedings have been served, the practitioner will have no option but to seek a voluntary interim payment from the defendant insurer in the early stages after an accident.

In cases involving a child or protected party the permission of the court must be obtained before any voluntary interim payment is made (CPR Part 25B PD

1.1). Any interim payments made to a protected party will be paid into the Court of Protection, who will decide how and when the money is to be spent. Any interim payments made to a child will be paid into court and dealt with in accordance with directions given by the court under CPR, r 21.11.

The prospect of an interim payment may be an issue from the moment of first instruction; indeed it may be the cause of a first instruction. The practical approach to be taken will, however, be dictated by the position on liability.

5.2.1 Liability admitted

In cases where liability is clear-cut, the defendant or its insurer should be asked for an open admission of liability in writing as soon as possible. If an admission is not forthcoming then it should be made plain that costs will be incurred on liability until an admission is made. Where an admission is made then the defendant should be told that in reliance upon that admission no further steps will be taken in relation to liability in order to make it harder for the defendant to resile from the admission at some future time.

Where liability is admitted the focus will be upon assessing and providing for the claimant's immediate needs. An immediate needs assessment should be prepared at a very early stage. Given the control that can be retained over the process, there may be an advantage in instructing this assessment privately (ie *outside* the Rehabilitation Code).[1] In addition, a feasibility report should be carried out in relation to the claimant's existing property from an experienced accommodation expert specialising in the claimant's type of disability.

Assuming the claimant and practitioner are happy with the content, these documents should be disclosed to the defendant insurer. If appropriate, the defendant insurer may even be invited to visit the claimant either in hospital or at home, in the presence of the claimant's solicitor, to witness the claimant's needs first hand.

If the claimant's reasonable needs can be addressed in the existing accommodation, an initial voluntary interim payment can be sought to carry out any immediate essential adaptations to the property and implement the care regime that has been identified by the case manager. If new accommodation is required, then a search can begin to find a suitable home. Estate agents and various internet websites such as www.rightmove.co.uk can assist with this process. There is as yet no national database of already adapted homes for sale or rent and the chance of finding the right property in the right place at the right time are slim. Some vendors are prepared to wait, but it cannot be taken for granted. It may be necessary to be prepared to undertake two searches: one to obtain indicative prices for the purposes of seeking an interim payment, and another to obtain a property that is available once an interim payment has been

---

[1]   The defendant insurer should be reminded that the claimant is likely to prepare his or her case more quickly with the assistance of a privately instructed case manager, thereby reducing legal costs.

received. As this may incur further costs the defendant should be put on notice and given the chance to provide funding for a property if and when it is available. The alternative may be to make expensive adaptations to an existing property that may only serve to increase the defendant's outlay in the event that new accommodation is ultimately required.

When a suitable property is identified (usually bungalow accommodation), the defendant should be invited to instruct their own accommodation expert to carry out a feasibility report so as to avoid any arguments regarding suitability or reasonableness further down the line. This process may also precipitate the making of a voluntary interim payment to cover the costs of purchasing such a property.

If the defendant insurer is reluctant to make a substantial voluntary interim payment that can be used to purchase new accommodation and/or set up a recommended care regime, the defendant could be told that the claimant will accept a *general* interim payment. Some insurers will feel more comfortable knowing that the interim payment is not stated for a particular purpose.

Once the immediate needs have been identified and addressed then work can begin on building the overall picture on quantum by instructing expert medico-legal, care and occupational therapy experts as soon as possible. Detailed quarterly updates should be prepared by the case manager and disclosed to the defendant insurer in order to keep them informed and to justify any top-up interim payments required. It is important not to lose sight of the fact, however, that the case manager should owe their duty to the claimant alone (see *Wright v Sullivan*)[2] and be answerable to the claimant and not the defendant or its insurers. The key for the practitioner is to try to foster a good working relationship with the defendant insurer. Regular informal progress meetings, telephone calls and/or emails should be encouraged. If matters are progressing amicably then one eye should be kept on any potential limitation period in order to avoid unnecessary problems.

The threat of issuing proceedings and making a formal application with cost consequences can be used if the insurer fails to respond constructively or refuses to make top-up payments. At the same time practitioners should consider serving the defendant with an issue-specific Part 36 offer in relation to the interim payment.

Ultimately, if all else fails, then proceedings will need to be issued and an application made.

5.2.2 Primary liability admitted but claimant contributory negligent

In these cases the practitioner will need to follow a similar approach to above, albeit that it may be more sensible to seek to rely upon the Rehabilitation Code

---

[2]   *Wright v Sullivan* [2005] EWCA Civ 656.

for immediate case management, needs assessment and recommended treatment due to the uncertain position on damages. The choice of care regime and accommodation will be dependent upon the level of contributory negligence to be applied. This will dictate the level of any interim payments sought.

5.2.3   Liability in dispute

The practitioner will need to adopt a different approach if liability is firmly in dispute. In these circumstances a voluntary interim payment is highly unlikely and the defendant insurer will be reluctant to abide by the provisions of the Rehabilitation Code. Furthermore, once proceedings have been issued, the court will not make an interim payment order unless the claimant can show that he or she has a very strong claim on liability.

Unless there are tactical reasons to do otherwise, the practitioner should seek to issue proceedings as soon as possible and seek a split trial on liability and quantum. This will allow the liability aspect to be determined quickly. In the meantime, it is likely that the claimant will require statutory assistance to meet his or her immediate accommodation, equipment and care needs. Medical needs will be met by the NHS.

5.3   JURISDICTION OF THE COURT

The court's power to make an interim payment is discretionary.[3] However, there are conditions to be satisfied and matters that must be taken into account. These are set out at CPR, r 25.7. Within the context of catastrophic injury litigation, the claimant will need to satisfy one of the following preconditions if such an application is to be entertained:

(a)   the defendant against whom the order is sought has admitted liability to pay damages (CPR, r 25.7(1)(a)); or

(b)   the claimant has obtained judgment against that defendant for damages to be assessed (CPR, r 25.7(1)(b)); or

(c)   the court is satisfied that, if the claim went to trial, the claimant would obtain judgment for a substantial amount of money (other than costs) against the defendant from whom he or she is seeking the order (CPR, r 25.7(1)(c)).

CPR, r 25.7(1)(a) and (b) require no explanation. These conditions will either be satisfied or not. However, the third category is not so straightforward, particularly where there are several defendants.

The leading authorities on this point, arising pre-CPR, are *Shearson Lehman Brothers Inc v Maclaine Watson & Co Ltd,*[4] *British & Commonwealth*

---

3   The Senior Courts Act 1981, s 32 and the County Courts Act 1984, s 50.
4   [1987] 2 All ER 181, CA.

Holdings plc v Quadrex Holdings Inc[5] and *Schott Kem Ltd v Bentley*.[6] These authorities tell us that the procedure is not suitable in a case where the factual issues are complicated or where difficult points of law arise and that when determining whether the claimant 'would obtain judgment for a substantial amount of money' if the claim went to trial, the court must apply the civil standard of proof. In *Schott Kem Ltd*, Neill LJ held that:

> 'Something more than a prima facie case is clearly required, but not proof beyond reasonable doubt. The burden is high. But it is a civil burden on the balance of probabilities, not a criminal burden.'

In practice therefore, it is highly unlikely that a claim with 51% prospects of success on liability will ever justify an interim payment. The practitioner must show that the claimant has a strong case and is very likely to succeed at trial.

The question of a *substantial amount of money* is vague and therefore not the most helpful of legal phraseology. However, in catastrophic injury claims, there will be no difficulties satisfying this test.

5.3.1 Multiple defendants

Provided there is a sufficiently strong case on the merits against an identified defendant, an order for an interim payment can be made against that defendant. It does not matter that there are other defendants named in proceedings (CPR, r 25.7(1)(c)). If there are issues of apportionment between defendants then they need not concern the claimant where liability is joint and several. It will not suffice, however, if the claimant is able to say that one of a number of defendants must be liable, but there is a real issue as to which one.

Equally, interim payment orders can be made against two or more defendants provided the court is satisfied as to the liability of each of the defendants against whom the order is made.[7]

Under CPR, r 25.7(1)(e), the court may also make an order for an interim payment where it is satisfied that the claimant would obtain judgment for a substantial amount of money against at least one of multiple defendants, but cannot determine which. However, this will only apply in cases where all the defendants are either:

(a) insured in respect of the claim;

(b) a defendant whose liability will be met by an insurer under s 151 of the Road Traffic Act 1988 or an insurer acting under the Motor Insurers Bureau Agreement, or the Motor Insurers Bureau where it is acting itself; or

---

5   [1989] QB 842.
6   [1990] 3 All ER 850 at 856E, CA repeating the words of Lloyd LJ in *Shearson Lehman Brothers Inc v Maclaine Watson & Co Ltd*.
7   *Schott Kem Ltd v Bentley* [1990] 3 WLR 397, CA.

(c)   a public body.

The construction of CPR, r 25.7(1)(e) was considered by the Court of Appeal in *Berry v Ashtead Plant Hire & Others*[8] where an application for an interim payment was made against two insured defendants, but not against a third uninsured defendant. It was contended that even if the Court were satisfied that one or other of two insured defendants would be held liable, an interim payment could only be obtained in a case where all the defendants were insured. This was rejected, the use of the word 'defendants' in CPR, r 25.7(1)(e)(ii) meant 'defendants against whom the application for interim payment is made' and the fact that an uninsured defendant was included in the claim did not preclude a successful interim payment application against other insured defendants.

5.3.2   Reasonable proportion of likely judgment

If the claimant satisfies one of the liability prerequisites, then the court will go on to consider whether to order an interim payment. The court has a wide discretion. However, under CPR, r 25.7(4) and (5), it must not order an interim payment of more than a *reasonable proportion* of the likely amount of the final judgment, taking into account any contributory negligence and any relevant set-off or counterclaim.

Before the advent of periodical payment orders in April 2005, the courts were able to make very large interim awards safe in the knowledge that the award for damages made at trial would generally be in the form of a lump sum payment. The judge would usually make a conservative preliminary estimate of the likely final award based upon the schedule of loss and counter schedule and order an interim payment which allowed a comfortable margin in case the preliminary estimate turned out to be too generous.

In these circumstances, it was not difficult for a catastrophically injured claimant to show that a sizeable interim payment represented a reasonable proportion of his or her final damages award. Unless the claimant was a child or a protected party (in which case all damages would be supervised), it was a matter for him or her to spend his or her award as he or she wished.[9] The only constraint was that the court needed to consider whether the interim payment prejudiced the trial or the position of the defendant in the proceedings (the so-called 'level playing field' principle).[10] Even then, the courts would generally give the possibility of such prejudice little weight.[11]

Since the arrival of periodical payment orders (PPOs), the practice has had to be modified. Under CPR, r 41.7, the court must have regard to whether a PPO is

---

[8]   *Donald Berry (a protected party) v Ashtead Plant Hire Co Ltd & Ors* [2011] EWCA Civ 1304.
[9]   See *Stringman v McArdle* [1994] 1 WLR 1653.
[10]   See *Campbell v Mylchreest* [1999] PIQR Q17.
[11]   See *Campbell v Mylchreest* and *Goode v West Hertfordshire NHS Trust* [2006] EWHC 2007 (QB).

likely to be the more appropriate form for all or part of an award for damages. The granting of a sizeable interim payment may affect the ability of the trial judge to weigh up the claimant's needs and award a lump sum or PPO accordingly. This has led to a host of reported cases including *Brewis v Heatherwood & Wrexham Park Hospitals NHS Trust*,[12] *Mealing v Chelsea & Westminster NHS Trust*,[13] *Braithwaite v Homerton University Hospitals NHS Foundation Trust*[14] and *Cobham Hire Services Ltd v Eeles*.[15]

In *Braithwaite v Homerton University Hospitals NHS Foundation Trust*, the claimant was a 3-year-old who had severe quadriplegic cerebral palsy caused at birth. She had obtained judgment for 100% of her claim and it was not disputed that she had extensive care needs. The claimant required money at an early stage in order to purchase suitable accommodation and therefore made an application for an interim payment of £850,000. The full capitalised value of the claim was in the region of £3.6m. Upon hearing the application, Stanley Burton J observed that, if all of the claimant's damages were going to be awarded at trial by way of lump sum, there would be no difficulty in making an interim order in the sum claimed. However, this was a case where it was clear that the trial judge may want to make one or more PPOs, particularly in relation to care needs. As a result, Stanley Burton J held that the proper approach was to calculate those parts of the claim that were bound to be awarded as a lump sum at trial. These included past special damages, general damages for pain and suffering and interest on both. These sums alone were unlikely to amount to £850,000 and would not be sufficient to permit an interim in that sum. However, his lordship considered that, in deciding the likely amount of the final judgment, he was entitled to predict what allocation as between capital and PPO the trial judge would make. In the circumstances of that case, there was no dispute that the claimant had an urgent need for accommodation and the trial judge would allocate a sufficient capital sum to enable the purchase of a suitable property. This sum would be significantly in excess of £850,000. Accordingly, he had jurisdiction to order an interim payment of that sum and exercised his discretion to do so.

The approach in *Braithwaite was endorsed in what has become the* leading authority in this area, *Cobham Hire Services Ltd v Eeles*. In this case the claimant had sustained serious head injuries in a road traffic accident at the age of 9 months. He was 11 years old at the date of the interim payment application and suffered from impairments to cognition and intellect, although life expectancy was not reduced. Liability was admitted and judgment had been entered. The claimant had already received interim payments of £450,000 and made an application for a further interim payment of £1.2m in order to purchase a suitable family home. At first instance, Foskett J considered that the

---

[12] [2008] EWHC 2526 (QB).
[13] [2008] LS Law Med 236.
[14] [2008] EWHC 353 QB.
[15] [2009] EWCA Civ 204.

total capital value of the claim, including the notional capital value of the PPOs that were likely to be awarded, was likely to be in the region of £3.5m. He therefore made the order as requested.

Upon appeal, the Court of Appeal agreed with the defendant that the judge had made an order outside his jurisdiction. Giving the leading judgment of the court Smith LJ held that, in a case in which a PPO is made, the amount of the final judgment is the actual capital lump sum awarded and does not include the notional capitalised value of any PPO that is likely to be made (this is irrelevant for the purposes of determining an interim payment in a case of this type). It was vitally important that any interim payment award did not fetter the trial judge's freedom to allocate the future losses in the way that would best meet the claimant's needs. In the circumstances, the interim payment of £1.2m was overturned. The Court of Appeal held that the only awards likely to be made on a lump sum basis at trial were general damages, past special damages, interest and accommodation costs. These could be conservatively valued at £590,000, meaning that there was very little room for any further interim payment beyond the £450,000 previously received. Smith LJ acknowledged that a number of additional heads of loss were frequently capitalised at trial, including therapies, equipment and Court of Protection costs. However, this may not prove to be the case and it was not normally appropriate to include such items in the assessment.

Smith LJ (paras 42–45) went on to summarise the approach that a judge should take when considering whether to make an interim payment in a case in which the trial judge may wish to make a PPO. It is widely accepted that the approach has two limbs.

(1) The judge's first task is to assess the likely amount of the final judgment, leaving out the heads of account the heads of future loss which the trial judge might wish to deal with by way of PPO. Thus, the allowable heads of loss ordinarily comprise (a) general damages including interest; (b) special damages to date including interest; and (c) capitalised accommodation costs, including future running costs. When conducting this assessment:
   (i)   a conservative approach needs to be adopted and, provided that is done, a reasonable proportion may be a high proportion;
   (ii) the judge need have no regard to what the claimant intends to do with the money. If he or she is of full age and capacity, he or she may spend it as he or she will. If not, expenditure will be controlled by the Court of Protection.

(2) If, having completed the above assessment, the interim payment requested exceeds a reasonable proportion of the likely award, the judge may include in the assessment the capitalised amounts of future losses. However, this is only permitted if the judge:
   (i)   can confidently predict that the trial judge will wish to award a larger capital sum than that covered by the items assessed under the first limb. This would include likely capitalised amounts for future losses, most commonly future loss of earnings; and

(ii)   is satisfied that there is a real need for the interim payment requested, for example, where the request is for a house purchase, the judge must be satisfied that there is a real need for accommodation now as opposed to after the trial and that the amount of money requested is reasonable.

There now exist a plethora of first instance decisions applying the principles expounded in *Eeles*. Of particular interest are the following.

FP v Taunton & Somerset NHS Trust[16] is an example of a court applying *Eeles* in the context of a claim where there was considerable uncertainty as to life expectancy. This case also illustrates the approach taken in relation to an interim payment application where there is a real and pressing need for the claimant to move into alternative accommodation immediately. Having already received voluntary interim payments of £500,000, the court initially awarded a further £1.2m in 2009. The claimant came back before the court in December 2011 when a further £500,000 was awarded, albeit that at that stage the claimant sought unsuccessfully to argue that the court was not bound by the approach in *Eeles* where there would be an inevitable shortfall in the capital sum compared with needs, or where the claimant can show a real or immediate need.

In *Kirby v Ashford & St Peter Hospital NHS Trust*,[17] the claimant had previously successfully applied for interim payments which had been extinguished by the purchase and refurbishment of accommodation. When making a further application the claimant was already in debt to the builders and they were not permitting the claimant to move into the property until these debts were discharged. The court reluctantly granted a further interim payment but regarded itself as being 'held hostage' and warned that applications for interim payments should be made in advance of binding contractual costs being incurred.

In *PZC v Gloucestershire Hospitals NHS Trust*,[18] the claimant suffered dyskinetic quadriplegic cerebral palsy at birth. She sought an interim payment of £845,000 for suitable accommodation but the court was not satisfied that there was an urgent need to move before the proposed trial date (6 months hence) nor that the expenditure of £845,000 for accommodation was reasonably necessary. As such, limb 2 of *Eeles* was not satisfied. In fact, the court declined to make any interim payment because the claimant's affairs were not yet administered by the Court of Protection.

In *Oxborrow (a protected party) v West Suffolk Hospitals NHS Trust*,[19] the claimant suffered severe disabilities as a result of quadriplegic cerebral palsy. It was conceded that the approach in *Eeles* applied but the approach to valuing

---

[16]   *FP v Taunton & Somerset NHS Trust* [2011] EWHC 3380.
[17]   *Kirby v Ashford & St Peter Hospital NHS Trust (no 2)* [2011] EWHC 624.
[18]   *PZC v Gloucestershire Hospitals NHS Trust* [2011] EWHC 1775.
[19]   *Oxborrow (a protected party) v West Suffolk Hospitals NHS Trust* [2012] EWHC 1010.

future accommodation was unusual. The defendant contended that the claimant could rent a suitable property at a cost of £10,000 per annum (he was renting at the time of the application). The claimant's primary contention was that the full capital cost of accommodation would be recovered at trial rather than a sum based on a *Roberts v Johnson*[20] calculation. The court rejected the defendant's submission and didn't need to express a view on the claimant's primary contention although it was suggested that the approach to accommodation using *Roberts v Johnson* was now so well established that to assess the likely value of the claim on any other basis was unlikely to succeed in an interim payment application.

In what may be regarded as a relaxing of the *Eeles* principles, Andrews J in *Griffin v Ponsonby*[21] was satisfied that the claimant's desire to have his future loss of earnings claim awarded in a lump sum was unlikely to be disturbed by the trial judge. Accordingly, she accepted that the trial judge was highly likely to make such an award and the lump sum value of his future loss of earnings was added to the sums assessed under the first limb of *Eeles*. This brought the total figure to just under £2m and she was prepared to award 80% of that figure by way of interim payment.

Finally, the case of *Sedge v Prime*[22] is significant. The claimant had suffered a parietal fracture and acute subdural haematoma in a road traffic accident. He had been left with severe physical disabilities together with limited cognitive and intellectual function. He had been discharged from hospital into residential care in October funded by the PCT. He needed 24-hour care. The evidence suggested he was physically well cared for and had not demonstrated unhappiness or frustration at being in the home he was in. However, the PCT did not fund any meaningful therapy. His existence was adjudged largely passive save for visits from his family. His life expectancy could be into his seventies.

An interim payment of £175,000 had been made in early 2011 to fund a case manager and support worker. Some of these funds were used to rent a bungalow at a cost of £13,200 pa and to adapt it (at a cost of just under £16,000). In January 2012 the claimant sought a further £300,000 to enable him to move, on a trial basis, into the adapted, rented bungalow with a 24-hour care regime. The claimant's experts considered the move to be a good idea, the defendant's experts did not. The judge observed that the decision was not for them. It has to be made by those who are responsible for him, subject to the supervision of the Court of Protection. To this end the claimant's advisers had ensured the issue was discussed before the interim payment application at a 'best interests' meeting between family, carers and the PCT. None of the claimant's legal team or medical-legal experts attended and no medico-legal evidence was submitted. Those at the meeting concluded that the trial would be a good idea.

---

[20]   *Roberts v Johnson* [1989] QB 878.
[21]   [2013] EWHC 3410 (QB).
[22]   *Sedge v Prime* [2012] EWHC 3460.

The judge concluded that although he was not bound by the outcome of this meeting he did not regard it as irrelevant as it suggested that a considerable body of experienced opinion did not reject community care as a potentially realistic option for the claimant. He went on to consider the test in *Eeles* and concluded that the costs of the trial were likely to be recovered and the fact that, as the application only sought the costs of the trial (rental plus adaptations), it was considerably less than the costs of buying alternative accommodation outright. Accordingly, the level playing field was not altered, the claimant being potentially disadvantaged if he attended the trial of the claim having not had the opportunity to trial community living albeit the judge sounded a note of caution indicating that his judgment should not be seen as 'encouraging trial runs of community living at insurer's expense'.

This claim subsequently settled for a sum in excess of £9m on a full liability basis, the defendant conceding that claimant was entitled to suitable accommodation in the community with a private care regime.

Clearly the result of the best interests meeting was given weight by the judge and the Court of Protection case of *Re SK*[23] confirms that it is right to exclude any medico-legal evidence/representation for either party from such a meeting.

5.3.3 Conditions attached to the award

The court has the power to attach conditions to any interim payment order or require the claimant to give undertakings. In *Harris v Ellen*[24] the court attached a condition (effected by an undertaking) that the claimant use an interim payment to purchase a suitable property and thereafter execute an equitable charge on the property in favour of the defendant. This provided the defendant with protection in the event that the interim payment was proven to be too high.

In *FP v Taunton & Somerset NHS Trust*,[25] Blair J was particularly concerned to ensure that the £1.2m interim payment awarded was properly expended for the purposes for which it was sought (ie accommodation and care needs). As the Court of Protection was not involved in this case, Blair J imposed a condition that the claimant's solicitor give an undertaking to hold the money in the firm's account and ensure that payments out were made only in respect of losses identified in the schedule of loss.

5.4 THE PROCEDURE

CPR, r 25.6 sets out the procedure that must be followed if an application for an interim payment is to be made. It is important to note that a claimant may make more than one application for such an order. This may be unavoidable in

---

[23] [2012] EW (1990).
[24] (Unreported) 21 December 1994, CA.
[25] [2009] EWHC 1965 (QB).

many catastrophic injury claims where the claimant's needs are constantly changing. However, practitioners should ensure that they do not face a situation where the costs of a further application are placed in issue because an earlier interim payment application could have identified and provided for ongoing needs.

Pursuant to CPR, r 25.6(7) the court may order an interim payment in one sum or in instalments. An instalment order is the equivalent of an interim PPO and can have obvious advantages in catastrophic claims. CPR Part 25B PD 3 confirms that where an interim payment is to be paid in instalments the order should set out:

(1)   the total amount of the payment;

(2)   the amount of each instalment;

(3)   the number of instalments and the date on which each is to be paid; and

(4)   to whom the payment should be made.

In all cases, the key will be to have a clear understanding of what is reasonably required to address the claimant's needs, both at the time of the application and in the period up to trial. The costs of meeting these reasonable needs will then have to be quantified and the interim payment application made accordingly. The claimant's expert evidence will be critical to this process.

If the claim is to proceed in the High Court, the application should be issued at the Masters Support Unit, Room E16.[26] In a District Registry or a county court it will be via the relevant court office.

The application must be served on the defendant at least 14 days before the hearing and must be supported by evidence in the form of a witness statement. CPR Part 25B PD 2.1 identifies the evidence that must be included in such a statement:

(a)   the sum of money sought by way of interim payment;

(b)   the items or matters in respect of which the interim payment is sought;

(c)   the sum of money for which final judgment is likely to be given;

(d)   the reasons for believing that the conditions set out in CPR, r 25.7 are satisfied;

(e)   any other relevant matters; and

(f)   details of special damages and past and future loss.

The witness statement should exhibit the claimant's schedule of loss, any counter schedule and copies of all relevant expert evidence that the claimant intends to rely on. All such evidence relied upon by the judge must also have been seen by the defendant otherwise the order will be at risk of being set aside (*Fred Perry (Holdings) Limited v Brands Plaza Trading Limited*).[27]

---

[26]   Queen's Bench Guide, para 7.13.6.

[27]   [2012] EWCA Civ 224.

Evidence of a payment into court made by a defendant is admissible as evidence in support of an application for an interim payment.[28] There is no good reason why the same approach cannot be taken in relation to Part 36 written offers, provided the interim payment application is not heard in front of the judge allocated to hear the trial (see CPR, r 36.13). In most cases, the interim payment application will be heard by a master or district judge so this will not be an issue. However, there will be some occasions when the value and complexity of the application warrants a hearing before a High Court or circuit judge.[29] In these cases, care must be taken to ensure that the same judge does not hear the substantive trial unless all the parties expressly agree in writing.

5.5 COMPENSATION RECOVERY PAYMENTS

Where there is an application for an interim payment other than by consent, the defendant must obtain a certificate of recoverable benefits (CRU certificate) and file this at the hearing of the application (CPR Part 25B PD 4). The order for an interim payment should set out the amount that is deductible in accordance with s 8 of, and Sch 2 to the Social Security (Recovery of Benefits) Act 1997. Thereafter, the payment made to the claimant will be the net amount but the interim payment for the purposes of any final judgment will be the gross amount.

5.6 POWERS OF THE COURT WHERE IT HAS MADE AN INTERIM PAYMENT

Once made, the court has wide powers to discharge or vary an interim payment order. This includes the power to: (i) order a claimant to repay all or part of an interim payment; or (ii) order one defendant to reimburse another (CPR, r 25.8). If all or part of the interim payment is repaid to a defendant, the court can award interest on the overpaid sum from the date when the interim payment was made (whether this be a voluntary interim payment or by court order) (CPR, r 25.8(5)).

Before the court gives its final judgment or order in a case, it may make such adjustments with respect to the interim payment as may be necessary in order to give effect to its determination of a defendant's liability. As between a claimant and defendant, the amount of the interim payment should be deducted from the total award of damages (including applicable interest) and judgment should be entered for the net difference. The form of judgment or order should recite the amount of the final judgment or the assessment of damages and should also recite the amounts and dates of the interim payments (whether

---

[28] *Fryer v London Transport Executive* (1982) *The Times*, December 4, CA as followed in *Bowmer & Kirland Ltd v Wilson Bowden Properties Ltd* LTL 10/12/97, (1997) 80 BLR 131.

[29] For examples of this see *Brewis v Heatherwood & Wrexham Park Hospitals NHS Trust* [2008] EWHC; *Mealing v Chelsea & Westminster NHS Trust* [2008] LS Law Med 236 and *Braithwaite v Homerton University Hospitals NHS Foundation Trust* [2008] EWHC 353.

made by court order or paid voluntarily by a defendant). The judgment or order should then provide for entry of judgment and payment of the balance (see CPR Part 25B PD 5).

Where the claimant has invested interim payments received from the defendant and earned interest, that interest should not be deducted from the sum allowed for interest in the final determination of quantum.[30]

5.7   RESTRICTION ON DISCLOSURE OF INTERIM PAYMENTS

Under CPR, r 25.9, any interim payment made by a defendant (whether voluntarily or by court order) shall not be disclosed to the trial judge until all questions of liability and quantum have been decided, unless the defendant agrees to this. This is to avoid a judge being unduly influenced by (a) the fact of interim payments when considering liability; and (b) the size of interim payments received when making a final assessment of quantum. The particulars of claim and schedule of loss should, therefore, make no reference to interim payments without agreement.

Where a master or district judge makes an order for an interim payment at the same time as any other order (eg at a case management conference), the order for the interim payment should be sealed as a separate order and not included in the trial bundle. If there are any concerns that reference to an interim payment remains on the court file then a formal request can be made to the court office in advance of the trial to remove any such references.

---

[30]   *Parry v North West Surrey Health Authority* (2000) *The Times*, January 5.

CHAPTER 6

DOCUMENTARY AND WITNESS EVIDENCE

6.1 DISCLOSURE

6.1.1 The duty to disclose

The process normally referred to as disclosure is in fact a two-part procedure more properly divided into disclosure and inspection. The first stage, disclosure, involves identifying the existence of a document. The second part, inspection, involves showing the document, and where appropriate providing a copy, to the other party. It does not follow, just because a document has been disclosed, that it will necessarily be shown to the other party in the course of inspection. Equally, it does not follow that just because a document will not be shown to the other party that its existence should not be disclosed.

Lord Woolf's Access to Justice reports that led to the CPR identified disclosure of documents, then referred to as 'discovery', as an area where cases became bogged down in unnecessary paper involving excessive cost and delay. The change in terminology was intended to emphasise that things had changed and that the courts were dealing with a different beast. The disclosure provisions in the CPR were intended to streamline the procedures for disclosure, to limit the extent of disclosure, introducing the idea of 'standard' disclosure, and to give the court greater control over the extent of disclosure. Lord Justice Jackson identified the same problems with disclosure, however, in his report on civil costs in most areas, except personal injury. As part of the Jackson reforms CPR Part 31.5 was amended for non-personal injury claims to remove standard disclosure as the default position and replace it with a menu of different disclosure options, from none to handing over the keys of the document warehouse, which will be chosen having considered disclosure reports submitted by the parties at the first case management conference and intended to reflect proportionality. Personal Injury disclosure was omitted from these provisions as it was thought that disclosure in such cases was largely dealt with under the pre-action protocol. Although the reforms do not expressly apply to personal injury claims, the menu of options may well influence the way in which courts exercise their discretion to make some other order than standard disclosure even in personal injury claims.

CPR Part 31 still deals with disclosure in catastrophic injury cases. The court retains its jurisdiction to order disclosure wherever necessary. It remains a key part of the CPR that discovery should be proportional to the nature of the action, a concept that has been reinforced by the Jackson costs reforms. In catastrophic injury claims, however, little has yet changed. Such claims remain document heavy. This is justified as being proportionate to the relatively high value of the claims. Whilst there still tend to be complaints from insurers and the NHSLA about proportionality of documentation, there are also still regular calls for all documentation to be produced to verify every item in schedules of loss, no matter how seemingly reasonable or trivial, and if it is called for it needs to be produced where practical.

Standard disclosure requires a party to disclose only:

(a)   the documents on which he relies; and

(b)   the documents which:
      (i)   adversely affect his own case;
      (ii)   adversely affect another party's case; or
      (iii)   support another party's case.

In many actions considerable disclosure will already have taken place before action under the pre-action protocol procedures. Where pre-action disclosure has been thorough, or liability is admitted and the defendant claims to have no documents relating to quantum there may be a temptation to do away with disclosure by the defendant in the action. This temptation should be resisted because an order for disclosure is required to trigger the duty to search and the continuing duty to disclose under CPR, r 31.11.

6.1.2   Gathering documents

It is unrealistic to expect parties, in particular injured claimants and their relatives, to produce all the necessary documents on demand, even if they are warned of the need to do so at the outset of a retainer. Claimants should be encouraged to keep diaries and logs of expenditure and events as they occur. One practical approach is the large brown envelope. At each meeting with the solicitor, the claimant or litigation friend can be given a large brown envelope in which to place any receipt or record coming to hand before the next meeting. The envelope is then handed in to the solicitor and a replacement envelope issued. Maintaining a running draft schedule of loss and expenses, and noting the documents relied on against each entry, will ensure ease of reference and limit the need to go over large amounts of receipts when finalising the schedule of loss. By gathering the evidence and collating it as it goes along there is some hope of collecting and preserving the supporting information.

In larger cases it may become difficult to keep a track of where documents have come from and who gave disclosure of a document and when they did so may become significant. For this reason many solicitors adopt a system of marking the documents received on inspection. Thus a document marked 'C123B' might signify that the document originated from inspection following the claimant's first supplemental list (A being the original list) and was document numbered 123. If, as they should be, documents are numbered consecutively and continuously from list to list (so that if the last document in the first list is 104 then the first document in the supplemental list is 105, and so on) then the last letter may be unnecessary, but this can ease speedy identification.

Disclosed documents should be retained separately in clearly marked folders (ring binders or lever-arch files). Where appropriate they should be kept in plastic folders with holes for insertion into lever-arch files rather than hole punched. Where there are a large number of documents it helps to mark the contents not just on the outside but also on the inside front cover so that it can be read when the folder is open. Thus when a folder is open the reader will be able to see, for example, that the folder is 'Claimant's main list docs 2nd folder docs 568 to 1240'. Similar labelling should be adopted at trial to cut down on the time spent dropping files whilst trying to see what they contain. Disclosure consisting of a few payslips and a few bills for over the counter painkillers does not need such elaboration, but catastrophic injury claims require more careful planning and housekeeping. It is, as always under the CPR, a question of finding a proportionate solution in each case, and being prepared to justify it at a costs management hearing and/or a detailed assessment of costs.

6.1.3 Disclosure of medical records

Medical records fall within the definition of disclosable documents. As a matter of good practice it is the claimant's solicitors who should obtain and collate the claimant's medical records, rather than give authority to the defendant to do so. Indeed the model directions used by the Masters assigned to clinical negligence actions at the Royal Courts of Justice provide:

> 'Legible copies of the medical (and educational) records of the Claimant/Deceased/ Claimant's Mother are to be placed in a separate paginated bundle at the earliest opportunity by the Claimant's Solicitors and kept up to date. All references to medical notes in any report are to be made by reference to the pages in that bundle.'

In such cases many of the key records will have come from the defendant in the first place.

Defendants normally seek and obtain disclosure to their own legal and medical advisers of medical records in the possession of third parties. Very often this creates no difficulty and the disclosure is arranged by the claimant's solicitors, but if objection is taken then disclosure is not automatic. Patient records are confidential as between a doctor and their patient and that confidentiality is underscored by the guarantee of respect for the patient's private and family life in Art 8 of the European Convention on Human Rights (ECHR). Even where it may be necessary for medical records to be disclosed to a defendant's expert by reason of the right to a fair trial under Art 6 of the ECHR, it does not follow that a defendant's legal adviser will be able to inspect the records.

In *Dunn v British Coal Corporation*,[1] the plaintiff sustained an injury at work. The plaintiff's medical expert concluded that the plaintiff was incapable of returning to work as a miner as a result of the accident. The defendant wished the plaintiff to be medically examined by their own expert and sought disclosure of the plaintiff's medical records. The plaintiff offered disclosure of only those medical records that related to the injuries sustained in the accident and any pre-existing similar injuries. The defendants wanted all the records to determine whether there were any pre-existing problems (related or unrelated) that might impact upon the future loss of earnings claim. On the facts of that case the court limited disclosure to the defendant's medical expert. Stuart-Smith LJ considered the position of medical records in the possession of third parties commenting:

> 'The judge was concerned that the plaintiff might justly object to some totally unrelated, but perhaps embarrassing condition being disclosed to the defendant. That is perfectly understandable and it is a legitimate concern. But it can be dealt with by limiting the disclosure to the defendant's medical advisers. The documents are disclosed to them in confidence and they must respect that confidence, except in so far as it is necessary to refer to matters which are relevant to litigation. Thus, for example, the fact that a plaintiff was or had been suffering from some sexually transmitted disease would be quite irrelevant unless it affected his future earning capacity, as might be the case if he was suffering from Aids.'

In *Hipwood v Gloucestershire Health Authority and others*[2] the claimant consented to disclosure of her medical records to the defendants' medical advisers, but not to their legal advisers. The Court of Appeal held that medical records had to be produced to the defendants' legal advisers. McCowan LJ repeated and agreed with the comments of the court below to the effect that:

> '... to my mind only a combination of the solicitors and medical consultants can gauge the relevance of medical records. It is in the experience of this Court that eminent medical consultants are not astute to see the legal implications of the matters before the Court. I therefore think it needs both lawyers and doctors to see the pre-existing medical documents and come to a good decision. It seems to me absurd for consultants to do it by themselves and to have conferences in which counsel does not know what documents have been seen by the medical experts.'

The application in *Hipwood* was, however, made under s 53 of the County Court Act 1984 (disclosure against a non-party) which specifically offered only three possibilities for disclosure to: (i) legal advisers; (ii) legal advisers *and* any medical or other professional adviser of the applicant; or (iii) in the absence of a legal adviser to a medical or other professional adviser. The Court noted that the application was made under s 53 and that it was essential to bear in mind

---

[1]   [1993] ICR 591, CA.

[2]   [1995] PIQR P 447.

the precise terms of s 53 which only provided the three options and not disclosure to medical advisers only, in circumstances where the party had legal advisers.

In *Bennett v Compass Group UK*,[3] the defendant did not accept the claimant's medical report and sought to have her examined by a different expert. For that purpose, the defendants wanted the claimant's medical records. The district judge ordered: 'The claimant do within 14 days supply both defendants all authority to enable them to obtain for their medical experts copies of both GP's and hospital records.' The principle issue on appeal was whether there was jurisdiction to make the order and whether the district judge had erred in the exercise of that discretion. Clarke and Chadwick LLJ (Pill LJ dissenting) upheld the district judge's decision ordering disclosure to the defendant's medical advisers in connection with examination of the claimant.

The Court of Appeal considered the effect of CPR Part 31 and provided the following guidelines:

(1) the medical report was an expert's report within the meaning of CPR, r 31.14(e). Therefore the defendants were entitled to inspect the documents referred to in that report;

(2) the defendants also had a right to inspect under CPR, r 31.3. The combined effect of CPR, r 31.3, r 31.6 and r 31.8 was to give the defendants a right to inspect the relevant medical records. Further the combined effect of CPR, r 31.3 and/or r 31.14 was to confer a right to inspect. So the rules contemplate ordering a party to permit inspection of a relevant document or documents;

(3) the effect of CPR, r 31.12(3) and r 3.1(2)(m) was to give the court power to order the relevant party, to permit a defendant to inspect any document that the defendant had a right to inspect. Accordingly the district judge had jurisdiction to make the order that he did and the appeal was dismissed on the jurisdiction point;

(4) where however an order was made requiring a claimant to authorise a third party to disclose medical records to an opposing party to litigation, the order had to be carefully worded to ensure that the claimant's rights were not infringed. The precise nature of the authority must be carefully delineated so that there is no doubt what it is that the defendants are permitted to see;

(5) the district judge had not erred in the exercise of his discretion, the Court of Appeal stating that there was no doubt that the records were to be obtained for the limited purpose of being submitted to the defendant's medical advisers in connection with the examination of the claimant.

Clarke LJ, at para 40, expressed the position thus:

---

[3]   [2002] EWCA Civ 642.

'... such an order should only be made in exceptional circumstances because in principle a patient should retain control over his or her own medical records. I entirely agree that a judge should think long and hard before making such an order because the defendant should only be allowed to see a claimant's medical records in carefully defined circumstances.'

Pill LJ (dissenting) at para 85 stated that there was no justification for such an order, a claimant was entitled, except in exceptional circumstances, to have the organisation and management of disclosure in the hands of her solicitor. The Rules contained ample penalties for non-disclosure. It was wrong to put control of a claimant's disclosure in the hands of the defendant, an order that gave the defendant the right to go to a claimant's GP or hospital and have authority to arrange the disclosure of the claimant's medical records should only be allowed in very rare cases.

6.2   SPECIFIC DISCLOSURE

If a party is dissatisfied with the disclosure that has been given then an application for specific disclosure may be made under CPR, r 31.12. On an application for specific disclosure the court can order a party to do one or more of the following things:

(a)   disclose documents or a class of documents specified in the order;

(b)   carry out a search to the extent stated in the order; and/or

(c)   disclose any documents located as a result of that search.

The considerations of reasonableness and proportionality, and the overriding objective, will guide the decision of the court as to whether it is necessary to order specific disclosure.

Specific disclosure applications are made under the Part 23 procedure that governs all interlocutory applications. The application must specify the order that the court is going to be asked to make and must be supported by a witness statement. The grounds for the application must be set out in the application notice itself or in the evidence in support. Where specific disclosure of a number of documents is being sought then it is often convenient to set them out in the form of a numbered schedule for ease of reference during the application and in any order that is made.

6.3   WITNESS EVIDENCE

Witness evidence provides the building blocks for any case before the courts. In order that the experts in a case are commenting on the evidence that will be placed before the court they should be provided with witness statements setting out the evidence that the court will be considering. It is not appropriate to leave experts to gather the evidence themselves from raw documents and talking direct to the claimant and their family. The parties cannot simply leave it up to their experts, however experienced or eminent they may be, to define what is relevant and admissible evidence. In *General Medical Council v Meadow*,[4] the Court of Appeal emphasised that it is for the parties' legal representatives, and ultimately for the judge, to identify before and at trial what evidence, lay or expert, is admissible and what is not.

The dangers of getting experts to obtain witness evidence were graphically illustrated in the Admiralty case of *Aquarius Financial Enterprises Inc and Delettrez v Lloyd's 970212, 'The Delphine'*.[5] A marine surveyor was sent to examine a yacht that had suffered a fire and took statements from the witnesses while doing so. At trial he was heavily criticised by Toulson J. Unbeknown to the surveyor he had been tape recorded taking the witness statements. The tapes disclosed that he had done so in a manner that was said to be intimidating and bullying. The particular problem there was the nature of the questioning but it is important to be clear with experts whether they are performing the role of investigator in the interests of a party or whether they are an independent expert assisting the court under CPR Part 35. If an expert does interview a witness, as opposed to carrying out a clinical examination, to prepare his report then the notes are not privileged.[6] It is surprising how often even the most eminent of doctors fail to transcribe the history they take accurately into their report. Inspection of the notes taken at the medical examination can help to clarify reported inconsistencies.

Care in the preparation of witness statements is especially important in catastrophic injury claims, where the story that a claimant may need to tell cannot be told in the 5 or 10 minutes that a clinical examination allows for a claimant to provide the previous history. There may also be communication difficulties due to serious injuries that need to be overcome with patience and time. Some brain-damaged claimants will be very unreliable historians, and will need to be protected from their own inability to convey what they mean and/or to recall accurately what has happened to them. In those cases the history given by a claimant will need to be checked with any objective or independent contemporaneous accounts and any differences dealt with either by correction or explanation. Obtaining a complete witness statement in a serious injury case may involve several home visits. These will give the claimant an opportunity to talk about the claim in his or her own environment, but will also allow the level of care to be seen and described with more confidence. It will also allow details to be checked directly with family, friends and carers, subject to the client's confidentiality. In head injury cases in particular the claimant may well have fallen out with family, friends and carers. In those circumstances getting witness statements from them may be difficult. If the claimant's behaviour is part of the case that needs to be made out, however, then the difficult task needs to be addressed, even if it causes embarrassment for the claimant.

Where the history of post accident recovery has been recorded in a series of witness statements there may be a benefit in serving the series of statements

---

4   [2006] EWCA Civ 1390 per Sir Anthony Clarke MR at para 89 and Auld LJ at para 206.
5   [2001] 2 Lloyd's Rep 542.
6   See *BCCI v Ali No 3* [1999] 4 All ER 83.

showing how matters have developed. In other cases it will be better to produce a single comprehensive statement for service covering the whole history up to date. It is a matter of judgment in each case which route to take, but the serial statement route should not be followed just because it is easier.

In order to convey the real effect of serious injuries it will often be essential to obtain more than the claimant's own evidence. It will normally require 'before and after' evidence from friends, family and colleagues. A photo gallery of before and after photographs, however casual, can often be very helpful in demonstrating the decline in the claimant due to the injuries, as well as helping to put a human face to the claim. In the case of children, evidence from school teachers supported by school reports and records may tell the story of how an injury affected the child's development.

It is unrealistic to expect a badly injured claimant and their family to recall the whole story faced with a solicitor and a blank sheet of paper. As soon as possible they should be asked to keep diaries of events so that when the time comes for making witness statements they have the material to go back to and base their evidence on.

Claimant's witness statements should descend into the particulars of a claim. This is required to support the schedule of loss with evidence upon which the court can properly award the sums claimed. Going into the detail of a claim is not just, however, a question of getting every last drop out of a claim. Providing details about the sort of expenditure that has become necessary helps to put the flesh on a claim and spell out how in very many small ways the claimant's life has been affected. Details about purchasing note pads for claimants whose memory has been affected, or long-handled scissors or back washers for claimants who can no longer bend provide a window in to the functional realities of a lasting serious injury, as well as adding a small amount to the claim. These details should be supported by disclosure of the bills, as discussed above

Sometimes the written word and photographs will not suffice to convey the impact of injuries on a claimant and their family. In such cases consideration should be given to a 'day in the life' video or DVD to show the defendant and the court what a claimant's life is like. This may be particularly important where a claimant is unable to give evidence either in court or by a witness statement due to the injuries that they received. Such videos can be prepared by firms specialising in such videos, but a home made video prepared by the family of the claimant can be just as effective and help deliver an important message that even the most detailed witness statement cannot convey. It is not a substitute for a witness statement from the family member, though, which it should supplement rather than replace. Care also needs to be taken that the video shows the reality of life and not a 'Sunday best' view of the claimant's life and difficulties.

Issues can arise as to whether it is appropriate for a treating doctor to be appointed as an expert or to provide factual evidence by way of a witness statement. This will depend on whether there is something in the relationship between the doctor and the claimant that might prevent, or appear to prevent, the doctor from complying with the duty to the court. In a straightforward case where there has been a full recovery with no ongoing relationship between the claimant and the doctor it might be perfectly acceptable and cost effective for the treating doctor to report for the court. At the other end of the scale in an exceptional case where the claimant was receiving ground-breaking treatment from the only expert with experience of that treatment, there may be no other option but to obtain a report from that expert. In many cases, however, there may be good reasons as to why a doctor's duty to the patient may, or may be seen to, interfere with a duty to the court. The necessary relationship of trust between patients and psychiatrists providing therapy, for example, may be inconsistent with providing a truly objective prognosis for the court. In *Wright v Sullivan*,[7] the court had to consider the position of a clinical case manager. She had been appointed to assist a severely injured person rather than for medico-legal purposes and the court held that she owed her duties to the patient alone and had to make decisions in the best interests of the patient. The court concluded that the role of the clinical case manager, if she was called to give evidence, would be one of a witness of fact and she would not be giving evidence of expert opinion. It followed that the representatives of both parties and their expert witnesses should have liberty to communicate with the case manager in relation to matters relevant to likely issues in the claim. If the clinical case manager considered that it was in the client's interests that she should attend a conference with legal advisers at which advice was being sought then the privilege would not be hers to waive and the court had no power to direct such a waiver. Nor could the court prevent the manager attending conferences with lawyers and experts where the contents remained privileged.

6.4 TRIAL

When considering the venue for a trial, consideration should be given to the practical difficulties of access, especially with claimants in wheelchairs who may need to be delivered to court in an adapted vehicle.

Where a long and complex trial depends on the timely attendance of witnesses, serious consideration should be given to the early service of witness summonses. They should not be regarded as hostile acts, but more a matter of good housekeeping. Courts have become unsympathetic to problems with witness, including expert witness, availability. In *Rollinson v Kimberley Clark*,[8] the Court of Appeal considered it was unacceptable for a solicitor to instruct an expert shortly before trial without checking their availability for the trial date. In *Matthews v Tarmac Bricks and Tiles Ltd*,[9] the Court of Appeal considered

---

[7]   [2005] EWCA 656.
[8]   TLR June 15, 1999.
[9]   TLR July 1, 1999.

that for proper case management the court would need to know specifically why an expert was not available for the trial date before even beginning to consider whether the date might be rearranged.

Witness summonses are provided for under CPR Part 34. If a summons is sought at least 7 days before trial, then permission from the court is not required. Some solicitors issue and serve witness summonses on their witnesses as a matter of course as soon as they know the trial date. This is no more than a way of trying to ensure priority over other court bookings that the witness may have. Some witnesses perceive it to be a hostile act and it can be counterproductive, unless the position is explained to them. Even where permission is not required, the court has a discretion to set aside a witness summons. In general courts will not permit an expert with no connection with a case to be summoned to court against his will.[10] Nor can a witness summons be used, save in very exceptional circumstances, to compel an expert witness to attend trial where a party has run out of funds to pay his fees.[11]

Complex trials require some timetabling, if possible by agreement between the parties. The trial bundle will need timely preparation in accordance with the trial directions not only to allow the court to pre-read them, but also to allow the preparation of skeleton arguments with page references in good time. A sensible trial timetable allows for the court to have some pre-reading time, maybe with the case listed at 10.30 am, but with the parties not required until 2.00 pm to allow the court to read in. This time can then be used by the parties for last minute negotiations, refining of issues or housekeeping.

It is now the norm for factual evidence to be taken first at trial. Whilst the witness statements stand as evidence in chief, some reasonable questioning in chief is normally allowed. The claimant's witnesses will be heard and cross-examined, normally with the claimant giving evidence first unless there is a good reason to depart from that. The defendant's witnesses of fact will then be heard and cross-examined. Thereafter the expert evidence is called. It is the norm now for experts in each field to be called 'back to back'. Thus the claimant's neurologist may be called followed by the defendant's neurologist, then the claimant's next expert followed by the equivalent expert from the defendants and so on until all the experts have been called. Closing submissions then follow.

Each trial creates an atmosphere and a short-hand language of its own. It can assist those giving evidence if they have sat in court and understood the individual flavour of each case. They will then have a better understanding of the questions being asked and what is required to assist the court. There are, however, dangers in getting a large 'team' together for a long period. Lord Justice Thorpe commented on these dangers, when considering the risks of experts losing their independence, in *Vernon v Bosley (No 1)*:[12]

---

[10]   See eg *Lloyd's v Clementson* TLR February 29, 1996.

[11]   See *Brown v Bennett* TLR November 2, 2000.

[12]   [1997] 1 All ER 577 at 612.

'The area of expertise in any case may be likened to a broad street with the plaintiff walking on one pavement and the defendant walking on the opposite one. Somehow the expert must be ever mindful of the need to walk straight down the middle of the road and to resist the temptation to join the party from whom his instructions come on the pavement. It seems to me that the expert's difficulty resisting the temptation and blandishments is much increased if he attends the trial for days on end as a member of the litigation team. Some sort of seduction into shared attitudes, assumptions and goals seems to me almost inevitable ... Not only does the daily attendance of the expert jeopardise detachment but it inflates the cost of litigation.'

Cost and independence need to be borne in mind, but so too must the need for experts to hear and understand the factual evidence that they are being asked to give their opinion on, as well as the views of other experts in the case.

CHAPTER 7

EXPERT EVIDENCE

7.1 INTRODUCTION

One of the main aims of the Civil Procedure Rules when they were first introduced was to control the use and expense of experts in providing evidence to the court. Suggestions that the court should appoint their own experts from panels of approved experts were rejected, but the right of parties to use reports was placed under the control of the court. In this chapter we consider the control mechanisms exercised by the courts and the effect they have on the use of expert evidence in catastrophic injury claims.

7.2 THE NEED FOR CONTROL

The need for control of experts can be seen in the potential that catastrophic injuries have for producing multiple reports at great cost.

A severe head injury will require a report from a *neurologist* or *neurosurgeon*, but it is most likely that that assessment will need to be supplemented by psychological testing (*neuro-psychologist*). It is likely that there will be ongoing problems that are psychiatric, rather than organic, in nature, with issues of capacity (*psychiatrist*). As the prognosis for severe head injuries does not begin to settle until 2 years after an accident it is likely that each of these specialties will have to report at least twice. Under the Mental Capacity Act capacity has to be considered on an issue-by-issue basis and at the time a decision has to be made. An attempt may be made at cognitive behavioural therapy (CBT) (*therapist*), which may alter the condition and prognosis. Accordingly there may need to be several psychiatric assessments and reports on capacity.

Very often there will be many other injuries that accompany a severe head injury. A blow to the head might damage the teeth, jaw bone and eye socket (*maxillo-facial surgeon*), eyesight (*ophthalmologist*), hearing, smell and taste (*ear, nose and throat (ENT) surgeon*) and leave scars (*photographer* and *plastic surgeon*). There may be other broken bones or soft tissue injury (*orthopaedic surgeon*) and if severe pain is experienced the cause and treatment may need to be considered (*pain consultant*). The effect of long periods of treatment on high drug doses may have disturbed (or the patient may fear that they have disturbed) a patient's hormones aggravating diabetes or thyroid problems (*endocrinologist*) or leading to hair loss (*tricologist*).

A patient in need of care will need that care assessed (*care expert*). This may follow attempts at rehabilitation (*rehabilitation expert*). They may need to move to a bungalow or have a lift fitted (*architect*) or require other appliances that they or their family may need training to use (*occupational therapist*). If their employment prospects are difficult to assess or they were in an unusual or very specific role and it is unclear what the prospects of returning to work are then some evidence on that may be needed (*employment consultant*). If they were running a business, were self-employed or had complex financial affairs then their financial loss may require expert input (*accountant*). If a periodic payment order is being considered then a report on the options may be needed (*financial consultant*).

Thus the number of experts can get into double figures very easily even if caution is exercised in deciding on the required fields. In the UK the maximum award for general damages for pain suffering and loss of amenity is under £300,000, and there comes a point where further reports on injuries will not add to the figure. It may be that one of the injuries alone is enough to render the claimant unable to ever work again and in need of constant care and so detailed reports on all the injuries will add little to the award that a court will make.

That is not to say that any of the injuries is unimportant. They are all important, but the detail required will depend on the context.

It may be that the loss of hearing, smell and taste, and even damage to eyesight, can be adequately recorded in a neurologist's report and will not be in issue and so no further report for legal purposes is required. It may be that the medical notes adequately evidence some secondary matters and they will not be challenged and need not be further reported on. An employment consultant may not be able to say more than the court can obtain by reference to the Annual Survey of Hours and Earnings (ASHE). In some catastrophic injury cases, however, there will be no substitute for a large number of expert reports to ensure that the court has the full picture of a claimant's injuries. Although a defendant can seek to limit the need for evidence by the making of early admissions, it is sometimes difficult to know whether to make or accept those admissions until the evidence has been obtained.

Limiting the number and cost of experts' reports is not only in the interests of hard-nosed defendants and insurers watching the purse. Excessive and unnecessary expert reports may eat into the funding available to get a case off the ground, and may delay or side track a claim from the main issues that need resolution before trial or settlement.

One way of attempting to control the number and cost of reports is to order a split trial of liability and causation, with quantum to be determined later. Not all cases are suited to a split trial. The issues may be too intertwined, for example where credibility is in issue in both liability and quantum and there is evidence relating to quantum that will be necessary in any event for credibility, or where causation is dependent on the precise breach of duty and the loss that it may or may not have caused. Where liability is very much in issue but the parties may be able to resolve quantum once they know where liability lies then the court may order a split trial and may order that liability experts' reports be served before the quantum reports. It does not follow from the fact that a split trial is ordered, however, that no quantum reports need be obtained. Although the courts have taken a sensible approach to 'preliminary' schedules of loss, containing the bare bones of a claim, but no detail until reports are obtained, the courts also recognise that the parties may need to obtain some evidence on quantum early on even where liability is to be tried first so that they can make some realistic assessment of the value of a case and have a chance of reaching a settlement.

7.2.1 Court control

CPR Part 35 places control of the extent of expert evidence in any proceedings firmly in the hands of the court. CPR, r 35.4 states in plain terms that no party may call an expert or put in evidence an expert's report without the court's permission. Further, when a party applies for permission under CPR Pt 35 he must provide an estimate of the costs of the proposed expert evidence and identify:

(a) the field in which expert evidence is required and the issues which the expert evidence will address; and

(b) where practicable, the name of the proposed expert.

If permission is granted it is only in relation to the expert named or the field identified in the court's order. In order to try and limit the cost of litigation under CPR, r 35.4(4) the court may specify the issues which the expert evidence should address and may limit the amount of the expert's fees and expenses that the party who wishes to rely on the expert can recover from any other party. Whilst the court had the power to do this before the Jackson reforms to the CPR, it was in practice little exercised. The post-Jackson amendments to the CPR include the express requirement to provide a costs estimate and it can be anticipated that the cost limiting powers will be more widely used by the courts.

An order that a party may rely on a report from an expert does not entitle that party to call that expert at trial, or the other party to insist on a right to cross-examine the expert. For that, an order granting permission to call oral expert evidence, or requiring attendance of an expert at trial is required. Just because a claim relates to a catastrophic injury and has a high value it does not follow that all experts will need to give oral evidence. In practice the same test is applied as in a fast-track case, ie, the court will not direct the attendance of an expert unless it is necessary in the interests of justice (CPR, r 35.5), but it will be easier to meet the test in multi-track cases where the cost of attendance is more proportionate to the value of the claim.

In many cases the court will be reluctant to grant permission for oral evidence from experts at the case management conference (CMC) stage. The court will want to see what the nature of any dispute between the experts is, if any, or whether any evidence from a single joint expert is controversial for any reason. It is easy to lose sight of the fact that permission for oral evidence has not been granted and it is worth noting and diarising that it should be reconsidered at a later CMC or at the listing questionnaire stage. In catastrophic injury cases the court faced with the possibility of a large number of experts may want to take the process gradually. It may start by allowing a report from experts in the fields of what appear at that stage to be the main injuries. There may be an initial umbrella condition and prognosis report that was obtained to serve with the proceedings to give the overall picture. Such a report may come from an accident and emergency consultant or an orthopaedic surgeon describing the injuries at an early stage in treatment and recovery. In those circumstances the court may order a report from, say, a neurologist or neurosurgeon to determine the initial extent of a head injury and a report from an orthopaedic surgeon to indicate the likely issues on condition and prognosis in that area. This may involve further CMCs to consider further directions for further experts thereafter, but the cost of those further hearings will be proportionate to the claim in a complex catastrophic case, and to the potential for saving cost and time with unnecessary expert evidence in a case that is going to take some time to reach a settled prognosis in any event.

The controls contained in CPR Part 35 apply to experts who have been 'instructed to give or prepare evidence for the purpose of court proceedings'. This wording provides an important limit on the activities that the court can control. The court cannot prevent a party from 'instructing' an expert beyond limiting the recovery of the cost of that expert on any assessment.[1] What the court can control is the use of expert evidence in proceedings. If the expert needs to examine a claimant, or a defendant's factory premises, then the court can refuse to order that such an examination be permitted if it concludes that the resultant expert report should not be used in the proceedings, but it cannot order a party not to instruct an expert. If an expert is instructed and then not used, either at the choice of the party or as a result of permission being refused then the party is at risk of not recovering the cost of that expert even if successful in obtaining an order for costs in their favour. Further, if the party attempts to obtain the costs of such an expert in an assessment of damages then it may be put to its election as to whether to disclose the report or abandon the claim for the cost of it.[2]

[1]   *Hajigeorgiou v Vasiliou* [2005] EWCA Civ 236.
[2]   *Gower Chemicals Group Litigation* [2008] EWHC 735 (QB).

7.2.2 Single joint experts

Where two or more parties wish to submit expert evidence on a particular issue, the court may give each party permission to produce its own expert evidence or, under the express powers of CPR, r 35.7, it may direct that the evidence on that issue is to be given by one expert only. The introduction of the 'single joint expert' has been a major innovation under the CPR. It has required a change of culture for all involved, legal advisers, experts and courts, but has become an established part of all personal injury practice, including catastrophic injury claims. Not all expert evidence is suited to single joint expert instruction, and there are practical problems that can arise, but the courts have now, after some initial over-enthusiasm in some quarters, come to realise this.

There is often some confusion over the concept of an expert agreed by a joint selection under the pre-action protocol and a single joint expert under CPR, r 35.7. They are not the same. Although a defendant may agree to the instruction of an expert under the pre-action protocol, that of itself does not convert the expert into a jointly instructed single expert. A claimant who obtains a report from an expert whose instruction has been agreed with a potential defendant under the pre-action protocol but then does not wish to rely on it may still claim privilege in the report and refuse to disclose it to the defendant, see *Carlson v Townsend*.[3] *Carlson v Townsend* was followed in the unreported case of *Sage v Feiven*,[4] in which the claimant obtained a report from an orthopaedic surgeon at the pre-action stage, which was not disclosed. When proceedings were issued the defendant invited the district judge to order a report from the same surgeon as a single joint expert, and the district judge did so, on proportionality grounds. On appeal this was overturned on the grounds that privileged information would be disclosed to the defendant and the parties were required to instruct a new expert. In *Edwards-Tubb v JD Wetherspoon plc*,[5] the Court of Appeal went so far as to hold that once the parties had engaged in a cooperative approach to obtaining expert evidence under the pre-action protocol then there was a discretionary power under CPR, r 35.4 to impose a condition that the claimant disclose a report prepared with a view to court proceedings that was not relied upon if they wanted to rely on a report from a different expert. The court nevertheless held that where there was a 'private' instruction to an expert at the claimant's own expense to advise the claimant rather than as a report to the court then privilege may be claimed as a bar to disclosure as in *Carlson v Townsend*.

There are limits on the extent to which the court can require single joint experts to be appointed and still provide an adversarial trial of the issues. These limits were recognised by the Court of Appeal in *Oxley v Penwarden*.[6] In this clinical negligence case causation was in issue. The judge at first instance ordered the parties, against their joint wishes, to agree on a vascular surgeon to prepare a

---

3   [2001] EWCA Civ 511.
4   [2002] CLY 430.
5   [2011] EWCA Civ 136.
6   [2001] Lloyd's Rep Med 347.

single joint expert report on causation, in default of which the court would appoint one. The Court of Appeal disapproved of the order and considered that it was necessary for each party to have an opportunity of investigating causation through an expert of their own choice and to have the opportunity to call that evidence at trial. In *S (a Minor) v Birmingham Health Authority*,[7] the judge had ordered a single joint expert to prepare opinion evidence on liability and causation in a clinical negligence claim. The claimant appealed on the basis that the issues to be covered in the expert's report were so important to the likely outcome of the case that the parties should be entitled to instruct an expert each: the Court of Appeal agreed. This is the line that the courts have followed subsequently and if the evidence is key to an issue in dispute then single joint expert evidence is not regarded as satisfactory. If the evidence relates to a matter that needs to be addressed but is not key to the real issue in the case then a single joint report is seen as the way to save time and costs. Thus in a catastrophic injury case where the real issue is liability but where there needs to be an assessment of care needs, a single joint care report may be ordered. A similar line may be taken where evidence is requested from an employment consultant. If employment prospects are not the real issue in dispute then the court will tend to order that if any employment reports are allowed then they will be by way of joint instruction. The courts have grown wary of allowing expert reports in areas where the court can make up its own mind on the basis on publicly available information. Thus in the field of employment prospects the court will not direct expert evidence where all the court needs to do is consider the information available from the government's Annual Survey of Hours and Earnings (ASHE). In the area of care the courts will not allow a care report where all that is needed is a British Nursing Association hourly rate for a particular area. Both of these sources of information, and many more, are summarised in the PNBA annual publication *Facts and Figures*, an essential tool for any personal injury practitioner and one that is recognised by the courts.

This approach to single joint experts is reflected in the Queen's Bench Guide:

> 'In very many cases it is possible for the question of expert evidence to be dealt with by a single expert. Single experts are, for example, often appropriate to deal with questions of quantum in cases where primary issues are as to liability. Likewise, where expert evidence is required in order to acquaint the court with matters of expert fact, as opposed to opinion, a single expert will usually be appropriate. There remain, however, a body of cases where liability will turn upon expert opinion evidence and where it will be appropriate for the parties to instruct their own experts. For example, in cases where the issue for determination is as to whether a party acted in accordance with proper professional standards, it will often be of value to the court to hear the opinions of more than one expert as to the proper standard in order that the court becomes acquainted with the range of views existing upon the question and in order that the evidence can be tested in cross-examination.'

---

[7]   [2001] Lloyd's Rep Med 382.

Although the court may limit the parties to producing expert evidence from a single joint expert, it will not itself instruct a single joint expert. It is the parties who instruct a single joint expert, although under CPR, r 35.7(3) if the parties cannot agree who to instruct the court may select the expert from a list prepared or identified by the parties, or direct some other means of selection. The fear at the outset of CPR that courts would have 'approved lists of experts' has not manifested itself. The parties may be able to agree the terms of the instruction, and it is best if they can do so. If they cannot then under CPR, r 35.8 each party may give instructions to the expert, but at the same time those instructions must be sent to the other instructing parties. It is not possible, therefore, for one party to give confidential or private instructions to a single joint expert that are kept from the other instructing party. If the parties are sending their own separate instructions to an expert it is nevertheless important that it is made plain to the expert by all parties that it is a joint instruction.

Instructing single joint experts does not remove practical problems. No party can withhold material from the other parties but give it to the single joint expert, as instructions to a single joint expert have to be disclosed to all parties. If the report of a single joint expert needs clarification then any party may put written questions to the expert under CPR, r 35.6. It is not possible, however, for one party to have a conference with a single joint expert without the other parties unless the other parties consent. In practice joint conferences are difficult to arrange and tend not to happen. This issue was raised in *P (a child) v Mid Kent Area Healthcare NHS Trust*,[8] a clinical negligence cerebral palsy case. A non-medical single joint expert had been appointed on quantum issues and the claimant wanted the expert to attend a conference with counsel in the absence of the other party. The Court of Appeal refused to allow the conference on the grounds that all contact with a single joint expert must be transparent and one party should not be permitted to test the evidence before trial without the involvement of the other party. However, some of the Court of Appeal's obiter comments in *P (a child) v Mid Kent Area Healthcare NHS Trust* have not been followed. In particular the suggestion that usually there should be no need to amplify or test the report of a single joint expert at trial by cross-examination has not stopped joint experts being called where CPR, r 35.6 questioning has been tried but there is still a need for oral amplification and explanation. The general view has reflected the comments of Colman J in *Voaden v Champion, 'The Baltic Surveyor'*,[9] in relation to an order for a joint single expert on valuation:

> 'Whereas there can be no doubt that the order for a single expert under CPR 35.7 was made with the interests of economy and proportionality in mind, the assumption that this important issue could be tried without that single expert being available in court for the purpose of explaining his views was, I have to say, misconceived. Certainly, in relation to trials in the Commercial Court and the Admiralty Court it will only be in cases where the sole expert is to report on discrete and substantially non-controversial matters, collateral to the main issues,

---

[8]   [2002] 1 WLR 210.
[9]   [2001] Lloyd's Rep 739.

that it should be assumed that the sole expert will not have to be present at the trial to explain the contents of his report. In any other case the absence of a sole expert may well prejudice the fair resolution of the expert issues in the light of all the other evidence before it.'

In *Austen v Oxfordshire County Council*,[10] on appeal it was ordered that a psychiatrist instructed as a single joint expert should give evidence at a disposal hearing because otherwise there could have been an injustice, reflecting the reasoning of Colman J in *The Baltic Surveyor*.

The appointment of a single joint expert does not remove or replace the role of the court as the decision-making tribunal on the issues before it. In *Coopers Payen Limited v Southampton Containers Limited*,[11] the Court of Appeal held that it was open to a court to make a considered choice between the evidence of a single joint expert and the evidence of a witness of fact where they were inconsistent. They considered that it would be unusual to disregard the expert evidence. Certainly the court would have to provide good reasons in its judgment for doing so. In *Regan v Chetwynd*,[12] the court agreed with a claimant that the single joint expert's accident reconstruction report should be treated with caution. In *Fuller v Strum*,[13] a chancery judge preferred the evidence of fact to that of a handwriting expert as to whether a will was forged on the basis that the expert was doing no more than drawing inferences from the facts given to him. In *Layland v Fairview New Homes plc*,[14] a summary judgment entered by a district judge on the basis of a disputed single joint expert report (concerning the alleged reduction in value of a property located close to an incinerator) was overturned. It was held that submissions and cross-examination on the report should have been allowed. In plain terms, therefore, the respect to be paid to a single joint expert's report depends on the circumstances, but departure from an unchallenged single expert's report will need to be justified. In *Armstrong v First York*,[15] the Court of Appeal held that where a trial judge had found that the claimants in a road traffic accident claim had been honest and reliable witnesses, he was entitled to find that it followed from that finding of honesty that there had been a flaw in the uncontroversial evidence of an expert, albeit that he could not identify the error, since there was always a possibility that an expert, particularly in a developing field, could have been wrong.

7.2.3 Lead experts

When the CPR was introduced one of the novel ideas that was mooted was that of a lead expert. The idea was that the court could direct that one expert take the lead in coordinating the evidence on a particular issue from the various disciplines involved. This idea did not find its way into CPR Part 35, but it does

---

[10] [2002] All ER (D) 97.
[11] [2003] All ER (D) 220.
[12] (Unreported) 15 December 2000, QB.
[13] [2001] 98 LSG 45.
[14] [2002] EWHC 1350.
[15] [2005] EWCA Civ 277.

appear in the Practice Direction to CPR Part 35 as a way of implementing an order for a single expert under CPR, r 35.7. PD 35, para 6 provides:

> 'Where the court has directed that the evidence on a particular issue is to be given by one expert only (CPR r 35.7) but there are a number of disciplines relevant to that issue, a leading expert in the dominant discipline should be identified as the single expert. He should prepare the general part of the report and be responsible for annexing or incorporating the contents of any reports from experts in other disciplines.'

In complex catastrophic injury cases the appointment of lead experts can prove a very useful tool when marshalling evidence. In a case where neurological evidence is required, for example, a neurologist could be appointed as the lead expert to prepare a report to the court that includes the input from a radiologist, a neuropsychologist and a psychiatrist if required. In a severe food poisoning case a gastroenterologist could be appointed to prepare a report that included the result of a barium meal scan by a radiologist and the input of a microbiologist if needed. This would not breach the requirement that experts should only comment within their own field of expertise as the reports of the other experts would be annexed or incorporated into the lead expert's report and if need be those experts could be called. It is, however, a way of avoiding the problem of experts reporting separately without any proper form of marshalling. Lead experts have not really caught on, but that is because parties very rarely think of asking for them. The provision is one that is capable of much greater use in appropriate cases where the 'following' evidence needs to be obtained but may prove not to be controversial. Once an area of controversy have been identified then the relevant following evidence can be moved out from under the lead expert and take its place in the ordinary way.

Even where all the experts are to be called to give evidence and no formal order is made for lead experts, it can help to treat one expert as the lead expert in the case. Where the experts on one side need to discuss matters before finalising their views, for example where the interplay between physical and psychological factors is complex, it can help to ask one expert to take the lead in the process. In complex cases it can help to get all the experts together, maybe for a conference with counsel, in order to ensure that the evidence is prepared in a coordinated way. It is normal for draft reports to have been prepared before such meetings, and for there to be draft pleadings for the experts to consider and approve as reflecting their views. Such meetings need to be planned well in advance, as the task of finding a suitable time convenient to all involved is never easy.

7.2.4 Multiple experts

Where single joint experts are not ordered the court may even be prepared to consider allowing a party more than one expert in a particular discipline where the circumstances warrant it, despite the contrary emphasis in CPR, r 35.4. In

ES v Chesterfield North Derbyshire Royal NHS Trust,[16] a claimant in a clinical negligence action was faced with a number of witnesses of fact for the defendant who were themselves experts in the discipline in issue. The claimant had to overcome the Bolam hurdle and argued that there would not be a level playing field if the defendant could in effect call additional experts. The claim was worth over £1.5m and the issues were complex, so additional expert evidence was proportionate to the size and nature of the claim, The Court of Appeal allowed the claimant additional experts. The key factor in *ES* was that the claimant faced a number of defence 'experts' as factual witnesses. Where the defendant will call only one doctor as a witness of fact then a level playing field can be achieved by limiting the parties to one expert each.[17]

7.3   DUTIES OF EXPERTS

The duties of experts are fundamental to their involvement in litigation. Although these duties are applicable to all experts we make no apology for covering them in this work given: (a) their fundamental importance; and (b) the persisting need to reinforce the principles involved. CPR, r 35.3 sets out that it is the duty of an expert to help the court on matters within his expertise. That duty overrides any obligation to the person from whom he has received instructions or by whom he is paid.

The effect of CPR Part 35 is to give some clout to the pre-existing case-law on the duties and responsibilities of experts. The leading statement of such duties and responsibilities is to be found in the judgment of Mr Justice Cresswell in the *Ikarian Reefer*:[18]

(1)   Expert evidence presented to the court should be, and should be seen to be, the independent product of the expert uninfluenced as to the form or content by the exigencies of litigation.

(2)   An expert should provide independent assistance to the court by way of objective unbiased opinion in relation to matters within his expertise.

(3)   An expert witness should state the facts or assumption on which his opinion is based. He should not omit to consider material facts which could detract from his concluded opinion.

(4)   An expert witness should make it clear when a particular question or issue falls outside his expertise.

(5)   If an expert's opinion is not properly researched because he considers that insufficient data is available then this must be stated with an indication that the opinion is no more than a provisional one. In cases where an expert witness who has prepared a report could not assert the report contained the truth, the whole truth and nothing but the truth without some qualification that qualification should be stated in the report.

---

[16]   [2003] EWCA Civ 1284.
[17]   *Beaumont v MOD* [2009] EWHC 1258 (QB).
[18]   [1993] 2 Lloyds Rep 68 at 81.

(6) If, after exchange of reports, an expert witness changes his view on the material having read the other side's expert report or for any other reason, such change of view should be communicated (through the legal representative) to the other side without delay and when appropriate to the court.

(7) Where expert evidence refers to photographs, plans, calculations, analyses, measurements, survey reports or other similar documents, these must be provided to the opposite party at the same time as the exchange of reports.

This statement of duties is reflected in the wording of CPR PD 35, with which all experts' reports must comply by reason of CPR, r 35.10. PD 35 provides that:

(1) It is the duty of an expert to help the court on matters within his own expertise: CPR, r 35.3(1). This duty is paramount and overrides any obligation to the person from whom the expert has received instructions or by whom he is paid: CPR, r 35.3(2).

(2) Expert evidence should be the independent product of the expert uninfluenced by the pressures of litigation.

(3) An expert should assist the court by providing objective, unbiased opinion on matters within his expertise, and should not assume the role of an advocate.

(4) An expert should consider all material facts, including those which might detract from his opinion.

(5) An expert should make it clear:
     (a) when a question or issue falls outside his expertise; and
     (b) when he is not able to reach a definite opinion, for example because he has insufficient information.

(6) If, after producing a report, an expert changes his view on any material matter, such change of view should be communicated to all the parties without delay, and when appropriate to the court.

Annexed to PD 35, but not specifically incorporated into it, is a Protocol for the instruction of experts to give evidence in civil claims. Experts and those instructing them are enjoined to have regard to the guidance contained in the Protocol by PD 35.1.

The court may, by specific order, impose particular duties on experts. These may include the timetable for producing reports and answers to questions as well as the holding of joint discussions. In order to assist in the compliance with such directions the court may expressly direct that a copy of its directions be served on the experts. This is now standard in the directions of the assigned clinical negligence masters at the Royal Courts of Justice, whose model direction includes:

> 'Experts instructed by the parties in accordance with this Order shall be provided with a copy of this Order within 7 days after it is sealed, or at the time of instruction, whichever is the later.'

This lead has been followed in the new para 6A of PD 35, which provides that:

> 'Where an order requires an act to be done by an expert, or otherwise affects an
> expert, the party instructing that expert must serve a copy of the order on the
> expert instructed by him. In the case of a jointly instructed expert, the claimant
> must serve the order.'

The independence of experts is underlined by the (little used) right of experts to
ask the court for directions. Under CPR, r 35.14 an expert may file a written
request for directions to assist him in carrying out his function as an expert. In
order to curb the enthusiasm of the more maverick expert, and in order to
ensure that the parties try and address an expert's concerns before the court
becomes involved, a proviso was added to CPR, r 35.14 that if an expert wants
to make a request to the court then he first has to provide a copy of the
proposed request to the party instructing him at least 7 days before filing a
request and then to all other parties at least 4 days before filing a request.
Where the court does give directions to an expert then it may direct that a copy
of the directions be served on a party under CPR, r 35.14. Presumably it will be
up to the court to determine which parties are served with copies, ie, whether it
is just the instructing party or all parties.

In *Vernon v Bosley (No 1)*,[19] Lord Justice Thorpe gave a graphic account of the
independent position of experts:

> 'The area of expertise in any case may be likened to a broad street with the
> plaintiff walking on one pavement and the defendant walking on the opposite one.
> Somehow the expert must be ever mindful of the need to walk straight down the
> middle of the road and to resist the temptation to join the party from whom his
> instructions come on the pavement. It seems to me that the expert's difficulty
> resisting the temptation and blandishments is much increased if he attends the trial
> for days on end as a member of the litigation team. Some sort of seduction into
> shared attitudes, assumptions and goals seems to me almost inevitable ... Not only
> does the daily attendance of the expert jeopardise detachment but it inflates the
> cost of litigation.'

An expert must be capable of, and must be seen to be capable of, fulfilling a
role independent of the interests of the parties. In *Liverpool Roman Catholic
Archdiocesan Trust v Goldberg*, Neuberger J[20] considered that there was no
reason in law or fact why a close friend and colleague of a defendant should not
give expert evidence in a professional negligence claim where the field of
experts was limited. At trial, however, Evans-Lombe J,[21] felt compelled to
disregard the evidence of the expert on public policy grounds that justice must
be seen to be done as well as done, and the expert could not appear with the
necessary independence because of his close ties to the defendant.

---

[19]   [1997] 1 All ER 577 at 612.
[20]   At an interlocutory stage reported at TLR, 9 March 2001.
[21]   Reported at [2001] 1 WLR 2337.

It is sometimes tempting to ask a treating doctor to provide an expert medico-legal report for use in court proceedings. This can arise particularly where there has been a very complex period of treatment for a combination of severe injuries and the interaction between the injuries is particularly well known to a specific treating doctor with a particular expertise in their field. The decision whether to use such a doctor as a Part 35 expert for court proceedings will depend on whether there is something in the relationship between the doctor and the claimant that might prevent, or appear to prevent, the doctor from complying with the duty to the court. In a straightforward case where there has been a full recovery with no ongoing relationship between the claimant and the doctor it might be perfectly acceptable and cost effective for the treating doctor to report for the court. At the other end of the scale in an exceptional case where the claimant was receiving ground-breaking treatment from the only expert with experience of that treatment, there may be no other option but to obtain a report from that expert. In many cases, however, there may be good reasons as to why a doctor's duty to the patient may, or may be seen to, interfere with a duty to the court. The necessary relationship of trust between patients and psychiatrists providing therapy, for example, may be inconsistent with providing a truly objective prognosis for the court. In *Wright v Sullivan*,[22] it was held that a clinical case manager, appointed to assist a severely injured person, owed duties to the patient alone and had to make decisions in the best interests of the patient and the appointment should not be an appointment by the parties jointly. The court concluded that the role of the clinical case manager, if she was called to give evidence, would be one of a witness of fact and she would not be giving evidence of expert opinion. It followed that the representatives of both parties and their expert witnesses should have liberty to communicate with the case manager in relation to matters relevant to likely issues in the claim. If the clinical case manager considered that it was in the client's interests that she should attend a conference with legal advisers at which advice was being sought then the privilege would not be hers to waive and the court had no power to direct such a waiver. Nor could the court prevent the manager attending conferences with lawyers and experts whose contents were privileged.

In the same way that it is not the task of an expert to be an advocate for a party, it is not the task of an expert to take witness statements for use in court proceedings. This can present difficulties where an expert is sent to examine the circumstances of an accident and then is asked to provide expert evidence to the court. In *Aquarius Financial Enterprises Inc and Delettrez v Lloyd's 970212, 'The Delphine'*,[23] a marine surveyor was heavily criticised by Toulson J at trial in the commercial court because he had taken witness statements but unbeknown to him he had been tape recorded doing so in a manner that was said to be intimidating and bullying. The particular problem there was the nature of the questioning but it is important to be clear with experts whether they are performing the role of investigator in the interests of a party or whether they are an independent expert assisting the court under CPR Part 35.

---

[22] LTL May 27, 2005, CA.
[23] [2001] 2 Lloyd's Rep 542.

If an expert does interview a witness to prepare his report the notes of the interview should be annexed to the report and are not privileged.[24] It is surprising how often doctors fail to transcribe the history they take accurately into their report. Inspection of the notes taken at the medical examination can help to clarify reported inconsistencies. In order that medical experts found their opinions on the evidence that will be before the court, they should be provided with witness statements from the claimant (where possible) and from friends, family and colleagues on the impact of the injury, and not left to obtain the facts unaided from the claimant and whoever happens to accompany them to an examination.

7.4   LETTERS OF INSTRUCTION

Care should be taken in the drafting of letters of instruction. There are limits to the extent that privilege from disclosure can be obtained. CPR, r 35.10(4) provides that a court shall not order disclosure of instructions to experts unless it is satisfied that there are reasonable grounds to consider the expert's statement of instructions to be incomplete, in which case privilege will not apply. Also at trial it may prove counter-productive to hang on to privilege if a real issue has arisen about the instruction given to an expert. A letter of instruction should, therefore, be drafted with one eye on how it would read in court. It is also important to think about how to get the best out of an expert.

It is common for the instruction of an expert to be a two-stage process. First a letter is sent setting out a brief description of the issues in the case and asking if the expert is willing to accept instructions. This request will need to ascertain whether the expert can report within the available timetable. If there is no timetable then it will need to ask for details of waiting times for an appointment for an examination, and then the timescale for preparation of the report. This request will also need to ask either whether the expert can report within the available budget, or ask for details of proposed fees if there is no budget. If the instructing party does not know the expert then it is worth spending some time checking out the expert before confirming instructions. It is not rude to check out an expert's credentials, and any expert who objects may well be unsuited to medico-legal work. A full CV should be requested, with details of relevant medical and medico-legal experience. It is quite usual post CPR for experts to be able to give rough breakdown of instruction from claimants, defendants and joint instructions. Some experts will even provide an anonymised sample report to aid with the selection process.

In clinical negligence cases what is needed is not just an expert in a particular field but one who has sufficient knowledge of the particular operation or treatment involved in the case to give a truly informed opinion on what is acceptable practice. In cases of treatment some years ago, such as a cerebral palsy case involving a birth incident to a now teenage claimant, knowledge of the standards at the relevant time will be needed. At the other end of the scale

---

[24]   See *BCCI v Ali No 3* [1999] 4 All ER 83.

avoid the expert who retired from clinical practice long before the incident involved. The status of 'Emeritus' or 'Honorary' Consultant may sound fine but it does not necessarily indicate up-to-date knowledge. Medical directories and website searches can help to reveal information about experts. If the solicitor does not do this background research then the chances are that either the client or the other side will, and it is better to be prepared.

Once the preliminary approach has had a favourable response, a full letter of instruction will follow. The matters that need to be included for consideration in a letter of instruction include:

- the name of the parties;
- whether the instructions are single joint instructions or from one party alone;
- the solicitor's details and references of each of the instructing parties;
- the identity of the court having case management control of the proceedings;
- the stage in the proceedings that has been reached with any timetable for reports, discussions and trial windows. Courts have become unsympathetic to problems with expert availability at trial, see below;
- the basis of any agreement as to payment of the expert's fees, including cancellation fees. In due course a time-limit for cancelling an expert's attendance at court without incurring a cancellation fee can provide a good opportunity to put pressure on the other side to settle a case, or at least start talking settlement. Contingency fee arrangements with experts are not permitted;
- a summary of the duties that the expert will be agreeing to abide by under CPR Part 35, PD 35 and the Protocol for Experts referred to in it if the instructions are accepted. An alternative is to send copies of all these documents if it is the first time the expert has been instructed since the latest amendment to any of the documents. It is helpful to set out the declaration that is required at the end of the report (see below);
- details of any court orders affecting the expert, with a copy of the order concerned;
- a summary of the case and of the issues involved, specifying the issues upon which the opinion is being sought, and if appropriate specifying the issues on which the expert is specifically not required to give an opinion. It is convenient for the expert if this is in a form that can be transposed into the report as the basis on instruction;
- an index of the documents enclosed together with an indication of the status of any enclosed chronology and/or bundle of documents, including specifically whether they are agreed. If privileged material is being enclosed indicate its status clearly, but for the reasons set out above be very careful before enclosing any privileged material;
- a request for a full CV, if one has not already been provided.

Counsel's opinions should not be sent to experts with letters of instruction.

7.5   FORM AND CONTENT OF EXPERT REPORTS

CPR, r 35.5 requires expert evidence to be given in a written report unless the court directs otherwise. In practice, permission to call an expert will normally be expressed to be by reference to a report already disclosed or conditional upon a written report having been served by a specified time. CPR, r 35.13 provides that a party who fails to disclose an expert's report may not use the report at the trial or call the expert to give evidence orally without permission from the court. This does not, however, require a party to have disclosed all draft reports written by an expert before the disclosed version of the expert report.[25]

CPR, r 35.10 requires experts to comply with the requirements for the form and contents of their reports laid down by the CPR PD 35. PD 35 requires that an expert's report must be addressed to the court and not to the party from whom the expert has received instructions. In the report the expert must:

(1)   give details of the expert's qualifications; a proper CV is generally of more use than a string of letters after the expert's name;

(2)   give details of any literature or other material which the expert has relied on in making the report; the suggested model directions used by the masters assigned to clinical negligence actions at the Royal Courts of Justice (RCJ) impose the useful additional requirement that:

> 'Any unpublished literature upon which any expert witness proposes to rely shall be served at the same time as service of his report together with a list of published literature. Any supplementary literature upon which any expert witness proposes to rely shall be notified to all other parties at least one month before trial. No expert witness shall rely upon any publications that have not been disclosed in accordance with this dissection without leave of the trial judge on such terms as to costs as he deems fit.'

This form of order was approved by the Court of Appeal in *Breeze v Ahmad*,[26] in which a judgment was set aside and the case remitted for re-hearing where the claimant's expert had not had a proper opportunity to consider literature referred to at trial by the defendant's expert;

(3)   contain a statement setting out the substance of all facts and instructions given to the expert which are material to the opinions expressed in the report or upon which those opinions are based; CPR, r 35.10(4) provides that the instructions to experts shall not be privileged against disclosure but that where a court is satisfied that there are reasonable grounds to consider the statement of instructions given in an expert's report to be inaccurate or incomplete the court may order disclosure of a specific

---

[25]   See *Jackson v Marley Davenport Ltd* [2004] EWCA Civ 1225.
[26]   [2005] EWCA Civ 223.

document containing material instructions and/or permit cross-examination of an expert as to the contents of his instructions;

(4) make clear which of the facts stated in the report are within the expert's own knowledge;

(5) say who carried out any examination, measurement, test or experiment which the expert has used for the report, give the qualifications of that person, and say whether or not the test or experiment has been carried out under the expert's supervision;

(6) where there is a range of opinion on the matters dealt with in the report:
  (a) summarise the range of opinion, and
  (b) give reasons for his own opinion;

(7) contain a summary of the conclusions reached;

(8) if the expert is not able to give his opinion without qualification, state the qualification; and

(9) contain a statement that the expert understands his duty to the court, and has complied with that duty and is aware of the requirements of Part 35, its Practice Direction and Protocol. This goes a little further than the requirement in CPR, r 35.10 that at the end of an expert's report there must be a statement that the expert understands his duty to the court and that he has complied with that duty. Some experts seem determined to put their declaration at the start of their report in case they forget it later. To be fair, CPR, r 35.10 does not say at which end of the expert's report the declaration has to go.

In addition to the declaration set out above, an expert's report must be verified by a statement of truth in the following terms:

> 'I confirm that I have made clear which facts and matters referred to in this report are within my own knowledge and which are not. Those that are within my own knowledge I confirm to be true. The opinions I have expressed represent my true and complete professional opinions on the matters to which they refer.'

The reference to the report containing the *complete* professional opinion of the expert was not in the original practice direction, which has undergone a number of amendments. The fact that it was felt necessary to add this to the statement of truth underlines the suspicion that some members of the judiciary appear to have that experts are still not acting as servants of the court but as servants of the paying party. In practice many experts appear to have developed very lengthy declarations at the end of their reports. Many of these are based on the form originally recommended by bodies such as the Expert Witness Institute and the Academy of Experts in pre-CPR efforts to regulate the efforts of expert witnesses, and appear to have been added to by a process of accretion as new suggestions were found in other reports. Very often, however, the wealth of declarations at the end of a report hides the fact that the declarations actually required by the rules are not there. It is worth including the correct from of declaration and statement of truth in the letter of instruction and checking that they are there before service of a report.

7.6   QUESTIONS TO EXPERTS

CPR, r 35.6 allows parties to put questions to an expert whose report has been served by another party, or as a result of joint instructions. One set of questions may be put as of right so long as they are put within 28 days of service of the report and are for the purposes of clarification of the report only. Further questions, other forms of questions, or questions outside the time-limit of 28 days, may be put if the other party agrees, or with permission from the court. The answers given by an expert are treated as part of the report. This can provide a form of paper cross-examination, and as such is particularly important in cases where the expert evidence will consist only of the written report without attendance at court by the expert. CPR, r 35.6 does not provide a time period within which the expert must respond to questions and very often in multi-track cases the court will include within the timetable provision for the asking of questions and the provision of answers. If an expert does not answer questions that a party was entitled to ask then, in addition to the general case management powers, the court has express powers under CPR, r 35.6(4) to prevent the party who served the expert's report from relying on the evidence of that expert, or to direct that the fees and expenses of the expert may not be recovered from any other party.

Where questions are asked of an expert that may go beyond mere clarification of a report objection is sometimes taken and it is asserted that such questions cannot be put. That sort of objection is misconceived. The questions cannot be put as of right, but they can be put and should be answered if to do so would assist the just disposal of the dispute. In *Mutch v Allen*,[27] a medical expert in a personal injury claim was asked by the defendant whether the claimant's injuries would have been less severe if he had been wearing a seat belt. At first instance it was accepted this was outside the scope of his instructions and report, and was not therefore 'clarification'. The Court of Appeal considered that for the expert to answer the question would assist 'the just disposal of the dispute', and therefore the question should be answered, but that the expert should be called to give evidence and be cross-examined at trial. If the question raises a significant new issue that needs to be addressed then the court could grant permission to obtain further expert evidence on the point.

In *MMR and MR Vaccine Litigation No 4*[28] the court held that questions relating to expert reports in group litigation under CPR Part 19 were not appropriate where they were prepared for an interim application hearing to decide the issues for trial, and were not intended to be relied upon at trial.

Ordinarily the questioning party will send its questions to the other side's solicitors for onward transmission to the expert, if only as a matter of courtesy. PD 35, para 5 anticipates, however, that this will not always be the case and

---

[27]   [2001] All ER (D) 121, CA.
[28]   [2002] EWHC 1213 (QB).

that questions may be sent direct to the expert. Where they are sent direct, however, a copy of the questions should be sent at the same time to the other party or parties.

PD 35, para 5.3 provides that it is the party who originally instructed the expert, not the questioning party, who pays the expert's fees for providing the answers. This is a reversal of the original provision in PD 35, and was altered to protect experts from being placed in difficulties recovering their fees from parties from whom they had not agreed to accept instructions. The rule as to payment of fees does not prevent the paying party from recovering those fees as part of the costs of the action. Indeed, where one party has put the other to the expense of getting answers to questions they had posed they may not be in very good position to complain unless the questions were only necessary due to inadequacies in the original report. If the questioning party does not have a right to put its questions, for example because they are out of time, or the questions go beyond clarification, then it may be possible to reach agreement that the questions be answered but on terms that the questioning party pays the fees for providing the answers. Where the questions are necessary for the just disposal of the case, however, it would not normally be reasonable to insist on the normal rule being reversed.

7.7 DISCUSSIONS AND JOINT STATEMENTS

It is now standard practice to require experts of like disciplines to hold discussions to try and reach agreement, or to narrow the issues before trial in order to prevent the calling of expert evidence, or narrow its scope. The power to order such discussions is in CPR, r 35.12. The discussions can be by telephone, they do not have to be meetings. The discussions can be ordered at any stage, but generally follow the exchange of experts' reports. The discussions are without prejudice and CPR, r 35.12(4) expressly provides that the content of the discussion is not to be referred to unless the parties agree. This provision is designed to encourage compromise and candour under the without prejudice protection. The fact that a discussion cannot be referred to, however, does not prevent the use of knowledge gained as a result of the discussion. Thus it may not be permissible to ask 'Is it right that it took Professor Smith 3 hours to persuade you that he was right and you were wrong on this point at the joint meeting', but it would be permissible to ask an expert in cross-examination why they had expressed their original opinion and how they had come to the new view in the joint statement, with a view to bringing out the vacillation and indecision that was demonstrated at the meeting. Judges vary in the stricture with which the rule is applied, and even without any desire to bend the rules it is all too easy for one expert in cross-examination to say something such as 'I believe Dr Jones had some difficulty in accepting this point when we met, but did eventually have to concede the point'. Caution is still needed, therefore, about what is said in the course of discussions.

Even if the experts reach agreement that does not bind the parties unless they expressly agree to be bound. It can be difficult to hold an expert to an agreement at trial, and impossible to hold a party to an agreement unless they have effectively made an admission, in which case the provisions of CPR, r 14.1(5) as to allowing a party to withdraw an admission apply. Very often the apparent unravelling of an agreement between experts at trial is in fact no more than the discovery that, despite appearances, they were never agreed in the first place. Conversely, although strictly a party may not be bound by an experts' agreement, there may be little the party can do to rescue the point if the agreement has destroyed the evidential basis for it.

The product of the discussions between experts should be a joint statement for the court. CPR, r 35.12(3) provides that such a statement should show:

(a)   those issues on which they agree; and

(b)   those issues on which they disagree and a summary of their reasons for disagreeing.

Some court orders require more from a joint statement. The suggested model directions used by the masters assigned to clinical negligence actions at the RCJ (see Annex 1 to this chapter), for example, require the experts to identify the action, if any, that may be taken to resolve the outstanding points of disagreement, and any further material points not raised in the agenda and the extent to which these issues are agreed.

Although the RCJ directions indicate that the use of agendas is not mandatory, the discussions will normally be better structured, and the joint statement more helpful, if there is a proper agenda. It will also help the legal representatives to comply with their duty, as expressed by the Court of Appeal in *GMC v Meadow*,[29] to ensure that experts' evidence is confined to what is relevant and admissible to the important issues in the case. As the legal advisers know the issues in the case it is helpful if the agenda is prepared by them, in discussion with the experts if need be. It should be possible to identify from the expert's reports the issues relevant to the trial that need to be discussed. Even if the order for discussions provides a timetable with a substantial gap between exchange of reports and holding of discussions it is worth tackling the issue of the agenda as soon as exchange has taken place. Very often the drawing up of the agenda is left too late and as a result the agenda is ill thought out, has not been the subject of proper consultation with experts, and is less likely to be agreed. The model directions used by the masters assigned to clinical negligence cases at the RCJ require the claimant's solicitors and experts jointly to prepare a suggested agenda and send it to the defendant's solicitors for comment at least 35 days before the agreed date for discussions. The defendants then have 21 days to agree the agenda or propose amendments. Within 7 days thereafter, and accordingly at least a week before the discussion, the solicitors should use their best endeavours to agree the agenda. Points of disagreement should be on matters of real substance and not semantics or on matters the experts could resolve of their own accord at the discussion. In default of agreement both agendas are to be provided to the experts, to be answered consecutively with

---

[29]   [2006] EWCA Civ 1390.

continuous numbering. The model directions provide that agendas should be reasonable in scope and directed to the remaining issues relevant to the expert's discipline. They should not include leading or hostile questions.

It is good practice to set out a preamble to an agenda to remind the experts of the task they are being asked to perform and remind them of their duties. The model directions indicate that a preamble should state the standard of proof, the Bolam test, a reminder that experts must not attempt to determine factual issues or stray outside of their field of expertise, and indicate the form of the joint statement. The model directions further suggest that it will be helpful to provide a comprehensive list of materials which each expert has seen, perhaps in the form of an agreed supplementary bundle.

The experts are not bound by the agenda and they can and should discuss whatever relevant issues they see fit within the scope of their duties. They will not be complying with their duty to the court, however, if they ignore the agenda provided to them and thus fail to assist the court with the issues that have been identified as relevant. It can help if the agenda provides some basic information. If there is an agreed chronology then that should be provided. If there is an agreed set of medical notes paginated in the way that will be used at trial then that should be provided so that references in the joint statement can be easily followed at trial. It can help to set out a brief summary of the duties of experts under CPR, r 35.10 and PD 35, as well as the requirements for discussions under CPR, r 35.12 and any order in the case for the joint discussion and the joint statement. If there are a lot of documents and reports it can help to provide a list of documents that the experts ought to have for their discussion, highlighting the ones that are new since they last considered the case. It is alarming how often experts respond that they had not seen a document at the time of their discussion when a query is raised.

Where there is a dispute between factual witnesses as to what happened then it is sometimes sensible to remind the experts that it is not their role as experts to resolve such a dispute, and that factual disputes are a matter for the trial judge. It may be helpful to the trial judge, however, if the experts identify the material facts upon which findings of fact need to be made and upon which their opinions are dependent. It can also be sensible to remind experts that they are not being invited to horse-trade and are under no obligation to arrive at a consensus if one does not genuinely exist.

Any questions should be related to the issues and for the purpose of progressing agreement. Questions such as ' Do you agree the claimant is lying', or 'Do you agree that the defence will lose' are not acceptable. The model direction used by the masters assigned to clinical negligence cases at the RCJ suggests that as far as possible the questions should be in a form capable of being answers 'yes' or 'no', but this is not always possible and can actually lead to confusion if experts feel restrained from adding the qualifications to their answers that they would otherwise wish to.

If the parties cannot agree on the agenda then two agendas should be prepared and submitted to the experts, and they should deal with both agendas even if this means some repetition. If there are two agendas then they should be numbered sequentially, ie, the claimant's questions may be numbered 1 to 10 and the defendant's 11 to 20.

The discussions are between the experts and not between the legal advisers and the experts. It is not appropriate for legal advisers to participate, although the experts may agree that certain points should be checked with the legal advisers as part of their discussion. Legal advisers should not attend the discussion unless the parties and experts agree. This can be a contentious point and there have been cases where one party has feared that there will be an inequality of arms between experts in the discussions. In *H v Lambeth, Southwark and Lewisham Health Authority*,[30] the Court of Appeal refused to allow legal advisers to attend the discussion even where there was a fear that one expert was more experienced than the other and might overawe him.

One idea that was raised by Lady Justice Hale in the case of *H v Lambeth, Southwark and Lewisham Health Authority*, which has excited some judicial interest, particularly in complex multi-party cases, is that a moderator should be appointed to chair the discussions. Although this may involve some cost, in cases where there are numerous experts to coordinate and to bring into the discussions, the appointment of a neutral chair may prove more efficient than leaving the experts to their own, sometimes rather disorganised, devices. In one unreported case a retired circuit judge was appointed as a moderator, and the appointment was regarded as a success. Recorders or accredited mediators may be suitable alternatives.

Thwarted of attendance at discussions, legal advisers sometimes ask for discussions to be taped. This is not so that the discussions can be referred to at trial, as this is not allowed without agreement under CPR, r 35.12, but so that the parties can understand what happened at the discussion and how any changes of opinion were brought about. The objections to taping, however, are similar to the attendance of legal advisers at the discussion. It does not really encourage candid discussion. It is also of limited use. What does a party do with the tape of without prejudice discussions if they do not like what they hear?

The real problem is that it can be very disappointing for a party if 'their' experts fold at a joint discussion, ruining their case, without any proper explanation. A number of complaints to the General Medical Council arise from dissatisfaction from this cause. The masters assigned to clinical negligence actions at the RCJ have addressed this problem in their suggested model directions. They now direct that if an expert radically alters his or her opinion then the joint statement should include a note or addendum by that expert explaining the change of opinion. That should at least identify if that is what the experts thought they were doing. If it was then it should make experts

---

[30]   TLR, 8 October 2001.

consider the matter carefully before changing their opinion. If they do change their opinion the party will have some explanation as to why. It may be that the joint statement has proceeded on a different factual basis than the basis that one expert was proceeding on at the time of an earlier report. This provision should help identify whether the experts really are changing opinions or whether in truth they are setting out different views dependent on the findings of fact made by the court.

ANNEX 1: MODEL DIRECTIONS FOR CLINICAL NEGLIGENCE CASES (2012)

MODEL DIRECTIONS FOR CLINICAL NEGLIGENCE CASES (2012) – before Master Roberts and Master Cook

Introductory note.

These are the Model Directions for use in the first Case Management Conference in clinical negligence cases before the Masters.

A draft order in Word format, adopting the Model Directions as necessary, is to be provided by email to the Master at least 2 days before the hearing.

Parties are required to use the form of order at the end of this document – adapted as necessary. From April 2013 CPR Rule changes will require parties to take as their starting point any relevant Model or Standard Directions.

The changes to the 2010 directions are to be found in paragraphs 4, 9, 10, 11, 19, 23, and 25. The changes are necessary but are not radical.

The email addresses of the clinical negligence Masters are:

master.roberts@judiciary.gsi.gov.uk

master.cook@judiciary.gsi.gov.uk

The Model Directions allow the court and the parties to be flexible. For example, sequential exchange of quantum statements (say, with schedule and counter-schedule of loss) may be appropriate. The sequential exchange of expert evidence on breach of duty and causation may sometimes be appropriate.

It would be helpful if dates appeared in bold type.

Please note: Solicitors must ensure that the claimant is accurately described in the title to the order: e.g., "JOHN SMITH (a child and protected party by his mother and Litigation Friend, JOAN SMITH). It is never permissible to refer to such a claimant as "JOHN SMITH".

The order should make it clear that it is made pursuant to a Case Management Conference or an application or both.

Please note the role of experts in the preparation of Agendas.

THE MODEL DIRECTIONS

The annotations in italics are to assist the parties and are not part of the Model Directions and should not appear in the order.

A draft order – without the annotations – appears at the end of this document. Parties are requested to adopt this draft.

***

Allocation

1. The case do remain on the Multi-track.

Allocation: The order states that "the case do remain on the Multi-track". Allocation may well have been dealt with before the CMC.

Preservation of Evidence

2. The Defendant do retain and preserve safely the original clinical notes relating to the action pending the trial. The Defendant do give facilities for inspection by the Claimant, the Claimant's legal advisers and experts of the said original notes upon 7 days written notice to do so.

Maintenance of records and reports etc

3. Legible copies of the medical (and educational) records of the Claimant / Deceased / Claimant's Mother are to be placed in a separate paginated bundle at the earliest opportunity by the Claimant's Solicitors and kept up to date. All references to medical notes in any report are to be made by reference to the pages in that bundle.

4. The parties do retain all electronically stored documents relating to the claim.

Amendments

The following is suggested:

Permission to Claimant / Defendant to amend the Particulars of Claim / Defence in terms of the draft initialed by the Master [or the draft served on   /   /12]; the Defendant to serve an amended Defence by   /   /12. Costs of and occasioned by the amendments to be borne by (usually, the party seeking permission to amend). [Where no draft is available, but the form of the amendments is not contentious] (Party wishing to amend) to serve draft amended [Statement of Case] by   /   /12. If no objection to the draft amendments, response to be served by   /   /12, if objection is taken to the draft, permission to restore.

Judgment

The following is suggested:

There be judgment for the Claimant with damages to be assessed.

Or

There be judgment for the Claimant for ...% of the damages as are assessed (or agreed by the parties) as due on a full liability basis.

Split Trial

[*An order "That there be a split trial" is inappropriate. The following is suggested.*]

5.   A preliminary issue shall be tried between the Claimant and the Defendant as to whether or not the Defendant is liable to the Claimant by reason of the matters alleged in the Particulars of Claim and, if so, whether or not any of the injuries pleaded were caused thereby; if any such injuries were so caused, the extent of the same.

Disclosure

6.   There be standard disclosure [on the preliminary issue] [limited to quantum] by list by   2012. Any initial request for inspection or copy documents is to be made within 7/14 days of service of the lists.

Where there is a large number of documents all falling into a particular category, the disclosing party may list those documents as a category rather than individually. See: para 3.2 to Practice Direction 31A.

Factual Evidence

7.   Signed and dated witness statements of fact in respect of breach of duty and causation [and quantum] shall be simultaneously exchanged by   2012. Civil Evidence Act notices are to be served by the same date. The witness statements of all concerned with the treatment and care of the Claimant at the time of the matters alleged against the Defendant shall be served under this paragraph.

8.   Signed and dated witness statements of fact in respect of quantum, condition and prognosis shall be served by   2012 (Claimant) and   2012 (Defendant). Civil Evidence Act notices are to be served by the same date.

Expert Evidence.

A.   Single Joint Experts.

9.   Each party has permission to rely on the evidence of a single joint expert in the following fields: *[state the disciplines; and identify the issues*]*. The experts are to be instructed by   2012 and the joint expert is to provide his/her report to the instructing parties by   2012. In case of difficulty, the parties have permission to restore before the Master.

If the parties are unable to agree on the identity of the expert to be instructed, the parties are to restore the CMC before the Master. At such hearing the parties are to provide details of the CVs, availability and the estimated fee of the expert they propose and reasoned objections to any other proposed.

* These words may be deleted where the issues do not have to be defined.

B.   Separate Experts.

10.   In respect of breach of duty and causation, each party has permission to rely on the evidence of an expert in the following fields: *[state the disciplines; and the names of the experts where known]*; permission being given to call the said experts on matters remaining in issue.

The reports of the said experts are to be simultaneously exchanged by   2012.

11.   In respect of quantum, condition and prognosis, each party (*[where there are several defendants]* the Defendants acting jointly, unless otherwise directed) has permission to rely on the evidence of an expert in the following fields: *[state the disciplines; and the name of the experts where known]*; permission being given to call the said experts on matters remaining in issue.

The reports of the said experts are to be served by:

Claimant: 2012
Defendant(s):   2012

Literature and CVs

12.   Any unpublished literature upon which any expert witness proposes to rely shall be served at the same time as service of his report together with a list of published literature. Any supplementary literature upon which any expert witness proposes to rely shall be notified to all other parties at least one month before trial. No expert witness shall rely upon any publications that have not been disclosed in accordance with this direction without the permission of the trial judge on such terms as to costs as he deems fit.

13.   Experts shall, at the time of producing their reports, produce a CV giving details of any employment or activity which raises a possible conflict of interest.

Experts' Discussions

14.   Unless otherwise agreed by all parties' solicitors, after consulting with the experts, the experts of like discipline for the parties shall discuss the case on a without prejudice basis by   2012. *(Usually 8 weeks after the exchange of reports)*.

Discussions between experts are not mandatory. The parties should consider, with their expert, whether there is likely to be any useful purpose in holding a discussion and should be prepared to agree that no discussion is in fact needed.

(a)   The purpose of the discussions is to identify:
    (i)   The extent of the agreement between the experts;
    (ii)   The points of disagreement and short reasons for disagreement;
    (iii) Action, if any, which may be taken to resolve the outstanding points of disagreement;
    (iv)   Any further material points not raised in the Agenda and the extent to which these issues are agreed;

(b)   Unless otherwise agreed by all parties' solicitors, after consulting with the experts, a draft Agenda which directs the experts to the remaining issues relevant to the experts' discipline, as identified in the statements of case shall be prepared jointly by the Claimant's solicitors and experts and sent to the Defendant's solicitors for comment at least 35 days before the agreed date for the experts' discussions;

Claimants' solicitors and counsel should note the obligation to prepare the draft Agenda jointly with the relevant expert. Experts should note that it is part of their overriding duty to the court to ensure that the Agenda complies with the following direction.

The use of agendas is not mandatory. Solicitors should consult with the experts to ensure that agendas are necessary and, if used, are reasonable in scope. The agenda should assist the experts and should not be in the form of leading questions or hostile in tone. An agenda must include a list of the outstanding issues in the preamble.

[Note : The preamble should state: the standard of proof : the Bolam test : remind the experts not to attempt to determine factual issues : remind them not to stray outside their field of expertise and indicate the form of the joint statement. It will also be helpful to provide a comprehensive list of the materials which each expert has seen, perhaps in the form of an agreed supplementary bundle (it is assumed that experts will have been provided with the medical notes bundle)]

(c)   The Defendants shall within 21 days of receipt agree the Agenda, or propose amendments;

(d)   Seven days thereafter all solicitors shall use their best endeavours to agree the Agenda. Points of disagreement should be on matters of real substance and not semantics or on matters the experts could resolve of their own accord at the discussion. In default of agreement, both versions shall be considered at the discussions. Agendas, when used, shall be provided to the experts not less than 7 days before the date fixed for discussions.

[Where it has been impossible to agree a single agenda, it is of assistance to the experts if the second agenda is consecutively numbered to the first, i.e. if the first agenda has 16 questions in it, the second agenda is numbered from 17 onwards]

15.   Unless otherwise ordered by the Court, or unless agreed by all parties, including the experts, neither the parties nor their legal representatives may attend such discussions. If the legal representatives do attend, they should not normally intervene in the discussion, except to answer questions put to them by the experts or to advise on the law; and the experts may if they so wish hold part of their discussions in the absence of the legal representatives.

16.   A signed joint statement shall be prepared by the experts dealing with (a) (i) – (iv) above. Individual copies of such statements shall be signed by the experts at the conclusion of the discussion, or as soon thereafter as practicable and provided to the parties' solicitors within 7 days of the discussions.

17.   Experts give their own opinions to assist the court and should attend discussions on the basis that they have full authority to sign the joint statement. The experts should not require the authorisation of solicitor or counsel before signing a joint statement.

[Note: *This does not affect Rule 35.12 which provides that where experts reach agreement on an issue during their discussions, the agreement shall not bind the parties unless the parties expressly agree to be bound by the agreement*]

18.   If an expert radically alters his or her opinion, the joint statement should include a note or addendum by that expert explaining the change of opinion.

19.   Experts instructed by the parties in accordance with this and any subsequent Order shall be provided with a copy of the Order by the instructing party within 7 days after it is sealed, or at the time of instruction whichever is the later.

Schedules and periodical payments

20.   Claimant do serve a final Schedule of loss and damage costed to the date of trial by   2012.

21.   The Defendant do serve a Counter-Schedule by   2012.

22.   The parties do set out their respective positions on the periodical payment of damages in the Schedule and Counter-Schedule of loss. [or, The periodical payment of damages is not appropriate to this case.]

Periodical Payments. Parties should, at the first CMC, be prepared to give their provisional view as to whether the case is one in which the periodical payment of damages might be appropriate.

Schedules. Parties are encouraged to exchange Schedules in a form which enables the Counter schedule to be based on the Claimant's Schedule i.e. by delivering a disk with the hard copy, or by sending it as an email attachment.]

Trial Directions

23.   The Claimant's Solicitors do by   2012 apply to Queen's Bench Judges' Listing in London / [the Listing Officer in the venue] for a listing appointment for a trial period for hearing within the trial window and give notice of the appointment to the Defendant. Pre-trial check lists to be filed as directed by Queen's Bench Judges' Listing.

Mode of trial: Judge alone; London; Category *[Usually]* B ; time estimate
   days.

Trial window:

[Certified fit for High Court Judge if available].

Trial Directions

The Claimant will usually be directed to apply to the Queen's Bench Judges' Listing for a listing appointment no later than 6 weeks after the CMC.

The Queen's Bench Judges' Listing, in order to maintain the necessary degree of flexibility for listing, will give a 'trial period' rather than a fixed date, but, in order to accommodate the parties' need for certainty as to dates for experts to attend, will, if an approach is made closer to the beginning of the trial period, confirm the date for the trial to begin as the first day of the trial period.

The trial period will usually be directed to begin at least 2 clear months after the last event besides ADR – this is to allow for ADR.

In relatively modest claims (in term of quantum), the Master may direct:

"If the parties reach agreement upon breach of duty and causation, the parties are to immediately restore the case before the Master so that alternative directions on the assessment of damages may be considered."

24.   Parties do agree the contents of the trial bundle and exchange skeleton arguments not less than 7 days before the hearing. Claimant to lodge the skeleton arguments and the Trial bundle under PD 39.3

Trial Bundles

Note: the object is to ensure that all the relevant material is provided at one time to the Clerk of the Lists to pass to the trial judge. The PD sets out both the contents of the bundle and the time when it must be lodged.

Alternative Dispute Resolution

25.   At all stages the parties must consider whether the case is capable of resolution by ADR. Any party refusing to engage in ADR by   2012 *[a date usually about 3 months before the trial window opens]* shall, not less than 28 days before the commencement of the trial, serve a witness statement, without prejudice save as to costs, giving reasons for that refusal. Such witness statement must not be shown to the trial judge until the question of costs arises.

26.   Such means of ADR as shall be adopted shall be concluded not less than 35 days prior to the trial.

[*'ADR' includes 'round table' conferences, at which the parties attempt to define and narrow the issues in the case, including those to which expert evidence is directed; early neutral evaluation; mediation; and arbitration. The object is to try to reduce the number of cases settled 'at the door of the Court', which are wasteful both of costs and judicial time.*]

Further CMC etc

27.   There be a further CMC on   2012 at   am/pm; Room E118/E112; time estimate 30 minutes. This hearing may be vacated by consent provided that all directions have been complied with; no further directions are required; and the Master is given reasonable notice.

28.   Permission to restore.

[*Note: A party may request the restoration of a CMC or application by letter or email to the assigned Master. If possible the Master should be provided with an agreed list of dates to avoid. Where the application is urgent and the time estimate is no more than 30 minutes, the Master will endeavour to list a hearing at 10.00am as soon as possible. Applications estimated to take more than 30 minutes should be applied for as private room appointments in the usual way.*]

[*Both Masters are willing, in appropriate cases, to hear applications by telephone link, provided sufficient notice is given directly to the Master concerned and the relevant papers are provided in advance. Emails are an acceptable means of communication, provided that they are copied to all parties.*]

[*Note: The Court File in cases proceeding before the Masters will not routinely be placed before the Master. Parties wishing for it to be produced should notify the Case Management Section FIVE CLEAR DAYS in advance of the appointment. In all other cases parties should bring with them copies of any filed documents upon which they intend to rely.*]

29.   Costs in case *[Or other costs order sought]*.

30.   Claimant to draw and file the order by   2012 and serve the Defendant (or Claimant to serve sealed order by   2012).

Dated the

DRAFT ORDER

See over

IN THE HIGH COURT OF JUSTICE   Claim No. HQ012X0ZZZZ
QUEEN'S BENCH DIVISION
MASTER [ROBERTS / COOK]

B E T W E E N:

ABC

Claimant

– and –

DEF NHS TRUST

Defendant

ORDER

UPON a Case Management Conference

[AND UPON the Claimant's / Defendant's application issued on   2012]

AND UPON hearing solicitor/counsel for the Claimant and solicitor/counsel for the Defendant

IT IS ORDERED that

1   The case do remain on the Multi-track.

2   The Defendant do retain and preserve safely the original clinical notes relating to the claim pending the trial. The Defendant do give facilities for

inspection by the Claimant, the Claimant's legal advisers and experts of the said original notes upon 7 days written notice to do so.

3   Legible copies of the medical (and educational) records of the Claimant / Deceased / Claimant's Mother are to be placed in a separate paginated bundle at the earliest opportunity by the Claimant's Solicitors and kept up to date. All references to medical notes in any report are to be made by reference to the pages in that bundle.

4   The parties do retain all electronically stored documents relating to the claim.

5   A preliminary issue shall be tried between the Claimant and the Defendant as to whether or not the Defendant is liable to the Claimant by reason of the matters alleged in the Particulars of Claim and, if so, whether or not any of the injuries pleaded were caused thereby; if any such injuries were so caused, the extent of the same.

6   There be standard disclosure [on the preliminary issue] [limited to quantum] by list by   2012. Any initial request for inspection or copy documents is to be made within 7/14 days of service of the lists.

7   Signed and dated witness statements of fact in respect of breach of duty and causation [and quantum] shall be simultaneously exchanged by   2012. Civil Evidence Act notices are to be served by the same date. The witness statements of all concerned with the treatment and care of the Claimant at the time of the matters alleged against the Defendant shall be served under this paragraph.

8   Signed and dated witness statements of fact in respect of quantum, condition and prognosis shall be served by   2012 (Claimant) and   2012 (Defendant). Civil Evidence Act notices are to be served by the same date.

9   Each party has permission to rely on the evidence of a single joint expert in the following fields: *[state the disciplines; and identify the issues]*. The experts are to be instructed by   2012 and the joint expert is to provide his report to the instructing parties by   2012. In case of difficulty, the parties have permission to restore before the Master.

10   In respect of breach of duty and causation, each party has permission to rely on the evidence of an expert in the following fields: *[state the disciplines; and the names of the experts, where known]*; permission being given to call the said experts on matters remaining in issue. The reports of the said experts are to be simultaneously exchanged by   2012.

11   In respect of quantum, condition and prognosis, each party (*[where there are several defendants]* the Defendants acting jointly, unless otherwise directed) has permission to rely on the evidence of an expert in the following fields: *[state*

the disciplines; and the names of the experts, where known]; permission being given to call the said experts on matters remaining in issue. The reports of the said experts are to be served by:

Claimant: 2012; Defendant(s):   2012.

12   Any unpublished literature upon which any expert witness proposes to rely shall be served at the same time as service of his report together with a list of published literature. Any supplementary literature upon which any expert witness proposes to rely shall be notified to all other parties at least one month before trial. No expert witness shall rely upon any publications that have not been disclosed in accordance with this direction without the permission of the trial judge on such terms as to costs as he deems fit.

13   Experts shall, at the time of producing their reports, produce a CV giving details of any employment or activity which raises a possible conflict of interest.

14   Unless otherwise agreed by all parties' solicitors, after consulting with the experts, the experts of like discipline for the parties shall discuss the case on a without prejudice basis by   2012.

Discussions between experts are not mandatory. The parties should consider, with their expert, whether there is likely to be any useful purpose in holding a discussion and should be prepared to agree that no discussion is in fact needed.

(a)   The purpose of the discussions is to identify:
   (i)   The extent of the agreement between the experts;
   (ii)   The points of disagreement and short reasons for disagreement;
   (iii) Action, if any, which may be taken to resolve the outstanding points of disagreement;
   (iv)   Any further material points not raised in the Agenda and the extent to which these issues are agreed;

(b)   **Unless otherwise agreed by all parties' solicitors, after consulting with the experts,** a draft Agenda which directs the experts to the remaining issues relevant to the experts' discipline, as identified in the statements of case shall be prepared jointly by the Claimant's solicitors and experts and sent to the Defendant's solicitors for comment at least 35 days before the agreed date for the experts' discussions;

The use of agendas is not mandatory. Solicitors should consult with the experts to ensure that agendas are necessary and, if used, are reasonable in scope. The agenda should assist the experts and should not be in the form of leading questions or hostile in tone. An agenda must include a list of the outstanding issues in the preamble.

(c)   The Defendants shall within 21 days of receipt agree the Agenda, or propose amendments;

(d)   Seven days thereafter all solicitors shall use their best endeavours to agree the Agenda. Points of disagreement should be on matters of real substance and not semantics or on matters the experts could resolve of their own accord at the discussion. In default of agreement, both versions shall be considered at the discussions. Agendas, when used, shall be provided to the experts not less than 7 days before the date fixed for discussions.

15. **Unless otherwise ordered by the Court, or unless agreed by all parties, including the experts,** neither the parties nor their legal representatives may attend such discussions. If the legal representatives do attend, they should not normally intervene in the discussion, except to answer questions put to them by the experts or to advise on the law; and the experts may if they so wish hold part of their discussions in the absence of the legal representatives.

16. A signed joint statement shall be prepared by the experts dealing with (a) (i) – (iv) above. Individual copies of such statements shall be signed by the experts at the conclusion of the discussion, or as soon thereafter as practicable and provided to the parties' solicitors within 7 **days** of the discussions.

17. Experts give their own opinions to assist the court and should attend discussions on the basis that they have full authority to sign the joint statement. The experts should not require the authorisation of solicitor or counsel before signing a joint statement.

18. If an expert radically alters his or her opinion, the joint statement should include a note or addendum by that expert explaining the change of opinion.

19. Experts instructed by the parties in accordance with this and any subsequent Order shall be provided with a copy of the Order by the instructing party within 7 days after it is sealed, or at the time of instruction, whichever is the later.

20. Claimant do serve a final Schedule of loss and damage costed to the date of trial by   2012.

21. The Defendant do serve a Counter-Schedule by   2012.

22. The parties do set out their respective positions on the periodical payment of damages in the Schedule and Counter-Schedule of loss.

23. The Claimant's Solicitors do by   2012 apply to Queen's Bench Judges' Listing in London / [the Listing Officer in the venue] for a listing appointment for a trial period for hearing within the trial window and give notice of the appointment to the Defendant. Pre-trial check lists to be filed as directed by Queen's Bench Judges' Listing.

Mode of trial: Judge alone; London; Category *[Usually]* B ; time estimate   days.

Trial window:

[Certified fit for High Court Judge if available].

24.   Parties do agree the contents of the trial bundle and exchange skeleton arguments not less than 7 days before the hearing. Claimant to lodge the skeleton arguments and the Trial bundle under PD 39.3

25.   At all stages the parties must consider whether the case is capable of resolution by ADR. Any party refusing to engage in ADR by   2012 *[a date usually about 3 months before the trial window opens]* shall, not less than 28 days before the commencement of the trial, serve a witness statement, without prejudice save as to costs, giving reasons for that refusal. Such witness statement must not be shown to the trial judge until the question of costs arises.

26.   Such means of ADR as shall be adopted shall be concluded not less than 35 days prior to the trial.

27.   There be a further CMC on   2012 at   am/pm; Room E118/E112; time estimate 30 minutes. This hearing may be vacated by consent provided that all directions have been complied with; no further directions are required; and the Master is given reasonable notice.

28.   Permission to restore.

29.   Costs in case *[Or other costs order sought]*.

30.   Claimant to draw and file the order by   2012 and serve the Defendant (or Claimant to serve sealed order by   2012).

Dated the

ANNEX 2: LETTER OF INSTRUCTION

Our ref:

Your ref:

[date]

Dear

Re: *A Claimant v A Defendant*

Further to your letter of [   ] confirming that you are able to accept instructions in this matter I am now writing to commission a report from you in this case dealing with [*my client's injuries and prognosis/causation of my client's injuries/the accommodation/orthotic needs/or as appropriate*] [*from a [neurological/as appropriate] perspective*].

Nature of Instructions

[Please note that in this case you are instructed to prepare a report for the court on behalf of the [*Claimant/Defendant*]. *This is not a joint instruction.*

or

[Please note that in this case you are instructed by both parties as a single joint expert. This means that you must please ensure that copies of all reports and correspondence are forwarded both to this office and to the [*Claimant's/Defendant's*] legal advisers. Their details are:-

[*Name, address and ref. of other party's Solicitors*]

Enclosures

I enclose herewith a bundle of documents for your consideration as particularised on the attached index/schedule of documents. These documents include [the Claimant's medical records that have been obtained, the witness statements of x and y, and the reports that have already been obtained from AC and B].

If you need any further information, including medical and/or educational records, to enable you to prepare your report in this case, then please let me know as soon as possible.

Nature of Report Requested

By way of introduction it is the Claimant's case in this matter that [   ]. The Defendants position is [   ]. I would ask you to please contact [*AC/AC's mother*] in order to arrange to see and assess/examine AC. The contact details are [   ]. Thereafter please provide a report in accordance with the following summary of your instructions:

[*Insert here a brief summary of the questions that the expert is being asked to give an opinion on.*]

Example 1

1. Please provide a brief summary as to the events which occurred at and around the time of AC's birth and subsequently.

2. Please provide a summary of the [neurological/as appropriate] disabilities AC exhibited following her birth.

3. Please provide information as to how those [neurological/as appropriate] disabilities progressed/developed and, in particular, how they have affected AC's activities of daily living and her need to rely upon input and support from others.

4. Please provide an up to date current position of AC's [neurological/as appropriate] disabilities, setting out what form they take and how they affect her activities of daily living.

5. Please provide a prognosis setting out how you consider her [neurological/as appropriate] disabilities will progress/develop in the future, how they are likely to affect her activities of living, her dependency upon others and her ability to live independently.

6. Please give your estimate of life expectancy with the reasoning therefore including any statistical sources.

Example 2

1. Can and should any adaptations be made to the present accommodation? If so:–
   a) What form should they take?
   b) What would be the purpose of such adaptations?
   c) What would be the cost of providing for them?

2. Do you recommend that the Claimant moves to alternative accommodation and if so, when?

3. If a move is recommended, please let us know where you consider would be reasonable for the Claimant to live. Also, please let us know the cost of purchasing suitable accommodation, bearing in mind the disabilities suffered by the Claimant and also the make-up of the family unit.

➡

4. Please provide a breakdown of the costs of such a move including, where appropriate, removal fees, legal fees, etc.

5. Please include details as to the approximate cost of purchasing an alternative more suitable property. If possible, please include a number of property particulars to support the assessment as to capital cost involved in purchasing alternative accommodation.

6. Please provide a breakdown as to the costs of adapting alternative accommodation, showing where appropriate capital costs and where appropriate VAT.

7. Please include details of the additional annual, running costs of alternative accommodation. These of course must be over and above 'normal' household costs that would have been incurred in any event. It is of course only the additional incurred as a result of A's disabilities which led to the move which can be recovered within the context of the claim.

8. If there are any other costs associated with the move, the acquisition of alternative accommodation, the running costs of that accommodation or any other outlays that should be included, either capital or repeat costs, then please include these in your report.

Scope of your Report

1. Please focus upon the [*nature and extent of disabilities*] that fall within your particularly area of expertise.

2. There is no need for you to consider the areas of [*as appropriate*] [*as liability/that issue has been agreed/these issues will be covered by other experts in the appropriate fields*].

3. *Please include in your assessment whether you consider AC should undergo regular neurological review. If so:–*
   a) How often?
   b) What form should this take?
   c) What should be the aims and objectives?
   d) What would be the cost of this neurological review if undertaken on a private, fee-paying, basis?

4. If there are any other aspects of the [*Claimant's disabilities*] that you consider should be addressed in your report then please do so.

5. If you consider that there are other fields of medical opinion that should be sought then please indicate the relevant field or fields.

I hope that you are clear as to the nature of the report that is requested. If not, please let me know as soon as possible.

Fee

Our client agrees to pay the fee that you have previously quoted for examination of our client and preparation of your report namely [£   ]

inclusive of vat. [We understand that in the event of further reports, joint discussions or attendance at conferences or court the basis of your charging would be [   ], with cancellation fees in the event that [   ]]. I would be grateful if you would provide me with an invoice upon delivery of your report.

The Proceedings

In this case proceedings have not yet been issued [and what we require at present is a preliminary report that will not be disclosed without further reference to you].

Or

In this case proceedings have been issued in the [court] and a copy of the order of that court dated [   ] relating to the evidence we are seeking from you is enclosed. You will notice that [*the trial window is confirmed at between [   ] and [   ] and we would be grateful for your dates of availability within that window*] [*the trial has been fixed for [date] and we are grateful for your confirmation that you are able to attend on that date and have marked your diary accordingly*].

Civil Procedure Rules

We would remind you that the instruction of experts in cases such as this is governed by Part 35 of the Civil procedure Rules, the Practice Direction thereto and the Protocol for Instruction of Experts, and I [*am grateful for your confirmation that you are familiar with these provisions/ enclose copies of these three documents for your perusal prior to completing your report/ enclose a note that I have drawn up for the guidance of experts*]. Further guidance can be obtained from the publication 'APIL Guide to Catastrophic Injury Claims'.

Specifically Part 35 provides that:

> Rule 35(3): It is the duty of an expert to help the Court on the matters within her expertise. This duty overrides any obligation to the person from whom the expert has received instructions or by whom she is paid.

Your report must contain a statement that you understand your duty to the court and that you have complied, and will continue to comply, with that duty. It must also be verified by a declaration in the following terms:

> 'I confirm that I have made clear which facts and matters referred to in this report are within my own knowledge and which are not. Those that are within my own knowledge I confirm to be true. The opinions I have expressed represent my true and complete professional opinions on the matters to which they refer.'

In the event that you should discover that you have any potential conflict of interest in this matter, whether by reason of any close personal or professional association with any of the doctors concerned in this case or otherwise, then you should inform me of that fact immediately but continue to respect the duty of confidence that is applies to the delivery of these instructions.

[*I am grateful for the CV that you have already provided to me, but in accordance with the Court requirements, would you please ensure that when you provide your report you attach a copy of your latest CV.*]

I thank you once again for agreeing to accept these instructions. I look forward to receiving your report by the [   ]. If any part of these instructions is unclear, or I can be of any further assistance then please do not hesitate to contact me using the contact details at the head of this letter.

Yours sincerely

ANNEX 3: AGENDA

IN THE . . . . COURT   Claim No ....

B E T W E E N:

A .... Claimant

Claimant

– and –

A .... Defendant

Defendant

[AGREED] AGENDA
FOR [Field of Expertise] EXPERTS'
DISCUSSIONS

PREAMBLE: PLEASE READ THIS PREAMBLE

1. Experts' Duty

The experts are reminded of their duty under the Court's Civil Procedure Rule relating to the duty of an expert:

Rule 35(3): It is the duty of an expert to help the Court on the matters within her expertise. This duty overrides any obligation to the person from whom the expert has received instructions or by whom she is paid.

2. Discussion between experts

In accordance with Civil Procedure Rule 35.12 the Court has in this case directed a discussion to take place between experts. A copy of the court order is enclosed. The purpose of the order is to require you as experts to:

a)　identify the issues in the proceedings; and

b)　where possible reach agreement on the issues.

The Court has further directed that following the discussion they must prepare a statement for the Court showing:

c)　those issues on which they agree; and

d)　those issues on which they disagree and a summary of their reasons for disagreeing;

e)　[What action, if any, may be taken to resolve the outstanding points of disagreement;]

f)　[Any further material points not raised in this agenda and the extent to which these issues are agreed.]

The content of the <u>discussion</u> between the experts shall not be referred to at the trial unless the parties agree (ie, the <u>contents</u> of the discussion, as opposed to the agreed statement which is prepared following the discussion). It follows that the discussion between experts is 'without prejudice', but thereafter the statement which the experts draw up and agree will be lodged with the Court and will be referred to at any trial.

It will be helpful to the Court if the joint statement is in the form of a schedule setting out the respective positions of the experts. It should be understood that there is no pressure upon the experts to reach a consensus – an expert should only agree to a statement that genuinely represents his or her own views. However, that said, an expert must feel free to modify previously expressed views if s/he feels it is appropriate to do so having considered colleagues' opinions. It is helpful [and required by the order dated ....] for experts to explain in the joint statement why they are changing their opinion if they do so.

Your Joint Statement should be supported by the same declaration as your earlier reports, namely, that for each of you:

> 'I confirm that I have made clear which facts and matters referred to in this report are within my own knowledge and which are not. Those that are within my own knowledge I confirm to be true. The opinions I have expressed represent my true and complete professional opinions on the matters to which they refer.'

3. Relevance

The experts are reminded that in General Medical Council v Meadow, [2006] EWCA Civ 1390, the Court of Appeal emphasised the importance of experts only expressing opinions that are relevant to the issues and within their field of expertise. Further, the Master of the Rolls emphasised that it is for the parties legal representatives, and ultimately for the judge, to identify before and at trial what evidence, lay or expert, admissible and what is not. In relation to expert evidence he said:

> 'it is critical that the legal representatives of the party proposing to rely on such evidence should ensure that the witness's written and oral evidence is confined to his expertise and is relevant and admissible to the important issues in the case on which he has been asked to assist. Equally it is incumbent on the legal representatives on the other side not to encourage, in the form of cross-examination or otherwise, an expert to give opinion evidence which is irrelevant to those issues and/or outside his expertise, and, therefore, inadmissible.'

4. Material

We enclose a schedule [supplementary/agreed bundle where appropriate] of the material that you should have in order to form the basis for your opinions.

5.   Factual disputes

Where there is a dispute between <u>factual</u> witnesses as to what happened then it is not the role of an expert to resolve such a dispute. Factual dispute is a matter for the Trial Judge. It may, however, be helpful to the Trial Judge to identify the material facts upon which findings of fact need to be made. If there are findings of fact on which opinions depend then please identify those finding of fact for the Court to make. You should feel free to comment on factual issues where your expertise may assist the Court in determining or interpreting the facts correctly.

6.   Breach of duty

When expressing a liability opinion in a clinical negligence context, the requisite standard of care, is that which would, at the time, have been accepted by a responsible body of professional opinion in the relevant field (the "Bolam" test). You should state if there is a range of acceptable practice or schools of thought.

7.   Causation

The Claimant must establish that the breach of duty that is alleged caused harm. This must be established on "a balance of probabilities" ie "more likely than not". [A possibility, or the loss of a chance will not suffice.]

8.   Timing

The Court has ordered that your Joint Statement be prepared by the [date].

ISSUES FOR DISCUSSION

1.   Have you read the above pre-amble?
2.   . . . .

CHAPTER 8

CARE AND CASE MANAGER EXPERTISE

*Maggie Sargent**

8.1 THE ROLE OF A CARE EXPERT

In all catastrophic injuries there will be a need for the care expert to assess past, present and future care needs. These care needs may range from emotional support for clients with brain injury, which is also known as the 'hidden disability', to direct physical help with all activities of daily living that clients with spinal injury may need. It is the role of the care expert to assess the need for past, present and future care and support. The report of the expert details hours and pay rates, which form the basis of the care claim. In order to do this it is necessary for the nursing consultant to visit the client either at home or in hospital or nursing home to assess the claimant's situation. Where the case involves a child, the role is more complex and may involve visiting the family, the case manager (if one is in post) and teachers. Clients with pre-existing problems are the most difficult of all to assess because it is necessary to establish what levels of support they needed beforehand, although it does not always follow that where professional care has become necessary due to a defendant's negligence credit will have to be given for pre-existing gratuitous care, see *Sklair v Haycock*.[1]

8.2 RELATIONSHIP OF CARE CONSULTANT/CASE MANAGER

The role of the care assessor is to try to provide an independent assessment of future care. I reiterate the views of Lord Blackburn, made 100 years ago that:

> 'The principle of the law is that consideration should as nearly as possible put the party who has suffered in the same position as he would have been if he had not sustained the wrong.'

Therefore it is necessary to obtain a very clear history of the situation both before and after the incident so as to be able to compare the claimant's life as it was before and as it is after the index event. This is possible only by visiting the claimant to form a relationship with the him or her and the family and to see their environment and thus assess and evaluate their care needs and really understand the position they are in. There can be confusion about the roles of

* Maggie Sargent & Associates, Darlingscott Farm, Darlingscott, Shipston on Stour, Warwickshire CV36 4PN.
[1] [2009] EWHC 3328.

the case manager and the care expert, and there is a clear difference. The care expert is either jointly or singly instructed to provide an 'expert report' on the care needs of the client. The claimant's case manager, whilst they may be expert in their own right, is *not* an expert witness in the case, but is instructed to provide an immediate-needs assessment in the first instance followed by a case management plan for rehabilitation, and it is not part of their role to comment on longer-term support of the client. In the personal injury court proceedings the case manager's role is one of providing factual evidence, and to guide the court, and this evidence is treated in a similar way to medical notes with full disclosure to both sides. The case management notes should include goals and objectives with details of reviews and activities carried out.

The roles of 'care expert' and 'case manager' are closely linked, and it is of note that many of the better-known care experts also work as case managers in care claims for clients. They are probably best placed to provide evidence on care costs because of the experience they have in the field of case management. The care expert must be suitably professionally qualified to be able to provide a detailed analysis of the client's care needs and must also have years of relevant working experience in the field that they are reporting on to the court. They need to be able to offer an independent assessment of the roles of the case manager, carers and their rehabilitation programme and they cannot do this if they lack the relevant experience. The danger of failing to provide independent advice is that, as happened in one recent case, the judge might conclude that the care expert is not really giving expert evidence on the care needs of the client, but instead is merely underwriting an existing care package without really challenging the necessity for the care package. In *C v Dixon*,[2] King J made exactly this finding. Similarly, in *Loughlin v Singh*,[3] the judgeKenneth Parker J found that the care and case management fell significantly below the standard that could reasonably be expected. In other words the objective value of what the claimant received was less than the amount of the charges made for the relevant services, and the judge made a reduction of 20% of the charges actually claimed. This left the claimant in the difficult position that he may need to look at recovering the loss from the case management company.

8.3   DETAILS OF INSTRUCTIONS

In order to provide in-depth assessment of need, it is necessary for the care expert to have adequate information and this includes medical reports, notes and written witness statements. In addition, detailed diaries for day care and night care are often necessary. Additional information will depend upon the exact nature of the client's disabilities and can include social services records, school reports, copies of benefit applications and case management notes. There may be independent nursing logs provided by paid carers or family diaries of a more narrative nature. Family can be just as involved in looking after clients who are suffering from a brain injury, but care needs are less

---

[2]   [2009] EWHC 708.
[3]   [2013] EWHC 1641.

obvious because they are suffering from cognitive impairment and have no physical needs. Similarly, this client group may need to have very high levels of case management yet relatively little support from carers. There are clients who will not engage with support workers and need to use a flexible, on-call service, as provided by case managers 24 hours a day. Many case managers offer this service, and this is usually necessary for those clients with little insight into their situation and who are importunate and create major crises. The case manager needs to form a close working relationship with the client and in some instances it will be necessary for a client and/or the family and medical advisers to interview several case managers before they appoint one. Considering the long-term nature of the appointment, it is perfectly reasonable to expect case managers to attend the first interview on a gratuitous basis, when the client decides whom to appoint as their case manager. Costs are in the region of £95 to £100 an hour (at August 2013), which is a therapeutic rate, and therefore all costs will be carefully scrutinised by the courts.

8.4 PAST CARE

On the subject of assessing children there has been much discussion as to the value of having a breakdown of figures for 'the normal care for children' and most experts have their own baseline figures, but to date it has not been possible to agree 'standard hours'. Children are very difficult to assess because the expert has to look at *all* of the stages of life, ie infancy, childhood, adolescence, adulthood and parenthood, and the consequences of the client deteriorating. Medical evidence is key, and account now tends to be taken of the years post-incident as opposed to actual age-bands for probable deterioration. From experience, the more physically damaged a client is, the less contentious are the care issues because of the undoubted high degree of support necessary. In the case of *Stevens*, in which I was involved in 1994, the issue of normal hours of care for a child was put forward by the defendants and a case made to deduct these from the care necessary for the future. However, it was accepted by the judge that because in this case the client was one of three children there should be no deduction from future care for 'normal hours of care' because it was impossible for parents to provide normal care in this case. This was confirmed in *Iqbal v Whipps Cross NHS Trust*;[4] Sir Rodger Bell came to the same conclusion, that in the case of a severely damaged child there is no such thing as a deduction for 'normal hours' when looking at future care for a child who needs 24-hour care, often from more than one carer.

Past care rates for gratuitous care and support are often an issue, and opinions diverge as to the appropriate rate between those who suggest the standard rate and those who recommend the aggregate rate. A major problem is that care experts are often attempting to use one standard rate to reflect all types of care within all areas of the country. Pay rates for experienced carers in catastrophic cases can vary from between £8 an hour and £15 an hour, and it is therefore very difficult to use one rate to reflect past rates. The standard National Joint

---

[4]   [2006] EWHC 3111 (QB).

Council Spinal Point 8 rate is much lower now than the rates paid to carers in so many of the cases, and it is something that needs to be reviewed. If the care expert is to try to reflect the 'commercial pay rate', as in *Housecroft v Burnett*,[5] then it makes sense for all experts to adopt the aggregate rate. This is an hourly pay rate calculated as an average of the weekday, weekend, and night-time rates, and in 2013 this is £9.24 an hour. Because there is no agreement on this, the different approaches are looked at on a case-by-case basis. There is a problem with the current system because, when looking at past care figures, we can see that the disparity between past care rates and future rates is too high and the current past care rates are just too low to reflect the levels of care provided in catastrophic cases.

8.5   ASSESSING FUTURE CARE NEEDS

Hours of care do need to be carefully evaluated and not just because they are being used specifically for support for the periods of past care, but also because they are a benchmark for future care. The assessment for past care should incorporate an estimate of just how many carers are necessary for each task. This then leads on to the future, and an assessment can be made of how many carers will be necessary to provide paid support in future. Furthermore, when we look at current Working Time Regulations, we can no longer expect carers to work excessively long hours and be on call day and night. A common-sense approach to assessment would in any event not allow for carers to work either day shifts or night shifts if there is need for regular night care, and it is generally accepted that a carer should not be asked to work both day and night. Details of the night care necessary should be carefully noted in a night log, and this would be clear then to any judge that there is night care involved. Usually a sleep-in carer is all that is required – this is a carer sleeping close by, who is paid, for example, for 6 hours to be on call for 10 hours. This is reassuring for the family and the patient even though the latter would need attention no more than twice a night and usually less often. Where more night care is necessary, a waking night carer has to be on duty and is paid for every hour worked.

Similarly, the issue of double-handling (that is whether one or two carers are needed to effect a manoeuvre or to help a client with some activity) often causes debate. This is a matter for 'risk assessment', and all care experts reporting on a catastrophic injury case should be trained in this area because they are having to make educated guesses for the future as to how many carers are going to be needed for manual handling purposes. Even when a mechanical hoist is used, two carers may be necessary, and this happens particularly when a client has strong spasms, which can put both client and carer at risk. From necessity the general risk assessment will be the first stage for any newly appointed case manager, who will then be able to provide relevant evidence as to the current situation. However, a more scientific approach is often needed for the future and looking at the equipment and therapy reports is necessary as well as discussing future accommodation with the relevant expert. This all needs to be

---

[5]   [1986] 1 All ER 332.

carefully checked by the care consultant to ensure that all measures have been exhausted before stating that a client is going to need double-handling in the future. In *Wakeling v MIB*,[6] the judgment confirmed that where a client needs to have two carers for all manual handling and where this means that there is one carer who is under-utilised, so be it, because the need for handling by two carers is unpredictable. One example of this problem is with toileting.

The role of the care expert will not be confined to reviewing domiciliary care options when assessing where the client will be living in future. It will often be necessary for care experts to evaluate any residential care that may be available for clients and the expert will have to form an opinion as to whether or not it is reasonable for a client to be discharged home. All care homes are registered, and therefore it is possible to obtain copies of the registration inspections, and discussions should take place with all interested parties to ensure that the best interests of the client are taken into account. Similarly, care in the residential unit needs to be reviewed and there will be cases when it is deemed necessary for clients to stay in a unit, but to have one-to-one or two-to-one staffing available to them. This can be difficult to organise if the staff are not part of the care home team, and it can be necessary to pay the home to increase their staffing levels so that it can cope. A case manager may also be necessary in these cases to provide specialist support to the home.

Over the years there has been much discussion as to whether it is in a client's best interest to leave a residential setting and move on and live in his or her own accommodation. An assessment may have been made by the defendant for the client to be looked after in residential care, and this has been argued out in court in a number of cases. In *Romy Smith v NHSLA*[7] and *Andre Crofton v East & North Hertfordshire Hospitals Trust*,[8] the courts provided judgments as to the best interest of the client and where they should be cared for. A care expert will look at whether or not it is 'safe' to do so, and it is for the medical experts to underpin their recommendations when looking at the evidence as a whole. There are clients who are best cared for in a group home situation and some of them may need extra support to help them have a proper quality of life and this may not be covered by the normal costs of funding a placement. These issues can often be difficult to 'bottom out' because the staff who work in the group home need to be seen to be providing a quality service that is cost-effective. Quality of life is very important, and this means that proactive carers should be looking after the client and that the client should not be left unable to follow activities just for the want of sometimes quite simple equipment or lack of one-to-one care.

Assessing future care is only the first part of the care expert's job. Next the care has to be costed at appropriate rates based on the type of care and the geographical area. Agency care is fairly simple because the expert uses the published client rates of the agency and adds some on-costs for food and

---

[6]   [2007] EWHC 1201.
[7]   [2008] EWHC 2234.
[8]   [2007] EWCA 71.

travelling where necessary. But direct-hire care packages have to take into account the carers' holidays, bank holidays, sickness, and staff training and so are currently calculated at 60 weeks a year. Then the various costs of running the regime have to be added. These include Employer's National Insurance (ERNIC) and allowances for food and related expenses, recruitment advertising, insurance, cost of training, pension contribution and payroll. Sometimes a team leader at an enhanced rate is part of the package and in nearly all cases provision must be made for a case manager.

Whiten v St George's Healthcare NHS Trust of 5 August 2011[9] is a very important case because Swift J. provided a detailed explanation of the thought process behind assessing the need for future care throughout the span of a client's life. The care costs were reviewed and comment made on all of the additional expenses and specifically costs of holidays and other recreational activities.

Further guidance on the presentation of care claims is provided in Chapters 17, 18 and 19.

8.6   LONG-TERM MANAGEMENT OF CLIENTS

Over the last 30 to 40 years, experience has built up on how to manage spinal injury clients and much research has taken place. However, acquired brain injury is still the least understood and most under-estimated area. There is very little research on the long-term management of these clients in the community and, with 20 years of brain injury case management, this research is only just now becoming feasible. There are recognised assessment tools, but they have difficulty in recording the need for prompting and this is best illustrated by using the risk assessment tool. There has been some discussion over the use of risk assessments when managing clients with an acquired injury, and currently there are no standardised documents available in the same way that there are for manual handling risk assessments. The Care Quality Commission, who regulate many case managers, will visit those who are registered with them and will meet their clients and ask the case manager to go through risk assessments and documentation on the service. They will assess the standard of the service on the basis of both the risk assessment process and feedback from the clients. All case managers must regularly review the risk assessments and document each review date.

Cases have gone to court because there has been a question about the effectiveness of the case manager. The solicitor can arrange for the care assessor to spend time with the case manager, either at the assessment or shortly afterwards. In all cases the case management notes should be fully disclosable, and in the case of *Wright v Sullivan*,[10] it was confirmed that the case manager has a technical role not dissimilar to the GP's. Therefore the assessment and

---

[9]   [2011] EWHC 2066.
[10]   [2005] EWCA 656.

notes are disclosable to both parties and are not legally privileged. Difficulties can be experienced when the case manager has not fully documented aims and objectives because he or she may not have the experience or may not have the information to provide for evidence. Goals need to be SMART (specific, measurable, achievable, realistic and time-based) and they need to include family, case manager, client and therapists if they are to be effective in the home environment.

The case manager will be held responsible by the court if the rehabilitation is felt to have been ineffective and not to have served the client's best interests, and more and more the role of the case manager is coming under the courts' scrutiny. Rightly so because the case manager is responsible and has a duty of care to provide an appropriate service for the client and to ensure that optimum progress is made. The case manager needs to review the situation if good progress is not being achieved and needs to take the appropriate actions. Quality of life is important and there is research detailing these issues for clients with acquired brain injury, who need the support of a companion/carer, often known as a buddy, because they are not motivated by themselves to take part in life's activities. It is very difficult for care experts to provide a proper assessment unless they are adequately prepared with copies of all the case management and carers' notes. With these they can then judge how worthwhile the case management and the input of the support package are see *Loughlin v Singh*, *above.*

8.7   CASE MANAGEMENT STANDARDS

There is no professional qualification for case managers and they currently have a professional registration in either nursing, occupational therapy, physiotherapy or social work. The British Association of Brain Injury Case Managers (BABICM) has set various standards and all advanced members have undergone a peer review. However, if a case manager is negligent and does not hold a professional qualification, there is no recourse if the services are not up to standard. It is hoped that the Health Professions Council (HPC) will in future offer a form of registration. All case managers should before taking on a new case be able to provide criminal record checks (CRBs) and also up-to-date references from clients they are currently working with. The UK has led Europe in advancing case management, and many European countries are now looking at the UK model as a way of developing their own rehabilitation services.

8.8   CASE MANAGEMENT PLAN

When a case manager has been engaged and has fully assessed the client's need, taking into account the assessments of the treating therapists, he or she should then provide an overall case management plan. This should include short-term costs and an action plan to meet the goals. The costs should be realistic for a budget to be agreed, and, if the budgeted hours and costs increase from those in the original plan, there should be written evidence as to why they have increased. Case management is now being provided for clients who have cerebral palsy, spinal injury and have lost a limb or had severe orthopaedic injuries, and these clients will all have capacity and will therefore be responsible for paying for services. Interim funds are provided on account for clients, and the case manager is responsible for insuring that a cost-effective service is being provided. Case management costs are based on therapeutic costs, and a support package should be closely monitored to include case management costs, and it is not reasonable to charge case management rates for jobs that are clearly administrative or clerical, when it is not necessary for a case manager to undertake the tasks.

Part of the role of the case manager is to look at cost-effective solutions to managing the client in the longer term. If a client lives in a remote location, this could include appointing an assistant case manager or it may be necessary for the client to visit the case manager on occasion. There are no hard and fast rules, and one case management company states on its website that they will do 'whatever it takes' and this sums up how case management works. In all cases, however, there should be an active plan, and all possible attempts should be made to provide effective rehabilitation. The goal of the rehabilitation is to help the client return to the highest levels of function and independence as possible while improving the overall clarity of life physically, emotionally, and socially, and this means engaging the relevant professionals for therapy in a timely and cost-effective manner.

8.9   IMPLEMENTING THE CARE PLAN

The case manager will be looking at accommodation, equipment and therapy because in some cases it is not possible to set up a care package until these issues have been sorted out. Some managers choose to use an agency, and then a Care Quality Commission (CQC) report should be obtained, and the case manager should ensure that they are recruiting the right levels of support for the client. There are cases where a trained nurse is needed because the agency organising the care cannot obtain the right level of insurance to take on an extended role for their support workers. Trained nurses are needed in cases where there is intense nursing care with procedures such as deep suction and naso-gastric feeding. Also clients suffering from brittle epilepsy may need a nurse's clinical judgment to administer medication. Many clients living at home and dependent on a ventilator to breathe do not need 24-hour nursing care because they can be looked after by skilled healthcare assistants taking on an extended role. In the longer term employing carers directly may be organised by the case manager with the client, the deputy or the client's family acting as the employer.

Case managers can now be registered with the CQC, which has extended the case management role, although not all local authorities will regulate case managers. The case manager takes over from the agency and recruits carers, organises their training and regularly appraises them, and this gives the client security. Furthermore, the CQC take up references from clients and provide a full report and evaluation of the case manager's services, and this is available to the public on the internet and is updated every year. When clients needs 24-hour support, there has to be emergency back-up to support them and their care teams. This is included in the basic case management costs and there is usually one case manager on call at all times to answer a telephone and be available in case of an emergency. This can be acutely necessary when the client has an acquired brain injury and is unpredictable, and the case manager has to provide very high levels of support. With mobile telephones this support network is much more easily available now and is a necessary part of the service to the clients or their representatives.

8.10   EVALUATING THE CASE MANAGEMENT PLAN: JOINT DISCUSSIONS

When the two care experts (claimant's and defendant's) have completed their reports, they will be expected to have a joint discussion. This is usually done by telephone or it can be done in person, and solicitors often now provide an agenda. It is important that each care expert has copies of all the relevant documents, and they should liaise before the joint discussion to ensure that they both have the same information and so are ready to proceed with the discussion.

The main benefit of the joint discussion is for the two experts to have a better understanding of the other expert's point of view and to share their views. Sometimes there is a need for the case manager to be party to the joint discussion, and in order to do this efficiently they may have to have a three-way telephone meeting set up. It may be possible to narrow the issues or it may not be possible to do so, and the case may proceed to trial. The more information available to both experts at this stage the better, and ideally the joint discussion between the care experts would not take place until the medical experts have met and provided their joint statement. This is not always possible because of timetabling issues, but it is always helpful and is really necessary in cases where the prognosis is not clear and there is a wide divergence of medical opinion.

There are cases where both medical experts and care experts agree that it is not possible to provide a final assessment of the client's future care needs within the timetable that the court has specified, and then the case has had to be adjourned. This may be in the case of a spinal injury because the client needs further surgery or where a brain injury client has not had enough time to complete rehabilitation. There are cases where the care expert has to put forward several options for the client's long-term need and this is because it will never be certain which of the choices will be the most appropriate for the future.

Further guidance on joint discussions by experts can be found in Chapter 7.

8.11   OVERSEAS CLAIMANTS

Occasionally a care expert may be instructed in a case where the claimant lives abroad but has a claim in the UK. In such cases the expert has to take into account the care available in the country in question as well as to be aware of any cultural issues involved. The expert will almost certainly have to visit the claimant and will need to investigate agencies and determine carer rates of pay in the country while considering that in many countries there is no concept of case management. This is only just developing in Europe and is not currently available in the Middle East, although the US and Australia have had case managers for some years. Some case management companies in the UK have managers based overseas.

CHAPTER 9

TRAUMATIC BRAIN INJURY

Nicholas Leng[*]

9.1 INTRODUCTION

Injury to the brain may occur as a result of a number of conditions, including trauma, cerebrovascular events, degenerative disorders, hydrocephalus, toxicity, infection, tumours, oxygen deprivation, metabolic and endocrine dysfunction and nutritional deficiencies. This chapter will focus on the commonest condition likely to be encountered in catastrophic personal injury litigation, namely traumatic brain injury. Much of what follows will apply, however, to other brain conditions giving rise to catastrophic personal injury claims.

The terms 'head injury' and 'brain injury' are often used interchangeably. The term that will be used here is 'traumatic brain injury' (TBI). A TBI is defined as a traumatically caused injury that produces physiological dysfunction of the brain. As we shall see, such physiological dysfunction is usually only temporary and, for practical purposes, reversible in milder cases, but in more severe cases there may be significant enduring cognitive, emotional and behavioural consequences.

TBIs are of two main types. The most common type is called a closed head injury, also sometimes referred to as a blunt head injury. In such injuries there may or may not be a skull fracture, but the dura mater (brain covering) and brain itself are not penetrated. The other type of TBI is called a penetrating head injury, also known as an open head injury, because in these cases the skull, dura mater and brain are penetrated, such as in a missile wound.

9.2 EPIDEMIOLOGY

TBI is the most common cause of brain damage in children and young adults. Studies vary in their estimates of incidence and prevalence because of the use of different criteria, for example whether deaths and all degrees of severity have been included, or where the study has been conducted. The incidence of TBI in the US, for instance, has been reported to be 220 per 100,000, but Chicago has about three times as many cases occurring as Maryland. In England it has been reported that 600,000 head injuries serious enough to cause attendance at hospital occur annually. Fortunately, the overwhelming proportion of head

[*] Nicholas Leng DPhil FBPsS, Consultant Neuropsychologist, London Medical Centre.

injuries involve little or no underlying TBI, and when a TBI has been sustained it is most likely to be mild (85% or so of cases) rather than severe, but 20% of cases are significant enough to be admitted to hospital, and although only 5% or less require transfer to specialised neurosciences units, some 4,000 individuals in England and Wales die each year from a TBI. Of course, these statistics should be taken as an approximation, since a significant number of head injured individuals either do not report to hospitals, or attend centres where epidemiological data are not kept.

TBI occurs more commonly in males than females, in younger rather than older adults, with the peak age range of 15–24, in lower rather than higher social classes and more often after alcohol consumption. Unemployment, alcoholism, previous head injury and lower educational level are also significant risk factors.

The major causes of TBI are road traffic accidents (RTAs), domestic falls, assaults, occupational injuries and recreational accidents.

In the case of RTAs, motorcyclists have a greater chance of death than those travelling in motor vehicles, although helmets have reduced mortality, but perhaps not surprisingly pedestrians are at greater risk.

9.3   ESTIMATING SEVERITY

If it is known, or suspected, that a physical injury has been sustained to the head, then an issue may arise as to whether or not there has been an underlying TBI. Assessing whether a TBI has occurred, and if so what the likely initial severity of it is, are important because of the implications for the medical care likely to be needed, and the outcome. Severity is usually estimated from the identification and measurement of two main indirect criteria: the depth and duration of coma, and the duration of post-traumatic amnesia (PTA).

Although it was developed primarily to monitor and detect deterioration in TBI patients, rather than to measure severity of injury, the Glasgow Coma Scale (GCS) is most often used as a measure of impairment of conscious level. It has the advantage of being simple and quick enough to use in a busy unit by staff at all levels of clinical expertise. The GCS has come into routine international clinical use and is therefore usually annotated in the hospital records.

TBI interferes with brain function at the time of the injury and creates a period of amnesia, starting from some point prior to injury, known as retrograde amnesia (RA), through to some time after it, referred to as anterograde amnesia or post-traumatic amnesia (PTA). RA is of less importance because it does not correlate as well with severity and outcome as does PTA. PTA ends not with the first post-accident memory, because patients still in PTA may have 'islands' of recall after the first memory, but with the reappearance of clear and continuous memory. PTA, unlike GCS, is almost never assessed in the hospital, which is unfortunate because it is generally accepted as providing the more accurate indication of severity. Scales do exist for the contemporaneous assessment of PTA and are occasionally applied by clinicians during the patient's hospital stay, but in almost every case it has to be assessed in retrospect. The assessment of PTA is by no means straightforward and requires a higher degree of theoretical knowledge and clinical skill than is the case with the GCS. Among the difficulties are that patients, like everyone else, forget with the passage of time, have gaps or 'islands' in their recall, display inaccuracies in their recall of events, convince themselves that things have happened when they have not, or conversely persuade themselves that things have not happened when they have, and often have difficulty differentiating between what they can remember as opposed to what they have reconstructed in their minds based upon what they have been told or assumed happened. There is an extensive literature on these phenomena, and anybody who is attempting to assess PTA should be familiar with it in order to minimise errors.

The GCS has a 15 point scale (though occasionally a 14 point scale is used) and the lowest score is 3. The lower the score, the worse the injury is likely to have been. Generally, a GCS of 13 or greater and a PTA of less than one hour indicate a mild traumatic brain injury (MTBI). A GCS of 9–12 and a PTA of 1–24 hours are taken to indicate a moderate TBI. A GCS of 8 or below and a PTA of greater than 24 hours imply a severe TBI. Some classification systems go further and specify that a PTA of more than one week indicates a very severe TBI and one of more than a month an extremely severe TBI. However, this system will not cover every eventuality. For example, in crush and penetrating injuries there may be little movement of the head to set in motion the mechanisms to cause coma and PTA, and coma and PTA may be short in these circumstances, even though significant brain damage might have occurred.

The above classifications are based in part upon their relationship with outcome statistics, but to some extent are arbitrary. Moreover, a difficulty not infrequently arises because the extent of impairment of the GCS and the length of PTA can be influenced by other factors such as the effects of psychological shock, alcohol, medication, sedation, analgesia and anaesthesia. For these reasons the author recommends the use of the Mayo system, as this is a system which is more comprehensive, taking into account a wider range of relevant variables, and is based upon a study of a large number of cases.

In this system, a TBI is classified as moderate to severe if one or more of the following criteria exist:
- death due to the brain injury;
- loss of consciousness of 30 minutes or more;
- PTA of 24 hours or more;
- worst GCS in the first 24 hours of 12 or less (unless explainable by other factors);

- one or more of the following: intracerebral haematoma, subdural haematoma, epidural haematoma, cerebral contusion, haemorrhagic contusion, penetrating TBI, subarachnoid haemorrhage or brain stem injury.

A TBI is considered as mild (probable) if one or more of these criteria are present:

- loss of consciousness of less than 30 minutes;
- PTA of less than 24 hours;
- depressed, basilar or linear skull fracture, without penetration of the dura mater.

If none of the above criteria apply, then a classification of symptomatic (possible) TBI is made if one or more of the following signs or symptoms are reported:

- blurred vision;
- confusion;
- dazed;
- dizziness;
- focal neurological symptoms;
- headache;
- nausea.

9.4   NEUROPATHOLOGY

For the purposes of this chapter we will focus upon closed rather than penetrating injury, since these are generally more common.

In closed injuries, a distinction is usually made between primary and secondary damage. The primary injury is caused by a mechanical force, which may be an impact force, such as when a stationary individual is struck a blow to the head, or an inertial force, which involves either translational acceleration, whereby the head moves in a straight line with respect to the centre of gravity of the brain, or rotational acceleration, whereby the head rotates around the centre of gravity. Such forces may result in contusional injury (bruising) to the brain either at the site of impact, known as the coup, or on the opposing side, called contrecoup. Another type of primary injury, known as diffuse axonal injury (DAI), may also occur, due to damage to the axons, or long fibres connecting nerve cells together. In association with DAI one may see petechial haemorrhages, most often in the frontal and temporal lobe areas. Haematomas (localised collections of blood, usually clotted) may form, and these may be either epidural, where the dura mater is torn from the skull; subdural, where the haematoma develops between the dura mater and the brain; or intracerebral, where they occur within the brain substance itself.

Secondary damage to the brain may be caused by raised pressure in the brain, oedema (swelling) of the brain, hypoxia, ischaemia and infection. Oedema has particular implications because of pressure on the brain stem which is involved in maintaining vital functions and it is thus of the essence that intracranial pressure is controlled during the acute recovery phase.

One might ask as to the relevance of brain imaging in these circumstances. CT and MRI scans will show macroscopic damage, but not necessarily microscopic damage, so although an abnormal scan provides positive evidence of a brain injury, a normal scan does not necessarily rule out that one has been sustained.

9.5 EFFECTS OF TBI

The effects of TBI of course depend upon the severity of the injury and the nature of any damage that has been caused, though there is also some degree of individual variability, so there is a wide range of possible outcomes.

Well-designed recent research carried out on 'pure' samples of individuals who have sustained a so-called mild uncomplicated TBI, which is to say individuals suffering a concussional injury when engaged in sport, where there are no 'contaminating' factors such as mental health, social, personality or motivational problems, has shown that they are not usually left with any adverse long-term cognitive, emotional or behavioural problems, with 95% or more making a full functional recovery as determined by a return to normal performance on all relevant tests within a relatively short time after injury.

Those who do not make a full recovery, and who are left with subjective complaints, which might include symptoms such as headaches, irritability, memory and concentration problems, fatigue, anxiety and depression, are often given a diagnosis of post-concussional syndrome (PCS). However, there have been criticisms of this formulation on the grounds that none of the symptoms of PCS are specific to it, they all occur in other disorders, and indeed have a surprisingly high frequency or base rate in the general population. Moreover, PCS is a descriptive rather than an explanatory term, because the actual cause of symptoms is not specified. The results of all relevant investigations, such as brain scans, neurological examinations and neuropsychological investigations are usually normal, and so the diagnosis is made solely on the basis of symptoms reported by the patient. The relevance of this is that symptoms are of course subjective and by definition cannot be seen or measured. When a diagnosis is made upon symptoms alone, errors will inevitably occur, because the diagnosis of another disorder, or indeed no disorder at all, may be just as probable. PCS is nowadays thought of as a form of somatoform disorder, which is to say a disorder characterised by symptoms that are not explained by an organic disorder. Clinically the picture can be quite complex in that PCS is inevitably enmeshed with psychological factors, the nature of which is very often unclear. It is commonly thought that the PCS patient responds to the original injury in a maladaptive way by, for example, falsely attributing 'symptoms', such as day-to-day memory lapses occurring in almost everybody, to brain damage, long after recovery from the original injury has actually occurred. In other cases the patient may develop an anxiety or depressive disorder, which can impair attention and concentration, and a negative, pessimistic style of thinking, leading to a belief that serious brain damage has occurred. Theoretically PCS is then treatable by means of cognitive-behavioural therapy (CBT), perhaps in combination with anti-depressant medication if there is a significant depressive disorder present, but some of these patients develop an *idée fixe* which can be very difficult to reverse.

In more severe TBIs the effects are more likely to be enduring.[1] Diffuse damage to the brain, known as diffuse axonal injury (DAI), as may occur in more severe TBIs, may lead to reduction in mental speed, attention, mental efficiency, reasoning and conceptual thinking. Patients often complain of 'fuzzy thinking', difficulties in concentrating, processing more complex information or dealing with problems involving multiple elements, and lack of clarity in thinking, in association with fatigue and irritability. Whilst TBI patients often complain about impairment of memory, it is often the case that they show normal ability to retain and retrieve material, and the underlying problem is more often one of disordered attention, concentration or inefficient mental processing.

Individuals who suffer a focal injury, which is to say a coup or contrecoup as described above, will be prone to present with a deficit in function relating to the particular area of the brain concerned, or at least in the function with which that part of the brain is involved. For example, there are two areas located in the dominant side of the brain, namely Broca's area and Wernicke's area, which are central to the use of language, damage to which may produce an aphasia. Changes in personality, behaviour, mood and insight often follow from damage to the front part of the brain, an area frequently implicated in TBI for reasons of anatomical vulnerability. Damage to the frontal lobes is often associated with anosmia (loss or impairment of the sense of smell), because the olfactory nerves pass directly beneath the undersurface of them.

Other physical problems, such as impairment of balance, is another not uncommon sequela to TBI, as is reduced ability to tolerate the effects of alcohol.

9.6   THE FRONTAL LOBES AND EXECUTIVE FUNCTIONS

Disorders of frontal lobe function are common enough following more severe TBIs to warrant a section of their own. The frontal lobes are the largest area of the cortex, accounting for about a third of it by volume, and are considered to be that part of the brain which most distinguishes humans from other primates. They are the last areas of the cortex to develop. This has particular implications for brain injuries in childhood, because such an injury occurs within the context of a brain which is yet developing and the injury may impede or prevent the

---

[1]   For an excellent description of the difficulties of coping with the effects of serious brain injury read *Touching Distance* by James Cracknell and Beverly Turner (Century, 2012).

development of higher mental control or executive functions over the ensuing years, an eventuality that may not become more fully apparent until late adolescence. For these reasons it is advisable not to settle such a case until a time has been reached when one can be more certain about the final prognosis.

The terms 'frontal lobe syndrome', 'dysexecutive syndrome' and 'organic personality disorder' are often used synonymously. Whilst it is true that the frontal lobes play a central role in the mediation of executive functions, other areas, notably the deeper regions of the brain, are also often implicated.

Executive or higher mental control functions allow the individual to plan and regulate behaviour. Put the other way round, an individual with a dysexecutive syndrome may even fail to realise when something needs to be done at all, let alone be able to work out what is to be done or how to do it. Recognising that a problem exists which requires a response, then planning or organising an action or series of actions, before putting the plan into effect, and then realising that the plan needs amendment if it is not working, may all be impaired to a greater or less extent.

Sub-divisions of the frontal lobes have been delineated, each of which seems to be more or less concerned with a particular aspect of executive functioning. The orbito-frontal region is implicated largely in the matter of behavioural control. Patients with damage to this region often have little insight into their behaviour or the effect that this might have upon somebody else. They may be prone to irrational or impulsive behaviour; they may be disinhibited, overly frank, emotionally, socially or sexually inappropriate; they may be prone to outbursts of anger or outrage often at minimal provocation. Behaviour may be obsessional or compulsive. Such individuals are often described as childish, unreasonable, egocentric, and unable to see others' points of view.

Damage to the dorsolateral area may produce more in the way of cognitive problems. Patients may have difficulty mentally juggling information, there may be inefficient recall of information from memory yet intact recognition of it. Fluency or word finding problems may be present. Thinking may be concrete, rigid, inflexible or 'tramlined'. They may find it difficult to find a solution to a problem, or to see more than one way of solving it. They may be impaired in their ability to make estimates or reasonable judgments.

The third region, referred to as the medial area, is more associated with lack of drive, initiative, apathy, and a flattening or absence of emotion.

In considering the above examples it must of course be borne in mind that there will be individuals who show these signs to a mild degree, whereas others will show more marked problems, and of course many different combinations of behavioural and cognitive problems can occur together.

9.7 THE MEANING OF FRONTAL LOBE DYSFUNCTION: THE CASE OF PHINEAS GAGE

On 13 December 1848, aged 25, Phineas Gage was working as a railroad engineer in New England. His job was to lay explosive and detonate it. This involved boring a hole, putting the explosive in place, covering it with sand, and then using a fuse and tamping iron to detonate an explosion. Accidentally, Gage placed the tamping iron directly on the explosive, and the resulting explosion sent the tamping iron through his skull and brain, out the other side, and 20 or so feet in the air. Gage remarkably survived this assault, a fact which is attributed to the hot tamping iron cauterising the wound as it passed through his brain, indeed he did not even lose consciousness and was able to walk to the cart that took him to hospital. In some ways the accident had few consequences: his physical abilities, memory and language were all unaffected. However, there were significant personality and behaviour changes. Prior to the accident he was described in these terms: 'strong', 'active', 'temperate habits', 'iron will', 'energy of character', 'a great favourite with his men', 'a most efficient and capable foreman', 'a well-balanced mind', 'a shrewd and smart business man', 'very energetic in executing plans'. He was considered an outstanding employee with excellent prospects. After the accident, however, he was described in these terms: 'fitful', 'irreverent', 'grossly profane', 'showing little deference for his fellows', 'impatient of restraint or advice that conflicted with his desires', 'obstinate', 'capricious', 'vacillating', 'plans no sooner arranged than abandoned', 'a child intellectually', 'the animal passions of a strong man'.

Gage did not regain his job as foreman. For a while he travelled around the country exhibiting himself before driving stagecoaches and then farming. He subsequently developed epilepsy and died 11 years later.

Almost certainly the damage involved the left frontal lobe, and probably also the right frontal lobe, and today we would diagnose a dysexecutive syndrome.

Sadly it is the case than many patients who suffer frontal lobe damage are left for the remainder of their lives unfulfilled in terms of their ability to hold down either employment or meaningful relationships with others.

9.8 THE MEDICAL EVIDENCE IN THE LITIGATION PROCESS

In the event that a TBI is suspected or known to have occurred, consideration will need to be given to the type of medical expert required to advise in the medico-legal process. Neurosurgeons, neurologists, neuroradiologists, neuro-otologists, neuropsychiatrists and neuropsychologists are all involved in either the diagnostic or treatment process, but it will often be a matter of proportionality as to which experts to approach. There is of course some overlap between specialists and if advice is needed only about the basic facts concerning the TBI, then it will be less important as to which expert to consult.

However, if the case is multi-factorial or complex, such that more detailed or specialised investigations in a particular area are required, then several experts may be needed.

Regarding the areas in which each of these experts has knowledge more specialised than the others, consideration may be given to the following. There is probably no need to specifically consider neurosurgical opinion unless there is an issue, let us say, as to whether a patient was managed neurosurgically in an appropriate way, or whether the correct operation was carried out in the right way or at the right time. Where there are issues to do with the more physical aspects of the case, such as hemiparesis or hemiplegia, migraine, damage to the balance mechanism or epilepsy, for example, then a neurologist would be the appropriate expert. The interpretation of brain scans is best addressed by the neuroradiologist. Disorders of mental health, particularly major mood disturbances and so-called organic personality disorders, lie within the province of the neuropsychiatrist. The neuropsychologist will add to the process by carrying out an objective assessment of mental abilities that will assist in quantifying the extent of brain injury and in assisting other experts, such as those involved in care or employment matters, in determining the extent to which there are losses of independence or barriers to certain kinds of work. An accurate neuropsychological assessment may also provide guidance as to rehabilitation and treatment needs, and contribute towards a decision as to the patient's mental capacity to manage their affairs or to deal with the litigation.

9.9 THE NEUROPSYCHOLOGICAL EXAMINATION

Although neuropsychologists usually examine the patient on tests which yield a measure of their intelligence (IQ), they tend to do so not so much because there will have been a loss of general intelligence, though in some cases some may have occurred, but because such tests also contain measures which indicate the extent to which the patient's ability to utilise their intelligence has been compromised, which is more commonly the case. TBI patients often present with an intact verbal IQ (VIQ) or verbal comprehension index (VCI), because this largely taps acquired information which is usually retained following injury unless the dominant (usually left) side of the brain has been damaged, whereas a reduction in their performance IQ (PIQ) or perceptual organisation index (POI) may reflect a loss in the ability to solve visual-spatial or novel problems as well as reflecting damage to the non-dominant (usually right) side of the brain. The use of VCI and POI are preferable to VIQ and PIQ because they provide purer measures. Tests of so-called 'working memory', yielding a working memory index (WMI), demonstrate how able the patient is to juggle information around in their mind, whereas tests of processing speed, giving a processing speed index (PSI), indicate whether the patient has become mentally slow. Performance on such tests can be compared with projected pre-morbid levels as determined from performance on tests known to 'hold up' against TBI, such as reading vocabulary or VCI and from demographic statistics.

Tests may be used to detect disorders of verbal memory which may arise from damage to the left side of the brain, and of visual memory arising from damage to the right side of the brain. Testing may also be carried out to reflect the fact that many TBI patients are often quite good at recognising that they have seen things before, but have difficulty acquiring information or recalling recently acquired knowledge because of attentional difficulties arising from damage to the frontal areas of the brain.

Executive functions, as noted above, arise largely from damage to the front part of the brain, and to some extent the sub-cortical regions. They are harder to measure than other brain functions because most tests are structured, at least in part, in such a way that patients may be able to comply with the test instructions, especially in a quiet, calm office, whereas their real difficulties in daily life lie in their inability to recognise or remember when something needs to be done, or to initiate or organise things without prompting. Moreover, disturbances of mood, temper control, fatigue, motivation, time keeping and so on are more difficult to measure objectively and do not necessarily present themselves during the clinical evaluation. Nevertheless, tests will be based on examining fluency and how well the patient is able to devise a plan and carry it out, see different ways of solving a problem, estimate things, divide their attention between one type of activity and another, or selectively attend to one kind of stimulus in the presence of another, distracting one that must be ignored.

The above is by no means exhaustive and the selection of tests will be guided by the clinical problems displayed, or thought likely to be present, in the individual patient. However, the advantage of the neuropsychological assessment over other types of clinical assessment which rely upon what the patient or somebody else says is wrong with them, is that it provides a reasonably objective measure of what the patient's level of performance is actually likely to be. This can be achieved because an individual's test scores can be compared with a normal control group matched for age, and a group of individuals who have incurred a known injury.

Whilst brain dysfunction undoubtedly affects performance on neuropsychological tests, there may be other factors that influence a patient's performance, such as mood state or pain, since anxiety and depression can impair attention and concentration for example. There is, however, one further problem not infrequently encountered and which needs to be brought into the equation.

9.10 EFFORT

Anybody can perform poorly on tests simply by not trying, and indeed effort has a greater effect upon test performance than TBI. Neuropsychologists have therefore devised tests specifically to address this issue, and indeed it is now considered mandatory to include such tests as part of any assessment, be it for clinical or medico-legal purposes. Such tests are not openly described for the obvious reason that once the purpose of the test has been made public its value as an indirect indicator of effort is lost.

Certain mental functions remain intact after TBI. Therefore such a test can be based upon an examination of such a function, such that even the most severely injured patient will pass it. A fail on the test must then be due to some factor other than brain damage. The second requirement is that the test should appear hard, when in fact it is easy, so as to minimise the possibility of the examinee detecting its real purpose.

A similar approach is taken with assessing the validity of symptom reporting by applying a scale which appears to consist of a series of 'symptoms' rarely endorsed by patients who in fact respond in such a way as to produce exactly the same low scores as normal individuals, so that high or abnormal scores indicate an over-endorsement of complaints, as may indicate exaggeration, whereas abnormally low scores conversely indicate an under-reporting or denial of 'symptoms'.

9.11   MALINGERING

Some clinicians argue that malingering is not a diagnosis, because by definition there is nothing wrong with the patient, and therefore there is no condition to diagnose. Others have difficulty in asserting that the patient might be malingering, because somehow it goes against the grain to suspect that they are being lied to, bearing in mind that clinicians are a group of professional people who are trained to listen very carefully to what the patient is telling them – and to believe them. And what is a more serious error – to diagnose malingering and miss a grave diagnosis which may deny the patient treatment, or to mistakenly diagnose an actual clinical condition and miss a diagnosis of malingering?

However, as neuropsychologists we are effectively behavioural scientists, and as such our job is to observe behaviour and try to explain it. Although recent advances in neuroimaging allow us to see which parts of the brain 'light up' when we get a subject to perform a particular task, thus shedding light upon which areas are concerned with a certain mental function, we cannot see into the brain or mind in such a way as to allow us to, for example, see what a person is thinking. We can only draw inferences from what we observe in behaviour, which is to say from the response to a given stimulus.

We also have to be quite clear in our definition of malingering, and how it differs from other behaviours which appear similar but may not be the same. We also need to ask at what point along the spectrum of exaggeration should we use the term malingering. For instance, if the patient is only slightly exaggerating a real symptom, which is thought to be quite common, does that qualify for a formulation of malingering, or do we reserve it for cases where there is complete fabrication and no symptom at all, which is thought to be rarer? Or do we place the cut-off somewhere in between those extremes?

Let us then look at how malingering might differ from other conditions. Effort and malingering, for example, are not necessarily the same thing, and whilst a patient may fail an effort or symptom validity test because they are grossly exaggerating, there may be other explanations. Whilst malingering is considered to be under conscious control, where the incentive is external and revolves around a financial reward or avoidance of duty, the clinician has to consider whether there is an alternative explanation, such as a conversion disorder. In this disorder, apparent exaggeration or abnormal behaviour is not considered to be under conscious control, but rather that there is a maladaptive response to managing stress or conflict. In another kind of disorder, called a factitious disorder, the patient's behaviour, like malingering, is considered to be under conscious control, but the incentive here is to adopt the sick role, in order to obtain care or attention, to maladaptively manage stress or to escape from duty, but not to obtain financial reward. In many cases there will be considerable debate as to exactly which disorder is present, if indeed they are mutually exclusive, but some clinicians have proposed a series of criteria to attempt to answer this often vexed question.

The American Psychiatric Association's *Diagnostic and Statistical Manual of Mental Disorders*, 4th edn, Text Revision, advises that malingering should be considered if any combination of the following are present:

- medico-legal context;
- marked discrepancy between reported problems and objective findings;
- lack of co-operation;
- anti-social personality disorder.

Unfortunately, none of these factors is diagnostic. It would be absurd to suggest, for example, that any individual presenting for a medico-legal examination is malingering just because there are discrepancies between reported problems and objective findings without further consideration of the circumstances. Discrepancies between reported problems and objective findings, or lack of co-operation could be due to something other than deliberately feigned illness.

Clinicians will therefore tend to look at a wider range of factors to see if a pattern emerges which would either strengthen or weaken the case for suspecting malingering.

First, does the history make sense? Was there a head injury in the first place? Were the impact or acceleration/deceleration forces sufficient to cause a brain injury? Is there something unusual about the account of retrograde or post-traumatic amnesia? Is there a significant discrepancy between what the patient says and what is recorded in the notes? Has the history changed over time, or has the patient given a different history to other clinicians?

Secondly, does the neuropsychological profile make sense? Has a mild traumatic brain injury produced deficits that are out of proportion? Is there an inconsistency between results from tests that measure the same thing? Are there deficits in areas known not to be adversely affected by the injury? Do test results vary from one occasion to another in a way that makes no sense? Does performance get worse over time instead of better as would be expected? Has there been a late of onset of symptoms? Is test performance good when required (eg the chance of job promotion), but bad when it might be advantageous (eg medico-legal assessment)?

Thirdly, does the patient's presentation make sense? Are the patient's emotional responses commensurate with the gravity of their condition? Is there gross or hyperbolic or simply absurd reporting of symptoms? Are there unusual symptoms? Is the pattern of symptoms unusual, illogical, atypical or inconsistent?

Sometimes the clinician may feel that the patient is exaggerating, but has difficulty putting forward the evidence. In these circumstances they may be provided with surveillance evidence. Whilst this may be useful in the assessment of physical injury, such as showing that a patient can walk quite normally when they do not know that they are being observed, as opposed to limping at the medical assessment, judgments about mental state can be far more difficult, unless there is something tangible, such as a demonstration that the patient, for example, frequently goes out alone to busy supermarkets when they have told the clinician that they suffer with agoraphobia and never venture out alone.

More recently, Slick and colleagues have proposed the following system for placing a probability on the formulation of malingering.

Definite malingered neurocognitive disorder (MND) is considered to be operative if the following are present:
- substantial external incentive (eg compensation claim, disability pension, evasion of criminal prosecution, release from military service);
- definite negative response bias as defined by below chance performance on forced choice cognitive tests;
- discrepancies between test data and known patterns of brain functioning, observed behaviour, collateral reports and documented background history not explainable by psychiatric, neurological or developmental factors.

Probable MND is diagnosed if the following are evident:
- substantial external incentive;
- two or more types of evidence from neuropsychological testing excluding definite negative response bias, or one type of such evidence, excluding definite negative response bias together with discrepancies between test data and known patterns of brain functioning, observed behaviour, collateral reports and documented background history not explainable by psychiatric, neurological or developmental factors;

- discrepancies between self-reported history or symptoms and documented history, known patterns of brain functioning, behavioural observations, collateral information and evidence of symptom exaggeration as from well validated symptom validity tests not accounted for by psychiatric, neurological or developmental factors.

Possible MND is diagnosed if the following are evident:

- substantial external incentive;
- discrepancies between self-reported history or symptoms and documented history, known patterns of brain functioning, behavioural observations, collateral information and evidence of symptom exaggeration as from well validated symptom validity tests not accounted for by psychiatric, neurological or developmental factors; or
- criteria for definite or probable MND are met except that primary psychiatric, neurological or developmental factors cannot be ruled out.

9.12   RECOVERY, TREATMENT, REHABILITATION AND PROGNOSIS

As we have already seen, all but a small number of patients who suffer a mild TBI can be expected to show a return to normal functioning as determined by relevant tests within a short time of sustaining injury. In cases of PCS, which is theoretically reversible, CBT is usually recommended. This is most commonly carried out by a clinical psychologist.

As we have also already noted, in more severe TBI, cognitive deficits, emotional and behavioural problems, and personality changes of varying degrees are more likely to persist into the long term. It is generally accepted that there is an inverse relationship between rate of recovery and time elapsed since injury, so that recovery in the early months tends to be more rapid than in the later months, with recovery tending to reach a plateau by about 2 years post-injury. These of course are generalisations and there are many exceptions, both in regard to the extent of recovery that occurs and the time that it takes. After 2 years it is then largely a matter of the extent to which the patient either learns to adapt to their environment by applying compensatory strategies, or alters their environment to suit their disability.

In many cases therefore it will be appropriate for the TBI patient to be offered treatment and rehabilitation to help in this adaptational process. The purpose of rehabilitation is to try to return the individual to a condition as close as possible to that which pre-existed the injury and to try to achieve a lifestyle that is as close to 'normal' as possible within the context of their disabilities. Sometimes there will be argument as to whether this should be offered on a residential or at home basis. In the event that the patient is being discharged from hospital, treatment or rehabilitation needs are multi-factorial. If specialist facilities that cannot be provided on a community basis are required, if there are severe behavioural problems or if community facilities are limited or just not available, then residential rehabilitation may be considered. In other instances, when the patient has already returned home, is well established there and a move to a residential setting may be disruptive or interfere with work and support networks locally, or if specialist residential facilities are not required and suitable community services are available, then a home based programme may be preferable, as it carries with it the further advantage that gains made in the residential unit do not then have to be transferred to the home setting.

The personnel involved with the rehabilitation programme will vary of course with the nature of the patient's problems, but may include physiotherapy, occupational therapy and speech therapy. From the neuropsychological perspective, consideration may need to be given to any role for psychopharmacological treatment to control disorders of mood, which will require neuropsychiatric management. Cognitive behavioural therapy, usually carried out by a clinical psychologist, may help with disorders of mood, anxiety, temper control, motivation and cognitive, behavioural and executive problems. There may be a role too in educating the patient and their relatives as to what has happened, what can be expected, and how particular problems are best managed.

The effects of rehabilitation may be no more than modest, and gains may need to be maintained by ongoing support input, and an assessment by a care expert may be helpful. Patients with dysexecutive syndromes are amongst the most difficult to rehabilitate, which is a particular problem given the frequency with which severe TBI patients suffer damage to the frontal lobe systems.

Finally, in terms of prognosis, the question is often asked as to whether patients with TBI deteriorate over time. Recent studies suggest as a possibility, rather than a probability, that in some circumstances TBI patients are more susceptible to developing dementia later in life, but further investigation of this is required. Some clinicians argue that, as a matter of common sense, TBI patients will show the effects of the normal ageing process earlier because they have lost a degree of 'brain reserve', in other words that the normal process of decline is now acting upon a brain whose function has already been reduced by injury, but this is another area that has not been sufficiently researched.

Following completion of rehabilitation consideration will need to be given to what, if any, long–term care and support needs there are. The main difficulty here is often how to strike the right balance between offering sufficient support on the one hand, but not being over-protective on the other. Just as it is the aim of rehabilitation to try to reach a normal as possible lifestyle, so it is with care and support that the aim should be to try to get the patient to live their lives as independently as possible.

9.13   EFFECT ON RELATIONSHIPS

Patients who have suffered a severe TBI often have difficulty establishing and maintaining relationships. The adverse behavioural, cognitive and emotional effects of severe TBI, particularly mood swings and poor temper control, have a negative impact upon those close to the patient and many patients end up without close friends or lasting sexual partners. Relationships with others are often temporary and shallow. Studies have produced differing probabilities of marital breakdown following TBI, but most suggest that this occurs in 50% or more cases. Clearly this has implications for care and support needs which will often increase if the spouse or partner leaves the family home.

9.14   EFFECT ON EMPLOYMENT

Not surprisingly there is a reasonable correlation between the severity of TBI as determined by factors such as PTA and neuropsychological deficits and the effect upon employment, but there are many factors to consider. A patient who is forgetful may commit an important error at work, another may repeatedly lose their temper with their boss or colleagues. A patient may show poor timekeeping, another may be slow and inefficient or unreliable. Some patients may be unproductive or require constant supervision which makes their employment economically non-viable. An individual who has been used to a managerial role might now be able to cope with a mundane, repetitive job, but psychologically may find this destructive of self-confidence and self-esteem. Reported rates of unemployment following severe TBI vary but have been found typically to be within the 22% to 66% range. Patients who do return to work often only manage at a reduced level of complexity or responsibility and only on a part-time basis. Others manage patchy employment, interspersed with periods of unemployment, some falling out of the employment market altogether. It will be appropriate in many cases to consider obtaining a vocational assessment and rehabilitation report, which may establish what the barriers to return to work are, whether they can be overcome and if so how, and whether support in the form of a job coach would be of assistance.

Patients who fail to return to or maintain employment need something to keep them occupied and to give life some kind of meaning, and in these circumstances a structured programme of occupational and social activity is required. This will need the employment of a support worker who can engage the patient in such a programme of activity devised with the assistance perhaps of an occupational therapist and neuropsychologist.

CHAPTER 10

BIRTH BRAIN INJURY

Dr Maggie Blott

10.1 INTRODUCTION

Electronic fetal heart rate monitoring was introduced into clinical practice in the 1960s in the hope that continuous monitoring of the fetal heart would facilitate early recognition of fetal hypoxia and ensure delivery of the baby before a hypoxic brain injury could occur. Unfortunately this has not been the case. Subsequent analysis has shown that the procedure of continuously monitoring the fetal heart in all women has led to an increase in interventions such as caesarean section and operative vaginal delivery without improving perinatal outcomes. There are many reasons for this and importantly it is now recognised that only about 10% of all cases of cerebral palsy are in fact due to intrapartum events and yet these claims form the largest number of obstetric claims by cause as reported by the NHSLA. Twenty per cent of these claims are due to the misinterpretation of the electronic fetal heart rate trace. For a claim to be successful the claimant will need to be able to demonstrate that the damage suffered was due to, or materially contributed to by, an intrapartum event and that there was a negligent failure of care such that a different action would have prevented or limited the damage.

10.2 INTRAPARTUM ASPHYXIA

There are two types of asphyxia that occur in labour. First, there is the sudden, largely unpredictable, event where urgent delivery of the baby within 20 minutes is needed if catastrophic damage is to be prevented. Such sentinel events include cord prolapse, massive placental abruption and rupture of the uterus. In many of these cases despite the swift actions of the obstetric team the baby will sustain a hypoxic brain insult which could not have been avoided. The other type of insult in labour is due to chronic partial hypoxia, which can take over an hour to lead to a hypoxic brain injury and should be largely preventable unless the patient is admitted from home with a pathological fetal heart rate pattern. When looking at these cases it is important to understand:

(1) How the healthy fetus copes with the physiological stress of labour.

(2) Why some fetus develop problems in labour.

(3) What the circumstances were by which the obstetric and midwifery team failed to identify the problem and or failed to act in time to prevent an hypoxic brain injury to the baby.

10.3   FETAL ADAPTATION TO INTRAUTERINE LIFE

The fetus is uniquely adapted to intrauterine life and has fetal reserve to cope with the physiological stress of labour. For the fetus the placenta is the organ of gas exchange. Oxygen diffuses across the placenta into the umbilical vein and deoxygenated blood is carried to the placenta in the two umbilical arteries. Carbon dioxide then diffuses across the placenta into the maternal circulation. This is one of only two situations where a vein carries oxygenated blood and an artery deoxygenated blood. The umbilical artery therefore is a reflection of the acid base balance of the fetus and the vein of the maternal and placental acid base balance. The amount of oxygen a fetus needs is determined by the fetal size, fetal activity and essential metabolic processes. The demand for energy is reduced by the fetus decreasing activity and growth, neither of which are essential functions. The amount of oxygen available to the fetus depends on the blood flow in the umbilical vessels, the haemoglobin concentration, the type of haemoglobin and the amount of oxygen carried by the haemoglobin within the red blood cells, known as the oxygen saturation. The fetus has a much higher haemoglobin concentration than it needs to enable it to carry extra oxygen and the type of haemoglobin the fetus has, known as Hb F, has a higher affinity for oxygen. The fetus also has a cardiac output four times greater, weight for weight, than it will have after delivery. This unique combination gives the fetus a reserve, ie it has more oxygen than it needs for normal intrauterine life and thus should be able to cope with additional physiological stresses such as labour.

10.4   ENERGY REQUIREMENTS

The fetus requires energy to grow. It derives this energy from glucose and oxygen that releases energy and forms carbon dioxide and water as waste products of this process.

Glucose and oxygen = energy + carbon dioxide + water

Carbon dioxide and water is carried in fetal blood as a bicarbonate ion HCO_3 and a hydrogen ion H+. At the placenta the H+ and HCO_3^- recombine as carbon dioxide, which then freely diffuses across the placenta. Hydrogen ions diffuse only very slowly across the placenta, so any problem with placental blood flow, such as can occur with cord compression, will lead to an accumulation of hydrogen ions and potentially affect the acid base balance of the fetus. When placental blood flow is normal, and the fetus has a sufficient supply of oxygen, it will continue with the steady state whereby the oxygen supply is sufficient for the energy requirements of the fetus.

10.5   WHY DO PROBLEMS DEVELOP?

In labour cord compression can occur in situations such as when the cord is wrapped around the neck or body of the fetus leading to additional physiological stress. Over a period of time this will start to cause problems in some babies.

If there is poor blood flow within the umbilical vessels this will have two effects.

(1)   there will be an accumulation of H+ ions;

(2)   there will be a reduced oxygen supply.

Initially the fetus will cope with the rise of the hydrogen ions by buffering or neutralising them. The fetus has a very well developed buffering system and has an excess of buffering capacity. In this situation the acidity of the blood (measured as a falling pH) may rise but as the system has sufficient buffering capacity there is no damage, this is known as a respiratory acidosis. A respiratory acidosis most frequently represents a very acute event, such as can occur at around the time of delivery. The fetal heart rate drops as the head is crowning and the baby is born with a low arterial pH, and a normal base excess in the umbilical artery cord gas and a normal venous sample. The baby will recover quickly from the insult and there will be no long-term damage. However, if the situation continues there are two further changes:

(1)   Gradually the excess of buffers will be used up and a base deficit will develop, often recorded as a negative base excess, the ability of the system to continue to neutralise or buffer the excess H+ will fall measured as a fall in the pH of the fetal blood and an enlarging base deficit.

(2)   With a continued reduced oxygen supply the fetus will switch from aerobic (using oxygen) production of energy to an anaerobic (does not require oxygen) production of energy. In this situation the fetus uses glycogen rather than glucose. This system produces energy but the waste product is lactic acid carried in the blood as lactate and hydrogen ions.

Glycogen = Energy and lactic acid (lactate and H+)

This system is designed to be protective to the fetus as it allows more time to delivery but it is very inefficient and high numbers of hydrogen ions are produced which rapidly use up the buffers. There is then an increase in the acidity of the blood (the pH falls) and there is an enlarging base deficit or negative base excess, this is known as a metabolic acidosis and is a very dangerous situation for the fetus. As the fetal cells become acidotic, ie they have a high concentration of hydrogen ions in the tissue, they die. While this is less important if it involves cells of the kidney or liver, it becomes very important when cardiac muscle cells start to die as this leads to cardiac damage, with a fall in cardiac output and therefore fetal blood pressure, with reduced cerebral perfusion and irreversible brain injury.

In an acute event such as a cord prolapse or a ruptured uterus there is an immediate suspension of blood flow in the umbilical vessels. The fetal reserve will protect the baby but unless delivery is effected very quickly the fetus will switch to anaerobic production of energy and become acidotic very rapidly. Hence the need to recognise the problem and deliver the baby within 10 to 20 minutes.

Some babies are more vulnerable to the effects of fetal hypoxia related entirely to how much fetal reserve they have and some maternal conditions will reduce the ability of the baby to cope with the normal physiological stress of labour.

10.6　FETAL HEART RATE MONITORING IN LABOUR

The NICE guideline Intrapartum Care, published in 2003 and revised in 2008 clearly describes the normal and abnormal features of the CTG. It is in use in the majority, if not all, of the maternity units in the UK. Earlier the International Federation of Obstetrics and Gynaecology (FIGO) published agreed terms and definitions which were published in the *International Journal of Obstetrics and Gynaecology* in 1987. Following this the Royal College of Obstetricians and Gynaecologists published 'The Use of Electronic Fetal Monitoring; The use and interpretation of cardiotocography in intrapartum fetal surveillance' in 2001, which was later replaced by the NICE intrapartum guideline in 2003.

Training and education is a key component of successful CTG interpretation. This training should be multi professional with midwives and doctors all training together. Training is important to both teach understanding of the features of the CTG and also to ensure a common language, so that the team members immediately understand the urgency of the situation.

While there is a correlation between certain features on a CTG and the condition of the baby at birth, the CTG is primarily a screening tool and cannot be used for the diagnosis of fetal asphyxia. The interpretation of a CTG must always be within the context of the clinical situation. Babies at high risk of developing fetal hypoxia should have continuous fetal monitoring in labour while those at low risk need only intermittent monitoring.

Common risk factors for fetal compromise in labour
Maternal conditions
- Pre eclampsia
- Antepartum haemorrhage
- Previous caesarean section
- Epidural anaesthesia
- Syntocinon augmentation
- Prolonged pregnancy
- Induction of labour
- Maternal diabetes
- Obstetric cholestasis

Fetal conditions
- Intrauterine growth restriction
- Breech presentation
- Meconium stained liquor
- Multiple pregnancy
- Prematurity

10.7   THE CARDIOTOCOGRAPH

In describing a CTG it is important firstly to identify the risk factors that require continuous fetal heart rate monitoring and then to note how many contractions are occurring, usually described as how many contractions there are in a 10-minute period of time. The CTG is then described feature by feature.

Reassuring features
- Baseline heart rate 110–160 beats per minute

- Baseline variability > 5 beats per minute

- Presence of acceleration

- Absence of decelerations

The presence of one non-reassuring feature makes a CTG suspicious and the presence of two non-reassuring CTG makes the CTG pathological. A suspicious CTG needs constant review to watch for further changes, a pathological CTG needs urgent action.

An image of a normal CTG appears on the following page.

A normal CTG

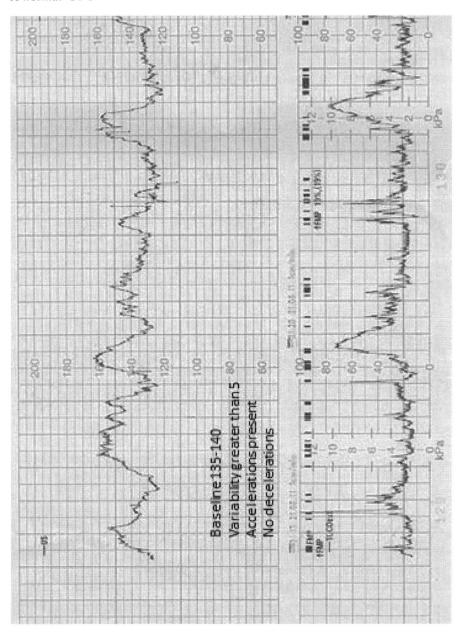

Non-reassuring features

- Baseline heart rate between 100–109 or 161–180
- Baseline variability <5 beats per minute for greater than 40 minutes
- The absence of accelerations if all other features reassuring is uncertain
- Presence of typical variable decelerations for over 50% of contractions for > 90 minutes decelerations

An image of a CTG showing reduced baseline variability appears on the following page.

Reduced baseline variability

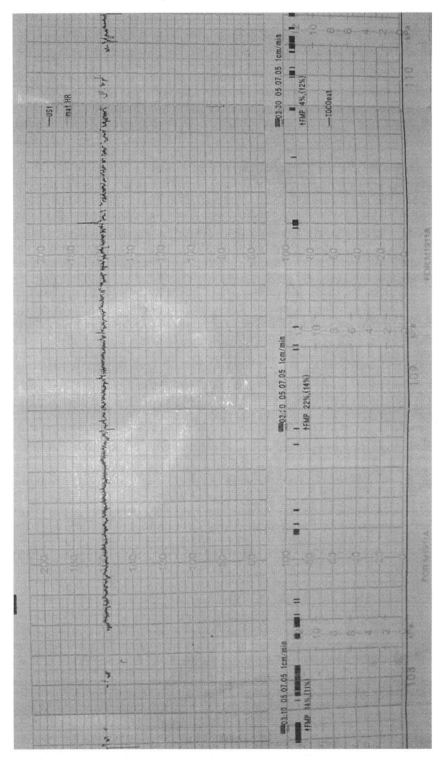

A pathological trace is one in which there are two non-reassuring features or one pathological feature.

Abnormal features

- Baseline heart rate <100 or >180
- Baseline variability <5 beats per minute for greater than 90 minutes
- The absence of accelerations if all other features reassuring is uncertain
- Presence of atypical variable decelerations for over 50% of contractions for >90 minutes decelerations or late decelerations

A pathological CTG

- Baseline >161-non reassuring feature
- Atypical variable decelerations are present-abnormal feature
- Baseline variability <5 for >40 minutes-non reassuring feature

---

An image of a CTG showing decelerations appears on the following page.

Decelerations

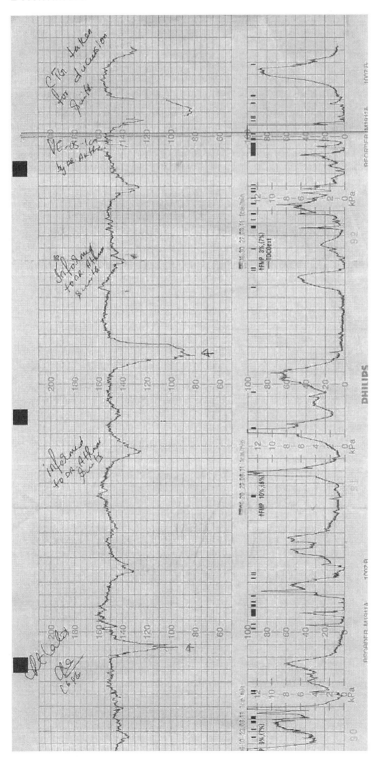

The most commonly seen decelerations are variable, so called as they vary in both morphology and timing with contractions. Once decelerations are present it is important to determine whether they are late, typical or atypical variable decelerations. So-called early decelerations are extremely rare. Typical variable decelerations are a normal response to cord compression, as the contraction starts and the umbilical vein is occluded the fetal heart rate increases, as the contraction increases and the umbilical artery is occluded the heart rate falls, then as the contraction eases and flow returns to the umbilical artery and vein the heart rate recovers to the baseline and increases slightly to compensate before quickly returning to the baseline, in the absence of any other non-reassuring features these decelerations are tolerated by the fetus which is why the NICE guideline have allowed them to be present for up to 90 minutes before they become a non-reassuring feature. Atypical variable decelerations occurring for 50% of all contractions over a 30-minute period are an abnormal feature of a CTG and classify the CTG as pathological. An atypical variable deceleration will have no shouldering, will have a slow return to the baseline, often the variability within the deceleration will be lost.

Typical variable deceleration

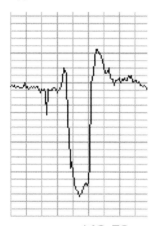

*13:50

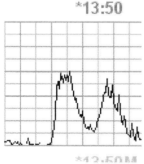

*13:50M

An atypical variable decelerations

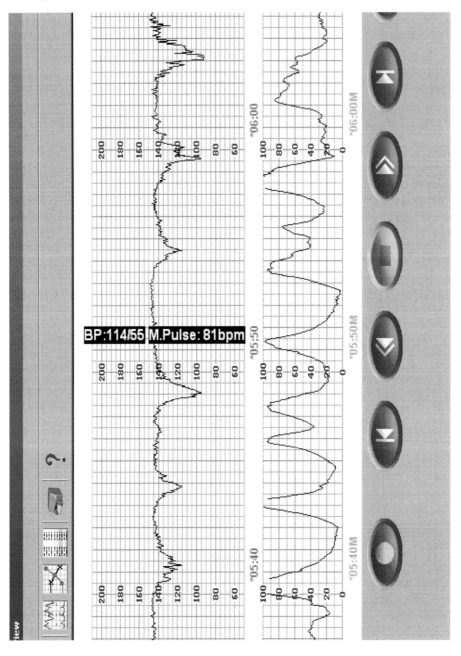

Late decelerations are also an abnormal feature; late decelerations look very similar and the timing will always occur after a contraction, it is sometimes difficult to distinguish a late deceleration from an atypical deceleration but in practice as they are both abnormal features they both render the CTG pathological so action is required.

An image of a CTG showing late decelerations can be found on the following page.

Late decelerations

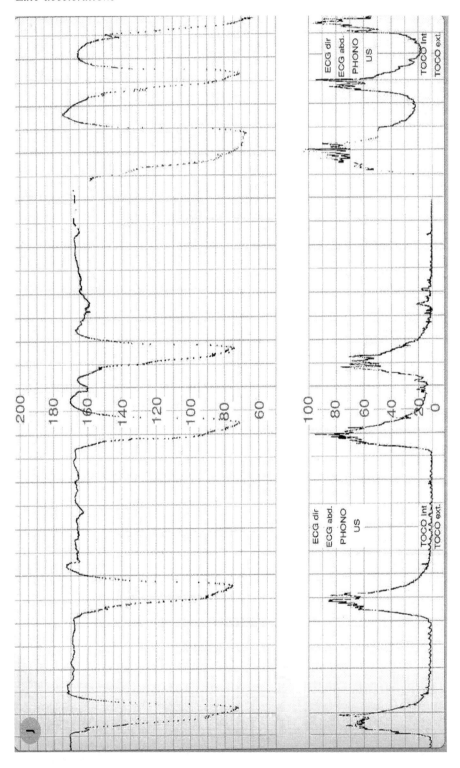

10.8   MONITORING OF LOW RISK PREGNANCIES

There is no evidence that women with babies at low risk of developing intrapartum hypoxia will benefit from continuous fetal heart rate monitoring and studies have confirmed that despite an increased number of obstetric interventions outcomes for babies are not improved. The nature of chronic intrauterine hypoxia is such that with careful intermittent monitoring any deviation from normal should be easily identified and electronic fetal monitoring commenced in plenty of time for an intervention to occur. The type of monitoring is clearly identified for low risk women in labour. In the first stage of labour the fetal heart should be listened to every 15 minutes for a minute after a contraction and in the second stage of labour for one minute every 5 minutes or after each contraction if they are more frequent than every 5 minutes. Any rise in baseline, deceleration or change in maternal condition should prompt continuous electronic fetal monitoring.

10.9   MANAGEMENT OF A PATHOLOGICAL CTG

The CTG is not a diagnostic tool, it is a screening tool for fetal hypoxia in labour. However, by the time a CTG is pathological it is important to take action to either confirm that the baby is not hypoxic by undertaking a fetal blood sample, or if this is not possible to move to deliver the baby. The decision to undertake a fetal blood sample must be taken within the clinical context. In a primiparous patient in very early labour with a pathological CTG and other risk factors such as meconium stained liquor where the likelihood of a delivery soon is low, it may be more reasonable to proceed straight to caesarean section. In a multiparous patient who is progressing rapidly a normal fetal blood sample result may give the time needed to complete the delivery. The fetal blood sample result reflects the condition of the baby at the time of the test and is not predictive, so if the CTG remains pathological the fetal blood sample will need to be repeated

Fetal blood sample result	Management
>7.25	Repeat if CTG remains pathological after 1 hour
7.21–7.24	Repeat or deliver depending on clinical situation
<7.20	Urgent delivery

10.10   ASSESSMENT OF THE BABY AFTER DELIVERY

APGAR scores (in a range of 0 to 10) evaluate the condition of the baby at birth to determine whether resuscitation is required, they are not a good prognostic indictor. In most maternity units it is now mandatory to take cord gases from both the umbilical artery and vein after all operative vaginal deliveries and after all emergency caesarean sections and in many units cord blood gases are taken after all deliveries. The cord gases at delivery, which as a minimum should record the pH and base excess in the umbilical vein and artery, are more useful particularly when correlated with any early neonatal problems.

10.11   EFFECTS OF FETAL ASPHYXIA

Fetal asphyxia due to impaired gas exchange will lead to hypoxaemia (a low level of oxygen in the fetal blood with a high carbon dioxide level) and if the insult continues to a fetal acidosis (high hydrogen ion concentration in the tissues) and a metabolic acidosis leading to cell poisoning and death. Birth brain injury due to intrauterine asphyxia will occur in up to 10% of babies born with a base deficit of 12-16 mmols/l and in up to 40% of babies born with a base deficit of greater than 16. There is a link between the presence of a fetal acidemia at birth and the development of cerebral palsy.

Criteria for the diagnosis intrapartum related cerebral palsy
- pH less than 7
- Base deficit greater than 12mmols/l
- Early onset moderate or severe neonatal encephalopathy in babies greater than 34 weeks
- Spastic quadriplegic or more rarely dyskinetic type cerebral palsy
- Exclusion of other causes

10.12   WHY IS A PATHOLOGICAL CTG NOT ACTED ON?

Despite extensive guidelines on the interpretation of fetal heart rate monitoring, a failure to recognise and act on a pathological CTG accounts for 20% of all claims by cause.

Factors include:
- failure to recognise a pathological CTG;
- failure to respond to a pathological CTG;
- delayed action once pathological CTG recognised.

Many of these failures will be system failures although this does not remove the individual accountability of the obstetrician and or midwife. System failures include:
(1)   Inappropriate delegation to junior medical staff
       Most maternity units in the UK have a different skill mix depending on the time of day, and while there has been great debate over the feasibility of senior medical staff presence overnight it remains a fact that most consultant obstetricians are on call from home at night. This is a common

occurrence. There is no consistency as to the grade of the most senior obstetrician in the unit at night. So while some units are well staffed with senior level trainees many are not.

(2) Poor supervision
Again most often at night a junior trainee may be left to handle a very difficult case and even if the consultant is on their way in from home there will be delay. Many maternity units are reliant on locum staff who may never have worked in that unit before and are not familiar with the policies and procedures.

(3) The teaching of the interpretation of CTG is essential and there is no defined systematic way to teach CTG interpretation.

(4) Staff shortages particularly will require midwives to look after more than one woman in labour.

10.13   SPECIFIC PROBLEMS

10.13.1   The use of oxytocin

Syntocinon, a form of synthetic oxytocin, is used to initiate contractions in a woman who is undergoing induction of labour and it is also used when there is delay in the progress of labour to increase both the strength and frequency of the contractions. Syntocinon will also increase the resting tone of the uterus reducing the amount of blood entering the utero placental space between contractions. A healthy fetus will tolerate this additional stress but if the contractions occur too frequently, ie greater than 5 in 10 minutes, there is little time for recovery from the contraction before the next one starts, which can lead to an increased risk of hypoxia. Every maternity unit should have a guideline outlining the use of syntocinon with the regime for increasing the dose. Mistakes occur when syntocinon is commenced in the presence of an already suspicious or pathological CTG or when the syntocinon is increased too rapidly. Syntocinon is sometimes increased too rapidly in the presence of a pathological CTG in the hope that the delivery will occur quickly. Syntocinon is also continued in the presence of a pathological fetal heart rate pattern, thereby increasing the effects of the asphyxia on the baby. Syntocinon should only ever be used when there is clear documentation of the fetal heart rate, and if there is a loss of contact the syntocinon should be stopped and the fetal heart rate located and recorded before the syntocinon is recommenced.

10.13.2   Maternal heart rate monitoring

When the maternal heart rate is high, as can happen due to pain or in the presence of infection, it can be very difficult to distinguish between fetal and maternal heart rate. It is very important that when CTG is commenced the maternal heart rate is simultaneously recorded to avoid such an event. More modern CTG machines have the capability to record both the maternal and fetal heart rate onto the CTG record simultaneously, where both can be easily seen.

In the CTG on the following pages the maternal heart rate was noted to be 120, the heart rate was recorded until delivery when a macerated stillborn baby was delivered. The baby had clearly died some time before labour but the CTG demonstrates how easy it is to misinterpret the maternal heart rate for the fetus. Figure A shows the heart rate at the beginning of the recording (maternal heart rate) and Figure B the recording just before delivery. The clue that the maternal heart rate is being monitored in Figure B is the response of the heart rate to the contractions and the difficulty in determining the baseline in the presence of normal baseline variability. In this situation, when there is difficulty in distinguishing the two heart rates, it is reasonable to apply a fetal scalp electrode to establish for certain the fetal heart rate.

Figure A

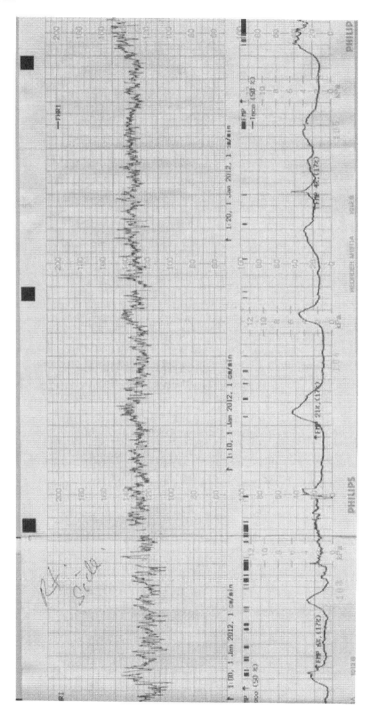

Figure B

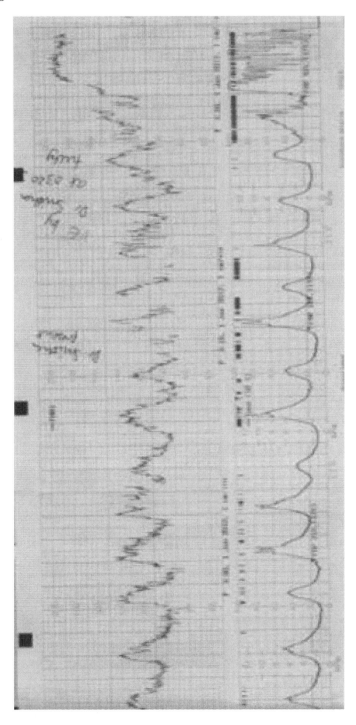

10.13.3 Monitoring of multiple pregnancy

Twins in labour are at high risk of intrapartum hypoxia as one or both twins have an increased risk of fetal growth restriction. The monitoring of twins in labour can be difficult and time consuming for the midwife. A twin monitor must always be used so that the two fetal hearts are recorded at the same time onto the same CTG strip. The most common problems are the monitoring of one twin twice with no recording of the second twin and difficulty in consistently monitoring the second twin. This is another situation when the use of a fetal scalp electrode can be very helpful.

10.14 SUMMARY

The delivery of a baby with irreversible brain damage is a tragic event. Only a small number of these cases are due to intrapartum hypoxia and in many of these cases the damage is unavoidable despite the best efforts of the obstetric team. There are a small number of cases where there was a missed opportunity to extract the baby from a hostile environment. In these cases careful analysis of the clinical case is required to establish whether the CTG was pathological and thence to determine why action was not taken. Issues to consider are:

(1) Were relevant risk factors identified clearly in the medical record?

(2) Was the team providing care competent to provide the care and was the delegation of the care to the doctor appropriate?

(3) Were there staffing issues that meant that the midwife and obstetrician were too busy with other cases to provide adequate care?

(4) If syntocinon was used was it appropriate to start it and then to continue to use it with a pathological CTG?

CHAPTER 11

ADULT NEURO-RADIOLOGY

Andrew Molyneux

11.1 INTRODUCTION: THE ROLE OF ADULT NEURO-IMAGING

Brain imaging is a crucial part in the assessment of patients with severe brain injury from a variety of different causes. It is possible, in some cases, to provide specific help to the courts in establishing the likely sequence of events leading to such injury, based on the brain imaging that is available.

The role of imaging in both the clinical and medico-legal context is to try to establish the causation of such damage and, in the clinical context, to guide appropriate treatment.

It may also be valuable in establishing the timing of such damage that might have occurred and whether, in the medico-legal context, but for a breach of duty of care such damage may have occurred in any event.

There are several pathological processes which lead to brain injury, the most common and widely known being acute strokes due to blockage of a blood vessel or haemorrhage in the brain.

11.2 NON-TRAUMATIC INJURY

11.2.1 Non-traumatic brain injury is caused by many different pathological processes

The commonest cause of a stroke is occlusion of a blood vessel, either within the brain itself or in the major blood vessels supplying the brain, this accounts for about 80% of cases. It leads to ischaemic stroke (lack of blood flow). When the neurons (nerve cells) are deprived of oxygen then rapid cell death and cerebral infarction occurs. The term ischaemia is used when cellular function is impaired but the cells may still be recoverable. Infarction is when cell death has occurred and cells are not recoverable.

20% of strokes are due to brain haemorrhage, which is usually spontaneous brain haemorrhage into the brain substance itself accounting for about 15% of strokes. The most common aetiological factor is hypertension, but rarely other underlying pathologies such as vascular malformation are the cause.

About 5% of stroke cases are due to rupture of an intracranial aneurysm causing a subarachnoid haemorrhage (SAH). This tends to occur in younger patients, often in their 50s and 60s, and is more common in females. It is significantly related to smoking. This is in contrast to the other types of stroke, which are much more common in the elderly population, particularly patients over 75, with the incidence rising dramatically in later decades.

Generalised hypoxic/ischaemic injury to the brain is most commonly seen following resuscitation after cardiac or respiratory arrest. It usually presents with different patterns of damage compared with ischaemic strokes, where focal blood vessel occlusion occurs.

Intracranial infections causing brain abscesses, meningitis which is infection spreading around the brain in the spinal fluid, or infection over the surface of the brain known as subdural empyema. These may all lead to focal or more generalised damage, depending on how promptly the infection is recognised and treated and its severity. Delayed diagnosis can have catastrophic consequences.

Brain tumours are relatively common however their presence is usually readily recognised if a CT or MRI scan is done and the prognosis for such tumours will depend entirely on the tumour type and location. See section below on brain tumours.

Modern brain imaging relies on both CT scanning and magnetic resonance imaging (MRI), both of which now provide extremely high quality and detailed imaging. The technique used depends on the clinical situation and the type of pathology that is sought.

11.3   MAIN PATHOLOGICAL CATEGORIES OF BRAIN INJURY

11.3.1   Stroke

Stroke is a clinical diagnosis; it is based on the sudden onset of a focal neurological deficit such as a hemiparesis, facial weakness and or speech disturbance. Public awareness of the importance of the recognition of stroke was increased several years ago with a national publicity campaign promoting early stroke recognition, the FAST test based on the Face, Arm, Speech, Time to increase public awareness. The aim was to get more patients into hospital in time to be eligible for intravenous thrombolytic therapy and to increase the proportion of patients arriving at the hospital receiving intravenous thrombolysis treatment.

Thrombolysis treatment has been shown in randomised trials to improve the outcome of patients with acute stroke due to blockage of an intracranial blood vessel, provided it is given within 4.5 hours of the stroke, although the size of the actual clinical benefit on outcome is quite modest (4–7% absolute benefit of a good outcome).

A National Stroke Strategy was implemented in the UK in 2008, designed at triaging patients to the correct emergency unit which could provide 24-hour stroke care, called Hyper-Acute Stroke Units (HASUs).

Acute stroke is divided into three main pathological types.

11.3.1.1 Ischaemic stroke

Ischaemic stroke is due to the blockage of an intracranial blood vessel or of one of the main blood vessels supplying the brain. This may involve the carotid artery in the neck, the intracranial portion of the carotid artery, or the main middle cerebral artery supply of the lateral side of the brain. Blockage of smaller arteries may either be more peripherally situated arteries supplying the cortex of the brain or those deep within the brain. When an occlusion affects one of the small arteries deep within the brain it may lead to deep strokes involving the white matter pathways, often called lacunar strokes because pathologically and on imaging they appear like small 'lakes'.

Depending on where the vessel occlusion occurs will determine the clinical signs in any given patient and which part of the body and whether speech is affected. Ischaemic stroke are responsible for about 80% of all strokes. They are much more common in later decades of life, with the incidence rising exponentially over the age of 75 and particularly over 85.

Figure 11.1: CT of ischaemic acute stroke

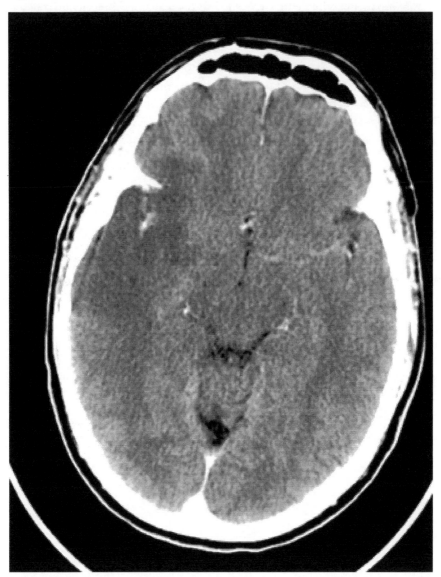

CT scan of acute cerebral infarct: This scan shows the presence of low attenuation in the right temporal lobe due to occlusion of the right middle cerebral artery about 24 hours earlier. The low attenuation area lies in the lateral aspect of the right temporal lobe.

Figure 11.2: MRI of ischaemic acute stroke: T2 sequence

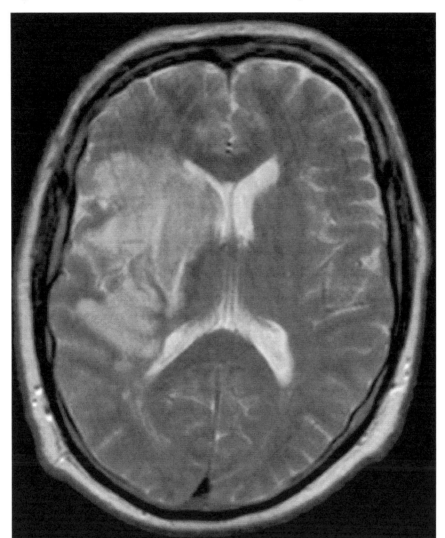

MRI scan T2 weighted sequence showing extensive early infarction in the right temporal lobe due to occlusion of the right carotid and middle cerebral artery 3 days' earlier.

Most ischaemic strokes affect the anterior part of the brain in the territory of the carotid arteries. However other parts of the brain may be affected.

Figure 11.3: MRI of ischaemic acute stroke: FLAIR sequence

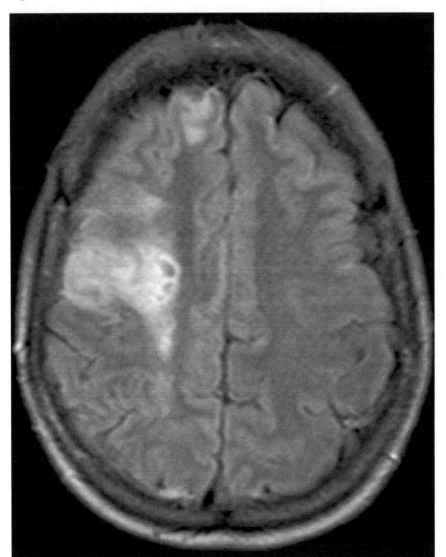

MRI Scan FLAIR: (Flow Attenuated Inversion Recovery) sequence of cortical infarct in a patient with multiple right middle cerebral hemisphere infarcts.

Posterior circulation stroke

A small but important proportion of strokes affect the arteries that supply the posterior part of the brain, the vertebral and basilar arteries.

These strokes may be more difficult to diagnose clinically because they do not immediately provide localised symptoms with a hemiparesis, hemiplegia or dysphasia. Not uncommonly they have prodromal symptoms, such as dizziness and unsteadiness, nausea and vomiting prior to a developing major stroke due to complete vessel occlusion.

If a basilar artery occlusion occurs then there is a rapid onset of coma and frequently respiratory depression. Without reopening of the basilar artery the clinical outcome is frequently catastrophic, with 85% of patients being dead or extremely disabled.

Strokes in this location also give rise to what is termed the 'locked in syndrome'. In this situation a patient can be fully alert and orientated, but they are only able to move their eyes. This tragic situation was illustrated and described in the well-known book and film, *The Diving Bell and the Butterfly*[1] written by Jean-Dominique Bauby, the editor-in-chief of French magazine *Elle*, who suffered from such a stroke. The book was written with the help of his occupational therapist.

This condition most frequently affects relatively younger patients, and is sometimes secondary to what is termed an arterial dissection, affecting the vertebral artery. Arterial dissection itself occurs when there is a split in the inner lining wall of the blood vessel and a haematoma forms between the layers of the arterial wall, and leads to acute narrowing or sometimes occlusion of the vessel, clot formation at the site which breaks off and blocks distal vessels.

Whilst the evidence base for acute treatment of basilar strokes due to basilar artery occlusion is incomplete, in many large UK centres both thrombolytic treatment and endovascular acute clot extraction by catheter techniques, similar to those used in cardiology in patients with acute myocardial infarction, is increasingly used in this group of patients. There is no good randomised data in respect of such treatment, however the outcomes observed in anecdotal series appear to show dramatic improvement over natural history, which as outlined above almost uniformly results in dreadful clinical outcomes with more than 85% of patients who suffer a basilar thrombosis being dead or catastrophically disabled.

---

[1]   Harper Perennial, 2008.

Figure 11.4: Basilar artery stroke: cerebellar infarction

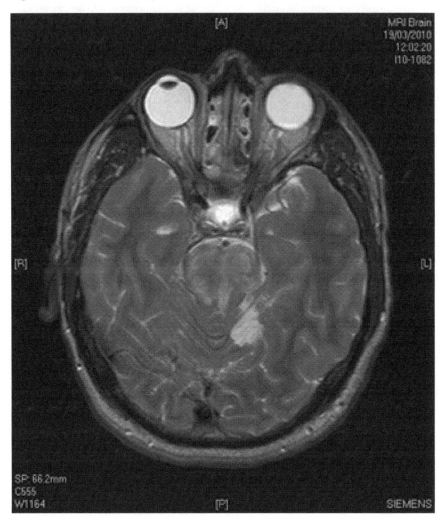

Large brain stem infarct and multiple cerebellar infarcts in patient with occlusion of vertebral and basilar artery. Resulting in locked–in syndrome.

Figure 11.5: Basilar artery stroke examples: brain stem infarction

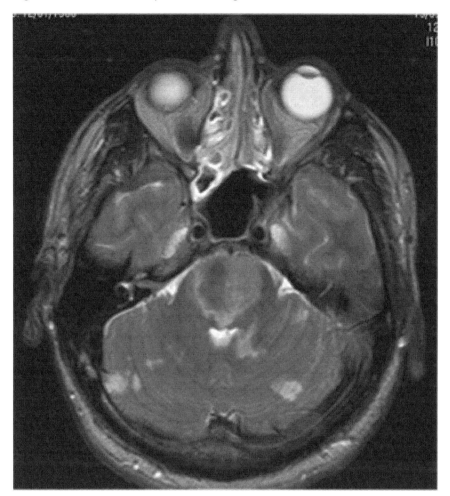

Same patient with images of the upper brain stem and cerebellum showing acute infarction.

11.3.1.2   Primary intracerebral haemorrhage

The second main type of stroke is primary intracerebral haemorrhage. This is due to rupture of a small blood vessel intracranially, it is associated with high blood pressure and advancing age; other risk factors include smoking and diabetes.

The diagnosis is made by CT scanning which will clearly demonstrate the presence of the intracerebral clot.

Figure 11.6. CT of Intracerebral clot

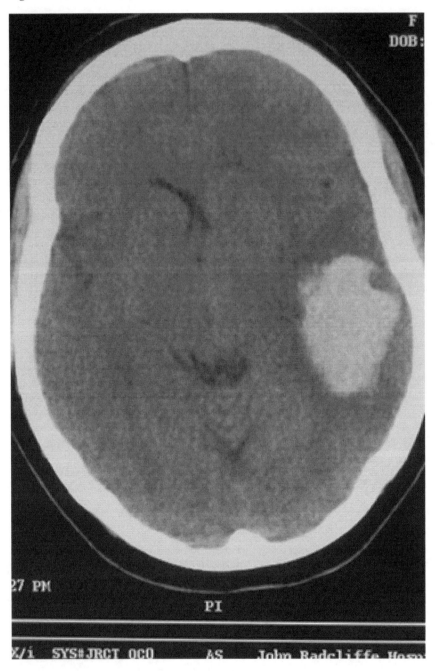

CT scan showing acute intracerebral clot in the left frontal lobe.

Treatment of acute ischaemic stroke

Urgent imaging prior to the use of intravenous thrombolysis is essential. Ideally this should be delivered as soon as possible and within a maximum of 4.5 hours after the stroke. It is not possible to distinguish acute ischaemic stroke patients from patients with intracranial haemorrhage clinically and thus when a patient is admitted with suspected ischaemic stroke who is potentially eligible for thrombolysis they need to have an emergency CT scan to exclude the presence of a haemorrhage. This is described by NICE Stroke guidelines as the next patient on the CT scanner or, if out of hours, within an hour.[2]

11.3.1.3   Subarachnoid haemorrhage and aneurysm rupture

The third and less common type of stroke, occurring in about 5% of patients, is subarachnoid haemorrhage. While this may be accompanied by neurological deficits at the time of onset, the cardinal feature of subarachnoid haemorrhage is the sudden onset of an extremely severe headache (coming on instantaneously or over a matter of minutes) usually described as the worst of the patient's life, and not uncommonly described as being hit on the head with a cricket bat (or other such object). The diagnosis of subarachnoid haemorrhage is particularly important, because the majority of patients who suffer this condition have an underlying intracranial aneurysm as the cause (approximately 85%).

If a patient survives the initial haemorrhage from an aneurysm rupture and recovers to a good clinical condition, with a Glasgow Coma score of 12–15/15 then urgent diagnosis and treatment of an aneurysm if it is present is essential to prevent re-bleeding from further rupture of the aneurysm. Re-bleeding occurs in about 30% of patients within the first 30 days of an initial haemorrhage. If an aneurysm does re-bleed then the likelihood of a catastrophic outcome, either death or major disability, is of the order of 80%.

---

[2]   2008, see www.nice.org.uk/guidance/cg68.

Figure 11.7: Acute subarachnoid haemorrhage due to aneurysm rupture.

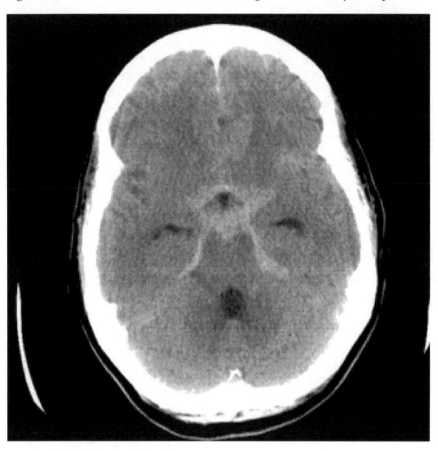

Acute subarachnoid haemorrhage with extensive blood shows as high attenuation surrounding the basal cisterns.

Figure 11.8: Cerebral aneurysm on CT angiogram

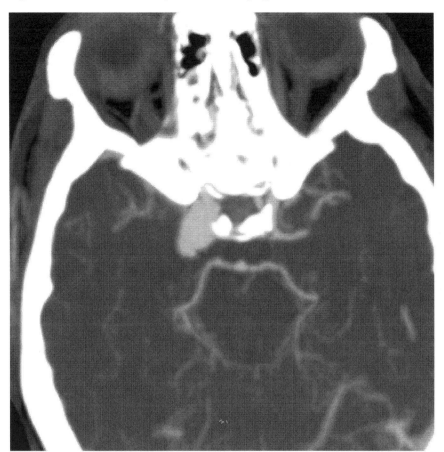

CT angiogram axial reconstructed image showing large aneurysm arising from the right internal carotid artery.

Complications of aneurysm rupture

Even when patients survive a subarachnoid haemorrhage, and despite proper management, significant complications can arise which have catastrophic affect on patient outcome. These include delayed cerebral ischaemia due to vasospasm, hydrocephalus due to blockage of the spinal fluid pathways by the presence of blood, or other medical complications. These complications may occur without any shortcomings in care, and are sometimes unavoidable.

Figure 11.9 Late complication of vasospasm following SAH

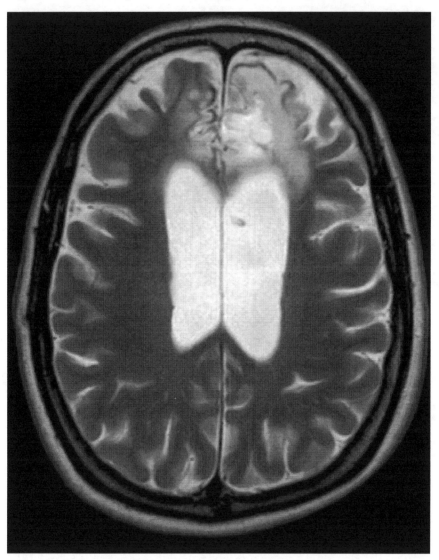

Patient 2 years after SAH whom suffered a re-bleed from an anterior communicating artery aneurysm and developed severe delayed cerebral ischemia due to vasospasm which resulted in bilateral frontal infarction. The ventricles are markedly enlarged due to local and generalised cerebral volume loss.

11.4 MEDICO-LEGAL ISSUES IN STROKE

11.4.1 Main issues arising in respect of clinical negligence cases in patients with stroke

11.4.1.1 Delayed diagnosis

The delay in diagnosis of acute ischaemic stroke usually results from a delay either by the ambulance service or in accident and emergency care with a failure to recognise that the stroke has occurred, or in achieving emergency brain imaging.

As noted above, following several prospective randomised clinical trials, there is good evidence that intravenous thrombolysis within 4.5 hours of an acute ischaemic stroke results in better clinical outcomes. However benefits of such treatment is very modest, approximately 4–7% absolute benefit in respect of preventing major disability for patients eligible for thrombolytic treatment.

This modest and unpredictable clinical gain in absolute benefit makes it difficult in many cases to show that even if there was a breach of duty of care, or failure to provide brain imaging sufficiently quickly, proving the effect of such a delay on the ultimate clinical outcome in any particular case is more difficult. Sometimes a delay in delivering thrombolysis, or being unable to give a patient thrombolysis because of a delay, gives rise to allegations of breach of duty, but proving causation is difficult.

11.4.1.2 Specific medico-legal issues in subarachnoid haemorrhage

The litigation situation is quite different in respect of subarachnoid haemorrhage. The failure to recognise the possibility of a SAH and to investigate can be catastrophic.

Delay in the diagnosis of a subarachnoid haemorrhage may occur either in primary care services, such as NHS direct and telephone consultations with out of hours services, general practice consultations or in accident and emergency departments. Less commonly it is in medical units once a patient is admitted to hospital.

If there is a failure to carry out the appropriate diagnostic test then it may result in discharge of the patient and the failure to investigate with an urgent CT scan. If the CT scan is normal but the diagnosis is suspected then it is mandatory to perform a lumbar puncture to exclude the diagnosis of subarachnoid haemorrhage. Blood is seen on the CT scan in the first 24 hours after a SAH and is present in about 95% of patients, however the blood rapidly disperses and may be no longer detectable within 2–3 days on the CT. In these circumstances examination of the spinal fluid is essential. The presence of blood products within the spinal fluid will last up to about 2 weeks and they will still be detectable using appropriate biochemistry.

Delay in making a diagnosis of possible SAH will expose a patient to the risk of recurrent aneurysm rupture with potentially catastrophic outcome. A second bleed from an aneurysm causes death or major disability in about 80% of patients. These are relatively young patients often in their 50s and 60s and the consequences of long-term care requirement for a totally dependent patient are obvious. Indeed the burden on families and society of ongoing disability associated with SAH is greater than that for ischaemic stroke because of the much younger age profile and the longer life expectancy of dependent survivors.

The second complication, absent re-bleeding, is the effect of dehydration and lack of the use of Nimodipine, a drug shown to have an effect in reducing the risks of cerebral vasospasm. This may expose the patient to a greater risk of developing delayed cerebral ischaemia due to vasospasm which may also result in a poor clinical outcome.

When a re-bleed from a ruptured aneurysm takes place several days after an initial presentation which has been missed then such cases may be very difficult to defend in respect to causation.

11.4.1.3   Cerebral venous sinus thrombosis

This is a rare cause of stroke-like damage in the brain. It occurs when a clot forms in the large veins draining blood from the brain and results in what is termed venous infarction with a rapid rise in intracranial pressure, and frequently haemorrhage into an area of infarction. It is most commonly seen in younger female patients and is associated with obesity and oral contraceptives.

11.4.1.4   Hypoxic-ischaemic brain injury

The principal role of brain imaging in adult patients with suspected hypoxic ischaemic injury is one of establishing causation and assisting in the determination of the extent of the brain injury. The patterns of ischaemic injury in patients who have suffered a cardio-respiratory arrest usually differ from embolic strokes due to blockage of a specific blood vessel. This is because certain neurones in the brain are more susceptible than others to hypoxic damage. This particularly applies to those nerve cells with the highest metabolic demands; usually in the basal nuclei of the brain, the basal ganglia and the hippocampal formations within the temporal lobes. This latter part of the brain plays a vital role in memory function, particularly laying down new memory and short-term memory. The other parts that are most vulnerable are those areas of the cerebral cortex where the collateral blood supply is the worst, known as the watershed areas. These are the junctional areas between the different cerebral artery territories, the anterior and middle cerebral arteries, and the posterior and middle cerebral arteries.

11.5   CAUSES OF HYPOXIC BRAIN INJURY

11.5.1   Cardiac and respiratory arrest

In any patient who has a cardiac or respiratory arrest when there is circulatory failure and low levels of oxygenated blood the most vulnerable organ is the brain.

External cardiac massage maintains a degree of brain perfusion but as time passes the metabolic demands of the nerve cells exceed the oxygen supply that is getting to the them and they start to fail and become ischaemic. Ultimately this leads to cell death, or infarction.

If circulatory failure lasts more than a few minutes then effects on the brain are likely to occur. Sometimes these are evident on late imaging, particularly follow-up MRI scans. However, not all damage is detectable on MRI scans and there may be significant damage which leads to cognitive change which is only detectable on objective neuropsychological examination.

Some of the features associated with brain damage due to ischaemia following cardiac arrest are shown in Figure 10.

Figure 11.10: Post cardiac arrest images showing multiple areas of infarction

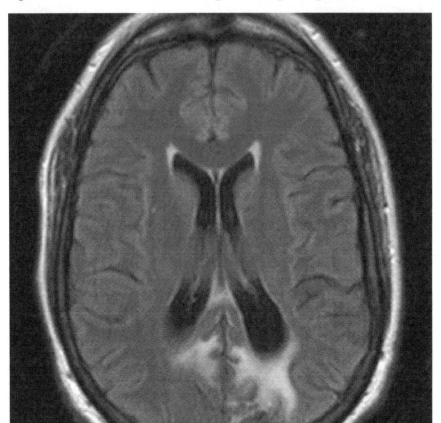

MRI scan showing 'watershed' infarction after cardio-respiratory arrest with cortical infarction in the distal arterial territories between the posterior middle and anterior cerebral arteries.

11.5.1.1   Cerebral air embolism

This is a rare cause of brain damage in adults. It is most commonly associated with poor management of central venous lines, in patients in intensive care or on wards. Air may be flushed in by accident, such as by emptying of an intravenous infusion bag. If a substantial volume of air enters the venous circulation it can pass through the lungs, or through unrecognised shunts between from the right side of the heart to the left, even in patients with otherwise normal heart and lungs. When air enters the systemic arterial circulation it can block small and intermediate sized arteries' circulation. If the patient is allowed to sit up on the removal of a central venous line then the negative venous pressure may allow air to be sucked into the large veins and to enter the right side of the heart in significant quantities.

Small quantities of air on the right side of the heart do not usually cause a problem. However, if the volume is large such volumes can pass from the right side of the heart into the left side and thence into the aorta and systemic circulation and to the brain.

Occasionally surgical errors such as might be associated with cardiac bypass surgery may result in significant air emboli reaching the brain.

The imaging findings most seen are as multiple scattered areas of infarction affecting the cerebral cortex.

Figure 11.11 CT scan soon after an acute cerebral air embolus

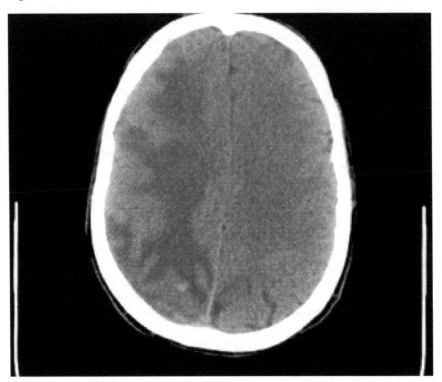

CT scan soon after an acute cerebral air embolus with widespread acute ischaemic damage in the right hemisphere.

11.5.1.2 Raised intracranial pressure and hydrocephalus

Hydrocephalus is the term used when the ventricles within the brain enlarge due to a failure of the cerebrospinal fluid (CSF) to drain properly from the brain. CSF is produced within the lateral ventricles of the brain and it flows from the lateral ventricles to the third and fourth ventricle and into the subarachnoid space around the brain and spinal cord, where it is absorbed. Hydrocephalus is caused whenever there is disruption to the flow and/or absorption of the fluid This may be because of an obstruction to the flow of the fluid by a mass lesion, such as a tumour pressing on the pathways of flow, or due to a failure to absorb the fluid after it has passed out of the ventricles into the subarachnoid space surrounding the brain. When the flow is blocked before it exits the ventricles it is called 'obstructive or non-communicating hydrocephalus'. When it occurs due to failure to absorb the fluid it is called 'communicating hydrocephalus'.

The clinical hallmark of hydrocephalus is headache, particularly if it is acute or sub-acute. If it is chronic then eye symptoms may develop with visual blurring and if not treated can lead to optic nerve atrophy and blindness.

11.5.1.3   *Severely raised intracranial pressure*

This can occur with a number of conditions, due to tumours, infection such as meningitis, brain abscess or infection over the surface of the brain – subdural empyemas.

Intracranial infections

Brain abscess. Whilst these are uncommon they may be seen associated with systemic infections such as septicaemia, immune compromised patients and patients in particular in some susceptible ethnic groups from South Asia, and Sub-Saharan Africa where tuberculosis is a relatively common cause of CNS infection.

Abscesses present most commonly with ring enhancing masses demonstrated on CT or MRI scanning and need emergency treatment. Sometimes, on imaging grounds alone it is not possible to distinguish brain abscesses from malignant brain tumours and there is a real danger that the much more common brain tumours are assumed to be the cause of a mass lesion and the presence of a brain abscess is not considered. It is essential in all cases where there is any doubt that a brain abscess may be in the differential diagnosis that a proper diagnosis is achieved urgently by biopsy.

Figure 11.12: Brain Abscess

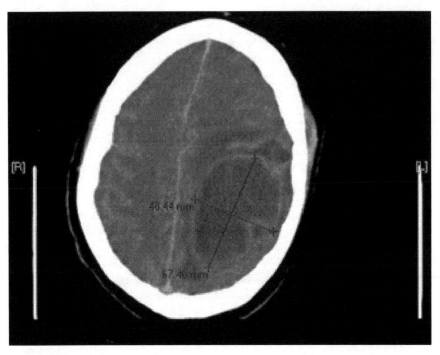

CT scan of brain abscess, showing very large ring enhancing mass, initially misdiagnosed as a tumour that resulted in delayed treatment of the abscess and a catastrophic clinical outcome.

Meningitis

Meningitis is usually diagnosed based on the history and the findings on lumbar puncture in the CSF. Sometimes, however, when meningitis is severe the infection may give rise to collections of infected material within the subdural space and causes the enlargement of the ventricular system because of the impairment of spinal fluid – hydrocephalus . This, combined with the brain swelling secondary to the infection, also gives rise to raised intracranial pressure. Under these circumstances lumbar puncture maybe hazardous because of raised intracranial pressure. Imaging prior to lumbar puncture is essential to exclude significant hydrocephalus in this situation. If a lumbar puncture is performed when there is hydrocephalus present with significantly raised intracranial pressure, then the brain can descend acutely and herniate at the foramen magnum causing brain stem compression, and sudden death in extreme cases.

Figure 11.13: Hydrocephalus associated with meningitis

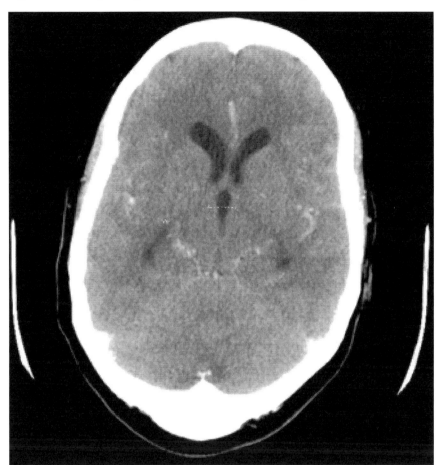

CT scan of a patient admitted with acute meningitis and hydrocephalus with moderate enlargement of the lateral ventricles.

Figure 11.14: Cerebellar infarction following coning after lumbar puncture

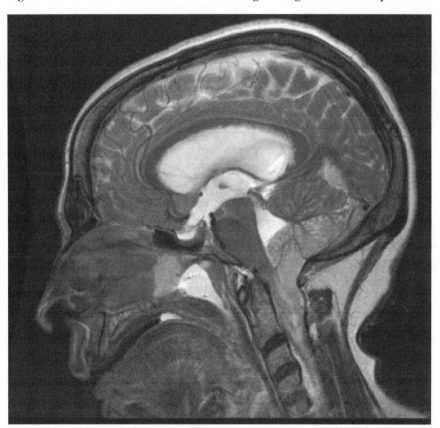

MRI scan done several hours after a lumbar puncture in the same patient who collapsed unconscious shortly after the LP and 'coned'.

A situation where the brain stem is forced downwards and is compressed into the foramen magnum causing severe brain stem compression leading to brain stem and cerebellar infarction. She died the following day.

Subdural empyema

This is a rare but easily missed intracranial infection which is often associated with spread from infection in the paranasal sinuses. It is often subtle in imaging appearances, but very characteristic and needs to be treated promptly and aggressively, requiring high dose antibiotics and surgery to evacuate the infected collection.

Brain tumours

Brain tumours divide into two distinct groups; those arising outside the brain itself, between the skull and the brain, usually from the lining meninges, and those from the cranial nerves, such as the auditory nerve. Most are benign meningioma, a tumour of the lining of the brain being the commonest. They are usually, but not always, surgically removable, depending on size and location. Tumours arising within the brain itself are mostly commonly glioma's which are usually malignant. Despite modern management techniques malignant glioma's frequently have a poor prognosis.

The most common source of medico-legal claims in respect of brain tumours is delayed diagnosis. This arises when there has been failure to refer a patient for a CT or MRI scan, although with good availability of modern imaging this is less common. Sometimes, particularly in district hospitals where the expertise in reporting brain scans is more limited, tumours may be missed on the scan. In some circumstances what are actually tumours maybe be misinterpreted as infarcts (strokes).

However, even when a breach of duty can be demonstrated, the success or otherwise of such actions will crucially rely on causation and whether the delay affected the ability to achieve satisfactory treatment of the tumour, and how the prognosis and outcome has been changed. This will very much depend on the type of tumour and the length of the delay concerned. For malignant glioma, it is unlikely in most cases that the ultimate prognosis is affected, although considerable distress may be caused to the family and patients. For benign meningioma's and acoustic nerve tumours there maybe circumstances when the difficulty and complications of tumour removal may be affected by such a delay, so the ultimate disability and intervening pain and suffering due to the delay are significant.

Figure 11.15: Primary Malignant Brain Tumour (Glioblastoma)

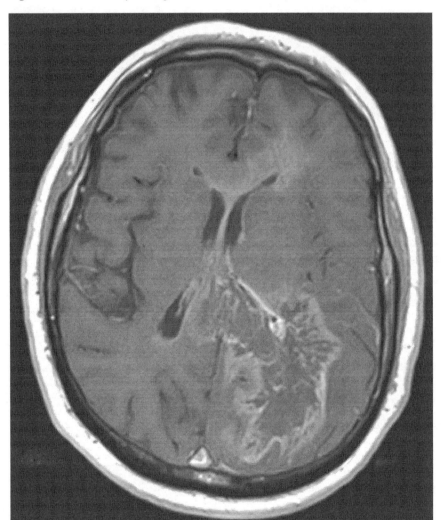

MRI scan: T1 contrast enhanced scan of a patient with a large malignant glioblastoma in the left hemisphere with extensive infiltration through much of the hemisphere and spread through the corpus callosum to the other side. Marked compression of the left lateral ventricle.

11.6   TRAUMATIC BRAIN INJURY

The incidence of severe brain injury, particularly due to road traffic accidents is declining. Nevertheless imaging may play a crucial role in the assessment of those patients unfortunate enough to sustain a head injury. It can provide objective evidence of damage in some patients and may help apportion the effects of the primary injury, or secondary effects from later aspects of head injury management.

11.6.1   Primary brain injury

Sudden deceleration of the brain, whether it be in a RTA, a fall such as striking the pavement, direct trauma from a collision between a car and a pedestrian, or direct blow to the head such as in an assault has the potential to cause direct damage to the brain. When severe rapid deceleration occurs, such as in a high speed road accident, damage to the brain is most commonly due to the disruption of the axons, the long nerve fibres that form the interconnections of the nerve cells or neurons. These pathways are what make up the white matter tracts of the brain, of which there are myriads. This type of injury is known as diffuse axonal injury, and it disrupts the communication between the neurons.

When a brain injury is severe enough these changes may be evident on acute imaging normally with CT scanning, with very small diffuse white matter haemorrhages, know as petechial hemorrhages. However many of these haemorrhages may be beyond the resolution of CT scans. Thus a normal CT scan immediately after an injury does not exclude a significant primary brain injury.

The other type of injury commonly seen with rapid deceleration when the head strikes a hard object is what is termed a 'coup/contrecoup' (see also Chapter 9). The coup injury, a local contusional injury (bruise) is at the site of the trauma, which may or may not be associated with a localised contusional (bruising) injury in the brain often associated with a small haematoma, this is the coup part and may be associated with a skull fracture in that region. The contrecoup injury is on the opposite side of the brain where the brain strikes the inner table of the skull on the rebound and leads to frequently worse localised contusional injury than that on the side of the direct blow. This is akin to a jelly bouncing and hitting the other side of the container.

The severity of primary brain injuries are a function of the causative trauma and of course this cannot be affected by medical care. The objective of acute care of head injury is to avoid the secondary effects of any primary injury.

Figure 11.16: Contusional coup/contrecoup Injury

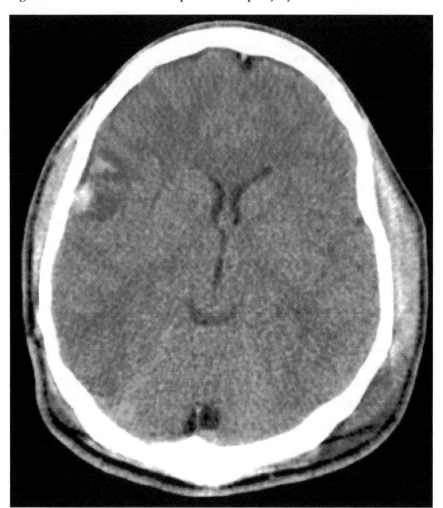

CT scan of patient with an acute head injury.

A contrecoup brain injury. Note the soft tissue swelling externally over the left side of the scalp but the brain injury is on the opposite side within the brain caused by the brain hitting the inner table of the skull resulting in local contusion.

11.6.2 Secondary brain injury

Whenever the skull or brain is injured secondary effects may develop. These can be divided into two distinct aspects.

11.6.2.1 Development of secondary blood clots after head injury

Extra-cerebral haematomas

The classical, but less common, lesion is an extradural haematoma. These may develop after relatively mild trauma, especially if a direct blow to the side of the head has caused a skull fracture which has involved one of the small arteries which lie between the skull and the outer lining membrane – the dura.

Patients with this condition may be fully conscious, or only experience a transient loss of consciousness, eg in a rugby match, after the initial injury, a so-called 'lucid interval', but they may rapidly deteriorate with reduced consciousness level due to accumulation of blood between the outer table of the skull and the dura with progressive increase in intracranial pressure leading to unconsciousness. This is the most pressing and urgent of neurosurgical emergencies. The sooner the clot is relieved by a burr hole or craniotomy the better the chances of a good recovery. Untreated, or with very delayed treatment, they may result in severe brain injury due to prolonged severely raised intracranial pressure, or even death.

Figure 11.17: Extradural haematoma

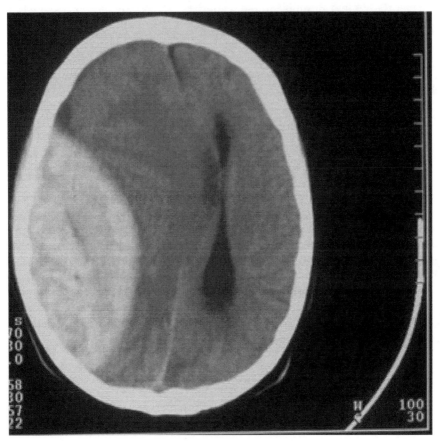

CT scan of a very large acute extradural haematoma with very severe midline shift and compression of the right lateral ventricle

Subdural haematoma

These develop between the inner lining of the dura and the brain itself. They may be acute and develop and enlarge soon after brain injury. Like extradural haematomas they may need emergency surgical evacuation. Alternatively they may be chronic (often so in elderly individuals) and develop after minor trauma, developing very slowly, over days or weeks in some cases.

Imaging, as in all acute head injury, is primarily reliant on CT scanning, which readily demonstrates the developing complications of haematomas.

11.6.2.2   Other secondary effects of head injury

Intra-cerebral haematomas and development of contusions

In many cases of severe primary trauma the appearances on the CT scan done a few days after the initial injury frequently shows more extensive changes, with larger more prominent contusions and frequently the development of surrounding secondary oedema and consequent swelling in the brain tissues which leads to either localised or diffuse brain swelling. It is these secondary effects of brain injury that acute neuro-intensive care is designed to limit. The crucial aspect being the management of the intracranial pressure, minimising the rise in the pressure which occurs after injury and maintaining the best possible perfusion and oxygenation of the brain.

To this end management involves direct monitoring of intracranial pressure with a direct 'intracranial pressure bolt' and maintenance of good arterial pressure to maintain cerebral perfusion pressure (the difference between mean arterial pressure (MAP) and intracranial pressure). If this falls too low then there is good evidence that additional neuronal damage will occur.

The role of imaging in this situation is the monitoring of any other complications, which may require surgical intervention, such as the development of haematomas, requiring evacuation, or in extreme cases decompressive craniectomy to remove a substantial amount of the bones of the skull to relieve the intracranial pressure.

11.7   IMAGING ASSESSMENT AFTER BRAIN INJURY

MRI plays a very valuable role in the late assessment after traumatic brain injury. Modern MRI studies can detect a range of pathology associated with brain injury. It is much more sensitive than CT in the detection of a number aspects of previous injury. Certain MRI sequences can detect the presence of previous haemorrhage with great sensitivity, due to detection of small amounts of iron deposition such as those which may be seen in the brain after diffuse axonal injury. These sequences known as gradient echo sequences detect the small quantities of iron which is are deposited in the brain after a haemorrhage, known as haemosiderin, with considerable sensitivity. Areas of previous contusion and local cortical damage are also readily detected on high quality MRI scans. Whilst the majority of MRI scanners in current clinical use operate at 1.5 Teslamagnetic field, 3.0 Tesla scanners, are now available. They have greater resolution and are superior in the detection of iron deposition because of what is called the susceptibility effects produced by the iron deposits, which are much greater at higher magnetic fields. Nevertheless, it must always be recognised that the even if MRI imaging is normal after head injury it does not mean that a significant brain injury has not occurred, and neuropsychological assessment is essential to detect objective effects on behaviour and performance which may have an organic basis. If evidence of damage is present on imaging then it provides strong evidence of specific structural injury.

CHAPTER 12

NEURO-REHABILITATION

Udo Kischka

12.1 INTRODUCTION

Catastrophic injury can cause a wide variety of symptoms that often occur in combination. Brain injury is present in many cases and can result in some of the most serious problems, with symptoms ranging from reduced level of consciousness to motor and sensory impairments to cognitive deficits. Other body parts may be injured or lost, and pain and emotional difficulties are common. These difficulties often render the person dependent on care and support from others, and prevent them from working and engaging in their normal social activities. The task of rehabilitation is, in general terms, to help patients regain their independence and improve their quality of life. Rehabilitation has been shown to be highly effective in achieving these aims. Timely provision of rehabilitation, therapies and support benefits not only the patients, but also their families (and their solicitors). It even benefits the defendants, because good rehabilitation has been shown to reduce complications and the long-term costs for care.

This chapter starts with an overview of common physical and mental difficulties after catastrophic injury that are typically encountered in rehabilitation.

12.1.1 The WHO Model of Functioning, Disability and Health (ICF)

This has been developed to help us understand the consequences of injury or illness by describing their impact on several levels: physiological, psychological and social. The model comprises not only bodily and mental functions, but also the consequences of the illness on the patients' everyday life, including their ability to care for themselves and the impact on their social roles.

The WHO Model of Functioning, Disability and Health

- Impairment: The symptoms and signs, such as weakness of an arm and leg, slurred speech, forgetfulness, or pain.
- Activity (also called disability): This looks at the ability of a person to independently perform activities of daily living (ADL) such as washing, dressing, feeding, continence and walking. ➡

> • Participation (also called handicap): It refers to changes in the person's social roles within their environment, for instance their work and their circle of friends.

Example

Impairment (symptom)	John Miller has a weakness of his right arm
Activity (disability)	Due to the weakness, he cannot dress and wash himself
Participation (handicap)	He cannot do his job as a plumber

Although the model may, at first sight, appear rather abstract, it actually has great practical value for the treatment and the prognosis of people after an injury. It demonstrates that even if the impairment (for instance, the arm weakness) is permanent, it is worthwhile providing rehabilitative therapies because the patient will be enabled to improve in their disability and handicap. They can learn dressing and washing themselves with their unaffected hand, and may even return to some kind of work.

In order to understand how rehabilitation can be used effectively after catastrophic injury, it is necessary to understand the nature and the range of challenges faced by patients and the people around them (including their lawyers). What follows is not a comprehensive description of all possible physical and mental difficulties that may be found after catastrophic injury, but the section focuses on those that are common and typically addressed by neuro-rehabilitation specialists.

12.1.1.1 Impairments (symptoms) after catastrophic injury:

Reduced level of consciousness is the most frequent symptom after head injury in the early stages, and it is the main indicator whether or not a traumatic brain injury has occurred. In the most severe cases, the person is in a coma. When coming out of coma, some patients go on to make gradual improvements in their responsiveness, mobility and communication. Others make a transition into the vegetative state, whereby the patient has no awareness of themselves and their environment around them, but vegetative functions such as heartbeat and breathing keep working, and a kind of sleep-wake-cycle develops. The injured person's basic reflexes continue to function, such as moving a limb to painful stimulation, or even appearing to look around the room. It is therefore often difficult for relatives to accept that the person who shows these reactions is, in fact, unaware of their presence. Standardised observations such as the SMART (sensory modality assessment and rehabilitation technique) and the Wessex Head Injury Matrix have been developed to try and clarify whether or not there is any evidence that the brain injured person is aware of their surroundings. The minimally conscious state (also called minimally responsive state or minimally aware state) describes individuals who have some, but little and only temporary, awareness of themselves and their surroundings. Examples of behaviour that indicates some awareness are following verbal requests repeatedly such as 'squeeze my hand' or 'open your mouth', or reaching out for an object. Detailed information about these states can be found in the recently published National Clinical Guidelines for Prolonged Disorders of Consciousness by the Royal College of Physicians.

Motor deficits

After catastrophic injury, difficulties with moving the different body parts are frequently found due to either injuries or loss of a limb, or due to damage to brain areas involved in motor control.

Loss of a limb: Following the amputation of a limb, patients do not only have to deal with the loss of function, but they also sometimes develop *phantom limb pain.*

Muscle weakness (paresis or plegia) in one or more limbs is the most common motor problem. Muscle weakness after injury can occur in different patterns: *Hemiparesis* means that the injured person has a weakness on one side of his/her body: the arm, the leg and sometimes the face is weak on the same side. *Tetraparesis* (or quadriparesis) is a state whereby an individual has weakness in all four limbs. *Paraparesis* refers to weakness of both legs. Sometimes the trunk muscles are also affected, particularly in the early stages after the injury. Patients then have difficulty sitting on their own and keeping their head upright.

Spasticity: In the days and weeks following the head injury, the paretic limbs sometimes become stiffer, which is called increased muscle tone or *spasticity.* Patients sometimes develop *spasms* whereby the limb jumps intermittently, and sometimes it shakes rhythmically, called *clonus.*

Ataxia and tremor: Ataxia is a motor disorder whereby the arm or leg performs jerky and clumsy, uncoordinated movements. It is often accompanied by *tremor* (rhythmic shaking) of the limb.

Swallowing problems may be dangerous and potentially life-threatening, as they may cause aspiration of food into the lungs, leading to *aspiration pneumonia.* A speech and language therapist will assess the quality of the patient's swallowing, and on whether or not the person is safe to eat and drink. Further investigations in an Ear, Nose and Throat Department may be needed, such as Fibreoptic Endoscopic Evaluation of Swallowing (FEES) or Videofluoroscopy.

Speech and language deficits.

The most common disorders of speech and language after acquired brain injury are:

Dysarthria: A disorder of speech caused by weakness reduced coordination of the muscles used for speaking. As a result the speech sounds slurred and may be difficult to understand.

Aphasia is a speech and language disorder that can affect all aspects of language including understanding what others say (receptive aphasia), the ability to find the right words to speak and to form sentences (expressive aphasia), and the ability to read and write (alexia and agraphia).

Sensory deficits

Visual deficits: Problems with vision can manifest themselves in different ways, depending on the site of the injury. *Loss of vision* in one eye can occur as a consequence of injury to the eye or the optic nerve that transports the visual information from the eye into the brain. *Visual field defects* in both eyes are usually caused by damage in the brain, not the eye. In these cases, patients cannot see what is on one side of their visual fields of both eyes: either on the right side in both eyes or the left side in both eyes. This visual deficit is called *hemianopia*. These patients sometimes walk into door frames or people on their left or their right side because they cannot see them. *Double vision* occurs when the coordination of the movement of both eyes is disrupted, and the eyes move independently of each other.

Hearing disturbance: Injury to the outer or inner ear can cause *hearing loss* on one or both sides.

Loss of smell: This occurs quite frequently after traumatic brain injury, and patients often experience not only loss of smell but loss of taste too. This can significantly reduce their quality of life as the person does not enjoy food and drink anymore. This deficit can also place the person in danger as they are not able to smell fire.

Deficits of sensation: Having reduced sensation in a hand or foot means that the person does not feel objects in his/her hand properly, and cannot feel the floor underfoot as usual. Reduced sensation therefore has a negative impact on moving the arm, and on walking safely. Patients who have lost the ability to distinguish hot and cold are at risk of burning themselves.

Cognitive deficits such as difficulties with memory, attention and executive functions are present in practically all patients with severe traumatic brain injury. They are described in Chapter 9, Traumatic Brain Injury.

Emotional and behavioural difficulties: Patients with severe injuries often have depression and/or anxiety. Irritability and aggressive outbursts are common in patients with injuries to the frontal lobes of the brain; they are discussed in Chapter 9. Those individuals who remember the accident may develop post-traumatic stress disorder (PTSD).

Fatigue: Many individuals after a severe injury, particularly after brain injury, feel less fit, have reduced stamina, and get tired easily after even mild physical or mental activity.

Headaches and other pain conditions are frequent after catastrophic injury and may significantly diminish the person's daily functioning and quality of life.

Vertigo and balance problems occur if the vestibular system in the inner ear is damaged during a head injury.

Epileptic seizures are a risk that people with severe brain injury live with. Seizures can manifest themselves in a variety of ways, and although some are obvious even to the non-expert, some are subtle and hard to notice. *Grand mal seizures* (or tonic-clonic seizures) are the most widely known ones, whereby the person loses consciousness, falls to the ground, the body stiffens up, and both arms and legs go into violent shakes. During *complex focal seizures*, the individual suddenly stops talking or whatever they were doing and stares into the air. They usually are not aware of what is happening, and they do not respond when spoken to. With *simple focal seizures* (or simple partial seizures), the affected person may develop rhythmic shaking of an arm or a leg or both, while being fully conscious.

Epileptic seizures can be life-threatening when they are long lasting (status epilepticus). The impact of post-traumatic epilepsy on the patient's life is great, in particular as they are not allowed to drive for one year after each seizure, and because it may prevent them from returning to their previous employment.

Specialist examinations such as an electroencephalogram (EEG) is sometimes helpful, but a normal EEG does not exclude epilepsy, as the EEG can be normal in periods between seizures. In these cases, a sleep-EEG or an EEG with video-telemetry can provide further information.

Bladder and bowel problems such as incontinence or urgency of micturition are common after catastrophic injury.

12.1.1.2 Impact of the patient's symptoms on his everyday life (disability and handicap)

The individual's physical and cognitive deficits can render them disabled in their personal care and their domestic activities. Apparently simple acts such as dressing and washing, walking from the bedroom to the kitchen, and making a cup of tea, may be difficult, slow or impossible, and the patient may rely on help from others for these activities. Patients may be restricted in their ability to access the community, including going shopping, using public transport, and driving. Their ability to talk to, and interact with, family members and friends may be greatly reduced, taking away pleasure and quality of life. Many patients cannot take up their previous hobbies.

Many patients are unable to resume their work. Consequently, not only do they lose their income, but they may also lose an important role such as breadwinner for their family or lead in an organisation. They might also suffer loss of the satisfaction, appreciation and self-confidence that comes with regular work.

12.1.1.3   Assessment of the patient's condition

It is clear by now that the assessment of patients' condition and rehabilitation needs can be complex, involving sometimes the evaluation of multiple physical conditions, cognitive and communication functions, but also emotional and social needs.

In most cases, an Independent Needs Assessment, also called Immediate Needs Assessment (INA) will be sought early in the litigation process. They are usually prepared by specialised nurses or occupational therapists. In many cases of catastrophic injury, it will be useful to instruct a consultant neurologist with experience in rehabilitation, or a consultant in neurological rehabilitation, early on. Such a specialist can not only advise on the patient's immediate rehabilitation needs, but can also comment on the prognostic significance of certain clinical symptoms or findings on CT scans, EEG etc. Furthermore, this specialist may sometimes discover symptoms that have been overlooked by the treating staff, because not all hospitals have specialised units for patients with catastrophic injury.

Condition and prognosis reports on clients with severe or moderately severe traumatic brain injury are usually provided by a consultant in neurological rehabilitation or consultant neurologist with experience in rehabilitation. These specialists typically work routinely within a multi-disciplinary team and are therefore in a good position to address all of a patient's physical and cognitive deficits, and his emotional and behavioural disturbances. They also take a patient's social situation into account, and the impact that the patient's symptoms have on his everyday life. Within a multi-disciplinary team there are specialists who can expand on specific aspects of assessment and treatment, for example:

Motor deficits are assessed further by a physiotherapist with a view to recommending the best possible physical therapy.

Deficits with speaking and swallowing are assessed by a speech and language therapist who will also comment on therapy. In some cases, an ear, nose and throat specialist will become involved.

A clinical neuropsychologist performs a comprehensive assessment of the different cognitive domains, compares the current deficits with an estimate of the pre-traumatic intellectual level, and draws up a cognitive rehabilitation plan. The neuropsychologist also addresses emotional and behavioural difficulties.

A consultant neuropsychiatrist should be involved in cases where the patient has significant mental health issues such as depression or PTSD.

Occupational therapists provide detailed information on the impact of the individual's deficits on his daily life, and recommend ways to help them regain as much independence in his activities of daily living as possible. They address a wide variety of domains including issues of personal care, domestic activities, money handling, community access, leisure activities and work.

Visual deficits require an examination by an ophthalmologist, and hearing deficits an assessment by an ear, nose and throat specialist.

Medical and paramedical experts sometimes use standardised assessment methods to establish the nature and extent of the individual's difficulties. Such assessment methods allow deficits to be quantified in an objective manner, which helps in determining the patient's rehabilitation needs. Furthermore, the recovery of functions through rehabilitation can be documented by repeating these assessments. Such assessments exist for mobility, speech and language, sensory and cognitive function, as well as activity (disability), quality of life, and pain.

Any intervention (for assessment of a condition or for rehabilitation purposes) requires the patient's consent. Because brain injury can significantly affect a person's mental function and thus their ability to give consent, mental capacity must be carefully reviewed.

12.1.1.4 Mental capacity

According to s 3 of the Mental Capacity Act 2005, a person is unable to make a decision for himself if he is unable:
(a) to understand the information relevant to the decision;
(b) to retain that information;
(c) to use or weigh that information as part of the process of making the decision; or
(d) to communicate his decision.

It is usually relatively uncontroversial to decide whether or not a patient fulfils the criteria (a), (b) and (d), as it can be obvious that a patient either has or does not have capacity in these areas. Most conflicts arise in judging whether a patient will be able to use or weigh relevant information when making a decision, or whether they have a dysexecutive syndrome that renders them prone to make decisions on impulse, and makes them vulnerable to being exploited by others. Mental capacity assessments are usually performed by consultants in neurological rehabilitation, neurologists, clinical neuropsychologists and neuropsychiatrists. In patients with aphasia, a speech and language therapist may be involved in this decision. See Chapter 3 for further information on the law of capacity.

12.2 REHABILITATION

In a general sense, rehabilitation aims to enable individuals to regain their maximum potential regarding their physical, psychological, social and vocational functions. Rehabilitation specialists work not only with the patients themselves, but also their family members and friends and, if possible, employers. In order to achieve the many levels of change necessary for successful rehabilitation, it must be provided by a multidisciplinary team. This usually comprises doctors, nurses, physiotherapists, occupational therapists, speech and language therapists, clinical neuropsychologists and social workers. Outside of a specialised rehabilitation centre, support workers and a case manager will also need to become involved.

These professionals work together with the patient and their family according to mutually agreed goals. To ensure that the patient's wishes and expectations are at the centre of all rehabilitative activities, goal-planning procedures should be followed that enable the patient to take an active and decisive role in this process. In most cases, the general goals of the rehabilitation process are to:

- maximise the recovery of impaired functions, such as limb weakness, speech difficulties and cognitive deficits;
- maximise the independence of the patient in their personal care, domestic activities and community access;
- maximise the patient's ability to resume their social roles including family life, leisure and work;
- maximise the patient's emotional well-being and minimise distress and pain (maximise quality of life);
- minimise the risk of medical complications, such as falls or pneumonia;
- minimise the distress of, and stress on, the patient's family and/or carers.

Rehabilitative therapies can follow one of two basic principles:

- Practice of an impaired function is usually characterised by repetition, starting with simple tasks and slowly increasing the level of difficulty. Examples are exercises to improve the movements of a weak limb, and practising to speak more clearly in a patient with dysarthria. The different impairments affect each other. For instance, pain in the hips will reduce a patient's ability to do walking exercises, and a person with severe memory deficits will require many more repetitions when practising a task than a person with good memory.
- An alternative approach is to use compensatory techniques in helping the patient to achieve the goal in a different way. This allows patients with physical or mental difficulties to improve in their ability to function independently in their everyday life even if their impairment does not recover. For example, a patient may learn to dress himself with his unaffected arm even if the mobility of his weaker arm does not return. Patients with memory deficits benefit from the regular use of diaries and reminders.

National clinical guidelines for the rehabilitation following acquired brain injury were published by the Royal College of Physicians and the British Society of Rehabilitation Medicine in 2003.

Evidence: Using standardised, internationally recognised criteria to determine the quality of research evidence, it has been found that there is strong evidence that rehabilitation is effective in restoring function and improving independence after acquired brain injury, and that it is most effective if it is well organised and starts early. There is a positive correlation between the amount of rehabilitative therapies and the clinical outcome: the more hours of therapy patients have, the better is their outcome. High quality, well organised multi-disciplinary rehabilitation has been shown to reduce long-term care needs and admissions to nursing homes. The costs of investing in high quality rehabilitation are therefore recovered relatively quickly by long-term savings in the cost of care.

Unfortunately, rehabilitation services in the NHS are seriously under-resourced. In the United Kingdom, there are only 0.2 specialists in Rehabilitation Medicine per 100k population, whereas in France there are 2.9, in Germany there are 2.0, and in Sweden there are 1.9 such specialists per 100k population. Many patients with traumatic brain injury are discharged home without any contact with a specialised rehabilitation team.

In this situation, funding for rehabilitation through litigation can greatly improve a patient's chances for a good outcome, and their own and their family's quality of life.

12.2.1   The Rehabilitation Code 2007

'The aim of this code is to promote the use of rehabilitation and early intervention in the compensation process so that the injured person makes the best and quickest possible medical, social and psychological recovery . . . The Code is designed to ensure that the claimant's need for rehabilitation is assessed and addressed as a priority, and that the process of so doing is pursued on a collaborative basis by the claimant's lawyer and the compensator.'

The Rehabilitation Code is a valuable framework to facilitate and speed up the assessment of a patient's rehabilitation needs, and to ensure that the individual receives the therapies they require at an early stage, when it is known to be the most effective. It is, however, not mandatory. See Chapter 2 for more on the Rehabilitation Code.

12.2.2   Rehabilitation of specific deficits

The following paragraphs give a brief overview of principles and techniques of rehabilitative therapies for some functions that are frequently defective after catastrophic injury.

12.2.2.1   Rehabilitation of motor deficits

Physiotherapists and occupational therapists help the patient regain his lost mobility by regular practice.

After the loss of a limb, prosthetic rehabilitation specialists offer the patient information about available prostheses and train him to use it in a functional way.

Following acquired brain injury, techniques employed in the treatment of motor deficits aim at improving the patient's limb function, posture and gait, reducing spasticity, alleviating pain, and preventing complications such as contractures. If the movement does not return in spite of the therapies, the patient will be trained to compensate for this loss by using the unaffected limb.

The therapist encourages the patient to perform an activity such as moving an arm or walking several steps, and gives feedback to achieve selective control of specific muscles. Further therapy techniques include positioning the patient in side-lying, sitting or standing in a support frame; and stretching exercises.

Several additional therapeutic techniques have been developed which can be used in conjunction with the methods described above. *Hydrotherapy* is physiotherapy performed in a swimming pool. In *treadmill training* with partial body weight support, the patient is strapped into a harness hanging above a treadmill on which he practises walking. *Constraint-induced movement therapy* immobilises the patient's unaffected arm in a sling or a splint for several hours per day, forcing him to use the affected arm for all activities. *Functional electrical stimulation* (FES) elicits muscle contractions with electric impulses. Patients with motor deficits often require *walking aids* such as splints, crutches or walking sticks, or they may need to use a wheelchair. If the motor impairment is severe, then they have to be transferred in and out of bed with the help of a hoist.

Medical treatments to reduce spasticity include drugs and injections with Botulinum toxin (botox).

12.2.2.2   Treatment of swallowing deficits

The speech and language therapists practise swallowing with the patient, which often starts with soft food such as yoghurt, and solid food is gradually introduced. Some patients require feeding through a PEG (*percutaneous endoscopic gastrostomy*) tube into the stomach.

12.2.2.3   Treatment of speech and language deficits

Speech and language therapists work with a wide variety of material to help the patient establish communication by any means. This includes verbal material and techniques, such as pronouncing words and sentences, repetition and sentence completion, but also non-verbal material such as gestures, pictures and photographs. In some cases, portable communication devices are used that transform words and sentences that the patient types on a keyboard into spoken language.

The patient spends only a small part of his time with the speech and language therapist. It is therefore important to train the family members and all rehabilitation professionals involved in the use of techniques to optimise the communication with the patient.

12.2.2.4 Treatment of sensory deficits

Depending on the nature of the visual deficit, an ophthalmologist can prescribe visual aids, such as glasses or an eye patch in the case of double vision. Patients with hemianopia can be taught to compensate for the defect by scanning with their eyes towards the blind side.

The treatment for *hearing loss* is obviously a hearing aid, but there is no rehabilitation technique to train the deaf ear to hear better.

No treatment exists to improve sense of *smell and taste*, so people with this problem need to be encouraged to check on food that is cooking and possibly adapt their environment to increase their safety, such as having smoke detectors installed.

Sensation that has been lost may gradually improve, but it cannot be restored by therapies or exercises in the same way that motor problems can. Treatment of sensory loss consists mainly of reminding the patient to pay attention to where they put their hand or foot, in order to avoid injuries.

Treatments of cognitive deficits are described in Chapter 9.

12.2.2.5 Treatment of psychological problems

Depression, anxiety and other mood disorders after head injury are the domain of a clinical neuropsychologist and sometimes a neuropsychiatrist. In addition to 'talking therapics', psychotropic drugs such as antidepressants (mostly SSRIs: selective serotonin reuptake inhibitors) and mood stabilisers (beta-blockers or anti-epileptic drugs) are often used successfully.

12.2.2.6 Fatigue management

Key aspects of fatigue management include instructing the patient to avoid exhaustion by taking regular breaks and spacing out activities.

12.2.2.7   Treatment of pain

The arsenal of pain management ranges from physical therapies such as positioning comfortably, movement education, massage and acupuncture to pain medication.

12.2.2.8   Epilepsy treatment

The treatment of epilepsy is based on avoiding the triggers, and on taking anti-epileptic medication. Frequently used drugs are Phenytoin (particularly in the acute stage), Carbamazepine, Levetiracetam and Lamotrigine. With these drugs, many patients remain seizure-free. They can have side effects in some patients, such as sleepiness, drowsiness and eczema. The doctor (neurologist or rehabilitation specialist) will review the patient regularly and, if he has remained seizure-free for several years, can discuss the possibility of gradually reducing the dose.

12.2.2.9   Treatment of disability and handicap

Helping the patient to overcome their difficulty with dressing and washing themselves is the domain of the occupational therapist, often in collaboration with the nurse or carer. If the patient has, for example, a weakness in one arm which is not recovering fast, then the therapists will introduce compensatory techniques, such as teaching the patient to achieve the intended goal by using the unaffected arm. Occupational therapists also practise domestic tasks such as cooking, and community activities such as going shopping and using public transport with the individual. Furthermore, occupational therapists help the patient prepare for their return to work or, if this is not possible, to identify meaningful leisure activities.

12.2.2.10   Rehabilitation providers

Names and contact details of rehabilitation providers can be found on the websites of the following organisations:

Association of Personal Injury Lawyers (APIL)

www.apil.org.uk

Bodily Injuries Claims Management Association (BICMA)

www.bicma.org.uk

Rehab Window

www.rehabwindow.net

12.3 PROGNOSIS: LIVING WITH CATASTROPHIC INJURY

The vast majority of patients who survive a severe brain injury will make some recovery. This is because the brain has some, albeit limited, capacity to repair the damage that occurred, and undamaged parts of the brain can take over some of the functions of the injured parts of the brain. This ability is called *plasticity* of the brain. The rate of recovery is the fastest in the first 6 to 12 months following the accident, but some further improvement, at a slower speed, can continue over years.

The severity of the head injury is the best predictor of the patient's future outcome. Other prognostic factors are the quality of their rehabilitation, the patient's age, their pre-traumatic intellectual function, and the support by their family.

When a patient is discharged from intensive hospital support, the costs to the carers – physical, psychological and financial – continue. Some patients have a lifetime of supported care ahead of them and this takes a financial toll: adaptations to the home, loss of income, cost of professional support and so on.

This final section addresses long-term issues that patients, carers and professionals face when a patient re-enters the community. These include potential psychological and medical risks and complications for the individual, a patient's domestic and social needs, and finally, occupational and educational needs.

12.3.1 Risks

Patients with catastrophic injuries live with increased risks of a range of possible medical complications, depending on the nature and severity of their impairments. Examples are:

- patients with severely reduced mobility are at increased risk of pneumonia, deep venous thrombosis and pressure sores;
- patients who walk with difficulty are at risk of injuries during falls;
- walking with an asymmetric gait due to weakness or loss of a leg can result in scoliosis and other secondary musculo-skeletal complications;
- contractures of the limb joints (an irreversible stiffening in the soft tissues around the joints) can form if a weak limb is not moved regularly;
- epileptic seizures can lead to injuries during falls;
- swallowing deficits can lead to aspiration of food or fluid in the lung, causing pneumonia;
- the experience of living with pain and/or disability can lead to depression;
- patients with cognitive deficits may get lost or hit by a car while crossing a road;
- cognitive deficits can render a patient vulnerable to being exploited by others;

- impulsive and aggressive behaviour as part of the dysexecutive syndrome (see Chapter 9) can elicit aggressive and violent reactions in others, potentially leading to physical altercations;
- the disability may lead to social isolation and loneliness.

The large number and potential seriousness of the risks listed above illustrates the need to prevent them, if at all possible, by appropriate ongoing therapies and care.

12.3.2   Care and support needs

After a catastrophic injury, many patients will remain permanently disabled and will require help from others in all or part of their daily activities such as dressing, washing, preparing meals, running the household, and going out into the community.

There are several possible scenarios to organise the care, depending on the nature and the severity of the patient's disability.

Patients with severe motor deficits who require help with most or all of their self-care can either be transferred to a suitable nursing home, or they may return to their own home with an appropriate package of care. The home will usually need to undergo adaptations such as the installation of hoists and ramps. If their own home is not suitable to the individual's needs, then a new home will need to be found.

There are advantages and disadvantages to each of these solutions. A nursing home provides certainty of availability of a team of carers around the clock, as well as opportunities for social contacts and activities with other residents. Setting the patient up in their own home, on the other hand, allows for more privacy, flexibility for instance with meal times, and, if the patient has a partner and family, enables them to be closer together.

A patient who lives in their own home (with or without partner) will have carers working with them regularly. Depending on their needs, the care can be organised as a series of visits from carers who come in several times per day, or as an arrangement of live-in care. It is the case manager's task to organise and review the care package.

If the patient is in a long-term relationship, then it will be up to them and their partner to decide whether the partner will take on the role of a carer. Many different issues have to be considered in this decision, amongst others the patient's and the partner's needs, the partner's own physical and mental health, and the prediction that the nature of a couple's relationship will be irreversibly altered from a more or less balanced partnership to an asymmetrical arrangement between a carer and a relatively helpless patient. As a principle, the ongoing future presence and active involvement of the partner can and should not be taken for granted, and the care package needs to be planned accordingly.

It is even more difficult to determine the type and intensity of care and support needed if the patient has regained the ability to walk and talk apparently without impediment, but has ongoing cognitive deficits and emotional and behavioural disturbances. In these cases, the patient and his family are initially relieved about his recovery, and become aware of difficulties only after he has returned home. The patient's ongoing cognitive deficits, in particular the dysexecutive syndrome including impulsivity, irritability, egocentricity and reduced insight, as described in Chapter 9 on Traumatic Brain Injuries, put a strain on the family relationships that worsens as time goes on. Appropriate support should therefore be organised as early as possible, to prevent a breakdown of communication within the family.

Carers or support workers can fulfil a wide variety of roles, depending on the nature and severity of the individual's impairments, disability and handicap. The roles may include:

- performing the personal care;
- feeding the patient;
- providing supervision to ensure the patient's safety;
- giving daily reminders and advice;
- practising the rehabilitation goals set by the rehabilitation experts;
- offering social companionship.

12.3.3   Accommodation

In many cases, patients will need to be rehoused. Their accommodation needs to be level access if they have motor deficits, and it needs to provide space not only for the patient's needs, but also for the family members and carers.

12.3.4   Work

Many patients will not successfully return to their previous workplace. In order to increase their chances of succeeding, the return to work should be prepared and facilitated by the therapists and the case manager. In most cases, an occupational therapist will take the lead in this process, but a clinical neuropsychologist, speech and language therapist and/or physiotherapist may also become involved. If the patient is not able to return to their previous work even with support, then a referral to a Specialist Vocational Rehabilitation Service may be helpful.

12.3.5   Education

Adolescents and young adults who have survived a catastrophic injury may require an educational programme to be combined with the rehabilitation and care as described above. Such a programme of combined rehabilitation and education can, in principle, be arranged at home. Alternatively, the patient can be placed in a college which is specialised in offering rehabilitation and education to young adults with acquired neurological disability. There are several such centres in the country.

12.3.6   Long-term aspects

While the patient is still making progress (even if it is slow) in their physical and cognitive functions, their speech and their independence in everyday activities, the therapies as described in the previous paragraph should continue with reasonable intensity and frequency in order to support, facilitate and accelerate this improvement. Once the progress has levelled out and the patient has reached a 'plateau', it is usually possible to reduce the amount of therapies and to change the rehabilitation programme into a maintenance programme. Its focus will be to consolidate the advances made, to sustain the individual's quality of life, and to prevent future deterioration and complications.

Patients with motor deficits often experience a slow deterioration of their mobility at higher age. This statement is based on clinical observation by rehabilitation specialists and reports from patients and their carers rather than scientific fact, as prospective clinical studies on the prognosis of patients with catastrophic injuries are missing. Such evidence does exist for people with cerebral palsy; it therefore appears reasonable to use these findings in analogy to some extent. Two explanations for this phenomenon have been offered: people with injuries to the brain have lost large numbers of brain cells and therefore have less reserve capacity to compensate for the natural progressive loss of neurones with advancing age; furthermore, secondary complications with hardening of the soft tissues over time may contribute to the deterioration.

CHAPTER 13

PSYCHIATRIC INJURY

Martin Baggaley

This chapter reviews typical psychological reactions found in catastrophic injuries. Psychiatric injuries can be of greater or equal importance as physical injuries. In addition, psychological injuries and reactions can complicate the rehabilitation and worsen the prognosis of physical injuries.

13.1 PSYCHIATRIC REACTIONS TO CATASTROPHIC INJURIES

13.1.1 What is a psychiatric injury?

A psychiatric injury is when an individual develops a recognisable psychiatric disorder in response to an event. A disorder is recognisable when a mental health professional (usually a psychiatrist or psychologist) determines that there is a sufficient range and severity of symptoms to satisfy the criteria for a particular disorder as defined in the psychiatric literature. There are two major psychiatric classification systems in use:

(1) the International Classification of Diseases, Version 10 of the World Health Organisation (ICD-10);[1]

(2) the Diagnostic and Statistical Manual of Mental Disorders, 5th edn, of the American Psychiatric Association (DSM-5).[2]

DSM-5 was released in April 2013 and replaced DSM-IV TR. Both systems are broadly equivalent and ICD-10 is used in the UK and DSM-IV TR and now 5 in the US. ICD-11 is due in the next few years. It is likely that it will be closer to DSM-5 than ICD-10 now is. Post traumatic stress disorder (PTSD) was first described in DSM-III and not in ICD-9 and therefore for historical reasons some UK psychiatrists use DSM when describing psychiatric injuries.

Individuals may experience psychological distress after a catastrophic event which is found not to satisfy criteria for a disorder. Uncomplicated bereavement, for example is not considered to be a psychiatric disorder.

---

[1] ICD-10: The ICD-10 Classification of Mental and Behavioural Disorders: Clinical Descriptions and Diagnostic Guidelines (World Health Organisation 1992).

[2] DSM-5: Diagnostic and Statistical Manual of Mental Disorders (Diagnostic & Statistical Manual of Mental Disorders) (American Psychiatric Association 2013).

13.1.2   Types of psychiatric injury frequently seen

A psychiatric injury can theoretically be any recognised psychiatric disorder, which is considered to have developed following a catastrophic event. However some are much more commonly seen than others. In general, the most serious chronic mental disorders such as schizophrenia or manic depression are not caused by a response to external events but are rather thought to arise in individuals with a genetic vulnerability. Catastrophic events can however trigger relapses of such disorders in pre-disposed individuals.[3]

The common types of psychiatric injury involve symptoms of anxiety and depression. There is often more than one psychiatric disorder found (co-morbidity); for example it is unusual to find a survivor of a traumatic event with just PTSD. In the majority of cases of PTSD, one or more additional psychiatric disorder can be diagnosed.

There is considerable overlap between different psychiatric disorders found after a traumatic event. On occasions different mental health professionals can use slightly different categories to describe very similar conditions (for example adjustment disorder F43.2, mixed anxiety and depression F41.2 and mild depressive episode F32.0 in ICD-10 can be used almost interchangeably in individuals who develop symptoms of anxiety and depression following a traumatic event).

13.2   SPECIFIC PSYCHIATRIC DISORDERS

13.2.1   Post traumatic stress disorder (PTSD)

Psychiatric disorders arising in response to traumatic events such as war, assaults and disasters have been described for many years, including in response to railway accidents, the American Civil War and subsequent World Wars.[4] However PTSD was first described only in 1980, following research into Vietnam veterans and the survivors of a number of civilian disasters.

PTSD can be diagnosed in both ICD-10 and DSM-5 and the definitions in each are broadly similar. The criteria for DSM-5 are more clearly defined than those in ICD-10 and therefore are often preferred by medical experts and lawyers.

PTSD is unusual in that it is one of the only disorders in either classification system which requires the presence of an external event to make the diagnosis; there has to have been a trauma of sufficient severity as one of the diagnostic criteria; this is clearly helpful in terms of the legal process and it reduces the argument over causation.

---

3   M Gelder, N Andreasen, J Lopez-Ibor, J Geddes *New Oxford Textbook of Psychiatry* (Oxford 2009).

4   E Jones and S Wessley *Shell Shock to PTSD: Military Psychiatry from 1900 to the Gulf War* (Maudsley Monographs 2005).

The diagnostic criteria for PTSD in DSM-5 are as follows.

Criteria A. Exposure to the actual or threatened death, serious injury or sexual violence in one (or more) of the following ways:

(1) directly experiencing the traumatic event(s);

(2) witnessing, in person, the event(s) as it occurred to others;

(3) learning that the traumatic event(s) occurred to a close family member or close friend. In cases of actual or threatened death of a family member or friend, the event(s) must have been violent or accidental;

(4) experiencing repeated or extreme exposure to aversive details of the traumatic event(s) (eg, first responders collecting human remains; police officers repeatedly exposed to details of child abuse).

Note: Criteria A4 does not apply to exposure through electronic media, television, movies, or pictures, unless this exposure is work related.

Criteria B. Presence of one (or more) of the following:

(1) recurrent, involuntary and intrusive distressing memories of the traumatic event(s), including images, thoughts, or perceptions. Note: in children older than 6 years repetitive play may occur in which themes or aspects of the trauma are expressed;

(2) recurrent distressing dreams of the event in which the content and/or effect of the dream are related to the traumatic event(s). Note: in young children, there may be frightening dreams without recognisable content;

(3) dissociative reactions (eg, flashbacks) in which the individual feels or acts as if the traumatic event were recurring (such reactions may occur on a continuum with the most extreme expression being a complete loss of awareness of present surroundings). Note: in children, trauma-specific reenactment may occur in play;

(4) intense or prolonged psychological distress at exposure to internal or external cues that symbolise or resemble an aspect of the traumatic event(s);

(5) marked physiological reactions to internal or external cues that symbolise or resemble an aspect of the traumatic event(s)

Criteria C. Persistent avoidance of stimuli associated with the traumatic event(s) beginning after the traumatic event(s) occurred as evidenced by one or both of the following:

(1) avoidance of or efforts to avoid distressing memories thoughts, or feelings about or closely associated with the traumatic events;

(2) avoidance of or efforts to avoid external reminders (people, places, conversations, activities, objects, situations) that arouse distressing memories thoughts or feelings about or closely associated with the traumatic event(s).

Criteria D. Negative alterations in cognitions and mood associated with the traumatic event(s) beginning or worsening after the traumatic event(s) occurred as evidenced by two (or more) of the following:

(1)   inability to recall an important aspect of the traumatic event(s) (typically due to dissociative amnesia and not to other factors such as head injury, alcohol or drugs);

(2)   Persistent and exaggerated negative beliefs or expectations about oneself, others or the world (eg, 'I am bad', 'no one can be trusted', 'the world is completely dangerous', 'my whole nervous system is permanently ruined');

(3)   Persistent, distorted cognitions about the cause or consequences of the traumatic event(s) that lead the individual to blame him/herself or others;

(4)   Persistent negative emotional state (eg, fear, horror, anger, guilt or shame);

(5)   markedly diminished interest or participation in significant activities;

(6)   feelings of detachment or estrangement from others;

(7)   persistent inability to experience positive emotions (eg, inability to experience happiness, satisfaction or loving feelings).

Criteria E. Marked alterations in arousal and reactivity associated with the traumatic event(s), beginning or worsening after the traumatic event(s) occurred as evidenced by two (or more) of the following:

(1)   irritable behaviour and angry outbursts (with little or no provocation) typically expressed as verbal or physical aggression toward people or objects;

(2)   reckless or self-destructive behaviour;

(3)   hypervigilance;

(4)   exaggerated startle response;

(5)   problems with concentration;

(6)   sleep disturbance (eg, difficulty falling or staying asleep or restless sleep).

The symptoms have to result in impairment of occupational and/or social functioning and have to be present for at least one month.

The ICD-10 definition is similar to the DSM-5, although there is less clarity in the number of symptoms required:

> 'This arises as a delayed and/or protracted response to a stressful event or situation (either short- or long-lasting) of an exceptionally threatening or catastrophic nature, which is likely to cause pervasive distress in almost anyone (eg, natural or man-made disaster, combat, serious accident, witnessing the violent death of others, or being the victim of torture, terrorism, rape, or other crime). Predisposing factors such as personality traits (eg, compulsive, asthenic) or previous history of neurotic illness may lower the threshold for the development of the syndrome or aggravate its course, but they are neither necessary nor sufficient to explain its occurrence. Typical symptoms include episodes of repeated reliving of the trauma in intrusive memories ("flashbacks") or dreams, occurring against the persisting background of a sense of "numbness" and emotional blunting, detachment from

other people, unresponsiveness to surroundings, anhedonia, and avoidance of activities and situations reminiscent of the trauma. Commonly there is fear and avoidance of cues that remind the sufferer of the original trauma. Rarely, there may be dramatic, acute bursts of fear, panic or aggression, triggered by stimuli arousing a sudden recollection and/or re-enactment of the trauma or of the original reaction to it. There is usually a state of autonomic hyperarousal with hypervigilance, an enhanced startle reaction, and insomnia. Anxiety and depression are commonly associated with the above symptoms and signs, and suicidal ideation is not infrequent. Excessive use of alcohol or drugs may be a complicating factor. The onset follows the trauma with a latency period which may range from a few weeks to months (but rarely exceeds 6 months). The course is fluctuating but recovery can be expected in the majority of cases. In a small proportion of patients the condition may show a chronic course over many years and a transition to an enduring personality change.'

The natural course of PTSD is slow and gradual recovery and approximately one-third of cases become chronic. Co-morbid disorder and lack of social support have been factors identified as leading to chronicity. Once chronic develops, the symptoms vary in severity with time in response to other life events.

PTSD is more likely following a trauma in females, those with previous psychiatric problems, low educational achievement, previous PTSD, family history of PTSD. The percentage of survivors of a traumatic event who go onto develop PTSD ranges from 30% – 70%.

It is not uncommon to see individuals who have a constellation of symptoms but whose range and severity are insufficient to achieve diagnostic significance for PTSD. Some use the term 'partial PTSD'. Using ICD-10 the term adjustment disorder F43.2 and in DSM-5 adjustment disorder 309 can be used.

It is unusual to develop PTSD alone. Commonly individuals satisfy the diagnostic criteria for other disorders, such as a depressive episode, panic disorder or substance misuse disorder.

PTSD can be delayed so that symptoms develop 6 months or more after the traumatic event. In some occasions the symptoms develop within 6 months but the individual does not present for medical attention until 6 months after the PTSD can be catorogised as simple or complex. Simple occurs typically after a single traumatic event. Complex occurs after multiple events and is often associated with childhood trauma including childhood sexual abuse. There is a significant overlap between the symptoms of PTSD and those of a personality disorder.

PTSD is not usually seen if there is a concurrent head injury with unconsciousness because the victim has no memory of the material event.

13.2.2   Adjustment disorder

An adjustment disorder (F43.2 in ICD-10 and 309 in DSM-5) is a syndrome consisting of a mixture of symptoms of anxiety and depression in response to a life event including trauma. It can be used to describe responses to trauma which fall short of the full diagnostic criteria for PTSD. The symptoms of either anxiety or depression are not of sufficient range or severity to achieve an individual diagnosis of anxiety or depression.

The symptoms of an adjustment disorder do not usually last for more than 6 months (24 months in the case of a prolonged depressive reaction). However if the stressor is a continuing event this can explain a prolongation of the syndrome.

13.2.3   Depression

Depression is one of the commonest diagnoses in psychiatry and is a frequent consequence of a catastrophic accident. Some individuals who experience depression also develop episodes of elevated mood (mania or hypomania) and this is classified as bi-polar affective disorder or manic depression. Bi-polar affective disorder is not thought to be caused by a traumatic event although an episode might be triggered by one.

The typical symptoms of depression include low mood, lack of pleasure in life (anhedonia), negative thoughts, poor concentration, guilt, disturbed sleep, reduced appetite, loss of interest in sex, feeling tired and experiencing suicidal thoughts. The symptoms disrupt normal occupational and social functioning. Some sufferers complain of physical symptoms (bodily pain, fatigue etc). Sleep disturbance can be difficulty getting to sleep (initial insomnia) or waking early (early morning wakening or emw). Appetite is normally reduced and associated with weight loss although it can be in rarer cases increased as can sleep. Mood is worse in the morning (diurnal variation in mood). The combination of emw, diurnal variation in mood and sleep and appetite disturbance is referred to as 'somatic' symptoms in ICD-10.

Depression has a lifetime prevalence of 17-20%. The cause is thought to be multi-factorial, with causative factors including genetic pre-disposition, early childhood experiences and adverse life events, including traumatic events in later life. Some factors such as having a close confiding relationship may be protective.

If there have been more than two discrete episodes of depression in a lifetime, the term recurrent depressive disorder is used. After one episode of depression the risk of a further lifetime event is increased to 40-50% and after two previous episodes to 60%.

DSM-5 296 uses the term major depressive disorder which can be mild moderate or severe. ICD-10 F32 uses the term mild moderate or severe depressive episode. Some very severe depression can have so-called psychotic features (delusions and hallucinations).

Anti-depressant medication is an effective treatment for depression, especially those of moderate to severe severity but can take several weeks of treatment before a response is experienced. Once the symptoms of depression have improved anti-depressant medication is continued for least 6 months. At this point the depression is said to be in remission. After a suitable period the medication can be stopped and if no symptoms reoccur the disorder is said to have recovered.

13.2.4   Mixed anxiety and depressive disorder

There are some psychological reactions which are a mixture of symptoms of anxiety and depression but with neither being sufficient to reach a separate diagnosis for anxiety or depression. ICD-10 defines mixed anxiety and depressive disorder, F41.2 as:

> 'when symptoms of anxiety and depression are both present, but neither is clearly predominant, and neither type of symptom is present to the extent that justifies a diagnosis if considered separately. When both anxiety and depressive symptoms are present and severe enough to justify individual diagnoses, both diagnoses should be recorded and this category should not be used.'

It will be more usual for a diagnosis of an adjustment disorder to be made instead but a mixed anxiety and depressive disorder is a possible alternative diagnosis, especially when the symptoms have lasted longer than 6 months after an injury when one would expect the symptoms of an adjustment disorder to have settled.

13.2.5   Travel anxiety

A common reaction to a catastrophic injury, which involves travelling by car, riding a motorbike or any other form of transport is a psychiatric disorder consisting of symptoms of anxiety associated with driving in a car/riding a bike together with avoidance of travelling by the relevant means. The avoidance can be partial or total. Individuals usually are more comfortable driving rather than being a passenger in a car (because they feel in greater control).

Travel anxiety can occur together with another disorder such as PTSD, an adjustment disorder or as the only psychiatric reaction. In ICD-10 it is classified as an isolated or specific phobia F40.2.

It is on occasions, difficult to separate what is avoidance due to anxiety from a rational, conscious decision to for example not to ride a motorbike again because it is too dangerous.

It can also be difficult to diagnose if the physical injury itself makes it difficult to ride the bike or drive the car and therefore the degree of avoidance cannot be easily tested.

13.2.6   Panic disorder and agoraphobia

A panic attack is a short lived but intense state of anxiety. Agoraphobia originally means fear of open spaces or the marketplace. Individuals with agoraphobia as a clinical condition have a fear of crowded places such as supermarkets.

Panic attacks can become associated with particular situations. Sufferers then avoid such situations. Panic attacks can occur with or without agoraphobia. If there is no associated agoraphobia the diagnostic term used is panic disorder without agoraphobia 300.01 and 300.21 with agoraphobia. ICD-10 describes agoraphobia F40.0 and panic disorder F41.0.

Panic attacks insufficient to reach the diagnostic threshold for a separate panic disorder diagnosis are common psychological reactions to catastrophic trauma and can be a component of PTSD, adjustment disorders and depression.

13.2.7   Obsessive compulsive disorder

Obsessive compulsive symptoms can be found following trauma. Obsessive compulsive disorder (OCD) is an anxiety disorder characterised by symptoms including intrusive thoughts that produce anxiety, by repetitive behaviours aimed at reducing anxiety, or by combinations of such thoughts (obsessions) and behaviours (F42 in ICD-10 and 300.3 in DSM-5).

These thoughts have common themes such as contamination with dirt, or sexual or religious themes. The sufferer recognises these thoughts as being irrational but belonging to themselves (in contrast to sufferers from schizophrenia who can experience such thoughts as being alien to them).

Obsessional symptoms can occur as part of a depressive disorder and can occur in cases of PTSD.

Obsessional traits are common in the general population and can pre-dispose to the development of a depressive disorder.

13.2.8   Personality disorder

A personality disorder is defined as 'an enduring pattern of inner experience and behaviour that deviates markedly from the expectations of the culture of the individual who exhibits it'. It is usually present from late adolescence. It is not therefore something that is caused by a catastrophic event but the presence of a personality disorder may either complicate or worsen the outcome of a psychological reaction to a catastrophic event or be mistaken for a psychological reaction.

Individuals who suffer from severe chronic PTSD may experience a permanent change to their personality and there is a category of enduring personality change in ICD-10. This is found in cases of complex trauma.

13.2.9 Alcohol and substance misuse

Alcohol and substance misuse is very common in the normal population. The psychiatric response to a catastrophic event can include the development of an alcohol or substance abuse disorder de novo or an exacerbation of an existing problem.

Alcohol and substance misuse are divided into harmful use (use that causes psychological, social or physical harm) and then dependence (addiction).

Individuals with PTSD and those with depression who find it difficult to sleep often self medicate with alcohol and use it to help them sleep. However chronic alcohol misuse can cause depression and rebound anxiety the morning after a heavy binge. In addition chronic alcohol problems can cause sleep disturbance and disruption to normal 'sleep architecture' and thereby increase the amount of dreams. Therefore some individuals who develop alcohol misuse problems after a catastrophic trauma can develop secondary depression and PTSD like symptoms.

13.2.10 Psychotic disorders

The most serious mental illnesses (eg, schizophrenia and bipolar affective disorder or manic depression) are not thought to be caused by a catastrophic event but are related to a genetic predisposition and early life experiences.

However a traumatic event can cause a relapse, an exacerbation of an episode or the triggering of the onset of the disorder in someone who was vulnerable to develop a disorder in any event.

13.2.11 Chronic fatigue/ME

Chronic fatigue syndrome (CFS), or myalgic encephalopathy (ME), is a collection of disorders characterised by persistent fatigue, widespread muscle and joint pain, cognitive difficulties, muscle weakness, hypersensitivity, digestive disturbances, depression, and cardiac and respiratory problems. There is a strong association between symptoms of chronic fatigue and various chronic pain syndromes.

The cause of CFS is poorly understood. There are various immunological theories partly because some cases seem to be related to viral infection (post viral fatigue). There is no good explanation as to why a catastrophic trauma should cause CFS. However it is accepted that a traumatic event can cause a relapse of CFS via 'nervous shock' (*Page v Smith*[5]).

The treatment of CFS can include cognitive behavioural psychotherapy, including a particular type known as 'pacing' and anti-depressant medication.

13.2.12   Chronic pain syndromes and somatoform disorders

It is not uncommon for victims of catastrophic accidents to develop pain and disability of greater severity and/or duration than can be easily explained by the relevant physical experts.

A somatoform disorder is a condition in which an individual does not consciously invent symptoms (this is malingering) but instead experiences physical symptoms for psychological reasons. A diagnosis of a persistent somatoform pain disorder, F45.4 in ICD-10 can be made. This is the term used for patients who experience chronic pain thought to be of psychological rather than physical causation. It is defined as:

> 'The predominant complaint is of persistent, severe and distressing pain, which cannot be explained fully by a physiological process or a physical disorder and which occurs in association with emotional conflict or psycho-social problems that are sufficient to allow the conclusion that they are the main causative influences. The result is usually a marked increase in support and attention, either personal or medical. The commonest problem is to differentiate this disorder from the histrionic elaboration of organically caused pain. Patients with organic pain for whom a definite physical diagnosis has not yet been reached may easily become frightened or resentful, with resulting attention-seeking behaviour. A variety of aches and pains are common in somatisation disorders, but without being so persistent or so dominant over the other complaints.'

Alternatively one could consider such symptoms to be hysterical in origin. Hysterical conversion disorder is now properly termed a dissociative disorder (F44.4-F44.7 Dissociative disorders of movement and sensation). Essentially the idea is that the individual presents with symptoms of physical illness, which are believed to be attributable to underlying unconscious psychological conflict. The definition of this in ICD-10 is as follows:

> 'There is a loss of or alteration in functioning of movements, or of sensations (usually cutaneous). The movements or sensations are changed or lost so that the patient presents as having a physical disorder, but one cannot be found that can explain the symptoms. The symptoms can often be seen to represent the patient's concept of physical disorder, which may be at variance with physiological or anatomical principles. In addition, the assessment of the patient's mental state and social situation usually suggest that the disability resulting from the loss of

---

[5]   *Page v Smith* [1995] 2 WLR 644, [1995] UKHL.

functions is helping the patient to escape from an unpleasant conflict, or to express dependency or resentment indirectly. Although problems or conflicts may be evident to others, the patient often denies their presence, and attributes any distress to the symptoms or the resulting disability. The degree of disability resulting from all types of these symptoms may vary from occasion to occasion, depending upon the number and type of other persons present, and upon the emotional state of the patient; in other words, a variable amount of attention-seeking behaviour may be present in addition to a central and unvarying core of loss of movement or sensation which is not under voluntary control. In some patients the symptoms usually develop in close relationship to psychological stress, but in others this link does not emerge. Calm acceptance ("belle indifférence") of serious disability may be striking, but is not universal; it is also found in well-adjusted individuals facing obvious serious physical illness. The diagnosis should be made with great caution in the presence of physical disorders of the nervous system, or in an individual previously well adjusted and with normal family and social relationships. For a definite diagnosis, (i) evidence of physical disorder should be absent, and (ii) sufficient must be known about the psychological and social setting and personal relationships of the patient to allow a convincing formulation to be made of the reasons for the appearance of the disorder. The diagnosis should remain probable or provisional if there is any doubt about the contribution of existing or possible physical disorders, or if it is impossible to achieve an understanding of why the disorder has developed. In cases which are puzzling or not clear-cut, the possibility of the later appearance of serious physical or psychiatric disorders should always be kept in mind.'

This is similar to a somatoform disorder and is an unconscious process but thought to be related (according to psychodynamic theory) to issues related to unresolved childhood anxieties.

Another way of explaining such a discrepancy between the expected and observed physical symptoms is the concept of abnormal illness behaviour. In this explanation, individuals obtain unconscious reward for adopting the sick role, ie if being ill avoids unpleasant activity (eg, doing a job one does not enjoy), the state of illness is rewarded and may continue.

Another explanation is the interaction between depression and physical pain/disability. That is pain makes depression worse and depression makes the perception of pain worse. This is a simple and easily understood explanation.

Finally a claimant may deliberately and consciously complain of pain and other physical symptoms, which he does not experience, for his gain. This is malingering.

13.3   SEVERITY OF PSYCHIATRIC INJURY

Clinical classification systems tend to divide severity into mild moderate and severe. This is usually determined by clinical judgment but as a general indication someone with mild disorder would have some impairment of work or social life, someone who was severe would be able to work or function to any extent socially and moderate somewhere in-between.

13.4   DIAGNOSIS OF A PSYCHIATRIC INJURY

A psychiatric disorder is diagnosed by an appropriate mental health profession (a psychiatrist or clinical psychologist) based on an interview, mental state examination of the individual and supported by other evidence such as contemporaneous medical records.

The interview should include relevant past and family history, as well as the material event and any relevant psychiatric symptoms.

The mental state examination usually includes a brief description of appearance and behaviour, an assessment of the subject's mood from the psychiatrist's perspective (objective mood) and how the subject describes their mood (subjective mood), whether they describe abnormal experiences (hallucinations), whether the psychiatrist elicits abnormal ideas (delusions), thought content, level of concentration and insight (how aware they are of their symptoms).

Some clinicians use psychometric tests. Unfortunately these are usually self-report instruments not designed or validated for use in a forensic setting. Some include subscales, which purport to detect unreliability or exaggeration, but again these are designed for normal clinical use.

13.5   RELIABILITY, MALINGERING AND EXAGGERATION

A psychiatric diagnosis is very dependent on the history from the claimant and there are few, if any, objective tests to prove someone is giving a true account.

Reliability of the claimant is therefore important. In non forensic settings doctors and other mental health professionals tend to take what is said by a patient at face value unless there are obvious discrepancies in the account. When assessing psychiatric injury after a catastrophic event it is important to consider that someone might be consciously inventing or exaggerating symptoms.

To complicate matters, there are some occasions where individuals do not consciously invent symptoms but experience symptoms for which there seems to be no physical cause but arise from psychological factors.

13.6   PSYCHIATRIC DISORDER AND HEAD INJURY

Psychiatric injury (usually a depressive syndrome) is common after a head injury. (Research indicates a prevalence of between 25–50%.) However, there are difficulties separating out cognitive problems from depression. Some cases of depression are similar to normal depressive episodes in that they may occur in response to external stresses and loss (ie a psychological reaction to an event) and may be pre-disposed to by some inherited vulnerability. Other cases of depression following head injury may differ in that they are caused by physical damage to those parts of the brain, which are relevant to emotions and mood. Such cases caused by a physical injury may be less responsive to normal psychiatric interventions.

In addition to depressive disorder caused by physical brain damage, some effects of brain damage cause symptoms, which can be confused with depression. This is because some of the signs and symptoms of physical brain damage, such as the dysexecutive syndrome which can occur after an injury to the frontal lobes, including symptoms of lack of drive, irritability, disturbed sleep and disturbed concentration, are similar symptoms to those of a depressive illness. As a result some individuals who do not have a depressive episode are misclassified as having one because of confusingly similar, but qualitatively different, symptoms caused by the brain damage.

A further complication is the neuropsychological assessment to determine the degree of any cognitive damage is affected by the presence of co-morbid depression due to the effects of the latter on concentration and attention.

One way to attempt to tease out the relative importance of depression versus cognitive damage is to have a trial of treatment with anti-depressant medication.

13.7   TREATMENT OF PSYCHIATRIC REACTIONS

The National Institute of Clinical Excellence[6] undertakes research into what is cost effective treatment and usually represents the 'gold standard' for what constitutes appropriate treatment.

The majority of psychiatric injuries following catastrophic trauma are treated with either medication (anti-depressants, mood stabilisers, anti-psychotic or hypnotic medication) or cognitive behavioural treatment (CBT). Treatment with medication is best supervised by a consultant psychiatrist but can be prescribed by a general practitioner. CBT is best administered by a clinical psychologist. CBT for PTSD is often referred to a 'trauma focused PTSD'. Other therapists may deliver CBT such as counsellors but clinical psychologists or trained psychiatrists are to be preferred.

Eye movement desensitisation and re-processing is a type CBT in which the subject, by following with their eyes a moving object at a particular frequency at the same time on focusing on recalling memories of a traumatic event. It is a recommended treatment for PTSD and found in the NICE guidelines.

CBT is usually delivered in weekly treatments (which may be spaced out as the treatment progresses). It usually is delivered in courses of 12 treatments.

---

6   See www.nice.org.uk.

The majority of treatment for psychiatric disorders which occur after a catastrophic reaction is usually given on an outpatient basis. There are occasionally reasons for inpatient care (eg, co-morbid alcohol or substance misuse which cannot be managed as an outpatient) but this is rare. Some medical experts affiliated to privately run psychiatric institutions are more likely to recommend inpatient treatment which is very expensive and in all probability unnecessary.

13.8   VULNERABILITY AND EXACERBATION OF A PRE-EXISTING PSYCHIATRIC CONDITION

The likelihood of a psychiatric reaction to a catastrophic event is related to a number of factors; including genetic make-up, early childhood experiences, previous adverse life events, previous psychiatric disorder, previous intellectual and occupational functioning and sex.

There are various ways of dealing with previous vulnerability in a medico-legal setting. The concept of 'egg shell' skull applies (ie one takes a victim as one finds one), although it is sometimes argued that the vulnerability is so great that the victim would have been liable to develop a psychiatric disorder in any event.

In the case where someone has had recurrent episodes of depression (or other psychiatric disorder) prior to the material event, it can be difficult to determine the amount of impact a catastrophic event would have on the course of the mental disorder. It can be instructive to review the medical records and question whether the pattern of attendance for psychological complaint has significantly changed before and after the index event.

13.9   TOP TIPS

- Psychiatric injuries are common and can be easily overlooked.
- Psychiatric injuries have important effects on occupational and social functioning.
- Psychiatric injuries significantly affect the prognosis of physical injury.

CHAPTER 14

SPINAL CORD INJURIES

*Brian Gardner**

14.1   INTRODUCTION

The effective resolution of a personal injury claim in a spinal cord injury (SCI) case is dependent on a comprehensive medical report that covers all aspects of the claimant's situation. Incomplete or otherwise inadequate reports prolong the litigation process. This not only increases costs but also, and more importantly, delays financial restitution to the severely disabled person at a time when he or she is in greatest need.

The medical expert will usually be required to act as lead expert in SCI cases. Even when this is not the case the court is unlikely to approve an item claimed without medical support. Only those doctors who are trained in comprehensive SCI care can advise the court in all relevant areas.

The purpose of this chapter is to help instructing lawyers to ensure that the medical expert constructs a report that incorporates all aspects relevant to the SCI claimant so that the rest of the legal team of experts, including specialists in care, therapy, psychology, housing, employment and special equipment, can be pointed in the correct direction from the outset. The headings in Annex 1 of this chapter indicate those areas that should be covered in a comprehensive report.[1]

14.2   COMPLETE AND INCOMPLETE SCI

A SCI is complete if there is no voluntary motor or sensory function below the level of injury. If the arms are spared the claimant has paraplegia. If they are involved the claimant has tetraplegia. The level of injury is the lowest intact spinal cord segment. If there is residual sacral sensation then the injury is incomplete. If there is voluntary motor power then the claimant has either paraparesis or tetraparesis.

---

*   Brian Gardner MA (Oxon), BM BCh, FRCP (Lond and Edin), FRCS, Consultant Surgeon in Spinal Cord Injuries, Stoke Mandeville Hospital, Aylesbury.
[1]   D Grundy and A Swain (eds) *ABC of Spinal Cord Injury* (BMJ Books, 4th edn, 2002).

The two classifications used to express the degree of SCI at a particular level are the Frankel and the ASIA (American Spinal Injury Association). Both classify patients as A–E. They are similar but not identical. The Frankel system has been in place for over 40 years.

Frankel A	Motor and sensory complete
Frankel B	Motor complete: sensory incomplete
Frankel C	Motor incomplete but non-useful: sensory incomplete
Frankel D	Motor incomplete and useful: sensory incomplete
Frankel E	Normal

14.3   CONTRIBUTORY NEGLIGENCE

14.3.1   Which event caused the disability

Medical experts can sometimes assist regarding the extent to which different negligent incidents have caused the disability, for example in multiple vehicle accidents or when there was inappropriate handling of the SCI person.

14.3.2   Seat belts

The accident reconstruction expert will describe how the patient would have moved during the accident if wearing or not wearing a seat belt. The medical expert will describe the injuries that could have occurred in these two scenarios as well as the mechanism of the spinal injury. This will help determine first whether or not a seat belt was being worn and second what injuries would have occurred if one was being worn.

14.4   CLINICAL BREACH OF DUTY WITH CAUSATION

14.4.1   Breach of duty

There is variation in opinion regarding the correct management of spinal cord trauma. The treatment selected must be reasonable, and carried out competently and with an acceptable degree of care. All are agreed that spine-in-line care, and adequate maintenance of oxygenation and blood pressure are essential.

Common sites of missed fractures include the cervico-dorsal junction and spinal fractures below the major injury; 9% of acute traumatic spinal cord injuries are missed.

If there are reasonable grounds for believing that a patient has sustained an unstable spinal injury then appropriate steps must be taken to protect the spine until such time as the diagnosis can be confirmed or refuted.

14.4.2   Causation

Causation is often a major area of dispute.

Although multiple secondary factors arise in the spinal cord after trauma, spontaneous neurological deterioration occurs in fewer than 5% of cases. Conversely, inappropriate movement at the injury site will cause neurological deterioration in the majority of cases.[2]

The key fact for the court to determine is whether or not the patient had voluntary movement below the injury level at any stage after the event. If the court concludes that there was voluntary movement that was subsequently lost then the most likely cause is inappropriate movement at the injury site.

The majority of acute traumatic SCI patients with some voluntary movement below the injury level will improve to gain useful function. Conversely, only a minority of those with no movement in the acute stages will gain useful function. In these latter cases, no causation will be demonstrated no matter how poor the care.[3]

Where movement is not observed there are indirect pointers to its presence, such as well-maintained blood pressure, normal pulse rates and absence of priapism, but these are poor substitutes for direct evidence of voluntary movement.

In cases where breach of duty has occurred, a careful perusal of the records is essential to determine if there was voluntary movement below the injury level at any stage. In the absence of such evidence the claimant is unlikely to receive compensation.

14.4.3   Avoidable SCI complications

Pressure sores can usually be avoided with good care. Minor sores are common. They have no long-term consequences provided they are well treated. Conversely, serious sores should never occur, and they can have significant long-term adverse results.

MRSA infection should not occur with good hand hygiene, but is nevertheless common.

---

[2]   Poonnoose, Ravichandran and McClelland 'Missed and mismanaged injuries of the spinal cord' (2002) 5(2) J Trauma 314-320. Marshall et al 'Deterioration following spinal cord injury' (1987) 66 J Neurosurg 400-404.

[3]   Kirshblum and O'Connor 'Predicting neurologic recovery in traumatic cervical spinal cord injury' (1998) 79 Arch Phys Med Rehabil 1456-1486.

14.5 QUANTUM

Relevant family, medication and past medical histories should be stated.

Smoking, alcohol and prohibited substance histories should be outlined, as these interact with and augment most of the important causes of morbidity and mortality in the spinal cord injured.

The history of the SCI person since injury should be described.

To clarify the quantum issues it is advisable to divide the consequences of SCI into categories. In each, acute and chronic aspects should be considered.

14.5.1 Associated injuries

Associated injuries can be very important in determining the quantum consequences of spinal cord damage.

14.5.1.1 Brain

The duration of unconsciousness and post-traumatic amnesia must be stated. The latter is the best guide to the severity of a brain injury though sometimes sedative drugs and artificial ventilation preclude an accurate estimation. Whenever significant brain damage has occurred a full psychological and psychometric assessment is mandatory.

Successful rehabilitation following SCI is dependent on the total involvement of the disabled person. Impairment of personality, memory, concentration and intellect can profoundly alter outcome. Good executive function is of particular importance in enabling the SCI person to lead a safe and well-integrated life. Relatively minor degrees of higher cerebral impairment can interact with the other problems associated with SCI to make employment more difficult.

The commonest cranial nerve abnormality following head injury, and the most frequently overlooked in SCI cases, is the loss of sense of smell and the altered taste sensation that result from olfactory nerve damage.

14.5.1.2 Limb joints, bones and soft tissues

Injuries to limb joints, bones and soft tissues should be described, in particular where residual deformity or loss of movement has occurred. An orthopaedic opinion is required when the prognosis for a joint or bone abnormality is uncertain.

SCI persons are more dependent on their arms than prior to their injury. Joint damage, and to a lesser extent long bone fractures, can severely impair transfers and wheelchair skills. Contractures are frequently very disabling.

Because arm joints, especially the shoulders, are put under stress by the routine activities of wheelchair life, problems commence in them at an earlier age. The onset of these joint problems is accelerated by joint damage sustained at the time of injury.

14.5.1.3   Peripheral nerve injuries, especially brachial plexus

The nature, degree and prognosis of any peripheral nerve or brachial plexus injury must be described.

Paraplegics require both arms for most activities. An affected arm cannot cope as well as an unaffected one with transfers and wheelchair control. The functional impact of a disabled arm can be reduced by trick movements, which are unnatural movements making use of other muscles to take over the function of affected muscles.

14.5.1.4   Chest and abdomen

Chest and abdominal injuries, though life threatening at the time of the original event, are seldom important in quantum terms because they do not often result in an increased requirement for care or equipment, and do not greatly alter life expectation after the acute stage.

14.5.2   Neurology

The level, degree of completeness and pattern of the SCI must be stated as they are of central importance in determining outcome and prognosis. There is no level of neurological disability, including ventilator dependency, which is incompatible with life in the community.

Incomplete injuries are associated with a longer expectation of life. Preserved sensation enables the paralysed person to become aware of complications as they arise below the level of injury. Complete SCI persons also learn to recognise signals coming from the paralysed and denervated parts of the body but these are less precise. When there is useful muscle as well as sensory function below the level of injury then life expectation is further improved.[4]

Every neurological level in the cervical region is of vital importance.

Patients with complete lesions at C3 and above usually require a greater or lesser degree of ventilatory support, such as intermittent positive pressure ventilation or phrenic nerve pacing. Non-invasive ventilation by mouth carries a lower risk to life, as tracheostomy-related complications are avoided.

---

[4]   Coll, Frankel, Charlifue and Whiteneck 'Evaluating neurological group homogeneity in assessing the mortality risk for people with spinal cord injuries' (1988) 36 *Spinal Cord* 275–279.

C4 level patients can almost always breathe independently but are otherwise totally dependent. Electric wheelchair mobility and control of the environment is achievable using retained head and neck control.

C5 level patients have good shoulder control as well as elbow flexion. With aids, such as feeding straps, limited function is possible. Assistance is required with every activity.

C6 level patients have good wrist dorsiflexion. Elbow extension is achieved by means of trick movements. By locking the elbow, transfers are sometimes possible. Wrist dorsiflexion is associated with passive tenodesis of the fingers and the thumb. Upper limb reconstructive procedures can be of great benefit at this level of injury. Active elbow extension can be achieved by the Moberg posterior deltoid to triceps transfer procedure. A stronger and more active key grip can be achieved by tendon transfers around the wrist. These procedures do not usually increase transfer capability but they do improve upper limb control and so lead to an improved quality of life.

Upper thoracic, T2 to T6, level patients lack the abdominal and lower paraspinal muscle control that is essential to achieve good truncal balance. Backwheel balance control and transfers are impaired as a result. Spontaneous spasms are likely to cause problems in transfers. Ambulation in long leg callipers is difficult and usually requires cumbersome braces to stabilise the upper body.

Lower thoracic, T7 to T12, persons have greater abdominal and paraspinal muscle control and hence better truncal balance. Higher kerbs can be negotiated because better backwheel balance can be achieved.

L1 level persons frequently achieve ambulation though this is seldom of functional benefit.

Mid-lumbar level persons have good quadriceps muscle control that usually allows functional ambulation.

14.5.2.1   Longer-term neurological consequences

The incidence of tertiary spinal cord change is much commoner than had previously been recognised. These changes continue to develop throughout the life of the SCI person. The most important tertiary change is the spinal cord syrinx. This affects 20% of tetraplegics and 30% of thoracic paraplegic SCI persons

If a person has a spinal cord syrinx he or she needs to take care so as to avoid those abrupt stresses, strains and other events that can cause serious spinal cord deterioration. Surgery may be necessary. In spite of optimum monitoring and optimum care, there is a circa 1 to 1.5% chance of the SCI person deteriorating neurologically at some stage during his lifetime to the extent that increased care and equipment are required.[5]

14.5.3 Spine

The SCI and its management should be described in the report. Great detail is seldom necessary because spinal problems are not usually a major concern following the acute event.

Arthritis may occur at an earlier stage in the mobile spinal joints above and below the injured segment. This can give rise to increased spinal pain and stiffness in older years.

Long spinal fixations can be very disabling. A young person with paraplegia and a long fixation is usually totally independent in his or her younger years but when older his or her loss of truncal mobility cannot be so readily compensated for by increased movement of the hips. Long fixations in the cervical region prevent the tetraplegic person from looking around.

Approximately 10% of spinal injured patients have fractures at multiple levels. Those below the level of the main fracture are important if they cause neurological damage or significant spinal deformity. A thoraco-lumbar fracture, for example, can damage the spinal cord conus giving rise to loss of bladder, bowel and sexual reflexes.

Progressive skeletal deformity is a particular problem in children. Regular careful spinal column review is required until skeletal maturity. Whereas a gibbus, the hump of a deformed spine, does not significantly increase disability, scoliosis, or curvature of the spine, can be a significant problem. Sitting posture, the pattern of pressure on the ischial buttock areas and transfers are impaired. Surgical correction may be required.

14.5.4 Pain

It is essential that the report gives a detailed description of any pain, its characteristics, its prognosis and the manner in which it affects the SCI person.

Musculo-skeletal and neurogenic pains are common following SCI. They can be intractably disabling. Treatment is frequently difficult as well as limited within the NHS, especially the non-pharmaceutical approaches. Pain clinics seldom have the resources required to provide the ongoing support that many SCI persons need.

---

[5] See for example *Kotula v EDF Energy Networks (EPN) Plc and others* [2011] EWHC 1546 (QB).

If pain makes it necessary for the SCI person to shift position or to lie down at intervals then care needs are sometimes increased and employment is difficult. Both pain and its medication can affect concentration.

14.5.5   Bladder

14.5.5.1   Lower urinary tract

The report should describe past, present and future urological care. The method by which urine is drained, urological complications to date and current uro-renal status should be stated.

Bladder sensation and control are impaired in the spinal cord injured. The precise pattern of bladder management varies with the individual.

All methods of bladder care are associated with events that can be distressing and inconvenient. With intermittent self catheterisation there is incontinence. Toilets are frequently inaccessible. With reflex voiding the urinary sheath occasionally comes off causing the SCI person to become soaked. Minor penile skin problems can prevent application of the sheath, forcing the person either to remain in bed or to insert an indwelling catheter. Upper urinary tract deterioration can occur due to elevated intravesical voiding pressures.

When partial control remains there is usually urgency and frequency that impairs the SCI person's quality of life, for example by forcing him to plan his journey according to the location of accessible toilets.

Bladder management in females is particularly difficult. There are no satisfactory external urine collection appliances. The risk of incontinence and the awareness that there may be a smell of urine impairs self-confidence and femininity.

14.5.5.2   Upper urinary tract

Continued vigilance of the upper urinary tract is required throughout the life of the paralysed person. Asymptomatic problems such as calculi produced by concretion of mineral salts or dilatation can occur.

Uro-renal causes of death were the most common. They are still important but much less so than previously as a result of better urological care.

14.5.6   Bowels

Bowel management can be distressing, time consuming and dependent on care. The report should include a full account of its impact on the claimant, including potential future problems.

Upper gastrointestinal problems are seldom significant.

Faecal evacuation is usually a major problem. A disciplined pattern of bowel control is essential. Most SCI persons require suppositories or digital stimulation. Some require aperients. Episodes of incontinence can be very distressing.

Most paraplegics are able to manage their bowels by transferring onto the toilet followed by suppository insertion or digital evacuation, then a rectal check.

Most tetraplegics need assistance. Bowel evacuation while seated on a shower chair over the toilet and followed by a shower at the end of the evacuation is a popular pattern. Toilet systems such as the Closomat offer a convenient way of cleaning the bottom.

In chronic SCI evacuation takes longer and aperients are less effective. Evacuation lasting several hours makes employment difficult. Colostomy and colonic irrigation, either antegrade or retrograde using the Peristeen system, are occasionally required. Sacral root stimulation can be beneficial.

14.5.7 Hygiene

Good hygiene helps to maintain the integrity of the skin. A description is required of the pattern of bathing, time taken and the level of care. Special equipment, such as shower chairs, specialised baths and driers, is often required.

14.5.8 Joints/limb soft tissues

Because of increased use, wear and tear on upper limb joints is increased. As paraplegic persons get older, episodes of upper limb pain and stiffness occur. Extra help is required.

Heterotopic ossification can occur in the early stage following injury. Hip mobility can be severely impaired. Transfers and activities of daily living are more difficult. The ossification process eventually becomes quiescent. Surgery is seldom required.

Contractures interfere with independent living, mobility and transfers. They cause pain. In tetraplegics, contractures of the shoulders, elbows and wrists are a particular problem. In paraplegics, lower limb contractures prevent ambulation and interfere with transfers.

14.5.9 Spasms

Spasms and spasticity are usual accompaniments of SCI. They are sometimes helpful but more usually a hindrance. They cause embarrassment. They can be dangerous if they occur abruptly during a transfer or when driving. Spasms throw the legs out of position in bed. The sleep of both the paralysed person and the partner may be disturbed. They can assist, but more usually impair, transfers and activities of daily living.

Eradication of precipitating causes and physical treatments, such as warm water immersion, swimming and functional electrically stimulated exercise, are preferred to drugs, such as Baclofen which causes drowsiness and interferes with concentration, and surgery.

14.5.10   Respiratory

Respiratory functional impairment is the most important increased risk to life in tetraplegics. Carers need to be fully instructed in the relief of choking, assisted coughing, postural drainage of the chest and clearance of secretions. The cough assist machine has an important role.

Permanent ventilator-assisted individuals (VAIs) can live safely in the community provided that they have sufficient care. A trained carer must be in-line-of-eye of the VAI at all times and capable of suctioning, bagging, reconnecting to the ventilator and re-positioning the tracheostomy tube. With a portable ventilator, supplemented where appropriate by the phrenic pacemaker and other systems, free movement of the VAI out of doors including aircraft travel is possible.

Mid and low cervical SCI persons have good diaphragmatic control but no intercostal or abdominal muscle function. Their cough is weak and may need to be assisted. Physiotherapy may be required during chest infections.

Mid-thoracic paraplegics lack a good cough because their abdominal and lower intercostal muscle control is absent. They may require help with chest infections in their older years.

14.5.11   Cardiovascular

Cardiovascular factors are an important source of morbidity and mortality in the spinal cord injured.

Postural hypotension is a common early problem. It is seldom disabling thereafter though tetraplegics may require occasional assistance with being tilted back. Postural hypotension can cause fatigue and pain in the neck and shoulders.

Autonomic dysreflexia is a serious potential problem in all patients with injuries at T6 and above. It can be precipitated by any stimulus arising below the level of injury, in particular from bladder and bowels. Carers must ensure that attacks are dealt with promptly and effectively.

In spite of immobility and leg dependency, anti-coagulation is seldom required following the acute stage.

Peripheral oedema and superficial lower limb skin changes are common. Careful attention must be paid to the feet so that cellulitis and other complications are avoided.

14.5.12   Skin

The history of the skin since injury, with particular reference to pressure sores, is a good guide to the quality of care that the SCI person has received. The report should deal with this and all the facets required to minimise the risk of skin complications in the future, including hygiene, seated posture, cushions, beds, mattresses, hoists, level and type of care, lifts in the wheelchair and repositioning in bed at night. The insensitive skin must be inspected morning and evening.

Minor red marks and skin abrasions necessitate bed-rest. This interferes with employment and quality of life.

With ageing, the skin and its underlying tissues become less resilient. The risk of pressure sores increases.

During the acute stage following injury 2-hourly turns in bed are necessary. Thereafter the gap increases. It decreases once more with ageing.

Paraplegics are usually able to turn in bed independently in their younger years. They require help as they get older. Tetraplegics usually require assistance with turns.

Variable height beds make transfers easier. The ability to elevate the head of the bed is useful. Turning beds are seldom used.

Most SCI persons prefer normal-looking double beds with double mattresses that they can share with their partners.

An appropriate mattress will increase the gap between turns.

The appropriate cushion is best selected in a posture and seating clinic. A spare cushion is essential.

The Jay Back helps maintain posture.

The Jay Protector surrounds the bottom, making climbing stairs and travel safer.

14.5.13   Sexual function

Sexuality is severely impaired following SCI. An SCI man sometimes feels incomplete because not only is normal sexual intercourse impossible but in addition he cannot be a full husband, father and breadwinner, or be involved in masculine activities.

SCI women can lose their self-respect. Wearing attractive clothes such as skirts is limited by the leg-bag and the wheelchair. Urinary incontinence is dreaded.

Although many approaches are available to achieve erections, sensation and orgasm are lost.

Fertility in SCI men is usually severely impaired. For an SCI person to become a genetic father it is usually necessary for the services of a fertility centre to be used, first to prepare the semen and second to treat the female partner to increase her fertility.

Methods for obtaining semen include the penile vibrator, rectal electrostimulated semen emission and micro-epididymal sperm aspiration. The quality of such semen is usually severely impaired.

Intra-cyto-plasmic sperm injection (ICSI) into oocytes has a high fertilisation rate. Because the take-home–baby rate per embryo replacement cycle is low, several such treatment cycles are usually required. A major benefit of ICSI is that non-motile sperm can be injected. As a result stored frozen sperm can be used.

In SCI women, intercourse is possible but passive. Normal orgasm does not occur except in lower levels of injury. Fertility is usually unimpaired.

Both male and female SCI persons are unable to be parents in the full sense. They cannot take their children out to the park or play with them as previously.

SCI persons who are not married at the time of injury have reduced prospects for developing firm and lasting relationships. Relationships already in existence are under increased stress following injury.

14.5.14   Mobility

Different wheelchairs are necessary for different purposes. For example, a sports wheelchair, a lightweight wheelchair and an electric wheelchair for outdoor use may all be required by the same person for use at different times.

The pattern of wheelchair requirement varies with the individual. It changes with age. A young tetraplegic can cope with a lightweight wheelchair indoors on level surfaces and up shallow slopes. In his or her older years, an electric wheelchair is required.

Before the appropriate wheelchairs for an SCI individual are selected they must be evaluated by him or her in a practical setting.

The most sophisticated wheelchairs permit environmental control, take portable ventilators and offer stand-up or reclining features.

The wheelchair must be integrated with an appropriate vehicle for satisfactory mobility out of doors. This often requires assessment in a specialised centre. Tall people have a restricted range of vehicle that they can use while seated in an electric wheelchair.

Tetraplegics at C5 usually require joystick control for driving. Some at C6 and most at C7 and below can cope with hand controlled vehicles. Ambulation is seldom a functional form of mobility for paraplegics or tetraplegics. It confers dignity and is a form of exercise. Those with poor truncal balance, such as low tetraplegics and high thoracic paraplegics, require orthoses with truncal support. Lower levels of thoracic and upper lumbar injury patients require the knee-ankle-foot orthoses or drop foot stimulators. Those with good quadriceps control usually cope with ankle-foot orthoses alone. The majority of SCI ambulators cease to walk after leaving the SCI centre. In spite of this, newer forms of orthotic ambulation are becoming commoner.

Public transport is difficult. Air travel is usually feasible.

There are a number of recreational mobility devices, such as the hand cycle. SCI persons involved in country pursuits may need an all-terrain vehicle.

14.5.15 Transfers

Nearly all paraplegics become independent in level transfers. Most achieve the more difficult ones as well, such as from low easy chairs into the wheelchair. The most difficult transfers, such as floor to wheelchair, are achieved by only the most able.

There is great individual variation between paraplegics in their transfer capability. Factors associated with reduced ability include increasing age, poor truncal balance, spasticity, spasms, obesity and upper limb problems such as muscle strains, nerve injury and joint contractures. Those with a low arm to trunk length ratio, for example achondroplastics, seldom achieve independent transfers.

A few low level tetraplegics become totally independent in transfers, usually with the aid of a sliding board. Most require help.

The minimum pattern of help required by each individual is best determined following a course of rehabilitation in a SCI unit.

Hoists are important. Portable ones are versatile. Ceiling mounted types take up less space. Strengthening of the ceiling is required with the latter. Risk assessment is required to determine the number of carers required to assist hoisted transfers.

14.5.16   Activities of daily living

The SCI person should describe both a typical day and one with unusual challenges.

In general, young paraplegics are fully independent and tetraplegics partially independent in activities of daily living.

Tetraplegics usually need help with lower-half washing, dressing and personal hygiene. Obesity, poor truncal balance, increasing age, upper limb musculo-skeletal problems, spasms, spasticity and short arms all impair ability.

Higher level tetraplegics require environmental control systems. Provided that the person can voluntarily control, in an accurate and predictable manner, a single muscle then he can control his environment, such as opening and closing curtains and using the telephone. Speech control is often the method of choice.

Most SCI persons benefit from a remote control door-opener.

14.5.17   Psychology

The effects of sudden paralysis, potential double incontinence, impotence, infertility, loss of relationships and all the other manifestations of spinal cord damage, affect every aspect of the person's life. The impact can be devastating. In spite of this, depression is not a major consequence of SCI and suicide is uncommon.

Most paraplegic and tetraplegic persons who have been through a SCI unit have learned to minimise the effect of their disability. They seldom concentrate on what they cannot do. It takes careful questioning to elicit the various ways in which the quality of their lives has been irretrievably altered by their condition.

14.5.18   Family

The enormous impact of paralysis on the family including parents, siblings, spouses and children must be described. Relationships can be destroyed. The old age of parents can be shattered by paralysis in their children. The ability of the SCI person to be a full partner or parent is severely impaired.

The view that family members should look after their SCI relative is no longer widely accepted. It is better for normal relationships to be retained. This will increase the likelihood of the integrity of the family being preserved. A partner should remain partner, parent and lover rather than become nurse and carer.

14.5.19 Home

Satisfactory housing is a very important pre-requisite for independence and quality of life following SCI.

Incomplete paraplegics who can ambulate and cope with stairs in their younger years find them increasingly difficult as they grow older. A single fall on stairs can be dangerous. Many eventually become wheelchair dependent.

Tetraplegics and complete paraplegics are safest in ground-floor wheelchair-accessible accommodation from the outset. Of particular importance are carer accommodation, exercise facilities and a guest bedroom.

SCI persons are less able to maintain their body temperature. Central heating is advised in all cases. Because tetraplegics can become overheated in hot weather, some rooms should have air conditioning.

14.5.20 Recreation and holidays

Re-engagement in life has both medical and psychological benefits. Upgraded seating in aircraft is sometimes required for comfort and safety.

14.5.21 Employment

In the UK one-third of SCI persons under 50 at injury, mostly paraplegics, achieve paid employment at some stage after injury. Those who had physical, outdoor or manual employment, or poor academic backgrounds pre-injury usually remain unemployed. SCI persons capable of desk bound work take longer to get up, need workplaces that are wheelchair accessible and facilities that allow for episodes of incontinence. Complications result in time off work. Drugs such as Baclofen interfere with concentration and mental agility. Fatigue is common.

14.5.22 Medical care

Good medical care is essential for the quality and duration of life of the SCI person to be optimal. The clinical needs of the spinal cord injured should be met by SCI centres.

Preventative maintenance is required to detect medical complications while they are at an early stage so that they can be treated effectively before they cause trouble. Problems can arise in many different areas including, among others, the spinal cord, spine, urinary tract, bowels and skin. The review should include medical, nursing, physiotherapy, occupational therapy and psychology input. Investigations for asymptomatic pathology that could arise are required so that it can be dealt with before it becomes a problem.

SCI persons should always be re-admitted into SCI centres whenever possible. Non-specialist centres lack the necessary knowledge and expertise in their care. The average annual readmission bed-days per SCI person is 5. As there are circa 35,000 SCI persons in the UK and only 450 SCI beds, two-thirds of which are for first admissions, the NHS readmission capacity is inadequate.

14.5.23   Ageing

People ageing with SCI require additional help to function at a satisfactory level. Changes in function due to age are superimposed and interact with the SCI.

Upper limb degenerative changes commence by 10 years post injury, with the onset tending to be earlier in females and those who are older. This is prior to the onset of clinical features and the need for extra care.

Both increased years post injury and current age are associated with increased need for help with ageing. Of these two, years post-injury is the more important. In general, age at SCI onset reflects ageing before SCI and years post-injury reflects ageing with SCI. The cumulative acquired effects of SCI are more important than the chronologic age of the person with SCI.

By 30 years post-injury most people living with SCI have reduced independence. To retain a satisfactory quality of life prior to this stage, the SCI person may need to have help to ensure that excessive time is not spent on functions such as bowel care etc.

The most common symptoms of ageing are fatigue, pain and new muscle weakness.

The activities of daily living most affected in ageing are bathing, transfers and dressing. Of these, difficulty with transfers is the commonest problem.

There is an evolving need for equipment with ageing.

The timing of onset of need for extra help with ageing is individual. Those with more weakness, more shoulder pain, greater weight, greater frequency of medical problems and greater postural changes tend to need more help with ageing. Other important factors include gender, the severity of spasms and spasticity, and the presence of upper limb pathology, such as upper limb injuries affecting mobility.

Women ageing with SCI tend to need more help than men with SCI, a factor reflected in the non-SCI population. Women have lower upper-body strength than men, lower arm to body length ratio, increased ligamentous laxity and wider elbow carrying angles. Transfers are often more difficult in women because they are bottom heavy.

14.5.24   Care

The purpose of care is to empower the SCI person to do whatever he or she reasonably wants to do and whenever he or she reasonably wants to do it and with reasonable safety.

Care need is increased by the superimposition of intercurrent situations such as illness, upper limb strains, child-bearing, altered environment and holidays.

Low-level paraplegics are usually independent when young, apart from needing help with domestic activities, shopping, certain obstacles out of doors, gardening, do-it-yourself work and home maintenance. They usually require stand-by assistance when ambulating in callipers or similar devices.

Mid-level paraplegics often require assistance with using the standing frame, getting out of the bath, getting in and out of the car and with lifting the wheelchair in and out of the car. Spasticity, intrinsic ability, obesity, truncal balance and age are important.

While a few low-level tetraplegics are almost independent, the majority require substantial assistance. For example, they can use a fork or spoon for eating but not cut up meat. They can drive vehicles but not transfer or lift their wheelchairs in and out.

Because tetraplegics can get autonomic dysreflexia or choke on food, someone should always at hand to deal with an emergency should the need arise. In general, one person is sufficient. A second should be present when there are activities that require two persons.

Ventilator assisted tetraplegics should always be in-line-of-eye of someone who can reconnect them to the ventilator, suck out secretions, reposition a dislodged tracheostomy tube and carry out bagging via the tracheostomy. The carers must be sufficiently experienced to ensure that problems are dealt with proactively rather than reactively.

Carer accommodation must be adequate if carer recruitment is to be assured.

14.5.25   Physiotherapy

In general, carers can carry out straightforward physiotherapy activities such as joint range of motion and assisting the SCI person into the standing frame. Training, supervision and more specialised physiotherapy tasks require a chartered physiotherapist.

14.5.26   Occupational therapy

The occupational therapist is helpful in bringing the SCI person up to date with modern developments in aids, equipment and recreations, as well as advising on housing.

14.5.27   Chiropody

Good foot care is essential, especially in the ageing SCI person, if lower limb infections and other complications are to be avoided.

14.5.28   Dental treatment

Good dental care is essential. If NHS access is difficult then private treatment is required.

14.5.29   Warm water therapy

An assessment will indicate if this provides significant benefits that cannot be achieved by land-based therapy.

14.5.30   Other therapy

SCI persons frequently have problems, such as pain, that are not relieved by conventional approaches. Alternative means, such as massage or acupuncture, may help.

14.5.31   Equipment

There is no such thing as a standard equipment list. The latter should be honed to the particular requirements of the SCI person being considered. As far as possible all equipment should be evaluated by the SCI person in conjunction with the appropriate therapist. Exhibitions, such as NAIDEX, can help. The medical expert can more readily support equipment that the claimant has personally evaluated and found useful.

14.5.32   Future developments

During the remainder of the life of each SCI person there will be developments from which he or she will benefit and for which he or she will need to pay. The NHS will pay for established treatments in some, but not all cases. With newer developments, funding is even less likely because it has to compete with claims for existing and more basic treatments, let alone newer advances.

14.5.33   Other experts

These are required if issues of liability and quantum cannot be fully resolved by the lead medical expert. Opinions on housing, equipment and care are always necessary.

14.5.34   Expectation of life

In arriving at an opinion on life expectation the following must be considered:

(1)   the projected life expectancy of the general population;

(2)   life expectancy after considering non-SCI factors;

(3)   the range of historical percentage remaining expected years of life in the UK and countries with similar healthcare systems, such as Australia;

(4)   where the claimant falls relative to this average range based on his or her SCI factors;

(5)   compensation improves life expectancy, provided that it is used to purchase those aspects, such as housing, equipment and care, that impact on life expectancy and that are insufficiently funded by the state to meet the reasonable needs of the SCI person;

(6)   whether life expectancy is static in relative terms for those with SCI, or increasing, as has been the case in the UK up to 1990.[67]

Annex 2 indicates the facts that must be obtained by the lead medical expert to assist in the determination of life expectancy after an SCI.

---

[6]   Middleton et al 'Life expectancy after spinal cord injury: a 50-year study' (2012) *Spinal Cord* 1-9.

[7]   Frankel et al 'Long-term survival in spinal cord injury: a fifty year investigation' (1998) 36 *Spinal Cord* 266-274.

ANNEX 1: HEADINGS IN A MODEL REPORT IN AN SCI CASE

(a) Introduction

Claimant's name and address

Date of report

Date of birth

Date of injury

Age at injury

Current age

Weight

Height

BMI

When and where client was examined

Who was present

Statement of duty to the court

Instructions of solicitor

List of material and literature relied upon

Abbreviated curriculum vitae

(b) General

Past medical history – especially that which is relevant to the current state

Family history – ages, causes of death, state of health, familial disorders

Medication history – pre and post injury

Alcohol, prohibited substance and smoking histories

Liability issues – seat belt, alcohol, medical

(c) History of presenting complaint

History from time of injury to the present

(d) Current condition and prognosis – considered under headings

(i) Associated injuries

Brain

Limb joints/bones/soft tissues

Peripheral nerves/brachial plexus

Chest/abdomen

(ii) SCI related

Neurology – level and completeness: syrinx.

Spine – deformity: arthritis.

Pain – musculoskeletal and neurogenic

Bladder – upper and lower urinary tract

Bowels

Hygiene – method of bathing, shower chair, bath

Joints/soft tissue – heterotopic ossification, strains, contractures, method of standing

Spasms and spasticity – ways in which these help or hinder

Respiratory

Cardiovascular – hypotension, fatigue, coat hanger pain, autonomic dysfunction

Skin – turns in bed, mattress, cushion, bed

Sexual function – fertility, intercourse, sexuality, relationships

Mobility – wheelchair, car, orthoses, recreational mobility, ramps

Transfers – level and split-level: hoists

Activities of daily living – environmental control systems

Psychology – counselling, suicide risk

Family – who live with, spouse, parents, children

Home

Recreation

Holidays

Employment – schooling, university, employment history: points of difficulty

Medical care – hospital, reviews.

Care needs – risk assessment of night care and transfers: domestic, gardening

Ageing issues

Physiotherapy

Occupational therapy

Chiropody

Dental

Other therapies – aquatherapy, acupuncture, dietician

Equipment

Potential developments in remaining years of life

Other experts

Life expectancy

(e) Summary

ANNEX 2: LIFE EXPECTANCY CHECKLIST

(a) Non-SCI factors

Age

Years since injury

BMI

Blood pressure

Past history

Family history

Smoking history

Alcohol history

Prohibited substances history

Socio-economic class status

(b) SCI factors – relative to the average SCI of claimant's age and neurological injury

Neurological status

Medication history

Abdominal surgery or condition

Urinary tract history

Respiratory tract history

Cardiovascular history

Physical exercise

Pressure sore history

Septicaemia risk

Housing

Engagement in life

Family support

Readmissions since injury

Care

Equipment

Suicide risk

CHAPTER 15

PROSTHETIC REHABILITATION OF TRAUMATIC AMPUTEES

Sellaiah Sooriakumaran

15.1 INTRODUCTION

Rehabilitation is a process by which an amputee is enabled to optimise physical, social and psychological state. Successful rehabilitation depends on team approach. The professionals include surgeon, rehabilitation physician, prosthetist, nurse, physiotherapist, occupational therapist, social worker, and psychologist. Good communication between all these professionals led by a rehabilitation physician, and liaison with appropriate colleagues in the community such as general practitioner and relevant agencies such as social services, is vital to achieve successful holistic rehabilitation. Key factors affecting rehabilitation outcome are: mental attitude and approach of patient; age and physical ability of patient; level of amputation; and rehabilitation programme. The typical traumatic amputee is often young, healthy, in manual occupation doing physically demanding sports and leisure activities. The index accident may also have caused other major injuries such as brain damage, multiple limb and internal injuries affecting their potential rehabilitation outcome. The amputation may lead to loss of employment, change in relationship/marital status, significant impact on previous lifestyle, housing requirements, driving etc.

It is crucial to do a holistic assessment and formulate a plan of comprehensive management of their prosthetic programme, taking account of their needs for pain control, psycho-social, and vocational aspects. The medico-legal claim and its timely settlement often play an important role in the rehabilitative process.

15.2 INCIDENCE AND PREVALENCE OF AMPUTATIONS IN THE UK:

The prevalence of amputees in England and Wales has been estimated at 65,000. The Limbless Statistics by United National Institute for Prosthetics & Orthotics Development (UNIPOD) provide details of new amputees referred to prosthetic clinics in England and Wales. An annual report is produced on data provided from the 44 prosthetic centres in the UK. The total number referred has remained fairly constant – about 5,500 per year. Lower extremity amputation accounts for 92% of the total. In lower-limb amputations there has been a welcome and increasing trend towards preserving the natural knee joint. The most common level of amputation referred now is transtibial. The upper limb amputee referrals remain very small. Upper limb patients tend to be in the younger age groups reflecting the aetiology of the condition (mainly trauma).

Amputations done for peripheral vascular disease and diabetes account for 70%. In the last two to three decades, the incidence of traumatic amputations in the UK has been contained at 7-9%. The enforcement of speed control, alcohol limits, seat belt use, compulsory helmets for motorcyclists, and improved surgical salvage techniques etc have all contributed to this. Similarly, health and safety implementation has reduced the incidence of industrial and home accidents reducing upper limb ablations. The commonest cause of traumatic lower limb amputation in the UK remains motorcycle accidents. The amputation may be carried out as a primary procedure for unsalvageable injury or electively for complications such as fracture non-union or chronic osteomyelitis.

15.3 AMPUTATION SURGERY AND RESIDUAL LIMB

The dictum of Sir William Ferguson that 'Amputation is one of the meanest yet one of the greatest operations in Surgery; mean when resorted to where better could be done – great as the only step to give comfort in life' is as true today as when first written in the 19th century. Trauma surgeons are now able to evaluate the injured limb in an objective manner (mangled extremity score) and make decisions in regard to salvage or primary amputation. The considerations differ in upper and lower limb. A salvaged upper limb with partial sensation and minimal active function may prove superior compared to amputation and prosthesis. In contrast, a lower limb, being mainly a weightbearing organ, is more easily replaced with prosthesis at times providing better function compared to a painful insensate non-functional leg. Amputation should not be considered a failure but rather another therapeutic modality.

Amputation, although ablative, should be considered as a re-constructive surgery, where the surgeon is fashioning the motor to drive the prosthesis. Introduction of formal education in amputation surgery as part of the curriculum for junior surgeons has improved the quality of amputation surgery. In the residual limb (amputation stump) the part remaining below the most distal joint is the lever, which controls the prosthesis. It is inserted into a socket and must be a long enough lever to function.

Amputation for trauma is dictated by level of tissue damage and proximal joint function. Amputation is through skin, fascia, muscles, ligaments and bones or joints.

Skin – The skin needs careful treatment to ensure as little scarring as possible. The incision should be planned so that if possible the scar is transverse to shear forces. The superficial and deep fascia is re-sutured to prevent the skin becoming adherent to deep structures. The amputation scar should be sensate, well healed, painless, pliable and non-adherent.

Muscles – The state of muscle balance is disturbed by amputation because the origins and insertions of the opposing groups are often at different levels. Divided muscle remnants in amputation should be sutured to the bone as distally as possible (myodesis) and over the end of the bone (myoplasty). Undesirable bulbousness of residual limb is avoided by tailoring the muscle bulk. The muscles thus restored would insulate the cut nerve endings and the bone from the prosthesis.

Nerves – Nerves have little mechanical significance in affecting prosthetic design. The healing process of a divided nerve produces a bulb (neuroma), which if exposed to pressure or tension can produce pain. Nerves should be divided as high as possible at operation and allowed to retract into the muscle mass.

Bone – Amputation can be through the shaft of a long bone or through a joint. Both have their advantages and disadvantages. Advantages of amputation through a joint (disarticulation): the expanded cancellous bone adapted to loadbearing in its natural state remains to provide end-bearing through the shaft with some degree of proprioceptive feedback; the skin and superficial fascia around joints are adapted to accept high loads; in children the cartilaginous growth plate is preserved; few muscle bellies are divided and divided tendons are easily re-attached; less vascular and control of bleeding is easier; the bulbous expansion provide suspension of prosthesis and an element of rotational control, the long bone preserved in its entirety provides a long lever; residual limb pain is rare. Disadvantages: some levels are fraught with delayed healing; ablated joint cannot be replaced with prosthetic joints at the same level; a bulbous end has to be accommodated in the socket and may compromise cosmesis. Advantages of amputation through shaft of bone: a useful joint above the level of amputation is preserved; a length of long bone is retained to act as a lever. Disadvantages: muscle bellies are sectioned with greater disturbance of muscle balance; reattachment of muscles is difficult; medullary cavity of the bone is opened with greater risk of the bone getting infected; divided bone cannot fully end-bear and load must largely be distributed at a higher level.

There is a distinction between surgeries done as emergencies as in accidents or war time compared to elective amputations. In the presence of contaminated wounds and infection amputation may be done at the most distal level by a guillotine type and left open initially for a formal revision at a later date.

15.4 PROSTHETICS

The earliest evidence available of a prosthesis is the cosmetic hallux found on a mummy circa 1000 BCE. Prosthetic innovations did not keep pace with that of amputation surgery and crude crutches and peg-legs were used until the 16th century. The French surgeon Pare made the first major advance in designing an inexpensive wooden knee walker peg-leg and a sophisticated transfemoral prosthesis, as well as a cleverly crafted prosthetic hand with locking fingers. In 1696 the Dutch surgeon Verduyn designed the transtibial prosthesis as well as the revolutionary posterior myo-cutaneous flap. This enabled the amputee to weightbear through the tightly laced leather thigh corset and mobilise with free knee motion. This prototype remained in use until the introduction of the patellar tendon-bearing (PTB) prosthesis in 1961 by Radcliffe and Foort at the University of California at Berkeley. The first body powered prosthetic hand was introduced around 1816. The concept of harnessing the remaining muscles to operate a terminal device was central to development in upper limb prosthetics until the introduction of myoelectrically controlled external power in 1958. Progress was made in the 19th and 20th centuries as a result of the wars. As prosthetics has always been a small field serving relatively few people it has not always been possible to devote the necessary time and financial resources to fully develop their concepts on any scale. Limited materials, namely wood, leather and iron, were used to construct early prosthetic limbs. By necessity prosthetists have had to borrow new techniques, devices, and materials as they became affordable from other fields and then adapt them to their own use. Significant advances have occurred in improving comfort of weightbearing through prosthesis by incorporating cushioned interphase liners especially for vulnerable skin.

Prosthetic construction and supply needs to be varied according to the patient group. For the active amputee the prosthesis must be functional, durable and of good appearance, and, above all manufactured and fitted as soon as possible after amputation. For the elderly the weight of the prosthesis becomes the prime factor in ensuring success, but it must still be cosmetically acceptable. The major cause of amputation is vascular disease, but the cause of limb loss in those who continue to attend prosthetic clinic for many years is mainly injury.

Normal gait is extremely efficient and any inefficiency, that is any alteration in the normal pattern of gait, decreases efficiency and increases energy consumption. A transtibial amputee consumes about 25%, and a transfemoral amputee about 60%, additional energy compared to normal walking. The additional energy spent walking with bilateral transtibial prostheses is 40%, and with bilateral transfemoral prostheses it is about 300%.

The design of a limb prosthesis, whose purpose is to replace a missing limb and to restore or provide function, is largely governed by the level of amputation and the remaining function, although residual pathology or unrelated disease may also affect it. The patient's age, physique, balance, sight and environmental or psychological needs may be of far greater importance than the cause of amputation. Prosthesis should aim to replace in every respect the performance of the natural limb. Prosthetic limb segments and joints must correspond to the equivalent natural levels.

The prime function of the lower limb is standing and walking. Other motor activities such as climbing, running, dancing etc are secondary. For the upper limb the problem is much more complex: first because the motor function is much more varied in the power used and the movement of joints; secondly because the hand is important as a sense organ, exploring the environment by touch; and lastly it is an important part of the body image. The hand is used in gesture as a supplement to speech, as an emotional outlet and in personal contact. In contrast to lower limb, one can lose the whole upper limb and still be able to wash, toilet, cook and eat, and follow many gainful and skilled occupations without any prosthesis. The gain from a prosthesis in body image, sensory feedback, and emotional outlet is poor, motor function is limited and crude and to gain in appearance with a life-like hand is usually to forfeit some motor function. There are many prosthetic devices that are useful but which do not resemble the human shape.

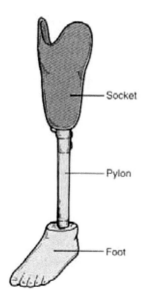

Socket

Pylon

Foot

Figure 15.1: Modular/endoskeletal prosthesis

Prosthetic components fall into five major groups:
(1) interphase (socket) components;
(2) terminal devices;
(3) joints, joint mechanisms and structure;
(4) alignment devices;
(5) cosmetic components.

15.4.1 Interphase components

These are the parts of prosthesis which are in direct contact with body tissues. All contact between the prosthesis and the body is through the skin, the body's interphase component. The prosthetic interphase component is the socket, which is the part of the prosthesis into which the residual limb in inserted. All the forces between the prosthesis and the body are transmitted through the socket. The skin has a limited tolerance to pressure, so the high forces which may be generated must be distributed over a wide area of skin. In addition, the impermeable socket prevents direct contact with the environment resulting in heat retention and sweating. Direct contact with skin provides some sensory feedback gathered by vibration and variation in the magnitude and direction of forces transmitted across the interphase. Sockets may be made from a range of materials; carved from wood, moulded from leather, shaped from metal. Today most sockets are made from plastic materials to a cast or computer aided imaging (CAD-CAM). A wrap-cast of the residual limb needs to be modified (rectification) to give a satisfactory fit. Progress has been made in developing the socket with compliant areas which accept changes under loading and active use while retaining rigidity where needed. The inevitable circumferential pressure from the socket should be less than arterial pressure but may be high enough to interfere with venous and lymphatic return and over a long period this may result in congestion and eventually eczema-like conditions of the unsupported soft tissues. It is now widely accepted that, whatever the site of amputation, major loading should be in total contact with the socket. Total contact also gives better sensory input. The design of socket brim is vital to preferentially load tolerant areas of residual limb and should be bevelled and flared to avoid skin problems from friction.

Suspension of prosthesis can be provided by pressure differential referred to as 'suction socket'. The original concept of suction socket was to maintain adhesion of the socket by negative pressure to the residual limb by providing a one-way exhaust valve below the residuum. Alternatively body contour suspension is used often in amputation by disarticulation at joints, where the bulbous end of residual limb is inserted into a socket shaped to the contour. Auxiliary harnesses attached to the socket and fastened to the body are another form of suspension. In recent times locking liner suspension has become more popular.

15.4.2   Terminal devices

These are the prosthetic representations of the hand and foot. They may be purely functional with no resemblance to a natural hand and foot such as split hook or peg-leg respectively.

15.4.3   Joints, joint mechanisms and structure

In modern times prostheses are made of modular components, which could be exchanged in repair or maintenance or to match patient's change in needs. The endoskeletal structure gives greater flexibility in the adjustment of axial rotation of one segment of the prosthesis with another and facilitates adjustment for length. Prosthetic joints replace an absent joint and contain mechanisms to control and stabilise range of movement. The joint may be rigid, allow movement in one axis (uniaxial) or about finite axes (multiaxial) or infinite number of axes (flexible). To be life-like the prosthetic joint needs to have extreme movement limited mechanically serving as natural ligaments giving static stability. Stability to maintain posture may be provided by a lock which when actuated prevents all movement of the joint. These may be automatic as in the lower limb prostheses for the elderly and feeble. In certain situations the lock may be operated to achieve different range of movements. There are three sources of power used to move parts of prostheses: the body's musculature, gravity and external power. Compression or stretching of springs and elastomers either by gravity or by an imparted movement is used to provide potential energy. Resistance is needed to decelerate a movement at the end of the desired range. There is friction, pneumatic and hydraulic mechanisms used to give this deceleration. These assisting and resisting mechanisms are intended to correspond to the accelerations and decelerations by which the normal musculature controls the movements of the natural limb. The prosthetic mimicry is poor although improving with introduction of microprocessor controls. The active person with a good amputation in the lower limb can walk on the level at a steady pace in a way which will deceive most people who are not trained observers, but the movements carried out in everyday life by the upper limb such as eating or combing the hair are so complex and individual that however efficient they are instantly recognisable as artificial.

15.4.4 Alignment devices

These are tools used in lower-limb fabrication to optimise loading. Traditionally prosthetists used 'bench alignment' and in recent years a number of devices have been developed to allow adjustment of spatial relationship of the socket relative to the foot to provide angular adjustments for flexion-extension, abduction-adduction and rotation. Alignment devices may be sited at one or both ends of a limb segment which can be adjusted in both static and dynamic use.

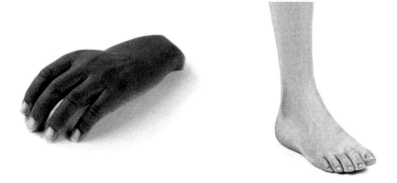

Figure 15.2: High definition life-like silicone cosmesis

15.4.5   Cosmetic components

These are parts of prosthesis which are used solely to satisfy the psychological loss. Various spongy materials such as foam plastic material are shaped to match the natural limb profile. Coloured plastic covers such as stocking is then pulled over the underlying shaped material to resemble the normal skin. Introduction of high definition life-like colour-matched silicone has improved satisfaction. The high definition silicone cosmetic cover is a bespoke item designed to mirror the sound side limb in terms of shape, colour and appendages. Discoloration by printer's ink and resistance to dirt vary with different materials.

15.5   PHASES OF LOWER LIMB REHABILITATION:

15.5.1   Pre-amputation stage

In the case of elective amputations, the patient would benefit from a pre-amputation consultation with the prosthetic team to understand details of relevant prosthesis, realistic potential rehabilitation outcome and possible complications related to amputation and using prosthesis. This would give an opportunity to the patient to be introduced to other age and amputation level matched established amputees. The physiotherapist should assess general strength, mobility, specific joint weakness and deformities and recommend appropriate pre-amputation exercise programmes. Patient's home conditions, employment, driving status, hobbies etc are assessed and appropriate advice given. Adequate pre-amputation pain control for 48 hours and continued for a few days post-operatively are known to reduce the incidence of severe phantom limb pain.

15.5.2   Post-amputation pre-prosthetic stage

The patient returns from theatre with a drain and light dressing over the suture line, held in place with light crêpe bandage. Pre-prosthetic physiotherapy should commence within a few days of amputation depending on adequate wound healing. Early post-operative pain and phantom limb pain should be adequately controlled to enable the patient to participate in physiotherapy, bed mobility, regain independence for personal hygiene and wheelchair mobility. The patient is encouraged to look at and handle the residual limb. The drain is removed by the third day, the wound dressing is changed and the patient dressed in his clothes to attend the physiotherapy department. An otherwise fit patient should be able to weightbear and mobilise between rails in the physiotherapy department using post-amputation pneumatic amputation mobility aid (PPAM aid) within 10 days from amputation. PPAM aid is a partial weightbearing prosthesis to be used within parallel bars or with crutches if the patient's balance is good. Active joint exercises and re-education of balance and core stability are commenced. Post-operative oedema is avoided by using special elasticated socks.

15.5.3   Prosthetic gait training

The prosthetic clinics within the NHS setting provide prostheses for all amputees who are eligible when clinically appropriate. Once the swelling on the residual limb is sufficiently resolved and wound healing is satisfactory, measurements or casts are taken and the first prosthesis is supplied to be used in the physiotherapy department within 3 weeks from amputation. The gait training starts in the parallel bars and once a good gait pattern is achieved a walking aid is supplied. During this period the patient learns the mechanics and maintenance of the prosthesis, to put on and take off the prosthesis independently, to sit and stand safely, walk correctly, and manage stairs, kerbs and slopes. If the patient is fit enough to manage transport they should be escorted on a journey and taught to get in and out of a car. As it is possible that the patient might at some time have a fall, they must be taught how to get up from lying. The prosthesis may or may not be completed with a cosmetic cover depending on the patient's wishes. At discharge, further therapy from colleagues in the community is arranged as needed.

15.5.4   Follow-up

Early recovery is then monitored at 4 to 6 weekly interval gradually reducing frequency to once in 3 to 4 months by the end of first year and less frequently afterwards. Appropriate adjustments of the prosthesis are made to match changes in residual limb. Patients may warrant a refresher course of physiotherapy when major changes are made in prosthetic components or when bad gait habits are detected. Higher level amputation and multiple limb amputations take a longer period to complete gait training programmes. The younger amputee should make greater efforts to walk with as normal a gait as possible.

Requirements of prostheses to fulfil daily walking, hobbies, sports, employment etc are taken into account in prescribing prostheses. The aim is to provide the range of prostheses and appropriate components to restore a near normal life as possible in the long term.

15.5.5   Wheelchair

At the early stages most amputees would depend on crutches or wheelchair until completing prosthetic fitting and training. They often fall back to using wheelchair when they are not able to use a prosthesis at later stages. Higher level or multiple limb amputees may consistently resort to wheelchair in addition to walking with prostheses. The suitable model wheelchair is prescribed by an occupational therapist. If the NHS is unable to provide an appropriate model the patient may have to part fund it using a voucher scheme or purchase it privately.

15.6   LONG-TERM MANAGEMENT

The time taken for the residual limb to resolve fully depends on the level of amputation and general medical condition and on average takes about 6 to 12 months. By this time the patient is ready to take on higher physical activities of their choice and the prosthetist considers appropriate components, socket design, interphase and suspension.

An active full time prosthetic user often requires more than one prosthesis to satisfy mobility and leisure/sports needs. It is the usual practice to provide a prosthesis for the purpose of daily walking and a second prosthesis to enable the amputee to resume the range of leisure/sports activities of choice. Depending on individual need supply of a third dedicated waterproof prosthesis may be warranted.

15.6.1   Sports prostheses

Traumatic amputees are more inclined to participate in recreational activities. Studies confirm that a high proportion of previously active amputees do return to recreational activities within a year after amputation. Delays may be attributed to prosthetic fitting, comfort, prolonged recovery, phantom pain and residual limb pain. Common recreational activities enjoyed by amputees are exercise with equipment, golf, swimming, fishing, walking, running, dancing, boating, bowling and bicycling. Middle-aged amputees may find recreational activities intimidating and would benefit from instruction and working with others in groups. A significant number of amputees experience prosthetic problems all of the time during physical activity. Persistent prosthetic problems can often be reduced with a variety of adaptations or ingenious modifications to meet the demands of a particular sport. Skin irritation and breakdown is the most common prosthetic problem. Amputees often perceive inability to run as the single most common factor limiting participation. It is a misconception that running is a prerequisite skill for sports. Able amputees should be exposed to basic running during rehabilitation so that they can pursue running if they wish. Prosthetic options for recreational activities and competitive athletes have grown tremendously through the years. Socket design, stability, suspension systems, shock absorbers, sports oriented prosthetic ankle/foot are all carefully explored at the time of prescribing to match individual amputee's requirements.

Figure 15.3: Sports/recreational prostheses

Level of aesthetic finish of prosthesis depends on patient's requirements. There is a range of off-the-shelf and custom-made cosmeses available to select from. They can vary from not having any cosmetic cover to high definition life-like silicone-made cosmesis.

15.6.2   Outcome measures

Progress in prosthetic rehabilitation and satisfaction with prostheses are regularly monitored by members of the team. Socket comfort score, nine-hole peg test, hospital anxiety and depression scale, numeric pain scale, 2-minute walking test, locomotor capability index, mobility grade classified by special interest group in amputee medicine (SIGAM) are examples.

15.7   LEVELS OF LOWER LIMB AMPUTATION AND PROSTHETICS

15.7.1   Amputations of foot and ankle and prostheses

In the forefoot, amputations can be done either transversely or longitudinally (ray) according to the degree of tissue damage with minimal disturbance of normal biomechanics of the foot. Necessary support is provided by shaped foam-filler in a supportive shoe with reinforced sole, and possibly 'rocker' profile if needed. Supply of silicone-made forefoot replacement provides improved cosmesis when worn with open shoes or sandals.

In mid-foot (tarsometatarsal or Lisfranc and midtarsal or Chopart) amputations, it is important to carry out a muscle balancing procedure to maintain balance of power in the hind-foot and avoid complication of equino-varus deformity.

If the residual foot is balanced to be plantar-grade then the patient may be able to manage with an ortholene back splint incorporating a sole plate and toe filler.

The advantage of this level of amputation is the ease of mobilising indoors without the need of prosthetic support and proprioceptive and sensory feedback, particularly in the elderly. Bulkiness of the prosthesis around the ankle may prove a significant disadvantage for young females conscious of choice of footwear.

15.7.2   Ankle disarticulation (Syme's) with retention of heel pad produces an end-bearing bulbous residuum

Prostheses for this level would need extension proximally to shin part of the lower leg to achieve stability during different phases of gait. As the natural ankle joint is destroyed a special ankle mechanism is placed below, or a solid ankle cushion heel (SACH) foot without any ankle is used. The appearance around the ankle part of a prosthesis may not be acceptable, particularly for women.

15.7.3 Transtibial (below knee) amputation and prosthesis

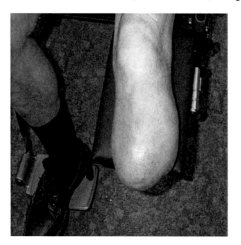

Figure 15.4: Transtibial residual limb

Amputation below the knee allows natural extension and flexion of the knee joint but requires a prosthetic ankle and foot. A long below knee amputation has no advantage and compromises fitting of a functional prosthesis. Utilising modern prosthetic techniques, residuum as short as 7 cm could be fitted successfully. The functional mobility outcome of a short below knee segment with intact extensor mechanism compared to knee disarticulation or transfemoral amputation would be superior. Incorporating thigh corset to below knee prosthesis for partial weight distribution and knee stability is favoured to sacrificing the natural knee and doing a proximal amputation. An optimal average length for transtibial amputation would be 16 cm from the knee joint axis. A below knee amputation transects all three muscle compartments, tibia and fibula. Bevelling of the tibial crest, chamfering of sharp bone edges and myodesis are recommended to produce a well contoured pain free residual limb. In cases of de-gloving type injury with extensive skin and soft tissue loss, cover is obtained by skin graft, myo-cutaneous free flap (such as latissimus dorsi muscle) or pedicled neuro-vascular flap. The amputation flaps are fashioned to position the scar away from weightbearing areas avoiding 'dog ear' formation.

Patellar tendon bearing (PTB) prostheses have become the prosthesis of choice throughout the world for this level amputation. The specific definition of weightbearing, relief on sensitive points, and alignment has been well described by Radcliffe and Foort. The trained prosthetist would modify the cast as it is taken to outline the patellar tendon and to provide counter pressure posteriorly. The positive male cast is 'rectified' with careful attention based on the findings on examination of the residual limb and the socket is fabricated using a foam plastic inner liner and a rigid outer plastic socket. A number of variations on this fundamental principle have been introduced in the last decade. The socket is set in 5–7 degrees of flexion and vertical load line to fall between anterior two-third and posterior one-third of the foot. The final alignment is adjusted after observing the patient's gait. At times additional alignment devices may be needed. Options of suspensions of transtibial prostheses are leather cuff strap around lower thigh, knee sleeve, supracondylar extension of socket, suction produced by expulsion valve or by the use of locking interphase liner.

15.7.4   Knee disarticulation and prosthesis

Amputation through the knee joint produces a bulbous end-bearing residual limb and should be considered as a viable clinical choice prior to considering a more proximal level amputation. As it is the least traumatic of any major lower limb amputation and does not involve any bone sectioning, it can be performed with minimal anaesthesia. The special merits of this amputation are proprioceptive feedback, full end-bearing, ability to self-suspend prosthesis using the condyles and lesser incidence of residual limb pain.

Prosthesis: The socket is end bearing and suspension is achieved by designing the socket to grip the residual limb above the femoral condyles. The residual limb is contained within the flexible inner liner and weight is transmitted via the laminated outer socket. Windows cut in the outer socket walls will allow a degree of flexibility of the inner socket in response to volume changes of the residual limb related to activity. A polycentric prosthetic knee joint would minimise discrepancy of knee joint axis and provide geometric stance stability. Swing phase control is provided by hydraulics.

15.7.5   Transfemoral (above knee) amputation and prosthesis

To lose the knee joint is a grave disadvantage to any patient and transfemoral amputation should not be performed where there is a possibility of an amputation at a lower level being successful. The longer the residual limb (within certain limits) the better the leverage. The recommendation is to section the bone 13 cm above knee joint line to provide adequate room to fit a prosthetic knee in the prosthesis. Equal anterior and posterior skin flaps are advocated. The muscles are separated into four quadrants. The adductor muscle and iliotibial tract are sutured to the bone end through drill holes (myodesis). The quadricpeps and hamstrings are sutured to each other in physiologic tension (myoplasty).

Prosthesis: The sockets of these prostheses are traditionally proximal-bearing and are ischial-bearing, although with an element of more distal loading and total surface-bearing is now common. There are a number of shapes which have evolved from different researchers. The shaped brim has to accommodate the adductor longus tendon at its origin, the ischial tuberosity and the greater trochanter. The soft tissues may be distorted to meet the mechanical requirements.

The socket is set in 5–10 degrees of flexion to optimise the loss of muscle balance between flexors and extensors. The tendency is for the residual limb to

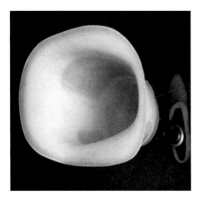

Figure 15.5: Transfemoral socket

abduct and this is corrected by setting the lateral wall of socket in adduction. The length of the residual limb and hip muscle strength would influence these adjustments to optimise gait and minimise the limp.

The type of suspension depends on hip stability and residual limb length. For those with hip instability a metal hip joint with pelvic belt is provided to control the prosthesis. A modified form of Silesian belt is an alternative in patients whose residual limb fluctuates in volume and cannot use a suction type socket. Self-suspension with locking liner or vacuum suction is the preferred option. The silicone Seal-In liner rolls over the residual limb and is in direct contact with the skin. A rubber hypobaric sealing membrane is situated around the circumference of the liner, once in contact with the socket a seal is created providing a suction suspension system. A valve is incorporated within the socket, to remove the socket the valve is opened letting air into the system.

15.7.5.1   Knees

The knee mechanisms may be divided into two groups: those concerned with stance-phase control and those concerned with swing-phase control.

Stance-phase control

Semi-automatic knee lock – This is the simplest and lightest of knee controls. The prosthetic knee automatically locks with full extension when the patient stands up and remains locked until positively released for sitting down. It is recommended for the elderly, feeble and those with short residual limbs who cannot control the prosthesis with alignment stability alone.

Hand-operated knee lock – This lock is applied voluntarily by the patient to the knee joint. It is usually combined with swing-phase control and is suitable for patients who wish to walk with a freely swinging knee but at times needs stability of a locked knee. The modern stabilising knee systems have made this requirement often obsolete.

Stance phase stability in a 'free knee' can be provided by hydraulic, friction or polycentric mechanisms. As weight is transmitted to the knee joint on stance the knee is locked up to about 30 degrees of flexion.

Figure 15.6: Polyaxial knee joint

Swing-phase control

The acceleration and deceleration mechanisms added to the prosthesis to modify the movements during the swing are referred to as swing-phase controls. Pneumatic and hydraulic swing-phase control with complex engineering incorporating microprocessor control have made significant advance in self-adjusting speed of walking.

There are single axis knee joints with electronically controlled hydraulic stance and swing phase controls. In the event of a stumble on the prosthesis the resistance to bending of the knee joint is increased, affording time to recover balance and regain posture. There are very stable knee joints offering inherent stability. There is ability to alter the swing phase control, rate of flexion and extension of the knee during gait. The hydraulic stance phase control offers 'yield' of the knee. This means that if a sudden flexion moment is applied to the knee the resistance to bending will increase. In the event of a stumble this affords a period of recovery time to regain posture and balance. There are knee joints that can be locked in one position if required, for instance if standing for a long period of time or all resistance can be eliminated from the knee for activities such as cycling.

15.7.5.2 Ankle and feet

There is a wide range of prosthetic ankle and feet available to match the need of the amputee. There are very lightweight stable feet for the elderly frail patient and energy storing carbon fibre made feet for patients aspiring to sports activities. Springs come in a range of stiffness and the appropriate spring is selected depending on the patient's body weight and the nature of activities. High impact could be absorbed by using pneumatic shock/torque absorbers. The torsion adapter absorbs rotational forces during gait, minimising stress on the residual limb and contributing towards a more natural gait.

15.7.6 Hip disarticulation, hindquarter amputation and prosthesis

In hip disarticulation the femur is detached at the hip joint and all muscles controlling the lower limb are severed. The stable bony pelvis remains and is capable of taking weight-bearing on the ischial tuberosity. In hindquarter amputation the lower extremity including the hip joint and the related hemipelvis is ablated. Success of mobilising with such a full length relatively heavy prosthesis at this level of amputation would depend on the patient's age, fitness and motivation.

Prosthesis: The socket embraces the whole pelvis and goes above the iliac crest over which it is closely moulded. This provides the needed suspension. The prosthetic hip joint is placed anteriorly giving stability on standing. Most patients would be fitted with a stable knee joint and the rest of the components would be decided according to the patient's mobility potential.

15.8 UPPER LIMB AMPUTATION, PROSTHETIC AND NON-PROSTHETIC REHABILITATION

Since the first reported arm replantation in 1962, microsurgery has advanced improving the results of upper limb salvage ranging from digits to entire arm replantation. The anatomic level of injury, age of patient, ischaemia time, general condition etc significantly impacts the outcome of a salvage attempt. In general amputation levels are more conservative in the upper extremity than in the lower extremity. Amongst certain cultures, social stigma is associated with loss of the hand or its parts so that retention of a painful, less functional part may be preferable to amputation for those individuals.

The hand has six types of prehension as well as being used to hold down or push. No prosthetic hand has been developed which can reproduce all these functions. The skin of the hand also changes colour, not only by exposure to sunlight, but also in response to elevation or dependency.

Arm prostheses are of general use for only a small number of patients, have a limited use (mainly cosmetic) for a much larger number, and are totally rejected by others. There has been a considerable reduction in upper limb amputation from trauma. In contrast to lower limb amputation a more detailed assessment of the patient is important prior to recommending prostheses. Factors such as dominance, level of amputation, age, hobbies, occupation, sports, driving, psychological impairment etc should be assessed and considered. There are different types of prostheses aimed at cosmetic and functional restoration. The higher level amputees tend to find the prostheses heavier and cumbersome and if at all tend to prefer lightweight cosmetically oriented prostheses. A transradial level amputee can often be successful in using a functional prosthesis, whether body-powered mechanical or electric powered prosthesis. A transhumeral level amputee, however, often ends up using a passive cosmetic prosthesis in preference to a functional prosthesis.

15.8.1 Digital amputations and prosthesis

Thimble-fitting, silicone made, high definition, colour matched, life-like digits can be fitted with high aesthetic satisfaction. However, they cannot be firmly attached to provide mechanical grip, and do not change colour to maintain the same appearance as normal skin. At times it proves to be a physical encumbrance and an advertisement of the loss after a trial gets rejected.

Amputation of all digits with retention of thumb would benefit from cosmetic hand for dress purpose and fitting of opposition plate for functional restoration.

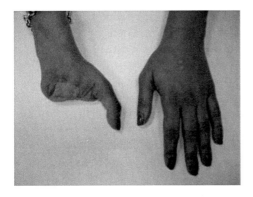

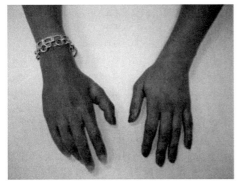

Figure 15.7: High definition life-like cosmetic/passive hand

15.8.2 Wrist disarticulation and prosthesis

Severe trauma to hand with considerable loss of tissue may lead to wrist joint disarticulation. It retains voluntary normal rotational (pronation-supination) movements of the forearm. Split socket could be used to retain this function and fit functional prosthesis.

15.8.3 Transradial (forearm) amputation and prosthesis

In an average adult an ideal residual limb length would be 17 cm from olecranon corresponding roughly to junction of proximal two-thirds and distal one-third of the forearm. Principles of optimal amputation technique should provide a powerful pain-free residual limb for prosthetic function.

Body-powered mechanical prosthesis: This is predominantly a functional working arm that utilises a harness system to open and close a mechanical terminal device, such as a split hook. The harness also serves to suspend the prosthesis and allows the transmission of heavier loads through the shoulder girdle. Because the harness is used to suspend the prosthesis the socket no longer extends over the elbow avoiding pressure over the bony structures. The wrist rotary mechanism allows the interchange of terminal devices such as a mechanical hand or split hook. A range of terminal devices are available to assist with occupational or sporting activities. Adequate power is generated from the triceps and some from shoulder flexion and tension of opposite pectorals to operate the terminal device. Most experienced users can perform delicate tasks and those needing considerable manipulative skill.

Myo-electric prosthesis: Electrodes are situated within the socket. The electrodes are able to pick up the action potential generated when a muscle contracts. The signal is then amplified and used to open and close the electric hand. One electrode is positioned over the extensor muscle in the residual limb and used to open the hand. The second electrode is positioned over the flexor muscle and used to close the hand. In the event that suitable electrode sites are unavailable the hand can be operated using a single electrode or a switch incorporated within an operating cord. A sensor situated within the thumb of the prosthetic hand will detect if an object held within its grasp is slipping and readjust the grip force of the hand accordingly. A Li-ion battery is situated in the forearm. Li-ion batteries take about 3 hours to fully charge. A fully charged battery will provide enough power for one day's use. The prosthesis is covered with a pre-fabricated cosmetic glove, selected to match the sound hand as closely as possible. There is an electric hand available with a quick disconnect wrist. This hand is opened and closed using a switch situated within the harness system. Minimal effort and movement is required to open and close the hand. Its operation is quieter and faster. There is an electric gripper available designed for maximum function.

Cosmetic/passive prosthesis: Commonly prescribed passive hands have bendable or spring loaded fingers that can provide a static grasp for objects. They are valued for their cosmetic appeal, light weight and basic function. A stock colour and size matched glove is pulled over the mannequin-like shell of a passive hand and replaced when worn out. The hands and gloves come in generic male, female, adolescent and child contours. The custom-sculpted glove offers most natural appearance. The glove is hand made from a sculptured reverse copy of the remaining hand. Calibrated photographs are used to match the skin tone. This artistic restoration is made of a specialised silicone elastomer that is more stain resistant than the polyvinyl chloride plastic used in the less expensive gloves.

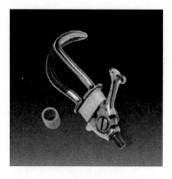

Figure 15.8: Split hook

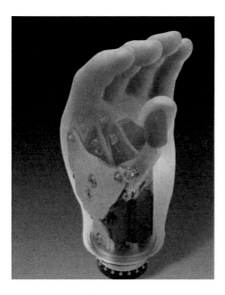

Figure 15.9: Electric hand

15.8.4 Elbow disarticulation and prosthesis

This level of amputation is generally avoided in those patients with prospects of using prostheses. The prosthesis will be bulky and cosmetically unacceptable. The joints have to be set outside the socket resulting in excessive width.

15.8.5 Transhumeral (upper arm) amputation and prosthesis

The ideal level of amputation is 10 cm above the elbow joint to incorporate the elbow mechanism in the prosthesis and to operate a functional prosthesis.

The socket extends up to the axillary fold and to the point of shoulder. The functional prosthesis could either be body-powered mechanical or myo-electrically powered electric hand and mechanical elbow (hybrid) prosthesis. The electrical signals from biceps would open the hand and triceps close the hand.

The elbow mechanism is composed of two parts – a simple uniaxial joint allowing 60 degrees of flexion and extension of 180 degrees at the elbow and an alternating elbow lock.

An alternative would be the elbow and forearm assembly, which contains an internal electronic elbow lock operated by a switch incorporated within the harness system. Minimal movement is required to activate the switch and lock the elbow into any position. Within the forearm is an automatic forearm balance (AFB). As the elbow is extended, the AFB stores energy that is later returned when the elbow is flexed, making bending of the forearm easier.

The section below the elbow would be as in transradial prosthesis.

15.8.6   Shoulder disarticulation and prosthesis

In amputations at shoulder level, it is advisable to leave the humeral head in situ when permitted to produce a better cosmetic appearance and more comfortable prosthesis. A true disarticulation, which empties the glenoid fossa, leaves the acromion and clavicle projecting laterally to present a sharp angle which it is difficult to protect from trauma.

Some patients with this level amputation require only prosthesis with shoulder cap and upper arm piece to provide a partial sleeve filler and others require total replacement. The rest of the prosthetic components would be as supplied for transhumeral amputation although the elbow lock must be operated by the opposite hand as there is no shoulder control. The prosthesis is held by means of straps. At this level the functional activities of the prostheses are very limited. Nevertheless, these prostheses are useful for steadying or holding down objects while writing, cutting etc and the flexed forearm can be used for carrying.

15.8.7   Forequarter amputation and prosthesis

This amputation is quite mutilating and is mostly performed for malignant tumours. The prosthetic need is for a speedy reduction in the deformity with provision of a light shoulder cap made of comfortable light material such as foam plastic held firmly on the sloping shoulder by webbing or plastic straps which encircle the chest wall. A full prosthesis can be made for cosmetic purpose if relevant to the patient.

Non-prosthetic rehabilitation: Adults and children with amputations and limb deficiencies can accomplish many activities without prostheses. Children with bilateral high level upper limb deficiencies are encouraged to capitalise on the tactile and prehensile capabilities of the feet to develop proficiency for daily living activities. Nonprosthetic techniques, home/office/driving adaptations, special equipments and assistive technology such as voice activation enable independent living, enjoy chosen leisure and vocations for those who do not wear prostheses. Amputee support groups such as Limbless Association, Amputee Coalition of America, REACH and STEPS can be resourceful in providing the relevant information.

15.9   THE CHILD AMPUTEE

In children about twice as many amputations are caused by trauma as by disease. The most common cause being power machinery such as lawnmowers. The management of an acquired amputation in a child is approached differently than in an adult as their bones continue to grow, they heal better and face different emotional and psychological issues.

It is usually better to perform a disarticulation than a transdiaphyseal amputation in a growing child to preserve the epiphyseal growth plate and ensure continued longitudinal growth of the remaining bone. This is especially true for the femur as 70% of growth occurs from distal physis.

A child amputee with transdiaphyseal amputation is prone for problems of bone overgrowth in the residual limb, especially at transtibial and transhumeral levels.

15.10 MULTIPLE LIMB AMPUTATIONS/DEFICIENCIES

It is not uncommon to come across multiple limb amputations in poly-trauma. Concurrent injuries and levels of amputations would often dictate the end result of rehabilitation. They may have to resort to alternative mobility aids in addition to using prostheses. The rehabilitation and prosthetic intervention is likely to be more intensive.

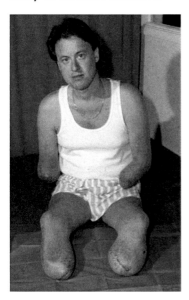

Figure 15.10: Multiple limb amputee

There are a number of people born with complete absence of both upper limbs and experience has proved that if they have good lower limbs *no* prostheses should be fitted since the feet are capable of excellent prehension.

To achieve the favoured outcome, management of multiple high level amputations/deficiencies would warrant input from enthusiastic, dedicated, experienced multi-disciplinary team resourced with a well equipped workshop manned by skilled technicians.

15.11   COMPLICATIONS

Amputation does not guard the residual limb against intercurrent diseases that afflict the normal limb. There are a number of pathological consequences secondary to long term prosthetic use.

15.11.1   Skin

Anaesthetic skin is always a hazard and does not withstand high loading. Split thickness skin grafts unless adherent to underlying tissue are surprisingly successful. Friction, high pressure and constriction are all causes of pathological changes in the skin and can usually be overcome by prosthetic changes. Cysts develop in the skin just above the brims of sockets when the skin laps over the edge and is subjected to friction. The condition can usually be overcome by bevelling or rounding the socket edge or using a flexible interphase liner. The cysts are inclusion dermoid cysts and common sites of occurrence are groin near the adductor tendon in a transfemoral amputee or in the popliteal fossa in a transtibial amputee. They may become infected needing antibiotics or even surgical removal. Similar pressure areas may arise as a result of mal-alignment of prosthesis. For example setting the foot too far from midline in a transtibial amputee would result in excessive ground reaction being directed laterally causing pressure on the fibular head. Proximal circumferential pressure on the residuum may result in discoloration, skin oedema, eczema and ulceration on the distal unsupported tissue. This can be cured by replacing the socket with uniform pressure and adequate tissue support at the distal end.

15.11.2   Muscles

Sometimes the attachment of opposing groups of muscles to residual bone is deficient leading not only to loss of effective power but also to the development of painful bursae. Suturing untailored bulky muscles to the bone end may result in a bulbous shape resulting in difficulty with insertion into the socket. The ideal residual limb should be cylindrical with slight tapering distally.

15.11.3   Nerves

Formation of neuroma is the normal process of healing of a cut nerve end. When pressed by prosthesis it may provoke pain. In the absence of relief with prosthetic adjustment it may warrant surgical removal. It is less of a problem in elective myoplastic surgery where the nerve is divided and allowed to retract into the muscle mass away from weightbearing areas.

15.11.4   Bone

There are no sharp angular surfaces in the palm of the hand or the sole of the foot and retained distal bone in residual limb which will function as a hand or foot should come as close to this natural state as possible. For example, in transtibial amputations, anterior cortical bevelling to remove the distal corner of the tibia is considered essential. All sharp cortical bone edges and irregularities should be contoured and rounded off. In traumatic amputations when the periosteum is at times peeled off the bone, the residual periosteal strips can slowly form irregular bone spurs resulting in painful pressure points.

15.11.5 Joints

In upper limb amputees, long term loss of symmetry tends to produce scoliosis of spine and overuse symptoms on the intact limb such as DeQuervain's tenosynovitis of thumb, carpal tunnel syndrome, tennis elbow and rotator cuff injury of the shoulder joint. It is widely accepted in the field that amputee patients due to longstanding asymmetric loading and altered biomechanics are prone to premature degenerative changes of major joints and spine.

15.12   PAIN MANAGEMENT

Amputation-related pain can become chronic, intense and, for some individuals, limit quality of life and functional capacity. Location, frequency, duration, severity, aggravating and relieving factors are typically assessed. Intensity is usually assessed using a numeric rating scale. It is crucial to distinguish non-painful phantom sensation, phantom pain and residual limb pain as the management differs significantly.

Phantom limb sensation is frequent and can present in varied forms such as touch, pressure, temperature, itch, location in space, movement etc. It often 'telescopes' so that the distal parts progressively move closer to the residual limb over time.

Phantom limb pain refers to painful sensation in the missing portion of the amputated limb. The reported incidence varies from 55% to 85%. It develops within the first few days of amputation, tends to be intermittent or episodic with only a few reporting constant pain. Most patients would describe phantom limb pain to be of moderate intensity. A number of central and peripheral mechanisms have been postulated to explain the phenomenon of phantom limb pain. Phantom limb pain is a form of neuropathic pain which often responds to specific medications (Gabapentin, Pregabalin, Amitryptilline), or therapy modalities (transcutaneous electric stimulation, acupuncture, mirror box therapy, relax liner).

Residual limb pain occurs in the portion of the amputated limb that is still physically present. There is wide variation of incidence depending on the study populations – clinic versus community as well as methodology used. Residual limb pain is typically of moderate intensity, episodic and often an underlying cause such as neuroma or bone spur could be elicited with prospects of successful management. Investigations such as x-ray, ultrasound, vascular and bone isotope imaging may be warranted to make a specific diagnosis. Careful assessment is needed to identify prosthesis-related pain and pain radiating from remote site such as lower back.

Chronic severe pain interfering with rehabilitation outcome may warrant management in a specialised pain clinic. Perception of pain is also known to be related to the psychological state of patient. Pain resistant to conventional pain management in a patient with adjustment reaction or post-traumatic stress disorder often benefits from combined pain and psychotherapy input such as EMDR or cognitive behavioural therapy (CBT).

15.13   PSYCHOLOGICAL MANAGEMENT

Whatever the cause amputation is mutilating and results in loss of function, sensation and body image. The psychological response to amputation is quite variable. It is creditable so many self-assured individuals adapt so well without needing formal assistance. Timid, self-conscious people with excessive concerns of their social standing are more likely to suffer. Some see it as a major assault on their dignity and self-worth. Conversely dependent people may cherish the role of patient and find it welcome relief from pressure and responsibility. Pre-morbid depression is known to increase susceptibility. Personality style, economic, vocational, psycho-social factors all affect emotional recovery. Restoration of body image and sexuality are important part of rehabilitation for some individuals.

Anxiety, depression, adjustment reaction and post-traumatic stress disorder are not uncommon. Treatment modalities such as counselling, psychotherapy, anti-depressant medication, CBT are established methods of treating such disorders with varying outcome.

15.14   RECENT ADVANCES IN AMPUTATION SURGERY

15.14.1   Osseointegration

Osseointegration provides a relatively new and original method for the direct attachment of prostheses to residual skeleton. It has enabled successful fitting of prostheses for certain levels of amputation which has proved difficult with socket prostheses. Two prime examples are short transfemoral amputation and thumb ablation. The trial of Branemark technique in the UK has been completed and a modified technique with prospect of both cutaneous and bone integration is in progress.

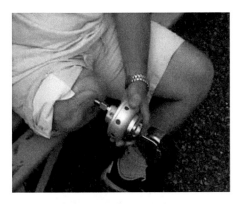

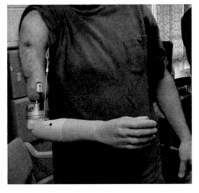

Figure 15.11: Direct skeletal attachment of prosthesis (osseointegration)

15.14.2   Targeted muscle reinnervation (TMR)

The Rehabilitation Institute in Chicago has been researching on a surgical technique to improve the control of myo-electric prosthesis in high level amputees. At transhumeral level several joints need to be controlled and only two sites (biceps and triceps) are available, which are not intuitive control sources for the wrist or hand. TMR takes advantage of intact residual nerves that previously connected to muscles distal to the amputation. These intact residual nerves are transferred to surgically denervated areas of unused muscles in the residual limb or chest. These new target muscle contractions correlate physiologically to the movements of the prosthetic device. The resulting control is more intuitive and thus requires less effort. Initial outcome measures have been very encouraging.

15.15   PROSTHETIC REPLACEMENT/MAINTENANCE

Frequency of replacement of socket and components would be dictated by factors such as activity level of the amputee, adjustments needed to match changes in residual limb/body weight, rehabilitation, recreational activities, ageing and intercurrent illness etc.

On average, socket replacement is likely to be needed once in 2-3 years and replacement of prosthesis once in 5 years. In the case of sleeves/liners two per year per prosthesis would be recommended.

15.16   NHS VERSUS PRIVATE PROSTHETIC CARE

There is variation in the essential resources for amputee care based at the various centres within the NHS setting. Most centres are adequately geared to treat elderly single limb amputees with sufficient confidence and satisfactory outcome. The expertise needed for more demanding situations such as for the management of multi-limb amputees, high level upper limb amputees, amputees warranting sports prostheses or high definition cosmeses, amputees looking for cutting edge technology may not be uniformly available in all the NHS facilities. Multi-disciplinary focus often led by a rehabilitation physician, access to investigations of complications and access to related specialities such as GP, diabetes, dermatology, orthopaedics etc are strengths in the NHS.

A young otherwise fit and healthy traumatic amputee wanting to make rapid progress in prosthetics may at times find the NHS pace and limited access to expensive components rather frustrating. They are looking for more a responsive service and a choice of components to match their needs rather than based on budget.

15.17   RECENT ADVANCES IN PROSTHETICS

15.17.1   Upper limb prosthesis

Research in the field focuses on developing a prosthetic hand that strives to imitate the natural hand. In recent years, for the first time, an electric hand with powered fingers and articulated rotatable powered thumb has been invented. Using the myoelectric principle, six different types of hand functions – key grip, power grip, precision grip, index point and thumb park has been achieved. State-of-the-art hands now have integrated sensors that reduce the need for the user to concentrate on grasping force. Miniaturising electromechanical components have now made it possible to fit levels of amputations at metacarpo-phalangeal level. Fitting programmable controls on electrically powered elbows and wrist rotators have proved beneficial in bilateral transhumeral amputees.

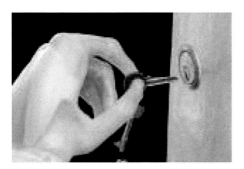

Figure 15.12: Multi-articulated electric hand

15.17.2   Lower limb prosthesis

Quality of socket comfort has been improved by introducing new casting and fabrication techniques. Use of innovative friction reducing interphase cushion liners have enabled high loading of residual limb.

Integration of microchips into 'smart' prosthetic joints has enabled amputees to achieve a near normal fluid gait with energy savings. Sensors and electronic components are better integrated into the prosthetic knee controls and are beginning to be trialled with ankle and hip units.

Otto Bock has introduced Genium, a highly advanced microprocessor controlled knee joint enabling a transfemoral amputee to walk smoothly with increased stability, climb up stairs step over step, cross obstacles more smoothly, walk backwards, stand more easily, and sit naturally. It is splash proof and offers an increased battery life lasting 5 days. A waterproof version called X-3 is in the process of being introduced to the UK market.

The OSSUR Power knee is the first knee joint in the market offering active knee extension. This assists the above knee amputee to climb stairs and inclines.

Enormous advances have been made in manufacturing a family of carbon fibre made feet and springs capable of storing and releasing energy for high impact sports and competitive running.

Figure 15.13: Hydraulic ankle and carbon fibre foot

15.18   REFERENCES

DG Smith, JW Michael and JH Bowker (eds) *Atlas of Amputations and Limb Deficiencies. Surgical, Prosthetic and Rehabilitation Principles* (American Academy of Orthopaedic Surgeons, 3rd edn, 2004)

International Society of Prosthetics & Orthotics – www.ispoweb.org

American Orthotics & Prosthetic Association – www.aopanet.org

Limbless Association – www.limbless-association.org/home

Amputee Coalition of America – www.amputee-coalition.org

CHAPTER 16

QUANTUM: SCHEDULES, PSLA, SPECIAL DAMAGES, HEADS OF LOSS AND PROVISIONAL DAMAGES

16.1 QUANTUM: SCHEDULES OF LOSS

The schedule of loss is of crucial importance in a claim involving catastrophic injuries. It is therefore important to ensure that the schedule contains the detail, and reflects the substance, of a claim in a way that all the parties and the court can understand.

16.1.1 The rules

Schedules and counter-schedules exist because the Practice Direction to Part 16 requires them in personal injury actions.

Particulars of Claim: paragraph 4

'4.2   The claimant must attach to his particulars of claim a schedule of details of any past and future expenses and losses which he claims.'

Defence: paragraph 12

'12.2   Where the claim is for personal injuries and the claimant has included a schedule of past and future expenses and losses, the defendant should include in or attach to his defence a counter-schedule stating:
(1)   which of those items he –
    (a)   agrees,
    (b)   disputes, or
    (c)   neither agrees nor disputes but has no knowledge of, and
(2)   where any items are disputed, supplying alternative figures where appropriate.'

Further, the Practice Direction to CPR Part 22 expressly provides that statements of truth are required in any schedule or counter-schedule.

Neither practice direction makes reference to 'preliminary schedules', but in reality in catastrophic injury cases the courts accept that the schedule served with the particulars of claim will be no more than 'work in progress'. A preliminary schedule should, however, provide an indication of the heads of claim and the extent of the claims made on the information available. However well advanced a schedule is at the issue of proceedings it will not be possible to finalise it until the trial date is known, for that will be dividing point between past and future losses, as well as the date of assessment for interest.

16.1.2   Style and form of schedules

The style of the schedule will be a matter for each individual drafter. Given the complexity of the claims that will be made, however, we would recommend that a clear structure is adopted and maintained through the various updatings that will be necessary. A precedent schedule is set out in the Annex to this chapter. A suitable structure is as follows:

(a)   an introduction to the claim comprising key facts such date of accident, claimant's date of birth, date of schedule, date of trial, claimant's age at accident/schedule/trial, position on liability and medico-legal evidence obtained;

(b)   a list of multipliers appropriate to the claim, with an explanation as to how they have been arrived at;

(c)   a summary of the pain, suffering and loss of amenity that the claimant has suffered, including a diagnosis and prognosis for the injuries;

(d)   a section dealing with all past losses/expenses, with a narrative recital of each individual head of loss and a calculation of the loss;

(e)   a section dealing with all future losses/expenses, with a narrative recital of each individual head of loss and a calculation of the loss (whether on a lump sum or PPO basis) (examples of both approaches are set out in the Annex);

(f)   a summary of all claims made at the beginning or end of the Schedule.

The following is a checklist of the types of claims commonly included in a catastrophic injury schedule:

- general damages for PSLA;
- loss of earnings;
- loss of pension;
- care;
- accommodation costs (including increased household expenditure);
- aids and equipment costs (including transportation);
- prosthetic/orthotic costs;
- DIY/gardening;
- travelling expenses;
- medical expenses/treatment;
- occupational therapy/physiotherapy/speech and language therapy fees;
- chiropody fees;
- case management fees;
- deputy/Court of Protection/professional trustee fees;
- increased holiday costs;

- disability subscriptions;
- miscellaneous expenses (including insurance excess, damaged clothing, telephone calls etc);
- interest;
- lost years.

Examples of these claims are provided in the precedent schedule in the Annex. Within this chapter we will discuss the critical items of loss that the practitioner must be familiar with.

A properly constructed schedule requires the collection of a great deal of detail. This causes real problems in cases of severely disabled claimants and may require a lot of work by an already hard-pressed relative acting as litigation friend. In serious cases, it is unlikely that a proper schedule can be prepared without at least one home visit, and sometimes several home visits may be required.

16.1.3 Gathering information

It is unrealistic to expect claimants and their relatives to recall all relevant matters at one sitting, even with the benefit of a questionnaire checklist. They should be encouraged to keep diaries and logs of expenditure and events as they occur. The invoices and receipts used to support a well-prepared schedule will be needed for disclosure in the list of documents. We consider in Chapter 6 some practical ways of dealing with gathering the necessary documentary evidence.

Some care needs to be exercised in deciding what to include. It is important to stand back from time to time and ask 'Does the picture given in this schedule tally with the injuries?'. Equally it is important not to ignore the minor items. This is not simply a question of maximising the claim, the smaller items can often give the real picture of the impact on the claimant's life, for example the incontinence pads, the heel replacements, the can openers and sock pullers.

Although the authors of care and occupational therapy reports will have a very important role to play in assessing a claimant's needs, it is unfair to them and to the claimant to expect the care report to be a complete substitute for, as opposed to a key aspect of, proper enquiry and investigation into the claimant's past and projected expenses.

Where the claimant's employment records are inadequate, then assistance can be obtained from tax and social security records, and from employers. If the employers cannot be identified, then assistance can be obtained from national insurance records. If employers, education bodies or other third parties prove difficult in providing information, then remember that the court has extensive powers to order third party disclosure under CPR, r 31.17. They are available to be used by claimant or defendant.

Thus possible sources of information include:

- pre-action protocol correspondence;
- GP and hospital notes;
- medical reports;
- care/occupational therapy reports;
- personnel files;
- national insurance records;
- Land Registry records;
- bank accounts;
- credit card statements;
- mortgage applications;
- employment applications and CVs;
- witness statements.

Help can be obtained from the CPR.

Part 18: requests for further information

'18.1

(1)   The court may at any time order a party to –
(a)   clarify any matter which is in dispute in the proceedings; or
(b)   give additional information in relation to any such matter,

whether or not the matter is contained or referred to in a statement of case.'

Part 31: disclosure

'31.8

(1)   A party's duty to disclose documents is limited to documents which are or have been in his control.

(2)   For this purpose a party has or has had a document in his control if –
(a)   it is or was in his physical possession;
(b)   he has or has had a right to possession of it; or
(c)   he has or has had a right to inspect or take copies of it.'

Part 31.17; Third Party disclosure

'31.17

(1)   This rule applies where an application is made to the court under any Act for disclosure by a person who is not a party to the proceedings.

(2)   The application must be supported by evidence.

(3)   The court may make an order under this rule only where –

(a)   the documents of which disclosure is sought are likely to support the case of the applicant or adversely affect the case of one of the other parties to the proceedings; and

(b)   disclosure is necessary in order to dispose fairly of the claim or to save costs.

(4)   An order under this rule must –

(a)   specify the documents or the classes of documents which the respondent must disclose; and

(b)   require the respondent, when making disclosure, to specify any of those documents –
  (i)   which are no longer in his control; or
  (ii) in respect of which he claims a right or duty to withhold inspection.

(5)   Such an order may –

(a)   require the respondent to indicate what has happened to any documents which are no longer in his control; and

(b)   specify the time and place for disclosure and inspection.'

16.1.4   Getting started

The thought of preparing a schedule can be frightening. It needn't be. Take a piece of paper and write down the heads you need to cover. Follow a structure such as that recommended above. By each head, write where the information is to be found and summarise it. Very quickly, you will find that this brief skeleton is fleshing itself out. When preparing a schedule remember:

(a)   tell the story;

(b)   make it user-friendly to the judge – the ultimate consumer; and

(c)   be realistic if you want your case to be credible.

You want your schedule to be the judge's preferred source for reliable data. There should be an easily accessible financial summary showing what it all amounts to, in such a way that the differences between the parties can also be identified speedily.

Appendices can be useful for setting out information that is bulky and/or tedious and which it is not necessary to read to follow the claim. Appendices are counter-productive if you have to go to them to follow the claim; it simply disrupts the consideration of the claim.

16.2   SCHEDULES OF LOSS: GENERAL DAMAGES FOR PAIN, SUFFERING AND LOSS OF AMENITY

The court will look towards the Judicial College Guidelines as the starting point for assessing general damages and we would encourage practitioners to identify the categories that are likely to be relevant in their schedule.

Although a comparison of similar case-law will form part of the assessment process in many cases, it is not usual practice to include reference to this in the schedule. Equally, unless the practitioner is completely confident in the level of award that he or she will be contending for, we would not recommend pleading a specific figure for general damages in the schedule as it may tactically rebound in the event that a higher award is sought at trial or settlement meeting.

There are now a large number of sources of case-law, including Kemp & Kemp, Current Law, Lawtel, Butterworths Personal Injury Services, Journal of Personal Injury Litigation, AvMA Journal, Westlaw, Butterworths PI online and the Law Reports.

Care should be taken with older cases that may not reflect the updated JC Guidelines and/or the current attitude of the courts. Equally, practitioners are reminded that many cases are reported with an ulterior motive (often because the award is particularly high or low). It is therefore no surprise that many judges assessing catastrophic injuries are now largely reliant upon the JC Guidelines as a reference tool for general damages.

Practitioners are reminded that, as a consequence of legislative changes introducing the Jackson reforms, there will be a 10% increase in the level of general damages for all judgments post-dating 1 April 2013 unless the claimant had entered into a Conditional Fee Agreement before that date.[1] It remains to be seen how the courts will approach general damages in cases where a CFA for litigation services pre-dates 1 April 2013 but the CFA for advocacy services post-dates it. This will no doubt form the basis of a test case in due course.

16.3 SCHEDULES OF LOSS: FINANCIAL LOSSES AND EXPENSES

16.3.1 Past loss of earnings/income

16.3.1.1 The starting point

A catastrophically injured claimant will ordinarily be deprived of the whole of his or her capacity for gainful earnings. Occasionally, therapeutic employment may have been achieved by the date of trial but any such source is likely to be modest. A set-off will be required from the net income that would have been received in the absence of the accident.

The assessment of the claim for past loss of earnings begins with the actual income which was being received at the time of the accident net of tax, national insurance and any pension contributions (usually assessed by reference to 13 weeks earning details/wage slips). If the income varied, or the work was of an intermittent or casual nature, the proper practice is to take an average over a longer period of time leading up to the accident, preferably using the claimant's P60s.

---

[1]   See *Simmons v Castle* [2012] EWCA Civ 1288 and [2013] 1 All ER 334.

For those cases where net earnings are not readily available from wage documentation (ie self-employed claimants), Table G1 in *Facts and Figures: Tables for the Calculation of Damages*[2] can be used.

Where the claimant would have received annual increases/increments in earnings between the date of the accident and the date of the trial, these increases should be accounted for (in contrast to the position with future inflation). Confirmation from the employer should be sought if possible. If not, consideration should be given to using the Average Earnings Index figures available from the Office of National Statistics.

16.3.1.2   Fringe benefits

In addition to loss of salary, practitioners should take care to ensure that any lost benefits available to the claimant in his or her employment are added to the claim. These benefits may include:

(a)   the loss of a company car;[3]

(b)   free fuel, insurance, servicing etc;

(c)   car parking;

(d)   free or reduced-cost public transport;

(e)   free board and lodging;

(f)   free or reduced cost air travel or holidays in the event of a claimant within the airline/travel industry;

(g)   cheap loans;

(h)   private medical insurance;

(i)   education allowances for children;

(j)   holiday pay;

(k)   bonuses, including performance-related, Christmas and long-service bonuses;

(l)   London living allowance[4]

(m)   subsidised meals;

(n)   share options or incentive schemes;

(o)   membership of sports clubs;

(p)   tips;

(q)   discounted goods (eg supermarket/shop workers).

16.3.1.3   Potential increases

In theory, past losses of earnings should be capable of precise calculation. However, the practitioner should always be alive to the following possibilities:

---

[2]   Sweet & Maxwell, 2013/14 edition
[3]   See *Facts and Figures*, Section L.
[4]   See *Crofts v Murton* LTL 10/09/2008.

(a)   in the absence of the accident, the claimant may have moved to a more lucrative job or received a position of promotion. If this was part of a normal career progression that does not lead to a significantly increased level of remuneration/salary, the full extent of this increase should be claimed and recovered on the basis that it represents a reasonable career model.[5] If the new position would have led to a significant increase in remuneration/salary, it is likely that the claim will need to be pursued on the basis of a loss of chance.[6] It is important for practitioners to remember that claims based on a loss of a chance are not only restricted to future losses;

(b)   substantial overtime, not available in the period prior to the accident, may have become available after the accident during the period of absence;

(c)   a self-employed claimant may have been on the verge of undertaking profitable new work or signing a lucrative contract.

In these circumstances, cogent evidence will be required from the claimant and from the third party/employer. In the case of increased overtime, the practitioner should ideally seek evidence in support by way of a comparator wage earner.

16.3.1.4   Potential discounts

There may be factors which reduce the claim for past loss of earnings.

Where the claimant had an inconsistent work history prior to the accident, a discount from past loss of earnings is likely to be made to reflect this fact. In *Clenshaw v Tanner*[7] the Court of Appeal endorsed a decision of Silber J to discount a claim for past loss of earnings by 30% to account for a pre-accident history of psychiatric problems impacting upon his ability to work.

Alternatively, if substantial redundancies/job losses have since occurred in the company which employed the claimant, there will be doubt about the continued receipt of earnings had the accident not taken place.

The key in both of these situations will be evidence. In the case of inconsistent work history, evidence from friends, family or employer should be obtained highlighting a change in direction and a new reliability for work. In the case of redundancies/job losses, inquiries will need to be made with the employer as to the claimant's personal risk of redundancy in the absence of the accident. In addition, practitioners should obtain evidence of finding alternative employment, with possible input from an expert employment consultant.

---

[5]   See *Herring v MOD* [2003] EWCA Civ 528.
[6]   See below under future loss of earnings/income for further guidance.
[7]   [2002] EWHC 184.

16.3.1.5 The unemployed or student claimant

In the event that the claimant was unemployed at the time of the accident, it will be necessary for the practitioner to obtain detailed instructions on the length of unemployment, qualifications/training/employment history pre-dating this period, the claimant's motivation to find work, any job applications made and the types of employment that he or she would have been interested in but for the accident. It may also be necessary to instruct an employment consultant to objectively assess the options that would have realistically been open to the claimant and the prospects of achieving such a position.

As with claims for career progression, it is possible to make a claim for the loss of a chance of obtaining paid employment provided that chance was 'real' or 'substantial' as opposed to 'speculative'.[8]

If the claimant was a student at the time of the accident, details of the education history will be required. This should include qualifications, school/college/university reports, witness statements from teachers/tutors. The family background of the student will also be important and supportive evidence about the career paths of siblings and other relatives should be obtained where possible.

16.3.1.6 Difficult cases

Problems of quantification for past loss of earnings may well arise where the injured claimant is a self-employed sole trader, in partnership or a shareholder-director of a limited company. Section F1 of *Facts & Figures* contains a very helpful summary of what is required to assess a claim for loss of earnings in such circumstances.

The self-employed sole trader/partner must be able to produce proper trading accounts in order to demonstrate his or her earnings before the accident. Ideally, these should be compared with the records held by HM Revenue and Customs. With the right evidence in support, it may be possible to argue that the claimant's business would have expanded in the absence of the accident, leading to greater profitability and earnings.[9] Evidence of new contracts or business opportunities should be sought.

Where a partner is injured and, as a result, the profits of the partnership are reduced, the injured claimant can only recover his or her share of the profits.[10] However, the court may be able to look beyond the presumption of equal shares in the event that the additional partner (often a spouse) contributed very little to the business and was used merely as a way of reducing tax liability.[11]

---

[8]   See below under future loss of earnings/income for further guidance.

[9]   See *Finnis v Caulfield* [2002] All ER (D) 353.

[10] As per s 24 of the Partnership Act 1890.

[11] *Ward v Newalls Insulation* [1998] 1 WLR 1722 and discussed further in *Neal v Jones* [2002] EWCA Civ 1731.

In the case of the claimant being both a director and shareholder of a limited company, with the injuries resulting in a cessation of employment thereby leading to a diminution/extinguishing of company profits, there are various ways in which he or she may recover damages:

(a)   if the lost profits would have been distributed by way of dividend, he or she can recover the net loss of such dividends;

(b)   if by way of salary or director's fees, net lost salary or fees;

(c)   if the claimant would have left profits within the company and made a capital gain by selling the shares, the damages should be the net loss of capital gain.

The growth of service companies for tax purposes means that practitioners need to keep a close eye on the potential losses in these cases. The input of a forensic accountant may be required.

16.3.1.7   *Deductions*

Obviously, any sums received by the claimant from his or her employer between the date of the accident and trial must be offset against the claim, in addition to any recoverable CRU benefits.

If there is a contractual obligation for the claimant to repay sick pay, a subrogated claim must be included on behalf of the employer for the value of this sick pay. Failure to do so may land the claimant with a very unwelcome bill at the end of the case.

16.3.2   Future loss of earnings/income

An analysis of the 7th edition Ogden Tables has been provided in Chapter 18 on multiplicands and multipliers. Unless there is evidence to the contrary, the court will assume that the claimant will continue to suffer the same net loss as at the date of trial. It is therefore vital that the potential for further advancement is fully investigated, with evidence obtained in support from the claimant and employer.

Equally, practitioners need to take careful instructions on the claimant's likely retirement date but for the accident. For many, this will be consistent with state pension age, which is steadily rising. The online government state pension age calculator is a very useful tool.[12] Practitioners are reminded that retirement beyond state pension age is now an unavoidable reality for some workers, particularly those who have suffered losses in occupational pensions.

As discussed earlier in this chapter, a claim can be made on the loss of chance of a future career, job opportunity or advancement. All that is required is a 'not

---

[12]   See www.gov.uk/calculate-state-pension.

insubstantial' chance of achieving such a position.[13] Once a chance is established by evidence, it is a matter for the court to assess the value of the chance.

Specific examples of how this works in practice within the context of a loss of earnings claim are provided by the cases of *Doyle v Wallace*,[14] *Langford v Hebran*,[15] *Herring v Ministry of Defence*,[16] *Appleton v El Safty*,[17] *Smith and another v Collett*,[18] *Clarke v Maltby*,[19] *XYZ v Portsmouth Hospitals NHS Trust*[20] and *Mann v Bahri*.[21]

In *Langford v Hebran*,[22] the Court of Appeal approved an increase in the claim for future loss of earnings based upon a chance of advancement assessed at 14%.

The loss of a chance approach should only be adopted when the career of the claimant would have taken a particular course leading to 'significantly higher' earnings. However, where the evidence shows that the claimant's career would have followed one of a number of models, all of which would have led to similar earnings, it is not appropriate to use the loss of chance method. In these circumstances the court will assume that the claimant had a 100% chance of achieving his or her pleaded earnings.[23]

In the event that a stepped multiplicand is appropriate for loss of earnings and a PPO is sought for such a claim, the schedule should identify the increase in earnings and the stage at which this will occur, along with the indexation that will be applied.

As a general rule, given the uncertainties involved, the court is likely to adopt an averaged multiplicand approach (as opposed to a stepped multiplicand) in the case of a claimant who has not yet entered the employment market at the time of the accident.[24]

The average earnings statistics set out at Section F7 of *Facts & Figures* provides a useful starting point when choosing the multiplicand for loss of earnings for

---

[13]   *Allied Maples v Simmons & Simmons* [1995] 1 WLR 1602.
[14]   [1998] PIQR Q146.
[15]   [2001] EWCA Civ 361.
[16]   [2003] EWCA Civ 528.
[17]   [2007] EWHC 631 (QB).
[18]   [2009] EWCA Civ 583.
[19]   [2010] EWHC 1201 (QB).
[20]   [2011] EWHC 243 (QB).
[21]   Lawtel 11/4/2012.
[22]   [2001] EWCA Civ 361.
[23]   *Herring v MOD* [2004] 1 All ER 44.
[24]   See *Sarwar v Ali and another* [2007] EWHC 1255 (QB), *AH v Powys HB* [2007] EWHC 2996, *Leesmith v Evans* [2008] EWHC 134 (QB), *Whiten v St George's Healthcare NHS Trust* [2011] EWHC 2066 (QB) and *Loughlin v Singh* [2013] EWHC 1641 (QB).

claimants who: (a) had yet to start employment; (b) were in the very early stages of their career; or (c) seeking to change career when the accident took place.

16.3.3 PPOs and loss of earnings

Historically, there seems to have been a general tendency to seek claims for future loss of earnings by way of lump sum as opposed to PPO. However, this is now changing. In *Sarwar v (1) Ali and (2) MIB*[25] Lloyd Jones J made an order that a PPO should be made for future loss of earnings indexed according to an earnings based index (ASHE) rather than RPI. The Court considered six options for indexing the loss of earnings in *Sarwar*, including the Average Earnings Index (AEI), the aggregated Annual Survey of Hours and Earnings (ASHE) for all male full-time employees, the aggregated ASHE for male full-time employees at the appropriate percentile of earnings corresponding with the multiplicand found by the Court, the disaggregated ASHE SOC1 (standard occupational classification) and disaggregated ASHE SOC2.On the facts of *Sarwar*, with the claimant yet to enter the labour market at the time of the accident, the Court found that aggregated ASHE at the appropriate percentile of earnings was most suitable. It was further noted that if the Court had felt able to determine the claimant's predicted occupation with greater certainty, an ASHE SOC index would have been more suitable.

More recently, in *Whiten (A Protected Party) v St Georges Healthcare NHS Trust*[26] a PPO for loss of earnings was made that was indexed to the ASHE earnings data for gross annual pay for all male full-time employees in the UK. Again, this generalised index reflected the fact that the claimant was a young child who had not yet entered the employment market. In a case involving a PPO for an *established employee*, a more specific ASHE measure relating to that position of employment can be applied and will have greater accuracy.

When making a PPO for loss of earnings, the parties and the court need to factor in the discount for contingencies that is ordinarily applied to the *multiplier*. In *Whiten v St Georges Healthcare* a 5% discount was applied to the multiplicand, albeit this was very much based on the particular facts of that case. In most cases it is likely that the methodology in Ogden 7 Tables A-D will be applied albeit that the discount will be applied to the multiplicand.

Of course, a PPO will not be suitable or acceptable to a lot of claimants. The claim for future loss of earnings on a lump sum basis will often provide the financial flexibility to purchase property or provide security of money in the bank. However, it is wrong to dismiss the option of a PPO in a claim for future loss of earnings without investigating this further and practitioners may be missing a very useful negotiating tool if they do so.

---

[25] [2007] EWHC 1255 (QB).
[26] [2011] EWHC 2066 (QB).

16.3.4 Loss of pension

The claimant may have been a member of a pension scheme at the time of his or her accident. This may have been:

(a) a final salary scheme (also known as a deferred benefit scheme) where benefits are defined in advance, usually by reference to final salary, number of years' service and a factor (often 1/60th or 1/80th for each year of service);

(b) money purchase scheme (also known as personal pensions and/or defined contribution pensions and/or occupational pensions) where the benefits depend on a combination of the amounts paid in by the member, his or her employer (if applicable), the investment returns achieved up to retirement and the annuity rates available on retirement.

The introduction of the Pensions Act into law in October 2012 means that employers (unless exempted) are legally obligated to make pension contributions into a qualifying occupational pension scheme (known as NEST pensions – National Employment Savings Trust) on behalf of employees over 22 years of age, earnings with qualifying earnings of between £5,668 and £41,150 per annum (2013/14 tax year – subject to annual review). Large employers (120,000+ employees) are first in line, and are required to start making contributions from 1 October 2012. However, employers with less than 50 employees, which will cover directly employed care teams, are on a phased implementation timetable, starting on 1 August 2014 and ending on 1 February 2016, depending on the last two letters of the employers PAYE scheme.

Qualifying earnings include a worker's salary, wages, overtime, bonuses and commission, as well as statutory sick pay, maternity, paternity or adoption pay. Minimum contributions are being gradually phased in over the next 5 years to help employers comply with their new duties. The combined minimum contribution rate until September 2017 is 2%, of which the employer must contribute at least 1%. From October 2017 to September 2018 this minimum contribution rate rises to 5%, of which the employer must contribute at least 3%. From October 2018 onwards the minimum contribution rate will rise to 8% of qualifying earnings, of which the employer must contribute at least 3%. Further details are available at www.nestpensions.org.uk. The important point for practitioners to consider is that pension loss calculations will now be the norm in most catastrophic injury claims.

16.3.4.1 *Final salary*

Claimants who were members of final salary schemes when injured will have a potential claim for damages for loss of future pension benefits, calculated on a conventional multiplicand/multiplier basis (as set out in Chapter 17) This pecuniary loss, which can be calculated with a reasonable level of certainty, may arise due to:

(a)   a reduction in the qualifying years of service, resulting in reduced annual pension;

(b)   a lower pensionable salary that would otherwise have been the case but for the injury or illness (particularly the case where the claimant would have been promoted, giving rise to a higher pensionable salary).

Details of the scheme must be obtained along with pension statements/predictions from the pension provider identifying the value of the pension: (a) but for the accident had the claimant remained in employment until normal retirement age; and (b) as a result of early retirement. Calculations of pension loss must be made net of tax. The tables at H1 and H2 of *Facts and Figures* can be used to find net equivalents to a range of gross annual pension figures.

If the claimant would have commuted part of his or her pension upon retirement in order to receive a tax-free lump sum and the value of this lump sum is reduced due to the accident, the difference in the respective lump sums should be ascertained and discounted for accelerated receipt. If the claimant receives a lump sum early under an ill-health pension, then the claim will be for the lump sum that would have been received upon normal retirement (subject to accelerated receipt and a discount for contingencies) minus a Longden credit (see below).

16.3.4.2   Discount for contingencies

The most important questions in catastrophic injury final salary pension loss claims will be: (a) life expectancy; and (b) the level of any discount made for contingencies. The discount for contingencies will be dependent upon a number of factors including the working record and pre-accident health of the claimant, the security of pre-accident employment and the chances of promotion. In practice, these discounts tend to hover around the 10–20% mark.[27] Occasionally a higher or lower discount will be appropriate.[28]

16.3.4.3   Early receipt of pension and lump sums

The claimant does not have to give credit for any payments made under an early/ill-health pension to the date of normal pension age.[29] However, credit should be given for part of a tax-free lump sum received early, as part of this lump sum represents a commutation in respect of the pension that would have been paid after normal retirement age. This is commonly known as the Longden credit. An example of this calculation is given in the precedent schedule in the Annex.

---

[27]   See *Wells v Wells* [1999] 1 AC 345; *Pratt v Smith* [2002] All ER (D) 322 (Dec); and *Anderson v Davis* [1993] PIQR Q87.

[28]   For an example of a higher discount, see *Smith v East and North Herts NHS Trust* [2008] EWHC 2234.

[29]   *Parry v Cleaver* [1970] AC 1, applied by the House of Lords in *Longden v British Coal Corporation* [1998] AC 653.

16.3.4.4 Money purchase

Future pension benefits under money purchase schemes are determined by the performance of the fund into which contributions are invested and the annuity rate that can be achieved to convert the fund into an annual pension at retirement age. These considerations inevitably mean that future pension benefits cannot be predicted with any level of certainty.

The basis of the claim will be that, had the claimant continued working, further contributions would have been made into the scheme and this would have produced a higher level of pension. Section H3 in *Facts and Figures* gives a breakdown of how this calculation can be carried out in practice and this is the approach often adopted in expert pension loss reports. However, the authors of this publication would point out that calculations of this type are problematic as they inevitably require assumptions about the level of investment return in the fund and the level of annuity achievable. Accordingly, the claim is usually calculated by adding the lost employer's contributions plus tax relief on any lost employee contribution onto the claim for loss of earnings, using the same Ogden 7 principles. There may also be a claim for the loss of additional growth that would have been achieved in the fund up to the date of trial had full contributions been made. This can be ascertained via the claimant's annual pension statements.

16.3.4.5 Complex pension loss claims

With complex pension schemes, expert accountancy evidence will be required.

As with claims for loss of earnings, practitioners should be alive to the prospect of a claim for loss of pension being based upon a loss of chance. In *Brown v MOD*[30] the court considered how to approach the valuation of loss of a military pension in a claimant who was injured during training 8 weeks into her basic service. The judge found that the claimant had a 50% chance of serving for 12 years and a 60% chance of serving for a further 10 years. Accordingly, the chance of obtaining an immediate pension after 22 years was assessed at 30% (50% of 60%). A similar approach had to be taken to possible levels of promotion to ascertain the true value of the pension upon retirement. The case *McKeown v Munday* provides another example of the loss of chance approach in practice.[31] As with loss of earnings, the loss of a chance approach should only be adopted in a claim for loss of pension when the career of the claimant would have taken a particular course leading to a significantly higher pension. If the career model is chosen because it is deemed an appropriate baseline and/or is one of a number of alternatives likely to give more of less similar results, then it is neither necessary or appropriate to adopt a percentage chance approach and any increase in pension entitlement should be recoverable in full as part of that reasonable career model.[32]

---

[30] [2006] EWCA Civ 546.
[31] [2002] EWHC 725.
[32] See *Herring v MOD* [2003] EWCA Civ 528.

16.3.5   Past medical expenses

A claimant can properly recover all medical expenses to the date of trial which have been reasonably incurred in the treatment and management of his or her injuries. These expenses may include the professional fees of medical and/or surgical practitioners, the charges of hospitals and nursing homes, and the cost of medical appliances, drugs and other prescriptions. It may also be possible to include the cost of a holiday, if taken on sound medical advice.

There may be a dispute as to whether the medical fees are reasonable or the treatment was appropriate. The resolution of the dispute will depend on the medical evidence called by each side, but experience tends to show that the court will allow the cost of treatment if the claimant proves that it was undertaken after express medical advice. The treating doctor may be prepared to support a particular line of therapy or surgery. Where the reasonableness of fees is challenged, a comparison with the approved BMA or Spire rates may assist.

Practitioners are reminded of the duty placed upon a claimant to mitigate loss. Accordingly, it is important to ensure that any medical expense or treatment is competitively priced.

In suitable cases, the costs of attending organisations such as Headway or the Spinal Injuries Association should be investigated (including the associated travelling costs).

It does not matter whether the claimed medical or hospital expenses could have been avoided had facilities provided by the NHS scheme been used.[33] A claimant is not bound to make use of the medical and hospital facilities of the NHS, and if he or she receives treatment as a private patient at his or her own cost, that expense is recoverable. Of course the impecunious party will usually only be able to take advantage of fee paying treatment with either the benefit of an interim payment, a loan, or an express undertaking by the insurer to pay the cost of treatment.

A particular area of practical difficulty for the catastrophically brain-injured claimant, and indirectly for the practitioner, is the limited availability of inpatient places at specialist long-stay head injury rehabilitation centres. The NHS may be unable to meet the demand in a particular case, yet the medical evidence obtained in the course of the litigation demonstrates that the plaintiff will greatly benefit from such treatment. Head injury rehabilitation is both skilful and resource intensive, and therefore expensive. A place at a privately run institution may be found for the claimant but at a very large cost. What is the practitioner to do in order to resolve the dilemma? The claimant will not have the funds to pay for the treatment. Some institutions will agree to defer their fees until the conclusion of the litigation, but this is obviously not satisfactory, save as a last resort. Deferment is likely to carry an interest penalty

---

[33]   Section 2(4) of the Law Reform (Personal Injuries) Act 1948.

which will not be recoverable, being caused by the claimant's impecuniosity. The better solution is to persuade the defendant's insurers to discharge the fees directly or to obtain the necessary funds by an interim payment of damages. The head injury treatment may bring significant improvements in the claimant's level of dependence and thereby ultimately reduce the total value of the claim as well as improving the claimant's well-being.

An increasing number of claimants have the benefit of private medical insurance. Where medical and hospital expenses resulting from the injury are discharged directly by the medical insurer and where there is a right of contractual recovery against the insured claimant, the practitioner must take care to include a claim for those expenses against the tortfeasor. The contract of medical insurance should be obtained and scrutinised. If a settlement with the defendant tortfeasor is proposed at a percentage of the claim, the medical expenses recovery should be resolved with the claimant's medical insurer at the same percentage.

The reasonable cost of the claimant's transport to and from the hospital or other institution at which the medical treatment is given will be recoverable. In addition, the travelling expenses of family members or close friends will be allowed, provided that they can be said to have facilitated the recovery of the injured claimant.[34] Travelling expenses, both direct and indirect, are customarily claimed as a head of damage which is separate from medical and allied expenses.

16.3.6   Future medical expenses

The claimant must prove:

(a)   the expected and reasonable cost of the medical and hospital services; and

(b)   that he or she is likely to make use of private, non-NHS medical treatment in the future.

The medico-legal experts will need to supply evidence of the claimant's probable continuing medical requirements and the likely cost of providing the necessary services in the private sector. An allowance will be made for regular outpatient attendance, investigations and tests, and inpatient treatment. Urinary tract infections are common in the wheelchair-bound so that regular investigation by means of intravenous pyelography or cystography may be essential; and in spinal injury cases there is often a small but definite risk of syringomyelia so that repeat investigation by magnetic resonance imaging is normally recommended in order to discover whether cavities in the spinal cord are forming or not. In catastrophic brain damage cases the risk of epilepsy, scoliosis and/or contractures of the limbs must be investigated.

The cost of treatments such as psychotherapy/CBT, physiotherapy, occupational therapy and chiropody will need to be accounted for in most catastrophic cases.

---

[34]   See *Bordin v St Mary's NHS Trust* [2000] Lloyd's Rep Med 287.

In brain injury cases, the costs of speech/language therapy, ophthalmic treatment, dentistry and orthotic/podiatry treatment should also be investigated. In spinal injury cases, dentistry, orthotic/podiatry and the costs of installing and maintaining a private hydrotherapy pool should also be considered.[35]

From the sourced medico-legal information, an annual composite multiplicand can be calculated. For example, the cost of an investigation which is required every 3 years at a cost of £1,500 may be apportioned into an annual sum of £500 and then multiplied by the multiplier for life. Alternatively, Tables A5 in *Facts & Figures* can be used.

In catastrophic injury cases, it is relatively common for the claimant's needs to change over time. In these circumstances, care should be taken to ensure that split multiplicands and multipliers are used.

The probable use of private medical treatment in the future will be determined by the pattern of pre-trial use, the expressed intentions of the claimant in his or her evidence with reasons for any private treatment preference, and the expert evidence concerning the non-availability of NHS care. The claimant will not recover future expenses which the court finds he or she will never in fact incur.[36]

16.3.7   Care, attendance and supervision

Claims for care in catastrophic injury claims will almost inevitably be subject to expert care/nursing evidence that will quantify the past and future level of care required. There are a number of different types of care available in any given case:

(a)   gratuitous care provided by family member or friend;

(b)   commercial carer(s) employed directly by the claimant;

(c)   commercial agency care;

(d)   residential care;

(e)   buddy/support worker care;

(f)   public statutory provision.

Ultimately, a claimant will be entitled to full compensation for his or her past and future care needs provided he or she can establish that the model of care chosen/advanced by the claimant is reasonable and the cost of that care is

---

[35]   For examples of cases involving hydrotherapy claims, see *Wakeling v (1) McDonagh and (2) MIB* (successful claim); *Burton v Kinsbury* [2007] EWHC 2091 (QB) (successful claim); *Iqbal v Whipps Cross University Hospital NHS Trust* [2006] EWHC 3111 (QB) (unsuccessful); *Smith v East and North Hertfordshire Hospitals NHS Trust* [2008] EWHC 2234 (QB) (unsuccessful); and *Noble v Owens* [2008] EWHC 359 (QB) (successful).

[36]   *Harris v Bright's Asphalt Contractors Ltd* [1953] 1 QB 617 at 635.

reasonable.[37] The test for judging the claimant's conduct ought not to be 'weighed in nice scales at the instance of the party which has occasioned the difficulty'.[38]

Practitioners are reminded that in many catastrophic injury claims, care needs are rarely static. It is therefore vitally important that a proper assessment of the claimant's care needs is carried out throughout the claimant's lifetime, with input from the medico-legal and care experts, and provision is made for any increased needs within the schedule.

In circumstances where the claimant and defendant both put forward care regimes that are deemed to be reasonable, the court must make an objective assessment of the claimant's short and long-term needs, then a subjective assessment of the reasonableness of the claimant's chosen regime. The reasonableness of the claimant's chosen regime requires an analysis of the alternatives available. Finally, if the claimant's regime is deemed reasonable, the court must make an objective assessment of the reasonableness of the costs claimed.

In *Sowden v Lodge*,[39] the Court of Appeal had to consider whether the claimant could claim the cost of care in the face of an argument by a defendant that an option of residential care should be taken up, for which there would be no charge. The impact of public statutory provision is considered below, but in the course of its judgment the court provided helpful guidance as to the basic principles to be applied when assessing care. The Court of Appeal held that, when a court was determining whether the claimant in a personal injury action was entitled to recover as damages the cost of proposed private care and accommodation, the test to be applied was whether the care and accommodation chosen by the claimant was reasonable. They rejected the 'best interests' test that had been applied in at least one first instance decision. The court concluded that paternalism did not replace the right of the claimant, or those with the responsibility for her, to make a reasonable choice. At start of his judgment in *Sowden v Lodge*, Longmore LJ noted that:

> 'It is common ground that if a person is negligently injured, he can, in principle, claim from the tortfeasor the reasonable expenses of dealing with the consequences of that injury.'

At para 10 of his judgment, Pill LJ stated as follows:

---

[37] See *Wakeling v McDonagh and another* [2007] EWHC 1201 (QB); *Massey v Tameside & Glossop Acute Services NHS Trust* [2007] EWHC 317; *Smith v East & North Hertfordshire Hospitals NHS Trust* [2008] EWHC 2234; *XXX v A Strategic Health Authority* [2008] EWHC 2727 (QB); *Smith v LC Fashion Windows* [2009] EWHC 1532 (QB) and *Whiten v St Georges Healthcare NHS Trust* [2011] EWHC 2066 (QB).

[38] See *Melia v Key Terrain Ltd* (1969) No 155B and *Morris v Richards* [2003] EWCA Civ 232.

[39] [2004] EWCA Civ 1370, [2005] 1 All ER 581.

'The basis on which damages are awarded at common law is not seriously in issue. Its history was traced by Stephenson, LJ in *Rialas v Mitchell* (1984) 128 Sol. Jo. 704, beginning with the statement of Lord Blackburn in *Livingstone v Rawyards Coal Co.* [1880] 5 App.Cas.25 at 39:

"... Where any injury is to be compensated by damages, in settling the sum of money to be given for reparation or damages, you should as nearly as possible get that sum of money which will put the party that has been injured, or who has been suffered, in the same position as he would have been in if he had not sustained the wrong for which he is now getting his compensation or reparation."

The relevance of *Rialas*'s case is that the issue was whether the tortfeasor was required to pay for a 12 year old boy to be cared for at home or whether he should live in an institution. That is a question similar to those in the present cases. On the facts of that case, the cost of caring for him in an institution was lower. Stephenson, LJ stated that "What has to be first considered by the Court is not whether other treatment is reasonable, but whether the treatment chosen and claimed for is reasonable." O'Connor, LJ stated:

"There may well be cases in which it would be right to conclude that it is unreasonable for a Plaintiff to insist on being cared for at home, but I am quite satisfied that this is not such a case and once it is concluded that it is reasonable for the infant Plaintiff to remain at home, then I can find no acceptable ground for saying that the Defendant should not pay the reasonable cost of caring for him at home, but pay only a lesser sum which would be appropriate only if it was unreasonable for him to live at home and reasonable for him to be in an institution."'

At para 38, Pill LJ stated:

'The test to be applied is in my judgment that expressed by O'Connor and Stephenson, LJJ in *Rialas*'s. That is different from the test applied by the Judge who repeatedly used the expression "best interests" where he equated that with a position which "most nearly restores her to the position in which she would be but for the accident". The Judge's good intentions with respect to the Claimant's welfare are not of course in question, and neither, in my view, is the perceptiveness with which he approached the medical evidence, but there is a difference between what a Claimant can establish as reasonable in the circumstances, and what a Judge objectively concludes is in the best interests of the Claimant. In this context, paternalism does not replace the right of a Claimant, or those with responsibility for the Claimant, making a reasonable choice. It was when dealing with a somewhat different argument that the objective approach was rejected in *Rialas*'s case.

The question is more complicated in a case such as the present where the Judge plainly had serious doubts about the evidence as to the Claimant's wishes. That is a very different situation from *Rialas*'s case, where the Trial Judge had held that "everyone agrees that for his own sake the Plaintiff ought to be accommodated at home".'

16.3.7.1 Gratuitous care

Gratuitous care will be quantified on a commercial basis but generally discounted to account for the fact that a gratuitous carer will not pay tax or national insurance and will ordinarily not have to incur significant expense travelling to/from the place of care. The conventional discount that has emerged over time is one of 25%.[40] However, there will be situations where no discount is applied given the special circumstances of the care provided, such as where the care provided has been of a very high quality,[41] where flat rates have been adopted in the commercial calculation that do not account for uplifts for unsocial hours or weekends,[42] where rates have been applied that are probably too low for the nature of the care provided[43] or where the care provider has given up highly paid employment in order to care for the claimant.[44]

An additional claim should be made for respite care, usually provided by an agency, to allow the gratuitous carer a period of recuperation from the significant demands that are placed upon them.[45] This is particularly important in cases where a partner or spouse is providing high levels of gratuitous care, so as to minimise the prospects of a relationship breakdown.

Practitioners should be aware of the risk that the claimant's current gratuitous carers may not continue to provide such care indefinitely, whether this be as a result of age, illness, marriage breakdown, death or voluntary decision. If placed in issue, it may be that a medical report needs to be obtained detailing the care provider's health and life expectancy.

An award for gratuitous care that is recovered is held on trust for the care provider(s). On this basis, any gratuitous care provided by the tortfeasor will not be recoverable and it is essential that an alternative care regime is put in place.[46]

If a claim for gratuitous care is made, credit must be given for any carer's allowance received by the person providing the care, pursuant to the principles laid down in *Hodgson v Trapp*.[47]

---

[40] See *Evans v Pontypridd Roofing* [2002] PIQR Q5; *Massey v Tameside & Glossop Acute Services NHS Trust* [2007] EWHC 317; *Noble v Owens* [2008] EWCH 359 and *Whiten v St George's Healthcare NHS Trust* [2011] EWHC 2066 (QB).

[41] See *Wells v Wells* [1997] 1 WLR 652; *Brown v King's Lynn & Wisbech NHS Trust* (unreported) 20 December 2000; and *A v National Blood Authority* [2001] Lloyd's Rep Med 187.

[42] *Newman v Folkes* [2002] EWCA Civ 591.

[43] *Parry v NW Surrey HA*, LTL 1 February 2000; (2000) *The Times*, January 5.

[44] *Fish v Wilcox* [1994] 5 Med LR 230; (1993) *The Times*, March 4.

[45] See *Evans v Pontypridd Roofing Ltd* [2001] EWCA Civ 1657.

[46] *Hunt v Severs* [1994] 2 AC 350.

[47] [1989] 1 AC 807.

16.3.7.2   Commercial care employed directly by the claimant

This can take the form of a single carer who meets all of the claimant's needs or, as is more common in catastrophic injury claims, a team of carers working shifts. Consideration must be given to the composition of the care team, including the potential need for a team leader at an enhanced rate,[48] the need for carers who are qualified nurses[49] and the overall number of carers. Once the composition of the care team is decided, subsidiary issues must be determined such as the appropriate regimes for daytime and night-time care, whether sleep-in as opposed to waking care is required at night, the appropriate hourly rates and whether there will be a need for double-up care at any time.[50]

Aside from salary costs, there are a number of additional costs to be factored into the calculation for employed care including recruitment and training costs, team meeting costs, holiday and sick pay, insurance costs, additional handover costs, supervision, liaison and team meeting costs, overlap in shifts, food and accommodation costs, travel costs, respite care and future compulsory NEST pension contributions. In catastrophic cases, it will now be common to cost the professional care regime based upon a 60-week year to cover factors such as training, sickness and holidays. The case of *Whiten v St George's Healthcare NHS Trust* is essential reading in this area.[51]

Given the high level of cost involved, is not uncommon for a defendant to argue that a directly employed care regime recommend by a claimant's care expert should instead be provided via a professional agency. However, this may not be satisfactory in cases where the claimant requires a stable, consistent and continuous regime that is likely to be better served by employed carers, who have been specifically chosen and trained to meet the claimant's individual needs. In these circumstances, it is essential that medico-legal evidence is in place (in brain injury cases, usually from a neuropsychologist) to support the proposals put forward by the claimant's care expert.[52]

16.3.7.3   Agency care

Under such a regime, a professional agency will supply the carers required by the claimant. The practitioner must ask the same questions regarding

---

[48]   See *Massey v Tameside & Glossop Acute Services NHS Trust* [2007] EWHC 317 (QB) and *XXX v A Strategic Health Authority* [2008] EWHC 2727 (QB) and *Whiten v St George's Healthcare NHS Trust* [2011] EWHC 2066 (QB).

[49]   See *A v B Hospitals NHS Trust* [2006] EWHC 1178 (QB) and *Ahsan v University Hospitals Leicester NHS Trust* [2006] EWHC 2624 (QB).

[50]   See *A v B Hospitals NHS Trust* [2006] EWHC 1178 (QB); *Corbett v South Yorkshire Strategic HA* [2007] LS Law Med 430; *Wakeling v McDonagh* [2007] EWHC 1201 (QB); *A v Powys Health Board* [2007] EWHC 2996 (QB) and *Whiten v St George's Healthcare NHS Trust* [2011] EWHC 2066 (QB).

[51]   It should be noted that the precise workings of the NEST pension scheme have been clarified since the judgment in *Whiten* and the pension contribution levels applied in the case are no longer applicable.

[52]   See *Lynham v The Morecambe Bay Hospitals NHS Trust* [2002] EWHC 823.

composition of the care team and the subsidiary issues such as daytime and night-time regime, appropriate hourly rates and the need for double-up care.

The advantages of such a regime are that the agency will generally have the resources to ensure that care is always available to the claimant and the agency will remain responsible for many of the additional costs associated with directly employed care. Such a regime is also unlikely to encounter difficulties with the Working Time Regulations 1998. However, the disadvantages are that the care is much more unlikely to be tailored to the claimant's individual needs and there will often be a lack of continuity and consistency as a result of different carers being provided at different times. The use of agency care is also particularly unattractive if the claimant requires live-in care.

If agency care is appropriate, it is important that practitioners ask their care expert to factor-in the likely increase in future costings when the Pensions Bill comes into force. Indeed, although the agency will be responsible for meeting such contributions on the part of their care staff, this is likely to be reflected in an increased cost to the customer.

16.3.7.4   *Residential care*

This can take a number of different forms, including residential care homes and long-stay residential catastrophic injury units dedicated to head or spinal injuries. If paid for privately, the costs of these placements will invariably be very expensive. It is therefore essential that there is clear medico-legal evidence justifying the provision for such intensive levels of care. In the event that residential care is appropriate, a deduction must be made for the savings that the claimant will make in not running his or her own home and buying his or her own food.[53]

16.3.7.5   *Buddy/support worker*

The use of a buddy/support worker is particularly common in head injury cases. It provides the claimant with a close, but specially trained, companion who can help improve quality of life through access to a number of different activities and interests.

If a live-in buddy is required then this may impact on, or give rise to, an additional accommodation claim as much as with any other type of carer.

16.3.7.6   *Public statutory provision*

This has been a particularly complex area of catastrophic injury litigation.

---

[53]   *Lim Poh Choo v Camden and Islington HA* [1980] AC 174 at 191.

The starting point is that the state has an obligation to provide care for those in need.[54] Problems have arisen because of the following competing factors:

(a)   defendants have sought to argue that a claimant's care needs should be met by the local authority under its statutory obligations hence there should be no recoverable loss for such services vis-à-vis the defendant;

(b)   claimants have sought to argue that it would be wrong to rely upon the local authority to satisfy reasonable needs (due to uncertainties surrounding the availability of such care into the future and question marks over the quality of such care when compared to a privately sourced regime);

(c)   in some circumstances, the local authority providing the care has the right to recover all or part of the cost of such care from the claimant;

(d)   there is always the risk of double recovery – ie the claimant recovering the costs of private care and then relying upon local authority provision.

There has been a considerable amount of case-law in this area.[55]

However, the most important case for practitioners to familiarise themselves with is *Peters v East Midlands Strategic HA &Nottingham City Council*,[56] being a decision of Butterfield J that was subsequently upheld by the Court of Appeal.[57] In *Peters*, the claimant had been born with congenital rubella syndrome and was seriously disabled, requiring specialist care in a private care home costing approximately £132,000 per annum. The defendant argued that the local authority should bear the cost of this placement in view of its statutory obligations under s 21 of the National Assistance Act 1948. The local authority (joined as a Part 20 defendant) refuted this and contended that it was entitled to look towards the claimant for a contribution to her care once a damages award had been made. For her part, the claimant sought damages for the private costs of providing the necessary care from the defendant tortfeasor so that she could guarantee good quality care for the remainder of her life irrespective of pressures on the public purse and without fear of changes in the criteria applied for local authority funding.

Butterfield J found for the defendant in relation to the law on s 21 of the National Assistance Act 1948 (NAA 1948). He concluded that, on a proper construction of the NAA 1948, the National Assistance (Assessment of Resources) Regulations 1992[58] and Sch 10 to the Income Support (General)

---

54   See s 21 of the National Assistance Act 1948; s 2 of the Chronically Sick and Disabled Persons Act 1970; s 17 of the Health and Social Services and Social Security Adjudications Act 1983; s 47 of the National Health Services and Community Care Act 1990 and s 57 of the Health and Social Care Act 2001.

55   See *Lim Poh Choo v Camden & Islington HA* [1980] AC 174; *Rialas v Mitchell* [1984] 128 SJ 704; *Avon County Council v Hooper* [1997] 1 WLR 1605; *Sowden v Lodge* [2004] EWCA Civ 1370; *Islington BC v UCH NHS Trust* [2005] EWCA Civ 596; and *Crofton v NHSLA* [2007] 1 WLR 923.

56   [2008] EWHC 778.

57   [2009] EWCA Civ 145.

58   SI 1992/2977.

Regulations 1987,[59] and on the assumption that the claimant's damages would be administered by the Court of Protection, the local authority was and (subject to any change in legislation) would in the future be, required to disregard as resources the following sums when assessing contributions payable under ss 22(3) and 26(3) of the NAA 1948:

(a) the capital sum constituted by an award of damages for personal injury (comprising the *whole* amount of all awards made, not just general damages);

(b) any interest or other income from the investment of that sum which is retained by the Court of Protection;

(c) any payments made out of monies held by the Court of Protection to the claimant, to her receiver, or any other person for the claimant's use;

(d) any payments made out of monies held by the Court of Protection to a third party on the claimant's behalf.

However, the defendant lost the second argument in respect of recoverability of damages for future care. Butterfield J found that the claimant did not have a placement for life whilst dependent on the local authority for funding, as this placement was subject to annual review and possible changes in legislation. The uncertainties created by this situation, particularly in the context of increasing financial demands placed upon local authorities, provided clear support for a claimant to be self-funding, as did the guarantee of quality care that a private regime would provide:[60]

> 'Whilst as the law presently stands C will have access to State-funded care in the future, that care is unlikely to provide her with the quality of care she presently enjoys for the rest of her life. The only way to ensure that she does receive such care in the future is for her to be self-funding. In my judgment there is no reason in principle why she should give up that option at the behest of the tortfeasor defendants and make herself dependent on the State. She has an immediate right to full compensation from the tortfeasor. She is entitled to look to the tortfeasor for such compensation. She is not obliged to make herself dependent on State resources.'

During the course of giving evidence in the case, the claimant's deputy had indicated that she would be prepared to give an undertaking not to claim for future state care so as to avoid the prospect of double recovery. However, Butterfield J found that any such undertaking would be undesirable, impractical and lacking in any proper legal basis. Instead, the learned judge was prepared to accept the evidence of the claimant's deputy that, barring some wholly unexpected development, the claimant would not require local authority care in the future. Accordingly, no question of double recovery would arise.

Four key issues arose upon appeal (the first issue being on appeal from the local authority, the following three issues being on appeal from the defendant):

---

[59] SI 1987/1967.
[60] Paragraphs 72–73 of the judgment.

(1) whether Butterfield J had been right to hold that the words 'an award of damages for personal injury' referred to all sums awarded in consequence of such an injury or whether this was restricted to general damages in respect of pain, suffering and loss of amenity;

(2) whether the claimant was fully entitled as a matter of law to choose to pursue the tortfeasor for funding as opposed to the local authority;

(3) whether the claimant had reasonably mitigated her loss by choosing self-funding care as opposed to local authority funded care;

(4) whether, if other issues were decided in the claimant's favour, her lifetime multiplier should be reduced to reflect the fact that the claimant would be entitled to state-funded care for at least a period of time into the future.[61]

The appeal failed on all four issues. In summary:

(1) the words 'an award of damages for personal injury' was clear, unambiguous and unqualified. It could not be construed as applying to some heads of damages and not others;

(2) provided there was no risk of double recovery, there was no reason in policy or principle which required the court to hold that a claimant who wishes to opt for self-funding and damages, in preference to reliance on the statutory obligations of a public authority, should not be entitled to do so as a matter of right;

(3) the risk of double recovery could be dealt with effectively by the claimant's deputy notifying the senior judge of the Court of Protection of the outcome of the proceedings and supplying him with copies of the judgments in the case. Thereafter, the Court of Protection could retain control over the deputy's ability to make any application for provision of the claimant's care and accommodation needs at public expense. There should also be provision for the defendant to be notified of any such application so that they are given the opportunity to make representations in response;

(4) although it was not strictly necessary to determine the third issue on appeal, the Court of Appeal decided that it was reasonable for the claimant to opt for self-funding rather than provision from the local authority. In arriving at this decision, the Court of Appeal highlighted that there was no certainty that the claimant would remain in the residential home provided by the local authority or that this would continue to be funded by the local authority. It was also held that Butterfield J had been right to have regard to the possibility of future legislative change as a relevant factor in deciding that it was reasonable for the claimant to opt for private funding;

(5) on the issue of the multiplier, this was not a case (unlike *Crofton v NHSLA*) where the claimant was envisaged to receive state-funded care into the future. In the circumstances, there would be no good reason for reducing the claimant's lifetime multiplier.

---

[61] As per *Crofton v NHSLA* [2007] 1 WLR 923.

Accordingly, a claimant can now elect self-funding over state-funding so long as the risk of double recovery is avoided. Although the Court of Protection was initially advanced as the mechanism for policing the risk of double recovery this practice has now withered on the vine and been largely replaced by a system of reverse indemnities. This requires the defendant to meet the claimant's reasonable care needs arising from an accident in return for an agreement that, in the event that any/all of the cost of the claimant's care is met by statutory funding in the future, then credit shall be given by the claimant for the same.

The decision in *Peters* clarifies the position for those who have recovered personal injury damages and seek public statutory provision in relation to residential care. The whole of the damages recovered under a claim will be disregarded when the local authority considers means, not just general damages. Furthermore, assuming the award is administered by the Court of Protection or in a personal injury trust, any interest or income arising from the damages award will be disregarded.[62]

The position with domiciliary care is different in that a local authority must continue to disregard capital held in a personal injury trust or administered by the court, but has discretion over the treatment of income derived on such capital, or by way of periodical payments. Consequently, whether a claimant will be entitled to statutory funding for domiciliary care, post-settlement, remains uncertain.

Further uncertainty has recently arisen with the publication of the NHS's Charging for Residential Accommodation Guide (CRAG) consultation in July 2012. This consultation paper moots the prospect of local authorities being allowed to take into account the care element of personal injury compensation in the financial assessment of what a care home resident can afford to pay for residential care. As yet, no decisions have been announced but practitioners will need to bear this possible development in mind.

16.3.8   Analysis of commercial rates

There are a range of commercial pay scales for qualified nurses and other carers, provided by different bodies, including the 'National Joint Council' rates, The 'Whitley scale' rates and 'Crossroads: Caring for Carers' rates. Within these pay scales there are different rates that depend upon the grade of carer, the nature of the care being provided and when the care is being provided.

The claimant's care expert will report upon the appropriate rates in the circumstances of each case. It is important to ensure that rates used are those that apply locally to the claimant, as prices can change significantly according

---

[62]   The position is more generous in Wales as a result of the Social Care (Charges) Wales Measure 2010 (Commencement) Order 2011, where the disregard extends to any capital 'under the order of the court'.

to geographical location.[63] In cases involving gratuitous care there is now uniformity in adopting the NJC Local Authority Spinal Point 8 rates. In most catastrophic injury cases involving round the clock care, the claimant should argue for the cost of the aggregate NJC Spinal Point 8 rates, as set out in Section K1 of *Facts and Figures* (subject to gratuitous discount).[64]

If an employed regime is required, it may be necessary to pay a higher rate to ensure that high quality and committed carers are put in place.

16.3.9   DIY, gardening and housekeeping assistance

Practitioners should ensure that their care report makes provision for DIY, gardening and housekeeping assistance and that this should be included within the schedule. Section K3 of *Facts and Figures* provides very helpful guidance on these claims. In *XXX v A Strategic Health Authority*, a small award of 4 hours per week was made to account for domestic cleaning over and above the claimant's care regime. A similar approach was taken in *Whiten v St George's Healthcare NHS Trust* (albeit a lesser award was made).

16.3.10   Case management

In many catastrophic injury claims a case manager will be required to implement and manage the claimant's care regime and ensure that the claimant's needs are being properly met (eg access to necessary healthcare professionals, carrying out risk assessments, attending multi-disciplinary team meetings, facilitating activities to add quality of life and ensuring entitlement to statutory benefits). Once again, the medico-legal and care experts will be crucial in determining the issue of reasonable need.[65] Practitioners should ensure that the costs of recommended case management are included within the schedule. In principle, there is no reason why the costs of gratuitous case management should not be recoverable.[66]

16.3.11   Double recovery

Any benefit payments that have been made in relation to past care that are not taken into account under the statutory scheme of recoupment, such as payments from the Independent Living Fund, will be deductible from damages.[67]

---

[63]   See *XXX v A Strategic Health Authority* [2008] EWHC 2727 (QB).
[64]   See *Massey v Tameside & Glossop Acute Services NHS Trust* [2007] EWHC 317; *Smith v East and North Herts NHS Trust* [2008] EWHC 2234 and *Whiten v St George's Healthcare NHS Trust* [2011] EWHC 2066 (QB).
[65]   See *XXX v A Strategic Health Authority* [2008] EWHC 2727; *Smith v LC Window Fashions Ltd* [2009] EWHC 1532 (QB) and *Whiten v St George's Healthcare NHS Trust* [2011] EWHC 2066 (QB).
[66]   *Massey v Tameside & Glossop Acute Services NHS Trust* [2007] EWHC 317 (QB); *A v Powys Health Board* [2007] EWHC 2996 (QB); and *Noble v Owens* [2008] EWHC 359 (QB).
[67]   *Dorrington v Lawrence* [2001] All ER 145.

16.3.12   Accommodation/increased household expenses

Unless subject to residential care, the catastrophically injured claimant will almost certainly require specially adapted accommodation. This is one of the most important heads of claim that needs to be reviewed at the very earliest opportunity.

The specialist accommodation can take many forms, including wheelchair-friendly facilities throughout the property, specially installed hoists/lifts, additional space for aids and equipment, purpose-built accommodation for carers and easy access garage facilities.

In some cases it may be possible to adapt existing accommodation. However, a large proportion of catastrophically injured claimants will need to purchase alternative accommodation. The input of the medico-legal experts, the care expert and an architect specialising in disabled accommodation should be sought when determining this issue.

As with care needs, practitioners are reminded that a claimant's housing needs may change over time. Accordingly, it is necessary to look at the clinical picture throughout the claimant's lifetime, not just up to the date of trial. The case of *Whiten v St George's Healthcare NHS Trust*[68] contains a tour de force analysis of accommodation issues within the context of a 7-year-old claimant with severe quadriplegic cerebral palsy and is essential reading.

The reality is that accommodation claims remain an enormous problem in catastrophic injury litigation, as the *Roberts v Johnstone* calculation (see below under 'New Accommodation') will rarely meet the capital required to purchase suitable accommodation, particularly when there is a short life expectancy. The law in this area is ripe for change (particularly if there is to be a reduction in the discount rate) but in the meantime practitioners are encouraged to consider all options when it comes to accommodation. In *Ryan St George v The Home Office*[69] a claim for a PPO was made to cover the *rental costs* of a suitable rental property. There are other known cases of insurance companies purchasing a suitable property for the claimant and charging a peppercorn rent for the remainder of the claimant's life. However, unless absolutely necessary, one can understand why most claimants would be unhappy with such arrangements.

16.3.12.1   Adaptations to existing property

The claimant will recover the cost of adaptations to an existing property provided he or she can establish that there is a reasonable need for such adaptations and cost is reasonable.[70] The capital costs of the adaptations

---

[68]   [2011] EWHC 2066 (QB).
[69]   [2008] 4 All ER 1039.
[70]   See *Cunningham v Harrison* [1973] QB 942 and *Whiten v St George's Healthcare NHS Trust* [2011] EWHC 2066 (QB).

should be included in the claim, along with the ongoing repair/replacement costs (see Chapter 17) and any additional household expenditure associated with the adapted property such as increased insurance and utility/maintenance costs.

16.3.12.2 New accommodation

In the event that a move to new accommodation is deemed reasonable, the claimant will recover:

(a)   the reasonable costs associated with the move such as estate agent fees, solicitors' fees, stamp duty, local authority searches and removal costs;

(b)   the reasonable cost of any alterations/adaptations reasonably required to that new property (both immediate and repair/replacement costs);

(c)   the reasonable cost of providing necessary furnishings and fittings;

(d)   damages for any additional capital spent in purchasing the new accommodation (known as the *Roberts v Johnstone* calculation).[71]

The *Roberts v Johnstone* claim is calculated by taking the difference in capital value of the old and new properties and applying a 2.5% interest rate (based on the prevailing discount rate) to the net sum to achieve an annual loss. This annual loss is then multiplied by the claimant's lifetime multiplier to achieve the lifetime loss. If the property has been purchased before the date of the trial, an additional claim should be made at 2.5% per annum for the period between purchase and trial. In the event that the claimant was a co-owner of the existing property, credit should only be given for 50% of the equity in that property when calculating the *Roberts v Johnston* claim.[72]

In the event that alterations/adaptations add value to a new property, Court of Appeal authority would suggest that the proven added value can simply be deducted from the claim that has been made for the cost of alterations/adaptations.[73] However, the better approach is to treat the capital cost of the expenditure which enhances value in the same way as expenditure which is incurred in the acquisition of the property and therefore part of the *Roberts v Johnstone* calculation.[74]

Where the costs of alterations/adaptations do not enhance the market value, the capital cost of such works will be recoverable in full. Where there is a reduction in capital value, the amount of that reduction can be added to the cost of such alterations/adaptations, with the figure used in the *Roberts v Johnstone* calculation based on the reduced value of the altered property after acquisition.

If the claimant was not a homeowner at the time of the accident but would have purchased a home at some point, credit must be given for the costs that

---

[71]   *Roberts v Johnstone* [1989] QB 878.

[72]   See *M (A Child) v Leeds HA* [2002] PIQR Q46 and *Sarwar v Ali* [2007] LS Medical 375.

[73]   As per the decision of the Court of Appeal in *Roberts v Johnstone*.

[74]   See *Willett v North Bedfordshire HA* [1993] PIQR Q166.

would have been incurred in doing so. If the claimant would have purchased such a home with a partner, then credit should only be given for a 50% share in the property.

If, in the absence of the accident, the claimant would have been renting property as opposed to purchasing, the costs of such rental should be offset against the *Roberts v Johnstone* calculation.

What about cases involving severely disabled children who live with their parents? Does credit have to be given for the accommodation costs that would have been incurred by the parents in the absence of looking after their disabled child? This was an issue addressed in the cases of *M (a child) v Leeds Health Authority*,[75] *Iqbal v Whipps*[76] and *Whiten v St George's Healthcare NHS Trust*.[77] At paras 465 and 466 of her judgment in *Whiten*, Swift J noted as follows:

> 'This is a difficult issue. If no allowance at all is made for the claimant's parents' accommodation costs, the effect will be that they (and, while they are living at home, their other children) will be provided with a home, free of charge, for as long as the claimant lives. Meanwhile, the defendant will be required to compensate the claimant for the whole of the annual interest on the capital value of the property. On the face of it, that result does not seem fair. The solution that is suggested is for the claimant to give credit, as against the capital value of the new property, for the value of the property that, had he not been injured, his parents would have owned and the family would have lived in. I agree with the judges in the cases of *M* and *Iqbal* that the problem with that solution is that the claim is brought on behalf of the claimant, not his parents. I consider that it is wrong in principle for the value of a property that would have been owned by the claimant's parents to be deducted from the value of the new property to be owned by him. To make such a deduction would also be unfair to the claimant. It would inevitably result in him being inadequately compensated for the loss of investment income on the capital value of the new property. It is not the claimant who has been relieved of the expense of purchasing a home; it is his parents. Yet the loss would fall on him. I recognise that, in *Roberts v Johnstone*, a deduction was made for the value of the claimant's parents' home. However, as I have already said, it appears that the claimant's advisers in that case had invited the court to make the deduction, so that the issue was not argued before the lower court or the Court of Appeal. The fact that neither court queried the concession made by the claimant does not necessarily imply that they "approved" it.'

In *Whiten* a claim was also successfully made for the costs of adapting the grandparents' home in Barbados to make it accessible for the claimant.

Finally it is important that the care and/or housing experts are asked to quantify the additional costs that are likely to be associated with the new accommodation, including insurance, council tax, utility rates, maintenance costs, new furnishings and carer furnishings/equipment etc. Once again, the

---

[75] [2002] PIQR Q46.
[76] [2007] LS Medical 97.
[77] [2011] EWHC 2066 (QB).

case of *Whiten* is hugely instructive on the issues surrounding these types of claim, with Swift J awarding £2,500 to cover the immediate costs of furnishing and equipping the carers' accommodation and allowing replacement of all relevant equipment every 10 years.[78]

16.3.13   Aids and equipment

Once again, this claim will be determined by a combination of medico-legal and expert care / OT evidence and the test will be reasonable need.

As with medical expenses and treatment, it does not matter that the aids or equipment are available free of charge on the NHS, provided the private purchase is deemed reasonable. This is a particular issue with prosthetic provision for amputees. It is not uncommon for a defendant to argue that suitable prosthetics are available on the NHS. However, the reality is that NHS provision is unsuitable in a number of respects, including of quality, design, availability, reliability, multiplicity and replacement. It is essential that the expert evidence highlights these problems.

In most catastrophic injury cases, the claimant's reasonable needs will be relatively clear and there will be strong grounds for recovering the private costs of aids and equipment. Instead the major issue is likely to be the reasonable cost of such items, the number of items required and the reasonable period of replacement.[79]

In the case of prosthetics, the battleground will often be the number of prosthesis required and the period of replacement. At the very least, a claimant should have access to an everyday and spare prosthesis that allows the claimant to continue as normal if repairs are required to the everyday limb. The claimant may also decide to rotate the use of his or her everyday and spare prosthetics for comfort reasons. At least one of these two prostheses should have a high-quality silicone cosmetic covering. If the claimant goes swimming or undertakes other sporting activities, an additional specialised prosthesis may be required. Again, the test is reasonable need and if the claimant can demonstrate the need for an activity limb used for sport this is likely to be deemed reasonable, albeit the period of replacement may be less regular than an everyday limb. Costs of travelling to/from regular prosthetic appointments/fittings need to be included in the claim.

It is important that all personal injury practitioners keep abreast of developments/advances within the field of prosthetics and neuro-prosthetics, including state-of-the-art multi-articulated prosthetic hands with integrated

---

[78]   The costs of purchasing and replacing a computer and printer for the care team and case manager to use were also deemed reasonable.

[79]   See *AH v Powys Health Board* [2007] EWHC 2996 and *Whiten v St George's Healthcare NHS Trust* [2011] EWHC 2066 (QB).

sensors, bionic knees and bionic eye implants. These are items that will no doubt become the norm over the coming years and should be investigated in all suitable cases.

Although practitioners will be led by their expert evidence on the issue of suitable equipment, they should also have an underlying level of knowledge about the types of equipment now available to enable and improve the quality of life of a catastrophically injured claimant. Examples will include manual wheelchairs and buggies, electric wheelchairs (including the SMART chair), beach wheelchairs, Tandem Flex ski equipment, all terrain vehicles/buggies, shower tables, bath seats and specialist beds.

Practitioners should ensure that the claimant's transportation costs are properly accounted for. This is likely to involve making a claim for a specially adapted motorcar, along with additional running costs, additional insurance costs (particularly if a carer/buddy is added to the policy), future replacements and breakdown cover. Higher mileage is likely to justify more regular replacement. Section L of *Facts and Figures* provides excellent guidance on these claims. If there is a need to transport a powered wheelchair/buggy or all terrain vehicle, a trailer may also be required. Consideration will need to be given to setting up and recovering the costs of a taxi account if a private vehicle is not pursued.

IT/technology is another area where claims are often not optimised. There may be items of technology that have a huge benefit to the injured party, such as computers, environmental controls, smart phones/tablets, eye gaze equipment, fingerprint recognition systems, specialist software programmes, security systems, remote control switches for household appliances etc. An IT consultant may be required to comment on these items. In the cases of *A v Powys Health Board* and *Whiten* awards of £180,000 and £134,000 were respectively awarded for this head of claim.

16.3.14 Holidays

If appropriate, the increased costs associated with taking the claimant on holiday should be included within the schedule. The care expert should deal with this issue in his or her report. Typical additional costs include travel and accommodation for the claimant, travel and accommodation for carers, business class seats on flights, increased insurance costs, increased vehicle hire and equipment hire, extra baggage, car parking and subsistence.

The claimant should be entitled to recover the reasonable costs of partaking in the type of holidays that he or she enjoyed prior to the accident.[80] Recent examples of awards being made under this head of damage can be found in *Sarwar v Ali and another* (£10,000 per annum), *AH v Powys Health Board* (£5,000 per annum), *Pankhurst v White & MIB* (£11,000 per annum) and *Whiten* (£6,265 reducing to £5,000 per annum after 12 years of age). In *Whiten*

---

[80] *Rialas v Mitchell* (1984) *The Times*, July 17.

a claim was also successfully made for the costs of adapting the grandparents' home in Barbados to make it accessible for the claimant. However, a claim for the costs of adapting a holiday home in France that the claimant's parents wished to buy were not recovered on the basis that the claimant did not have a reasonable need for such a holiday home. Instead, Swift J concluded that the claimant's needs would be met satisfactorily if his parents and case manager sourced a rental property that already had the specialist fittings required. The additional costs of this formed part of the £5,000 per annum awarded for holidays.

There is likely to be an additional claim for increased travel insurance (for the claimant and any accompanying family members/carers) and this should be investigated. There may also be a recoverable claim for an increase in carers' expenses with meals and drinks etc over holiday periods. In *Whiten*, an annual sum of £350 was allowed to cover the increased expenses of the claimant's care team whilst on holiday.

16.3.15   Cost of future legal representation

In *Whiten v St George's Healthcare NHS Trust*, a claim was made for the costs of future legal representation at a Disability and Special Needs Tribunal. The basis of this claim was that the family were going to move to an area served by a different local education authority (LEA) and this LEA may have subsequently refused to fund the claimant's one-to-one classroom assistant. Swift J accepted that this was a risk facing the family and made an award of £20,000 to cover such costs, subject to accelerated receipt. The claimant also recovered a small award to cover the small risk that tribunal proceedings were unsuccessful and the claimant would be forced to pay privately for such one-to-one assistance.

16.3.16   Cost of managing claimant's affairs/investment advice

Where the claimant is a protected party under the jurisdiction of the Court of Protection, the past and future fees charged by the Court of Protection must be included in the claim.

Additional fees will be incurred if a deputy has been appointed to make decisions regarding the claimant's property and financial affairs.

Section J of *Facts and Figures* provides examples of the type of fees/costs that should be included in the schedule. If there is a professional deputy in place, he or she should be asked to provide a witness statement setting out the past and future cost of managing the claimant's affairs and dealing with the Court of Protection. If no deputy has yet been appointed then a report on future costs should be obtained from a prospective deputy.

A useful analysis of Court of Protection/Professional Deputy costs is provided at 52 of the judgment in *Whiten v St George's Healthcare NHS Trust*.[81] It is noteworthy that the judgment in this case made provision for the costs of the professional deputy to be replaced every 10 years throughout the lifetime of the claimant.

If the claimant is deemed to have capacity but there are concerns regarding his or her ability to safeguard the damages award, the possibility of appointing a professional trustee should be investigated and the costs of such an appointment can be included in the schedule.[82] It needs to be borne in mind that capacity under the Mental Capacity Act can depend on the nature and timing of the decision being made. Thus in theory, but also in practice, a claimant could have sufficient capacity to make a decision on liability, but not on a financial settlement/making of a periodical payment order.

The costs of investment advice are irrecoverable pursuant to *Eagle v Chambers*, the rationale being that recoverability would form an indirect attack on the discount rate (which assumes that damages will be invested in ILGS and be risk free, hence there is no need for investment advice). However, this may change if the recent discount rate consultation process leads to the ILGS approach being abandoned and the discount rate being set on the assumption that a claimant will invest in a mixed portfolio of assets/equities. In these circumstances it is difficult to see how a claimant could properly or safely invest their damages without investment advice and the costs of this professional advice should therefore be recoverable in the claim.

16.3.17   Interest

Interest on general damages will run at 2% per annum from the date of service of proceedings to the date of judgment or sooner payment.

In cases of continuing special damages, the appropriate rate will be half the special account rate[83] from the date of the accident until trial or sooner payment. The court will retain a discretion to award interest at the full special account rate on discrete losses that were limited to a finite period of time.[84] However, this is unlikely to be applicable in a catastrophic injury claim where losses are likely to be ongoing.

As things stand, the special account rate is set at 0.5% per annum. The following is a breakdown of the full special account rates from 1 August 1999 onwards:

---

[81] [2011] EWHC 2066 (QB).
[82] In *A v Powys Local Health Board* [2007] EWHC 2996 (QB) a claim for the costs of setting up and running a trust for a 17-year-old girl with cerebral palsy who had capacity was rejected but an alternative claim for the costs of a premier banking service was allowed.
[83] Set by the Court Funds Office.
[84] *Prokop v Department of Health and Social Security* [1985] CLY 1037.

1.8.99:	7.0%
1.2.02:	6.0%
1.2.09:	3.0%
1.6.09:	1.5%
1.7.09:	0.5%

In the likely event that a defendant has made interim payments towards the claimant's damages, these payments must be taken into account when calculating interest. This is done as follows:[85]

Step 1: Calculate how much loss has accrued between the accident and interim payment.

Step 2: Calculate the interest due over that period at half the special account rate applicable at the relevant time.

Step 3: Reduce the loss that has accrued by the amount of the interim payment.

Step 4: Calculate the interest due on the above sum combined with any further damages accrued until the next relevant date, be it a further interim payment, settlement or trial.

Any interest earned on interim payments should not be set-off against the final sums awarded.[86]

16.4 PROVISIONAL DAMAGES

Pursuant to CPR, r 41.2, a court may award provisional damages if such a claim is pleaded and it is satisfied that s 32A of the Senior Courts Act 1981 or s 51 of the County Courts Act 1984 applies. Section 32A of the Senior Courts Act states as follows:

> 'This section applies to an action for damages for personal injuries in which there is proved or admitted to be a chance that at some definite or indefinite time in the future the injured person will, as a result of the act or omission which gave rise to the cause of action, develop some serious disease or suffer some serious deterioration in his physical or mental condition.'

Under the provisions of the Damages Act 1996 (implemented in April 2005) the court has the power to make a provisional periodical payments order.[87]

The leading case in this area is that of *Curi v Colina*,[88] in which Roch LJ identified the following approach to the question of provisional damages:

---

[85] *Bristow v Judd* [1993] PIQR Q117.

[86] See *Parry v North West Area HA*, LTL, 1 February 2000; (2000) *The Times*, January 5.

[87] See art 2 of the Damages (Variation of Periodical Payments) Order 2005, SI 2005/841.

[88] LTL, 29 July 1998; (1998) *The Times*, October 14.

(1) first, the claimant had to satisfy the court that the chance of developing the disease or deterioration in physical or mental condition was measurable and more than fanciful (but less than *probable*, as this would merit a once and for all award);

(2) thereafter, it was necessary for the claimant to prove that the disease or deterioration could be described as serious. This would be measured against its effects on the activities of the injured claimant, life expectancy or on financial consequences;

(3) if the claimant satisfied both of the above tests, the court needed to consider whether to exercise its discretion to award provisional damages. One such consideration would be whether an award of damages in full and final settlement, which included a sum for the chance of the disease or deterioration occurring, would be wholly inadequate to compensate the claimant for the position in which he or she would find him or herself once the chance had materialised.

In *Wilson v MOD*,[89] Scott Baker J found that a clear-cut future event was required in order to satisfy the test of serious deterioration and that the risk of this event needed to be more than de minimis. Gradual deterioration in a claimant's condition is not sufficient to merit a provisional award.

Perhaps unsurprisingly, the courts have been seen to exercise this discretion inconsistently within the context of catastrophic injury claims. For examples of the approach taken in practice, the practitioner is referred to the cases of *Mitchell v Royal Liverpool & Broadgreen NHS Trust*,[90] *H (A Child) v Thomson Holidays Ltd*[91] and *Davies v Bradshaw and another*.[92]

The more recent decisions in *Kotula v EDF Energy and Others*[93] (involving future risk of syringomyelia) and *Loughlin v Singh*[94] (involving a future risk of epilepsy consequent to head injury) are particularly important in the context of catastrophic injury litigation.

What seems clear is that the consequences of the deterioration are of critical importance to the exercise of the discretion. Equally, the court will be slow to accede to a request for provisional damages where it is in a position to make a reasoned judgment on future developments of the injury for which damages are being assessed, thereby enabling this to be taken into account in a full and final settlement.

---

[89] [1991] 1 All ER 638.
[90] LTL, 11 September 2008.
[91] [2007] EWHC 850 (QB).
[92] [2008] EWHC 740 (QB) (this decision of Wilkie J was subsequently appealed by consent, leading to an award for provisional damages).
[93] [2011] EWHC 1546 (QB).
[94] [2013] EWHC 1641 (QB).

ANNEX: SCHEDULE OF LOSS AND EXPENSE

IN THE HIGH COURT OF   CLAIM No. HQ12345
JUSTICE

QUEEN'S BENCH DIVISION

B E T W E E N:

xxxxxxxxxxxx

(A Protected Party by his Litigation Friend

yyyyyyyyyy)

                                                          Claimant

–and–

zzzzzzzzzzzzz

                                                          Defendant

---

SCHEDULE OF LOSS & EXPENSE

A. Relevant Dates/Information

Date of Accident:	9 December 2011
Date of Schedule:	10 October 2013
Position on Liability:	Admitted 21 January 2012
Claimant's date of birth:	9 May 1973
Life Expectancy:	Reduced by 2 years
Date of Disposal:	5-day trial concluding 10 May 2014
Claimant's age at Accident/Disposal:	38.59/41
Period between Schedule and Disposal:	0.58 years
Period between Accident and Disposal:	2.43 years
Expert Evidence:	See Appendix 1

B. Background

(i)   At the age of 38 the Claimant was involved as a passenger in a head-on collision with the Defendant's vehicle and sustained a very severe closed head injury complicated by an acute subdural haematoma, burst temporal lobe and the need for a second craniotomy due to secondary haemorrhage into the brain;

(ii) The Claimant has been left significantly handicapped, with major cognitive defects, memory and executive function deficits, poor intellectual functioning, epilepsy, loss of smell/taste, poor eyesight, severe expressive and receptive dysphasia, a residual right hemianopia and a chronic right hemiplegia. The Claimant also has major psychological, behavioural and emotional difficulties;

(iii) The Claimant's medical status is permanent and there are no treatments that will improve his outlook;

(iv) The Claimant is profoundly disabled and will be permanently unemployable, having previously been a skilled fibre-optics technician. The Claimant's life expectancy has been slightly reduced on account of his catastrophic injuries;

(v) The Claimant lacks capacity and will remain dependent upon others for personal care for the remainder of his life. An appropriate care and case management regime will be required for life. Specialised equipment, accommodation and orthotics are required to accommodate the Claimant's disabilities.

C. Summary

Item	Claim
General Damages	TBA
Past Losses	
Past Loss of Earnings	£36,245
Past Care & Assistance	£91,035
Past Case Man/OT	£30,427.86
Past Aids & Equipment	£14,257
Past Travel Expenses	£6,000
Past Medical Expenses	£5,838
Past Accommodation	£51,563.66
Past Increased Bills	£7,507.97
Past Miscellaneous	£3,750
Past Deputy/Court of Protection Fees	£31,255.96
Total Past	
Interest	TBC
Future losses	
Future Loss Earnings	PPO £22,946 p a
Future Loss of Pension	£54,250
Future Accommodation etc	£491,207.41

Item	Claim
Future Care & Assistance	PPO £82,340.32/ £138,814.64/ £178,832.96 pa
Future Case Management	PPO £8,340 pa + £13,234 lump sum
Future Physiotherapy Costs	£38,426.10
Future Occupational Therapy	£30,540
Future Aids, Appliances & Equipment	£62,684.27
Future Vehicle Costs/Adaptations/ Expenses	£244,734.68
Future Laundry	£7,635
Future DIY/Decoration/ Gardening	£27,049.76
Future Holidays	£52,847
Disability Subscriptions	£250.00
Future Chiropody	£6,362.50
Carer Furnishings	£12,154.79
Opthalmic Costs	£10,413.25
Orthotic Costs	£3,970.96
Future Deputy/Court of Protection Fees	£316,085
Lost Years	£4,033.08

D. Multipliers (Taken at date of Disposal as at age 41 years)

Lifetime Multiplier: 25.45

(i)   The Claimant notes the agreed reduction in life expectancy of 2 years outlined in the joint statement of Mr. W and Dr. O;

(ii) As at the date of disposal, the Claimant will be 41 years of age. For the purpose of this exercise, the Claimant will be treated as if he is 43 years of age;

(iii) Table 1 of the Ogden Tables highlights that the lifetime multiplier for a 43-year-old male at 2.5% discount rate will be 25.45.

Base Loss of Earnings Multiplier: 18.95

(i) But for the accident, the Claimant would have continued working until a retirement age of 68;

(ii) The appropriate base multiplier for loss of earnings for a 41-year-old male to retirement age 68 is 18.95 [interpolating between the figures for a 41-year-old male outlined in Tables 9 and 11].

E. General Damages

JC Guidelines

(1) The Claimant's injuries fall in the category of (A)(a) Very Severe Brain Damage [£ to £].

(2) *An appropriate award would be [ ].*[95]

F. Past Special Damages

I. Loss of Earnings Claim

1. Recital

(1) As a result of the catastrophic injuries sustained in the accident, the Claimant has been unable to return to any form of employment;

(2) At the time of the accident the Claimant was employed by the Defendant as a skilled fibre-optics technician. His wage details for the 13-week period immediately prior to the accident reveal average net earnings of £352.00 per week, equating to approximately £18,300 per annum;

(3) But for the accident, the Claimant would have continued to earn approximately £18,300 per annum. Allowing for inflation upon earnings, at 2% per annum historically, the Claimant's earnings would have been as follows:

(i)	10th Dec 2011 to 9th Dec 2012:		£18,300
(ii)	10th Dec 2012 to 9th Dec 2013:		£18,666
(iii)	10th Dec 2013 to 10th May 2014:		£7,933

= £44,899

(4) As it is, the Claimant received only £8,654 in sick pay before the Defendant formally terminated his employment on incapacity grounds. This equates to a net loss of earnings totalling £36,245.00.

2. Calculation

(1) Total Past Loss of Earnings is **£36,245.00.**

---

[95] If appropriate.

II. Care & Assistance

1. Recital

(1) The Claimant requires extensive care & assistance as a result of his profound disabilities;

(2) The Claimant refers to and relies upon the Needs Reports prepared by Mrs U dated 9th July 2012 and 9th July 2013. The Claimant also relies and refers to the figures provided by Mrs U in the joint statement dated 10thAugust 2013;

(3) Thus far, the Claimant has insisted on all aspects of daily care being provided by the Litigation Friend (wife) and other family members;

(4) Mrs U has calculated the cost of this care at £104,913.33 to the date of disposal reflecting the aggregate NJC Spinal Point 8 rate;

(4) All of this gratuitous care & assistance should be reduced by a factor of 25% to account for the fact that no tax or national insurance is paid on these commercial rates. This equates to a net figure of £78,685;

(5) In addition, a claim is made for the costs of a Buddy/Support Worker that has been recommended (both by the Case Manager, Care Experts & Neuropsychological Experts). The costs of this Buddy/Support Worker to the date of disposal totals £12,350.

2. Calculation

(1) Total for past Care & Assistance, including Buddy/Support Worker costs is **£91,035.00**.

III. Case Management/Occupational Therapy

1. Recital

(1) The Claimant refers to and relies upon the witness statement on behalf of the Case Manager, Mrs A, and the witness statement from Mr B (Professional Deputy);

(2) Up to the date of the Schedule, the total costs of Case Management have been £18,658.39;

(3) In addition, the total costs of the privately instructed occupational therapist have been £6,450.47;

(4) On the basis of predicted future case management fees of £8,340.00 pa plus £520.00 pa travelling costs, additional fees of £5,319.00 will be incurred between the date of this Schedule and disposal (£8,860.00 × 0.58 years);

(5) The care experts agree the past costs of Case Management.

2. Calculation

(1) Total for past Case Management/Occupational Therapy Fees is **£30,427.86**.

IV. *Aids, Appliances & Equipment*

1. Recital

(1) The Claimant has required an extensive list of aids, appliances and equipment, as set out in the Needs Reports prepared by Mrs U dated 9th July 2012 and 9th July 2013;

(2) These items, agreed in the joint statement of the care experts, total £14,257.00.

2. Calculation

(1) Total for past aids, appliances and equipment is **£14,257.00**.

V. *Travelling Expenses*

1. Recital

(1) As a result of the catastrophic injuries sustained in the accident, the Claimant is wholly dependent upon others for transportation;

(2) Unfortunately, the Claimant's wife is not yet able to drive, meaning that the Claimant and his wife are dependent upon taxis or other members of family for transportation;

(3) A record of the various expenses has been kept and is exhibited at [attach appendix]. These expenses total £4,860 to the date of the Schedule, being approximately £2,000 per annum. A claim for £6,000 will be made to account for additional expenses to the date of disposal.

2. Calculation

(1) Total for Past Travelling expenses is **£6,000.00**.

VI. *Medical Expenses*

1. Recital

(1) A record of medical expenses has been kept and is exhibited at [attach appendix].

(2) These expenses total £5,338 to date. A further allowance of £500.00 is made for the costs that are likely to be incurred to trial, as set out in the witness statement of the Claimant's Litigation Friend.

2. Calculation

(1) Total for past medical expenses is **£5,838.00**.

VII. *Accommodation*

1. Recital

(1) There is no dispute that, as a result of the catastrophic injuries sustained in the accident, the Claimant requires specialist bungalow accommodation.

This was purchased on 12th September 2012 at a cost of £318,000 with the agreement of the Defendant and his accommodation expert;

(2)   The Claimant's previous property was sold for £213,000, meaning that the additional Roberts v. Johnstone capital spent purchasing this property was £105,000;

(3)   2.5% of £105,000 = £2,625.00 per annum;

(4)   The new property was purchased on 12th September 2012, a period of 1.66 years prior to the date of the Disposal in May 2014. 1.66 × £2,625.00 = £4,358;

(5)   In addition, the Claimant has incurred the following fees/expenses associated with the move [see witness statement of Mr B]:
  (i)   £9,600.00 Stamp duty
  (ii)   £470.00 Surveyor's fees
  (iii) £220.00 Land Registry Fees
  (iv)   £54.00 Local Search Fees
  (v)   £913.63 Solicitors Fees
  (vi)   £13,143.60 Furniture costs
  (vii) £349.98 Fridge Freezer
  viii) £302.00 Skip and Van hire for move

(6)   Finally, the Claimant makes a claim for the following required adaptations that have been carried out thus far in relation to the new property:
  (i)   £1,862.52 Architects Report (22.01.12)
  (ii)   £12,706.80 Deposit for new kitchen (07.11.12)
  (iii) £2,185.00 Fencing for garden and kennels (16.04.13 & 29.05.13)
  (iv)   £1,000.00 Ancillary expenses for new property (19.09.12)
  (vi)   £2,675.23 Pond maintenance (02.07.13 & 07.07.13)
  (vii) £104.90 Replacement door (27.07.13)
  (viii) £1,250.00 Internal decorating (10.08.13)
  (ix)   £368.00 Tree Services

2. Calculation

(1)   Total for past accommodation is £51,563.66.

VIII. *Increased Utility/Council Tax/Insurance/Laundry Costs*

1. Recital

(1)   The Claimant relies upon the joint statement of the accommodation experts, in which Mr T estimates the additional running costs of the new property at £2,487.00 per annum. 1.66 years × £2,487.00 = £4,128.42;

(2)   In addition, a claim is made for council tax at £491.48 per annum [agreed by accommodation experts]. 1.66 years × £491.48 = £815.86;

(3)   Increased insurance costs/home cover costs to Disposal total £1,834.69 [see witness statement of Mr B];

(4) Additional laundry costs, associated with episodes of incontinence and night sweats, are calculated at £300.00 per annum [see report of Mrs U dated 9th July 2013]. 2.43 years × £300.00 = £729.00.

2. Calculation

(1) Total for past Increased Utility/Council Tax/Insurance/Laundry Costs is £7,507.97.

IX. *Miscellaneous*

1. Recital

(1) Since the accident, the Claimant and his family have incurred numerous non-receipted miscellaneous expenses including telephone calls and postage charges;

(2) It is conservatively estimated that these charges will have totalled at least £250.00 at Disposal;

(3) In addition, costs of £3,500.00 have been incurred on several short holidays/breaks [see witness statements of Litigation Friend, Mrs A].

2. Calculation

(1) Total for past Misc. is £3,750.00.

X. *Deputy/Court of Protection Fees*

1. Recital

(1) A breakdown of the Receiver/Deputy and Court of Protection fees incurred to the date of the Schedule is set out in the witness statement of Mr B. These fees total £25,255.96;

(2) Additional estimated fees of £6,000.00 will be incurred between the date of the Schedule and Disposal.

2. Calculation

(1) Total for past Deputy/ Court of Protection costs is £31,255.96.

XI. *Interest*

1. Recital

(1) A claim is made upon all items of past special damages at 1/2 special account rate. To the date of disposal, interest on special damages totals 0.61%.

(2) Interest on general damages for PSLA is claimed at 2% per annum from the date of service of the Claim Form. To the date of disposal, this totals 2.54%.

2. Calculation

(1) TBC.

G. Future Losses

I. Loss of Earnings

1. Recital

(1) But for the accident, it is submitted that the Claimant would have continued to work within the fibre-optics industry earning at least £19,420.00 per annum;

(2) Evidence has been obtained from the Claimant's work colleagues and section manager which confirms that the Claimant had a 1 in 3 chance of achieving promotion to a managerial position within a period of 5 years. This would have given rise to net earnings of approximately £30,000 per annum;

(3) A claim will be made for the loss of chance of achieving such a role. The claim for future loss of earnings will be pleaded on the basis of net earnings at £22,946 per annum representing 33% of the additional earnings that the promotion would have attracted based upon the 33% chance of achieving such a position;

(4) As it is, the Claimant will never return to any form of gainful employment;

(5) The Claimant intends to seek the claim for future loss of earnings by way of PPO indexed according to the appropriate ASHE SOC;

(6) For the purpose of a lump sum illustration, the base multiplier for loss of earnings until retirement age of 68 [being the Claimant's predicted date of retirement but for the accident] is 18.95;

(7) The discount for contingencies according to Ogden 7 is 0.88 [Table A of explanatory notes to Ogden Tables – age 40-44 – category GEA educational attainment]. This results in a revised multiplier 16.68 × £22,946 = £382,739.

2. Calculation

(1) A claim is made for a PPO for loss of earnings in the sum of £22,946 per annum to age 68, indexed according to the appropriate ASHE SOC;

(2) On a lump sum basis, the claim for future loss of earnings would be **£382,739** (16.68 × £22,946).

II. Loss of Pension

1. Recital

(1) At the time of the accident the Claimant was a member of a final salary pension scheme with his employer;

(2) Had the Claimant continued to work for his employer until retirement age 68, he would have been entitled to a tax-free lump sum of £18,000 and an

annual pension of £12,000 based upon a final salary of £19,420 [see letter from employer's pension department dated 14.07.12]. Had the Claimant achieved promotion to a managerial position, this tax-free lump sum would have risen to £25,000 and the annual pension would have risen to £16,000 per annum see letter from employer's pension department dated 14.07.12];

(3) Based upon a 33% chance of achieving the position of promotion, a claim will be made on the basis that the Claimant would have received a tax-free lump sum of £20,333 and a gross annual pension of £13,333 [approximately £12,500 net of tax – see Section H1 *Facts & Figures* 2009/10];

(4) As a result of the accident, the Claimant was medically retired and received a tax-free lump sum of £10,000 and an incapacity pension of £6,000 per annum [below personal allowance];

(5) Based on his reduced life expectancy, the Claimant's lifetime multiplier is 25.45. The Claimant's multiplier to retirement age is 18.95. The base multiplier for loss of annual pension will therefore be 6.5;

(6) The Claimant's wife is entitled to 50% of his pension in the event that she outlives him;

(7) The Claimant's wife will be 36 at the date of Disposal. According to the Expectation of Life Table at Section A3 of *Facts & Figures*, the Claimant's wife is likely to live another 54 years. This is another 27 years beyond the time that the Claimant reaches 68 years of age;

(8) The multiplier for this period of 27 years is 19.71 [Table 28]. This figure must be discounted for accelerated receipt by a period of 27 years by applying a factor of 0.5134 [Table 27], resulting in a revised multiplier of 10.12;

(9) Given that the Claimant's wife is entitled to 1/2 of his pension for the period that she outlives him, the Claimant's multiplier of 6.5 should be increased by 1.81 [representing 50% the difference in multipliers of 3.62]. This results in a final multiplier of 8.31;

(10) The claim for annual loss of pension will therefore be 8.31 × £6,500 [£12,500 – £6,000] = £54,105;

(11) In addition, a claim is made for the loss of potential lump sum;

(12) But for the accident, the Claimant would have been entitled to a potential tax-free lump sum of £20,333. This must be discounted for accelerated receipt over a period of 27 years to account for the fact that the Claimant will receive the monies 27 years early. The appropriate discount is 0.5134 [Table 27], resulting in a revised loss of lump sum at £10,438.96;

(13) A discount must be made for part of the lump sum received early by way of incapacity pension [Longden Credit]. The Claimant's whole life multiplier is 25.45. The multiplier to pension age is 18.95. The Claimant must therefore give credit for 18.95 divided by 25.45, ie 74% credit for the lump sum received of £10,000. This equates to £7,400.00;

(14) £54,105 + £10,438.96 – £7,400 = £57,143.96;

(15) The Claimant will reduce this claim by approximately 5% to account for contingencies. A figure of £54,250 is claimed for loss of pension.

2.   Calculation

(1)   Total for future loss of pension is <u>£54,250.00</u>.

III. *Accommodation/Increased Utility/ Maintenance/Insurance/Council Tax*

1.   Recital

(1) A claim for a Roberts v Johnstone Award will continue in the sum of £2,625.00 per annum, representing 2.5% of the additional capital of £105,000 spent;

(2) The Claimant's lifetime multiplier is 25.45, equating to a future Roberts v Johnstone claim for <u>£66,806.25</u>;

(3) A claim is made for the one-off costs calculated by Mr T in the joint accommodation report:
   (i)   £195,955.00 adaptations
   (ii)   £79,900.00 extension for carer/buddy accommodation
   (iii) £10,310.00 conservatory
   (iv) £5,000.00 moving costs for carer
   (v)   £2,520.00 additional floor finishes
   (vi) £4,250.00 additional curtains
   (vii) £400.00 additional lighting
   (viii) £5,000.00 repairs and improvements

(4) Deducting the £12,706.80 deposit that has been paid for the kitchen, this equates to one-off costs totalling <u>£280,628.20</u>;

(5) In addition, a claim is made for the following ongoing costs:
   (i)   £2,787.00 per annum additional running cost
   (ii)   £1984.21 per annum additional insurance/home cover (matter of record)
   (iii) £150.00 per annum additional premium for carer's suite
   (iv) £691.48 per annum Council Tax

(6) Accounting for a lifetime multiplier of 25.45, this equates to ongoing costs of <u>£142,842.96</u>

(7) Finally, a claim is made for the immediate maintenance work required to the oak tree in the Claimant's garden at £930.00 [see letter from XTree Services dated 04.09.2013].

2.   Calculation

(1)   Total for future Accommodation/Increased Utility/Maintenance/Insurance/ Council Tax is <u>£491,207.41</u>.

IV. *Care & Assistance*

1. Recital

(1) The Claimant refers to and relies upon the reports of Mrs U and the joint statement of the care experts;

(2) The reality is that the Claimant's family is unlikely to be able to cope with the Claimant's future care needs without professional assistance and the reliance upon professional care will increase as time goes on;

(3) In this respect, the Claimant notes:
    (i) The opinion of Mrs U in her addendum report dated 07.08.2013, where she confirms that '*paid professional support will be increasingly required*';
    (ii) The opinion of the Defendant's care expert in her report dated June 2013, where it is stated that '*a time will come in the foreseeable future when Mrs C is no longer the primary carer and the gratuitous support she provides will need to be converted to employed support*' [p 18 report];
    (iii) The opinion of both experts in the joint statement where they '*agreed the need to provide proper professional support for the client via an agency and the reality that the client's wife cannot cope with providing care on a long-term basis*';

(4) The Claimant relies upon the opinion of Mrs U that it would be reasonable for the Claimant to receive 50% family care and 50% professional agency care for a period of 5 years post disposal. Thereafter, it would be reasonable to assume that all care will need to be provided professionally by an agency;

(5) In her report dated 9th July 2012 Mrs U values the future cost of family care at £25,821.96 per annum [£19,366.47 net 25% discount], plus buddy support worker at approximately £125.00 per week = £6,500.00 per annum. The cost of agency care is calculated at £132,314.64 per annum for the foreseeable future (first 10 years) and £172,332.96 per annum in later life [inclusive of daytime and night-time care provided by a team of agency carers];

(6) The Claimant will seek a Periodical Payments Order in relation to the claim for future care indexed according to ASHE 6115 on the following basis:
    (i) From 10th May 2013 to 9th May 2018 @ £82,340.32 pa [50% family + 50% agency + buddy]
    (ii) From 10th May 2018 to 9th May 2023 @ £138,814.64pa [agency + buddy]
    (iii) From 10th May 2020 for life @ £178,832.96 pa [agency + buddy]

(7) For the purpose of illustration only, the Claimant pleads the claim on a lump sum basis within this Schedule:
    (i) Lifetime multiplier of 25.45, split into three individual segments representing the different periods of care:
    First 5 years: 4.70 [term certain 5 years – Table 28]

Following 5 years: 4.16 [being the difference between the figure for a term certain of 10 years (namely 8.86) and a term certain of 5 years (namely 4.70)]

Remaining Lifetime Period: 16.59 [25.45 – 4.70 – 4.16];

(ii) First 5 years: £9,683.24 family care [50% of £19,366.47] + £6,500.00 buddy care + £66,157.32[50% of £132,314.64] × 4.70 = <u>£387,000</u>;

(iii) Following 5 years: £132,314.64 agency care + £6,500.00 buddy care × 4.16 = <u>£577,469</u>;

(iv) Remaining Lifetime Period: £172,332.96 agency care + £6,500.00 buddy care × 16.59 = <u>£2,966,839</u>;

(v) = <u>£3,931,308</u> total.

2. Calculation

(1) The Claimant will seek a **PPO** in relation to the claim for future care & assistance (subject to indexation on the basis of ASHE 6115):

(i) From 10th May 2013 to 9th May 2018 @ £82,340.32 pa

(ii) From 10th May 2018 to 9th May 2023 @ £138,814.64 pa

(iii) From 10th May 2020 for life @ £178,832.96 pa

(2) On a lump sum basis, the claim for future care would total <u>£3,931,308</u>.

V. Case Management

1. Recital

(1) As outlined in the recent report of Mrs U, the Claimant will require long-term assistance from a Case Manager;

(2) The care experts have agreed the cost of future case management at £8,340.00 per annum, plus travel, on the basis that agency care is utilised;

(3) The Claimant will seek a PPO in relation to the costs of future case management, indexed according to ASHE 6115 at £8,340.00 per annum;

(4) A claim will be made for the mileage costs associated with such case management on a lump sum basis. Mrs A has confirmed that mileage of 1,300 miles is likely to be incurred on an annual basis. Accounting for a rate of 40p per mile, this equates to £520.00 per annum;

(5) The Claimant's lifetime multiplier is 25.45. Accordingly, the claim for future case management travel costs will total £13,234.00 on a lump sum basis.

2. Calculation

(1) The Claimant will seek a **PPO** of **£8,340.00 per annum** in relation to future case management costs subject to indexation on the basis of ASHE 6115;

(2) Travelling expenses are claimed on a lump sum basis in the sum of <u>£13,234.00</u>.

VI. *Physiotherapy Costs*

1. Recital

(1) The Claimant refers to and relies upon the jointly instructed physiotherapy report prepared by Ms K dated 30th April 2013;

(2) Firstly, the Claimant requires a formal graded physiotherapy programme for the remainder of his life. On the basis of a lump sum payment, split multipliers are required for the calculation of the claim:
   (i) First 2 years: £2,340 per annum × 1.95 [Table 28] = £4,563.00;
   (ii) Following 5 years: £1,620 per annum × 4.48 [being the difference between the multiplier for a term certain of 7 years (namely 6.43) and 2 years (namely 1.95)] = £7,257.60;
   (iii) Ongoing Maintenance Physiotherapy: £900.00 per annum × 19.02 [25.45 – 1.95 – 4.48] = £17,118.00;
   (iv) Musculoskeletal physiotherapy: £180.00 per annum × 25.45 = £4,581.00;

(3) In addition, the Claimant will require physiotherapy aids & equipment, as set out in the report;

(4) The purchase cost of the recommended pieces of physiotherapy equipment totals £992.79. The replacement costs total £160.07 per annum × 24.45 [multiplier 25.45 minus 1 for immediate capital outlay] = £3,913.71;

2. Calculation

(1) Total for the future costs of physiotherapy and equipment is £38,426.10.

VII. *Occupational Therapy*

1. Recital

(1) The Claimant requires a twice-yearly home review from an occupational therapist, as set out in the report of Miss I dated 16th June 2013;

(2) The annual cost will be £1,200.00;

(3) Over the Claimant's lifetime, the claim will total £30,540 [25.45 × £1,200.00].

2. Calculation

(1) Total for future Occupational Therapy is £30,540.

VIII. *Aids, Appliances & Equipment*

1. Recital

(1) The Claimant refers to and relies upon the report of Mrs U dated 9th July 2012 together with the joint statement of the care experts;

(2) The joint statement agrees virtually all of the required items of aids, appliances and equipment save for some minor difference on insurance and replacement costs;

(3) The following items of aids, appliances and equipment are required immediately:

(i)	Lightweight manual wheelchair:	£1,600.00
(ii)	Spare manual wheelchair:	£1,600.00
(iii)	Controlled Powered Wheelchair:	£5,000.00
(iv)	Walking Trolley:	£102.70
(v)	Ferrules:	£1.94
(iv)	Electric Tin Opener:	£20.95
(vi)	Swedish Workstation:	£43.75
(vii)	Cooking baskets:	£30.60
(viii)	6 in-one multi-opener:	£9.70
(ix)	Spillnot Jar and Bottle Opener:	£16.34
(x)	Lightweight Reacher:	£12.85
(xi)	Long-Handled Gardening Implements:	£110.00
(xii)	Bath Lift:	£1,800.00
(xiii)	Grab Rails:	£110.00
(xiv)	Shower Chair:	£500.00
(xv)	White Board & Pens:	£25.00
(xvi)	Multi-fold aluminium wheelchair ramp:	£275.00
(xvii)	Bio Bidet:	£499.00
(xviii)	One-handed knife and fork:	£12.00
(xix)	Non-Vinyl bedding protectors:	£25.00
(xx)	Postage & Packing:	£75.00

= £11,869.83

(3) The cost of replacing and, where required, insuring items of aids & equipment totals £2,078.30 per annum [see joint statement];

(4) On the basis of a lump sum payment, adopting a multiplier of 24.45 [25.45 minus 1 to reflect immediate capital purchase], this equates to a figure of <u>£50,814.44</u>.

2. Calculation

(1) Total for future aids, equipment and appliances is <u>**£62,684.27**</u>.

IX. *Vehicle Costs/Adaptations/Travelling Expenses*

1. Recital

(1) As a starting point, provision needs to be made for the Litigation Friend to take driving lessons and pass her driving test;

(2) A claim for £925.00 is made for these costs, as outlined in the report of Mrs U dated 9th July 2012;

(3) The care experts agree the purchase, replacement and running costs of a suitably adapted vehicle. This is claimed as follows:

    (i) Initial cost of purchasing and adapting Ford Galaxy vehicle: £30,690.00

    (ii) Proportion of price lost at each replacement: 64% [Table 1, *Facts & Figures* 2012/13 p 330]

    (iii) Cost of each replacement: £30,690.00 × 0.64 = £19,641.60 Replacement period: 4 years = multiplier of £4,910.40

    (vi) Cost of future replacements: 25.45 × £4,910.40 = £124,969.68

    (vii) Additional running costs, over and above the costs of running a small second-hand car in the absence of the accident, are estimated at £3,500 per annum inclusive of increased costs of petrol, insurance and AA subscription. £3,500 × lifetime multiplier of 25.45 = £89,075.

2. Calculation

(1) Total for future vehicle/travelling expenses is **£244,734.68**.

X. Increased Laundry Costs

1. Recital

(1) The Claimant adopts the figures calculated by Mrs U, in her report dated 9th July 2012, totalling £300.00 per annum. These costs are agreed in the joint statement;

(2) Accounting for a lifetime multiplier of 25.45, this equates to a future claim for £7,635.00;

2. Calculation

(1) Total for future increased laundry costs is **£7,635.00**.

XI. DIY/Decoration/Gardening

1. Recital

(1) The Claimant adopts the recommendations outlined in the report of Mrs U dated 9th July 2012, where she makes an allowance of £772.00 per annum for DIY/Maintenance and £400.00 per annum for gardening costs;

(2) These claims should be reduced by 50% as from the Claimant's 70th birthday to reflect the fact that such assistance may have been required from this point onwards irrespective of the accident;

(3) The multiplier for a fixed period of 29 years to 70 years of age is 20.71 [Table 28]. £1,172.00 × 20.71 = £24,272.12;

(4) Thereafter, £586.00 × 4.74 [25.45 − 20.71] = £2,777.64.

2. Calculation

(1)   Total for future DIY/Decoration/Gardening is **£27,049.76**.

XII. *Increased Holiday Costs*

1. Recital

(1)   The care experts agree a cost of £2,000.00 per annum towards future increased holiday costs [see joint statement];

(2)   25.45 × £2,000.00 per annum = £50,900;

(3)   In addition, a separate provision should be made for attending on a sailing holiday with the Jubilee Trust. The costs of this are estimated to be £1,947.00 (the Claimant and 2 carers) and are agreed by the care experts.

2. Calculation

(1)   Total for future holiday costs is **£52,847**.

XIII. *Disability Subscriptions*

1. Recital

(1)As recommended in the report of Mrs U dated 9th July 2012, a claim is made for the cost of lifetime membership with Headway at £250.00. This claim is agreed in the joint statement.

2. Calculation

(1)   Total for Disability Subscriptions is **£250.00**.

XIV. *Chiropody*

1. Recital

(1)   As recommended in the report of Mrs U dated 9th July 2012, a claim is made for the cost of chiropody at £250.00 pa. This claim is agreed in the joint statement.

(2)   25.45 lifetime multiplier × £250.00 = **£6,362.50**.

2. Calculation

(1)   Total for future chiropody is **£6,362.50**.

XV. *Carer/Support Worker Furnishings*

1. Recital

(1)   The Claimant's property is being specifically adapted to incorporate carer's accommodation. This area will require furnishing;

(2)   The Claimant relies upon the costs outlined in Mrs U's report dated 9th July 2012, repeated in the joint statement;

(3) A claim will be made for the immediate capital cost of furnishings at £1,995.86. A claim for annual replacement is made at £399.17 [£1995.86/5 year replacement]. Adopting a lifetime multiplier of 25.45, this equates to a further claim for £10,158.93.

2. Calculation

(1) Total for future carer/support worker furnishings is **£12,154.79**.

XVI. *Opthalmic Costs*

1. Recital

(1) As a result of his head injuries, the Claimant suffers from a right sided loss of visual field and a divergent strabismus, causing a loss of 3 dimensional vision;

(2) The jointly instructed ophthalmic expert, Mr L, recommends an orthoptic assessment at a cost of £50.00;

(3) Thereafter, Mr L recommends glasses and an annual ophthalmic assessment. The initial consultation will cost £150.00 and the repeat consultations £100.00. Including the cost of glasses at say £300.00 every 3 years, a claim will be made for these ongoing costs at £200.00 per annum. 25.45 × £200.00 = £5,090;

(4) Finally, Mr L recommends strabismus surgery to straighten the Claimant's eyes, at a cost of £3,750.00. This has an 80% chance of straightening the Claimant's eyes. However, there is a 20% chance of further surgery being required within a period of 3–6 months [£3,750 × 20% = £750.00] and a further 20% chance of surgery being repeated within 5–10 years [£3,750 x. 20% × 0.831 discount factor of 7.5 years [Table 27] = £623.25.

2. Calculation

(1) Total for future ophthalmic costs is **£10,413.25**.

XVII. *Orthotic Costs*

1. Recital

(1) The court is referred to the Orthotic Report prepared by Mr J (Senior Orthotist) dated 27th August 2013;

(2) The costs of supplying 2 suitable Ankle Foot Orthosis (AFOs) will be £624.12 every 4 years, equating to £156.03 per annum;

(3) £156.03 per annum × life expectancy of 25.45 = £3,970.96.

2. Calculation

(1) Total for future Orthotic costs is **£3,970.96**.

XVIII. *Deputy/Court of Protection Fees*

1. Recital

(1) The court is referred to the witness statement of Mr B for a breakdown of future Deputy and Court of Protection fees;

(2) The Professional Deputy Fees are estimated to be £12,500 per annum for say 2.5 years post disposal and £8,500 thereafter;

(3) A split multiplier is required. 2.42 for the first 2.5 years and 23.03 for the remaining period [25.45 – 2.42]. This equates to the following claim:
  i)   £12,500 × 2.42 = £30,250
  ii)   £8,500 × 23.03 = £195,755

(4) The Court of Protection Fees are as follows:
  (i)   Annual Supervision Fee: £320.00 pa × 25.45 = £4,576.25
  (ii)   Account Fees: £220.00 pa × 25.45 = £5,230.00
  (iii) Security Bond Fees: £625.00 pa × 25.45 = £9,152.50
  (iv)   Costs Draughtsman's fee: £550.00
  (v)   Statutory Will: £600 pa [£6,000 every 10 years] × 25.45 =£15,270
  (vi)   General disbursements: £200.00 pa × 25.45 = £5,090.00
  (vii) Transaction Fees: say £300.00 pa (£100.00 each × 3 pa) × 25.45 = £7,635
  (viii) Solicitors costs and disbursements for appointing new Deputy/ Obtaining new order: £225 pa [£2,250 every 10 years] × 25.45 = £5,726.25
  (ix)   Winding-up fee on death of patient: £1,850
  (x)   Contingency Sum: £35,000.

2. Calculation

(1) Total for future Deputy/ Court of Protection costs is **£316,085**.

H. Lost Years

1. Recital

(1) A claim is made for the lost pension income during the 2-year period where the Claimant's life expectancy had been reduced on account of his catastrophic injuries;

(2) This pension income comprises loss of final salary pension (the difference between spouses pension upon his death and the amount that the Claimant would have been received if alive, namely £6,250.00) plus loss of state pension at £4,953.00;

(3) As the Claimant is married with no children, it is appropriate deduct 50% this income for living expenses, providing a net loss of £5,601.50;

(4) The Claimant's lifetime multiplier in the absence of the accident would be 26.17 [Table 1 – 41 years of age]. As it is, the multiplier is 25.45, representing a multiplier loss of 0.72;

(5) 0.72 × £5,601.50 = £4,033.08.

2. Calculation

(1) Total for lost years is **£4,033.08**.

A Practitioner QC

B Practitioner

Statement of Truth

I believe that the contents of this schedule are true.

Signed by Litigation
Friend. . . . .

Print Name. . . . .

Date. . . . .

Served by the Claimant's Solicitors:

Hughton, Wolfswinkel & Bassong

11, Carrow Road

Norwich

Ref: FA/11v11,1.0

Appendix 1: Expert Evidence

Claimant's Expert Medical Evidence:	(i) Mr Z (Consultant Neurosurgeon) dated 28.03.2012 & 08.06.2013
	(ii) Professor Y (Consultant Neuropsychologist) dated 18.03.2012
	(iii) Dr X Consultant Psychiatrist) dated 06.05.2009 & 15.07.2012
	(iv) Mr W (Consultant General Surgeon) dated 20.03.2012
Claimant's Additional Expert Evidence:	(i) Mrs U (Care & Needs) dated 09.07.2012 & 07.08.2013
	(ii) Mr T (Accommodation) dated 15.04.2012
	(iii) PPO Viability Report from Mr S dated 15.09.2013
Defendant's Medico-Legal Evidence:	(i) Dr R (Consultant Neurosurgeon) dated 22.09.2012, 27.07.2013 & 18.08.2013
	(ii) Dr Q (Consultant Neuropsychologist) dated 28.05.2012
	(iii) Dr P (Consultant Psychiatrist) dated 20.02.2012

	(iv) Dr O (Consultant Physician) dated 27.05.2012 & 03.08.2013
Defendant's Additional Expert Evidence:	(i) Mrs N (Care & Needs) dated Sep 2012 & June 2013
	(ii) Mr M (Accommodation) dated 29.04.2012
Jointly Instructed Medico-Legal Evidence:	(i) Mr L (Consultant Ophthalmic Surgeon) dated 15.07.2012 & 08.09.2013
	(ii) Ms K (Chartered Physiotherapist) dated 30.04.2013
	(iii) Mr J (Orthotist) dated 27.08.13
	(iv) Miss I (Occupational Therapist) dated 16.06.2013

Joint Statements:
 (i)   Dr Z and Dr R (Neurological) dated 10.09.2013
 (ii) Prof Y and Dr Q (Neuropsychological) dated 20.09.2013
 (iii) Dr X and Dr P (Psychiatric) dated 29.08.2013
 (iv) Mr W and Dr O (Life Expectancy) dated 18.08.2013
 (v)   Mrs U and Mrs N (Care) dated 01.10.2013
 (vi) Mr T and Mr M (Accommodation) dated 29.08.2013

CHAPTER 17

FUTURE LOSS: LUMP SUM AWARDS, MULTIPLICANDS AND MULTIPLIERS

17.1 INTRODUCTION

The compensation objective in all personal injury litigation is the same, namely to place the injured party, as best as is possible, in the same financial position as they would have been in the absence of the accident.

The quantification of past loss is a question of assessing the costs that have already been incurred and the losses already suffered. Future loss post-trial involves large elements of guessing at the unknown. Although science and actuarial analysis can be brought to bear it is by definition an imprecise science that involves educated guess work. This is particularly so in catastrophic injury cases. The problems that have faced practitioners and judges historically are perfectly encapsulated in the well-known words of Lord Scarman in *Lim PohChoo v Camden and Islington Area Health Authority*:[1]

> 'The course of the litigation illustrates, with devastating clarity, the insuperable problems implicit in a system of compensation for personal injuries which (unless the parties agree otherwise) can yield only a lump sum assessed by the court at the time of judgment. Sooner or later, and too often later rather than sooner, if the parties do not settle, a court (once liability is admitted or proved) has to make an award of damages. The award, which covers past, present and future injury and loss, must, under our law, be of a lump sum assessed at the conclusion of the legal process. The award is final; it is not susceptible to review as the future unfolds, substituting fact for estimate. Knowledge of the future being denied to mankind, so much of the award as is to be attributed to future loss and suffering (in many cases the major part of the award) will almost surely be wrong. There is only one certainty: the future will prove the award to be either too high or too low.'

Since 1 April 2005 the landscape of quantifying future pecuniary loss has fundamentally changed with the introduction of periodical payment orders.[2] The courts now have the power to make a variable or non-variable periodical payment order that will cover any anticipated future loss or expense. This development, which is now the norm in catastrophic injury litigation, has gone a long way towards addressing the concerns highlighted by Lord Scarman in *Lim PohChoo*. However, the fact remains that some claimants continue to

---

[1] [1980] AC 174 at 192; [1979] 2 All ER 910 at 914.
[2] Section 2 of the Damages Act 1996 as substituted by s 100 of the Courts Act 2003.

prefer a traditional lump sum calculation for some or all of their future losses. For others, such as where there is a high degree of contributory negligence or pre-existing disability that will dictate the use of local authority care and meaningful indemnities unworkable, a lump sum may be the only workable arrangement. In this chapter we consider the calculation of future losses on a lump sum basis. Relatively small changes in the multiplicand or multiplier can, once multiplied up give rise to significant changes in the overall award and for that reason we will set out in some detail the rationale, limitations and practical explanation of the multiplicand/multiplier approach. The individual heads of claim are considered in Chapter 16 and periodical payment orders are considered in Chapter 18.

17.2   THE LUMP SUM

The traditional method of assessing future pecuniary loss and expense is based upon the application of a multiplicand and multiplier formula. The multiplicand is the annual sum required to replace a loss or need at a defined rate. The multiplier is the period by which the multiplicand is multiplied in order to arrive at a lump sum which, if invested, should last for a period equivalent to the future period of loss or expense. The lump sum effectively operates theoretically as an annuity that will be extinguished at the very end of the period of loss, be it:

(a)   a finite period of years to cover, for example, medical treatment;

(b)   a full life;

(c)   a working life lost as a result of the injuries;

(d)   a loss of pension between retirement and end of life;

(e)   a loss over the course of childhood until 18 years of age;

(f)   some other period adopted by the court.

17.3   THE MULTIPLICAND

The multiplicand is the annual loss or expense calculated at the date of the trial. In most catastrophic injury cases where a lump sum award is sought there will be a series of different multiplicands required for the various individual heads of loss such as care, case management, aids and equipment, therapies, medical expenses, loss of earnings and pension. No account is taken of future inflation in prices, which is worked into the discount rate applied to the multiplier (see 17.4 and 17.5 below). This was the focus of the conjoined appeals in the case of *Cooke v United Bristol Health Care*[3] where three severely and permanently disabled claimants sought to introduce expert evidence from a chartered accountant to the effect that the future cost of care in each case would be significantly underestimated on a traditional multiplicand/multiplier basis since care costs increased at a greater rate than the retail prices index (RPI). In order to address this potential shortfall, the chartered accountant argued that it was

---

[3]   [2004] 1 WLR 251.

necessary to use various different multiplicands with stepped increases over time. Dismissing the appeals, Laws LJ concluded that:[4]

> 'Once it is accepted that the discount rate is intended in any given personal injury case to be the only factor (in the equation ultimately yielding the claimant's lump sum payment) to allow for any future inflation relevant to the case, then the multiplicand cannot be taken as allowing for the same thing, or any part of it, without usurping the basis on which the multiplier has been fixed. And it must be accepted that the discount rate was so intended.'

However, the fact that the multiplicand is fixed at the date of trial without reference to future inflation does not mean that different multiplicands cannot be used for different periods of future loss. In catastrophic injury cases, claims for care and/or case management will often increase on a stepped basis. There may also be evidence that a claimant's earnings would have increased at certain ages in line with career development or promotion. In these circumstances, it is perfectly permissible to stagger the multiplicands for these claims, using split multipliers.

When deciding the multiplicand(s) to be adopted for future loss or expense, the court has to assess the *possibility* of the loss occurring after the trial and attempt to value that loss. The exercise is one of evaluating chances:[5]

> 'You can prove that a past event happened, but you cannot prove that a future event will happen and I do not think the law is so foolish as to suppose that you can. All that you can do is to evaluate the chance. Sometimes it is virtually 100%, sometimes virtually nil. But often it is somewhere in between. And if it is somewhere in between I do not see much difference between a probability of 51% and a probability of 49%.'

Specific examples of how this works in practice within the context of a loss of earnings claim are provided by the cases of *Doyle v Wallace*,[6] *Langford v Hebran*,[7] *Herring v Ministry of Defence*,[8] *Appleton v El Safty*,[9] *Smith and another v Collett*,[10] *Clarke v Maltby*,[11] *XYZ v Portsmouth Hospitals NHS Trust*[12] and *Mann v Bahri*.[13] In *Doyle*, a case involving a brain-damaged 19-year-old girl, the Court of Appeal upheld a decision of the trial judge to assess the claimant's loss of earnings multiplicand on the basis of the mid-point between the salary of an administrative worker and the salary of a teacher. This decision had been based upon a finding that the badly injured claimant would

---

[4]   At para 30.
[5]   Per Lord Reid in *Davis v Taylor* [1974] AC 207 at 213.
[6]   [1998] PIQR Q146.
[7]   [2001] EWCA Civ 361.
[8]   [2003] EWCA Civ 528.
[9]   [2007] EWHC 631 (QB).
[10] [2009] EWCA Civ 583.
[11] [2010] EWHC 1201 (QB).
[12] [2011] EWHC 243 (QB).
[13] Lawtel 11/4/2012.

certainly have achieved a position as an administrative employee and had a 50% chance of achieving the more financially advantageous role of a teacher.

In *Clarke v Maltby*, Owen J was required to assess a number of alternative career scenarios involving a solicitor who had suffered a traumatic brain injury in an accident. Each of these scenarios was based upon the claimant attaining a higher level of success and higher earnings but for the accident, with percentage chances being allotted to each scenario. The award for loss of earnings was calculated by reference to the claimant's baseline income (ie a baseline salary that would have undoubtedly been achieved) plus a percentage of higher earnings based on the percentage chance of attaining the higher levels of success.

The same logic will apply to other heads of claim. For example, if the medical evidence concludes that a brain-damaged claimant has a 20% chance of requiring an increased care and case management regime within a period of say 5 years, then the multiplicand applied for that cost of care and case management from 5 years forwards will be the base level plus 20% of the additional cost that would be incurred if the increased regime was in place.

17.4   THE MULTIPLIER

There are three fundamental features to be taken into account when assessing the appropriate multiplier for future losses and expenses:

(1) the arithmetical calculation of the actual period of loss or expense, commencing at the date of trial;

(2) the appropriate discount rate to be applied for early receipt of the lump sum, determined by the likely rate of interest to be earned on the lump sum in the future;

(3) the contingencies which may have affected the claimant in the future had he or she not been injured.

The first of these features will be a relatively straightforward exercise dependent upon the circumstances of each individual case.

The second feature is much more contentious and continues to dominate personal injury litigation to this day. In summary, the greater rate of return that one assumes on a lump sum investment, the lower the lump sum needs to be to produce enough income to meet the loss over the required period. Therefore, if one assumes a rate of return at 2.5% per annum (after inflation), the multiplier will be less than if the rate of return is assumed to be 1.5%. The following table, which illustrates the lump sum cost of a £50,000 a year future lifetime loss for a female claimant aged 15 at trial, is a stark example of how serious the implications of the discount rate are, both for a catastrophically injured claimant and the insurer who meets the claim.

Discount rate	Current 2.5%	At 1.5%	At 0.5%	At -0.5%
Multiplier	33.91	45.12	63.21	93.86
Lump sum amount (£)	£1,695,500	£2,256,000	£3,160,500	£4,693,000
% increase		+33%	+86%	+276%

Traditionally, multipliers were assessed in a rather rough and ready way using a discount rate of between 4% and 5% and a reduction from the multiplier chosen to account for contingencies in general. A system of actuarial tables, the Ogden Tables, had been in place since 1984, providing a ready means of calculating multipliers for both loss of earnings and lifetime losses. However, these tables were used inconsistently and more as an aid to checking multipliers calculated by conventional or intuitive means. The result was highly unsatisfactory, both in terms of the level of return that was assumed upon the lump sum investment and the unpredictability of the multiplier chosen in the first place.

These concerns gave rise to the seminal decision of the House of Lords in the conjoined cases of *Wells v Wells, Thomas v Brighton Health Authority and Page v Sheerness*,[14] where it was held that, save in exceptional circumstances such as a marked change in economic climate or exceptionally high taxation leading to lower return, the discount rate should be fixed on the basis that the claimant would invest in index-linked government securities (ILGS) and yield a return in the region of 3% net of tax per annum.

The critical reasoning behind this decision was that investment in ILGS represented a low risk and reliable investment strategy. Although it was accepted that a prudent investor could achieve a return of more than 3% per annum with a more risky equity-based investment strategy, the House of Lords found that it was unreasonable to place a claimant in such a position. Lord Steyn summarised the position as follows:[15]

> 'The premise that the claimants, who have perhaps been very seriously injured, are in the same position as ordinary investors is not one that I can accept. Such claimants have not chosen to invest: the tort and its consequences compel them to do so ... Typically, by investing in equities an ordinary investor takes a calculated risk which he can bear in order to improve his financial position. On the other hand, the typical claimant requires the return from an award of damages to provide the necessities of life.'

The second ground-breaking consequence of the House of Lords decision in *Wells v Wells* was the endorsement of a system of actuarial tables (the Ogden Tables) as a starting point for determining future multipliers. In his judgment to the House, Lord Lloyd of Berwick described the use of the actuarial tables as follows:[16]

---

[14]   [1999] 1 AC 345.
[15]   [1999] 1 AC 345 at 353D and F.
[16]   [1999] 1 AC 345 at 346b.

'A judge should be slow to depart from the relevant actuarial multiplier on impressionistic grounds, or by reference to a "spread of multipliers in comparable cases" especially when the multipliers were fixed before the actuarial tables were widely used.'

Lord Lloyd of Berwick went on to highlight that there was no longer any room for judicial discount when calculating the lifetime multiplier for a claimant from the Ogden Tables (unless there was clear medical evidence of a reduction in life expectancy) as the contingency of falling short of or exceeding this multiplier could work in either direction. In contrast, the courts would retain the right to reduce the multiplier for loss of earnings on the basis that the risk of contingencies materialising in relation to a claimant's working life would generally only work in favour of the defendant.

17.5   THE DAMAGES ACT 1996 AND THE LORD CHANCELLOR'S DECISION ON 25 JUNE 2001

Following on from *Wells v Wells*, there was concern amongst practitioners and commentators alike[17] that a discount rate of 3% was not in line with the average (and falling) rate of return upon ILGS. In *Warren v Northern General Hospital NHS Trust (No 2)*[18] some £2.5m was awarded at trial for future loss based upon a discount rate of 3%. On appeal, the claimant relied upon evidence to show that the average rate of return on ILGS had fallen to closer to 2% per annum. The appellant also contended that the rate of return should be reduced because the incidence of taxation on higher awards distorted the rate of return and led to under-compensation. The Court of Appeal rejected the appeal on the basis that the rate of return upon ILGS was liable to fluctuate and the discount rate would stay at 3% until the Lord Chancellor exercised his power to set a different rate under the Damages Act 1996. The Court of Appeal further concluded that it would only be in the most exceptional circumstances that a lower discount rate would be appropriate, such as where the claimant was subject to an unusually high level of taxation that served to distort the income received from the award.

In March 2000 the then Lord Chancellor, Lord Irvine of Lairg, initiated a consultation process that resulted in the Damages (Personal Injury) Order 2001[19] coming into force on 25 June 2001. Under this order, for the first time, the Lord Chancellor decided to exercise his right to fix the discount rate under the Damages Act 1996 and did so at a figure of 2.5%. In the notice accompanying the decision, the Lord Chancellor provided the following background to his decision:

'In determining the discount rate, I have applied the appropriate legal principle laid down authoritatively by the courts, and in particular by the House of Lords in *Wells v Wells* [1999] 1 AC 345.

---

17   Including Sir Michael Ogden QC.
18   [2000] 1 WLR 1404.
19   SI 2001/2301.

I also consider that it is highly desirable to exercise my powers under the Act so as to produce a situation in which claimants and defendants may have a reasonably clear idea about the impact of the discount rate upon their cases, so as to facilitate negotiation of settlements and the presentation of cases in court. In order to promote this objective, I have concluded that I should:

a.　set a single rate to cover all cases. This accords with the solution adopted by the House of Lords in *Wells v Wells*. It will eliminate scope for uncertainty and argument about the applicable rate. Similarly, I consider it is preferable to have a fixed rate, which promotes certainty and which avoids the complexity and extra costs that a formula would entail;

b.　set a rate which is easy for all parties and their lawyers to apply in practice and which reflects the fact that the rate is bound to be applied in a range of different circumstances over a period of time. For this reason, I consider it appropriate to set the discount rate to the nearest half per cent., so as to ensure that the figure will be suitable for use in conjunction with the Ogden Tables, which are a ready means for parties to take into account actuarial factors in computing the quantum of damages;

c.　set a rate which should obtain for the foreseeable future. I consider it would be very detrimental to the reasonable certainty which is necessary to promote the just and efficient resolution of disputes (by settlement as well as by hearing in court) to make frequent changes to the discount rate. Therefore, whilst I will remain ready to review the discount rate whenever I find there is a significant and established change in the relevant real rates of return to be expected, I do not propose to tinker with the rate frequently to take account of every transient shift in market conditions.'

The Lord Chancellor's basis for setting the discount rate at 2.5% was that the average gross yield on ILGS in the 3 years leading up to June 2001 was 2.61%. Accounting for tax, this justified a discount rate of between 2 and 2.5%, with 2.5% preferred.

Within a matter of weeks, the Lord Chancellor had revisited this decision as a result of questions about the 3-year average yield figure upon which he had relied. This led to a formal statement from his department published on 27 July 2001. A full copy of this statement can be found in *Facts and Figures: Tables for the Calculation of Damages*[20] and the Ministry of Justice website.[21] However, in summary, the Lord Chancellor endorsed his decision to set the discount rate at 2.5% for the following reasons:

(1)　It was accepted that the gross redemption yield figure for ILGS was 2.46% per annum, not the 2.61% previously stated. However, the 2.46% figure assumed an inflation figure of 3% extending into the future. In fact, it was likely that inflation would remain close to or below a figure of 2.5%, in line with government policy, and this was likely to lead to a higher rate of return than 2.46%.

(2)　The prevailing rate of return on ILGS did not produce a pure and undistorted measure of the real rate of return which could be achieved on the market. Having taken financial advice, the Lord Chancellor concluded

---

[20]　Sweet & Maxwell; 2013/14 edition.
[21]　www.justice.gov.uk.

that continuing high demand for ILGS and scarcity of supply had led to artificially low yields and there was a reasonable prospect of a reversion to higher rates of return in the future when the government's plans to abolish the minimum funding requirement introduced by the Pensions Act 1995 came into effect.

(3)   It was noted that the Court of Protection had continued to invest in multi-asset portfolios, comprising a mixture of equities, gilts and cash, producing rates of return well in excess of 2.5%. It therefore appeared that there were sensible, low risk investment strategies available that would enable claimants to achieve a rate of return above 2.5% without being exposed to undue risk.

(4)   It remained open to the courts under s 1(2) of the Damages Act 1996 to adopt a different discount rate in any particular case if there were exceptional circumstances justifying a departure from 2.5%.

17.6   DAMAGES ACT 1996, SECTION 1(2)

In *Warriner v Warriner*[22] a brain-damaged claimant was given permission at a case management hearing to rely upon forensic accountancy evidence to the effect that a 2.5% discount rate was insufficient for those awarded substantial sums of money that had to last a long time. It was asserted that the claimant, who had a life expectancy of 46 years, would achieve a return (after tax) of only 2.12% on an award of £1m, 1.97% on £2m and 1.86% on £2.75m. In the circumstances, it was argued that the discount rate set down by the Lord Chancellor was too simplistic and should be varied by the court under s 1(2) of the Damages Act 1996.

The Court of Appeal subsequently overturned the decision to allow the claimant to rely upon expert accountancy evidence. It was held that the intention of the Lord Chancellor had been to eliminate the need to call such expert evidence and the claimant had not identified any special features of her case that had not already been taken into account when the Lord Chancellor set the discount rate at 2.5%. Accordingly, there were no exceptional circumstances that justified applying a lower discount rate. A similar decision was made by the Court of Appeal in *Cooke v United Bristol Health Care*[23] and highlighted again in the case *of Flora v Wakom (Heathrow) Ltd*.[24]

Section 1(2) of the Damages Act 1996 recently resurfaced in the case of *Harries (A Child) v Stevenson*,[25] in which it was said that a PPO to cover substantial future care and accommodation needs would not be available at trial because the defendant and his funder (the Medical Defence Union) were unable to provide reasonable security for payments under a PPO. The claimant's case was that, if a discount rate of 2.5% was adopted he would be undercompensated by

---

[22]   [2002] 1 WLR 1703.
[23]   [2004] 1 WLR 251.
[24]   [2005] PIQR Q7.
[25]   [2012] EWHC 3447 (QB).

an amount in excess of £2m and therefore a lower rate was justified using s 1(2). Having considered the relevant authorities (outlined above), Morgan J concluded that before the claimant could bring his case within s 1(2), he had to show that it either: (a) fell into a category which the Lord Chancellor did not take into account; or (b) had special features which were material to the choice of the rate of return and were shown from an examination of the Lord Chancellor's reasons not to have been taken into account. In his judgment, neither of these applied and the claimant's case was a direct attack on the prescribed rate that could not be permitted. At para 55 of his judgment Morgan J accepted that *Helmot v Simon*, below, reflected the common law position, but held that given the terms of the Damages Act the relevance of *Helmot* was that where a judge was entitled to depart from the prescribed rate then he might well do so.

17.6.1   Helmot v Simon and the discount rate consultation

Since 2001 the economic data has shown that ILGS do not yield an average income of 2.5% after inflation. In fact, the return has been considerably lower over the past 10 years. This means that the assumption of a claimant investing his damages in ILGS and achieving the required rate of return to meet future losses is flawed. As an alternative, it has not been possible for a claimant to achieve anywhere close to the required rate of return by putting money in a bank/building society as interest rates remain so low. In effect, an injured claimant has been left with very little option but to take investment risks (usually by way of investing in the stock market) if he/she is to have any chance of a lump sum meeting future needs. This cannot be satisfactory. Indeed, there will be a sizeable number of claimants in this position who will have lost money (hence their ability to meet their future needs) by taking such risks.

The problem is compounded as there are certain heads of damages (notably care and case management) where prices on earnings are demonstrably increasing at a higher rate than conventional RPI inflation. This means that it is even harder for lump sum damages to meet the rising costs of such future outlay. In fact it is nigh on impossible. Similar considerations apply if the claimant is a higher rate taxpayer who is required to pay 40-50% tax on any investment returns achieved on their lump sum damages.

The introduction of PPOs have heralded an easy solution to the problem. You can seek a tax-free PPO to meet future care, case management and loss of earnings and uprate this every year in accordance with a suitable *earnings based index* that keeps in line with rises in inflation on earnings. However, as we have previously discussed, PPOs are not available in every case and sometimes a claimant will prefer the flexibility of a lump sum – particularly if there is a need for large capital expenditure. If so, the reality is that a lump sum based on a discount rate of 2.5% is very unlikely to produce adequate future compensation.

17.6.2   Helmot v Simon [2012] UKPC 5

The case of *Helmot v Simon* was determined in Guernsey, which is not subject to the jurisdiction of the Damages Act 1996 and the imposed discount rate of 2.5%. The claimant also did not have the opportunity to argue for a PPO as legislation had not been passed to enable the courts to make such an order in Guernsey. It was therefore a perfect opportunity for a claimant to demonstrate that a lower discount rate was required if lump sum damages were to be sought – particularly in relation to earnings based damages (such as care and loss of earnings).

The case was initially determined in the Royal Court in Guernsey in early 2010 before a Deputy Bailiff and three Jurats. The claimant relied upon extensive financial/actuarial evidence to justify lower discount rates for specific heads of loss (evidence that was barely challenged in cross examination). In response the defendant argued for the straightforward application of the 2.5% discount rate imposed by the Lord Chancellor in England, Wales and NI. At the end of a 6-week hearing the court awarded global damages of £9,337,852.27 plus interest, with a 1% discount rate applied to all elements of future recurring loss.

On appeal to the Guernsey Court of Appeal both parties argued that the 1% discount rate was wrong. The claimant/appellant argued that a lower discount rate was justified and the defendant maintained its support for application of the Lord Chancellor's prescribed rate of 2.5%. Sitting as the presiding judge in the Guernsey Court of Appeal, Jonathan Sumption QC (now Lord Sumption) found that a discount rate of 0.5% should apply for non-earnings related losses and -1.5% for earnings related losses. This made an enormous difference to the resultant lump sums, with global damages increasing to circa £14m.

The defendant subsequently (unsuccessfully) appealed the decision of the CA in Guernsey to the Privy Council. The judgment of the Privy Council given in 2012, which should be read in full, is of significant consequence to PI/clinical negligence practitioners, as it highlights the potential inequities of the current discount rate and challenges the assumption that a single discount rate always has to be adopted:

> 'It would be wrong to do that if the evidence showed that, if that were to be done, a given head of loss would not be fully compensated [per Lord Hope at para 53 of the judgment]'

17.6.3   The consultation period

In late 2010, on the back of the decision of the Guernsey Court of Appeal in *Helmot v Simon* and persistent lobbying by interest groups such as APIL, the Lord Chancellor/Minister of Justice (then Ken Clarke MP) agreed to conduct a review of the discount rate under the Damages Act 1996. Unfortunately, a lengthy period of prevarication and delay thereafter occurred on the part of the government (leading to Judicial Review Proceedings by APIL) and a discount rate consultation paper was only published in August 2012. This consultation paper broadly considered two options:

(1) carrying on as before and using the assumption that ILGS investment is appropriate (on this basis, given historical returns over the past 10 years, it would be hard to justify anything other than a discount rate deduction);

(2) consideration should be given to the assumption that a claimant will invest their damages in a mixed portfolio of assets/investments and yield a higher return (on this basis, an argument could be made for preserving the present discount rate).

Of course, the problem with the second option is that it assumes a degree of investment risk on the part of an injured claimant, contrary to *Wells v Wells*.

In February 2013, following the end of the first consultation process in October 2012, the Ministry of Justice announced the publication of a second consultation paper: 'The Discount Rate – Review of the Legal Framework'. The contents of this paper appear to reinforce the view that the MOJ is potentially looking to change the parameters used to set the discount rate away from the approach advocated under *Wells v Wells* – namely that the rate of investment return should be based on potential returns available from ILGS because this exposes a claimant to minimal investment risk. The most recent consultation paper suggests that the MOJ is now actively considering two options:

(1) setting the discount rate based on the assumption that an injured claimant will invest in a mixed portfolio of financial assets rather than ILGS alone. This could lead to a higher or lower discount rate depending upon how the portfolio is defined. If anything, the consultation paper hints at an increase being most likely;

(2) encouraging greater use of periodical payment orders.

The suggestion that a catastrophically injured claimant should have to invest their damages in a risk-laden mixed portfolio of financial assets is a most alarming proposition. Furthermore, the MOJ appears to be ignoring the fact that PPOs are not always a viable option in PI litigation. Ultimately, it is impossible to avoid the conclusion that politics + economics = the driving force behind the decisions that will be taken under the consultation.

What about the prospect of differing discount rates? This has also been addressed in the consultation papers, no doubt on the back of the decision in *Helmot v Simon*. Although there are good arguments in favour of such an approach (it is logical that different heads of loss should be prescribed different discount rates to account for different indices of future inflation), it would also prove complex, liable to regular variation and impracticable for practitioners and courts to operate. The general expectation, therefore, is that we will continue to operate within the confines of a single discount rate.

Where does that leave us? As things stand, until a decision on the discount rate is made, the only advice that one can properly give is to plead and seek a PPO in all substantial cases where applicable and attempt to argue for an over-inflated lump sum to buy off the PPO if that is what the claimant wants. It is also important to advise solicitors and clients that an *increase* in the discount rate remains a real possibility.

17.7   SPECIFIC MULTIPLIERS IN CATASTROPHIC INJURY CASES

The Ogden Tables have changed the calculation of multipliers completely. The tables are set out in a user friendly manner and with helpful explanations as to their use in *Facts and Figures*.[26] With this in mind, we have focused upon the core principles relevant to the multipliers commonly used in catastrophic injury litigation.

17.7.1   Multipliers for life

The initial presumption is that a claimant has a normal life expectancy, calculated by reference to 'Expectation of Life' tables produced by the ONS[27] using projected changes in mortality assumed in 2010-based population projections. The multiplier for normal life expectancy will be obtained from Tables 1 (male) and 2 (female) of the Ogden Tables at a current discount rate of 2.5%. Tables 1-26 of the 7th edn Ogden Tables are based on the projected mortality rates underlying the 2008-based population projections. This means that the Ogden Tables are currently slightly out of kilter with the Expectation of Life Tables.

One potential area of contention is that the tables relate to life expectancy in the UK as a whole, whereas life expectancy does differ between each constituent country within the UK and within different geographical components of each constituent country (by way of example, a typical resident of the South East England will statistically have a longer life expectancy than a resident of South West Scotland). Arguments of this type have yet to be tested in the courts but will no doubt come to the fore in due course.

The presumption of normal life expectancy will be rebutted if there is cogent evidence to suggest a shorter or longer life expectancy. Claimants should be careful before acceding to arguments fora reduced life expectancy on the basis of lifestyle factors such as drinking or smoking. The fact remains that the Ogden Tables are based on the average life expectancy of a cross section of society including those that drink and smoke. Arguments of this type cut both

---

[26]   Sweet & Maxwell; 2013/14 edition.

[27]   As set out at section A3 of *Facts & Figures*.

ways and will inevitably undermine the consistent application of life expectancy calculations in the majority of personal injury/clinical negligence cases.[28]

Although advances in science and medicine have continued to improve the outlook, it is a sad fact that the victims of catastrophic injuries will very often be left with a shortened expectation of life as a result of their continuing disability. The factors which may prejudice longevity will depend upon the precise nature of the injuries which have been suffered and should be addressed in the medico-legal evidence. If a claimant is not able to self-feed then that may have an adverse effect upon life expectancy. The risk factors for wheelchair-bound claimants include:

(a)   skin problems, including pressure sores leading to chronic sepsis;

(b)   chest infections, consequent upon the paralysis of the intercostal muscles;

(c)   urinary tract infections and/or ascending cystic degeneration of the urinary bladder;

(d)   kidney infection;

(e)   osteoporosis and bone fractures;

(f)   ascending syringomyelia;

(g)   high blood pressure with the risk of intracranial haemorrhage;

(h)   depression.

Where a claimant's life expectancy is placed in issue, it will be a matter for the court to determine that life expectancy, using a combination of medical and statistical evidence.[29] In *Lewis (A Child) v Royal Shrewsbury NHS Trust*,[30] His Honour Judge MacDuff QC (now MacDuff J) rejected the approach put forward on behalf of the 11-year-old claimant (who had been born with athetoid cerebral palsy) which relied solely on medical evidence, using the life tables as a starting point for the calculation of life expectancy and then making deductions for each risk factor affecting the claimant. His Honour Judge MacDuff QC held that this method lacked any scientific or statistical support and was prone to uncertainty. Instead, the appropriate starting point for a patient with cerebral palsy was a specific life table constructed for that segment of the population. Thereafter, it was appropriate to have regard to the clinical evidence and, if appropriate, adjustments would be made in light of clinical opinion one way or another.

In *Arden v Malcom*,[31] Tugendhat J held that clinicians should be the normal and primary route through which statistical evidence was put before the court. It was only if there was a disagreement between clinicians on a statistical matter that the evidence of a statistician would be required. The point being that clinicians have the opportunity to tailor life expectancy on a case-by-case basis,

---

[28]   See *Edwards v Martin* [2010] EWHC 570 (QB) for an example of a case where the court rejected the defendant's argument for a reduction in life expectancy based on lifestyle factors.

[29]   *Royal Victoria Infirmary NHS Trust v B (A Child)* [2002] EWCA Civ 348.

[30]   LTL, 14 June 2007 (unreported elsewhere).

[31]   [2007] EWCH 404.

with the use of statistics forming part of this process. Where statistical analysis is used to determine life expectancy it is important to consider whether the statistical basis used is appropriate without any adjustment. In some cases, such as the determination of life expectancy for cerebral palsy patients relying on the work in California of Professor Strauss and his colleagues, the published papers will be based on US general population life expectancy rates. It is easy to assume that US life expectancy rates are at least as good as those in the UK given that the US is an advanced economy with good health care. It can, however, be dangerous to do so as the figures do differ. Furthermore, the Strauss papers do not contain data relating to individuals aged between 3½ and 15 years of age.[32]

Where the clinical evidence provides for an agreed life expectancy, or the trial judge makes a determination on actual life expectancy (usually the case in cerebral palsy and spinal cord injury cases), Table 28 of the Ogden Tables should be used to calculate the applicable life expectancy without any further discount (using the 2.5% rate of return column).[33] The logic behind this process is that a clinical judgment has already accounted for mortality risk factors and therefore the use of Tables 1 (male) or 2 (female), which account for mortality, would involve a double discount.

By way of example, if there is an agreed life expectancy of a further 25 years at trial, the appropriate multiplier using Table 28 will be 18.65 (2.5%).

In contrast, where the clinical evidence results in an agreed reduction of years from a normal life expectancy, it has generally been appropriate to use Tables 1 or 2 of the Ogden Tables, treating the claimant as X years older (X being the period of agreed reduction of years). This approach was taken in *Smith v LC Window Fashions Ltd*,[34] where the medical experts agreed that the life expectancy of a brain-damaged 52-year-old claimant had been reduced by 6.5 years. Cranston J held that the medical evidence in the case did not decide for how long the claimant would live, but instead determined by how long his pre-morbid statistical life expectancy had been reduced. Accordingly, there was no double discount in the use of Table 1.[35]

By way of example, if a 28-year-old male claimant has an agreed reduction in life expectancy of 5 years, it will be necessary to use Ogden Table 1 and treat the claimant as a 33-year-old man at trial, leading to a multiplier of 28.75.

It is important to point out that, where the agreed reduction in life expectancy is substantial, involving 'massive permanent disability', the use of Tables 1 and

---

[32]   See *Whiten v St George's Healthcare NHS Trust* [2011] EWHC 2066 (QB) for further analysis of these issues.

[33]   See *Whiten v St George's Healthcare NHS Trust* [2011] EWHC 2066 (QB), *Davies v Bradshaw* [2008] EWHC 740 (QB), *Burton v Kingsbury* [2007] EWCH 2091 and *Sarwar v (1) Ali and (2) MIB (No 1)* [2007] EWHC 274 (QB).

[34]   [2009] EWHC 1532.

[35]   See also *Crofts v Murton*, Lawtel 10 September 2008 (unreported elsewhere).

2 as a reference point is not satisfactory.[36] In these circumstances, the medical experts should be asked to provide a figure for actual life expectancy so that Ogden Table 28 can be used.

The clinical evidence required to determine life expectancy will be dependent upon the precise nature of the injuries sustained. It is now common practice for a consultant general surgeon or physician to report on the issue of life expectancy, but in catastrophic injury cases it is important to obtain the input from the experts in the relevant field of injury, usually neurology, spinal cord injury and/or rehabilitation.

17.7.2 Multipliers for loss of earnings/income

Until the introduction of the 6th and then 7th edn of the Ogden Tables, the calculation of future loss of earnings was a relatively simplistic process:

(1) take claimant's age at date of trial;

(2) identify claimant's retirement age;

(3) choose the relevant multiplier using Tables 3–14 at a discount rate of 2.5%;

(4) make a discount from the multiplier to account for contingencies other than mortality including age, gender, type of occupation, geographical location and economic climate (using Tables A–C in earlier editions of the Ogden Tables);

(5) identify the appropriate multiplicand for loss of earnings;

(6) multiply the discounted multiplier by the multiplicand to calculate income but for the accident (the 'but for' figure);

(7) carry out the same process for any residual earnings that the claimant may have and then deduct this figure (the 'residual' figure) from the 'but for' figure to produce a net loss of future earnings;

(8) add a lump sum *Smith v Manchester* award to make up for any additional weakness faced by the claimant on the labour market.

The 6th edition of the Ogden Tables heralded a significant change in the way in which the multipliers for future loss of earnings were calculated and claims were made. The introduction to these tables highlighted the inclusion of a new Section B, based upon research carried out by Professor Richard Verrall, Professor Steven Haberman, Mr Zoltan Butt and Dr Victoria Vass into the impact of contingencies other than mortality on working life. This research demonstrated that people without disabilities spend more time out of employment than earlier research had suggested. As a result, it is appropriate to apply a higher discount for contingencies other than mortality than was previously recommended in the earlier Ogden Tables. The research also demonstrated that, other than gender, the factors that had most effect on a person's future employment status are: (i) whether the person was employed or

---

[36] As per Thorpe LJ in *Royal Victoria NHS Trust* [2002] PIQR Q137 at para 46.

unemployed at the outset; (ii) whether the person is disabled or not; and (iii) the educational attainment of the person. In contrast, the factors previously relied upon to justify contingency discounts (ie gender, age, occupation, geography and economic climate) were relatively insignificant.

The starting point is now to calculate the earnings that the claimant is likely to have achieved but for the accident. The following is an example:

The claimant, who has been catastrophically injured, is 35 at trial and intended to retire at 60 but for the accident. At the time of the accident she was earning £20,000 per annum net and these earnings would have continued into the future. The claimant was in full employment, not disabled and had A-Level qualifications. She has no residual earning capacity due to her injuries/ disabilities.

Step 1: Appropriate table for loss of earnings for a 35-year-old female with retirement age of 60 is Ogden Table 8.

Step 2: The base multiplier for loss of earnings for a 35-year-old female at 2.5% is 18.43.

Step 3: The appropriate discount for a 35-year-old female assuming that the accident had never occurred and she had remained not-disabled is 0.86 (Table C in Section B, not-disabled, aged 35-39 at trial, employed, category GEA educational attainment).

Step 4: 18.43 × 0.86 = discounted multiplier of 15.85.

Step 5: Loss of Earnings is £20,000 × 15.85 = £316,800.

The sad reality is that, in the majority of catastrophic injury claims, the claimant will have no residual earning capacity. However, in the event there is some residual earning capacity, the calculation for that residual earning capacity must follow the same process. Let us say that the same 35-year-old catastrophically injured female claimant remained unemployed at the date of trial but was seeking some part-time therapeutic employment providing a small income of say £5,000 per annum net. This residual earning capacity would be calculated as follows:

Step 1: Appropriate table for loss of earnings for a 35-year-old female with retirement age of 60 is Ogden Table 8.

Step 2: The base multiplier for a 35-year-old female at 2.5% is 18.43.

Step 3: The appropriate discount for a 35-year-old female accounting for the accident and resultant disability, leading to her current unemployment will be 0.28 (Table D in Section B, disabled, aged 35-39 at trial, non-employed, category GEA educational status).

Step 4: 18.43 × 0.28 = discounted multiplier of 5.16.

Step 5: Residual earnings £5,000 × 5.16 = £25,800.

Step 6: £316,800 – £25,800 = £291,000 net loss.

In the event that the same claimant may have gained promotion in the future in the absence of the accident, it may be possible to present the claim on the basis of a loss of chance of achieving that position. If the evidence points towards a 1 in 4 chance of achieving that position (25%) within a period of say 5 years, leading to an increased salary of £30,000 per annum net, the calculation would require a split multiplicand and multiplier as follows:

Step 1: Appropriate table for 35-year-old female with retirement age of 60 is Ogden Table 8.

Step 2: The base multiplier for a 35-year-old female at 2.5% is 18.43.

Step 3: The multiplier for a term certain of 25 years (ignoring mortality risks) is 18.65 (Ogden Table 28).

Step 4: The term certain multiplier needs to be split so that each individual segment of the whole working life period (25 years) is represented by a figure. This is achieved as follows:

Step 5: Split multiplier into two periods:
(i)   first 5 years: Multiplier for fixed period 5 years = 4.70 (Ogden Table 28);
(ii)   remaining period: 13.95 (18.65 – 4.70).

Step 6: Each of these split multipliers needs to reflect a percentage of the whole term certain. On this basis, 4.70 represents 25.20% of 18.65 (4.70/18.65) and 13.95 represents 74.80% (13.95/18.65).

Step 7: The working life multiplier from Table 8 can now be split into identical proportions in which the Table 28 multiplier has been treated. The first 5-year period is now represented by a multiplier of 4.64 (18.43 × 25.20%) and the remaining period is represented by a multiplier of 13.79 (18.43 × 74.80%).

Step 8: The appropriate discount for a 35-year-old female assuming that the accident had never occurred and she had remained not-disabled is 0.86 (Table C in Section B, not-disabled, aged 35-39 at trial, employed, category GEA educational attainment).

Step 9: Apply discount to split multipliers:
(i)   4.64 × 0.86 = 3.99;
(ii)   13.79 × 0.86 = 11.86.

Step 10: Split multiplicands:

(i)   first 5 years: £20,000 per annum;

(ii) remaining earnings: £22,500 per annum (based on 25% chance increased promotion to £30,000 per annum).

Step 11: Multiply split multiplicands by split multipliers:

(i)   £20,000 × 3.99 = £79,800;

(ii) £22,500 × 11.86 = £266,850.

Step 12: £79,800 + £266,850 = £346,650.

The cases of *Al Conner v Bradman*,[37] *Hunter v Ministry of Defence*,[38] *Garth v (1) Grant (2) MIB*,[39] *Hunter v MOD*,[40] *Hopkinson v MOD*,[41] *Peters v East Midlands SHA*,[42] *Leesmith v Evans*,[43] *McGhee v Diageo plc*,[44] *Huntley v Simmonds*,[45] *Fleet v Fleet*,[46] *Watson v Cakebread*,[47] *Clarke v Maltby*,[48] *Edwards v Martin*,[49] *XYZ v Portsmouth Hospitals NHS Trust*,[50] *Connery v PHS*,[51] *Johnson v Fourie*,[52] *Hindmarch v Virgin Atlantic*,[53] *Higgs v Pickles*,[54] and *Whiten v St George's Healthcare NHS Trust*,[55] all provide examples of how the courts have applied this approach in practice. The case-law in this area reflects the recommendations given in the guidance notes to Ogden 6/7, namely that Tables A to D provide a ready reckoner, but the individual circumstances of each case will be critical to the approach that will be taken by the court and it may be appropriate to argue for higher or lower adjustments. This has inevitably led to a level of inconsistency and unpredictability in the valuation of loss of earnings claims (to be discussed further in Chapter 18).

In catastrophic injury claims, there will be no difficulty satisfying the court that the claimant satisfies the criteria of disabled and that the options for future employment are seriously limited, if not extinguished. The most likely areas of contention will be whether there should be any allowance for residual capacity, and if so, whether the contingency discount should be higher than the Table B

---

[37] [2007] EWHC 2789.
[38] [2007] NIQB 43.
[39] Lawtel 17/7/2007.
[40] [2007] NIQB 43.
[41] [2008] EWHC 699 (QB).
[42] [2008] EWHC 778 (QB).
[43] [2008] EWHC 134.
[44] [2008] CSOH 74.
[45] [2009] EWHC 405 (QB).
[46] [2009] EWHC 3166 (QB).
[47] [2009] EWHC 1695 (QB).
[48] .[2010] EWHC 1856 (QB).
[49] .[2010] EWHC 570 (QB).
[50] .[2011] EWHC 243 (QB).
[51] .[2011] EWHC 1685 (QB).
[52] .[2011] EWHC 1062 (QB).
[53] .[2011] EWHC 1227 (QB).
[54] .[2011] PIQR P15.
[55] .[2011] EWHC 2066 (QB).

and D figures to account for the substantial level of disability affecting the claimant's prospects on the labour market.

It should be noted that Tables A–D at Section B of the explanatory notes to the 7th edition Ogden Tables cover claimants of between the ages 16–54 at trial. There is no reason why the tables cannot be used for claimants outside this age bracket and *Facts and Figures* provides an extrapolation to higher ages. Outside of the Ogden bracket, however, the discount may more readily be determined by individual circumstances.[56]

It is hoped and anticipated that Ogden 8 will provide further guidance/clarification on the application of Ogden contingency discounts.

17.7.3   Multipliers for loss of pension

An analysis of pension loss is provided in Chapter 18. The multiplier for loss of pension (final salary) is assessed as at the future date of retirement. There are two different ways of calculating this.

The first method, known as the 'Auty' approach,[57] involves using the life tables[58] and working out the claimant's life expectancy as at the date of his or her normal retirement. This figure is then converted into a multiplier using Ogden Table 28 at 2.5% rate of return. By way of example:

The claimant is a 40-year-old male at trial who would have retired at 65 but for the accident. As a result of his injuries, the claimant will not be able to return to work and this has resulted in a loss of his final salary pension. The loss of this final salary pension (calculated as a net loss on an annual basis) will commence as from 65 years of age to death.

Step 1: Life expectancy for 40-year-old male: 46.2 (Table A3) – ie 21.2 years beyond 65.

Step 2: Appropriate multiplier for period of 21.2 years is 16.50 (Ogden Table 28 – interpolating between the multipliers for 21 and 22 years fixed using 2.5%).

Step 3: Apply multiplier of 16.50 × net loss multiplicand.

Step 4: Discount sum achieved for accelerated receipt of monies using Ogden Table 27 (in this case, by a factor of 25 years = 0.5394 using 2.5%).

Step 5: Discount for contingencies (dependent upon individual circumstances).

---

[56] .See *Fleet v Fleet* [2009] EWHC 3166 (QB) and *Watson v Cakebread* [2009] EWHC 1695 (QB).

[57] *Auty v National Coal Board* [1985] 1 All ER 930.

[58] Section A3 of *Facts and Figures*.

In the event that the same male claimant is married and his spouse is entitled to a widow's pension upon his death, this needs to be reflected in the multiplier. Let us say that the wife is 35 years of age at trial and is entitled to 50% of her husband's pension upon death. The calculation along Auty lines will be as follows:

Step 1: Life Expectancy for 40-year-old male: 46.2 (Table A3) – ie 21.2 years beyond 65.

Step 2: Appropriate multiplier for period of 21.2 years is 16.50 (Ogden Table 28 – interpolating between the multipliers for 21 and 22 years fixed using 2.5%).

Step 3: Life Expectancy for 35-year-old female: 55.1 (Table A3) – ie 25.1 years beyond 65.

Step 4: Appropriate multiplier for period of 25.1 years is 18.70 (Ogden Table 28).

Step 5: Since the spouse's pension is 50% of the value of her husband's pension for the period that she outlives him, the claimant's multiplier should be increased by 1.1, representing 50% of the difference between his multiplier (16.50) and her multiplier (18.70). This equates to a revised multiplier of 17.6.

Step 6: Apply multiplier of 17.6 × net loss multiplicand.

Step 7: Discount lump sum achieved for accelerated receipt of monies using Ogden Table 27 (in this case, by a factor of 25 years = 0.5394 using 2.5%).

Step 8: Discount for contingencies.

The second method, which is perhaps easier, is to use Ogden Tables 15–26 that are specifically designed to produce multipliers for loss of pension in male and female claimants at retirement ages of between 50 and 75 years of age.

The appropriate retirement table should be chosen, with the multiplier found by reference to the claimant's age using the 2.5% column. A discount for contingencies will be required, but no further discount for accelerated receipt should be made as the tables already account for acceleration. It is generally accepted that the discount for contingencies should be less than that applied for loss of earnings because ill-health contingency may give rise to significant ill-health rights. A bigger reduction may be necessary in cases where there is significant doubt whether pension rights would have continued to accrue in the absence of the accident.

The disadvantage of the method using Tables 15–26 is that it is not so easy to factor-in any spouse's pension.

Obviously, if there is a reduction in life expectancy, the multiplier needs to be tailored accordingly. The Auty approach particularly lends itself to such a situation. Practitioners should be aware of the potential for a lost years claim in these circumstances (see Chapter 18).

In cases involving an automatic enrolment occupational pension (NEST pensions) it is possible to adopt an Ogden 7 approach and add loss of employer pension contributions plus tax relief onto the calculation for loss of earnings.

17.7.4 Multipliers for care/case management/professional deputy/Court of Protection/accommodation costs

The multiplier for care, case management, professional deputy, Court of Protection and accommodation costs in catastrophic injury claims will ordinarily be the multiplier for life. Accordingly, the principles set out earlier in this chapter should be followed in order to determine the appropriate multiplier.

Section A of the explanatory notes to the 7th edition Ogden Tables provides a step-by-step guide of how to split the multiplier for future costs. The same principles apply as with split multipliers for future loss of earnings, save that the lifetime multiplier is the appropriate starting point (Tables 1 or 2) and there will be no discount for contingencies.[59]

17.7.5 Multipliers for DIY/gardening/domestic help

The position is not quite so straightforward in claims for DIY/gardening/ domestic help. With these claims, the court is likely to account for the fact that a claimant's ability to carry out such activities will diminish towards the later part of their life irrespective of the accident.

A cut off point of between 65–75 years of age has historically been seen as realistic in these claims.[60] In these cases, the relevant multiplier can be obtained by calculating the fixed number of years between the claimant's age at trial and 65–75 years of age using Ogden Table 28.

However, increasing life expectancy and increased state retirement age towards 70 remain strong arguments for seeking a longer multiplier beyond 65-75 years of age and most care/OT reports obtained on behalf of a claimant will tend to support a graded claim for DIY/gardening/domestic help over the claimant's lifetime.[61]

---

[59] As per *Wells v Wells* [1999] 1 AC 345.
[60] See *Smith v McCrae* [2003] EWCA Civ 505, *Smith v East and North Hertfordshire Hospitals NHS Trust* [2008] EWHC 2234 (QB) and *Beesley v New Century Group* [2008] EWHC 3033 (QB).
[61] See *Crofts v Murton* LTL 10/09/2008 where an award for DIY and gardening was made in the sum of £1,500 per annum to age 70 and £1,095 per annum thereafter.

17.7.6 Multipliers for medical treatment/aids and equipment

If required over a lifetime, the principles set out under the heading Multipliers for Life should be followed.

In the event that treatment, aids or equipment are required over a fixed period of time, Ogden Table 28 can be used.

17.7.7 Multipliers involving child claimants

The multiplier for care for a catastrophically injured child will be determined in the same way as an adult. However, the selection of a multiplier for loss of earnings can be extremely difficult in view of issues over accelerated receipt of loss and uncertainties over whether the child would have found and stayed within employment.

It is vitally important that detailed instructions are taken from the family in relation to educational achievement attained by the child pre-injury (if applicable) and the family background of education and employment (both parents and siblings). This evidence will assist in maximising the multiplier and multiplicand.

The starting point when identifying the suitable multiplier for loss of earnings will be to determine an assumed age at which the claimant would have commenced work and to find the appropriate multiplier for that age using Tables 3–14 according to the assumed retirement age. This multiplier will then need to be discounted using Table 27 for the period between the date of the trial and the date it is assumed the claimant would have started work. Thereafter, if the child is to be treated as having a consistent work history but for the accident, they will be subject to the same 7th edition Ogden Table discounting factors (for contingencies other than mortality) as an adult claimant, applying as at the date the child would have started work.[62]

Further examples of these claims are provided by *Croke v Wiseman,*[63] *Almond v Leeds Western HA,*[64] *Cassel v Hammersmith HA,*[65] *M (A Child) v Leeds HA,*[66] *McKeown v Munday,*[67] *Lewis v Royal Shrewsbury NHS Trust*[68], *Whipps CrossUniversity NHS Trust v Iqbal,*[69] and *Whiten v St George's Healthcare NHS Trust.*[70] The case of *Whiten* (where a 5% contingency discount was applied to the multiplicand for loss of earnings) reminds us that individual circumstances will be key to the process.

---

[62] See *AH v Powys Local Health Board* [2007] EWHC 2996.
[63] [1982] 1 WLR 71.
[64] [1990] 1 Med LR 370.
[65] [1992] PIQR Q168.
[66] [2002] PIQR Q46.
[67] [2002] EWHC 725.
[68] LTL, 14 June 2007 (unreported elsewhere).
[69] [2008] PIQR P9.
[70] [2011] EWHC 2066 (QB).

17.7.8   Multipliers involving periodic losses/expenses

There are two recommended means of calculating periodic losses that occur at intervals.

The first and easiest method involves taking the cost of the item and then dividing this cost by the period of replacement (in terms of years).[71] The resulting figure is then multiplied by the multiplier for the duration of the loss. By way of example, if a 40-year-old claimant with an agreed life expectancy of 25 years requires a motorised buggy at a cost of £3,000 and this will need replacing every 5 years, the claim will be as follows:

Step 1: Immediate capital outlay of initial buggy: £3,000.

Step 2: £600 replacement multiplicand (£3,000/5) × 18.11 (multiplier for fixed period of 24 as opposed to 25 years used because assumed immediate capital purchase of buggy) = £10,866.

If the claimant already has a buggy and there will be no immediate capital purchase, the claim will be:

£600 replacement multiplicand × 18.65 (multiplier for fixed period of 25 years) = £11,190.

The second method is outlined at Section A5 of *Facts and Figures* where there are defined multipliers for fixed periods and at intervals along with detailed guidance of how to apply these in practice. This method has the advantage when calculating items of loss that may arise at irregular periods of time.

It is important to point out that, in both methods, it is assumed that yearly loss is incurred at the end of each year in which the loss arises. Therefore, using the buggy as an example, a 5-year lifespan does not mean that the loss occurs in the sixth year. Claimant practitioners should be alive to defendants raising such arguments, which would inevitably reduce the value of the claim.

17.7.9   Lost years

If the life of a living claimant has been shortened as a result of his or her injuries, he or she is entitled to seek compensation for the pecuniary benefit which he or she would have received during the period of his or her life of which he or she has been deprived: the *lost years*. Practitioners should note that, under CPR, r 41.8(2), a periodical payments order can continue after a claimant's death for the benefit of his or her dependants. Within the context of a catastrophic injuries claim where the claimant's life expectancy has been

---

[71]   This approach is commonly used by care experts in their reports.

reduced, the critical losses are likely to be loss of earnings (if the reduction in life expectancy is substantial) and loss of pension[72] (including state pension).[73]

A deduction from the lost pecuniary benefit needs to be made to account for the claimant's probable living expenses during the lost years. In *Harris v Empress Motors Ltd*,[74] O'Connor LJ offered the following practical guidance on this subject:

> 'In my judgment three principles emerge: 1. The ingredients that go to make up "living expenses" are the same whether the victim be young or old, single or married, with or without dependants. 2. The sum to be deducted as living expenses is the proportion of the victim's net earnings that he spends to maintain himself at the standard of life appropriate to his case. 3. Any sums expended to maintain or benefit others do not form part of the victim's living expenses and are not to be deducted from the net earnings.'

In cases where there is a proportion of the earnings/income expended on shared expenditure, such as rent, mortgage, council tax, utility bills and the costs of running a vehicle, then a pro-rata proportion of those expenses should be allocated for deduction.

The deduction for living expenses (known as the 'available surplus') will be accounted for in the multiplicand. The following conventional approaches have been adopted by the courts:

(1) Married claimant with no dependent children: assume 33% of income spent on claimant, 33% on spouse and 33% on joint expenditure. Accounting for the pro-rata deduction for joint expenditure (one-half of 33%), a deduction of 50% should be made to account for living expenses.

(2) Married claimant with dependent children: assume 25% income spent on claimant, 33% on joint living expenses and remainder on family. The joint living expenses need to be apportioned in equal measure depending upon the number of children. For example, if there are two dependent children (ie family of four), the 33% will be apportioned four ways, giving a figure of 8.25% attributable to the claimant. 25% + 8.25% = 33.25% deduction.

(iii) Unmarried claimant: a young man/woman living at home with parents may be regarded as having deductible living expenses of 67% of net income, rising to 75% if he or she gets a place of their own. However, recent case-law has shown a willingness to reduce this figure towards 50% reflecting the fact that, but for the accident, the claimant may have married and had children.[75]

---

[72] See *Marley v MOD* (unreported) 30 July 1984 (QBD); *Phipps v Brooks Dry Cleaning Services Ltd* PIQR Q100, *Jeffrey v Cape Insulation Ltd* [1999] CLY 1536 and *Crofts v Murton*, LTL, 10 September 2008.

[73] *Whyte v Barber* (unreported) 18 February 2003.

[74] [1984] 1 WLR 212.

[75] See *Warren v Northern General Hospital NHS Trust* [2000] 1 WLR 1404 and *Eagle v Chambers* [2003] EWHC 3135 (QB).

(iv) Young child claimant: following *Croke (A Minor) v Wiseman*,[76] no loss of years claim can be made in relation to a young child claimant with no dependants. In *Iqbal v Whipps Cross University Hospital NHS Trust*,[77] the Court of Appeal concluded that the decision in *Croke* was inconsistent with the decision in *Pickett* (which did not restrict a claim for lost years to adults with or without dependants). However, any such error had to be corrected by the House of Lords. This will no doubt be the subject of further litigation.

The multiplier for a loss of earnings lost years claim will be the conventional multiplier for the loss (assuming no lost years) minus the multiplier to early death. By way of example, if the claimant is a 45-year-old degree-educated male (in employment at the time of the accident) who would have worked to 65 but instead is going to die at age 55, the multiplier would be calculated as follows:

Step 1: Take conventional loss of earnings multiplier for 45-year-old male to retirement age 65: 15.27 (Ogden Table 9).

Step 2: Discount for contingencies: Table A, 45–49 age bracket, category D education: 0.86 discount.

Step 3: 15.27 × 0.86 = 13.13.

Step 4: Take loss of earnings multiplier for 45-year-old male to age 55: 8.74 (Ogden Table 5).

Step 5: Apply same discount for contingencies of 0.86: 8.74 × 0.86 = 7.52 (there may be some creative argument here as to the level of discount applied as Table A assumes a retirement age of 65).

Step 6: Appropriate multiplier for calculation = 5.61 (13.13 – 7.52).

The calculation of a lost years claim for pension loss is even more straightforward. If the same claimant would have been entitled to a pension from expected retirement date of 65, this would be calculated as follows:

Step 1: Take conventional pension loss multiplier for 45-year-old male commencing age 65: 9.43 (Ogden Table 21).

Step 2: Discount for contingencies (case specific – assume 10%).

Step 3: Appropriate multiplier for calculation = 8.49 (9.43 × 0.90).

---

[76] [1982] 1 WLR 71.
[77] [2007] EWCA Civ 1190.

17.7.10 Broad brush awards: calculating loss where multiplicand/multiplier is not appropriate

If there is evidence that a loss will be sustained, but there are too many imponderables in a claim to allow a reliable calculation of the loss on a multiplicand and multiplier basis, the court may prefer to make a broad brush assessment of the loss in question and award a lump sum to compensate the loss.[78] However, recent case-law has seen a shift away from judges making such awards unless 'they really have no alternative'.[79] Where the court does adopt a broad brush approach the Court of Appeal will be loathe to interfere with the trial judge's decision as to the amount.[80]

---

[78] See *Blamire v South Cumbria Health Authority* [1993] PIQR Q1, along with *Michael v Ashdown*, LTL, 2 February1998 (unreported elsewhere); *Willemse v Hesp* [2003] EWCA Civ 994; *Crouch v King's Healthcare NHS Trust* [2004] EWCA Civ 853; *Smale v Ball*, LTL, 6 June 2007 (unreported elsewhere).

[79] Per Keen LJ in *Bullock v Atlas Ward Structures Ltd* [2008] EWCA Civ 194 and followed in *Palmer v Kitley* [2008] EWHC 2819 (QB), *Hiom v WM Morrison Supermarkets* [2010] EWHC 1183 (QB), *Ward v Allies & Morrison Architects* [2012] EWCA Civ 1287.

[80] *Morgan v UPS* [2008] EWCA Civ 375.

CHAPTER 18

PERIODICAL PAYMENT ORDERS

Richard Cropper

18.1 LUMP SUM OR PPO?

The Ministry of Justice's (MOJ) consultation paper, published on 12 February 2013 entitled 'Damages Act 1996: The Discount Rate, Review of the Legal Framework' states the following aim of any award of damages for personal injury:

> 'Awards of damages are intended to compensate claimants for the losses they have suffered as a result of wrongful actions. This principle of full compensation – neither more, nor less – is a cornerstone of the law of damages. It is, however, not a precise concept ...

> The inherent uncertainty as to whether a lump sum award will fully compensate the injured person's losses, which is at least partly attributable to the application of a discount rate, can, however, be avoided because compensation can be taken wholly or partly in the form of periodical payments to meet the losses as they arise. These payments clearly have to be funded and come with their own advantages and disadvantages but they do avoid problems attributable to the application of a discount rate.'

In fact, there are three risks for each and every claimant with a conventional lump sum for future losses:

- the mortality risk of living longer than the duration for which the claimant is compensated;

- the investment risk of not achieving the discount rate; and

- the quantum risk that the annual needs as estimated at the point of settlement were underestimated, and the claimant's true needs are far higher.

Although actuarial tables are used to make an allowance for projected life expectancy, it is almost certain that death will not occur 'on time'. Actual investment returns will not be 2.5% per annum each and every year, net of costs and taxation and above inflation, and will fluctuate. Furthermore, an actual average return of 2.5% per annum real and net return does not guarantee success if worse returns are achieved in the early years post-settlement, with the catch-up being later on, when much of the award has already been spent.

Therefore, a lump sum is likely to lead to one of three outcomes:

(1) over-compensation, with damages remaining upon the claimant's death;
(2) under-compensation, with the damages being exhausted with life; or (most likely);
(3) compromise, with the claimant managing the award to meet their most important needs, within the reality of investment returns actually achieved and the state of their actual health.

Whilst 'guaranteed for life' periodical payments transfer the mortality and investment risks of a conventional lump sum to the defendant (more usually, the insurer), there is still room for error. With periodical payments, the main risk stems from the measure applied to update any periodical payments being so inaccurate as to lead to under-compensation (referred to in this chapter as the 'indexation risks'). The quantum risks remain with the claimant and are heightened: whilst there is the certainty and security of a guaranteed income for life, if it proves insufficient, the claimant cannot draw from future payments to meet current needs.

It is also important to note that the factor that has the greatest impact on both the risks involved with a conventional lump sum and periodical payments is time. For example:

•   the present value of the mortality risks of living longer reduce with time;
•   investment risks with a lump sum reduce with time;
•   the uncertainty with regard to the impact of taxation and inflation increase with time;
•   the quantum risks that the current estimates of the claimant's needs will prove to be wrong increase with time;
•   the impact of the indexation risk increases with time.

With all of the risks set out above, there is also opportunity. However, it is appropriate to focus on the risks more than the opportunities, as the opportunities tend not to result in actual benefits to the claimant (for example, in not living as long as expected is not an opportunity and better than expected investment returns are often held back rather than spent in case of worse economic times in the future).

Consequently, when assessing the viability of periodical payments in respect of any element of the claim for future loss it is key to keep in mind that only hindsight will tell which form of award will actually be the most appropriate and there is inherent risk in attempting to predict that result in advance, especially over very long periods of time.

18.2   THE IMPETUS FOR CHANGE

Historically, most personal injury claims have been concluded by way of a once and for all lump sum payment of damages from the defendant to the claimant.

This system's inherent problems were highlighted by the Master of the Rolls' Working Party Report entitled 'Structured Settlements'[1] which concluded:

> 'The Working Party considers that of the features we have identified that of accuracy is the most important. We are concerned that a consequence of a system of once and for all lump sum awards is that there will be under or over-compensation (in some cases considerable) and particularly concerned that a proportion of claimants whose life expectancy is uncertain, and who need significant continuing care, might be left with significant uncompensated need. It adds to our concern that this is likely to occur later in life when the consequences will be particularly hard to manage. It is also of concern that appreciation of this may give rise to excessive prudence and under expenditure in earlier years.'

At that time, the alternative to the traditional 'once and for all' award of damages was the 'structured settlement', the origins of which can be traced back to *Kelly v Dawes*.[2]

However, this system faltered because it was reliant upon both the consent of parties[3] and upon the financial viability of annuities available in the open market. If the cost of an annuity to provide a given level of future income by way of a structured settlement were greater than the conventional lump sum, the defendant would simply not agree. Alternatively, if the claimant were to look to apply an amount of capital that otherwise would have been awarded by way of a conventional lump sum to an annuity, in order that the cost to the defendant was the same, the annual income was often reduced by such an amount as to make it unattractive.

The Courts Act 2003[4] was designed to revolutionise the old structured settlement approach by removing both the need for consent and the reliance upon the availability of open market annuities.

The rules relating to periodical payments apply from 1 April 2005 to all existing cases. Variable periodical payments orders can only be made in respect of claims issued after 1 April 2005. The Department of Constitutional Affairs (DCA) has also provided a Guidance Note on periodical payments, designed for practitioners and the judiciary.

This DCA Guidance stated that the government's policy intentions in introducing these provisions were:

> 'based on the belief that the existing system of compensation for future losses by way of lump sums is unsatisfactory, and that periodical payments are usually a much better and fairer way of compensating those facing long term future loss and

---

[1] August 2002.

[2] (1990) *The Times*, September 27, QBD (14 July 1989, Potter J).

[3] See *Burke v Tower Hamlets Health Authority* (1989) *The Times*, August 10, [1989] CLY 1201.

[4] The relevant law is to be found in ss 100-101 of the Courts Act 2003, amending the Damages Act 1996, amendments to the Civil Procedure Rules 1998 (CPR) Parts 41 and 36 and PDs 21, 29, 36 and 41b, a new Practice Direction to CPR Part 41 and the Damages (Variation of Periodical Payments) Order 2005.

care needs. As the Law Commission recognised in its 1994 report "Structured Settlements and Interim and Provisional Damages", the principles of tort law do not create a right to compensation in the form of a lump sum to compensate for future loss in advance of that loss being incurred. Ministers adopted this analysis during passage of the Courts Act, indicating that the claimant's needs should be paramount, and not the claimant's wishes.'

To avoid confusion over terminology the term 'periodical payments' is used rather than 'structured settlements', which was the previous and now obsolete nomenclature (the legislation dealing with structured settlements having been repealed).

18.3 OVERVIEW OF THE POST-2005 REGIME

The key provisions areas follows:

- The court has the power to award damages for future financial loss in the form of periodical payments even if one or both of the parties objects.

- Other damages can be the subject of a periodical payments order where the parties consent.

- The court can only make a periodical payments order when satisfied that the 'continuity of payment under the order is reasonably secure' as defined in s 2(4)-(5) of the Damages Act 1996.

- If so satisfied, then in considering whether to make a periodical payments order the court will have principally in mind what is the more appropriate form of award of damages for all or part of the award, having regard in particular to the form of award which would best meet the claimant's needs as assessed by the court.

- This assessment is informed, but not determined, by the parties' preferences as to the form of award, the reasons for such preferences and the nature of any financial advice obtained by the claimant.

- The order will be for periodical payments to increase by reference to the retail price index (RPI) unless otherwise ordered by the court.

- The claimant can only convert any periodical payments back to a lump sum award in special circumstances by assignment or charge. It requires approval by the court which made the original order.

- There is a power to make a variable periodical payments order where there is a chance that at some definite or indefinite time in the future the claimant will, as a result of the relevant act or omission, develop some serious disease or suffer some serious deterioration or have a significant improvement. Both claimant and defendant may apply for such an order. This only applies to cases where proceedings have been issued on or after 1 April 2005.

- There is no minimum value for periodical payments orders.

18.4 THE REQUIREMENT OF 'REASONABLE SECURITY'

The court can only make a periodical payments order where it is satisfied that the continuity of payment is 'reasonably secure'. Therefore, before considering the relative merits of periodical payments it is imperative that consideration is given as to whether or not suitable periodical payments can even be achieved, which may not be certain.

What is meant by reasonable security is defined under s 2(4) of the Damages Act 1996.

The DCA Guidance states:

'In order that the court does not have to give specific consideration to the future security of periodical payments in every individual case, section 2(4) provides that the continuity of payment can automatically be considered to be reasonably secure where:
(a) it is protected by a Ministerial guarantee under section 6 of the 1996 Act,
(b) it is protected by a scheme under section 213 of the Financial Services and Markets Act 2000, or
(c) the source of the payments is a government or health service body.'

The Damages (Government and Health Services Bodies) Order 2005 defines those entities covered by section (c) above.

However, there are a number of bodies that do not fall directly within these criteria to be considered automatically secure. In such circumstances, it is open to the court, under s 2(5)(b) of the Damages Act to rely on an alternative to the requirements of s 2(4). CPR Part 41, PD 41b states the following at para 3:

'Before ordering an alternative method of funding under rule 41.9(1), the court must be satisfied that the following criteria are met –
(1) that a method of funding provided for under section 2(4) of the 1996 Act is not possible or there are good reasons to justify an alternative method of funding;
(2) that the proposed method of funding can be maintained for the duration of the award or for the proposed duration of the method of funding; and
(3) that the proposed method of funding will meet the level of payment ordered by the court.'

No guidance is given with regard to what would qualify as being 'good reasons' to justify an alternative method of funding, but one assumes that it would not be unreasonable to apply a method of funding that clearly allows for the same level of security as a method under s 2(4).

The following are bodies that are not covered by s 2(4) in every case:

18.4.1   Health authorities, NHS Trusts and Foundation NHS Trusts in England

Section 2(4)(c) of the Damages Act 1996 'deems' that there is reasonable security if the source of the payment is a government or health service body, ie the National Health Service Litigation Authority (NHSLA) or the Department of Health.[5] This presents real difficulty if neither of these two bodies are named in the periodical payments order as the source of the payment.

The solution to this problem for claims under the Clinical Negligence Scheme for Trusts (CNST)[6] was found in *YM v Gloucestershire Hospitals NHS Foundation Trust* (*YM*)[7] whereby the NHSLA agreed to be named as the source of the payments in periodical payments orders in circumstances where it had entered into agreements with NHS trusts allowing it to take on such liability. This provides claimants with practical effective security of periodical payments because the NHSLA is a Health Service Body. A model order was attached to the judgment and is the preferred model order to be used in cases where the claim is brought against an NHS trust or NHS foundation trust. It provides for a means of enforcement against the NHSLA in the event of future disputes.

Where the claim arises not under the CNST but under the Existing Liabilities Scheme (ELS)[8] any periodical payments are funded directly by the Department of Health. The source of funds is therefore a government body named in the Order referred to above, and periodical payments can be regarded as reasonably secure.

On 17 January 2007 the Department of Health wrote to the Chief Executive of the NHSLA to confirm that the Secretary of State is responsible for all payments made under the ELS, specifically in the context of Foundation Trusts, drawing these claims under s 2(4)(c).

18.4.2   Medical Protection Society (MPS) and the Medical Defence Union (MDU)

The MPS and the MDU have historically been indemnifiers rather than insurers. Therefore, both bodies are unable to provide reasonably secure periodical payments, except by way of an annuity. However, from 2001 the MDU issued insurance policies to members. On 14 January 2005, MDU Services Ltd (MDUSL) was established as a joint venture company between the MDU and Converium AG (formerly known as Zurich Reinsurance) specifically to arrange and administer the insurance policy which is issued by Converium's specialist underwriting arm, Converium Insurance (UK) Ltd.

---

[5]   Ibid.
[6]   Claims where the incident in question took place on or after 1 April 1995.
[7]   [2006] EWHC 820 (QB), [2006] PIQR 432.
[8]   Claims where the incident in question took place before April 1995.

In effect, the MDU issued contracts of insurance and is authorised and regulated by the FCA, thereby attracting the protection of a scheme under s 213 of the Financial Services and Markets Act 2000. In other words, MDU claims under a policy of insurance would now be covered by the requirements of s 2(4), whilst claims under the MPS would not. However, this policy is limited in cover to £10m in the aggregate, including both sides' legal expenses. Therefore, cover under s 2(4) is available to the limit of the indemnity.[9] Furthermore, the writer understands that the MDU will not be renewing expiring insurance policies after 1 April 2013, which will revert the MDU to being an indemnifier in respect of claims notified after that date.

18.4.3   Motor Insurers' Bureau (MIB)

Since the implementation of the Courts Act 2003, the MIB has successfully illustrated to the courts that it is suitably secure to allow it to self-fund periodical payments, even though they are not covered by any of the options as set out in s 2(4) of the Damages Act 1996. This is allowed for under s 2(5) of the Damages Act 1996.

18.4.4   Lloyd's syndicates

Where the claim falls under the Lloyd's policy that was issued after 1 January 2004, s 2(4)(b) applies and reasonable security can be established. However, this section does not apply where the policy under which the claim falls was issued prior to that date.

For reasons set out in the judgments in *Bennett v Stephens*[10] it has been established that, as long as certain criteria have been met, in the event that the policy was issued prior to 1 January 2004 and the policy is for motor insurance, the terms of the current MIB Uninsured Drivers' Agreement would mean that the MIB would be required to continue to pay any periodical payments in the event of default.

18.4.5   Insolvent insurers

Some insolvent insurers may benefit from protection under s 213 of the Financial Services and Markets Act 2000. This depends upon the date of the insolvency of the insurer and the date the policy of insurance under which the claim falls was issued. For example, Independent Insurance became insolvent prior to the implementation of the Act and, therefore, it does not benefit from the necessary protection. However, the writer is aware that the FSCS has consented to the implementation of periodical payments on behalf of an insolvent insurer, where the insurer became insolvent after the implementation of the Act.

---

9   Issues surrounding limited indemnity cover are considered in further detail later.
10   [2010] EWHC 2194 (QB), [2012] EWHC 1 (QB) and [2012] EWHC 58 (QB).

18.4.6   Private defendants

Whilst these defendants may be extremely large and secure in nature, they are not covered by the regulations. It is open for them to ask the court to consider them suitably secure, but the court could not order periodical payments unless satisfied. The judgment of Mackay J in Bennett states:

> 'If matters rested there, however, I would be reluctant to pronounce myself satisfied under s.2(3). Without in any way denigrating the current status or stability of Faraday as a going concern, taller trees than it have fallen in the financial forest before now and unless it could claim the backing of s.2(4), which it cannot as I am presently invited to assume, I would hesitate to say that I could sufficiently discount the risk that it might fail sometime in the next 50 years or so, which is the period I have to consider covered by the proposed order in this case.'

18.4.7   Non-individual or small company defendants

The protection of the FSCS is only afforded to individuals and small companies. Therefore, if the defendant is a large company, the protection of the FSCS does not apply. However, in correspondence on 29 March 2012, the FSCS set out the following:

> 'The analysis communicated by FSCS to date and as set out above relates to the position under the COMP Rules. However, FSCS has now been able to consider the security position in further detail, and with the benefit of Counsel's advice. My understanding is that the Damages Act 1996, as amended by the Courts Act 2003, effectively enhances the protection available [to] claimants (who would otherwise be unprotected under the COMP Rules) in two ways:
>
> 1. In cases where a claimant has a right to periodical payments, sub sections 4(1) and 4(2) of the Damages Act 1996 will extend FSCS protection to 100% of the value of the payment. Therefore, where a liability for periodical payments arises in the context of non-compulsory insurances, FSCS's usual protection of 90% of the payment under the COMP Rules will be extended to 100%.
>
> 2. Sub sections 4(3) and 4(4) appear to provide a narrow abrogation of the eligibility requirements in person or fatal injury cases where the claimant has a right to periodical payments. Under these subsections, where an insurer is required to meet the defendant's periodical payments to the claimant, the claimant is to be treated as having entered into an "arrangement of the same kind" with the insurer. This has the effect that the eligibility or otherwise of the defendant under the COMP Rules is no longer relevant, as the claimant is deemed to have a direct route to claim on FSCS in respect of the failed insurer. Therefore, provided that the claimant themselves is eligible under the COMP Rules (i.e. as an individual or a small business), and the arrangement is covered by FSCS, then FSCS can protect the claim.
>
> If this interpretation of section 4 of the Damages Act (as amended) is accepted by the court then, in the event that the defendant's insurers were declared "in default", FSCS would consider the claimant (as an individual) eligible to claim on FSCS, notwithstanding the size of the policyholder-defendants.'

The response on behalf of the FSCS is understood to mean that instead of the claimant being put 'in the shoes of the defendant' (as policyholder), he would be given 'a new pair of shoes' in his own right, thus passporting him to FSCS protection as an individual. However, that could only be the outcome where the original policy would otherwise have been protected under the FSCS.

18.4.8 Policies with limited indemnities

It is often the case with employers' liability insurance, public liability insurance and professional negligence policies (including MDU policies referred to above) that the indemnity under the policy is not unlimited as it is with compulsory insurance.

However, there is currently uncertainty as to how periodical payments are dealt with under such a policy of insurance. The judgment of Irwin J in *Kotula v EDF Energy*,[11] states:

> 'What is the value of the claim and how does that relate to the available sums? The court was invited by those representing the claimant to consider what should be the approach to calculating the available sums under the policies of insurance. Clearly, if the value of the claim, that is to say the capitalised value of the liability to make these payments, were the basis of calculating liability under the policies, then that would not be the total of all of the aggregated future payments which will have to be made. The very purpose behind capitalising a claim is to assess the current cost of buying the future stream of payments. In law, the value of the claim, it seems to me, could be regarded as the cost of purchasing the agreed payments. That is so because in law, by operation of statute for the purpose of personal injury claims, there is a fixed assumption as to the applicable rate of interest.

> However, I am told here that these insurers do not take such an approach. They do not regard the limit of liability under the policy as being set by reference to the capitalised cost or value, depending on which side of the notional sale one is considering, of all the payments. Rather they do regard the limit as applying to the aggregated mathematical sum of all of the payments anticipated. Hence, if simply totting up the future payments reaches the mathematical sum of the liability under the policy, that would be the end of the exposure of a given insurer and the end of the contribution from that insurer to the payments to the claimant.

> It seems to me that it is appropriate to consider the security of the future payments, assuming that analysis of the limit of liability under the two relevant policies of insurance will be binding. I should stress I make no ruling. I have not heard argument on whether that is legally correct. I make no ruling as to whether that is legally correct. I gave no indication as to whether that is legally correct. Anything that I have said and do say during this judgment should not be taken by anyone to be precedent on that point. I have, I hope, for good reason declined to enter into those lists. Were I to have done so, it seems to me I would have been wrong not to ask for representations from within the industry and from the professional body representing insurers within Britain. The point may have very great implications

---

[11] [2011] EWHC 1546.

for other cases and for the approval of streams of periodical payments in other cases; because that point alone might often set such a limit to the capacity of insurers to meet streams of periodical payments, that unless it was resolved, no judge could reach of the position of concluding that the future payments were secure. That is an argument I have to put to one side and, in the interests of the claimant and of the proper exercise of this jurisdiction, assume on a cautious basis that the approach taken by these insurers is correct.'

Clearly, whether or not the indemnity limit will be breached during the claimant's lifetime under the 'totting up' approach will depend upon the following factors:

- the amount of the indemnity limit remaining having accounted for the conventional lump sum element of the claim, costs and potentially other claims (if the limit of the indemnity is in the aggregate);
- the initial amount of annual periodical payments;
- the level of growth in respect of the measure applied to uprate any periodical payments; and
- the claimant's life expectancy.

Therefore, in such cases there is a need for careful analysis as to whether it is likely that the indemnity limit will be breached during the claimant's lifetime.

18.4.9   Foreign insurers issuing policies to cover risks situated in the UK

This remains an untested area and may depend on the type of policy. For example, if the policy is for compulsory insurance, such as road traffic insurance, and the defendant's insurer is situated within the EU, then unlimited protection, akin to that provided by the MIB in the UK, is afforded. As a result, it would seem unlikely that in such circumstances 'reasonable security' could not be established. The position is less clear if the defendant's insurer is outside of the UK and/or the insurance is not compulsory.

As a result of the above, the nature of the defendant or the defendant's insurer may impact upon whether the court can order periodical payments.

The DCA Guidance set out the following in respect of such circumstances:

'This does not mean that courts cannot Order periodical payments against these defendants and insurance bodies [those that cannot be considered automatically secure]. They may be able to provide statutorily secure periodical payments by purchasing an appropriate annuity from a life office for the benefit of the claimant, thus attracting the full protection of the FSCS under section 4(1) and (2) of the 1996 Act (but see para 52 below). Alternatively, it is open to these bodies to satisfy the court that they can offer a method of funding, other than one of those deemed secure under section 2(4) that is reasonably secure.'

However, there are no suitable annuities currently available in the market.

Furthermore, even if providers were to enter this market, an earnings-linked annuity that would meet the terms of an ASHE 6115-linked periodical payments order, for example, is presently not available. Until recently an earnings-link was a precluded link under Financial Conduct Authority (formerly the FSA) regulations. However, the FSA Policy Statement 07/77 entitled 'Permitted links for long-term insurance business' states:

> **'Approved Indices**
>
> 2.41 Our proposal to retain the current definition of "approved index" for index-linked benefits was not challenged by respondents. However, there were requests for the Average Earnings Index (AEI) to be allowed as a permitted index.
>
> 2.42 The context for this request is that of bulk purchase annuity business. Firms writing this business can find that Guaranteed Minimum Pension (GMP) benefits included within defined benefit pension schemes are revalued in line with the AEI as is allowed by the Department for Work and Pensions rules. But the AEI is not a permitted index because of the difficulty in finding suitable assets to match their liabilities to the standards required by INSPRU 3.1.58. This may prevent firms from accepting such business.
>
> OUR RESPONSE: We intend to consult on a proposal to include AEI as a permitted index in a forthcoming QCP.
>
> In the meantime, any firm wishing to link benefits to the AEI will need to apply for a waiver. Any such application should include a detailed analysis of how the firm would intend to comply with the requirements of INSPRU in respect of this business.'

Following this policy statement, the FSA has approved earnings-linked annuities for a limited class of pension business (Guaranteed Minimum Pensions), although the writer understands that no waiver has either been applied for or granted at this time for an earnings-linked annuity that is suitable to be used to fund periodical payments.

18.5   FEATURES OF PERIODICAL PAYMENTS

Periodical payments have a number of features that differentiate them from a conventional lump sum award, the principal of which are considered below.

18.5.1   Guarantee of payments for life

In calculating a conventional lump sum award, a decision must be made in respect of the duration of future loss. This means obtaining a view with regard to the claimant's future life expectancy. This view is likely to be either too long or too short, with the claimant carrying the responsibility of investing the award and making it last an unknown lifetime.

As periodical payments are usually guaranteed for the claimant's lifetime[12] regardless of how long that may be, it means that this portion of the damages award can never run out.

The Lord Chancellor's Department's initial consultation paper, entitled 'Damages for Future Loss: Giving the courts the Power to Order Periodical Payments for Future Loss and Care Costs in Personal Injury Cases',[13] stated that periodical payments:

> 'place the risks associated with life expectancy and investment on defendants rather than claimants. This ensures that claimants who live longer than expected enjoy the quality of life they are entitled to, and do not have to fall back on social security when the money runs out.'

The DCA Guidance also states:

> 'The lump sum system is based on predictions about the future life expectancy of a claimant which are inevitably uncertain and almost always lead to over-compensation or under-compensation. In contrast, periodical payments ensure that people receive appropriate compensation for as long as it is needed.
>
> Periodical payments should also avoid the need for argument about life expectancy during the litigation. This is often unpleasant and stressful for the claimant. It will not be necessary to assess life expectancy to decide the value of periodical payments that will meet the claimant's future needs (an actuarial judgment on life expectancy will still be relevant to the issue of how payments are to be funded by the defendant; but this should not form part of the litigation or concern the claimant).'

However, periodical payments only overcome the need to obtain life expectancy evidence if all of the future losses are paid in the form of periodical payments. Given that it is unlikely that all of the future losses are appropriate to be paid in the form of periodical payments,[14] the question of life expectancy still has to be addressed in the vast majority of cases.

18.5.2   Certain level of future income

In calculating the level of a conventional lump sum award, it is presently assumed by the court that the claimant can achieve a real and net return that is after tax, investment charges[15] and above inflation, of 2.5% per annum.[16] The

---

[12]   Unless otherwise stated to meet a particular need the claimant may have that is for a specific period of time.

[13]   Published in March 2002.

[14]   For example, it is unlikely that the future accommodation claim should be paid in any other form than a conventional lump sum. The *Roberts v Johnstone* calculation (*Roberts v Johnstone* [1989] QB 878, [1988] 3 WLR 1247, [1989] 5 LS Gaz R 44, CA) requires the application of a conventional multiplier to the annual loss.

[15]   *Page v Plymouth Hospitals NHS Trust* [2004] EWHC 1154 (QB), [2004] 3 All ER 367.

[16]   'Setting the Discount Rate: The Lord Chancellor's Reasons', 27 July 2002.

investment of a conventional lump sum may give rise to greater or lesser returns over time. Either way, this investment risk is carried by the claimant.

The amount paid each year under periodical payments is set at the point of settlement. Therefore, these payments are not affected by future fluctuations in the interest rates or stock market volatility. The future payments only vary by way of the index they are linked to.

The investment of a conventional lump sum may be illustrated to give rise to greater returns over time. However, this can rarely be guaranteed. Furthermore, a conventional lump sum award requires active management, with associated costs. The DCA Guidance states that:

> 'Claimants will not have to bear the risks associated with investing and managing a lump sum award. These risks will fall on defendants, who are generally far better able to bear them. This should remove the need for claimants to obtain detailed financial advice on the investment and management of the award ...'

This often means that periodical payments are only suitable when applied to elements of the claim that are themselves known and certain, in respect of the annual loss and duration. If a claimant's future needs are uncertain, which is particularly the case with young claimants with long life expectancies, then periodical payments could provide nothing more than a financial straitjacket over time.

The flexibility inherent with a conventional lump sum award means that the income stream provided in the future can adapt over time to increases and decreases in need as and when actually required. Periodical payments cannot.

Furthermore, whilst recent investment returns illustrate that a return in line with the assumed discount rate of 2.5% per annum after tax and above inflation is improbable over the short term, returns over the longer term show that it is possible. Periodical payments take away the ability to do better or worse than the amount fixed at outset, into the future.

18.5.3 Enhanced protection

Periodical payments, as long as they are funded in an appropriate manner, benefit from 100% protection. This means that if the provider of periodical payments were to become insolvent or cease to exist, the payments would continue to be paid without deduction. No other investment vehicle has such protective guarantees.[17]

However, that is not to say that conventionally invested lump sum damages would be inherently insecure. Risk in relation to financial security can be

---

[17] The issue of security will be considered in greater detail below.

significantly reduced by ensuring wide diversification of investments, particularly through collective schemes, such as unit trusts and OEICs (open-ended investment companies).

18.5.4   Tax-free income

The Income Tax (Trading and Other Income) Act 2005, sets out the following:[18]

> **'731 Periodical payments of personal injury damages**
>
> (1) No liability to income tax arises for the persons specified in section 733 in respect of periodical payments to which subsection (2) applies or annuity payments to which subsection (3) applies.
>
> (2) This subsection applies to periodical payments made pursuant to—
> (a)   an order of the court, so far as it is made in reliance on section 2 of the Damages Act 1996 (c. 48) (periodical payments) (including an order as varied),
> (b)   an order of a court outside the United Kingdom which is similar to an order made in reliance on that section (including an order as varied),
> (c)   an agreement, so far as it settles a claim or action for damages in respect of personal injury (including an agreement as varied),
> (d)   an agreement, so far as it relates to making payments on account of damages that may be awarded in such a claim or action (including an agreement as varied), or
> (e)   a Motor Insurers' Bureau undertaking in relation to a claim or action in respect of personal injury (including an undertaking as varied).
>
> (3) This subsection applies to annuity payments made under an annuity purchased or provided—
> (a)   by the person by whom payments to which subsection (2) applies would otherwise fall to be made, and
> (b)   in accordance with such an order, agreement or undertaking as is mentioned in subsection (2) or a varying order, agreement or undertaking.
>
> (4) In this section "damages in respect of personal injury" includes damages in respect of a person's death from personal injury.
>
> (5) In this section "personal injury" includes disease and impairment of physical or mental condition.
>
> (6) In this section "a Motor Insurers' Bureau undertaking" means an undertaking given by—
> (a)   the Motor Insurers' Bureau (being the company of that name incorporated on 14 June 1946 under the Companies Act 1929 (c. 23)), or
> (b)   an Article 75 insurer under the Bureau's Articles of Association.'

The persons referred to in s 733 are:

---

[18]   This Act replaced ss 329A and 329AB of the Income and Corporation Taxes Act 1988.

- the person entitled to the damages under the order, agreement, undertaking or to the compensation under the award in question ('A');
- a person who receives the payment in question on behalf of A; and
- a trustee who receives the payment in question on trust for the benefit of A under a trust under which A is, while alive, the only person who may benefit.

It is important to note that if periodical payments are paid into a trust where the claimant is not the sole beneficiary during his lifetime, the periodical payments will not benefit from the taxation exemption.

A conventional lump sum award is paid without deduction of any taxation. However, interest, income and capital gains generated on the capital will fall to be taxed in the usual manner, regardless of the claimant's age or whether he is a child or a protected beneficiary under the Court of Protection. Therefore, with periodical payments, the claimant does not carry the future risk of how a detrimental change to taxation regimes or rates may affect the claimant's ability to achieve a 2.5% per annum real and net rate of return on a conventional lump sum.

18.5.5 Index-linking of the future payments

Prior to the landmark case of *Thompstone and others* the vast majority of periodical payments were escalated in line with price inflation, as measured by the General Index of Retail Prices (all items) ('the RPI') for the claimant's lifetime.

This erosive effect of inflation has been less of an issue in recent years due to an unprecedented period of low and even negative inflation. However, history indicates the levels of inflation that have been seen and that could return in the future.

If inflation were to return to such high levels again in the future, RPI-linking would stop the real value of the annual payments being eroded relative to retail prices.

However, data also indicates that care costs have not tended to increase in line with retail prices, as such costs are predominantly driven by wages. All reasonable data indicates that earnings inflation consistently rises above price inflation over the longer term. As a result, RPI-linked periodical payments are unlikely to increase enough to meet the increasing care costs over time. This will invariably create a shortfall. The solution is to link periodical payments to an index (or indices) that more closely matches the loss. The courts have a power to do this under s 2(9) of the Damages Act 1996.

The Court of Appeal judgment in *Thompstone and others* states the following:

'The court is seeking to provide an answer which, on the information it has at the trial, will, through the use of a PPO, best provide the claimant with 100% compensation. If, in the context of future care, of which the main element is the wages of the carers, the RPI is not suitable for the purpose of tracking wage inflation, the question is whether a more suitable index or measure is available. Suitability should be tested against the criteria set out by Mackay J quoted above. If an alternative is more suitable, it must be open to the court to accept that alternative even if some criticisms can be made of it. If the alternative is less suitable than RPI it obviously could not be chosen. But this is not a "stand alone" exercise under which the court would have to disqualify an alternative because of criticisms of its suitability even though the alternative was more suitable than RPI ...

His Honour Judge Bullimore took the view that the exercise is bound to be a comparative one but that any alternative that was unsuitable would have to be rejected. That must be right, and before Mackay J the criteria for suitability were hardly an issue. He identified them in the following words:

"[70] Before considering individual measures proposed I should consider the criteria that should be applied when making what I consider to be a comparative assessment as to whether each meets the test of fairness of appropriateness defined above.

[71] The experts helpfully agreed the criteria for the suitability of an index as being:

(i) accuracy of match of the particular data series to the loss or expenditure being compensated;

(ii) authority of the collector of the data;

(iii) statistical reliability;

(iv) accessibility;

(v) consistency over time;

(vi) reproducibility in the future;

(vii) simplicity and consistency in application."

This appears to me an entirely appropriate and sensible list of the qualities which are to be looked for. Mr Hall sought to add that the candidate measure should be "free of distorting factors". Dr Wass, more realistically in my view, said that that is in effect asking for the impossible though it should be as free as possible ...

We hope that as a result of these proceedings the National Health Service, and other defendants in proceedings that involve catastrophic injury, will now accept that the appropriateness of indexation on the basis of ASHE 6115 has been established after an exhaustive review of all the possible objections to its use, both in itself and as applied to the recovery of costs of care and case management. It will not be appropriate to re-open that issue in any future proceedings unless the defendant can produce evidence and argument significantly different from, and more persuasive than, that which has been deployed in the present cases. Judges should not hesitate to strike out any defences that do not meet that requirement.'

Therefore, in respect of future care and case management, an earnings link has been established. This means that when comparing periodical payments in respect of care and case management with a conventional lump sum, one must achieve 2.5% per annum after taxation, charges and above carers' earnings growth rather than price inflation.

Further, as ASHE 6115 captures 'pay-drift' it is unique in that it will reflect future qualitative change, rather than assume that the present level of need remains over the claimant's lifetime.

This is clearly a very attractive feature of such periodical payments.

However, the application of ASHE 6115 has not been without its problems. The model Schedule to the Order has required amendment on three occasions.[19] The most recent alteration was caused by the reclassification of the ASHE data in 2010, which had an impact on the 2012 data. Details with regard to these issues were set out in the article entitled 'A Senior Moment'.[20] The Judgment of Swift J was accompanied by the following summary:

'The case of RH was one of the original "test" cases on the issue of the indexation of periodical payments. The periodical payments order in RH was made by Mackay J in July 2007 and was subsequently modified slightly at a hearing before Sir Christopher Holland in December 2008. Since then, the "model order" based on Sir Christopher's modified order in RH has been used in every case involving the National Health Service Litigation Authority (NHS LA) in which a periodical payments order for care and case management has been made. To date 643 such orders have been made.

Periodical payments for care and case management in cases involving the NHS LA are index-linked by reference to the Annual Survey of Hours and Earnings (ASHE) 6115 published by the Office for National Statistics (ONS). The model order contains formulae based on the ASHE 6115 data to be used when calculating the annual increase in the periodical payments to be made to a claimant.

In 2010, the ONS changed its methodology, as a result of which certain data which were required to calculate the increases in the periodical payments payable to claimants in December 2012 were not available to the NHS LA. Periodical payments were made on the basis of the data that were available and claimants/Deputies were informed that balancing payments would be made, if appropriate, once the problem caused by the missing data had been solved.

With the assistance of the three experts who had been instructed for the claimant and the defendant in RH and other "test" cases and who had both been involved

---

19 [2008] EWHC 2424 (QB), [2008] EWHC 2948 (QB) and [2013] EWHC 229 (QB).
20 APIL's PI Focus magazine (Vol 22, issue 9).

in the development of the model order, the defendant/NHS LA succeeded in identifying a solution to the problem of the missing data. That solution and the proposed amendments to the order in RH (which amendments are to be replicated in the model order) have been carefully considered by the experts, together with solicitors and leading counsel, and are agreed by the parties in RH.

I am entirely satisfied that the proposed solution is fair and reasonable and will achieve justice as between the parties. I am satisfied also that the proposed amendments are both necessary and appropriate to meet the problem which has arisen in giving effect to the existing order.

It is the NHS LA's intention to use the amended model order in all future cases where periodical payments orders for care and case management are made. It is also necessary that the amended provisions should be applied to all cases involving the NHS LA in which there are existing periodical payments orders for care and case management so as to enable the periodical payments made in December 2012 to be recalculated and any balance owing to claimants to be paid, and also so as to ensure that there is a process in place to deal with any similar problems that might arise in the future.

I would strongly encourage all claimants and Deputies in cases with existing periodical payments for care and case management to accept the NHS LA's proposal that the amended provisions of the model order should be applied to their case. Whilst it is open to an individual claimant or Deputy to object to that course and to contend that the problem that has arisen should be solved in some other way, he/she should be aware of the implications of doing so. If an objection is raised, the claimant or Deputy will have to be prepared to demonstrate, to the satisfaction of a court and on the basis of sound expert evidence, circumstances such as:

a)   the existence of some technical or other flaw in the solution that has been adopted in the case of RH which has gone undetected and will affect the future operation of the model order; and/or

b)   an alternative proposed solution to the problem of the missing data which has very significant advantages over the solution adopted in RH such that a further amendment to the model order would be just and proportionate; and/or

c)   some specific feature of the claimant's case that makes the solution adopted in RH unworkable.

In the event that the objection is dismissed, the claimant will be at risk of paying the costs of what may have been a very expensive exercise.

The NHS LA proposes to write to the claimant or Deputy in every case in which the NHS LA is involved and where there is an existing periodical payments order for care and case management:

a)   identifying the problem that has arisen and explaining the way in which it intends to solve it;

b) enclosing and explaining the revised calculation and the financial consequences for the claimant;

c) enclosing a copy of the amended model order, with track changes so that the amendments can be clearly seen; and

d) informing him/her that the NHS LA intends to apply the provisions of the amended model order to the claimant's case in the future unless, within 28 days of receipt of the letter, the claimant or Deputy gives notice in writing to the NHS LA's solicitors that he/she disagrees with the proposed solution and/or the amendments to the order, setting out his/her proposed alternative solution, together with any relevant calculation(s) and/or proposed technical adjustments.

The proposals set out above do not of course apply to cases in which periodical payments orders for care and case management have been made and the NHS LA is not involved. I am told that there are many such cases currently in existence. The compensators in those cases include government and public bodies, insurers, the Motor Insurers' Bureau and Lloyd's syndicates. I am told that the form of periodical payments orders used in non-NHS LA claims varies, some being based on the NHS LA's model order and others not.

I would urge compensators in all cases where a periodical payments order for care and case management has been made and the NHS LA is not involved to review the terms of their existing order(s) and, in the event that the terms of the orders require it and the same problem of calculation arises, to seek acceptance by claimants and Deputies to amendments similar to those which have been made to the NHS LA model order.'

In *Olivia v Mahmood and Liverpool Victoria*[21] the court approved Brazilian Real denominated periodical payments linked to a measure of the costs of medical care in Brazil, as the claimant is resident there, having been satisfied that the measure met the Mackay J requirements.

In respect of other elements of the claim, in *Sarwar*[22] the court awarded damages in the form of periodical payments for the future loss of earnings element of the claim, linked to the 90th percentile of aggregate ASHE. The judgment states:

'For these reasons I conclude that if an award of periodical payments is to be made in respect of loss of future earnings the index most likely to secure that the periodical payments maintain their value is ASHE aggregate for male full-time employees at the 90th percentile. Accordingly, if the award in this case in respect of loss of future earnings is to be in the form of periodical payments, section 2(8), Damages Act 1996 should be modified to the extent that such periodical payments should be linked not to RPI but to ASHE aggregate for male full-time employees at the 90th percentile.'

---

[21] Unreported.
[22] [2007] EWHC 274 (QB).

In *Whiten*,[23] the Judgment of Swift J states:

> 'There was a dispute as to whether the award for loss of earnings should be paid by way of lump sum or periodical payments. I decided today that it was in the claimant's best interests for a periodical payments order to be made. It is agreed that the award should be uprated annually by reference to the ASHE earnings data for the gross annual pay for all male full-time employees in the United Kingdom (currently Table 1.7a).'

Aggregate ASHE is the earnings levels for all occupations, rather than a specific occupation.

These are the only cases where the court has awarded damages in the form of periodical payments and applied an alternative to the RPI for an element of the claim other than for future care and case management.

Under the Mackay J test it may well be difficult to find suitable alternatives to the RPI for many other elements of the claim, such as aids and equipment, transport, prosthetics, holidays, etc. However, the writer understands that cases have compromised by consent with alternative measures being applied in respect of loss of earnings (utilising specific occupational classifications), professional deputy fees (utilising the occupational classification for 'legal professionals) and therapies.

It is likely that the issue of indexation will continue to develop over time.

A conventional lump sum gives the claimant the opportunity to invest some of the damages in assets that tend, over time, to rise in value above the retail price index. As noted by Senior Judge Lush,[24] whilst it cannot be guaranteed that this will be achieved, this option is removed by periodical payments linked to the RPI. The longer the period of loss, the more significant this problem becomes.

However, the dimension of time is critical here. Hedging against inflation by investing in, say, equities requires a long view, as time is needed to withstand the ups and downs in value. In a case where life expectancy is relatively short, such an approach is too risky. The guarantee of inflation proofing even from RPI-linked periodical payments in this scenario may well look a far more attractive option for the non-future care and case management elements of the claim than the lump sum alternative. For example, in *St George v The Home Office*[25] RPI-linked periodical payments were agreed by consent to be the most appropriate form of award in respect of the claimant's accommodation need (rent), taking into account the claimant's short and uncertain life expectancy and his wish to remain in an area where property values are very high.

---

[23]   *Whiten v St George's Healthcare NHS Trust* [2011] EWHC 2066 (QB).

[24]   London Law Review, Vol 1:187 [2005].

[25]   (2010) unreported.

These positive features need to be considered alongside the negative features of periodical payments, the principal of which are set out below.

18.5.6 Immediate capital needs

By their very nature, periodical payments provide a future stream of income. Therefore, they are not suitable to meet any capital expenditure (such as a property, a vehicle and equipment etc). It is most often the case that due to the claimants' immediate capital needs, particularly that of accommodation, and requirement for future flexibility, that periodical payments cannot be appropriately applied to meet all of the claimant's future needs.

It is important to consider the implications of the application of the *Roberts v Johnstone* approach to accommodation in this case. Clearly, most claimants do not have access to the required level of capital outside of the claim to purchase the required property. Therefore the capital needed is not 'spare' and can only be set aside by capitalising elements of future losses and locking that capital into the house.

The result is that the application of the *Roberts v Johnstone* approach to accommodation can often distort the 'form of award' decision, as without the capital hole created in respect of accommodation, more elements of the claim may be better met by way of periodical payments.

18.5.7 Inflexibility

Once the periodical payments have been agreed, they cannot be altered or encashed in any way.[26] Therefore, it is important to ensure that there are sufficient monies available in more conventional investments to provide for future changes in circumstances.

One must accept that, whilst the elements of the future loss claim are assumed to be certain, based on 'the balance of probability' assumption, in reality any claimants' future may not precisely reflect what can be foreseen today. This uncertainty increases with longevity, as there is more likely to be imprecision of estimate over the longer-term.

Therefore, in order to provide a suitable financial balance between certainty and flexibility, certain elements of the claim for future loss may well have to be paid in the form of a conventional lump sum (in addition to the immediate capital needs referred to above).

---

[26] Unless the terms are made under the Damages (Variation of Periodical Payments) Order 2005 or there are exceptional circumstances in which the court is persuaded to allow assignment under s 2(6) of the Damages Act.

18.5.8   The impact of less than 100% recovery

It is clear that where there is any deduction in the award, due to liability or causation issues or pre-existing conditions, any periodical payments can, at best, only be expected to provide for the recoverable proportion of the claimant's future needs.

The claimant has the following options in reality:
(1)   provide for the recoverable proportion of the annual needs for life; or
(2)   provide for all the annual needs for the recoverable proportion of life; or
(3)   provide for the most important needs in full, as and when they occur, for as long as the funds last.

Periodical payments can often only be appropriately applied to follow the first of these three options.

With regard to the second option, this would only be appropriate if the claimant had resources outside of the claim (whether that be monetary or gratuitous help) to meet all of the needs for the duration from the point of settlement that represents the irrecoverable proportion of life post-settlement.

With regard to the third option, as this could only be met by accepting a conventional lump sum, there remains the problem of achieving a 2.5% per annum real and net return and the uncertain duration of loss.

18.5.9   Impact on statutory funding

For reasons clearly set out in the Court of Appeal Judgment in Crofton,[27] in respect of local authority home care services, whilst the capital conventional lump sum is to be disregarded (if held in trust or held under the Order of the Court), the income generated on a conventional lump sum may be assessed at the discretion of the local authority (under the Health and Social Services and Social Security Adjudication Act 1983 (HASSASSA Act 1983)). This was further confirmed by Mr Justice Holman in the case of Collins v Plymouth County Council.[28]

However, neither of these cases specifically considered the treatment of periodical payments income.

It is the writer's experience that some local authorities take into account income derived from either the capital sum or periodical payments in full, other local authorities take only some of this income into account (by applying a maximum contributory level) and some local authorities continue to disregard income. Furthermore, policy with regard to income can change from time to time.

---

[27]   [2007] EWCA Civ 71.
[28]   [2009] EWHC 3279 (Admin).

Whilst a conventional lump sum can be legitimately invested in order to limit income (which is not onerous in the present economic climate) since SI 2002/2531, all of any periodical payments are to be treated as income.

The Explanatory Note to the statutory instrument states:

> 'Regulation 2 allows all periodical payments received by virtue of any agreement or court order to make personal injury payments to the resident, to the extent that they are not a payment of income, to be treated as income.'

Therefore, periodical payments are likely to have a greater adverse impact on the claimant's future entitlement to such funding.

That said, the Department of Health have recently published a paper on care and support funding reform. It is suggested that the most any individual will be asked to contribute towards their future domiciliary care is £75,000 and the cap is set to £0.00 if the needs present prior to age 18.

In the event that this legislation is implemented and applied to personal injury damages in the same way as any other capital, the playing field between the treatment of a conventional lump sum and periodical payments might be levelled.

Whilst the above sets out the most important factors to take into account generally, each claimant needs an 'in principle' consideration of whether the advantages of a periodical payment order outweigh the disadvantages of a periodical payment order for them.

The individual factors are specific to each case and will depend upon the following factors:
- that claimant's life expectancy issues;
- the resulting mortality risks;
- the claimant's attitude towards investment risk;
- the need for financial certainty;
- the stability of income need;
- the need for flexibility;
- any uncertainty surrounding the claimant's future needs;
- the impact of the *Roberts v Johnstone* claim on capital need;
- the nature of the defendant;
- indexation issues;
- any deduction from full recovery;
- state benefits and support entitlement;
- the immediate capital expenditure;
- the wishes of the claimant;
- any existing assets, liabilities and other income; and

• the impact of the claimant living abroad (either now or in the future).

It is likely that a proportion of the above factors will not be known at an early stage. Therefore, it may be appropriate to consider setting out to the court the factors that will need to be known in order to give the 'in principle' indication. The court has the power to order that further evidence is given in respect of this issue at some point in the future.

18.6 VARIABLE ORDERS

A variable order means an order for periodical payments which permits variation in the payments where it is proved or admitted to be a chance that at some definite or indefinite time in the future the claimant will, as a result of the relevant act or omission, develop some serious disease or suffer some serious deterioration.[29]

Conversely, where there is proved or admitted to be a chance in the future that the claimant will enjoy some significant improvement in his physical or mental condition, where that condition had been adversely affected as a result of that act or omission (which gave rise to the cause of action), then the court may make a variable order.[30] This is a significant innovation. It allows a defendant to apply for a form of reverse 'provisional' periodical payments order. This stands in stark contrast with the position in relation to provisional damages.

The variable order:
• must specify the disease or type of deterioration or improvement;
• may specify a period in which an application for variation may be made;
• may specify more than one disease or type of deterioration or improvement and may, in respect of each, specify a different period within which an application for variation is to be made;
• must provide that a party must obtain the court's permission to apply for it to be varied, unless the court otherwise orders.[31]

Where a period is specified for an application to vary, a party may make more than one application to extend time for an application to vary. There is only permission to apply to vary once in relation to each specified condition and within the specified period.[32]

Where a variable order is made, the case file documents must be preserved by both the court and the parties for the duration of the order or any extension to it.[33]

---

[29] Articles 1(2)(f) and 2(a) of the Damages (Variation of Periodical Payments) Order 2005.
[30] Article 2(b) of the Damages (Variation of Periodical Payments) Order 2005.
[31] Article 5 of the Damages (Variation of Periodical Payments) Order 2005.
[32] Articles 6–7 of the Damages (Variation of Periodical Payments) Order 2005.
[33] Article 8 of the Damages (Variation of Periodical Payments) Order 2005.

With regard to the application of a variation, it is interesting to note the following extract from Hansard:[34]

> 'Lord Goodhart ...
>
> I have one small query. I note that the order in Article 13 does not appear to provide for the possible termination of a periodical payment where the claimant has fully recovered, which will happen no doubt from time to time. But, presumably, it could, without being terminated, be reduced to a nominal sum. Can the Minister confirm that that is the position?
>
> ...
>
> Lord Triesman ...
>
> I shall deal briefly with the point about full recovery. It is right to say that the order does not appear to provide for termination, but I agree with the noble Lord that the order could be reduced to a nominal sum if that were appropriate. We must make sure that that point is understood as well.

Parallel provisions allow the parties to make a variable agreement for periodical payments. The agreement must, in effect, contain the same provisions as a variable order.[35] A party who is permitted by an agreement to apply for its terms to be varied must obtain the court's permission to apply for it to be varied. This precludes actual variation by agreement unless the court is not to be involved at the point of settlement, or subsequently.[36]

18.7 CONCLUSIONS

Periodical payments remain a relatively new tool, which continue to develop in many areas. Their appropriate use has been limited to the highest value claims, where the need to secure financial funding for care for life is critical. The use of variable orders has been even more limited.

However, the Impact Assessment report to the MOJ's 2013 consultation paper previously referred to states the following:

> '2.47   Under this option greater use of periodical payment orders would be encouraged. The mechanism through which this would be achieved is not firmly established at this stage and the consultation associated with this IA seeks evidence to help inform this ...
>
> 2.49   It is understood that periodical payment orders are not currently used in a large proportion of cases, although it is possible that their use may change if the discount rate changes as part of the review of the methodology (the August 2012 consultation).'

---

[34]   House of Lords, 26 October 2004 vol 665 cc 1239-47.
[35]   Article 9 of the Damages (Variation of Periodical Payments) Order 2005.
[36]   Articles 5(e) and 9(3) of the Damages (Variation of Periodical Payments) Order 2005.

There is the spectre that there will be an attempt to encourage the use of periodical payments by using the stick of adjusting the discount rate to make conventional lump sum even more unattractive.

As a result, claimants may be forced into accepting periodical payments for elements of the claim that require the flexibility only afforded by a lump sum or for which there is no accurate measure that could be applied to best ensure that the need will be met in full for life. Furthermore, in those cases where periodical payments are either not achievable (for security reasons) or inappropriate (due to far less than 100% recovery), these claimants would be clearly penalised.

What does seem clear is that the use of periodical payments is likely to widen with time.

ANNEX: DRAFT MODEL PERIODICAL PAYMENTS ORDER AND SCHEDULE

IN THE HIGH COURT OF JUSTICE   Claim No: 6NG00547

QUEEN'S BENCH DIVISION

BETWEEN

C

(A protected party who proceeds by his Litigation Friend, CLF)

Claimant

and

D

Defendant

ORDER

BEFORE The Honourable Mr Justice [   ] sitting in the High Court of Justice Queens Bench Division in the [   ] District Registry on the [   ].

UPON HEARING [   ] on behalf of the Claimant and [   ] on behalf of the Defendant.

WHEREAS the Claimant has made a claim (the 'Claim') against the Defendant for personal injuries suffered by him arising out of the Defendant's negligence on or about [   ] and in respect of which proceedings were commenced by the Claimant against the Defendant in the High Court of Justice, on [   ].

AND WHEREAS the Claimant is a protected party and brings the claim by his Mother and Litigation Friend [   ].

[*AND WHEREAS Judgment was entered for the Claimant against the Defendant by the Honourable Mr Justice [   ] on [   ], with damages to be assessed.*]

AND WHEREAS [*by letter dated [   ] on behalf of the Secretary of State for Health it has been confirmed that the Secretary of State for Health (and any successor to that office) is the source of the proposed periodical payments (set out below) pursuant to the National Health Service (Existing Liabilities Scheme) Regulations/or as appropriate.*]

Or

[*AND WHEREAS the Defendant's insurer, has agreed to be responsible for and make the payments set out in the First Schedule to this Order for the benefit of the Claimant (referred to below as 'periodical payments'), in the sum of*

£[   ], *index linked to ASHE 6115 80*th *centile, subject to a deduction in respect of certain benefits as specified, as set out in the First Schedule attached.*

AND WHEREAS *the Defendant's insurer have confirmed that the periodical payments are protected by a scheme under section 213 of the Financial Services and Markets Act 2000 in accordance with section 2(4)(b) of the Damages Act 1996 as amended.*

AND WHEREAS *the Defendant and the Defendant's insurer agree with the Claimant that without prejudice to the Claimant's rights of enforcement of this Order generally, any failure to make the periodical payments in accordance with the First Schedule hereto, or any alteration in the method or change in the identity of the source of payment not in accordance with the Schedule, shall give rise to a direct right of the Claimant to enforce this Order and all rights arising under it against the Defendant's insurer in consideration of the Claimant agreeing to the terms of this Order.*]

Or

as appropriate

AND UPON READING the Advice from [Leading] Counsel for the Claimant dated the [   ] and the financial report of [   ], an independent financial adviser, dated [   ].

AND UPON the Claimant and the Defendant having agreed in full and final settlement of the claim the terms set forth herein.

AND UPON the Court being satisfied that:
(1) The continuity of payment under the Order is reasonably secure pursuant to section 2(3) of the Damages Act 1996 and/or pursuant to section 2(4)(c) of the Damages Act 1996 and under the terms of the Order as herein set out because *[the source of payment is a government body, namely the Secretary of State for Health (the Department of Health being a designated government body under the Damages (Government and Health Services Bodies) Order 2005) or as appropriate]*.
(2) The periodical payments are to be paid free of taxation under section 731–734 of the Income Tax (Trading and Other Income) Act 2005.
(3) The Order set out below is agreed by the Claimant and the Defendant as being the preferred Order that should apply.
(4) The form of the Order is that which best meets the Claimant's needs and the parties have complied with CPR 21 & 41.

AND UPON the Claimant having given the following undertakings to the Court:
(1) A Deputy has been appointed for the Claimant.

(2) The Claimant whether acting by his Litigation Friend or his Deputy will take all necessary steps to seek to stay the Claim in any proceedings which have begun or have been threatened against the Defendant in connection with the claim.

(3) The Claimant, his Litigation Friend and/or his Deputy will not institute any proceedings against the Defendant or any other party or person whomsoever in connection with the claim save by way of enforcement of this Order.

AND UPON the parties having agreed in full and final settlement of the claim that the Defendant shall pay to the Claimant the sum of £[ ] inclusive of interim payments of £[ ] and CRU of £[ ] and interest to 28 days after the date of the order approving the agreement together with the periodical payments contained in the Schedule annexed to this Order.

AND UPON the Court having approved the terms of this Order and the Schedule and Agreement annexed to this Order.

BY CONSENT

(1) **IT IS ORDERED** that the Defendant shall make payments to or for the benefit of the Claimant as follows in full and final settlement of the claim.

(a) By the [ ] the Defendant shall pay (having taken into account any interim payments and CRU and interest to that date) the sum of £[ ] into the Court of Protection in the Protection Division into account numbered [ ] [subject to a first charge pursuant to section 16(6) of the Legal Aid Act 1988 or section 10(7) of the Access to Justice Act 1999 if appropriate], there to be dealt with as a fund of a protected beneficiary and as that Court in its discretion shall think fit.

(b) By the [ ] the Defendant shall pay to the Claimant's solicitors free of any statutory charge the sum of £[ ] which sum shall include interest thereon to 28 days after the date of this order in respect of damages to be held on trust for the Claimant's parents in respect of gratuitous past care.

(c) The Defendant shall pay to the Department of Work and Pensions the CRU benefits amounting to £[ ].

(d) Further, the sums as specified in the attached Schedule be paid by the Defendant as stipulated in the Schedule and be funded in accordance with section 2(4)(c) of the Damages Act 1996 with the sums payable to comprise damages for future care and case management.

(2) **AND IT IS FURTHER ORDERED** that the Defendant do pay the Claimant's costs of this action on the standard basis such costs to be the subject of a Detailed Assessment if not agreed.

(3) **AND IT IS FURTHER ORDERED** that there be a Detailed Assessment of the Claimant's costs in accordance with Regulation 107 of the Civil Legal Aid (General) Regulations 1989 as amended, Article 5 of the Access to Justice

Act 1999 (Commencement No. 3) Order 2000, Article 4 of the Community Legal Services (Funding) Order 2000 and the Civil Legal Aid (General) (Amendment) Regulations 2000 as amended, save that in the event that the Claimant's Solicitors waive any claim to any further costs beyond those referred to above, they have permission to dispense with any Legal Aid assessment.

(4) **AND IT IS FURTHER ORDERED** that all further proceedings in this action be stayed except for the purpose of implementing the terms of this Order and the terms set out in the attached Schedule.

(5) **AND IT IS FURTHER ORDERED** that there be permission to restore.

Dated this [   ].

SCHEDULE TO THE ORDER

Part 1 of the Schedule to the Order

Each sum payable under part(s) 2 and 3 of this schedule is a "periodical payment" subject to the conditions set out in paragraphs 1-8 of this part

1   Unless specifically stated, all the periodical payments under part(s) 2 and 3 of this schedule will continue during the lifetime of the Claimant.

2   No minimum number of periodical payments under part(s) 2 and 3 of this schedule shall be made.

3   The Defence Insurer shall be entitled to require the Claimant to undergo medical examinations at their request upon reasonable notice being given to the Claimant at any time during the Claimant's life time, such medical examinations to be limited to obtaining a medical opinion as to the Claimant's general health for the express purposes of reviewing their reserves and/or obtaining a quotation for the purchase cost of an annuity to fund the periodical payments. The Claimant shall have permission to apply to the Court in the event of reasonable concern with regard to the frequency of any such examinations. The cost of any such examination and/or application to the court, to include any reasonable costs incurred by the Claimant in attending the examination, shall be paid by the Defence Insurer who has required the Claimant to undergo the examination or examinations unless the Court otherwise orders.

4   Payment of the periodical payments under part(s) 2 and 3 of this schedule will cease on the death of the Claimant.

5   The final periodical payment under part(s) 2 and 3 of this schedule will be pro-rated for so much of the final year that the Claimant had survived and any balance owing to the NHS LA or its successor will be repayable to it out of the Claimant's estate, subject only to deduction by the Claimant's estate of such sums as the Claimant's estate may be liable for in respect of the termination of the employment of any persons employed to care for the Claimant.

6   The NHS LA shall be entitled to require the Claimant to produce evidence in a form reasonably satisfactory to the NHS LA that the Claimant remains alive before making any periodical payment.

7   The periodical payments under part(s) 2 and 3 of this schedule are to be made by BACS to the Court of Protection (or its successor) for the benefit of the Claimant under reference [   ] (where applicable).

8   Under part(s) 2 and 3 of this schedule the NHS LA shall provide to the Claimant and/or the Deputy in writing:

   8.1 At the time of each periodical payment an explanation of how it has been calculated;

   8.2 If reclassification or a change of methodology occurs within the meaning of part 3 of this Schedule then when a periodical payment is made or in the event of a deferred periodical payment as soon as practicable following such a reclassification or a change of methodology, the relevant calculation(s) under paragraph 6 and the numerical value of '*AR*' as defined in paragraph 7.1.4 of that part applicable to any current and/or future periodical payment to be made under that part.

9   The NHS LA shall pay the relevant annual sums set out in part(s) 2 and 3 of this schedule on 15 December of each year, save that:

   9.1 If the Office for National Statistics ['*ONS*'] does not publish by 17th November in the relevant year all the relevant data and as a result the NHS LA is unable to perform the relevant calculations under part(s) 2 and 3 to recalculate the periodical payment(s) due to the Claimant before 15 December of the relevant year, the NHS LA shall on 15 December of the relevant year make the periodical payment(s): (a) in the same sum as that paid in the previous year; or (b) in the increased/decreased sum recalculated in accordance with the relevant data for the previous year where in the relevant year the annual sum was due to be increased or decreased or commenced under the relevant sub-paragraph of paragraph 1 of part(s) 2 or 3.

   9.2 Any balancing payment due to the claimant or the NHS LA shall be made within 28 days after the publication of all the relevant data by the ONS.

   9.3 The NHS LA shall pay interest at the then applicable Judgment Act rate on any outstanding periodical payment or part of a periodical payment not paid on 15 December in any year from 16 December in that year until full payment is made, except that in the circumstances contemplated in paragraphs 8.1-2 interest due on any balancing payment shall only be payable by the NHS LA from 28 days after publication of all the relevant data until full payment is made.

10   For the period from [the date when the future loss period accrues assuming periodical payments relate only to future loss] to [14 December of the relevant year when the periodical payments will commence] to represent the periodical payment under part(s) 2 and 3 of this schedule for

that period the Defendant do pay the sum of [£   ] (   ) due as the balance of the periodical payment for the above period and that sum shall be paid 4.00 pm on the [   ].

Part 2: The RPI-Linked Periodical Payments

1.   The following present value annual sums as recalculated in accordance with paragraph 3 shall be paid in advance:

    1.1 The annual sum of [£   ] (   ) payable on the 15th of December in each year from 15th December [   ] until 15th December [   ] inclusive, with the first such payment to be made on 15th December [   ]

    1.2 The annual sum of [£   ] (   ) payable on the 15th of December in each year from 15th December [   ] until 15th December [   ] inclusive

    1.3 The annual sum of [£   ] (   ) payable on 15th of December in each year from 15th December [   ]

The expiry of one period and the commencement of another period under the above sub-paragraphs constitutes a "step change" under this Schedule.

2.   The index to be applied is the United Kingdom General Index of Retail Prices for all items ['RPI'] published by the ONS (January 1987 = 100) or any equivalent or comparable measure which in the parties' reasonable opinion replaces such index from time to time. In the event of a dispute between the parties as to the appropriate alternative measure and/or the formulae to be applied in the event of a rebasing of RPI the same shall be determined by the court.

3.   Each periodical payment referred to in paragraph 1 *[1.1 to 1.3]* above shall be recalculated annually in November in each year prior to payment on 15th December of the same year from November [   ] in accordance with the following formula

$$PP = C \times \frac{NF}{A}$$

    3.1 Where

        3.1.1 'PP' = the amount payable by way of periodical payment in each year, the first PP being the payment made on 15th December [ ]

        3.1.2 'C' = the relevant annual sum set out in paragraph 1 *[1.1 to 1.3]* above respectively

        3.1.3 'NF' = the index applicable to September in the year in which the calculation is being carried out, the first NF being in respect of September [ ]

        3.1.4 'A' = the index applicable to [the index applicable to three months prior to the date of settlement or judgment]

Part 3: The ASHE 6115-Linked Periodical Payments

1   The following present value annual sums as recalculated in accordance
     with paragraphs 3-10 shall be paid in advance
     1.1 The annual sum of [£   ] (   ) payable on 15th December in each
          year from [   ] until 15th December [   ] inclusive, with the first
          such payment to be made on 15th December [ ]
     1.2 The annual sum of [£   ] (   ) payable on 15th December in each
          year from [   ] until 15th December [   ] inclusive
     1.3 The annual sum of [£   ] (   ) payable on 15th December in each
          year from [   ]

The expiry of one period and the commencement of another period under the
above sub-paragraphs constitutes a "step change" under this Schedule

2   The relevant earnings data are the gross hourly pay for "*all*" employees
     given by the present Standard Occupational Category ['SOC'] for (Care
     assistants and home carers) ['*6115*'] at the relevant percentile shown
     below (currently in table <u>26.5a</u> at the tab for "*all*" employees) of the
     Annual Survey of Hours and Earnings in the United Kingdom ['*ASHE*']
     published by the ONS. The original relevant percentiles are:
     2.1 [   ] percentile shall be applied to paragraphs [   ] above
     2.2 [   ] percentile shall be applied to paragraphs [   ] above

First payment of periodical payments under each step

3   Unless paragraphs 5-10 below apply, the annual periodical payments
     referred to in paragraph 1 *[1.1 to 1.3]* above shall be recalculated in
     November prior to payment on the 15th December of the same year from
     November [   ] in accordance with the following formula

$$PP = C \times \frac{NP}{A}$$

3.1 Where
     3.1.1 '*PP*' = the amount payable by way of periodical payment in each
            year being calculated in November and paid on the 15th of December
            the first '*PP*' being the payment on the 15th of December [   ]
     3.1.2 '*C*' = the relevant annual sum set out in paragraph 1 *[1.1 to 1.3]*
            above respectively
     3.1.3 '*NP*' = the "*first release*" hourly gross wage rate published by the
            ONS for the relevant percentile of ASHE SOC 6115 for "*all*"
            employees for the year in which the calculation is being carried out,
            the first *NP* being the figure applicable to the year [   ] published in
            or around October [   ]
     3.1.4 '*A*' = the "*revised*" hourly gross wage rate for the relevant
            percentile of ASHE SOC 6115 for all employees applicable to [   ]
            and published by the ONS in or around October [   ]. In the event
            of a correction by the ONS it will be the replacement "*revised*" figure
            issued by the ONS

Subsequent payment of periodical payments under each step

4   Unless paragraphs 5-10 below apply, the annual periodical payments referred to in paragraph 1 *[1.1 to 1.3]* above shall be recalculated annually in subsequent years in November in each year prior to payment on the 15th December of the same year from November [   ] in accordance with the following formula

$$PP = C \times \frac{NP + (NF - OP)}{A}$$

4.1   Where in addition to the definitions previously set out

    4.1.1   '*NF*' = the "*revised*" hourly gross wage rate published by the ONS for the relevant percentile of ASHE SOC 6115 for "*all*" employees for the year prior to the year in which the calculation is being carried out, the first *NF* being that applicable to the year [   ] and published in or around October [   ]

    4.1.2   '*OP*' = the "*first release*" hourly gross wage rate published by the ONS for the relevant percentile of ASHE SOC 6115 for "*all*" employees for the year prior to the year in which the calculation is being carried out, the first *OP* being the figure applicable to the year [   ] published in or around October [   ].

Payments upon reclassification of the SOC or a change of methodology by the ONS

5   Reclassification for the purposes of paragraphs 6-9 below, and subject to paragraph 6.1.2, occurs when the ONS publishes for the same year "*revised*" hourly gross wage rates for both:

    5.1   the previously applied SOC (for which the "*revised*" wage rate is defined as '*AF*' in paragraph 6.1.1 below) and

    5.2   for a new SOC (for which the "*revised*" wage rate is defined as '*AR*' in paragraph 7.1.4 below) that includes those currently defined as "*home carers*" in ASHE SOC 6115

Or alternatively, where the ONS publishes *AR* for a new SOC that includes those currently defined as "home carers" in the previously applied SOC but does not publish *AF* for the same year, then reclassification is nonetheless deemed to have occurred.

Unless the Court otherwise orders pursuant to paragraph 11 below, in either event the new SOC shall be applied.

6   The relevant annual sum referable to the sums at paragraph 1 *[1.1 to 1.3]* above following reclassification shall be known as '*CR*' and shall be calculated only in each year of reclassification, in accordance with the following formula

$$CR = C \times \frac{AF}{A}$$

6.1 Where in addition to the definitions previously set out

    6.1.1 '*AF*' = the final published "*revised*" hourly gross wage rate for the relevant percentile of the previously applied SOC for "*all*" employees

    6.1.2 If, for the year of reclassification, the ONS does not publish *AF*, then the "*first release*" hourly gross wage rate published for the relevant percentile of the previously applied SOC for "*all*" employees (which is defined as '*OPF*' in paragraph 7.1.3 below) shall be applied in its place

    6.1.3 If reclassification has previously occurred then C will be the numerical value of CR calculated when reclassification last occurred

7   When reclassification occurs the first payment only shall be

$$PPR = [CR \times \frac{NPR}{AR}] + [C \times \frac{AF - OPF}{A}]$$

The second bracket of the above formula shall not apply where at the time of reclassification, either (a) there has been no periodical payment made in the previous year or (b) where at that time a step change in the annual sum is due under paragraph 1 above and in those circumstances the first payment shall be calculated in accordance with the following formula

$$PPR = [CR \times \frac{NPR}{AR}]$$

Where reclassification has occurred on more than one occasion prior to the first payment then successive applications of paragraph 6 above must be carried out first to arrive at the present numerical value of CR and C shall represent the numerical value of CR previously calculated

7.1 Where in addition to the definitions previously set out

    7.1.1 '*PPR*' = the amount payable by way of periodical payment in each year following reclassification

    7.1.2 '*NPR*' = the "*first release*" hourly gross wage rate published for the relevant percentile of the new SOC following reclassification for the year in which the calculation is being carried out

    7.1.3 '*OPF*' = the final "*first release*" hourly gross wage rate published for the relevant percentile of the previously applied SOC for "*all*" employees

7.1.4 '*AR*' = the "*revised*" hourly gross wage rate for the <u>published</u> percentile of the new SOC, <u>which,</u> when first published, is closest to *AF*, and the <u>relevant</u> percentile <u>of the new</u> SOC shall be the percentile to which *AR* corresponds

8 Until further reclassification the formula for calculating subsequent values of *PPR* shall be

$$PPR = CR \times \frac{NPR + (NFR - OPR)}{AR}$$

8.1 Where in addition to the definitions previously set out

8.1.1 '*NFR*' = the "*revised*" hourly gross wage rate published for the relevant percentile of the new SOC following reclassification for the year prior to the year in which the calculation is being carried out

8.1.2 '*OPR*' = the "*first release*" hourly gross wage rate published for the relevant percentile in the new SOC following reclassification for the year prior to the year in which the calculation is being carried out

9 Further reclassifications shall be dealt with in the same way by the application of paragraphs 5-8 above

10 For the purposes of this part a change of methodology occurs when the ONS publishes two sets of data for the applied SOC. In that event, the same process as set out in paragraphs 6-9 above shall be undertaken. However, in these circumstances references to

10.1 '*reclassification*' shall be treated as being a reference to '*a change of methodology*',

10.2 '*the new SOC*' shall be treated as being a reference to '*the existing SOC using the new methodology*', and

10.3 '*the previously applied SOC*' shall be treated as being a reference to '*the existing SOC using the old methodology*'.

Miscellaneous

11 In the event of a dispute between the parties arising out of the application of this part, there be liberty to apply.

CHAPTER 19

STATUTORY BENEFITS (INCLUDING RECOUPMENT) AND SERVICES

19.1 INTRODUCTION

Statutory assistance and catastrophic injury litigation often go hand-in-hand. However, this is a topic that many practitioners struggle to get to grips with. In this chapter we aim to provide guidance on the assistance available to catastrophically injured claimants from the state and how these benefits and services interact with a claim for damages. We will also provide practical assistance on how to protect entitlement to such statutory assistance following an award of damages.[1]

19.2 SOURCES OF STATUTORY ASSISTANCE

There are a number of sources of statutory assistance, including social security benefits, local authority care (both residential and domiciliary), NHS care, children's services and Supporting People grants.

The law relating to social security benefits, found in primary and secondary legislation, is relatively rigid in its operation and interpretation. By contrast, the law in relation to community and healthcare assistance is complex, convoluted and largely subject to discretion. The higher courts have not been slow to point out the problems facing all of those involved in attempting to analyse, interpret and apply the law in this area. Indeed, in *Crofton v NHS Litigation Authority*,[2] Dyson LJ felt compelled to state:

> 'We cannot conclude this judgment without expressing our dismay at the complexity and labyrinthine nature of the relevant legislation and guidance, as well as (in some respects) its obscurity.'

19.2.1 Social security benefits

A clear understanding of social security benefits is needed for practitioners involved in catastrophic injury litigation as they can impact on a claim in two

---

[1] For a detailed explanation of the law in this area, practitioners are referred to Paul Stagg's chapter (Chapter 5) in Kemp & Kemp, Vol 1, 'Impact of entitlement to state services and benefits' (Sweet & Maxwell, loose leaf).

[2] [2007] EWCA Civ 71, [2007] 1 WLR 923 at para 111.

important ways. A seriously injured claimant may be reliant upon state benefits to help meet his or her needs and entitlement to means-tested benefits is usually a prerequisite for entitlement to state funded care. Practitioners must also understand the circumstances in which social security benefits will be offset from the claimant's damages so as to avoid miscalculating or under-settling the claim.

A distinction needs to be drawn between social security benefits that are means-tested and non means-tested. Non means-tested benefits will not be affected by the receipt of an award of damages.[3] Quite the contrary is true of means-tested benefits.

Sections I1 and I2 of *Facts and Figures: Tables for the Calculation of Damages*[4] provide a detailed breakdown of these benefits and the amount that is payable at current rates. Useful guidance is also given on the DWP website.[5]

The whole system of welfare benefits is currently undergoing a process of radical change and this chapter seeks to point out the key points for practitioners to be aware of.

19.2.1.1 Non means-tested

(1) Employment and support allowance (ESA): this has replaced incapacity benefit (IB) and income support (IS) and is paid on incapacity grounds for new claimants from October 2008 onwards. It includes both contributory and income related (means tested) benefit based on either limited capability for work or limited capability for work-related activity. Benefit is paid at a basic rate during a 13-week assessment phase. Youth ESA was abolished for new claimants from April 2012. Existing claimants are able to go on claiming but only for one year from entitlement, disregarding time in the support group. Contributory ESA benefit is time-limited to one year for those in the work-related activity group and is taxable. Income related ESA (IRESA) is a passport to additional benefits including housing benefit (HB) and council tax benefit (CTB). Pensioner premiums are also applicable. Contributory ESA is taxable. Means-tested ESA is not.

(2) Incapacity benefit (IB): existing claimants paid IB pre-October 2008 will move to ESA over a transitional period with all surviving IB claimants to move to ESA by March 2014. IB is contributory (save for those incapacitated in youth) and payable to those who are incapable of work. Personal capability assessments apply. IB is paid on sliding scale depending on age and whether a short-term or long-term claimant. It is taxable save for short-term lower rate and transitional benefits.

(3) Industrial injuries disablement benefit (IIDB): this is paid if an employed claimant has suffered from an accident at work or contracted certain

---

[3]   However, in certain circumstances entitlement may be affected where the claimant is in hospital or local authority residential care.

[4]   Sweet & Maxwell, current edition 2012/13.

[5]   See www.gov.uk/browse/benefits.

industrial diseases and it is shown that the claimant is at least 14% disabled as a result of that accident or disease. The amount of benefit is dependent on age and seriousness of disability (assessed by doctor on a scale of 1–100%). It is non-taxable and non-contributory.

(4) Carer's allowance: this is paid to those over 16 who spend at least 35 hours per week caring for a recipient of higher or middle rates of disability living allowance (DLA) (care component) or attendance allowance (AA) or constant attendance allowance (CAA). It is not payable if the claimant is earning more that £100 per week. It is non-contributory and taxable.

(5) Disability living allowance (DLA): this comprises two components, care and mobility. The care component is awarded at three different rates depending on level of assistance required by claimant during day and night. The mobility component is paid at higher or lower rates depending upon level of immobility. The claimant must qualify before reaching 65. Available to under 16s. It is non-contributory and non-taxable. It is due to be replaced by the Personal Independency Payment (PIP) from 2013 onwards (see **19.2.1.3**).

(6) Attendance allowance (AA): this is the equivalent of the care component of DLA for those over 65.

19.2.1.2 Means-tested

(1) Income support (IS): this is available to under 60s working less than 16 hours per week on low income. It is not for unemployed or new claimants post October 2008 who have no or limited capacity for work (these claimants will qualify for ESA). IS brings automatic entitlement to additional benefits such as maximum housing benefit (HB) and council tax benefit (CTB). Excluding the value of the claimant's home, capital up to £6,000 is disregarded in the means-testing process. There is no entitlement if capital exceeds £16,000. Capital between £6,000 and £16,000 is deemed to produce tariff income of £1 for each £250 (or part) over £6,000.[6] Capital of the claimant's partner counts as belonging to the claimant. Different capital limits apply for those in residential homes. Premiums are payable for disability, enhanced disability and specific family circumstances. It is non-contributory and non-taxable, save for exceptional circumstances.

(2) Housing benefit (HB) and council tax benefit (CTB): these assist with the claimant's payment of rent and council tax. It is administered by local authorities. The award is dependent on money coming in, the amount of the claimant's savings and eligible charge. Excluding the value of the claimant's home, capital up to £6,000 is disregarded (£6,000 increases to £10,000 for pensioners as from November 2009). There is no entitlement if capital exceeds £16,000, save if the claimant is on pension credit (PC) guarantee. Capital between £6,000 and £16,000 is deemed to produce tariff income of £1 for every £250/£500 depending upon whether claimant

---

[6] By way of example, if a claimant has £7,000 assessable capital, a tariff income of £4 will be assumed.

is under/over 60. Capital of the claimant's partner counts as belonging to the claimant. Different capital limits apply for children and those in residential homes. They are non-contributory and non-taxable.

(3) Pension credit (PC): this comprises two elements: 'guarantee credit' for those 60 and over whose income is below the standard minimum guarantee and 'savings credit' for those 65 and over with modest savings or income. It is administered by the Pensions Service. As from November 2009, excluding the value of the claimant's home, capital of £10,000 is disregarded (£6,000 before this date). Thereafter, capital above £10,000 is deemed to produce tariff income of £1 for each £500 (or part). There is no upper capital limit. Guarantee credit is a passport to HB and CTB. It is non-contributory and non-taxable.

(4) Working tax credit (WTC) and child tax credit (CTC): these provide support for families with children. They are based on gross annual income. If the claimant has a partner, they are based on joint income. They taper as income rises. Additional premiums are payable if the claimant worker is disabled or claimant's child is disabled. They are administered by HMRC.

Assessable capital includes cash, money in the bank or building society, National Savings accounts and certificates, income bonds, stocks and shares, property (other than the claimant's own home), premium bonds and the value of any trust fund that is available to the claimant (which does not comprise a personal injury trust).

19.2.1.3   Reform

Universal Credit is a new benefit that has started to replace six existing benefits with a simpler, single monthly payment if you are out of work or on a low income. Universal Credit will help you to be better off in work, start a new job or work more hours.

Universal Credit will eventually replace:
- Income-based Jobseeker's Allowance;
- Income-related Employment and Support Allowance;
- Income Support;
- Working Tax Credit;
- Child Tax Credit;
- Housing Benefit.

Universal Credit was introduced on 29 April 2013 in selected areas of Greater Manchester and Cheshire. At this time, the eligibility to claim Universal Credit will depend on where the claimant lives and their personal circumstances. Universal Credit will be gradually rolled out to the rest of the UK from October 2013 and will be completed by 2017.[7]

---

[7]   Further details are available at www.gov.uk/universal-credit/overview.

In addition to the Universal Credit reform, Disability Living Allowance (DLA) will be replaced for working age claimants (age 16 to 64) with the new Personal Independence Payments (PIP). As from 10 June 2013 all new claims for anyone within working age will be for PIP instead of DLA throughout the entirety of the UK, with the exception of renewal claims from a fixed term DLA award which is due to expire before the end of February 2014. From October 2014 the DWP will begin to select existing DLA claimants and converting them to PIP. This conversion process is likely to last until at least 2018. Children turning 16 will have to claim PIP when their existing fixed term award is coming to an end.

PIP is made up of a Mobility Component and a Daily Living Component, each payable at two weekly rates, namely standard and enhanced. Unlike DLA, PIP does not assess a claimant's disabilities but considers the impact that a person's health condition has on their daily lives and their ability to undertake a number of specified everyday activities. The assessment takes account of physical, sensory, mental, intellectual and cognitive impairments and developmental needs. PIP carries the same benefits as DLA: it is non means-tested and non-taxable. Any award of the Daily Living Component will be a gateway to Carer's Allowance and the Enhanced Rate Mobility Component will entitle the claimant to the Motability Scheme.

For personal injury/clinical negligence practitioners, the key points to look out for are that there is no equivalent to the existing lower rate care component of DLA and to qualify for the higher rate Mobility Component a claimant must be unable to walk a short distance (the regulations saying 20 metres) before the onset of severe discomfort.

Housing Benefit and Council Tax Support are also due for reform. As from April 2013 social housing tenants (who are claiming housing benefit) with spare bedrooms will receive less housing benefit and will either have to pay the difference to their landlord or move to a home that has the appropriate number of rooms for their family circumstances (commonly known as the 'Bedroom Tax'). There will be no new claims for Housing Benefit after April 2014, with current claimants transferred to Universal Credit by 2017. Council Tax Support is replacing Council Tax Benefit. This allows local authorities in England to design their own Council Tax Support Schemes. The result is that the level of council tax benefit/support is likely to reduce, albeit there will be protection for people over pensionable age and claimants who are entitled to disability premiums and those with a dependent child under 6 years of age.

In cases involving members of the armed forces injured in the line of duty, the Armed Forces Independence Payment will apply as an alternative to DLA, the PIP and Attendance Allowance.

19.2.2 The temporary disregard/personal injury trusts/structured settlements

The first payment made to a claimant in consequence of any personal injury (not a fatal accident claim) will be disregarded for a period of 52 weeks when assessing that claimant's entitlement to means tested IS, ISESA, HB and CTB.[8] The rules relating to this temporary disregard are complex and far from satisfactory. If an interim payment is made, the disregard is triggered. If part of the award is spent, then the amount disregarded must be reduced by the amount of the expenditure.

In catastrophic injury cases, if the claimant is not a protected party, a personal injury trust should be set up in good time during the first year after receipt of any interim payment or damages without those funds being mixed with any other funds in the meantime. Any lump sum or periodical payment paid into the trust will then be disregarded for benefit purposes and the entitlement to claim means-tested benefits will remain unaffected by the receipt of funds.[9] This will avoid the practical difficulties surrounding the 52-week disregard. Even if the claimant is a protected party (in which case damages administered by the Court of Protection, county court or High Court will be disregarded for the purposes of means-tested benefits) there may still be practical advantages of setting up a personal injury trust. An application to the court would be required to set up such a trust in these circumstances and the Court of Protection does not encourage such applications. Guidance was given by the Court in *Re HM*,[10] where, despite granting the setting up of a PIT on the facts of that case, the Court said that there should be some prima facie factor of 'magnetic importance' to warrant setting up a PIT where funds would otherwise be within the Court of Protection. The Court would look for a major advantage, such as a major or unusual tax advantage, and a high level of trustee control to counteract the loss of Court of Protection supervision, control of costs and requirements for security bonds and professional indemnity insurance.

The existence of a personal injury trust does not affect entitlement to means-tested benefits of a claimant's partner or family members in the same household.[11]

Detailed guidance on the implementation and operation of personal injury trusts is provided at Section I4 of *Facts & Figures*. In all cases the safest course

---

[8]   Paragraph 12A of Sch 10 to the Income Support (General) Regulations 1987, SI 1987/1967; the Social Security (Miscellaneous Amendments) (No 4) Regulations 2006, SI 2006/2378 and the National Assistance (Sums for Personal Requirements and Assessment of Resources) Amendment (England) Regulations 2008, SI 2008/593 – note: temporary disregards do not apply for PC or HB and CTB for people over 60 as these disregard payments made in compensation for personal injury anyway.

[9]   Provided he or she satisfies the criteria of low income and capital under the relevant threshold limit.

[10] Court of Protection, 4 November 2011, 11870543, HHJ Marshall QC.

[11] Income Support (General) Regulations 23(1) 1987 – mirrored by regulations for other means-tested benefits.

of action for the practitioner must be to take advice from an independent financial expert before the first payment is made under a claim (whether this is an interim payment or final judgment/settlement).

19.2.3 Recovery of social security benefits

Social security benefit recovery is governed by the Social Security (Recovery of Benefits) Act 1997 (SS(RB)A 1997) and administered by the Compensation Recovery Unit (CRU).

The basic aim of the SS(RB)A 1997 is that a defendant should repay the state for the social security benefits received by a claimant as a consequence of his or her accident, whilst at the same time allowing the defendant to offset such benefits against the claim for damages, thereby ensuring no double recovery on the part of the claimant.

However, a deduction should only take place on a like-for-like basis. In *Lowther v Chatwin*,[12] Hale LJ summed up the purpose of the legislation as follows:

> 'Under the 1997 Act, the sums paid to the state to recoup certain benefits can only be deducted from the equivalent head of damages awarded. The object is to "ring fence" the general damages for pain, suffering, loss of amenity, or for loss of congenial employment, or the like, while enabling the state to recoup its expenditure on benefits paid in respect of loss of earnings, the cost of care and loss of mobility. Another important qualification is that the state can only recover benefits paid, and accordingly such benefits can only be deducted from the damages, for the "relevant period", which is a maximum of five years.'

Section 13 of *Facts & Figures* provides excellent guidance on the operation of SS(RB)A 1997 as it applies to personal injury claims. For the purpose of providing a quick reference guide, the following updated table sets out the relevant heads of compensation and corresponding listed benefits that are recoverable against such claims:[13]

---

[12] [2003] EWCA Civ 729 at para 3.
[13] Taken from the DWP website at www.dwp.gov.uk.

Type of claim affected	Deductible Benefits
Compensation for loss of earnings	Disablement pension payable under section 103 of the Social Security Contributions and Benefits 1992 Act (also known as Industrial Injuries Disablement Benefit) Employment and Support Allowance Incapacity Benefit Income Support Invalidity Pension Allowance Jobseeker's Allowance Reduced Earnings Allowance Severe Disablement Allowance Sickness Benefits Statutory Sick Pay Unemployability Supplement Unemployment Benefit
Compensation for the cost of care incurred during the relevant period	Attendance Allowance Care component of Disability Living Allowance Disablement pension increase for Constant Attendance Allowance Exceptionally Severe Disablement Allowance Living Component of Personal Independence Payment (PIP L)
Compensation for loss of mobility during the relevant period	Mobility Allowance Mobility Component of Disability Living Allowance Mobility Component of Personal Independence Payment (PIP M)

The 'relevant period' during which benefits are deemed recoverable is a maximum of 5 years from the date of the accident or injury or, in the case of disease, 5 years from the date of the first claim for benefit on the basis of the disease. The relevant period may be brought to an end sooner if a payment is made in final discharge of the claim.

Practitioners are reminded that the compensator's liability to make CRU payments arises on the making of the first compensation payment. Accordingly, an interim payment will trigger the liability (see Chapter ?on interim payments).

Interest is payable on the full amount of special damages before allowing for recoupment. As a general principle, therefore, benefits do not reduce the interest payable.[14]

---

14   *Wadey v Surrey County Council* [2001] 1 WLR 820.

'Compensation' in Sch 2 to the SS(RB)A 1997 includes interest, so an offset can be made against any interest payable on a claim for loss of earnings, cost of care or loss of mobility.[15]

19.2.4   Recoupment and Part 36 offers

CPR, r 36.15 provides for the effect of recoupment on settlement offers. *Williams v Devon County Council*[16] provides further guidance in this area and highlights that the Part 36 offer will not be effective unless it: (a) states the gross amount of compensation that is being offered; (b) the name and amount of any deductible benefits by which the gross amount is being reduced; and (c) the net sum in compensation.[17]

19.2.5   Exempted payments

A host of payments that may have been made to the claimant are exempted from the operation of the SS(RB)A 1997 by way of primary and secondary legislation. These can be found on the DWP website.[18]

19.2.6   Benefits outside the SS(RB)A 1997

By virtue of s 17 of the SS(RB)A 1997, any listed benefits paid after the relevant period are to be disregarded. Accordingly, there is no right to offset listed benefits paid after the relevant period.[19]

The position is different vis-à-vis those benefits that are not listed in the SS(RB)A 1997. Any such benefits fall to be assessed in accordance with the common law principles set out in the case of *Hodgson v Trapp*.[20] Accordingly, unless the unlisted benefit would have been received in any event, the claimant will have to give credit against his or her claim on a like-for-like basis, both in terms of the past and future receipt of such benefits.[21] Examples of this in practice include HB,[22] CTB[23] and payments received from the ILF.[24] If the defendant argues for the deduction of such benefits into the future, the claimant should contend for a discount to the multiplier applied to reflect the prospect that benefits may not be payable on an ongoing basis.[25]

---

[15]   *Griffiths v British Coal Corporation* [2001] 1 WLR 1493.
[16]   [2003] EWCA Civ 365.
[17]   In accordance with s 8 and Sch 2 to the SS(RB)A 1997.
[18]   See www.dwp.gov.uk.
[19]   See *Jackman v Corbett* [1988] QB 154 and *Eagle v Chambers (No 2)* [2004] EWCA Civ 1033.
[20]   [1989] AC 807.
[21]   If the benefit relates to an aspect of damages that is not claimed, no credit need be given.
[22]   *Clenshaw v Tanner* [2002] EWCA Civ 184.
[23]   *Smith v Jenkins* [2003] EWHC 1356.
[24]   *Dorrington v Lawrence* [2001] All ER (D) 145.
[25]   By way of example, in *Smith v Salford HA* (unreported) 4 August 1995, Potter J applied a multiplier of 15 for the future care claim and a reduced multiplier of 10 for the future receipt of DLA that was to be offset against the claim (pre 1997 Act).

19.3   NHS CARE

Under Part 1 of the National Health Service Act 2006, care provided by the NHS must be free of charge. This includes an obligation to provide for ongoing nursing care, as opposed to 'ordinary personal care' that is to be provided by a local authority.

Under s 49 of the Health and Social Care Act 2001, nursing care is defined as:

> 'any services provided by a registered nurse and involving—
> (a)   the provision of care, or
> (b)   the planning, supervision or delegation of the provision of care,
>
> other than any services which, having regard to their nature and the circumstances in which they are provided, do not need to be provided by a registered nurse.'

In practice, given that a claimant may be required to pay for care provided by a local authority, the distinction can have enormous consequences. Unfortunately, however, it is not always easy to delineate between the two, and local authorities do not always do so consistently.

19.3.1   Continuing care

NHS care delivered outside primary healthcare facilities is known as 'continuing care'. This is distinct from the term 'continuing healthcare', which is a specific type of 'continuing care'.

There are four types of assistance provided by an NHS trust on a continuing care basis.

19.3.1.1   *Continuing Healthcare*

Continuing Healthcare is governed by the National Framework for NHS Continuing Healthcare and NHS Funded Nursing Care ('the National Framework')[26] and supplemented by the NHS Continuing Healthcare (Responsibilities) Directions. A service user will be entitled to Continuing Healthcare if his or her 'primary need is a health need'.[27] A service user will only be required to fall back on local authority assistance if continuing healthcare is not required.

As from 1 April 2013, Clinical Commissioning Groups (CCGs) and the NHS Commissioning Board ('the Board') assumed responsibilities for NHS continuing healthcare and NHS-funded nursing care. CCGs will have the same responsibilities as were previously held by Primary Care Trusts (PCTs), except in specified circumstances.

---

[26]   Published by the Department of Health (November 2012, Revised).
[27]   Paragraph 23 of the National Framework and applied in *R v North and East Devon HA ex p Coughlan* [2001] QB 213.

As from April 2014, people who have been assessed as eligible for NHS Continuing Healthcare services will have the 'right to ask' for a Personal Health Budget (PHB) and by 2015 it is expected that everyone who could benefit will have the option of a PHB.

Under the National Framework, a service user does not comply with the primary need test if the nursing or other health services that he or she requires are:

'(i)   no more than incidental or ancillary to the provision of accommodation which Local Authority social services are under a duty to provide; and

(ii)   are not of a nature beyond which a Local Authority whose primary responsibility is to provide social services could be expected to provide.'

It is not surprising that difficulties have arisen in relation to the application of this test. Within the National Framework a 'decision support tool' is provided to assist practitioners in determining whether the test is satisfied or not. This incorporates a number of practical considerations including the nature of the service user's needs, along with the intensity, complexity and unpredictability of those needs.

The duty to provide Continuing Healthcare is not enforceable by way of an action claiming damages[28] and a service user must therefore use the extensive rights of review available and judicial review if necessary.

19.3.1.2   *Care provided jointly by NHS trusts and local authorities*

Under the National Health Service Act 2006, NHS trusts and local authorities can enter into partnership agreements to meet the needs of a service user. This applies where a service user does not qualify for fully funded continuing healthcare but continues to have extensive needs for services that only the NHS can provide. Money can be pooled between health bodies and health-related local authority services, functions can be delegated and resources and management structures can be integrated.

Ordinarily, services are commissioned by the local authority, who then receives reimbursement from the NHS trust. In these circumstances, the service user will receive the proportion of services paid for by the NHS trust free of charge, but he or she remains eligible for charge vis-à-vis the proportion funded by the local authority.

19.3.1.3   *Local authority care where there is a nursing contribution from the NHS trust*

In cases where a service user has a need for nursing care that satisfies the primary need test but this can be provided in local authority residential care, the NHS trust will pay a contribution towards the nursing care. The

---

[28]   See *Jones v Powys Local Health Board* [2008] EWHC 2562 (Admin).

implementation of the National Framework for NHS Continuing Healthcare on 1 October 2007 heralded a single standard rate of payment for nursing contribution in place of three separate bands of payment that were at the discretion of the NHS trust. At the date of this publication, this standard rate is £109.79 per week in England and £120.55 in Wales.

19.3.1.4   Standard NHS services provided within residential care facilities

If a resident in local authority accommodation has no ongoing nursing care needs and does not require continuing care from the NHS, he may still access ordinary NHS services. The National Framework for NHS Continuing Healthcare makes it clear that local authorities and care home owners must not charge for the provision of such services that should be provided free of charge on the NHS.

19.3.2   Assessment of needs

Under the NHS Continuing Healthcare (Responsibilities) Directions, CCGs should use a checklist[29] to make a preliminary decision as to whether a full assessment for continuing healthcare is required. If a full assessment is recommended, it must involve multidisciplinary input and the use of the 'decision support tool' outlined above. If continuing healthcare is not required, an assessment must be made of whether a joint care arrangement or nursing contribution is appropriate.

NHS trusts are under a responsibility to carry out a proper assessment of whether a patient is fit to be discharged from an NHS hospital or institution.[30] This assessment must include consideration of continuing healthcare.

Under the National Framework, a review of the initial assessments must be carried out within 3 months and then yearly thereafter. If there is to be any change in NHS services, the service user and the local authority must be consulted first. Decisions regarding continuing healthcare can be challenged by referral to a review panel of the relevant Primary Care Trust and thereafter to an independent review panel of the Strategic Health Authority. If that fails, the health service ombudsman can be approached.

Given the significant level of resources involved, it has been relatively common for disputes to emerge on eligibility for continuing care. The decision of a NHS trust/CCG may subject to judicial review by the courts.[31]

---

[29]   The NHS Continuing Healthcare Checklist – issued by the Department of Health in 2012.
[30]   Delayed Discharge (Continuing Care) Directions 2009.
[31]   *St Helens BC v Manchester Primary Care Trust* [2008] EWCA Civ 931.

19.4 LOCAL AUTHORITY CARE

This has been one of the most contentious areas of catastrophic injury litigation. Further commentary is provided in Chapter 9 on Damages. For the purpose of this chapter, we simply aim to provide a summary of the relevant statutory rules and regulations relating to local authority assistance. It should be noted that, as with reform to welfare benefits, social care will inevitably be subject to review and change over the coming years. It is therefore essential that all practitioners keep abreast of developments in this area and seek expert advice from a suitable financial/welfare expert when appropriate.

Local authorities are under a duty to carry out an assessment of a person's needs for community care services. Detailed guidance is provided by the Community Care Assessment Directions 2004. The sad reality is that financial constraints have led many local authorities to adopt a policy of only meeting the most critical of needs.

Services can either be provided directly by the local authority, using its own staff, or by outside contracts with private care/service providers. Direct payments can be made to the claimant covering the costs of such services.[32]

If direct payments are made, conditions may be imposed and the local authority has the right to demand repayment if they are misused.

A local authority is not able to recover any of its outlay directly from a tortfeasor defendant. This means that (if applicable) the claimant will be charged directly for such services and then have to seek recovery of such charges as a head of loss in their personal injury claim.

19.4.1 Residential care

Under s 21(1) of the National Assistance Act 1948 (NAA 1948) (as amended by the National Health Service and Community Care Act 1990) a local authority is obliged to provide residential accommodation for adults who 'by reason of age, illness, disability or any other circumstances are in need of care and attention which is not otherwise available to them'. The leading case of *R v Slough Borough Council*[33] sets out the meaning of 'care and attention', which was described as 'doing something for the person being cared for which he cannot or should not be expected to do for himself'.

A local authority also has an obligation to charge for those services in accordance with the National Assistance (Assessment of Resources)

---

[32] Health and Social Care Act 2001, s 57, as amended by the Health and Social Care Act 2008 and Community Care, Services for Carers and Children's Services (Direct Payments) (England) Regulations 2009, SI 2009/1887; In Wales, SI 2011/831 and *Guidance on direct payments: For community care, services for carers and children's services* (Department of Health, 2010) apply.

[33] [2008] 1 WLR 1808.

Regulations 1992 (as amended) (NA(AR) Regulations).[34] When charging for residential care, local authorities must take account of the provisions of the Charging for Residential Accommodation Guide (CRAG).[35]

Special rules apply where an individual is not normally resident in the local authority's area or where the individual is in care through the provision of intermediate services (ie where there is a requirement for short-term therapy or treatment).[36]

The NA(AR) Regulations means-test is an individual means-test comprising both income and capital-based criteria. If the resident has over £23,250 in assessable capital he or she must pay for all their fees. Any capital below £14,250 is disregarded. Capital between £14,250 and £23,250 is accounted for on a sliding scale. The income aspect of the NA(AR) Regulations means-test needs to be viewed in conjunction with the Social Security (Miscellaneous Amendments) (No 4) Regulations 2006.[37]

Wales differs in that they have their own set of Regulations under which there is only one capital threshold of £23,250 above which claimants pay the costs of their care in full (until or unless their capital is reduced to that threshold amount). No tariff income scheme applies.

In *Peters v East Midlands Strategic HA and Nottingham City Council*,[38] Butterfield J found that, on a proper construction of the NAA 1948, the NA(AR) Regulations and Sch 10 to the Income Support (General) Regulations 1987, and on the assumption that the claimant's damages would be administered by the Court of Protection, the local authority was and (subject to any change in legislation) would in the future be, required to disregard the following sums as resources when assessing contributions payable under ss 22(3) and 26(3) of the NAA 1948:

(a)   the capital sum constituted by an award of damages for personal injury (comprising the whole amount of all awards made, not just general damages);

(b)   any interest or other income from the investment of that sum which is retained by the Court of Protection;

(c)   any payments made out of monies held by the Court of Protection to the claimant, to his or her receiver, or any other person for the claimant's use;

(d)   any payments made out of monies held by the Court of Protection to a third party on the claimant's behalf.

---

[34]   As amended by the National Assistance (Sums for Personal Requirements and Assessment of Resources) (Amendment) Regulations 2008, SI 2008/593.

[35]   Published by the Department of Health.

[36]   In these circumstances the residential care will be free.

[37]   SI 2006/2378.

[38]   [2008] EWHC 778.

This decision, subsequently upheld by the Court of Appeal,[39] clarifies the position for those who have recovered personal injury damages and seek public statutory provision in relation to residential care. The whole of the damages recovered under a claim will be disregarded when the local authority considers means, not just general damages. Furthermore, assuming the award is administered by the Court of Protection or in a personal injury trust, any interest or income arising from the damages award will be disregarded. The position is more generous in Wales as a result of the Social Care (Charges) Wales Measure 2010 (Commencement) Order 2011, where the disregard extends to any capital 'under the order of the court'.

Although periodical payments arising from personal injury awards are disregarded in the calculation of income under the NA(AR) Regulations, it makes good administrative sense to pay any such payments into a personal injury trust in any event.

Some uncertainty has recently arisen with the publication of the NHS's Charging for Residential Accommodation Guide (CRAG) consultation in July 2012. This consultation paper moots the prospect of local authorities being allowed to take into account the care element of personal injury compensation in the financial assessment of what a care home resident can afford to pay for residential care. As yet, no decisions have been announced but practitioners will need to bear this possible development in mind.

19.4.2 Care at home (domiciliary care)

Section 29 of the NAA 1948 relates to domiciliary care and the provision of services to the injured party in their home.

Under s 17 of the Health and Social Services and Social Security Adjudications Act 1983 (HSSASSA Act 1983) the local authority may use its discretion to recover such charges as it considers reasonable for adult non-residential care services.[40] The Department of Health has issued mandatory guidance on the operation of such charging schemes entitled *Fairer Charging* and a local authority may only depart from this guidance if there is good reason to do so.

A local authority can recover sums spent in respect of past domiciliary care if it is deemed reasonable to do so.

In the case of *Crofton v NHSLA*[41] the Court of Appeal held that the Fairer Charging Guidance incorporated CRAG but only in terms of how it dealt with capital. The position with domiciliary care is different in that a local authority must continue to disregard capital held in a personal injury trust or

---

[39] [2009] EWCA Civ 145.
[40] See *Collins v Plymouth City Council* [2009] EWHC 3279 (Admin) where this discretion was described by Holman J as 'very broad'.
[41] [2007] EWCA Civ 71, [2007] 1 WLR 923 followed in *Collins (A Protected Party) v Plymouth City Council* [2009] EWHC 3279.

administered by the court, but has discretion over the treatment of income derived on such capital, or by way of periodical payments. Consequently, whether a claimant will be entitled to statutory funding for domiciliary care, post-settlement, remains uncertain. Early advice from an expert in this field should be obtained in all cases where this might be an issue.

The Fairer Charging Guidance no longer applies in Wales, having been replaced in April 2011 by new statutory guidance. In Wales, charges for domiciliary care are subject to different rules provided under the Social Care Charges (Wales) Measure 2010 and associated regulations. This provides a power to charge for chargeable care services at a maximum level of £50 per week.

19.4.3   Risk of double recovery

The issue of double recovery within the context of local authority care remains a very important one. Following the decision in *Peters*, a claimant can now elect to recover the full cost of future care from the defendant as a matter of right. This leaves open the possibility of a claimant receiving a windfall if he/she subsequently seeks to force a local authority to provide for their care needs in any event.

In *Peters*, the claimant sought to address this difficult issue by suggesting that the Professional Deputy appointed in the case give an undertaking to the court not to seek statutory funding for the claimant's care needs in the future. Butterfield J rejected this suggestion as being fraught with difficulty. Instead, he was prepared to accept and find as a fact that the claimant would not seek state provision in the future and he could properly dispense with the issue on this basis. On appeal, the Court of Appeal concluded that this was not a satisfactory way of dealing with the possibility of double recovery and that some sort of policing mechanism was necessary. The Court of Appeal concluded that this could be achieved by amending the court order under which the professional deputy was appointed to include an undertaking on the part of the Deputy to notify the senior judge of the Court of Protection about the outcome of proceedings and supply him with copies of the judgments given. Thereafter, the Deputy could seek from a Court of Protection a limit on the authority of the Deputy to pursue further public funding of the claimant's care without further order or direction of the Court of Protection (and provision for the defendants to be notified in advance of any such application to obtain such an order or direction).

19.4.4   Double recovery: policing

In essence, therefore, the Court of Appeal felt that the Court of Protection was the appropriate mechanism for policing the issue of double recovery, with a new phrase of 'Peters Promises' entering legal parlance.

In practice, however, Peters Promises have not proved a satisfactory method of dealing with the problem. In the matter of *Re Mark Reeves*[42] the senior judge in the Court of Protection (Denzil Lush) expressed grave doubts as to whether that court was the appropriate means of resolving issues about the scope of a Deputy's authority. Furthermore, a Peters Promise does not work in a case involving a claimant who retains capacity. As a result, practitioners have had to devise alternative approaches, with reverse indemnities now becoming the norm in cases of this type. Under this approach, a claimant will receive monies from the defendant to pay for future care on a private basis but will give an undertaking to refund the defendant for the value of any local authority care provision that is subsequently obtained. Once again, it is essential that practitioners take independent expert financial advice in all suitable cases.

19.4.5   Mental health aftercare

Under s 117 of the Mental Health Act 1983, if the claimant has previously been detained in hospital under ss 3, 37, 47 or 48 of the Act and is then discharged into residential care, the NHS and local authority are obliged to provide 'aftercare services' and cannot charge for the same.[43] This aftercare provision does not have to continue indefinitely, but it must continue until the NHS and local authority are satisfied that the individual no longer needs such services.[44]

19.4.6   Services for children

Under the Children Act 1989, a local authority must provide services to children 'in need'. This includes disabled children. The local authority is under an obligation to provide 'a range and level of services appropriate to those children's needs'.[45] There is a qualified duty to provide children with accommodation. If the child is over 16, local authorities have powers to recover the costs of services and accommodation provided.[46] If under 16, parents can be charged.

19.4.7   Supporting People grants

Under this system grants are provided to help deliver 'housing-related services' to those in need. Monies are provided by the Secretary of State[47] and must be used by local authorities in accordance with guidance provided under the Local Government Act 2000. Supporting People grants cannot be used to pay for services provided in residential nursing/care homes, nor can it be used for services that the local authority is already obliged to provide under statute.

---

42   [2010] WTLR 509.
43   See *Tinsley v Sarkar* [2005] EWHC 192 (QB).
44   *R v Richmond LBC and others, ex p Watson and others* [1992] 2 CCLR 402.
45   Children Act 1989, s 17(1), Part 1, Sch 2 provides examples.
46   Children Act 1989, s 29(1) and Sch 2, para 21.
47   Under the Local Government Act 2000.

19.4.8   The Independent Living Fund

One of the consequences of recent welfare reform is that the ILF (previously available to help disabled people live independently in the community rather than in residential care) is now permanently closed to new applications. It is anticipated that the fund will close completely by 2015, with any remaining funds transferred to local authorities with responsibility for existing users.

19.4.9   Assessment of local authority needs

Under s 47 of the National Health Service and Community Care Act 1990, local authorities are under general duties to carry out an assessment of an individual's needs for community care services. This is commonly referred to as a 'section 47 assessment'. The assessment involves the local authority:

(1)   identifying those who need to be assessed for services;

(2)   ascertaining the needs;

(3)   determining how those needs will be met; and

(4)   providing for those needs by way of services.

Assessments and care plans must be kept under constant review. Those who provide care must also have their needs assessed.[48]

If a child is involved, the provisions of the Children Act 1989 will apply in relation to the assessment of needs.

If a patient is to be discharged from an NHS hospital and does not qualify for NHS funded continuing healthcare, the local authority owes a duty under the Community Care (Delayed Discharges) Act 2003 to carry out a prompt assessment of the patient's needs and, if appropriate, produce a care plan to meet those needs upon discharge.

---

[48]   Carers (Rights to Services) Act 1995 and Carers and Disabled Children Act 2000.

CHAPTER 20

FRAUD AND MALINGERING

20.1 INTRODUCTION

A broken bone can be seen on an x-ray. The effects of the injury can be harder to judge. Not all brain injuries can be seen on brain scans, and a scan does not indicate the extent of functional damage. The assessment can turn on the validity of a claimant's reported symptoms and functional difficulties. It is difficult to invent a catastrophic injury completely and such cases are fortunately rare. Some degree of alleged exaggeration is, however, a common feature of litigation in this area. Sorting out where the truth lies in such cases can occupy considerable time and money and keeps lawyers and the courts busy.

Various of the psychometric tests that clinical psychologists use are designed to catch out the claimant who tries to fake the result of tests by failing to make sufficient effort in the test. Thus some claimants will be reported to have faired badly in tests that even severely brain damaged people can normally manage. That will be offered as evidence of deliberate faking of symptoms. In the orthopaedic field reference is often made to the presence of Waddell signs that are said to indicate inappropriate symptoms that are inconsistent with, or not explained by the claimed injury. These are sometimes advanced as indications of faking, although Waddell himself was careful to emphasise that they were indication for caution about progressing to surgery without further investigation, but not necessarily signs of malingering.

The tool most commonly used by insurers to catch out malingerers and exaggerators of injury is the covertly taken video or DVD. This is often timed to coincide with the visit to the defendant's medical experts, as the contrast between what has been said to the experts and the contemporaneous behaviour of the claimant outside the consulting room is often relied on as the clearest evidence of bad faith. How such enquiry agent evidence should be handled before the courts is an issue that the courts have had to consider on many occasions. Judicial attitudes have changed, and the Human Rights Act 1998 changed the language in which the debate was conducted. In this chapter we consider how the courts deal with evidence of malingering and fraud.

20.2   DISCLOSURE OF VIDEO EVIDENCE

Videos are disclosable 'documents' under CPR Part 31. There was a time, however, when the courts accepted that defendants should be allowed to ambush claimants, then called plaintiffs, at trial with undisclosed evidence. The rationale for this approach was that plaintiffs would tailor their evidence if they knew what the defendants had on them. In *McGuiness v Kellog*[1] the Court of Appeal, including Woolf LJ as its junior member, upheld the first instance exercise of discretion under the pre-CPR Rules of the Supreme Court (RSC) that permitted a defendant to withhold video evidence of an allegedly malingering plaintiff taken by enquiry agents until the trial of the action, even though a video tape was a disclosable document under the RSC, just as it is under CPR Part 31. By 1994, however, the cards on the table approach had taken hold and in *Digby v Essex CC*[2] and *Khan v Armaguard*,[3] the Court of Appeal considered that it would not normally be appropriate to allow video evidence to be withheld in order to allow a plaintiff to be ambushed at trial.

20.3   PERMISSION TO RELY ON VIDEO EVIDENCE

The Human Rights Act 1998, and the incorporation of the European Convention on Human Rights (ECHR) into English law, created a new debate about whether evidence obtained by covert surveillance should be permitted by the courts. By this time the methods used by private investigators had also developed with the times. A favoured ruse was to call at the house of the claimant and tell him that there was a promotion in the area for TV dishes and that he could have a free dish so long as he fitted it himself. This led to a number of claimants being videoed up ladders.

Under the Human Rights Act two competing rights are engaged. On behalf of claimants reliance is placed on the right to privacy under Art 8 of the ECHR. There is no direct duty on defendants, insurers or private investigators as a result of this right, but there is a duty on the court as a public authority to ensure respect for the right on the basis that Art 8.2 requires that:

> 'There shall be no interference by a public authority with the exercise of this right except such as is in accordance with the law and is necessary in a democratic society in the interests of national security.'

It has thus been argued that the courts, in order to carry out their duty to protect the right, ought to prevent defendants from relying on evidence that was obtained in breach of the claimant's right to privacy, particularly where it was obtained otherwise than 'in accordance with the law' by reason of some trespass or other tort.

---

[1]   [1988] 1 WLR 913.
[2]   [1994] PIQR P53.
[3]   [1994] 1 WLR 1204.

On behalf of defendants it has been argued that they have a right under Art 6 of the ECHR to a fair trial and that that right would be infringed if they were prohibited from revealing wrongdoing on the part of a claimant.

Thus the issue of whether to allow evidence obtained by covert videoing requires the courts to consider two competing public interests; the interests of the public that in litigation the truth should be revealed and the interests of the public that the courts should not acquiesce in, let alone encourage, the use of unlawful means to obtain evidence.

The solution that the courts have found to this dilemma has been to decide that the court respects each right not by blind enforcement of it but by giving due respect to it in reaching a balance in each case between the two rights so as to find a fair solution to achieve the overriding duty of the court to achieve justice.

In finding this solution the courts under the CPR have followed Strasbourg jurisprudence on the ECHR to be found in case-law such as *Schenk v Switzerland*,[4] and *Khan v UK*.[5] A similar approach is to be found in the jurisprudence on the written constitutions of commonwealth countries, many of which are based on the ECHR. In cases such as *Allie Mohammed v The State*,[6] the Privy Council has held that the court had a discretion to include or exclude the evidence. The civil courts have also followed the route taken by the criminal courts in the UK in a number of cases including *R v Wright and McGregor*,[7] and *R v Loveridge*.[8] In the latter case the Court of Appeal went so far as to say that secret filming was objectionable because those being filmed could not prevent it but that it could be justified despite the right to privacy under Art 8 of the ECHR if it was done 'in accordance with the law' and was necessary for the prevention of disorder or crime. In *Loveridge* the secret filming by police was unlawful and was a contravention of Convention rights but was nevertheless held to be admissible, as it did not prevent a fair trial.

20.4 LATE DISCLOSURE

In *Rall v Hume*,[9] the Court of Appeal allowed the defendant to rely on video evidence in a personal injury action even though it had been disclosed late. The claimant had been involved in a road traffic accident for which the defendant had admitted liability. The claimant submitted a substantial claim for future loss. Directions were given for disclosure and the matter re-listed for further directions/disposal. Shortly afterwards, the solicitors for the defendant obtained a covert video film containing footage of the claimant's movements. It showed an apparent lack of difficulty with movement. The video evidence was not disclosed until after updated medical evidence had been obtained. A further

---

4   [1988] 13 EHRR 242.
5   TLR, 23 May 2000.
6   [1999] 2 AC 111.
7   [2001] EWCA Crim 1394.
8   [2001] EWCA Crim 1034.
9   [2001] EWCA Civ 146.

video obtained later by the defendant's solicitors was also disclosed. Initially both parties overlooked the need for permission to rely on this evidence prior to the hearing, but in due course the defendant applied to rely on the video evidence. At that hearing, the judge refused the application on the basis of it being made too late and the defendant appealed. The court of appeal confirmed that a video film or a recording was a document within CPR, r 31.4, and that a defendant who proposed to use such a film to attack a claimant's case was therefore subject to the rules as to disclosure and inspection of the documents contained in CPR Part 31. As the evidence was being adduced for the purposes of cross-examination of the claimant, rather than as part of the defendant's own case, it was held that justice required that the defendant be given an opportunity to cross-examine on the contents of the video. In giving the reasons of the court Potter LJ, with Sedley LJ agreeing, stated:

> 'In principle, as it seems to me, the starting point on any application of this kind must be that, where video evidence is available which, according to the defendant, undermines the case of the claimant to an extent that would substantially reduce the award of damages to which she is entitled, it will usually be in the overall interests of justice to require that the defendant should be permitted to cross-examine the claimant and her medical advisors upon it, so long as this does not amount to trial by ambush. This was not an ambush case: there had been no deliberate delay in disclosure by the defendant so as to achieve surprise, nor was the delay otherwise culpable, bearing in mind the mutual muddle over the 9 October hearing date. Nor is this the comparatively rare kind of case in which the film has to be independently adduced because what it shows goes beyond what can be established by cross-examination, and where different directions may be needed.'

It can be prejudicial, therefore, to obtain video evidence too early and risk sitting on it for so long that the delay counts against permission to rely on it. A favourite time for defendants to video claimants is about the time of exchange of medical evidence, often starting with the claimant's journey to and from the appointment with the defendant's expert. It is then served after exchange of the medical evidence, by which time the claimant has committed him or herself as to the extent of his or her disabilities, but service of the videos will not prejudice the trial date.

If a defendant makes a tactical decision not to serve its expert evidence in time, but to benefit from the delay to obtain surveillance evidence then it risks being refused permission to rely on expert evidence served late, even where there has been inaction by the claimant and the trial date would not be effected, see *Dass v Dass*.[10]

20.5   THE BALANCING EXERCISE

At first instance in the county courts, objection to the tactics of some enquiry agents has persisted. In the summer of 2001 *Hesketh v Courts*, unreported, was

---

[10]   [2013] EWHC 2520.

heard in Weymouth County Court and video evidence was excluded under Arts 6 and 8 where it had been obtained by 'deception and, trickery and trespass'. Enquiry agents had befriended the claimant, arranged a trip to a London hotel for him and his family and then carried out video surveillance. Thus the claimant got the trip, but the defendant could not use the evidence.

The issue of admissibility of covert video evidence returned to the Court of Appeal in February 2003 in *Jones v University of Warwick*.[11] The claimant claimed to have ongoing disabilities as a result of an episode of extensor tenosynovitis caused by an accident for which liability was admitted. The defendant obtained video evidence from enquiry agents who obtained access to the claimant's home twice by posing as market researchers and videoed her in her home without her knowledge. It was common ground that the enquiry agent was guilty of trespass. The videos had been shown to the defendant's medical expert, who took the view that they showed that there was no ongoing disability. The claimant's advisers initially did not show the videos to their medical expert as they objected to their admissibility. By the time the case came to the Court of Appeal, however, the videos had been shown to the claimant's medical expert, who concluded that they showed the claimant on good days and that on other days there was still significant disability. In the Court of Appeal it was common ground that if the video evidence was excluded then new experts would have to be instructed, with additional cost and delay, and that potentially illuminating evidence would have to be kept from the new experts. The Court of Appeal allowed in the video evidence. Lord Woolf, who was now presiding, gave the lead judgment of the court and concluded:

> 'The court must try to give effect to what are here the two conflicting public interests. The weight to be attached to each will vary according to the circumstances. The significance of the evidence will differ as will the gravity of the breach of Article 8, according to the facts of the particular case. The decision will depend on all the circumstances. Here, the court cannot ignore the reality of the situation. This is not a case where the conduct of the defendant's insurers is so outrageous that the defence should be struck out. The case, therefore, has to be tried. It would be artificial and undesirable for the actual evidence, which is relevant and admissible, not to be placed before the judge who has the task of trying the case.'

Interestingly the Court of Appeal considered that it had been sensible for the claimant's advisers to withhold the video evidence from the claimant's medical expert until the issue of admissibility had been resolved. In doing so they disagreed with the circuit judge who had been critical of that decision.

What made the video evidence objectionable in *Jones* was the fact that it had been obtained by a deceit that gave rise to a trespass. One of the issues that the courts have to decide before entering into the balancing exercise outlined in *Jones* is whether the actions of the enquiry agents do in fact amount to a breach of privacy. In *Law Debenture Trust Group v Malley and the Pensions*

---

[11] [2003] EWCA Civ 151.

Ombudsman,[12] Alliott J held that covert surveillance was a legitimate course to pursue on appropriate occasions in the investigation of personal injury claims and did not breach Art 8. On appeal in *R v Broadcasting Standards Commission ex p BBC*[13] the Court of Appeal held that secret filming in a place to which the public had access (in that case a shop) could amount to an infringement of privacy. They were not, however, considering the issue of admissibility of evidence. In *R v Press Complaints Commission ex p Ford*,[14] Silber J held that Anna Ford, the newsreader, could have a reasonable expectation of privacy on a public beach. There is a limit, however, to the extent to which celebrity privacy cases inform the decision in relation to 'ordinary' claimants. In *Rall v Hume*, the Court of Appeal excluded any footage of the claimant within her own home or within the nursery visited with her children from the permission to rely on video evidence.

It follows from the approach adopted by the courts that a video taken in a bedroom by a camera planted by someone who broke into the premises would be treated more seriously, and thus be more likely to be rejected, than a photograph taken by a cameraman who inadvertently stepped onto private property. It is the exercise by the court of its discretion that prevents there being a denial of a remedy for any breach of ECHR rights in this, and in many other instances under the CPR, as stated by Lord Woolf in *Ford v GKR Construction*.[15] The complainant would not be deprived of a remedy for the breach of his Convention rights if the evidence were admitted. The court would have afforded an adequate remedy by taking the right into consideration in the balancing exercise.

In many cases, where the video evidence though covert does not involve any great intrusion into the claimant's privacy, it will be counter-productive for the claimant to object and it is better to get on with dealing with the contents of the video on its merits rather than making a fuss and thereby appearing to give more weight to the video than it deserves. If there is an explanation for what appears on the video, then it should be given in a witness statement.

20.6   DISCLOSURE OF ALL VIDEO EVIDENCE

Where some video evidence has been disclosed the claimant may seek confirmation as to whether the defendant has other video evidence that may be of less assistance to the defendant and more favourable to the claimant. If the defendant refuses to disclose any additional video evidence then that may be a matter for the court to weigh up in deciding whether permission should be granted to the defendant to rely on the video evidence which it wants to produce, or for the court to draw its own inferences at trial.

---

[12]   Ch D 23 July 1999, ILR 25 October 1999.
[13]   [2000] 3 WLR 1327.
[14]   [2001] EWHC Admin 683.
[15]   TLR, 5 November 1999.

Sometimes the editing of the disclosed video evidence raises suspicions about whether it is a complete and accurate version of what was observed. In *Samson v Ali*[16] the defendant's insurers admitted liability in a personal injury action and served video evidence purporting to undermine the claimant's asserted injuries. The claimant's solicitors obtained expert counter-surveillance evidence which analysed the video and suggested that some important footage had been omitted or withheld and that the video tape was speeded up by the operatives. The insurers sought to debar the claimant from relying on the evidence, but Mr Justice Stadlen granted permission for the claimant to call the evidence at trial.[17]

20.7   ADMISSIBILITY ISSUES RAISED AT TRIAL

There are practical difficulties that arise if the discretion has to be exercised by the trial judge. In *Official Receiver v Stern*,[18] the Court of Appeal upheld Sir Richard Scott's decision[19] that it was not necessarily a breach of Art 6(1) to use in director's disqualification proceedings answers obtained under the powers of s 235 of the Insolvency Act 1986. This was on the basis that such proceedings are not criminal proceedings and are primarily for the protection of the public. The court considered that the admissibility of the evidence was a matter of fairness to be judged at trial as a question of substance not form. Although questions of admissibility of video evidence are dealt with before trial, so as to prevent defendants from ambushing claimants, the balance of interests could change during a trial. If video evidence was excluded but then a claimant gave evidence that could be flatly contradicted by the video, it might be appropriate to reopen the admissibility of the evidence before the trial judge. In those circumstances even if the trial judge ruled that the evidence was inadmissible, it might still have been seen.

20.8   SANCTIONS: COSTS

In *Jones v University of Warwick* the Court of Appeal allowed the video evidence in but imposed terms to reflect its disapproval of the way the evidence had been obtained. The Court of Appeal considered that it was right for the defendant to pay the costs of determining the admissibility issue before the district judge, circuit judge and Court of Appeal, even though they had succeeded. The problem had arisen from the conduct of the defendant's enquiry agents and accordingly the defendant should pay the bill for resolving it.

The Court of Appeal also indicated that the trial judge should take account of the defendant's conduct in deciding the appropriate order for costs. They suggested that the costs of the enquiry agents could be disallowed. If the trial

---

16   [2012] EWHC 4146.

17   See 'Eye Spy' by Jeff Simm of http://dontbewatched.com PI Focus Vol. 23 Issue 8 October 2013.

18   ILR, 10 February 2000.

19   TLR, 19 January 2000.

judge concluded that there was an innocent explanation for the apparent control of movement by the claimant as shown in the video then they suggested that it might be appropriate to order the defendant to pay the costs on an indemnity basis. Where the video evidence is of marginal benefit, therefore, then defendants may be well advised not to seek to rely on it.

In *Rall v Hume*, the defendant was also ordered to pay the costs of the appeal, even though permission to rely on the video evidence was granted, on the basis that they had delayed in raising the issue of the video evidence.

Even if the court does not impose any particular sanction, if the video evidence does not in fact show anything that is of great significance then all it will do is increase the claimant's costs that the defendant may end up having to pay. The costs involved in the claimant's solicitor viewing the video, obtaining copies, comparing it with previous statements and medical reports, taking instructions, obtaining the views of experts, considering issues of admissibility, questioning its provenance and completeness, and finally responding to the defendant on its contents could outweigh the probative effect of a video that in fact reveals very little.

If, however, a claimant is found to have been intentionally exaggerating a claim then it is likely that they will be penalised in costs, even if ultimately they have been successful. A good illustration of the application of this rule can be seen in the Court of Appeal decision in *Painting v University of Oxford*.[20] The claimant sought damages of £400,000. The defendant had admitted liability and paid into court the sum of £184,442 shortly before trial. Rather belatedly, the defendant then realised it had video surveillance evidence which significantly undermined the claimant's case. The defendant applied for and was granted permission to withdraw all but £10,000 of the payment into court. At trial the judge found that the claimant had deliberately exaggerated her injuries and awarded her £23,331 by way of damages. On the basis that the claimant had still beaten the payment into court she was awarded all of her costs. On appeal the Court of Appeal held that although the judge had found that the claimant had exaggerated her injuries he had not given that factor sufficient weight when considering his discretion as to costs. Were it not for the exaggeration the claim would probably have settled. The court should have regard to the conduct of the parties (CPR, r 44.3(iv)(a)) and whether the claim had been exaggerated (CPR, r 44.3(v)(d)). Whilst the CPR did not draw a distinction between intentional and unintentional exaggeration, the court should have regard to intentional exaggeration in any assessment of costs. The costs order was set aside. The defendant was ordered to pay the claimant's costs to the date of the payment in with the claimant paying the defendant's costs thereafter. At para 22 Maurice Kay LJ said:

> '... at no stage did Mrs Painting manifest any willingness to negotiate or put forward a counter-proposal to the Part 36 payment. No one can compel a claimant

---

[20]　[2005] EWCA Civ 161, TLR, 15 February 2005.

to take such steps. However, to contest and lose an issue of exaggeration without having made even a counter-proposal is a matter of some significance in this kind of litigation.'

Agreeing, Longmore LJ at para 27 said:

'... it is relevant that Mrs Painting herself made no attempt to negotiate, made no offer of her own and made no response to the offers of the University. That would not have mattered in pre-CPR days but, to my mind, it now matters very much. Negotiation is meant to be a two-way street, and a claimant who makes no attempt to negotiate can expect, and should expect, the courts to take that into account when making the appropriate order as to costs.'

A similar approach was taken in *Carver v BAA plc*.[21] A claimant who had rejected an offer of £3,486 was found to have exaggerated her claim and awarded £4,686.26. Although she had recovered more than the offer she was ordered to pay the defendant's costs after the time for accepting the offer had expired. The Court of Appeal upheld the costs order, but emphasised that CPR Part 36 in its then amended state permitted a wider review of all the circumstances of a case, and the court would not interfere with a judge's exercise of his discretion in doing so. Post Jackson Part 36 has been amended to reduce the discretion that the court will exercise so as to give Part 36 more force even where an offer is only beaten by a 'whisker'. This reflects the view that Part 36 should offers an effective way to deal with the behaviour of parties and put them on risk as to costs, a view that was also expressed by the Supreme Court in *Summers v Fairclough Homes*[22] when refusing to strike out a claim where it was held that there had been deliberate exaggeration of the claimant's injuries.

20.9   SANCTIONS: CONTEMPT AND THE CRIMINAL LAW

A fraudulent claimant (or indeed defendant) exposes themselves to prosecution under the criminal law, including perjury and perverting the course of justice, as Jeffrey Archer and Jonathan Aitken have both discovered. Whilst not every discrepancy between a witness's evidence, whether in the witness box or in a witness statement verified by a statement of truth, and some other evidence such as a video will be a contempt of court, if the court should conclude that there has been knowing and deliberate falsehood it may amount to contempt of court and the court could impose a penalty for the contempt, see, for example, *Walton v Kirk*.[23]

20.10   PLEADING MALINGERING

One objection that is still sometimes raised to evidence of malingering is that there is no express allegation of fraud in the defence. It is sometimes suggested

---

[21]   [2008] EWCA Civ 412.
[22]   [2012] UKSC 26.
[23]   [2009] EWHC 703 (QB).

that the absence of such an allegation precludes a defendant from raising issues of malingering. This objection had its origins in the per incuriam, obiter dicta to this effect in the pre-CPR Admiralty case of *Cooper v Stena Line Limited*.[24] Unfortunately the point was not in fact argued before the court in that case, and accordingly it provided no binding authority. In *Kearsley v Klarfeld*,[25] the Court of Appeal confirmed the correct position, namely that it was sufficient to set out fully any facts from which the defence would be inviting the judge to draw the inference that the claimant had not in fact suffered the injuries he asserted, and that there was no burden on the defence to prove fraud. The defendant does not have to put forward a substantive case of fraud in order to succeed so long as he followed the rules in CPR, r 16.5.

---

24   [1999] 1 Lloyd's Rep 734.
25   LTL, 6 December 2005.

CHAPTER 21

SETTLEMENT AND ADR

21.1 INTRODUCTION

Most cases settle, and most parties would like to achieve a mutually acceptable settlement if they can rather than go to court for a trial. Catastrophic injury claims are no exception, though the process of settlement may be more complex depending on the issues, the amount of evidence required for the parties to make an informed assessment, the need for a settled prognosis and the type of settlement envisaged. One of the significant cultural changes brought about by the Woolf reforms was to include the reality that parties will want to achieve a cost effective settlement in the process of case management. Cases are no longer just case managed with a view to trial, they are case managed in a way that allows them to be settled at whatever stage appears sensible and possible. To this end the courts now encourage alternative dispute resolution by a number of means otherwise than through the normal trial process. Together these methods are referred to as alternative dispute resolution (ADR). CPR, r 1.4 requires the court to further the overriding objective by active case management, which includes, under para (2)(e), encouraging the parties to use an ADR procedure if the court considers that appropriate, and facilitating the use of such procedure. To this extent ADR is no longer truly 'alternative', but could more properly stand for accelerated dispute resolution.

21.2 FORMS OF ADR

The most common forms of ADR in catastrophic injury cases are without prejudice discussions, including, round table meetings (RTMs) and mediation with an independent mediator. Other methods of ADR, including early neutral evaluation by an independent third party and arbitration before an independent arbitrator or panel of arbitrators, are rarely used.

21.3 PUBLIC BODIES

In March 2001 the Lord Chancellor gave an 'ADR Pledge' on behalf of all public bodies that ADR would be considered and used by public bodies in all suitable cases wherever the other party accepts it. In July 2002, the Department for Constitutional Affairs published a report as to the effectiveness of the government's commitment to the ADR Pledge. The report stated that the Pledge had been taken seriously, and identified a number of initiatives that had been introduced as a direct result of it. These included an initiative on the part of the National Health Service Litigation Authority (NHSLA):

> 'The encouragement of greater use of mediation, and other forms of alternative dispute resolution, is one of the options considered by the NHSLA, who are responsible for handling clinical negligence claims against the NHS. The NHSLA is working with the Legal Services Commission to develop a joint strategy for promoting greater use of mediation as an alternative to litigation in clinical negligence disputes.
>
> Since May 2000 the NHSLA has been requiring solicitors representing NHS bodies in such claims to offer mediation in appropriate cases, and provide clear reasons to the authority if a case is considered inappropriate.'

21.4 WITHOUT PREJUDICE DISCUSSIONS

Discussions to settle a case can occur at any time under without prejudice protection. Building provisions for without prejudice discussions into the case management timetable removes the possible barriers to fruitful discussions that can occur if neither party feels that it should make the first move. 'The Court has told us we should consider ADR, shall we have a meeting' can break the ice.

The Model Directions for Clinical Negligence actions developed by the Queen's Bench Assigned Masters at the Royal Courts of Justice provide expressly that consideration of ADR should include 'round table' conferences in the following terms:

> ### 'Alternative Dispute Resolution
>
> The parties shall by [a date usually about 3 months before the trial window opens] consider whether the case is capable of resolution by ADR. If any party considers that the case is unsuitable for resolution by ADR, that party shall be prepared to justify that decision at the conclusion of the trial, should the trial judge consider that such means of resolution were appropriate, when he is considering the appropriate costs order to make.
>
> The party considering the case unsuitable for ADR shall, not less than 28 days before the commencement of the trial, file with the Court a Witness Statement, without prejudice save as to costs, giving the reasons upon which they rely for saying that the case was unsuitable. The Witness Statement shall not be disclosed to the trial Judge until the conclusion of the case.
>
> [*"ADR" includes "round table" conferences, at which the parties attempt to define and narrow the issues in the case, including those to which expert evidence is directed, early neutral evaluation, mediation and arbitration. The object is to try to reduce the number of cases settled "at the door of the Court", which are wasteful both of costs and judicial time.*]'

This form of order is known as an Ungley order, after John Ungley the former Master assigned to clinical negligence action at the Royal Courts of Justice. It was approved by the Court of Appeal in *Halsey v Milton Keynes General NHS Trust*.[1]

21.5 ROUND TABLE MEETINGS

Without prejudice discussions can vary from a quick telephone call, or chat outside the case management conference, to a formal round table meeting of all the parties arranged as part of the timetable to try and reach a compromise of the action. Getting all the clients and their legal advisers together to discuss settlement, whether at a mediation or a round table discussion, can create a momentum towards a settlement that is acceptable to all parties. The preparation for the meeting will have focused all parties' attention on the case at the same time, and will have helped all parties to 'buy in' to the idea of settlement and the opportunity to bring the dispute to an end. As with mediations, a round table meeting can speed up the process of offer and counter-offer that might otherwise require weeks or months of correspondence, over which time costs will be increasing.

In catastrophic injury actions considerable thought needs to be given to the psychology of round table discussions, in particular discussions involving the claimant. This is so whether the meeting is in the form of a mediation or a without prejudice meeting of the parties without outside facilitation. In cases of PTSD or other psychiatric vulnerability the need for preparation of the client will be more obvious, but in all cases clients will need to be educated in preparation for a without prejudice discussion. The nature of without prejudice confidentiality will need to be explained. The principle that what is said without prejudice cannot be referred to in court is important, but so too is the fact that what is said cannot be 'unsaid' and that the other side may use it to colour their view of the case or to stimulate other enquiries that could result in admissible evidence.

Explanations of matters such as funding, Part 36 offers and payments, provisional damages, periodical payment orders and interest will need to be given. Clients may sometimes need to be prepared for the task of making a decision to end litigation. That can be daunting when, for example, what is being decided is the funding to enable someone to provide care for the rest of their life.

Thought will also need to be given to the physical constraints on holding meetings and reaching decisions. This can involve more than ensuring adequate wheelchair access, with parking close to hand and access for wider powered wheelchairs where necessary. A claimant in receipt of high levels of care will need to bring adequate carers with them. That can involve delicate discussions about who is present for various parts of the discussions in order to maintain

---

[1]   [2004] EWCA Civ 576.

privacy and confidentiality and to ensure that decisions are made freely and without undue influence from family, friends and carers. In many cases a settlement will not work unless the family support network has had an opportunity to be heard and to 'buy in' to the settlement.

Very badly injured claimants can find the process of attending a meeting and discussing settlement emotionally over powering and physically demanding. Issues such as temperature control, fluid intake, medication and toileting need to be prepared for. In order to allow informed decision making a meeting may need to be paced so that a claimant has time to take in the various stages in negotiations. This will be easier if they have been prepared for what might happen in advance. In many cases a badly injured claimant will get to a point where it is unwise to ask them to make a final decision without further time for thought without the pressure of making an immediate decision. It is for this reason that the parties should try and pace a meeting to make the best progress in the time available, but realising that a final decision may need to await another day. Better use of the time available will be made where adequate preparation has been undertaken.

In most serious cases proper preparation will involve a preliminary meeting with the client in advance of the date of the round table discussion. It may be possible to be more objective in setting agreed parameters for settlement, and in agreeing the negotiating strategy in a meeting when the other side are not sitting in another room waiting to talk to you. Negotiation preparation should include matters such as whether to make an opening offer and what the opening position will be, as well as where to be prepared to end up by way of a settlement. The costs implications of settling and not settling should also be discussed. Other non-cash possibilities can also be discussed, such as apologies, undertakings to change safety or training practices and undertakings as to future employment or assistance.

Such a meeting allows the clients to take in the information at their own pace without feeling under pressure, and to go away and prepare themselves, and often their family, for the prospect of settlement. The client will then arrive for the meeting having had less of a sleepless night through worry of the unknown, and will feel more in control of the process and able to make sensible decisions as a result. Clients should, in particular, be asked whether they wish to have a say at the meeting. If need be they can be given gentle encouragement and reassurance about having their say. They can then begin to think about what it is they do want to say. It is important to bear in mind that this may be just another meeting for the lawyers and insurers, but an important once in a lifetime occasion for the claimant.

It may be sensible, in the right case, to include the claimant in part of the face-to-face meetings with insurers, but this is a decision ultimately for the claimant and they should not be coerced into a meeting that they do not want, or thrown into it unprepared. It can sometimes help, however, to get the claimant and the claim handler from the insurer to speak openly to each other in the presence of their legal advisers. This way each gets to realise that they are dealing with a real person on the other side. They can also convey what is really troubling them about the case. Clients can be very powerful advocates in their own cause if given the opportunity to speak direct to insurers at a mediation or round table meeting. They can talk about feelings and concerns that they will not get to talk about when giving evidence and it can have a dramatic effect on the views of opponents but also a cathartic effect for the client. A well-managed round table meeting can provide both sides with a welcome sense of having 'had their day' and 'their say' without the need for a trial. If the parties feel that such a discussion would be useful but that it should be moderated by the presence of a neutral party, then that is one of the roles that a mediator can fulfil.

As with mediation, the timing of round table meetings can be important. The Model Directions for Clinical Negligence actions developed by the Queen's Bench Assigned Masters at the Royal Courts of Justice suggest that consideration should be given to ADR about 3 months before the start of the trial window. In some cases there may be a benefit in holding a round table meeting earlier, as the prospects for settlement may be improved if the parties have not yet incurred large costs that could be saved by an early settlement. Where liability is the real issue it may be sensible to hold a meeting once the evidence, including expert evidence on liability is disclosed. Sometimes where the parties are apart on liability a cash settlement can break the log jam. The parties need to have made some assessment of quantum in order to achieve that even if they have been concentrating on liability, maybe because there has been an order or agreement for a split trial. Where quantum is in issue the point for a meeting may come after exchange of schedules and counter-schedules. As with mediation, there can be real benefit in holding a round table meeting before the parties' positions have become entrenched by Part 36 offers or payments into court.

21.6 AUTHORITY TO SETTLE

Whether at a round table meeting or a mediation one of the issues that needs to be addressed in advance, but which even then can cause problems, is authority to settle. In a dispute between two individuals who are present the position is simple but other cases can present problems.

For claimants, problems can occur in multi-party actions. Obtaining prior written binding authority from all claimants can be difficult. It is harder to manage client expectations with a large group. The group may be unwilling, for understandable reasons, to give unlimited authority to negotiators. If authority is sought to settle on a particular basis or above a set sum then there may be concerns that the bottom line position set out in the authority will leak out to the other side. Some action groups elect representatives to reach agreement, but very often all that can be achieved is a provisional agreement that will be recommended to the group as a whole.

In cases where a settlement requires court approval, ie because it involves a child or a protected party (formerly referred to as a patient before the Mental Capacity Act), any settlement will need to be subject to the approval of the court. Since the Mental Capacity Act the Court of Protection does not give official prior approval of settlements, but there may be issues, such as how the damages will be invested and/or used that it would be helpful to consult the Court of Protection on before a settlement.

For defendants problems can arise if the defendants in a multi-defendant action have nominated one defendant's solicitors to enter into negotiations. A claimant needs to know in those circumstances whether they have authority to bind all the defendants, or whether they may be left with a defendant who is unwilling to join a settlement and may, for example, refuse to pay their own costs to walk away where the other parties have settled.

Problems may also arise where more than one insurer is involved. If different syndicates at Lloyd's are involved the problem is normally overcome by the nomination of a lead underwriter to represent them all. Where part of a claim is reinsured, however, problems of authority can arise. In the course of negotiations the figures being discussed could move out of the layer covered by one insurer to enter into the layer reinsured with another insurer. Such problems need to be anticipated so that at least a contact number for the reinsurer is available and the person who is to be contacted is prepared and ready to make a decision. Much of the benefit of getting the parties together can be lost, however, if the person making the final decision has not been part of the process.

A mediation agreement will normally require the parties to confirm that they have authority to settle the dispute. The mediator will normally seek reconfirmation of such authority at the start of the mediation. In the situations discussed above any confirmation of authority may need to be qualified. One area of frustration can be where a defendant's insurer attends a round table meeting or mediation on the basis that the person attending has authority to settle, only to say mid-afternoon as negotiations progress that they have reached the limit of their authority and either they can go no higher or they need to speak to the reinsurer or their boss who is in a meeting/fishing/playing golf. In practice, given the confidential nature of anything said without prejudice, especially in mediation, there is little that can be done except to be patient and use the embarrassment involved in admitting the claimed lack of authority as part of the negotiations. It is because such problems can and do arise, however, that it is important to address the issue of authority to settle in advance.

21.7 MEDIATION

Mediation means using an independent person, the mediator, to facilitate the process of resolving a dispute. The mediator does not act as a judge to determine the dispute nor make rulings, but assists the parties to explore the strengths and weaknesses of their cases and tries to find if there is a point at which the parties' needs and expectations can be brought together to form a settlement. In some cases a mediator will not be necessary and the parties will be able to reach agreement without independent help, but where that has not happened then experience shows that mediation does work.

Mediation provides a confidential and relatively quick and cost effective way of resolving disputes without trial. It has the benefit that the parties remain in control of the process, and issues can be addressed that are outside the narrow scope of litigation. Thus matters such as apologies or undertakings as to future treatment or care provision can feature in mediation in a way that litigation cannot handle once the matter gets into court. These are matters that may not be central in the litigation process but can be of fundamental importance to a party, and if addressed can assist the process of settlement. The Legal Services Commission (LSC) recognises the benefits of mediation and does provide funding, but prior authority should be requested for the cost of mediation in accordance with the LSC guidelines, either as part of the case plan or by a request for specific authority.

The more complex a dispute the more appropriate it is for mediation, as mediation can be a way of cutting through the web of issues to find an acceptable outcome that reflects the litigation risks. It can provide litigants with a feeling of closure, without risk of appeal, but also a feeling that they have 'had their day' and 'their say' without the cost, and risks, of trial. In multi-defendant cases it can allow defendants to negotiate with each other with the claimant on hand to consider any joint approach that may result. Mediation has proved particularly fruitful in multi-party cases.

21.7.1 Agreeing a format

Before a mediation starts the parties enter into a mediation agreement. The agreement confirms that the parties have authority to settle their claims and that they will keep the discussions private and confidential, the whole process being without prejudice to any court proceedings unless and until agreement is reached, just like a without prejudice meeting between the parties. The psychological preparation for a without prejudice meeting or round table meeting referred to above is just as important for mediations.

Confidentiality is an important part of the process of mediation, so that parties can feel free to talk and to explore ideas for settlement. If need be the courts will enforce the duty of confidentiality by injunctive relief, as in *Venture Investment Placement Ltd v Hall*,[2] in which HHJ Reid QC, sitting as a deputy judge of the Chancery Division, granted an injunction restraining a party from referring to any part of the discussions that took place during the mediation process, where that party had allegedly made statements to others concerning the mediation discussions.

---

[2]   LTL, 16 February 2005.

A normal mediation will last a day. In commercial disputes it is not uncommon for mediations to go on late into the night to thrash out a compromise. This is rarely appropriate in catastrophic injury claims as the claimant is normally not physically able to make an informed decision under such pressure. In those circumstances it is more common for a mediation to end for the day and either be resumed by telephone discussions between the parties or via the mediator, or for the mediation meeting to be resumed on another day if agreement is still possible but has not been reached despite progress being made.

21.7.2   How to set up a mediation

To set up a mediation the parties can go to one of the organisations offering mediators, such as the Centre for Effective Dispute Resolution (CEDR), ADR Group, Trust Mediation or In Place of Strife. Alternatively the parties can go direct to a mediator and book them, just as if they were booking counsel for a court hearing. Some mediation providers have taken the view in the past that what a mediator needs is mediation skills, rather than detailed expertise in the area of the dispute. Some mediators are so skilled and experienced that they can mediate a dispute in any area, but that should not be taken for granted. Some research should be undertaken into the background of proffered mediators to gauge their suitability. Catastrophic injury work, as this book confirms, has become a highly technical area, and a thorough understanding of personal injury law, damages and practice will assist a mediator to bring the parties to a settlement. The main mediator providers are increasingly appreciating that such specialism is what the market for mediators wants, and are reacting to market pressure by offering suitable personnel as mediators.

A suite of rooms is needed for the mediation (normally it helps to have at least three rooms, or one per party plus one large enough to hold all parties). Either the parties can make an arrangement to host the mediation, or if that is a problem then arrangements can be made with the mediator to find a convenient location. Hiring of space, whether via a mediation provider or direct, can work out to be a significant expense. If you do not have the facilities it is worth exploring options with all solicitors and counsel in the case, or with the parties. Bear in mind, however, that you may be in the rooms for quite some time and it is worth finding rooms that the parties can feel comfortable in.

The mediator will need to be provided with some background information about the dispute. Normally the equivalent of a case management conference hearing bundle will suffice. The parties need to agree the mediator's fees before the mediation. The fee will normally be a fixed fee to include the day set aside for the mediation and any reasonable pre-reading and liaison with the parties. An hourly rate may be agreed for any additional work. Ordinarily either one party agrees to pay the mediator's fees or they are divided equally between the parties and then can be the subject of costs recovery as costs in the case as appropriate (just like the costs of a without prejudice meeting).

21.7.3   Costs of mediation

A typical standard mediation agreement may contain a provision such as:

> 'The parties agree to pay their own costs of the mediation unless otherwise agreed.'

This means no more than would be the case with a without prejudice meeting, that the parties pay their own costs but that the cost is recoverable on an assessment of costs if there is a paying party either by agreement or by court order, and that is how the courts interpret such clauses. This general approach was confirmed in *Natwest Bank v Feeney*.[3] That case, however, involved a mediation using the old, 9th edition, CEDR Solve agreement, which had guidance notes indicating that parties may amend the agreement to identify that the costs of the mediation may be taken into account in any court orders if there is no settlement at the mediation. It was arguable that the guidance notes did not affect the construction of the agreement, but Eady J considered that they should be taken into account in deriving the intention of the parties, and where no amendment had been made the agreement, with the guidance notes, indicated the intention of the parties that the costs of the mediation would not be recoverable unless expressly made so as a result of the mediation. In that case the action had been resolved by a Tomlin order following a mediation. The order made provision for the claimant to pay the defendants' costs of the counterclaim, waived the claimant's entitlement to costs under various interim orders relating to the counterclaim and ordered legal aid assessment of the defendants' costs but did not deal expressly with the costs of the mediation. The defendants argued that the mediation agreement did not, and should not be read as, restricting the result the parties might arrive at by way of mediation. Thus it was argued that the Tomlin order took precedence over the agreement, and did not restrict the definition of costs, and by necessary implication therefore the costs of the mediation were included in the costs order. Eady J, as had costs judge Campbell below,[4] rejected that submission and held that the mediation agreement was binding on the parties and was not discharged by the Tomlin order, as that would be to read too much into the Tomlin order.

Some mediation agreements now reflect the normal practice in catastrophic injury mediations. For example, the CEDR mediation agreement was amended from its 10th edn to provide that:

> 'Unless otherwise agreed by the Parties and CEDR Solve in writing, each Party agrees to share the Mediation Fees equally and also to bear its own legal and other costs and expenses of preparing for and attending the Mediation ("each Party's Legal Costs") prior to the Mediation. However, each Party further agrees that any court or tribunal may treat both the Mediation Fees and each Party's Legal Costs as costs in the case in relation to any litigation or arbitration where that court or tribunal has power to assess or make orders as to costs, whether or not the Mediation results in settlement of the Dispute.'

---

[3]   SCCO No 9 of 2007, May 14.
[4]   See EWHC/Costs/2006/90066.

This makes it clear that costs of mediation can be recovered as costs in litigation. In the interest of clarity it is wise to amend the wording of any agreement that does not so provide to some clearer formula such as:

> 'The parties agree to pay their own costs of the mediation, and those costs and the cost of the Mediator shall be costs in the case of the proceedings unless otherwise agreed.'

In order that the costs can be recovered on an assessment it is also wise to amend any confidentiality clause, such as 'No party to this mediation shall make any reference to this mediation in Court proceedings', to the following effect:

> 'No party to this mediation shall make any reference to this mediation in Court proceedings *save for the purposes of any assessment of costs, or as ordered by the Court.*'

In general, courts would regard as unreasonable a refusal to mediate save on terms that each party pays their own costs of the mediation in any event, particularly where there was an inequality of bargaining positions by reason of funding differences.

21.7.4   On the day

The mediator will normally hold telephone discussions with each side before the day fixed for the mediation in order to agree practical arrangements and also to begin understanding what the dispute is really about. Even if a dispute does not settle within the time set for the mediation, the mediator will normally follow up the dispute in the subsequent days to see if any outstanding matters can be agreed and a resolution reached to end the dispute. Experience indicates that many cases settle soon after the mediation.

On the day of a mediation the mediator will usually meet the parties separately and finalise the agreement and any questions about the process that have not been sorted out in advance. The parties will often have been asked to provide brief written summaries of the case and of their positions to help the mediator and also to help focus discussions. These may be private briefings to the mediator, or exchanged with the other parties, or a combination of the two, as agreed between the parties and the mediator. The mediator will normally then start with a joint session in which each party will be invited to make a brief opening statement of their position for 5 or 10 minutes. The mediator will then hold private discussions with each party separately to explore each party's position before engaging in some shuttle diplomacy to explore the room for settlement. That process may go on until agreement is reached or the attempt is abandoned, but where the mediator thinks it appropriate the parties may be brought back together to address issues with each other, or the lawyers, or the clients, or the funders may be put together for discussions as the mediator thinks might assist.

A mediator may well want to ask questions about the issues in the case, and as to whether the parties have given consideration to them, but it is not the role of the mediator to go into the detail of a case that would be explored at trial. The mediator does not come to conclusions on the issues in case and it is important to prepare clients for this approach in case they feel that the mediator is ignoring their case. The mediator's view of the issues will be far broader than a trial judge's and it is not the mediator who produces the settlement. The mediator is there to help the parties come to their own settlement. It is the parties' dispute and it must be the parties' settlement. It is this aspect that is one of the benefits of mediation as it leaves the parties in control of the dispute whilst allowing the mediator to guide the process of settlement.

It helps to have at the mediation a current schedule of costs to date and of prospective costs to trial. This is for the purpose of assessing litigation risks and in case there is an opportunity to negotiate a costs inclusive deal. Sometimes the mediator will have asked for this information in advance. If not then the mediator will ask for it on the day. It is worth being ready with the information.

Standard learning has it that mediations begin with an opening phase where the process is established and then move on to an evaluation phase where the issues are explored and discussed, either in joint sessions or in private sessions with the mediator. Then comes a negotiation phase, often with the mediator operating a sort of shuttle diplomacy. Then finally comes a conclusion phase, when the parties are brought to an agreement and the terms are worked out and set down in writing. In truth these phases are not fixed periods and a mediation can ebb and flow with phases of evaluation interspersing phases of negotiation. One of the roles of a mediator is to keep this process going where otherwise the parties on their own would call it a day and give up.

If agreement is reached at the mediation then it will be set out in writing. The mediation agreement will normally provide that no agreement will be binding until it is in writing and signed by or on behalf of the parties. This allows parties to raise settlement proposals for discussion knowing that they will not be committed until an agreement is signed. The parties will be encouraged to draft the agreement themselves but the mediator will assist in the process.

21.7.5 Refusal to mediate: adverse costs orders

In February 2002 the Court of Appeal refused a successful defendant its costs because it had rejected mediation, despite being encouraged to mediate by the single Lord Justice who granted the claimant permission to appeal to the Court of Appeal. In giving judgment in *Dunnett v Railtrack plc*,[5] Brooke LJ said:

> 'Skilled Mediators are now able to achieve results satisfactory to both parties in many cases which are quite beyond the power of lawyers and Courts to achieve. This Court has knowledge of cases where intense feelings have arisen, for instance in relation to clinical negligence claims. But when the parties are brought together

---

[5] [2002] 1 WLR 2434.

on neutral soil with a skilled Mediator to help them resolve their differences, it may very well be that the Mediator is able to achieve a result by which the parties shake hands at the end and feel that they had gone away having settled the dispute on terms with which they are happy to live. A Mediator may be able to provide solutions which are beyond the powers of the Court to provide.'

The decision in *Dunnett v Railtrack plc* prompted an increase in the number of mediations for fear that an adverse costs order would be made against even a successful party if mediation was refused. The argument in favour of an adverse costs order against the party refusing mediation appeared even stronger in the case of public bodies who are subject to the ADR Pledge described above.

In May 2004, however, the Court of Appeal in *Halsey v Milton Keynes General NHS Trust*, reaffirmed the principle that a successful party would only normally be deprived of its costs for refusing mediation where the refusal was unreasonable. They held that the court had no power to compel parties to undertake mediation and that to require parties to mediate rather than litigate would be in breach of Art 6 of the ECHR. The court could, and should, encourage mediation, and unreasonable conduct is refusing to mediate could be reflected in an adverse costs order. The burden was on the unsuccessful party to show that the successful party had been acting unreasonably in refusing ADR:

'The burden should not be on the refusing party to satisfy the Court that mediation had no reasonable prospect of success. As we have already stated, the fundamental question is whether it has been shown by the unsuccessful party that the successful party unreasonably refused to agree to mediation. The question whether there was a reasonable prospect that a mediation would have been successful is but one of a number of potentially relevant factors which may need to be considered in determining the answer to that fundamental question. Since the burden of proving an unreasonable refusal is on the unsuccessful party, we see no reason why the burden of proof should lie on the successful party to show that mediation did not have any reasonable prospect of success. In most cases it would not be possible for the successful party to prove that a mediation had no reasonable prospect of success. In our judgement, it would not be right to stigmatise as unreasonable a refusal by the successful party to agree to a mediation unless he showed that a mediation had no reasonable prospect of success. That would be to tip the scales too heavily against the right of the successful party to refuse a mediation and insist on an adjudication of the dispute by the Court. It seems to us that a fairer balance is struck if the burden is placed on the unsuccessful party to show that there was a reasonable prospect that mediation would have been successful. This is not an unduly onerous burden to discharge: he does not have to prove that a mediation would in fact have succeeded. It is significantly easier for the unsuccessful party to prove that there was a reasonable prospect that a mediation would have succeeded than for the successful party to prove the contrary.'

The factors that could be relevant to the issue of unreasonableness in this context were:

- the nature of the dispute;
- the merits of the case;
- the extent to which other settlement methods had been attempted;

- whether the costs of ADR would be disproportionately high;
- whether any delay in holding ADR would be prejudicial;
- whether ADR had a reasonable prospect of success.

Just as some after *Dunnett* had wrongly concluded that mediation was effectively compulsory, some after *Halsey* wrongly concluded that they no longer needed to bother about mediation or ADR. In fact the effect of the judgments is to require parties to behave reasonably against a background in which it is no longer considered reasonable to turn a blind eye to the benefits of mediation. This was emphasised post-*Halsey* by the Court of Appeal in *Burchell v Bullard*,[6] in which Lord Justice Ward, at para 43, said:

> 'Halsey has made plain not only the high rate of a successful outcome being achieved by mediation but also its established importance as a track to a just result running parallel with that of the court system. Both have a proper part to play in the administration of justice. The court has given its stamp of approval to mediation and it is now the legal profession which must become fully aware of and acknowledge its value. The profession can no longer with impunity shrug aside reasonable requests to mediate . . . These defendants have escaped the imposition of a costs sanction in this case but defendants in a like position in the future can expect little sympathy if they blithely battle on regardless of the alternatives.'

As Lord Justice Ward emphasised, the main reason for using mediation is because experience has shown that it works. This was reinforced in the psychiatric stress through over-work case of *Vahidi v Fairstead House School Trust Ltd*,[7] in which the Court of Appeal expressed its exasperation with parties who engage in long trials and appeals where the Court of Appeal has already laid down settled principles. In the words of Lord Justice Longmore:

> 'One shudders to think of the costs of this appeal and of the trial which apparently took as long as 9 days. As the courts have settled many of the principles in stress at work cases, litigants really should mediate cases such as the present.'

In *Malmesbury v Strutt & Parker*,[8] the court even held that a party who agreed to mediation but then took an unreasonable position in the mediation was in the same position as a party who unreasonably refused to mediate. It is difficult to see how this will be enforced very often, however, due to the confidential nature of mediation proceedings.

The Halsey guidance was extended further by the Court of Appeal in *PGF II SA v OMES Co 1 Limited*[9] when they held that as a general rule silence in the face of an invitation to participate in ADR amounted to unreasonable conduct which could be reflected in costs. In doing so the court expressly endorsed the Judicial College's Jackson ADR Handbook.

---

[6]   [2005] EWCA Civ 358.
[7]   LTL, 9 June 2005, (2005) *The Times*, June 24.
[8]   [2008] EWHC 424 (QB).
[9]   [2013] EWCA 1288.

APPENDIX

BIOGRAPHIES

GRAHAME ALDOUS QC

Grahame is a Queen's Counsel at 9 Gough Square, London (www. 9goughsquare.co.uk). He is recommended for both Clinical Negligence and Personal Injury in Legal 500 and Chambers & Partners, who have described him as:

> 'one of the most approachable barristers and really understands what being a modern silk is all about. Attentive to the needs of both solicitor and client, he understands client care whilst also being a pedigree performer in court who is known for his fearsome cross-examinations.'

His other publications include *Clinical Negligence Claims: A Practical Guide*, *Work Accidents at Sea* and *Kemp & Kemp*. He is a Fellow of the Association of Personal Injury Lawyers, a member of the CEDR Lead Mediators' Panel and sits as a Recorder. Grahame has served as Head of Chambers at 9 Gough Square and as Chairman of the PNBA Clinical Negligence Conference. He is a Governing Bencher of the Honourable Society of the Inner Temple.

STUART MCKECHNIE

Stuart is a barrister at 9 Gough Square, London and is listed as a Leading Junior in the Chambers and Partners and Legal 500 Clients' Guides where he is variously described as 'widely considered to be a future silk', 'admired for his amazing service', 'a rising star', 'seriously talented' and 'a real specialist in catastrophic injury cases'. Stuart was awarded the title of 'Personal Injury Barrister of the Year' at the 2011 Eclipse Proclaim Personal Injury Awards and in September 2012 it was announced that Stuart had been shortlisted as Personal Injury/Clinical Negligence Junior of the Year, at the Chambers & Partners Bar Awards. In 2012, Stuart was appointed as one of only three Barrister members of the working party responsible for the Judicial College Guidelines for the Assessment of General Damages in Personal Injury Cases. Stuart has extensive experience in a complete range of personal injury and clinical negligence work but specialises in high value catastrophic claims involving complex issues and multiple experts. Much of his practice is at the High Court. Stuart writes for *Kemp: Practice and Procedure on the subject of Periodical Payment Orders*. In 2013, Stuart has advised and represented claimants in cases with a combined value in excess of £35 million. In addition to the high value cases that he undertakes on his own, Stuart is currently instructed as junior counsel on a number of catastrophic injury claims.

JEREMY FORD

Jeremy is recommended as a leading personal injury junior in Legal 500 (2014) and in Chambers & Partners (2014). Comments highlight his bold approach; sound judgment; effectiveness; and client care. He conducts cases in all aspects of personal injury litigation with an emphasis on serious brain injury; multiple orthopaedic injury; and fatal accident cases. He also has a particular interest in cases with an underlying psychiatric component and cases involving the Motor Insurers' Bureau, being editor of Butterworth's Personal Injury Litigation Service on issues of road traffic insurance and the MIB.

Jeremy conducts cases in his own right and as a junior counsel working with leading silks. In the last 12 months he has achieved settlements that exceed £30 million in value. Most recently, in a case as junior to Grahame Aldous QC, what was probably one of the highest ever personal injury settlements was achieved for a gravely brain-injured client. A record settlement of £1.9 million was also achieved for a 57 year old above the knee amputee, settlement being founded on provision of prostheses with computerised knee joints.

Jeremy is the secretary to the APIL Brain Injury Special Interest Group, responsible for organising meetings and lectures on brain injury topics. He has also contributed to publications including *APIL Road Traffic Claims* (2nd edn, Jordan Publishing, 2012) and *Clinical Negligence* (9 Gough Square, 2012). He regularly contributes articles to leading journals such as *New Law Journal*.

TERRY LEE

Terry has been qualified as a Solicitor for over 30 years. He was Partner and then Senior Partner in the Firm of Evill and Coleman. Following the merger of that Practice with the Practice of Russell-Cooke in 2005 he is now a Senior Consultant.

Throughout his legal career he has only undertaken work representing the interests of victims who have suffered accidents at work, on the roads, in hospital and whilst undertaking sporting activities. Terry has undertaken clinical negligence claims for over 25 years and has been involved in ground-breaking decisions including *Brown v Merton, Sutton and Wandsworth Health Authority, Hall v Piri* and *Joyce v Wandsworth Health Authority* and *Dudley v East Dorset Health Authority. Joyce v Wandsworth Health Authority* provided clarification of the judicial approach to causation in clinical negligence cases. Recently (2013) Terry successfully settled a claim against Network Rail arising from the deaths of two young females who were killed when crossing a railway track in Cambridgeshire, when they were struck by an express train. This claim was defended strenuously by Network Rail but a settlement in the claim was achieved shortly before the trial was due to commence.

In *Dudley v East Dorset Health Authority* he was involved in a contested application to remove the litigation friend who had abused his position and after a lengthy hearing the Judge ordered the removal of the litigation friend, who was replaced by a representative from the Court of Protection. The case was reported following the successful settlement of the claim, which was achieved by way of structured settlement payments for the remainder of the claimant's life.

Terry has, over the years, focused upon claims involving catastrophic injuries including claims arising from birth asphyxia leading to cerebral palsy. He has extensive experience in dealing with claims of considerable complexity including asbestosis and mesothelioma claims, 'one vehicle' accidents, sporting injuries and claims leading to severe head and spinal injuries.

He is a member of the Law Society Personal Injury and Clinical Negligence Accreditation Scheme and an assessor to the Personal Injury Accreditation Scheme. He has investigated a number of complex sporting injury cases, including the ground-breaking decision in *Smolden v Whitworth and Nolan* which was the first case of its kind brought against a rugby referee and which was successful both at first instance and in the Court of Appeal.

He has dealt with multi-million pound value claims and those which involve settlement by way of periodic payments. He also has extensive experience in dealing with the Court of Protection and in a reported judgment of the Court of Protection he was referred to as one of the country's leading personal injury solicitors.

In 2000, he was honoured by being the first solicitor to be selected for the prestigious 'Lawyer of the Year' award by the Association of Personal Injury Lawyers. He is a member of a number of organisations, including the Association of Personal Injury Lawyers, Actions for Victims of Medical Accidents and FOCIS. In addition, he is a member of the Ethics Committee of the Royal Hospital for Neurodisability, Putney and a member of the Board of Management of the Royal Hospital. In 2007, he received the highest level of accreditation by the Association of Personal Injury Lawyers, which is the level of Senior Fellowship.

He has also undertaken a further literary project for the Association of Personal Injury Lawyers in their *Personal Injury Law Practice and Precedents* publication in providing details as to the function and role of the Court of Protection.

As a Consultant in the merged practice of Evill & Coleman and Russell-Cooke he maintains a case load of complex clinical negligence and personal claims.

For relaxation, Terry has been known to play the occasional game of golf!

LUCY WILTON

Lucy is a Senior Associate solicitor in Russell-Cooke's Clinical Negligence and Personal Injury team. Her expertise covers cases involving alleged negligence on the part of hospitals, individual doctors or other medical practitioners and nursing or care homes. Lucy's work also includes a wide range of personal injury cases, including road traffic and work-related accidents and 'slip and trip' claims.

Lucy has a degree in law from Oxford University and qualified as a solicitor in 2007, having previously trained at Russell-Cooke. She is recommended in the Legal 500 (2012) directory, which described her as 'meticulous' and 'hardworking', and she was selected by Corporate INTL Magazine 2013 for one of their 'Clinical Negligence Rising Star of the Year in England' awards.

Lucy is experienced in helping those who have suffered catastrophic injuries as a result of negligence, including brain injuries sustained at birth, to recover substantial compensation. Lucy also specialises in 'fatal' claims arising from a person's death, where this has allegedly been caused by medical negligence or an accident. Lucy has particular interest in cases relating to delayed diagnosis of cancer, negligent obstetric and gynaecological treatment and care of the elderly.

Lucy also represents individuals and organisations in relation to inquests in the coroners' courts. She has acted for bereaved families at inquests involving deaths in hospital, road traffic accidents and apparent suicide.

MAGGIE SARGENT

Maggie is a Registered General Nurse with over 30 years of experience and is an advanced member of BABICM. This followed a career in management of clients in the community. She is nursing adviser to Headway National. In 2004 she published a paper at the European Brain Injury Symposium at the Vatican on caring for clients in the community with PVS and has published other papers on costs of care in the community. Maggie was an invited speaker on case management at the 'Fifth World Congress for NeuroRehabilitation', which took place in Brasilia in September 2008 and the PEOPIL Conference in Malta in 2009. In 2011 she established the Oxford Group of the Silver Lining Charity providing social opportunities and challenges for clients with brain injury, which has a client group of 20 to 30 service users at present. She also lectures at seminars across the country on costs of care both in the public and private sectors.

Maggie is a director of Community Case Management Services Limited covering both the United Kingdom, Europe, and worldwide. She has her own current case load and is involved in actively supporting and mentoring case managers in the organisation. Maggie is an accredited risk assessor and Manual Handling People Trainer.

NICHOLAS LENG

Dr Nicholas Leng qualified as a clinical psychologist in 1981. He holds the academic qualifications of Bachelor of Science (Honours), Diploma in Clinical Psychology and Doctor of Philosophy. He is a Fellow of the British Psychological Society, a Fellow of the Royal Society of Medicine and he is registered with the Law Society and with the Academy of Experts as an expert witness, and is a member of the Society of Expert Witnesses. He has held posts in the NHS and was the Head of the Department of Clinical Neuropsychology and Consultant Neuropsychologist to the Brain Injury Unit at the Royal Hospital for Neuro-disability in London until 1991. He has held undergraduate and postgraduate teaching and research appointments at the University of London and University of Sussex. He is currently an independent Consultant Neuropsychologist whose practice is divided between clinical and medico-legal cases. He has published a number of papers in international refereed journals, many on organic amnesia, presented various papers at conferences and has written two books. He has prepared over 5,000 expert reports for the courts under the instructions of insurers and solicitors acting for both claimants and defendants, and as a single joint expert, since he was first asked to do so over 20 years ago. Instruction percentages are currently 70% claimant, 30% defendant and single joint instruction.

MAGGIE BLOTT

Dr Maggie Blott graduated from the University of Newcastle upon Tyne in 1982 and undertook all her postgraduate training in London where she was appointed as a consultant obstetrician and gynaecologist in 1994 to the staff of King's College Hospital. In 2003 she moved back to Newcastle upon Tyne to work at the Royal Victoria Infirmary before moving in 2007 to University College Hospital London. Dr Blott has always had an interest in postgraduate training and for 3 years, between 2006 and 2009 was the Vice President of the Royal College of Obstetricians and Gynaecologists with responsibility for Postgraduate Medical Education and Training. Dr Blott moved to the Corniche Hospital in Abu Dhabi in 2011 and has set up a 5-year structured OBGYN residency training programme. Dr Blott has always worked clinically and has a particular interest in the management of labour, fetal heart rate interpretation and shoulder dystocia.

ANDREW MOLYNEUX

Dr Andrew Molyneux graduated from Cambridge and spent most of his professional career in Oxford.

He has been working in the field of stroke and interventional treatment of brain vascular lesions for more than 25 years and pioneered the treatment of intracranial aneurysms by endovascular techniques for more than 20 years.

He has published widely in many aspects of stroke, interventional treatment of brain lesions and intracranial aneurysm treatment in particular, with a personal experience of well over 1,000 cases over the last 14 years.

He was a Consultant Neuroradiologist at the Radcliffe Infirmary, Oxford for 25 years and at Frenchay Hospital, Bristol for 4 years. He was until recently a Senior Clinical Research Fellow, at the Nuffield Department of Surgery, University of Oxford. He led the MRC funded International Subarachnoid Aneurysm Trial (ISAT).

He is first author on two major publications in the *Lancet* in 2002 and 2005 reporting the results of the ISAT study, which has transformed the management of patients with ruptured brain aneurysm in many countries of the developed world.

He was on the Royal College of Physicians, Stroke Guidelines Group published in 2003 and on the National Institute for Clinical Excellence (NICE) Guidelines development group which issued national guidelines for acute stroke care published in 2008.

He has been providing expert witness evidence for medico-legal cases for over 15 years in the field of neuroradiology, both diagnostic (reading scans) and in cases of Interventional procedures and stroke and spinal disease.

He continues in active research as well as medico-legal work.

PROFESSOR UDO KISCHKA MD FRCP

Professor Udo Kischka studied Medicine and Psychology at the Universities of Amsterdam and Heidelberg, and trained as a Neurologist in Switzerland and Germany. He spent 2 years doing medical research at the Harvard MIT Division of Health Sciences and Technology, and the Massachusetts General Hospital in Boston, USA.

Since 1994, he has been a Consultant Neurologist and Consultant in Neurological Rehabilitation at hospitals in Switzerland, Germany and the United Kingdom. Since 2001, he has been Consultant in Neurological Rehabilitation at Rivermead Rehabilitation Centre and the Oxford Centre for Enablement, which is part of the Oxford University Hospitals.

He is an Honorary Consultant Neurologist at the Oxford University Hospitals and a Clinical Advisor for the Parliamentary and Health Services Ombudsman. Since 2003, he has been a Visiting Professor at Oxford Brookes University, the

University of Hertfordshire, and the University of Basel, Switzerland. He is also a senior clinical researcher and honorary senior lecturer at the Department of Neurology, University of Oxford.

He is the author and editor of three books and numerous publications, and has been on the editorial board of two medical journals.

His special interests are neuropsychological deficits and behavioural disorders following injury to the frontal lobes of the brain, motor control and its recovery after brain injury, spasticity, neuropharmacology, as well as other topics related to neurological rehabilitation.

DR MARTIN BAGGALEY MB, BS, BSC, FRCPSYCH

Dr Baggaley qualified from St Bartholomew's Hospital in 1984. He served in the British Army from 1985 until 1997. He trained as a psychiatrist in the Army and at Guy's Hospital, London. He has been a full-time psychiatrist from 1986 and has been a consultant from 1993.

He left the British Army in 1997 and was appointed to the post of consultant psychiatrist for the Lewisham & Guys Mental Health NHS Trust.

He was appointed Executive Medical Director of the South London & Maudsley NHS Foundation Trust in August 2007. He undertakes his NHS practice on an acute admission ward at Lambeth Hospital.

He has been a General Medical Council (GMC) Health Examiner and Health Assessor since 2010.

He has extensive experience in the assessment, treatment and management of post traumatic stress reactions and the management of psychological trauma after accidents and disasters. He worked as Senior lecturer in Military Psychiatry for 4 years and for 2 years was Head of Division at the Defence Services Psychiatric Centre, Catterick. Whilst at Catterick, he was in charge of the Post Traumatic Stress Disorder (PTSD) programme, specialising in the management of treatment resistant PTSD. He has served on operational tours in Bosnia and Northern Ireland.

Dr Baggaley has extensive experience in providing expert psychiatric evidence in civil courts, mental health tribunals, employment tribunals and criminal courts.

MR BRIAN GARDNER, BM, BCH, MA (OXON) FRCS, FRCP (LOND&EDIN)

Brian Gardner qualified as a doctor in Oxford in 1973. After completing his basic medical training, mainly in London and Cambridge, and achieving the higher qualifications of both the Royal College of Surgeons and the Royal College of Physicians, he undertook higher specialist training in neurosurgery in Belfast and later in spinal cord injuries in Southport.

In 1985 he was appointed Consultant Surgeon in Spinal Cord Injuries in Stoke Mandeville Hospital. He retired from the NHS in July of 2011.

He has authored or co-authored over 100 publications of various types. He has taught locally, nationally and internationally on aspects related to spinal cord injury. He has contributed to the development of the speciality of spinal cord injury both nationally through the British Association of Spinal Cord Injury, where he was Chair up to 2011, and internationally via the International Spinal Cord Society, as Treasurer and Editorial Board Member.

Brian is able to advise on the medical and medico-legal aspects of the spinal cord injured, in relation to both quantum issues and liability matters.

SELLAIAH SOORIAKUMARAN

Dr Sooriakumaran, MBBS, FRCP(Eng), FRCS(Eng, Edin&Glas), is Consultant in Rehabilitation Medicine at Queen Mary's Hospital, Roehampton, having been appointed in 1990.

Working in the world-renowned rehabilitation centre at Roehampton for over 10 years, he has gained expertise in the management of upper and lower limb amputees of all age groups. He is the Clinical Director for an experienced multidisciplinary team representing physiotherapy, occupational therapy, nursing, clinical psychology, social workers, prosthetists, orthotists and rehabilitation engineers. The centre has a registered caseload of 2,600 amputees with a hardware budget of £1.6 million. There is a purpose built in-patient unit (Douglas Bader Unit), a 12-bedded ward for management of complex problems in amputees such as chronic stump pain, multiple amputations, and patents with concurrent medical problems who need intensive rehabilitation programmes. Numbers of patients are referred annually for second opinion from other regions and from abroad. The workshop has the expertise to fabricate the full range of hardware both modern sophisticated prostheses using hi-tech components and conventional prostheses using leather and metal, on site to cater for the wide range of clinical situations.

RICHARD CROPPER

Richard Cropper is a Consultant at Personal Financial Planning Limited, a company dedicated to providing expert independent financial advice exclusively in personal injury cases. A graduate of the University of Birmingham, Richard is a fully qualified and authorised independent financial adviser, and has been involved in providing expert advice since 1993. He is accredited as a 'First Tier' expert witness by APIL.

Richard regularly advises on periodical payments, bespoke investment planning, Local Authority and Social Services provision and Personal Injury Trusts, and has acted in claims with a value in excess of £10 million, both in the UK and abroad.

Richard has provided expert evidence and advice to the court in many of the milestone periodical payments cases in recent years, including *YM, Thompstone, Corbett, De Haas, RH, Bennett, Peters* and most recently *Oliva*. His work in these areas is widely acknowledged, for example most recently by Swift J in *RH* [2013]:

> 'Mr Cropper had been involved at all stages of the development of the model order and the formulae contained in the Schedule to the model order originate from work carried out by him. He was clearly the right person to consider what could be done to solve the problem caused by the missing data.'

Richard is also approved by the Court of Protection to manage investments for claimants who lack capacity.

He is a regular speaker at events for lawyers, and regularly contributes to legal journals and textbooks. He is instructed on behalf of claimants, defendants and jointly.

INDEX

References are to paragraph numbers.